Ibn Taymiyya's Theological Ethics

Ibn Taymiyya's Theological Ethics

SOPHIA VASALOU

OXFORD
UNIVERSITY PRESS

OXFORD
UNIVERSITY PRESS

Oxford University Press is a department of the University of Oxford. It furthers the University's objective of excellence in research, scholarship, and education by publishing worldwide.

Oxford New York
Auckland Cape Town Dar es Salaam Hong Kong Karachi
Kuala Lumpur Madrid Melbourne Mexico City Nairobi
New Delhi Shanghai Taipei Toronto

With offices in
Argentina Austria Brazil Chile Czech Republic France Greece
Guatemala Hungary Italy Japan Poland Portugal Singapore
South Korea Switzerland Thailand Turkey Ukraine Vietnam

Published in the United States of America by
Oxford University Press
198 Madison Avenue, New York, NY 10016

Library of Congress Cataloging-in-Publication Data
Vasalou, Sophia.
Ibn Taymiyya's theological ethics / Sophia Vasalou.
pages cm
Includes bibliographical references and index.
ISBN 978-0-19-939783-9 (hardback: alk. paper)
1. Ibn Taymiyah, Ahmad ibn 'Abd al-Halim, 1263–1328. 2. Muslim scholars—Biography.
3. Islamic ethics. I. Title.
BP80.I29V37 2016
297.5092—dc23
2015004821

1 3 5 7 9 8 6 4 2
Printed in the United States of America
on acid-free paper

To my family

Contents

Acknowledgments

THIS BOOK'S BIGGEST—LITERALLY life-giving—debt must be to Gregor Schwarb, who nearly five years ago refused to take no for an answer when inviting me to take part in a meeting of the ERC project Rediscovering Theological Rationalism in the Medieval World of Islam and gave me a pretext for responding to the curiosity that my still cursory readings of Ibn Taymiyya had excited in me. I set sail for the *Collected Fatwas* and was soon hooked on the thread that would lead me through its mazes. That meeting was one of several events that would provide me with occasions for developing and refining my ideas, and I am grateful to the organizers and participants of conferences in Istanbul, Marburg, Göttingen, Edinburgh, and London for these opportunities over the past few years. Materially, this book owes a debt to several sources. Begun during my term as a teaching fellow at the European College of Liberal Arts in Berlin and during the sunset of my junior research fellowship at Gonville and Caius College in Cambridge, it was then made possible by a grant from the Deutscher Akademischer Austausch Dienst in 2011 and even more substantially by a research fellowship at the Orient Institut in Beirut in 2012. The final stage of the writing of this book took place during a research fellowship at Oxford Brookes University in 2014. I am grateful for all these forms of support.

Among the conversations that stand in the background of this book, the one that did the most to catalyze its reflections at an early stage was my exchange with Frank Griffel, who generously shared his insights and his better knowledge of many of the textual sources that entered my paper trail, and then also critically read an earlier draft of this manuscript from cover to cover. This book is deeply indebted to his close reading, as well as to the invaluable criticisms of my two readers for Oxford University Press, without which it simply would not have assumed its current shape. (For its shortcomings, it goes without saying, they stand absolved.) All other debts are to my close family, who have their own reasons to be rejoicing that this book is finally complete. I would also like to thank my editor, Theo Calderara, for his support and his efficiency in leading the book through the Press.

Ibn Taymiyya's Theological Ethics

Introduction

AMONG THE MANY messages Muslims have put out in engaging their religious faith in the contemporary context, there is one that stands out with special tenacity. *Al-Islām dīn al-fiṭra*, it runs. "Islam is the religion of our original nature." It is a catchphrase that has grown to be ubiquitous in the contemporary setting, appearing in a broad spectrum of writings, particularly popular ones, among authors who might otherwise be divided by important differences in intellectual orientation. We hear it among stakeholders of more traditional educational environments. We hear it among members of the broad Islamist movement and others who stand for the new religious approaches spawned by the circumstances of modernity. And when we hear it, its sound is that of a refrain whose presence has come to be so pervasive in the acoustic field that it no longer invites pause. Take the tract by the late Saudi cleric Muḥammad ibn Ṣāliḥ al-ʿUthaymīn, for example, running under the title *Ḥuqūq daʿat ilayhā al-fiṭra wa-qarrarathā al-sharīʿa* (Rights Demanded by Our Original Nature and Confirmed by the Sharīʿa), which offers an enumeration of different kinds of rights filed under familiar headings: the rights of spouses, of children, of neighbors; the rights of God. More remarkable than these contents is the fact that the language of *fiṭra*, having appeared in the title, never once appears in the body of the text itself, its function apparently complete in this elliptical gesture and wholly comprehensible (we may suppose) to its readers.

And toward what, one may ask, might this gesture be? Considered more closely, the notion of *fiṭra* here and elsewhere would seem to point us to a particular matrix of relationships or correspondences. At its heart, and most immediately, lies the claim of a correspondence between the demands of our nature and the demands and principles of the Islamic faith. It is a message of harmony that stands out, for example, in the characteristic expression found in a recent popular work on ethics by the prominent Damascene scholar of law Wahba al-Zuḥaylī: "Islam does not conflict with human nature or innate desires because it is the religion of our original nature [*fiṭra*] and the religion of moderation."[1] Yet joined to this first correspondence as its implicit alter ego would seem to be another: the message of a correspondence between the prescriptions of the faith and the nature of the prescribed actions themselves. A good illustration of the latter is provided by a remark that appears in a highly popular work by the well-known Egyptian cleric and member of the Muslim Brotherhood, Yūsuf al-Qaraḍāwī. "Out of mercy for His servants," al-Qaraḍāwī writes in *al-Ḥalāl wa'l-ḥarām,* "God Almighty has made permissibility and prohibition dependent upon intelligible grounds [*ja'ala al-taḥlīl wa'l-taḥrīm li-'ilal ma'qūla*], which relate to the welfare of human beings themselves. It thus became known in Islam that the prohibition of something follows upon [or depends on: *yatba'u*] its malignancy and harmfulness [*al-khubth wa'l-ḍarar*]."[2] We may notice that al-Qaraḍāwī here accentuates considerations of utility in explaining this correspondence; al-'Uthaymīn, on the other hand, had sounded the deontological accent with the notion (*ḥaqq*) that figured as his organizing term.

It is this twofold correspondence—connecting the commands of the Islamic faith with our own nature, on the one hand, and the nature of actions, on the other—that would appear to underlie the pervasive catchphrase as we find it. And with this matrix out in the open, now, those considering this intellectual scene against the classical theological tradition might respond with a certain sense of surprise. For certainly the notion of *fiṭra* as such had hardly been a foreign one in the Islamic tradition, given the deep scriptural roots that grounded it. The notion of *fiṭra* ("the natural disposition" or "constitution," "our original nature") makes a key appearance in the Qur'an in the verse that reads: "So set your face to the religion, a man of pure faith [*ḥanīfan*]—the nature (framed) of God, in which He has created man [*fiṭrat Allāh allatī faṭara al-nās 'alayhā*]." This scriptural base had been enriched by several prophetic traditions taking *fiṭra* as their central term, the most familiar being the one that states: "Every child is born with the natural disposition ['*ala'l-fiṭra*], and it is its parents that render it a Jew, or a Christian, or a Magean." Picking up on the connection forged in the Qur'anic text between human nature and the religion of the original monotheists (*ḥunafā'*), this hadith was part of a pool of rich (though not uncontested) resources that had been used to theorize about the positive religious impulses built into the material of human nature. Drawing on these resources, the most important way in which the notion of *fiṭra* had been developed by Muslim writers was as a base disposition for religious belief, or indeed, as some would argue the point more thickly, for the Islamic faith.

Yet the conceptual matrix underlying modern usage would seem to go beyond this intellectual tradition, bringing out a set of connections belonging to the evaluative rather than the more narrowly theological field. And in doing so, it would stir up old ghosts that our readings of Islamic theological history would appear to have laid to rest. Because taken together, the series of correspondences just outlined as the subtext of that well-worn catchphrase—*al-Islām dīn al-fiṭra*—point to an understanding of the relationship between God's command and human reason that we regard as having been largely rejected by Sunni Muslim theologians in the classical period, when questions about the nature of value and our epistemic access to it had come up for heated debate. It was a debate that came to be known as that of *al-taḥsīn wa 'l-taqbīḥ*—literally, the determination of good and bad—and one that, in the telling most familiar to us, was defined by a binary opposition between the vantage point of Ashʿarite and Muʿtazilite theologians. Notions of right and wrong, the latter had argued, are intuitively available to the human mind and yield objective moral standards that apply across agents, as much to human beings as to God. It is a position we have often understood through its contrary, which was the Ashʿarite claim that God authors the values of actions by attaching consequences—reward and punishment—to their performance or omission. Right and wrong are constituted through God's word; and it is through the same means that they can be exclusively known.

In the classical debates, the notion of *fiṭra* was not known to have made an appearance. It was rather the notion of reason (*ʿaql*) that figured as the central term of dispute. Yet if we hold our hand over this change of register, the modern notion of *fiṭra*—carrying with it the idea of a correspondence between what the Sharīʿa commands and what is already present within us naturally or independently of religious input—would seem to involve a semantic freight not at all far removed from what the Muʿtazilites had been concerned to claim. In doing so, it would reopen the door of a debate that had long ago appeared to close in the face of Muʿtazilism and its rationalistic commitments. Whether we call it nature or reason, Muʿtazilite moral rationalism would not lie far in the distance.

This study began as a desire to reopen that door and discover where it leads. How to understand the historical origins of the characteristic turn of thinking codified in the notion of *fiṭra*? How seriously to take the message of moral rationalism that appears to buoy it? How to relate this message to the premises and outcomes of the theological discourse inherited from the classical period?[3] As so often in Islamic thought, however, questions about the present lead back to the past, and they sometimes retain one there with a tenacity unanticipated by the searchlights of one's initial investigation. In this case, the return to the past took the form of a return to the terms of the classical debate itself, to consider more directly the contribution of one of its more maverick participants. For standing just outside the familiar perimeter of this debate was a figure who has often been felt to cast a particularly tenebrous shadow over contemporary Islamic thought: the Ḥanbalite theologian Taqī al-Dīn Ibn Taymiyya.

And accosted with the uncertain curiosity of the present, his writings seemed calculated to provoke a twofold reaction of recognition—and a new surprise. Recognition, because it was soon clear that the notion of *fiṭra* so amply attested in the contemporary scene was one that assumed critical dimensions in his thought, including his writings on ethics. Surprise, because probed more closely, Ibn Taymiyya turned out to articulate a view that appeared to run cross-beam to the shape of the traditional debate on the nature of value as we have often narrated it. Disavowing the binary opposition of Muʿtazilism and Ashʿarism that has supplied such narratives with their backbone, Ibn Taymiyya called for a new position that would overcome it: not Muʿtazilism, not Ashʿarism, but something in between. Yet this *via media* was one that Ibn Taymiyya appeared to spell out in explicitly rationalist terms. Right and wrong, he claimed, are known by reason. And while the language of reason would indeed be deployed in couching this claim, Ibn Taymiyya in many places replaced it with another—that of *fiṭra*. The claim then became: We know what is right and wrong by the human *fiṭra*.

Taken seriously, it is an intellectual development that would appear to subvert everything we thought we knew about the shape of this theological debate and to call for a brand new chapter in this well-rehearsed history. A new chapter, a new answer, and one that holds out a double excitement to the reader of the classical theological tradition: in offering a fresh synthesis in an old debate, and in offering a synthesis distinctly framed in rationalist terms. Before us would seem to stand nothing less than the promise of a new claim of moral reason.

It was this surprise that gave the present book its immediate impetus. As it progressed, the historical questions that provided the original impetus quickly transformed themselves into a deeper engagement with Ibn Taymiyya's ethical thought. Thus, while these questions continue to shadow the present study as its distant framework, and while I hope to be offering some of the material needed for answering them, the study that follows is an effort to engage directly and on his own terms a thinker that still remains—remarkably given his wide influence in the contemporary context—understudied. At the heart of this engagement stands a question about the claim of reason announcing itself in Ibn Taymiyya's works. How to understand the promise of this claim and how to judge its fulfillment?

Questions about Ibn Taymiyya's engagement of reason have formed a prominent theme in scholarly appraisals of his intellectual legacy. Only until recently Ibn Taymiyya appeared in narratives of the history of Islamic theological and philosophical thought as the herald of a new era of decline and the augur of an antirationalist retrenchment following several centuries of efflorescence in the rationalist sciences. The new age of antirationalism, Majid Fakhry could write in his recent introduction to the Islamic intellectual tradition, was marked by a "return to the Ḥanbalite position which rejected all philosophical, and even theological, methods of discourse, and clung to the sacred text, literally interpreted."[4] And it was Ibn Taymiyya who was identified as one of the salient contributors to this Ḥanbalite re-implosion. More recent writings on Ibn Taymiyya—notably by Jon Hoover, Yahya Michot, and Ovamir Anjum—have sought to reverse this facile judgment, emphasizing the significance of his engagement with the discourses forming the object of his supposed rejection. Taking the question of Ibn

Taymiyya's rationalism to one of its most important seats, the present study can be read as a contribution to this larger debate concerning the nature of his legacy.

The focus of this study falls on Ibn Taymiyya's ethical outlook relative to two key questions that shaped classical theological debates about ethics: a question about the nature of ethical value and a related question about the nature of ethical knowledge and the role of reason in achieving this. Piecing this account together involves tackling several separate tasks. Given the long life such questions had led within classical debates, and given the crucial significance of these historical debates in framing Ibn Taymiyya's own enterprise, clarifying his ethical views must in part be pursued as an effort to recount their relationship to preexisting theological topography. This book is thus as much a window into classical theological debates about ethics—particularly Muʿtazilite and Ashʿarite approaches to ethics—as it is a window into Ibn Taymiyya's own thinking. Muʿtazilite theologians, of course, have often been celebrated for having pressed a bold claim of reason in ethical matters. Yet what has received less attention among readers of this region of Islamic theological history is the claim of reason that Ashʿarite thinkers had articulated in both their theological and legal writings.

Shedding clearer light on Ashʿarite ethical thought is important in its own right, giving us new resources for recalibrating our understanding of classical debates. But it is equally important for telling the more specific story that forms the subject of this book. For one of the things I hope to show is that the story of Ibn Taymiyya's ethical views can be told far more compellingly as a story about his relationship to the Ashʿarites than as a story about his affinities to Muʿtazilism. It is also a story, as I hope to show, that must partly be told as an account of Ibn Taymiyya's fraught engagement with the philosophy of Avicenna, the perception of whose towering intellectual presence Ibn Taymiyya shared with late Ashʿarites but was far more concerned to contest. It may seem both surprising and unsurprising, in this respect, to discover that it is Avicenna's denial of the connection between ethical judgments and human nature (*fiṭra*)—a denial that had made deep inroads into Ashʿarite ethical thought—that provides Ibn Taymiyya with a critical context for developing his own view of this connection and of ethical judgments more broadly.

Probing Ibn Taymiyya's ethical outlook thus involves engaging a wider series of intellectual contexts, bringing into view the trajectory of key ethical ideas across the fields of theology, philosophy, and indeed law. Yet classical debates about ethics had always been profoundly anchored in an underlying structure of theological concerns. Questions that on the surface revolved around matters of value as these pertain to human existence—questions about what *human beings* know regarding right and wrong or what is right and wrong for *human beings* to do—ultimately pointed beyond human life and translated into fundamental questions about the moral life of God himself. A fuller appraisal of Ibn Taymiyya's ethical views must thus also involve transposing his views about human morality into their theological context and considering the understanding of God's morality that complements them and lends them their significance.

Set against this nest of intellectual contexts, one of the conclusions of this book can be stated simply: Ibn Taymiyya's claim of moral reason, examined more closely, turns out to be a rather misleading one. Reason, when it comes to determining right and wrong, carries a far less substantive and far less substantially articulated content than at first sight appears and than the prima facie resemblance between Ibn Taymiyya's position and the Muʿtazilites' may lead one to anticipate. Restated in terms of the theological possibilities as we know them, Ibn Taymiyya's view of moral reason in fact coincides with Ashʿarism in most of its basic features and with the more limited brand of rationalism expounded by Ashʿarite writers.

I speak of stating conclusions "simply." Yet one of the chief messages I hope readers will take away from this book is that simple conclusions are not so easy to wrest from Ibn Taymiyya's work. If Ibn Taymiyya's ethical view, upon closer consideration, turns out to be different from what an initial consideration leads us to expect—if "appearances" can be "misleading" and the realities can surprise our expectations—this already suggests that something unusual must be afoot. Interpretive work, of course, is often about digging more deeply beneath appearances and ferreting out what is not immediately plain to view. Wonder has frequently been thought of as the passion of intellectual inquiry; surprise seems to me a good candidate for one of the main passions that move us not only *to* but *through* the effort to reconstruct a thinker's viewpoint. On one level, this simply reflects the fact that interpretation is an activity that unfolds in time. The web of interpretation begins to weave itself from the very first line of the very first page ("Can it be . . . ?" "Does he really mean . . . ?" "It would be interesting if . . ."); and the progress of interpretation as we pursue our journey through a body of extended writing is partly a matter of partial impressions and early expectations ceding to more holistic perspectives, as more and more of this body comes into view. At the same time, what the notion of surprise seems to flag is our inescapable investment in a particular conception of what interpretation involves—a conception in which the notion of discovery, and ideals of unity, occupy a central place. When we ask "What does *A* think about . . . ?," that part of us that remains untouched by sophisticated literary scruples cherishes the prospect of discovering an answer that we could present with reasonable coherence, telling it without being too self-conscious about the act of telling and without needing to lay the nuts and bolts on the table one by one to show how the story was pieced together, what was accepted and what thrown out.

It is an ideal of discovery and self-effacing interpretive unity that comes under special strain when one brings it to Ibn Taymiyya's work. For his views—on the topics that form the subject of this book certainly—turn out to require effort of a particularly concerted kind to be pieced together. The journey into Ibn Taymiyya's account often has all the excitement, yet also all the precariousness, of detective work undertaken under challenging conditions: the conflict of testimonies, the statement made only to be retracted, the circumstantial evidence here, the witness who unintentionally misleads the jury. Key positions (like the ethical positions of Muʿtazilite thinkers just referred to) are described in ways that appear like mis-descriptions and have to be carefully winnowed apart. Central distinctions are obscured and have to be dug up. Clear statements are made in one place that appear to be contradicted by the clear implications of others, making the evidence harder to unify. Theses are offered with promissory terseness but never extensively developed, leaving one wondering how seriously they were intended to be taken. Theses are voiced in polemical contexts, leaving one wondering whether they would have been voiced in others. Sifting through these elements exacts a high degree of textual focus and a far more self-conscious attention to the way one relates the different pieces that enter the story one tells. If readers of texts might sometimes be able to avoid dwelling too much on their own form-making activity, the form of Ibn Taymiyya's works places that self-forgetfulness out of reach and often forces one to show one's hand.

Such unselfconsciousness is of course never a virtue (if indeed it is even a possibility), and thinkers who place our interpretive fantasies under strain pay us a valuable service in forcing us to interrogate these fantasies and to reflect on the standards and aims that drive our activity. Yet to the extent that certain thinkers expose these fantasies to greater strain than others, this will be important to bring out in limning the character of their intellectual contribution. I would thus argue more strongly that those elements of the *how* of Ibn Taymiyya's writing that thematize the painter's hand by hindering it are ones that, far from being mere hindrances or disturbances to the *what* of his views, form an essential and substantive lesson to be learned about his oeuvre. They certainly compel us to ask a more pointed question regarding Ibn Taymiyya's aims in pressing the claim of ethical reason. They also provide us with resources for understanding why Ibn Taymiyya's legacy, speaking in elusive voices, may allow itself to be appropriated in plural ways and play host to competing interpretations.

My own conclusions about the principal tendency of Ibn Taymiyya's ethical thought and about the limited claim of reason that shapes it need to be read against this more complex appreciation of what it means to form conclusions about Ibn Taymiyya's thought. Although several of the moments of surprise that moved my own investigation forward have been filtered out of view in presenting the story that follows—faithfully to the tradition of inquiry, in its characteristic drive to purify the product of inquiry from the temporality of its process—I hope these actuating surprises, and the way they thematize the act of storytelling, will still be palpable.

So let me say something about how the discussion unfolds. In chapter 1 I set the stage for the discussion by first isolating certain features of Ibn Taymiyya's intellectual outlook that are of special relevance for approaching his ethical views—namely his advocacy of the *via media*, his engagement of rationalist methods, and his claim of harmony between reason and revelation—and by framing a broad comment about the nature of his writing and the significance of this particular subject in the structure of his concerns. I then turn to my main topic, Ibn Taymiyya's understanding of the nature of ethical value. Ibn Taymiyya proposes to carve a *via media* between Muʿtazilite and Ashʿarite approaches, but he appears to draw far nearer to the Muʿtazilite pole of this intellectual field in espousing an objectivist view of ethical value. Yet the Muʿtazilites, for their part, had given a prominent place to deontological considerations in spelling out their ethical ontology. A closer study of a number of Taymiyyan texts, by contrast, suggests that Ibn Taymiyya's objectivism is construed in overwhelmingly consequentialist or utilitarian terms. The central ethical concept for Ibn Taymiyya is utility (*manfaʿa, maṣlaḥa*), and the value of seemingly deontological types of acts is reduced to their utilitarian tendencies, not only for the individual but indeed for the social community.

With this insight in place, in chapter 2 I go on to address Ibn Taymiyya's ethical epistemology, focusing on two salient epistemic notions that he appeals to in his ethical remarks: reason (*ʿaql*) and nature (*fiṭra*). I begin by schematizing the argument (or thought experiment) articulated by Avicenna against including moral judgments in the perspective of human nature, an argument that can be taken to mark a broad distinction between nature and convention. I then turn to Ibn Taymiyya's counterclaim. In his evaluative deployment of the notion of *fiṭra*, I argue, Ibn Taymiyya primarily approaches *fiṭra* as a desiderative principle—as a principle of natural desire, alternately construed as a desire for what is pleasurable and as a desire for what is beneficial. Mined more carefully, this construal reveals that nature cannot be taken to carry the positive status or constitute the source of ethical guidance that Ibn Taymiyya's remarks invite us to assume, reflecting the positive scriptural connotations of the notion of *fiṭra*. Similar limitations attach to the resources of reason. While in certain writings Ibn Taymiyya shows an interest in developing the idea that moral judgments are the product of naturalistic empirical reasoning (*tajriba*), elsewhere he lays strong emphasis on the limitations of reason as a source for knowing the consequences of actions that constitute their ultimate value. The evaluative guidance available to us through our natural or internal epistemic resources thus turns out to be subject to serious limitations. For the full criterion of ethical value, we instead need to look to the revealed Law.

In chapter 3 I make an approach to Ibn Taymiyya's elusive relationship to Ashʿarite ethical thought. Ibn Taymiyya often appears to be locked in relations of bitter conflict with Ashʿarite theology, and this extends to questions of ethics.

A closer scrutiny of the facts, however, paints a different picture. A more nuanced survey of the evolving Ashʿarite view of ethics, particularly with regard to the ethical role of reason, and of the Ashʿarite assimilation of Avicenna's ethical ideas reveals Ibn Taymiyya's relationship to Ashʿarism to be one of concealed indebtedness. Some of Ibn Taymiyya's central contentions—not only his claim that right and wrong are known by reason but also his claim that they are known by (desiderative) nature and indeed his claim that value comes down to utility—find their immediate counterparts in Ashʿarite theology.

Turning away from questions about human morality, in chapter 4 I turn to consider what Ibn Taymiyya has to say about the morality of God. A positive emphasis on God's morality—on the fact that God's action is responsive to reasons, that God is just and indeed wise—is central to the ethical *via media* Ibn Taymiyya intends to chart, as it is also crucial for appraising his chief point of friction with the Ashʿarites. This friction expresses itself partly as a contestation of the notion of God's wisdom (*ḥikma*) and of the role of welfare (*maṣlaḥa*) among the aims of the divine Law. While Ashʿarite theorists had foregrounded considerations of welfare in their legal works, in doing so they had appeared to create tension for views they had expressed in a theological context—notably their conservative view of the evaluative grasp of human beings and their denial that concepts of purpose apply to God. I begin by offering a closer reading of this apparent tension within the Ashʿarite viewpoint and the strategies Ashʿarites devised to resolve it. I then detail Ibn Taymiyya's competing conception of God's morality by investigating two questions that respectively thematize God's wisdom and God's justice: Why does God command the actions He does? And why must God punish? Both topics reopen questions about the nature of ethical value broached in earlier chapters in relation to human morality and reinforce (but also problematize) the understanding of the primacy of utility that emerged there.

Turning back to the domain of human morality, in the first part of chapter 5 I seek to broaden the earlier inquiry into Ibn Taymiyya's ethical epistemology by transposing it to his legal writings and by addressing his understanding of how considerations of welfare stand to be engaged within the legal context. Examining Ibn Taymiyya's stance as expressed on three main levels—in his appeal to "pragmatic" grounds of need in his practical legal rulings, in his emphasis on preponderant utility as a determinant of legal rulings, and in his theoretical remarks about unattested interests (*maṣāliḥ mursala*) as a source of Law—an initial reading bespeaks a robust embrace of the human mind's ability to engage considerations of welfare directly and substantively in isolation from textual safeguards. Yet a closer reading holds up a different picture, displaying the textualist commitments of Ibn Taymiyya's thinking. This reading is supported by an analysis of his position on a debate that forms the hidden backbone of his legal appeal to pragmatic considerations, the debate about the value of actions prior to the advent of revelation (*ḥukm al-afʿāl qabla wurūd al-sharʿ*). The conclusion reached here dovetails with the understanding of Ibn Taymiyya's limited rationalism articulated in chapter 2. Having broadened the bases for this understanding, in the second part of the chapter I seek to locate it against two additional foils by raising a question about Ibn Taymiyya's deeper motivations for pressing the claim of moral reason and by raising a larger question about the relation between reason and revelation within his thought. Once again, there seem to be competing messages at work within Ibn Taymiyya's writings, but I argue that reason must be understood as possessing limited independence and as largely conditioned by, and departing from, the vantage point of religious revelation.

And while my aim in this book is not to effect the historical leap from past to present, in chapter 6 I conclude with some heuristic thoughts about how some of the bridges between past and present might be built.

I

Ethical Value between Deontology and Consequentialism

Framing Ibn Taymiyya's Project

"The best things are those that lie in the middle." They are not the kind of words that first come to mind when we open a discussion about that Ḥanbalite theologian whose legacy has cast such a long shadow on modern times.

Icon of extremist Islamist ideologues from Sadat to Bin Laden, revered spiritual leader of Wahhabi and salafi movements known for their religious rigorism and conservative bent, the Ibn Taymiyya we have come to know in our own times is a thinker we associate with hard attitudes that would appear to be worlds away from the message of moderation that stands out in these words.[1] The Ibn Taymiyya who looks back at us through the lens of history would seem to share in the spirit of his epigones. A member of the Ḥanbalite community of Damascus, displaced from Harran as a young boy as a result of the Mongol invasion, his life is full of conflict and upheaval that mirror the upheaval of the Islamic world around him as Mamluk rule comes under Mongol threat and betoken a thinker who does not mince trenchant views. Looking across the sixty-five years of his life's work from 1263 to 1328 CE in Syria and Egypt, we see the firebrand reformer and indefatigable polemicist who launches himself on the dominant intellectual schools and spiritual practices of his time in a spirit of tireless critique, antagonizing many of his contemporaries with controversial positions that challenge prevailing views and call for wide-ranging reform. He decries the visitation of saints' tombs, antagonizing popular Sufi practice; he denounces legal stratagems and the common use of divorce oaths, antagonizing widespread legal practice; he rallies to a literalist, seemingly anthropomorphist view of God, exciting the animus of Ashʿarite theologians. He composes polemics against the monistic theosophy of Ibn ʿArabī and his followers, yet more polemics against the *falāsifa*, and still has energy left over for the Ashʿarite *mutakallimūn*. Sidelining time-honored religious authorities, he calls for a return to the purer sources of the faith: to the insight solely available to the early generations of the Muslim community (*salaf*) who stood closest to the age of prophetic inspiration, to the revealed text itself unmediated by artificial interpretive accretions and school allegiances. His life a never-ending stream of controversies, he is put on trial and imprisoned several times in his life in both Syria and Egypt, eventually dying in prison in the citadel of Damascus, the fitting end to a life of defiance that "opposed by word and deed almost every aspect of religion practiced in the Mamluk Empire," in the words of one commentator.[2]

Both as his image has been projected in the present and as it has often been historically understood, Ibn Taymiyya has seemed to speak not for the middle but for the extremes. And yet the notion of a balance, or a middle road, is one that runs the length of his sprawling work and provides it with one of its organizing motifs. In his landmark study of Ibn Taymiyya in the middle of the twentieth century, Henri Laoust was emphasizing the centrality of this notion when he connected it to Ibn Taymiyya's construction of the privileged religious grouping designated as *ahl al-sunna wa'l-jamāʿa*, which represents the truest repository of the thought of the Prophet and the *salaf*, albeit a repository less real than ideal. On Laoust's reading, it refers to "an ideal grouping whose doctrines, still waiting to be created rather than already constituted, form a kind of mean between diverse opinions."[3] It is this notion likewise that Yahya Michot recently sought to highlight in a self-conscious effort to restore the image of a thinker tarnished by his self-proclaimed disciples in the modern age, who have cast him as the patron saint of everything modernity abhors—of an "opposition to reason and mysticism, of fundamentalism and intolerance, of radical extremism"—and thereby blinded us to his character as a "master of the *via media*, the middle way that is at the heart of traditional Islam."[4]

Ibn Taymiyya as a master of moderation—of what he himself refers to widely in his works as *al-wasaṭ* or *al-qawl al-mutawassiṭ*. It is not the only revision of popular perceptions or immediate impressions that a closer consideration of his works would invite. Recent scholarship has slowly begun to prise loose a set of earlier perceptions of Ibn Taymiyya not unrelated to the image of his extremism, which, beguiled by the surface of his traditionalist commitments and his polemics against the rational sciences, overlooked the subtler relationship in which he places scripture and human reason and the depth of his engagement of the rational sciences against which he wages his wars. Since its earliest history Ḥanbalism has often been associated with a fideistic attachment to the text and a suspicion of rationalist methods encapsulated in Aḥmad ibn Ḥanbal's famed motto that "we do not ask how" (*bilā kayfa*) regarding scriptural descriptions of God. In the same century that Ibn Taymiyya was born, the eminent Damascene Ḥanbalite scholar Muwaffaq al-Dīn ibn Qudāma (d. 1223) would issue a book-length admonition against perusing works of speculative or dialectical theology (*kalām*) typical of the traditionalist stance.[5] Ibn Taymiyya's polemics against the philosophical mysticism of Ibn ʿArabī, the views of the *falāsifa* and the *mutakallimūn*, by contrast, attest to a depth of reading that flouts received commonplaces about traditionalist attitudes toward such works and point to the multiple ways in which their resources seep into his own thought. It is not without justice that the Shāfiʿite scholar Shams al-Dīn al-Dhahabī (d. 1348) would exclaim, in an oft-cited passage, that Ibn Taymiyya had "repeatedly swallowed the poison of the philosophers and their works."[6] This is, after all, one of the reasons, as has been recently suggested, why Ibn Taymiyya—contrary, once again, to popular perceptions of his prominence throughout Islamic religious history—had a troubled relationship to the traditionalists of his time and was regarded with an attitude of "fluctuating scepticism" within Damascene Ḥanbalite circles. Both during his life and after his death, Ibn Taymiyya's influence remained limited until the eighteenth century, when his legacy witnessed a sea-change and he was catapulted from "a little-read scholar with problematic and controversial views" to a central figure in the Islamic religious tradition for both Ḥanbalite and non-Ḥanbalite Sunni scholars.[7]

For some, the aspects just outlined—Ibn Taymiyya's emphasis on the *via media* and his openness to rational methods of inquiry—are intrinsically linked. Ibn Taymiyya's notion of the *via media*, as Merlin Swartz suggested some time ago, has to be understood less as a matter of what it excludes than what it includes. For it "does not mean simply or primarily that truth (or the truth) somehow lies in the middle ground between two opposing extremes. It means rather that truth has a bi-polar character so that the two opposing extremes, instead of being excluded, are actually included within the truth in something of a dialectical fashion.... *Wasaṭ* means that doctrinal error or heresy results when one element of the truth is elevated to the level of the whole." This notion of the mean, Swartz continues, provides the basis for Ibn Taymiyya's polemical or critical confrontations with different movements. Yet what is more important is that it also provides the basis for his more positive engagement with these movements. For it allows the recognition that "even though their systems of thought contained error, they also contained elements of truth," and to that extent "they were to be taken seriously," thereby justifying "at least a limited openness vis-à-vis the heterodox ideologies, and ... the incorporation of elements of their thought."[8]

In thematizing the relationship between the negative and positive aspects of Ibn Taymiyya's task, Swartz's remarks pick up on an important space of questioning that opens out from Ibn Taymiyya's work. But what is more relevant here is to connect this synthetic description to yet another facet of Ibn Taymiyya's understanding of his task which ties in with the facets already highlighted. For Ibn Taymiyya's engagement with rationalist methods must be seen additionally in light of a broader headline that stamps his entire work with its special character and gives the content of his distinctive intellectual vocation. "The sound view," he writes in his creedal commentary *Sharḥ al-ʿAqīda al-Iṣbahāniyya*, "is the one that agrees with sound revelation and plain reason [*ṣaḥīḥ al-manqūl wa-ṣarīḥ al-maʿqūl*], which unites the elements of truth that different views contain and steers clear from the error they contain."[9] The explicit theme of some of Ibn Taymiyya's best-known works, the constant refrain of almost all others, it is this claim of harmony between reason and revelation that provides his readers with yet another context for his engagement with rationalist methods and yet another hallmark of his synthetic aims. For this claim cannot be held down without confronting the competing ways in which other thinkers have proposed to relate the two terms of the equation and the ways they have specified the content of reason.

It is this plexus of interconnecting headlines—Ibn Taymiyya's espousal of a *via media*, his positive engagement of rationalist methods, his claim of harmony between human reason and the divine word—that provides the framework for the particular questions that form the topic of this book. The task of this book will be to follow these headlines to one of their most important theological lairs in order to consider their significance more closely and to deepen the way we understand them. For it is precisely under these headlines that Ibn Taymiyya invites us to read his contribution to a debate that had sent up a high flame among Muslim thinkers from the earliest days of *kalām* and whose heartland was constituted by a set of interlinked questions about the standards of value that govern the actions of human beings and the actions of God. Are there things that we can count on God to do? Are there limits to what God can do? Can God, for example, punish the innocent, fail to reward the virtuous? Can He determine our actions and then punish us for them? What notion of justice do God's actions answer to, and how does this relate to the notion of justice we are familiar with from the ordinary human world? Are there real, objective standards of action common to all intelligent beings—standards universally accessible to human beings by reason? How do these standards relate to the actions prescribed by scripture? How can God be answerable to moral standards without this undermining His omnipotence? How can our freedom to act, for that matter, be squared with God's omnipotence?

The possibilities of response held out by these kinds of questions were riven with difficult conflicts. This was a conflict between different demands generated by the conception of God—His justice against His power. It was also, more implicitly, a conflict between the demands of God and the needs of human beings, for whom the ability to have faith in a just God represents a deep-seated psychological and spiritual need. Such conflicts would seem to be deeply inscribed in this field of possibility, as attested by their frequent recurrence in other monotheistic traditions of theological inquiry, notably in Christianity. As we often tell the history of these debates in the Islamic context, Muslim theologians responded to the conflict by resolutely seizing the competing horns and pulling, producing the two dominant factions that appear as ideal types in any reading of Islamic theological history. Mu'tazilite theologians pulled in the direction of divine justice and the primacy of human reason; Ash'arite theologians in the direction of divine power and the primacy of the divine word.

Sketched in broad brush strokes, the theological positions articulated by these two sides have often seemed easy to capture in a few telling formulations. The Mu'tazilites argued: certain kinds of actions—such as lying or injustice, gratitude or ingratitude—are inherently good or bad and are known by reason to be so; the divine Law merely confirms and particularizes that native knowledge. These standards apply no less to divine than to human actions, and God, being wise, never does evil and only does good, as these notions are commonly understood. God, thus, does not punish the innocent; reward the undeserving; fail to reward those who have deserved it through their works; impose obligations that people cannot fulfill. In these and other ways, God is just in His dealings and never fails in His moral obligations. Performing a volte-face against this view, the Ash'arites had responded: reason gives us no such information; actions are instead rendered good or bad through the divine command or prohibition that attaches to them. In legislating actions, God does not respond to values that are already in the world—to intrinsic characteristics of actions—but rather creates value by the very act of commanding. The answer to the question "Why does God command the particular things He does?" comes down to God's arbitrary will. God Himself could never be subject to any Law. If God is just, it is not in a sense that would place Him and human beings under a shared yoke. Neither obliged to reward nor obliged to spare from punishment, His dealings with human beings are as free as those of a master disposing his chattel.[10] On this story of half-heard conversations and theological reversals, it is Ash'arite voluntarism that became ascendant in much of the Sunni world—though not the Shi'i world, where Mu'tazilism continued to flourish—and Mu'tazilite ethical rationalism was by and large decisively sidelined.

Either justice *or* power; *either* the demands of divinity *or* the needs of human beings. Yet the conflict between these terms was too strong to be entirely expunged, and this was particularly in evidence when it came to the question of the human freedom to act. For while a robust acknowledgment of human freedom might conflict with a robust assertion of God's power, a thoroughgoing determinism also conflicts with the demands implicit in God's own promulgation of the Law. If human acts are determined by God, what sense does it make for God to command us to act in certain ways against others? Even those who pulled in the direction of God's power, such as the late Ash'arite theologian Fakhr al-Dīn al-Rāzī (d. 1210), would at times retreat before such questions and declare them a mystery (*sirr*) inaccessible to a satisfying rational resolution.[11]

Reprising the debate, Ibn Taymiyya would describe it using several overlapping dichotomies: as a conflict between God's dominion (*mulk*) and God's praiseworthiness (*ḥamd*), between the Law (*sharʿ*) and divine determination (*qadar*), and also between two types of monotheism: what he terms the acknowledgment of God's lordship (*tawḥīd al-rubūbiyya*) and the acknowledgment of His divinity (*tawḥīd al-ilāhiyya*). Accusing both parties of failing to produce a fruitful conciliation between these conflicting demands and distancing himself from al-Rāzī's surrender to mystery, he would call for a new, comprehensible conciliation.[12]

The focus of this book falls on a set of questions that formed one of the central threads of the debate just outlined and that concern the nature of moral standards and the nature of our epistemological access to them. Such questions were traditionally grouped under the rubric that came to be known as *al-taḥsīn wa'l-taqbīḥ* or "the determination of good and bad" (or "right and wrong").[13] In revisiting this strand of the debate, as in its conceptual partners, what is crucial is that Ibn Taymiyya's contribution presents itself as an affirmation of a *via media* and also as a claim parsed in distinctively objectivist and rationalist terms. Good and bad are objective qualities, and they can be known by reason, Ibn Taymiyya suggests, articulating a position that had earlier counted the Muʿtazilites as its most vocal exponents.

In this chapter my aim will be to present this moderating claim, focusing on the first aspect—the nature of ethical value, or moral ontology—and deferring to the next chapter the second aspect—our knowledge of ethical value, or moral epistemology. It is a task, as we will see, that turns out to confront an unusual set of challenges deriving from Ibn Taymiyya's own presentation of the issues. These are challenges that have something significant to tell us about the character of Ibn Taymiyya's engagement with the topic and indeed of his writing as a whole and about the difficulties of establishing a unified account of his views. Given these difficulties, it is important to begin with some preliminary orienting comments on the nature of his writing and what it means to look for his views; and by another comment about the place of the topic in the structure of his concerns and written output.

"FROM ONE DAY to the next," al-Dhahabī tells us, "he would write four quires or more of exegesis, jurisprudence, the principles of Islamic religion, and refutation[s] of the philosophers and of the speculative sciences. It is no exaggeration [to say] that up to now his writings have reached five hundred volumes." This description of Ibn Taymiyya's writing habits may reflect a degree of hyperbole that was common practice in scholarly biographies, with their peculiar mixture of eulogy and fact.[14] Yet in foregrounding the explosiveness of Ibn Taymiyya's writing, it captures one of the familiar challenges faced by readers seeking to ascertain his views on any given subject. It is not so much the explosiveness in the quantity of his work, however, as of its quality that presents the gravest challenge.[15] The thirty-seven volumes of Ibn Taymiyya's *Collected Fatwas* (*Majmūʿ Fatāwā*) may be rather misleadingly titled, as it includes not only fatwas but also a number of longer and more autonomous works. Yet this choice of title appropriately reflects his predilection for the literary format of short compositions—for what his foremost biographer, Ibn ʿAbd al-Hādī (d. 1343), classifies variously as principles (*qawāʿid*), epistles (*rasāʾil*), and responsa (*ajwiba*), conveying a disciple's mixture of eulogistic intention and understandable helplessness when remarking that "it is hard to fix with precision and enumerate" these works.[16] It also reflects, more specifically, his reliance on the fatwa—traditionally a response to laymen's requests for legal opinions about concrete situations—as a vehicle for the expression of his views, using it to discuss not only legal topics but also a wider range of subjects, notably theological ones. It is this expanded significance of the fatwa that Michot picks up on when he describes Ibn Taymiyya as a "theologian-mufti."[17]

In adopting the fatwa as a vehicle for the expression of theological views, Ibn Taymiyya to a great extent transforms the genre. Practical legal fatwas are not literary productions in the first instance, as Bernard Weiss observes. Ibn Taymiyya's collection of fatwas, by contrast, displays him as "very much a *writer* of fatwas, a writer who adopts the fatwa as a literary form." His fatwas, similarly, often abandon the brevity typically associated with legal opinions and run to the length of self-contained treatises. Yet however Ibn Taymiyya might transform the genre, his use of it preserves some of its limitations, particularly its circumstantial character—the compositional occasion is provided by a question that happens to be posed by an interested party—and its unsuitability for systematically developed reflection.[18] The circumstantial nature of Ibn Taymiyya's output posed barriers to its efficient collection after his death and continues to impede efforts to produce a reliable chronology for his works.[19] Yet even more troubling for his readers is the barrier this poses to the ambition of arriving at a coherent and unified understanding of his thought.

There is much to suggest, however, that this barrier is not merely a construction of Ibn Taymiyya's preferred literary format. His shorter works, including his fatwas, after all take their place next to an impressive series of independent works running into several volumes each. These include, notably, *Darʾ taʿāruḍ al-ʿaql wa'l-naql* (Averting the Conflict between Reason and Revelation), criticizing the relationship between reason and scripture as viewed by *mutakallimūn* but also *falāsifa; Bayān talbīs al-jahmiyya* (Exposing the Jahmite Deceit), confronting the Ashʿarite view of the divine attributes; and the *Minhāj al-sunna* (The Way of the Sunna), directed against the Shīʿites and more specifically the work of the Shīʿite theologian al-ʿAllāma al-Ḥillī (d. 1325). Yet readers of these long works have often found themselves faced with a separate set of challenges in trying to piece together a cohesive understanding of Ibn Taymiyya's views, this time deriving from his style. For the forward-moving unfolding of these works may often be guided by a certain general script, but the discussion often progresses like floodwater, bursting into every available nook and cranny along the way before returning to its course and engaging in multiple sideshows that weaken the cohesion of any argument under way. As with Russian dolls (as Michot has suggested in a more vivid image) or as in the *1001 Nights*, one argument always pops open for another to appear within it, and one plot always gives way to another and another.[20] The reader's experience, already fractured by such digressiveness, is fractured again by what we may call, as positively as possible, the responsiveness of Ibn Taymiyya's writing. Many of his texts bear the aspect of a mosaic of apostrophized words: bringing up his subject, he proceeds to quote a head-spinning array of writers at length, to then comment, question, and subject to critique. His own thinking takes place in the interstices—interstices all the slimmer for the scriptural quotations with which they are heavily laced. His positive views are often framed by a context of doxographical report, commentary, and critique that sometimes makes it hard to decisively tell apart what is in his own voice and what is in others' or what is positively as against dialectically affirmed, and that certainly makes for meager pickings when it comes to isolating the direct expository discussion of any subject.

Those of Ibn Taymiyya's readers who have remarked such features in the past have wavered between whether to count them as signs of intellectual weakness or as interpretive keys to his underlying intellectual program. Wael Hallaq, thus, has suggested that the repetitiveness and lack of a "systematic and orderly mode of exposition" in Ibn Taymiyya's work reflect the negative act of dissuasion, as against the positive act of persuasion, at which he fundamentally aims. For Ibn Taymiyya, "a systematic and complete presentation of a body of thought was not a significant concern." More recently, Ovamir Anjum has contrasted Ibn Taymiyya's "deconstructive project" with the "synthetic impulse" of theologians like al-Ghazālī (d. 1111) and al-Rāzī, whose project of harmonizing reason and revelation he otherwise sees him as continuing.[21] Michot, on his part, does not tie his characterization of Ibn Taymiyya's status as a "theologian-mufti" to an explicit statement of Ibn Taymiyya's intellectual program. Yet the effect of this designation is the same, namely to interrogate the expectations of unity and systematicity with which we approach Ibn Taymiyya's work. "Influenced by/responsive to circumstances as they are," he writes, "the opinions of a theologian-mufti cannot be expected to constitute a comprehensive, integrated system of thought. How can a road, even a straight road, not be intimately connected to the contours of the landscape it is traversing?"[22]

Such perspectives, and the features of Ibn Taymiyya's work they respond to, would seem to call into doubt the wisdom of aspiring to produce unified accounts of Ibn Taymiyya's views. The challenge seems far greater than is the case with theologians who adopt more systematic, expository forms of writing, such as al-Ghazālī or al-Rāzī, or prolific Muʿtazilite writers like ʿAbd al-Jabbār and his disciples. These contrasts, of course, are instructive precisely in reminding us of the sheer pervasiveness of this type of interpretive challenge. Al-Ghazālī is a case in point, his seemingly conflicting pronouncements about the nature of causality across different works having given rise to vexed debates about the perspective that could unify them. Similarly, for all their formidable literary production, as I have suggested elsewhere, the Baṣran Muʿtazilites present their readers with no mean interpretive task, offering an exiguous amount of positive exposition as against dialectical engagement and sending their readers hunting among the dialectical sections of their work for evidence that can be forcibly marshaled together to constitute what might then be self-consciously called "the Muʿtazilite view."[23]

Here and elsewhere, the interpreter's hand cannot be easily removed from the painting. Yet even if we allow the contrast between Ibn Taymiyya and such thinkers to stand—and there will be much in what follows to support that contrast—it seems to me that it would be a mistake to exaggerate the fragmentation and negative character of Ibn Taymiyya's thought. That his intellectual project must be read in more positive terms, after all, is strongly suggested by the very headline of a *via media* that organizes it, which architecturally demands a moment of thesis or (as Swartz emphasizes) synthesis. Similarly, what prevents Ibn Taymiyya's readers from swooning when faced with the vertiginous plotlessness with which he often proceeds is the fact that certain general plots recur with unfailing regularity, that his writing keeps gravitating toward a set of thematic clusters and theses with distinct internal relations to one another. Taken together, these revisited theses add up to a robust overall vision sustained with impressive consistency throughout his work. The concern with the fruitfulness of looking for Ibn Taymiyya's theological views would partly play itself out in the question whether, peering closer to such thematic clusters and theses, we find that he develops them with sufficient unity and in sufficient detail—whether "theses" become sufficiently "theories"—to make them the worthwhile subject of investigation. But as this last evaluative accent ("a worthwhile subject") betrays, our judgments of what counts as "sufficient" detail or unity, like our sense of the general "fruitfulness" of the effort, may also depend on broader judgments about the significance of the specific subject at stake.

What can we say about the topic of ethics ("the determination of good and bad") in these terms? Taken narrowly, it is a topic to which Ibn Taymiyya does not appear to have devoted a single independent text—none, at least, that survived.[24] The most concentrated discussions of the topic include a short epistle in volume 8 of the *Majmūʿ Fatāwā* and an exchange with the *falāsifa* in his work against the logicians, *al-Radd ʿala'l-manṭiqiyyīn*. Yet outside these texts it appears throughout his work as a recurrent motif, revisited in a variety of thematic clusters and argumentative contexts. The relative poverty of its independent textual appearances cannot be translated into a sign of its marginality within the structure of Ibn Taymiyya's concerns. I have already mentioned one higher-level thesis with which this topic is linked, the claim of concordance between reason and revelation. The theological problematic with which it is more immediately linked is the thematic cluster that concerns the relationship between God's justice (or wisdom, in Ibn Taymiyya's more usual parlance) and God's power, a theme of colossal significance within his work. Thus, it is under the discussion of this tension, using the dichotomous terms of *shar'* and *qadar*, that Ibn Taymiyya brings up the topic in his creed *al-'Aqīda al-Tadmuriyya*. It is in the same thematic vicinity that he brings it up again in many of the short epistles and fatwas collected in volume 8 of his *Majmū' Fatāwā*, which are notably organized by the theme of *qadar*. Construed less narrowly, the question of ethics puts out a rich set of thematic feelers into topics of crucial importance for Ibn Taymiyya's outlook explored in a variety of textual locations—his discussion of prophecy, his understanding of the natural human constitution (*fiṭra*), his view of the role of welfare (*maṣlaḥa*) in the Law. These richer thematic affinities will form a key print of the story that follows.

The topic of ethics and the conceptual filaments with which it is affiliated are addressed with varying degrees of depth within Ibn Taymiyya's work, and it must be admitted that even in the best of times, the theses we receive do not rise to the analytical rigor of fully developed theories. When one seeks to peer closer to the detail of the views Ibn Taymiyya expresses in order to pull their weave into sharp focus, the threads often begin to thin, and the burden of argument turns out to be carried by solitary threads—by what scholars of hadith may have called *āḥād*—that appear in unexpected locations and often fail to reappear. As I will also show, his discussions of value are at times riven by textual tensions, and his ethical views are obscured by the intellectual compass he himself offers for locating them within the classical debates on the topic. The most immediate defense of nevertheless striving for a unified narrative will seem psychological: where appearances are in disaccord, or where what immediately meets the eye begins to suggest something different, interpreters feel compelled to push the heuristic of interpretive coherence as far as it can go and to follow through with their surprises.

Yet on the one hand, it is clear that this interpretive pursuit does not go unrewarded. It reveals Ibn Taymiyya's ethical understanding to be organized by a number of definite contours, even if some of its features could be the subject of debate. In this respect, the balance of definite and indefinite, of detail and unity, within his account—taken in combination with the centrality of the subject for his vision as a whole, the interest of the contribution it appears to promise, and the contemporary influence of his ideas—seems sufficient to warrant a concerted interpretive attention that pushes this account as far as it allows. At the same time, I would suggest that the very interpretive tensions and indeterminacies carried by Ibn Taymiyya's work provide their own kind of warrant for such attention. If his work invites conflicting interpretations, and if what meets the eye may demand digging beyond the appearances, this is a point that is important to bring out in engaging his legacy. This means, however, that the problems of form have to be kept in view throughout the effort to determine the content, making the self-conscious thematization of the form of Ibn Taymiyya's writing and the obstacles it sets to one's form-making activity integral to the interpretive task.

Ibn Taymiyya's Moral Objectivism: A Revised Muʿtazilism?

With these orienting remarks in place, we are ready to grab hold of the main thread of our discussion in this chapter: What makes actions good? In considering Ibn Taymiyya's understanding of ethical value, I will seek to make a first approach to his relationship to his interlocutors and more immediately to the views of the Muʿtazilites with which his own views seem prima facie to be most closely partnered. My argument, to preview it here, will be that this initial similarity belies fundamental underlying differences. The shape of Ibn Taymiyya's conception of value and the differences that separate him from Muʿtazilite ethics reveal themselves most starkly in a tension between the deontological and consequentialist components of his account. This tension, I will suggest, resolves in favor of the latter: the primary notion that organizes Ibn Taymiyya's conception of ethical value is that of utility or welfare. In this section, I will begin by placing on display a key passage in which Ibn Taymiyya outlines his ethical position. It is a position, as already previewed, that arrives as an avowal of a *via media*. Taking my cues from this passage, the task will then to be to flesh out his position more fully and, zooming out, to re-create some of his theological topography in order to determine more accurately where he stands within it. Having brought out the main tension at stake in Ibn Taymiyya's conception of value, I will devote the next section to resolving it by bringing a wider range of his writings into the conversation.

"The question of whether reason determines what is good and bad," states Ibn Taymiyya, "is the subject of notorious controversy." On this subject, people divide into three positions: "two extremes and a middle" (*ṭarafān wa-wasaṭ*). Here they are, in sequence:

> One extreme is the position of those who affirm good and bad, and who make these out to be essential attributes of acts that are inseparably attached to them [*ṣifāt dhātiyya li'l-fiʿl lāzima lahu*], and make out the Law to have the sole task of revealing those attributes, not of causally producing any of them. This is the view of the Muʿtazilites, and it is a weak one. And if in addition to this one transfers to God what applies to His creation [*qiyās al-rabb ʿalā khalqihi*]—thus saying that what is good for created beings to do is also good for the Creator, and what is bad for created beings to do is also bad for the

> Creator—one is led to the falsehoods of the [exponents of free will][25] and what they have said regarding the determination of justice and injustice. These are assimilationists with respect to acts [*mushabbihāt al-afʿāl*], assimilating the Creator to His creatures and creatures to the Creator on the level of their acts. This is a false view, just as it is false to liken the Creator to His creatures and the creature to the Creator on the level of their attributes [*ṣifāt*].

A few lines down, the second extreme comes into view:

> The other extreme in the question of the determination of good and bad is the position of those who say that actions do not contain attributes that constitute [evaluative] qualifications [*aḥkām*] nor attributes that constitute the causes [*ʿilal*] of qualifications. Rather, [God] issued a command for one of two [equally possible] similar actions [*mutamāthilayn*] out of sheer arbitrary will, not due to any wise purpose, and not in order to promote any welfare [*maṣlaḥa*] in either the realm of creation [*khalq*] or command [*amr*]. And they say that it is possible that God might command one to polytheism, or forbid one from worshipping Him alone, and it is possible that He command injustice and foul deeds, and forbid righteousness and piety, and that the qualifications that attach to acts[26] are only a [contingent or extrinsic] relation and association [*nisba wa-iḍāfa*]. And what is right [*maʿrūf*] is not right in itself [*fī nafsihi*], in their view, nor is what is wrong [*munkar*] in itself wrong. Thus, when God says, "[The Prophet] commands them that which is right and forbids them that which is wrong, he makes lawful for them all good things and prohibits for them only the foul" [Q 7:157],[27] the real meaning of that, for them, is that He commands them what He commands them and forbids them what He forbids them, makes lawful for them what He makes lawful for them and prohibits for them what He prohibits for them. Command and prohibition, making lawful and prohibiting, are in their view not [about] what is right or wrong, good or foul in itself [*fī nafs al-amr*], unless this is taken to refer to that which agrees with people's natural appetites [*mā yulāʾimu al-ṭibāʿ*], and this does not entail, according to them, that God loves what is right and hates what is wrong.

This view too "is weak, and in conflict with the Qur'an and the Sunna, the consensus of the *salaf* and the jurists, in addition to conflicting with plain reason [*ṣarīḥ al-maʿqūl*]." Having outlined these two extremes, Ibn Taymiyya turns to articulate the alternative:

> The jurists and the majority of Muslims say: "God promulgated the prohibition of prohibited things," and "they are prohibited"; and "God promulgated

the obligation to perform obligatory things," and "they are obligatory."[28] Here we have two things: the act of promulgating obligation and prohibition, which is God's act of speech and His address [*khiṭāb*]; and obligation and prohibition, which are attributes [*ṣifa*] of acts. God is knowing and wise [*ḥakīm*], and knowing the benefits that qualifications comprise [*mā tataḍammanuhu al-aḥkām min al-maṣāliḥ*], He issued commands and prohibitions based on His knowledge of the benefits and harms that commands and prohibitions, and the things commanded and forbidden, involve for His servants. He established the qualification of an act; as for its attribute, this might already have been actual [*thābit*] prior to the divine address. There are then . . . three types of acts:

[1] One is the case in which an act contains benefit or harm [*maṣlaḥa aw-mafsada*], [and it would do so] even if the Law had not come to report that, the way it is known that justice serves the good of the world [*maṣlaḥat al-ʿālam*] and injustice tends to its harm. This type is [in itself, respectively,] good and bad, and the fact that it is bad may be known by reason and by revelation [*al-sharʿ*], without meaning that an attribute was assigned to the act that had not existed before. But from the fact that this is bad, it does not follow that one who performs it will be punished in the hereafter if the Law has not informed us of that. This is where the hard-line advocates of [reason's] determination of good and bad went wrong. . . . [For] God said, "We never chastise, until We send forth a Messenger" [Q 17:15]. . . .

[2] The second type is the one in which the Lawgiver commands something and it becomes good, and forbids something and it becomes bad, and acts acquire the attributes of goodness and badness through the Lawgiver's address.

[3] The third type is the one in which the Lawgiver commands something in order to put His servant to the test, to see whether he will obey or disobey Him, without it being [really] desired that the act commanded be performed. An example is the way Abraham was commanded to sacrifice his son.[29]

There will be much to take in in this long passage, even for those familiar with the topic and its habitual turns of phrase and organizing distinctions. Yet the best place to begin is the most rudimentary, by considering just how the identity of the sides that frame Ibn Taymiyya's *via media* on the topic should be filled out. The most basic identification may seem obvious, and it is indicated clearly in the first excerpt quoted ("the view of the Muʿtazilites"), which invokes a bifurcation of intellectual landscape that will be familiar to students of this region of

Islamic theological history. The two sides represent the views respectively adopted by Muʿtazilite and Ashʿarite theologians. Yet the opening of the epistle adds further texture to this bifurcation. The view that reason declares what is right and wrong, Ibn Taymiyya states, has been taken by the Ḥanafites and by "many" of the Mālikites, Shāfiʿites, and Ḥanbalites; and "it is the view of Muslims of most stripes, of the Jews, the Christians, the Mageans and others."[30] The opposing view, the Ashʿarite one, is likewise adopted by "many" of the Shāfiʿites, Mālikites, and Ḥanbalites. This richer specification of the sides offers us an important reminder of the diffusion of theological views among the legal schools and of the regular conjunction established between certain legal schools and certain theological creeds, notably between Ḥanafism and Muʿtazilite theology, and Shāfiʿism and Ashʿarite theology. And in doing so, it also invites a question about the relationship of Ḥanbalism to such creeds, and thus a question about the genealogy of Ibn Taymiyya's own positioning.

The traditional hostility shown by Ḥanbalite scholars to the practice of *kalām* would seem to close up the space for such questions in advance. Yet there had been prominent scholars within Ḥanbalite history who had overcome this traditional suspicion to engage in more rationalistic forms of theological inquiry, including the Qāḍī Abū Yaʿlā (d. 1066), whose *al-Muʿtamad fī uṣūl al-dīn*, as Michael Cook suggests, followed "an intellectual style which is Muʿtazilite rather than Ḥanbalite in inspiration." In this work Abū Yaʿlā had in fact adopted an Ashʿarite position, disavowing the view that reason offers ethical deliverances.[31] His eminent student Ibn ʿAqīl (d. 1119) had followed in his footsteps, opening himself to this mode of theological inquiry with even greater gusto, and having put his flirtation with Muʿtazilism behind him, he would later align himself with the Ashʿarite view in claiming that value is determined by the Law and that "reason is not ruler but subject [*maḥkūm ʿalayhi lā ḥākim*] when it comes to these [i.e., evaluative] judgements."[32] In constructing his context, on the other hand, Ibn Taymiyya calls attention to a number of Ḥanbalites who had adopted a rationalist view of ethical judgments, including Abuʾl-Ḥasan al-Tamīmī (d. 982) and Abuʾl-Khaṭṭāb al-Kalwadhānī (d. 1116), also a student of Abū Yaʿlā.[33]

More arresting than this particularization of the sides will be the bold claim of majority that Ibn Taymiyya pins to the rationalist view ("Muslims of most stripes")—a claim of majority promoted to one of consensus in his later dismissal of the Ashʿarite position as conflicting with "the consensus [*ijmāʿ*] of the *salaf* and the jurists," besides the dictates of "plain reason." This claim, tirelessly repeated throughout Ibn Taymiyya's writings, may fall on our ears with some surprise. Ibn Taymiyya is speaking to us, after all, from the end of the thirteenth century and the beginning of the fourteenth, at a time when Ashʿarism had become a redoubtable force, and the rejection of ethical rationalism had been central to its theological program. Whence, then, these confident descriptions of the intellectual demographic?[34] One answer to this question will have to wait until a later stage of our discussion to be considered, but the simplest may lie in recalling that claims of such kind often have a rhetorical function distinct from their factual accuracy. This is a point that Ibn Taymiyya's own predecessors, al-Kalwadhānī and Ibn ʿAqīl, had earlier brought home when each had claimed majority for their conflicting positions on the topic.[35] What is particularly significant for our context is to note the even richer specification of the sides that Ibn Taymiyya contributes in dismissing the Ashʿarite view when he invokes the authority of the *salaf*, the support of scripture, but also the congruence with reason—a congruence that can partly be taken to interpret his reference to the views of non-Muslim communities.

And it is certainly a claim of reason, and a strong affirmation of the objective reality of the values of actions, that stands out limpidly in this passage. The values of certain acts "may be known by reason and by revelation [*al-sharʿ*]"; they may be "actual [*thābit*] prior to the divine address" and actual "even if the Law had not come to report that." Reason can tell us what is right and wrong; right and wrong exist independently, and revelation does not constitute them. The epistemology of value and its ontology—two questions that had always been deeply intermeshed in the classical debates yet which we will need to address in sequence, deferring the first thesis to the next chapter and devoting this chapter to an investigation of the second.

Now, approaching the subject with traditional theological divisions in mind, Ibn Taymiyya's view would immediately seem to lay down strong bridges to the rationalism and (more relevantly here) the objectivism that we have come to associate with the Muʿtazilite school. For this—to slowly begin conjuring the theological field into view—was a conception of value that had formed a distinctive feature of the Muʿtazilite ethical outlook as this had been honed across many generations of thinkers, from the early expressions of faith in divine justice to the sophisticated theories of later members of the Baṣran school who often provide us with the sharpest window into Muʿtazilite ethical thought. Looking through that window, the moral universe we see described by the Baṣran Muʿtazilites is one in which acts divided into two chief evaluative categories: good (*ḥasan*) and bad (*qabīḥ*), the former subdividing again into the obligatory (*wājib*), the recommended or supererogatory (*nadb* and *tafaḍḍul*), and what we may call "plain good" or permissible (*mubāḥ*). In articulating their view of these attributes, the Muʿtazilites had made a point of highlighting the real ontological features of acts that provide them with their anchor. Acts possess their qualifications (*aḥkām*), Ibn Mattawayh (d. 1076?) would write, on account of "something to do with them and an attribute that exclusively attaches to them [*li-amr yarjiʿu ilayhā wa-li-ṣifa takhuṣṣuhā*]."[36] When acts are seen to carry a certain value, his teacher ʿAbd al-Jabbār (d. 1025) had earlier argued, there has to be a reason for this fact that distinguishes them from other acts that lack this value. There must be a certain something that "exclusively attaches to them" (*amr yakhtaṣṣu bihi*) and "necessarily entails" (*yaqtaḍī*) their status—something, moreover, that constitutes an intelligible (*ma ʿqūl*) component.[37] If the evaluative status of acts depends on their intrinsic features, it is clear that it does not derive from God's command and prohibition. Ibn Mattawayh would again furnish a hallmark expression of this point when stating that God's prohibition "reveals the badness of what is bad—it does not causally necessitate it to be so; His command, likewise, reveals what is good—it does not causally necessitate it."[38] The affirmation of the reality of value, couched in the objectivist language of rationally apprehensible *ṣifāt*, was central to the Muʿtazilite case that standards of value do not vary across agents and do not depend on their particular features. The status of God as creator and master, and of human beings as creatures and subjects, in particular, are morally irrelevant features. Moral standards apply as much to God as they do to human beings.

In responding to this view, Ashʿarites had offered two main proposals for how the meaning of "good" and "bad"—and thus the nature of value—should be understood. The proposal most familiar to their readers is the one that grounded moral concepts in God's command and prohibition. "Good" and "bad," in the definition offered by al-Ghazālī in his legal work *al-Mustaṣfā min ʿilm al-uṣūl*, are, respectively, those acts that "the Law declared to be good by praising those who perform them" and those acts that it declared to be bad by blaming those who perform them.[39] One of al-Ghazālī's contemporaries, Abuʾl-Qāsim al-Anṣārī (d. 1118), had brought out the ontological commitments of this stipulative proposal even more clearly when stating: the qualifications of acts "do not derive from the acts themselves nor from their attributes [*lā tarjiʿu ilā anfusihā wa-lā ilā ṣifātihā*] but rather stem from God's word [*āyila ilā qawl Allāh*]." He had then spelled out more positively what this understanding excludes, in a stroke that brought into view the close imbrication into which questions of epistemology and ontology were drawn in such discussions: "A thing is not good on account of itself [*li-nafsihi*] or its class or an intrinsic attribute that is inseparably attached to it [*ṣifa nafsiyya lāzima lahu*]; and this is why reason falls short of perceiving it."[40] Several Ashʿarites had fearlessly pressed this view to its natural conclusions and declared that God could have issued an entirely different set of commands and prohibitions.[41]

Yet to this stipulative religious meaning of "good" and "bad," later Ashʿarites from al-Ghazālī onward had added another. Synthesizing in his *Mustaṣfā* many of the elliptical notes that had appeared in the writings of his predecessors, al-Ghazālī had offered an empirical and naturalistic account of ordinary usage of evaluative vocabulary. "Good," as people ordinarily use it, refers to "whatever agrees with an agent's purposes" (*mā yuwāfiqu gharaḍ al-fāʿil*), and obversely, "bad" refers to whatever conflicts with these purposes.[42] This definition reflected a conceptual move that would come to play a seminal role in the Ashʿarite response to the Muʿtazilite view, with its special imbrication of a rationalist epistemology with an objectivist ontology. For the Muʿtazilites had insisted that reason gives us access to the intrinsic values of actions: the grounds of value must be *intelligible* (*maʿqūl*); the values of acts are known by every *rational* being (*ʿāqil*).[43] Rejecting these claims, the Ashʿarites had displaced the notion of reason with that of desire or the appetitive self (*ṭabʿ*), in a manner—as Sherman Jackson glosses the point—"similar to the development of Western ethical thinking after the egoistic naturalism of Hobbes."[44] The purposes that form the touchstone for our ordinary usage of "good" and "bad" represent the egoistic, particular, *ṭabʿ*-based desires and interests of individual subjects. These, of course, are desires that may often be in conflict, so that what is deemed good by one person may be deemed bad by another. Crucially, thus, both accounts of evaluative vocabulary—religious and naturalistic—reveal evaluations to be merely relative (*awṣāf iḍāfiyya*) and to have no purchase in objective reality. Equally crucially, neither conception of evaluative standards allows us to extend their application to God, who has neither self-interested purposes to pursue nor commands to respond to. God, as the founder of the school Abu'l-Ḥasan al-Ashʿarī (d. 935) had proclaimed, is under no *sharīʿa*.

In openly embracing the objectivity of values, Ibn Taymiyya thus takes a decision that appears to place him in orthogonal opposition to the Ashʿarite viewpoint. Most features of his critical documentation of the Ashʿarite view in this passage, we may now notice, center on their contestation of this thesis. He highlights the Ashʿarites' denial that God's command reflects the intrinsic qualities of acts (what an act is "in itself": *fī nafsihi* or *fī nafs al-amr*) as against their relative features (*nisba wa-iḍāfa*). Having picked out the claim that God's command attaches contingently to its objects and the implication that God's command could have been different—recalling the Ashʿarites' first semantic proposal—he picks out the claim that good and bad are merely a matter of what agrees with people's appetites (*mā yulāʾimu al-ṭibāʿ*)—recalling the second semantic proposal.

By the same token, Ibn Taymiyya's view may already appear to concede so much to the objectivism we associate with the Muʿtazilites that we may be tempted to pronounce it a revised Muʿtazilism at once and close the subject, discounting the architectonic implications of a *via media* and declaring this a middle ground that leans heavily toward one of its extremes. Yet this would be to overlook the radical impact that revisions—even revisions in the spirit of a *via media*—can have on the terms they seek to reconcile. And just how profoundly changed Ibn Taymiyya's revisions leave the Muʿtazilites' view will become evident once we have adumbrated more distinctly the points on which he distances himself from the latter, taking our cue from the passage we have heard.

One point stands out clearly, and it may remind us of Swartz's dialectical construal of Ibn Taymiyya's notion of the *via media* ("the sound view . . . unites the elements of truth that different views contain"). While the value of acts may not *always* depend on revelation, as the Ashʿarites claim, *sometimes* it will. On a more inclusive view, some acts carry objective value, some depend on divine command, and others test obedience; Ibn Taymiyya offers no examples of the second class but elsewhere suggests he is thinking of ritual obligations.[45] Yet besides this key claim, Ibn Taymiyya outlines a number of points on which he dissociates himself from the Muʿtazilites' position. For the Muʿtazilites had coupled their view of ethical judgments to a claim that moral standards apply equally to God as to human beings ("what is good for created beings to do is also good for the Creator," as the text frames this). Here and elsewhere, Ibn Taymiyya categorically condemns this as a failure to respect God's otherness and an unconscionable act of anthropomorphism or assimilation (*tashbīh*).[46] To this he adds the distinguishing claim that while acts may be good and bad, and known by reason to be such, God will not punish people for them until revelation has arrived. The most critical affirmation, however, through which Ibn Taymiyya distinguishes himself from the Muʿtazilite view is not present in the translated passage but has appeared right before it: and this is the affirmation of the divine determination of human acts (*qadar*).[47]

The foundation for each of these revisions is fully Qur'anic in origin and inspiration: divine otherness, in the spirit of *laysa ka-mithlihi shayʾ* ("Like Him there is naught," Q 42:11); suspension of punishment until the advent of revelation: *wa-mā kunnā muʿadhdhibīn ḥattā nabʿatha rasūlan* ("We never chastise, until We send forth a Messenger," Q 17:15); embrace of *qadar*, in the spirit of *Allāhu ʿalā kulli shayʾ qadīr* ("God has power over all things," Q 3:29). Among these claims, it is Ibn Taymiyya's insistence on God's determination of human acts that bears the most visible imprint of his intention to recalibrate the way the familiar conflict between God's power and God's justice had been settled, honoring the former term far more than the Muʿtazilites had done before him. The *ahl al-sunna*, as Ibn Taymiyya states elsewhere, seek to affirm both sides of the equation, in doing so affirming what God has said about Himself in scripture: "God has power over everything"; "What God wills comes to pass, and what God does not will, does not"—yet also "God is just in all He creates"; "He puts things in their proper places."[48] The affirmation of God's determination supplies the former term with a backbone that the Muʿtazilites, in upholding human beings' creative authorship of their acts, had refused it.

Ibn Taymiyya thus takes the decision to sunder the question of the ethical qualities of acts from the question of God's determination of human acts.[49] Yet the latter was a thesis that Muʿtazilite theologians had taken to bear an internal and not merely contingent relation to their ethical claims. A just God would not punish human beings for evil deeds He himself had creatively determined them to perform. Faced with such action on the part of God, we would not call it just. What this brings out more clearly, at the same time, is the significance of the second distinguishing move that Ibn Taymiyya has performed by driving a wedge between the moral standards applicable to human action (what "we" would call "just") and the standards applicable to God. To claim that moral standards are objective, on these terms, is not to claim they give us the standards of justice to which God Himself must answer. To know right and wrong in the human domain is still to know nothing about how God must act.

It takes little to see that, with these distinctions in place, Ibn Taymiyya's claim of objectivity has been prised free from the entire web of relations in which the Muʿtazilites had embedded it; and one already has good reason to think that this disembedding cannot have taken place without seismic shifts in its conceptual content. Ibn Taymiyya himself provides us with what looks like a well-labeled map of these shifts, nailing to the Muʿtazilites' door a brisk catalogue of his countertheses and revisions. Yet the question to consider now is whether the map he has provided offers an entirely adequate account of the most telling differences that divide him from the Muʿtazilite position, and thus a fully satisfactory description of his location within the classical debates about value. Ibn Taymiyya's own characterization of these intellectual differences, I will argue, obscures differences that readers of Muʿtazilite ethics will find rather more egregious. Bringing these into focus has a far-reaching effect on the way we construe Ibn Taymiyya's relationship not only to the Muʿtazilites but also to the larger theological field he inhabits. And the Ariadne's thread that leads us to the heart of this alternative construal is a notion with a linchpin role in Ibn Taymiyya's ethics: that of utility or welfare (*maṣlaḥa*).

For turning back to the stage-setting passage that opened our discussion, let us lend a closer ear to the content of Ibn Taymiyya's positive arbitrating statement. It was a *via media: some* acts have their value independently of revelation, *other* acts do not. Ibn Taymiyya's objectivism was vested in the first claim, which he framed by referring us to the type of case "in which an act contains benefit or harm [*maṣlaḥa aw-mafsada*], [and it would do so] even if the Law had not come to report that, the way it is known that justice serves the good of the world and injustice tends to its harm."[50] For certainly the language of objective attributes (*ṣifāt*) is there; and so is a notion that had figured prominently in Muʿtazilite preoccupations, namely justice and injustice. Yet these appearances should not distract us from certain other conceptual ingredients in this vicinity—ingredients that will be easier to pick out once we have leaned a little more deeply into our earlier window to sketch out more of the moral universe the (Baṣran) Muʿtazilites had envisaged.

My decision to focus on the Baṣran Muʿtazilites at this juncture may seem to require defense. The Muʿtazilites, after all, had historically comprised not one but two main schools, Baṣran and Baghdādī, and they had flourished across several geographical regions and over a period of several centuries in which their thought had undergone important developments, even if the fundamental theological tenets codified as God's "unity and justice" remained constant.[51] Abū Hāshim al-Jubbāʾī's (d. 933) theory of states left Baṣran Muʿtazilism transformed; Abuʾl-Ḥusayn al-Baṣrī's (d. 1044) and his disciples' engagement of philosophical thought likewise. In crafting intellectual comparisons, it is important to ensure we have the right terms. And this is partly a way of asking: Which thinkers was Ibn Taymiyya himself engaging in conversation? It is a question that it will be more fruitful to defer until we have run through the next stage of our discussion. The decision to look through this particular window can be justified most immediately by pointing to the prominent role the Baṣran Muʿtazilites had occupied as interlocutors in *kalām* debates about ethics, as also to their status as title holders to one of the most richly developed ethical theories within the broader school—and as one of the most serious contenders therefore to be engaged in criticizing the Muʿtazilite ethical outlook.

And looking into this window, all we need to do is draw a little closer to the objectivist language that already came before us to consider its larger environment more acutely. For when ʿAbd al-Jabbār had insisted on the existence of something that "exclusively attaches" to actions (*amr yakhtaṣṣu bihi*) and "necessarily entails" (*yaqtaḍī*) their evaluative qualifications in an intelligible (*maʿqūl*) manner, what he in fact had in mind was a certain ontological element termed *wajh* (pl. *wujūh*), which we variously translate as "aspect," "ground," or "act-description." "Ground" captures the causal force attaching to this element, the way it serves to *explain* value: it is due to their instantiation of these aspects that acts are rendered good or bad. These aspects in fact act as "necessitating causes" (*ʿilal mūjiba*) of the evaluative status of acts.[52] "Act-description" captures the fact that explanation goes only so far, for what is at stake is an intuitionist epistemology in which it is sufficient to perceive that a given act instantiates one of these aspects in order to immediately know (by way of *ʿilm ḍarūrī* or "necessary knowledge") the value of the act.[53] The works of the Baṣran Muʿtazilites were replete with detailed tabulations of the grounds that account for different types of values. Thus, the act-descriptions that make acts bad (*qabīḥ*) include the fact that an act is a lie, that it constitutes injustice (*ẓulm*)—understood as an act of harm that is undeserved or is not outweighed by greater benefit—or that it constitutes ingratitude (*kufr al-niʿma*). The act-descriptions that make acts obligatory (*wājib*) include the fact that it is an act of gratitude, that it is the act of returning a deposit or repaying a debt (acts of owed justice or *inṣāf*, more broadly), or that it involves repelling harm from oneself (*dafʿ al-maḍarra*).

These examples may seem an odd bag, reminding us of a complaint frequently voiced against intuitionist theories in our own times. Such theories, critics have argued, present us with a wild garden of plural and irreducible values without structure or system—an "unconnected heap of duties with no underlying rationale."[54] There is certainly something of this list-like spirit of "heaping," as I have suggested elsewhere, that also clings to the Baṣran Muʿtazilite enterprise. There is a terminus to the "Why?" questions that the Muʿtazilites admit in matters of ethics. If someone asks "Why?," all that can be done is to call their attention to the fact that a certain action instantiates a certain description—and it can sometimes take extra reflection for us to determine *that* a certain description is realized.[55] Yet if, having determined its presence, they go on to contest the value that attaches to the act, they are contesting a self-evident truth, and nothing more can be done by way of rational persuasion.

Despite these limitations, the Muʿtazilites provided one crucial way of sifting the contents of this intuitive list of moral do's and don'ts. For one of the most important theoretical distinctions *we* would like to draw within this list is between those of its act-descriptions that concern utility or consequences (like the prudential obligation to repel harm from self or the prohibition of harm to others unless outweighed by greater utility) and those that do not (like the prohibition of lying or of undeserved harm). Settling on this distinction a more recognizable pair of terms, we might call the first teleological or consequentialist considerations; we might call the latter deontological. While the Baṣran Muʿtazilites' own way of labeling the distinction would never attain the terminological clarity of modern usage, they would make several notable bids to signpost it throughout their writings. This was the distinction that ʿAbd al-Jabbār and Ibn Mattawayh would draw in different locations when dividing actions into those that owe their value to their intrinsic attribute, form, or class (*ṣifa takhtaṣṣu bihi, ṣūra, jins*) and those that owe it to their instrumental relationship to benefit or harm (*mafsada, maḍarra*).[56]

Given the recognition that Muʿtazilite ethical theory offers to a number of ethical considerations, it would be a mistake to label it exclusively as "deontological" or "consequentialist" in kind. Yet it is important—and it will be important for the later stages of our story—to be clear on the seminal role played by deontological considerations in this theory. This is already evidenced by the centrality of the notions of justice and injustice within it. The deontological principle of desert (*istiḥqāq*) provides a moral limitation to—and conversely a moral justification for—the harm one may justly do to others that is separate from utility.[57] Digging more deeply into the category of justice and injustice, in fact, one uncovers the once again deontological notion of *ḥaqq* (pl. *ḥuqūq*)—"right" or "claim"—which underlies many of the obligations that the Baṣrans itemize as discrete act-descriptions. The return of a deposit is a claim (*ḥaqq*) another person has upon me, as is the repayment of a debt. This relationship is brought out plainly in certain definitions of justice (*ʿadl*), such as the one provided by the Zaydī Muʿtazilite Mānkdīm Shashdīw (d. 1034), who defines it as "rendering another his right, and exacting one's right (or claim) from another [*tawfīr ḥaqq al-ghayr wa-istīfāʾ al-ḥaqq minhu*]."[58]

Yet the deontological notion of desert has an even more fundamental role to play within Baṣran Muʿtazilite theory, to the extent that it forms the defining term for the moral attributes or *ṣifāt* mentioned earlier, such as "bad" (*qabīḥ*) and "good" (*ḥasan*) in its different subdivisions. For an act to be bad is for the agent to deserve blame for committing it and praise for omitting it; for an act to be obligatory is for its agent to deserve blame for omitting it and praise for performing it; for supererogatory acts, to deserve praise for performing and no blame for omitting. To say that these desert entailments (*aḥkām*) "define" moral concepts is to make a stronger claim than may be immediately evident, for it means recognizing that these entailments form the ultimate epistemological and ontological bedrock of the moral world. It is these deserts that form the real object of our moral knowledge, and also these deserts (to give this epistemological claim its ontological form) that constitute the real "stuff" of moral reality. To know that an act is bad *is* to know that its agent deserves a certain response on account of it. The words "bad" or "good" are just that, words, about which people might disagree in a way that they cannot disagree about the realities that define them. The primacy of desert in the mind and reality is laid bare in such formulations as ʿAbd al-Jabbār's: "It belongs to mature reason [*kamāl al-ʿaql*] to know that injustice is something we deserve blame for."[59] In claiming that God's command follows the real value of acts, the more specific claim the Baṣran Muʿtazilites were defending was that God's command follows their desert entailments. "God's imposition of obligation [*taklīf*]," in the words of ʿAbd al-Jabbār again, "does not confer on an act an attribute it does not possess, but rather indicates the state of the act, and that it has an attribute for which reason necessitates specific desert entailments [*annahu biʾl-ṣifa allatī yaqtaḍī al-ʿaql lahā al-aḥkām al-makhṣūṣa*]."[60]

The significance of deontological considerations, finally, is also evident on the level of moral psychology. For an act to be morally fertile—to generate desert, and desert of reward in particular—it must be undertaken at least in part due to its intelligible moral ground (*li-ḥusnihi, li-wujūbihi* or *li-wajh ḥusnihi, li-wajh wujūbihi*). "Were one to do what is obligatory for some other purpose [*gharaḍ*]," as Ibn Mattawayh writes, "one would be like one who acts out of impulsive desire [*shahwa*]"—and such people do not deserve praise.[61] Truly meritorious action is action undertaken out of duty, not out of inclination.

The relations between the deontological and the consequentialist components of Muʿtazilite ethics, it must be admitted, are far from unambiguous, and even the strongest deontological affirmations turn out to have roots that are watered by deeper consequentialist considerations. The claim that lying is unconditionally bad regardless of its utility or disutility is a case in point, as it is necessitated by an ultimately teleological reflection on what the project of divinely instituted Law requires for its success.[62] Even more pointed, while merit depends on acting for the sake of the intrinsic value of the act, the projected consequences of one's actions and the way these impact on one's interests—above all, the prospect of otherworldly reward and punishment—are acknowledged by the Muʿtazilites as by all Muslim thinkers as crucial factors in exacting obedience or disobedience to God's Law. *Liʾl-mustaḥaqq biʾl-afʿāl ḥaẓẓ al-duʿāʾ waʾl-ṣarf*: what is deserved serves to attract and repel, as Ibn Mattawayh characteristically says.[63]

Yet even if not watertight, it is a distinction that does not entirely give way. Given the fundamental theological function of Muʿtazilite ethical theory—the purpose of talking about human morality is to get a grip on what we can say about God—one of the foremost locations where this distinction has to hold is unsurprisingly in accounting for divine action. For to the extent that God is inaccessible to considerations of personal utility or disutility, His motivation to abstain from certain actions can only be grounded in the intrinsic disvalue of these actions as this derives from their act-descriptions.[64] His motivation to perform certain acts, conversely, must be grounded in their intrinsic value (*li-ḥusnihi*). Given His inaccessibility to benefit, in fact, all of God's acts have to be transitive or other-directed (*tataʿaddā liʾl-ghayr*), and most have to be subsumed under the concept of acts of grace or beneficence (*tafaḍḍul, iḥsān*).[65]

The later stages of our discussion will present further opportunities for sketching out the Muʿtazilites' ethical understanding from additional angles. Yet even this rapid look through the Muʿtazilites' windows has provided us with many of the ingredients we need in order to turn back to Ibn Taymiyya's position and consider it with new eyes. And looking back at his statement of the objectivity of value—"An act contains benefit or harm [*maṣlaḥa aw-mafsada*], even if the Law had not come to report that, the way it is known that justice serves the good of the world and injustice tends to its harm"—we can now allow ourselves to be surprised. For the most natural way to receive Ibn Taymiyya's positive affirmation of the independent reality of moral values was to read it as an attempt to dialectically synthesize into his view that "element of truth" which the Muʿtazilite ethical position had contained. Yet this affirmation, it will be clear, sits remarkably awkwardly against the ethical claims articulated by the Muʿtazilites in some of their most sophisticated works.

Certainly, here are the notions of justice and injustice that had preoccupied the Muʿtazilites so intensely within their theological and ethical vision. Yet what is one to make of the immediate conversion of such notions into those of benefit and harm? Benefit and harm, to be sure, had figured prominently in the way these notions had been articulated by the Muʿtazilites. Injustice is harm that is then submitted to critical judgment, a judgment partly of utility (Is this harm outweighed by greater utility?) but also, crucially, of desert (Is this harm deserved?).[66] The notions of justice and injustice, as explained earlier, rested on a backbone constituted by deontological concepts such as that of *ḥuqūq*-claims and desert. What this means, among other things, is that some harm can turn out to be just, all things considered, and some benefit can turn out to be unjust. In leaving such complex conceptual points out of view, Ibn Taymiyya's swift and unmarked passage between the notions of justice and injustice and the notions of benefit and harm can only seem bewildering. To ask the obvious question: What is going on?

What Can Our Love of Fine Acts Tell Us about the Nature of Ethical Value?

This response of surprise and the question it generates, I would suggest, holds the key to the way we understand Ibn Taymiyya's ethical claims (including the epistemological claims deferred to the next chapter) and their relationship to their intellectual context. Stated more positively, this is a question about how Ibn Taymiyya understands the real form or nature of ethical value. Stated more derivatively, it is a question about the story his understanding of ethical value has to tell us about his location within the classical debates about value. With this derivative question in the background, in this section and the next I will attempt to marshal the evidence for the positive question, with the aim of clarifying the relationship between deontology and utility within Ibn Taymiyya's thinking. It is the notion of utility, I will be arguing, that appears to carry moral ultimacy within Ibn Taymiyya's scheme; yet this conclusion has to be gained in the teeth of several puzzles and tensions within Ibn Taymiyya's discussion and by sifting through fragmentary evidence that does not always wear its interpretation on its sleeve.

One puzzle has already come before us: How might Ibn Taymiyya mean us to take the unglossed transition from talk of justice to talk of utility? It is a puzzle that we can work through only by first allowing it to deepen. And the best way of doing so is by surveying a wider range of evidence and taking stock of what Ibn Taymiyya has to say about the nature of value elsewhere. Coming from the direction of Muʿtazilite theory, Ibn Taymiyya's translation of justice and injustice into utility may have struck us as extraordinary. Yet the emphasis on utility, we quickly discover, coheres with much of what he has to say about ethical value.

Throughout his work, Ibn Taymiyya's remarks on this subject display a remarkable consistency. Out of the pages of his critique of philosophical logic, *al-Radd ʿala ʾl-manṭiqiyyīn,* we hear: "The goodness and badness of human actions is a matter of the benefit and harm that actions involve [*al-ḥusn wa ʾl-qubḥ min afʿāl al-ʿibād yarjiʿu ilā kawn al-afʿāl nāfiʿa lahum ḍārra lahum*]."[67] Out of the pages of his *Fatāwā,* we hear again: "The only kind of good that exists is in the sense of what is agreeable, and the only kind of bad that exists is in the sense of what is disagreeable [*laysa fi ʾl-wujūd ḥasan illā bi-maʿnā al-mulāʾim, wa-lā qabīḥ illā bi-maʿnā al-munāfī*]." Restating and amplifying: "There are things that are agreeable and beneficial to human beings which thus give them pleasure [*mā huwa mulāʾim li ʾl-insān nāfiʿ lahu fa-taḥṣulu*[68] *lahu bihi al-ladhdha*], and there are other things that are contrary and harmful to them and give them pain [*mā huwa muḍādd lahu ḍārr lahu yaḥṣulu lahu bihi al-alam*], so the distinction reduces to the difference between pleasure and pain and their respective causes ... and if we affirm the difference between good deeds and misdeeds, which is the difference between good and bad, the difference reduces to that."[69] These quotes are but a minute sample of a view we find replicated widely across Ibn Taymiyya's writings. Taken together, their import seems unmistakable: what is good is equivalent to what is pleasurable; or beneficial; or agreeable.[70] Utility is here identified as the sole good-making feature of actions. The Muʿtazilites had offered a number of plural and irreducible considerations; Ibn Taymiyya offers only one. It is not even a matter of weighing different possible grounds against each other and deciding which to privilege. Here and elsewhere Ibn Taymiyya grants the title to utility without contest.

The primacy of utility, pressed so directly in this context, emerges no less brilliantly in several others. If the remarks above have told us what is the value at which our actions *should* aim, another set of remarks tells us that this is the value at which our actions in fact *do* aim. "Every living being," states Ibn Taymiyya in his *Qāʿida fiʾl-maḥabba*, "strives for what brings it enjoyment [*tanaʿʿum*] and pleasure."[71] Pleasure is the "final end of voluntary actions" and "desired in itself" (*maqṣūd li-nafsihi*); couching it again in more normative tones: "that living beings should attain what benefits them and what gives them pleasure" forms the "objective of life."[72] The close imbrication just observed between what is desired and what is desirable—the smooth glide from a description of actual human desires to a more normative characterization of the proper object of human desires—will remind us of a long history of similar imbrications, from Aristotle to utilitarian philosophers such as Bentham and Mill. Yet given the baldness with which this double characterization of utility appears in Ibn Taymiyya's work—utility forms the ground of value and the object of human motivation—the effect in this context must be to make us wonder just how it might help us understand those other claims that appear no less baldly in his work, where value is ascribed to acts such as justice and injustice and immediately construed in consequentialist terms. "Justice is good," we hear elsewhere, "*that is to say*, it brings about benefit and good; and injustice is . . . bad, that is to say, it brings about harm and corruption."[73] For like the Muʿtazilites, these are not notions we would intuitively think to translate into consequentialist terms, and with the adventures of philosophical utilitarianism behind us, we might indeed be wary of presuming they could be entirely reduced to utility without remainder. At the very least we will want to ask: Benefit to whom? What about *ḥuqūq*-claims? And: What is the argument?

Ibn Taymiyya nowhere seems to offer an explicit argument that would explain in detail how justice and utility stand to be related, yet there are several occasions within his works where his discussion poises itself to shed light on the topic. One of the most important—and the one that will form the focus of this section—is the discussion of ethics that appears in his critique of logic, *al-Radd ʿalaʾl-manṭiqiyyīn*. There is an interesting story to be told at this location as to why one of Ibn Taymiyya's most concentrated treatments of ethical questions should have appeared in a work engaging not works of *kalām*—where such questions had historically found their primary habitat—but rather views of the *falāsifa*. This story will come more fully into view in the next chapters, but we can anticipate it by recalling the close intellectual embrace into which *falsafa* and *kalām*—notably Ashʿarite *kalām*—had been drawn by Ibn Taymiyya's time. This embrace, as we will later see, had been cemented with special tenacity in the philosophical view of moral propositions that provides Ibn Taymiyya with his immediate target and with the foil against which he articulates his own views. All we need to remark at present is that it is as a response to, and a refutation of, a view of moral knowledge that he ascribes to both the philosophers and their Ashʿarite commentators, respectively represented in the *Radd* by Avicenna and al-Rāzī—namely the view that moral propositions do not belong to the class of epistemic certainties (*yaqīniyyāt*)—that Ibn Taymiyya crafts his own position. And this consists in an emphatic declaration of the ironclad certainty of human ethical knowledge.

No less important, among the narrative threads leading out of this particular text, is the fact it forms the prime scene for one of the most distinctive developments of Ibn Taymiyya's approach to ethical questions. It is here, and for reasons once again connected to his argumentative context, that Ibn Taymiyya deploys with the highest intensity a key notion, that of *fiṭra*—often translated as the "natural disposition or constitution" or our "original nature"—as an idiom for couching his ethical claims. These claims will center on certain core types of moral acts that, crucially for our purposes, fall on both sides of the rough deontological-consequentialist divide and notably include justice (*ʿadl*), injustice (*ẓulm*), truth-telling (*ṣidq*), lying (*kidhb*), and beneficence (*iḥsān*).[74] Ibn Taymiyya's argument will be that the moral propositions we frame concerning such acts—as in our claim that "injustice is evil" or that "justice is good"—are such that they are not only known with certainty but are indeed among the greatest certainties known by reason (*min aʿẓam al-yaqīniyyāt al-maʿlūma biʾl-ʿaql*).[75] *ʿAql*, or—in this new idiom that will shadow the language of "reason" in a series of slippery epistemological transitions—the human *fiṭra*.

Yet for our context, the focus must once again fall not on what this text has to tell us about how we know ethical values, but (in this far-from-hermetic division) what it has to tell us about their nature, and more specifically about the nature of the benefit we derive from them. For in the slippery transitions that stamp this text with its special character, the glide from "reason" to "nature" that stands out as a notable signature is accompanied by another and no less notable glide from the notion of "reason" to that of "desire." In several of Ibn Taymiyya's statements against his interlocutors, it is not as objects of knowledge but more saliently as objects of desire—indeed of a passionate response dignified with the language of "love"—that we are invited to consider our relationship to ethical acts. The argument that we know the value of these acts is executed as an argument about how strongly we desire them. And while Ibn Taymiyya's focus falls on deontological types of acts in this discussion, his argument is heavily couched in consequentialist terms. Digging deeper beneath such responses and the consequentialist language that frames them would seem to hold the promise of new insight into the question—Why benefit?—that we have raised. Although the discussion in this chapter is premised on sequestering questions about the nature of value from questions about its epistemic access, it is a token of the close conjunction in which ontology and epistemology are drawn in classical debates that one of the best ways of investigating the former should have to lie in approaching it as the object of intentional states.

> When people say "justice is good and injustice is bad," what they mean by this is that justice is beloved to our nature [*al-ʿadl maḥbūb li ʾl-fiṭra*], so that its realization causes it [i.e., one's nature] pleasure [*ladhdha*] and joy [*faraḥ*], and that it is beneficial for its bearer [*ṣāḥibihi*] and for those other than its bearer. . . . And when they say "injustice is bad," what they mean by this is that it is harmful for its bearer and those other than its bearer, and that it is hateful [*baghīḍ*] and that it causes pain [*alam*] and grief [*ghamm*] and torment to the soul [*mā tataʿadhdhabu bihi al-nufūs*].

Reformulating and expanding:

> One naturally [*min nafsihi*] finds in justice, truthfulness, knowledge, and beneficence a pleasure and happiness [*surūr*] which one does not find in injustice, lying, and ignorance. And [both?] the people whom this has reached [*alladhīna waṣala ilayhim dhālika*] and those it hasn't experience [*yajidūna fī anfusihim*] a sense of pleasure, joy, and happiness at the just man's justice, the knowledgeable man's knowledge, and the benefactor's beneficence which they do not experience with injustice, lying, ignorance, and offenses. That is why they experience love for those who do these things and a desire to praise them and wish them well, and they are naturally formed [*mafṭūrūn*] to love and take pleasure in this . . . just as they have been naturally formed to take pleasure in food and drink and to experience pain upon hunger or thirst.[76]

Present in these two passages are two separate claims that are placed in relations of mutual dependence. There is a semantic claim about the meaning of moral propositions: "justice is good" *means* "we love justice," "justice brings us pleasure or happiness," "justice is beneficial." Notice the presence of two related yet distinct components within this claim: one an ascription of subjective emotive states, the other a more objective claim about benefit. Yet this semantic claim, it will be obvious, is linked to an empirical claim: this is how human beings in fact respond to justice and injustice and similar acts.

Taking it as a semantic claim, readers familiar with philosophical history may here be reminded of Hume and his sentimentalist analysis of moral notions (specifically "virtue" and "vice"). "When you pronounce any action or character to be vicious," he would write in his *Treatise of Human Nature*, "you mean nothing, but that from the constitution of your nature you have a feeling or sentiment of blame from the contemplation of it." And while Hume specifically refers to the moral response of blame (and praise or admiration), elsewhere he focuses precisely on the emotions of love and hate that Ibn Taymiyya picks out in this passage.[77] The comparison bears further scrutiny; Hume's objective in this analysis—to question the view that "the immutable measures of right and wrong impose an obligation, not only on human creatures, but also on the Deity himself" (*T* 456)—is one he shares with Ibn Taymiyya and one of many superficial similarities that light the way to even deeper and more instructive ones.

It is a comparison we will be revisiting in what follows. Yet more relevant for our purposes will be a different kind of comparison that Ibn Taymiyya's second, empirical claim more immediately evokes. For in the context of Islamic debates about value, the claim that human beings are intrinsically drawn to justice will remind us of a very specific position that had been taken within those debates—a view of human motivation that had once again been associated with Muʿtazilite theologians. In that peculiar interweaving of epistemology and ontology that had typified these debates, empirical claims of moral psychology had often been in turn drafted to play a crucial supplementary role. The argument that values are objective (an ontological claim) had passed through the argument that human beings in fact rationally know what is right and wrong (an epistemological claim) and had been linked to an audacious empirical claim about human behavior and its deeper drives. Look around you, the Muʿtazilites had said, and you will see ordinary people, even people who know nothing of revealed religion, running after the blind to rescue them from their next misstep, leaping with alacrity to the assistance of those who have lost their way. Looking a bit harder, you will see the death-defying determination with which people cling to their oaths and convictions even when faced with the sword. Ordinary people act in such ways even when they expect no praise, even when they are unbelievers (*mulḥid zindīq*) and expect no heavenly reward, and even indeed (here Kant would have broken into a broad smile) when they are hard-hearted (*qāsī al-qalb jāfī al-fuʾād*) and have no passionate inclination to benefit others. They do so for no other reason than that they know such acts to be good. Purely moral or "deontological" motivation—motivation grounded not in need, *ḥāja*, but in goodness, *ḥusn* or *iḥsān*—may be rare, but it is real.[78] And—here the argument closed in on its real quarry through a typical leap of *qiyās al-ghāʾib ʿala'l-shāhid*, a transfer from the seen to the unseen—if human beings can act for moral reasons, so, a fortiori, does God.

Ashʿarites had responded to this starry-eyed view of the possibilities of human nobility with a reductive cynicism that we, nourished on an ethical history still laboring under the reality check it received from Hobbes, will find uncannily familiar. The heart that Muʿtazilites declared to be stocked with disinterested impulses in fact pulses to a rather different beat—the beat not of reason but of desire, and more specifically self-interested desire. *Kull insān majbūl ʿalā ḥubb nafsihi*, "every person is formed by nature to love himself," al-Ghazālī would write in his reprise of the debate in the *Mustaṣfā*, in an epigram that summarized many of his most potent arguments against the Muʿtazilite showcase of high-minded good-doers. Or in a more pregnant rephrasing: "Everyone is by nature besotted with himself, and contemptuously indifferent to others [*kull ṭabʿ mashghūf bi-nafsihi wa-mustaḥqir li-ghayrihi*]."[79] If we lead the blind and jump after the drowning, it is because of our love of praise, which we have unconsciously learned to associate with such actions, or because of the discomfort we experience when we imagine ourselves (and the focus here is on *ourselves*) in another's predicament. Central to this deconstruction, as the second rephrasing reveals, was a notion that already came into view earlier as a core aspect of the Ashʿarite scheme, that of *ṭabʿ* or human nature taken as a set of appetitive egoistic drives.

In avowing our natural attraction to moral acts like truth-telling and justice in the *Radd*, it is the Muʿtazilite conception of human nature that Ibn Taymiyya seems to be resuming, offering a flat disavowal of al-Ghazālī's psychological egoism. Al-Ghazālī had said: *kull insān majbūl ʿalā ḥubb nafsihi*. Ibn Taymiyya's claim registers as a precise inversion: *al-nufūs majbūla ʿalā maḥabbat al-ʿadl wa-ahlihi* ("people are naturally formed to love justice and those party to it").[80] The Muʿtazilites, of course, had not used the emotive language of love in couching their view; they had used the cognitivist language of approval and disapproval (*istiḥsān, istiqbāḥ*) and of knowledge and ignorance. They had also, crucially, not used the language of utility or benefit. And it is partly these differences that create the space for a question within Ibn Taymiyya's account—a question not unlike the one the Ashʿarites had carved open within the Muʿtazilites' discussions in a more polemical spirit when they had asked for a deeper explanatory "why" of the surface moral phenomena. It may be the spirit of self-doubt we have inherited from Hobbes: we cannot help asking "Why?" when things seem too good to be true. In this case: "Why love?" "Why joy?" And resuming our initial parsing: "Why benefit?"

In fact it may not seem all that paradoxical to say that Ibn Taymiyya invites this question by the very fact that he fails to pose it directly himself. What's more, much of what he says seems to paper over the most important distinctions that would need to be drawn in answering it. For the question "Why benefit?" can be addressed only by considering more closely the different ways of answering the question "To whom?" More specifically, are we thinking of the first-person perspective of the *agent* of the relevant acts (justice, beneficence, truth-telling, and so on)? Or are we thinking of the third-person perspective of those on the receiving end of such acts? Ibn Taymiyya's language appears to slide between the two perspectives without marking the significance of this transition. He speaks about "the bearer" of justice—which would seem to refer us to its agent—but he also speaks of "those other than the bearer." Overall one's impression is that it is the third-person perspective—that of the beneficiary of such acts—that dominates Ibn Taymiyya's remarks, as in the reference to "the just man's justice," to our love "for those who do these things," and to those whom such actions reach (*alladhīna waṣala ilayhim dhālika*), which must mean those who are on the receiving end of these actions.[81]

Yet whether we take ourselves to be considering the perspective of the agent as against the recipient would make a tremendous difference to the way we answer the question "Why?" we have posed. Because from the latter perspective—the perspective of the one who receives back deposits or has his debts repaid, who is treated to the generosity or honesty of another—it is obvious that questions such as "Why joy?" and "Why pleasure?" can be readily answered in straightforwardly self-interested, nonmoral terms. Ibn Taymiyya makes this clear in an important passage whose immediate topic is the different ways of loving God and that addresses the love that is based on divine beneficence. "People are naturally formed [*majbūla*] to love those who act beneficently toward them and to hate those who act badly toward them"; but in this type of love, "what one only really loves is oneself."[82] Yet the perspective that has often seemed to require the most pressing attention is not this one. It is the perspective of the person who must herself decide whether to return a deposit or undertake a beneficent act. And it is the awareness of the fact that justice, beneficence, and other ethical actions come at a cost that has been the enduring source of inspiration for efforts to justify them and defend their rationality ever since Plato's *Republic*, in the backdrop of a fear that ethical action may turn out, not only not to further one's interests, but to openly conflict with them—that happiness and duty (or virtue) may fail to coincide.

It was this sense of the cost of acting rightly, certainly, that Muʿtazilites had signaled when they had foregrounded the notion of hardship (*mashaqqa* or *kulfa*) in their ethical account. The term *kulfa* is in fact etymologically linked to the notion of *taklīf*, the divine imposition of obligations on human beings, in both its rationally known (*ʿaqlī*) and revelationally known (*samʿī*) forms. Obeying the moral Law is difficult: it involves "doing something that one's nature [*ṭabʿ*] is averse to, and abstaining from something that one covets." Yet it is precisely the difficulty one sustains in obeying the Law that is then commuted into reward by way of requital or correspondence (*muqābala*).[83] Ibn Mattawayh brings the point even closer to our own context when he openly states: "One suffers harm [*ḍarar*] by returning deposits, paying back debts, and undertaking justice [*inṣāf*] in its different forms, and one suffers hardship also through [performing] all obligations."[84] This open statement indeed offers us a cue for returning to one of the core evaluative notions that we connected to justice earlier—the notion of *ḥaqq*—for a crucial clarification. I called this a "deontological" notion; yet better-versed readers of Muʿtazilite texts will note the striking fact that the Muʿtazilites elsewhere specify *ḥuqūq*-claims in terms of utility. ʿAbd al-Jabbār thus characterizes *ḥuqūq* as consisting of "either benefit or the repulsion of harm." In doing so he echoes the words of other writers on the topic, such as the Mālikite jurist al-Qarāfī (d. 1285), who states in his *Kitāb al-Furūq: ḥaqq al-ʿabd maṣāliḥuhu*—a person's right/claim is their welfare, benefit, interests.[85] The reasoning behind this equation seems obvious if we are considering things from the perspective of the *owner* of the right: the property I rightfully own, for example, is to me a good I enjoy. Yet when this good faces others, it does so as a limit to their own enjoyment and as a source of obligation: the property I own is a good you are obligated to return if you have borrowed it or taken it into safekeeping.[86]

In describing our affective response to morally good acts, as I have suggested, the perspective that Ibn Taymiyya foregrounds is that of their third-person recipient. Yet the first-person perspective is not absent, and it is this perspective with regard to which the question "Why?" seems most meaningful and most significant (because more costly). So it is worth focusing our question on this perspective and asking again: "Why pleasure?" Here it will be helpful to take a step back and, drawing on the history of philosophical and theological ethics, to consider some of the types of answers that might be possible. Why might I take pleasure in an act of justice or beneficence I perform? One answer might be the Aristotelian one: if I am virtuous, I take pleasure in such acts because they are intrinsically fine, and I count the external costs of virtuous action differently than most people (and may not even experience them as costs). Another is what we may call broadly Humean: I take pleasure in such acts because of the natural sympathy that connects me to others. A third is the prudential one: I take pleasure not in these acts themselves but in their consequences, which outweigh their immediate perceptible costs.

Quickly eliminating one of the contenders from the field, we may simply observe that the second answer suffered an unlucky defeat in the *kalām* debates about value, where the notion of sympathy came to be associated with the egoistic perspective to which Ashʿarites sought to reduce all ethical responses.[87] What is also worth remarking is that Ibn Taymiyya himself does not appear to have developed his understanding of *fiṭra* in a way that would incorporate other-regarding desires directed to the good of other human beings. We will be returning to this particular answer in what follows from a different direction. Yet it is the first answer, or something along its lines, that would involve taking Ibn Taymiyya's claims at face value, resealing the space for asking "Why?" of this pleasure and ruling the pleasure to be irreducible and inaccessible to further explanation. The pleasure or benefit we find in moral action is simply the intrinsic pleasure in the good—discouraging our use of "utility" as a potentially misleading choice of term and, crucially for our overarching argument, leaving open the possibility that the (objective) features of actions to which we (subjectively) respond with such delight may not reduce to their utility.

Yet the key question now is this: Can this view be reconciled with those other descriptions of human motivation that Ibn Taymiyya offers us elsewhere? We have heard some of these descriptive statements already: "every living being strives for what brings it enjoyment and pleasure"; pleasure is the "final end of voluntary actions" and "desired in itself." What these statements spell out in unmistakable terms is a thesis of psychological hedonism. If the space for asking "Why?" opens up at all within Ibn Taymiyya's prima facie rehearsal of the Muʿtazilites' high-minded depiction of humanity, we can now state more clearly, this owes in no small part to the depiction of humanity that Ibn Taymiyya himself offers us in other parts of his work. The claim that human beings are naturally pleasure-seeking, of course, may still seem to leave many options open. There can be different kinds of pleasures, some higher and some lower, as Plato had recognized in the *Republic*; and we know that Aristotle also made pleasure central to his understanding of the ethical life. The virtuous person takes pleasure in acting well. ("Just things are pleasant to the lover of justice," as he had put it in the *Nicomachean Ethics*, "and in general, things in accord with virtue are pleasant to the lover of virtue.")[88] Yet in developing this notion, Aristotle—whose ethical viewpoint, in various refractions and amalgamations, was available in the Islamic milieu and had been reworked by several writers with whom Ibn Taymiyya was familiar, such as Avicenna (d. 1037) and al-Ghazālī—had been specifically concerned to *dismantle* the type of hedonism expressed by Ibn Taymiyya. His aim, as Dorothea Frede notes, had been to "integrate pleasure in his moral philosophy and to assign an intrinsic value to it *without treating it as the ultimate motive of our actions*." This was the context of Aristotle's articulation of his distinctive view that pleasure is a "characteristic of the performance" of actions rather than an end at which we aim.[89]

The strongest evidence for the "intrinsic" reading of the pleasure we take in moral acts, in fact, appears in an extraordinary epistle that Ibn Taymiyya devotes precisely to the topic of the human attraction to the good, where he proposes to investigate whether "human beings have a love for what is good and right and praiseworthy in itself, so that they do it out of the love they have for it . . . the way one might love acting beneficently to those in need, love practicing forgiveness toward delinquents, love learning . . . and telling the truth [*ṣidq*], keeping promises and rendering back trusts," as well as justice (*ʿadl*). The first-person perspective of the agent is here foregrounded with remarkable clarity, and Ibn Taymiyya's immediate response to this question registers as a strong claim that this kind of motivation in fact characterizes the majority of people (*hādhā ḥāl akthar al-nufūs*). The next remark presses this home even more forcefully, rehearsing a claim about the purity of moral motivation that will remind us of the Muʿtazilites' characteristic formulations, but also adding a notable new gesture. "One performs these actions," Ibn Taymiyya explains, "not by way of ingratiating oneself with any person nor by way of soliciting anyone's praise or for fear of incurring their blame, but rather because living beings enjoy these perceptions and movements and take pleasure in them [*yatanaʿʿamu bihā al-ḥayy wa-yaltadhdhu bihā*], and experience joy [*faraḥ*] and happiness [*surūr*] in them, just as they take pleasure in merely hearing beautiful sounds or seeing joyous things and in merely [smelling] lovely fragrances."[90]

This passage will seem remarkable for many reasons, not only for its unambiguous attribution of disinterested action to human beings, but also for comparing moral pleasure to aesthetic forms of enjoyment—a startling maneuver in a debate in which the aesthetic-moral comparison, suggested by the term *ḥusn* itself, had been used by *opponents* of Muʿtazilite-style objectivism seeking to call attention to the *subjectivity* of moral responses.[91] The philosophical associations of this comparison will seem equally resonant, in a tradition of reflective inquiry where the good and the beautiful had often been found entwined. We may be reminded once again of the particular comparison sparked by Hume when remarking that "there is no spectacle so fair and beautiful as a noble and generous action" (*T* 470). The language of this passage throws out multiple bridges to the language of the passages of the *Radd* we surveyed. No less remarkable is the bridge it throws out to the statements tagged earlier as expressions of psychological hedonism: "Every living being strives for what brings it enjoyment and pleasure [*kull ḥayy innamā yaʿmalu limā fīhi tanaʿʿumuhu wa-ladhdhatuhu*]." That enjoyment, this passage suggests, can include the intrinsic and irreducible pleasure we take in ethical acts.

Here we have it, the shard-like nature of some of the texts that enter into our comprehension of Ibn Taymiyya's thought: a *unicum* that offers to nuance the hedonistic view of human motivation expressed elsewhere, contributing a new interpretive thread that would unravel the pattern assembled by other, seemingly more numerous threads. All that can be done is to highlight the isolation of this thread and to emphasize the evidence that resists it. This perspective—whose natural affiliation with an ethics of virtue Ibn Taymiyya flags directly when he refers to the "noble character traits" (*makārim al-akhlāq*) in the same context[92]—simply does not seem to be developed elsewhere. Moreover, when the opportunity arises when he might have integrated the viewpoint of this shard-like epistle more deeply into his thinking, Ibn Taymiyya passes it by. Writing in his *Qāʿida fi'l-maḥabba*, he offers us a threefold classification of (mundane) pleasures, dividing them into bodily pleasures (typically deriving from food, drink, and sex), pleasures of honor (deriving from the esteem we receive from others), and pleasures of the mind or spirit (such as those deriving from the knowledge of God or the knowledge of truth).[93] This scheme is significant in presenting an expressly pluralistic view of human pleasures, and it will put us in mind of its counterparts in the Greek philosophical tradition and of the Arab philosophers who reworked it. Yet what is more relevant for the present point is that in setting out this scheme, Ibn Taymiyya gives us no tools for locating moral pleasure (or aesthetic pleasure, for that matter) within this scheme and leaves us to fill in the gaps ourselves.

Left to our own devices, I would argue, it is an emphasis on sensory pleasures that we are likely to pick out within Ibn Taymiyya's ethical remarks, and a related emphasis on the agent's natural self-interest that often directly resumes the wording of al-Ghazālī. "Human beings are naturally formed to love themselves [*al-insān majbūl ʿalā maḥabbat nafsihi*]," we hear.[94] Transposed to the question of morally good actions, this results in a view of our motivation that is framed in the strong terms of egoistic hedonism. People, Ibn Taymiyya states in another epistle, "act beneficently toward others in order to obtain a benefit or repel harm."[95] But in that case we are back where we started. "Why pleasure?" we asked, and put our ear to the possibility that this could take an Aristotelian type of response, tying our pleasure to the intrinsic attraction exercised by the moral character of the acts.[96] Having put this answer aside, I would suggest that it is the third answer outlined earlier—the prudential perspective that looks to the consequences of acts—that Ibn Taymiyya appears to presuppose in his account of the first-person pleasure taken in fine acts that carry immediate costs. As he puts it later in the *Radd* with reference to the reverse case of first-person displeasure in wrongful acts that carry immediate gains: "Even if we suppose that one takes pleasure [in such things] in the present, one will experience pain at their evil consequences [*qubḥ ʿāqibatihi*]." The point is spelled out more programmatically elsewhere: "One endures what is painful on account of a greater pleasure or pain that outweighs it," just as "one desists from what is pleasurable on account of a greater pleasure or pain that outweighs it."[97]

These consequences include the ones implicit in Ibn Taymiyya's own discussion in the *Radd*: the love we provoke in others by acting well and the hatred we provoke by acting badly. For we experience pleasure and joy in being the objects of others' love and praise; it is "agreeable" (*mulāʾim, muwāfiq*) to us—terms that significantly resume Ibn Taymiyya's earlier schematization of moral value ("the only kind of good that exists is in the sense of what is agreeable," we heard above).[98] This is one of several beneficial consequences Ibn Taymiyya elsewhere pins to ethical acts, which include increased intellectual understanding and physical well-being and a greater propensity to good actions.[99] These consequences represent the worldly or mundane (*ʿājil/dunyā*) domain; they predictably but crucially find their complement in the consequences relating to the otherworldly domain (*ʾājil/ākhira*). For we might derive an immediate pleasure from ethically bad acts such as adultery (*zinā*) or injustice, yet these then serve as the "cause [*sabab*] of torment that exceeds the pleasure of the act itself," like delicious food that is poisoned and leads to illness and death.[100] Mutatis mutandis with ethically good acts. If human beings love those who act well, so does God—for reasons to be considered in greater detail in chapter 4—and He metes out an appropriate reward for such acts ("Whoso brings a good deed shall have ten the like of it," Q 6:160). This is the logic implicit in the Qur'anic dictum "If you do good, it is your own souls you do good to [*in aḥsantum aḥsantum li-anfusikum*], and if you do evil it is to them likewise" (Q 17:7) and unpacked by Ibn Taymiyya in several locations in his own work.[101]

Yet I would argue that there is something more to be exhumed from Ibn Taymiyya's discussion of the utility of morally good actions in the passages of the *Radd* we are considering—a broader conception of utility that forms a crucial motif in his thinking and that involves a rather more complex specification of the first-person perspective that we have been pursuing. In order to bring this into the open, however, we need to connect several dots that Ibn Taymiyya does not himself pull into the most convenient proximity. For turning back to the passage from the *Radd* translated earlier, our attention may be caught by the striking comparison that concluded it. People feel "love ... and a desire to praise" the just and the beneficent, Ibn Taymiyya had written, "and they are naturally formed [*mafṭūrūn*] to love and take pleasure in this ... just as they have been naturally formed to take pleasure in food and drink and to experience pain upon hunger or thirst."[102] The comparison will seem curious next to the aesthetic comparison that terminated that other brief epistle that recently came before us. Here Ibn Taymiyya crafts a comparison calculated to put us in mind of the agent's self-interest; there he had struck an analogy calculated to put us in mind of utter disinterest. Yet the more illuminating textual collocations, in my view, lie elsewhere.

For in comparing the pleasure of justice with the pleasure of food and drink here, the "they" with which Ibn Taymiyya frames the second claim ("they have been naturally formed to take pleasure in food and drink") will most readily be heard as inviting the kind of interpretation we have already seen. The "they" is the first-person singular, the individual agent whose motivation for acting justly comes up for question given the prima facie gap between the two sets of pleasure at stake. Yet that this is not the only way of receiving the present "they" is intimated by Ibn Taymiyya in a remark of rather different vintage, whose broader context we may here leave out of view. "The need of Muslims for food and clothing and the like," he states in his treatise *al-Ḥisba*, "belongs to the general interest [*maṣlaḥa ʿāmma*]."[103] The "they," this tersely suggests, can be taken at face value as a first-person plural, and may speak not for the individual agent, but for the community as a whole. The interest at stake, correlatively, may be the interest of the whole. Having opened ourselves to this distinction, we may be better prepared for the discussion of ethical norms to which Ibn Taymiyya regales us in several other writings and may find ourselves slightly less astonished at the proposal we hear there. In this proposal, the social community is presented as the genetic origin, no less, of ethical norms, and it is the connection of ethical norms with communal welfare that lies at its heart.

"For all human beings endowed with reason," Ibn Taymiyya writes in one place of his collected *Fatāwā*, "there are things that they must command and things they must prohibit, for their welfare [*maṣlaḥa*] cannot be achieved without that, and they cannot live in the world [*fī 'l-dunyā*]—indeed, even a single one of them, taken on his own, cannot live—without doing things that bring them benefit [*manfa 'a*] and doing[104] things that repel harm from them."[105] The enumeration of ethical actions that succeeds this remark will be familiar to us: justice, truthfulness, beneficence, the return of trusts. In the *Qā 'ida fī 'l-maḥabba*, the notion of the community's self-command is recalibrated using the significant notions of a "convention" and "contract." It is through a mutual pledge and contractual agreement (*al-ta 'āhud wa 'l-ta 'āqud*) that human beings place themselves under obligations in order to collaboratively pursue what benefits the community as a whole and to repel what harms it.[106] The focal categories of justice and truthfulness appear again in this context. So does an affective notion familiar to us from the *Radd*: people thereby "agreed and contracted themselves to bring about what they *love*, and repel what they find *repugnant* [*ittafaqū wa-ta 'āqadū 'alā ijtilāb al-amr alladhī yuḥibbūnahu wa-daf' al-amr alladhī yakrahūnahu*]."[107] Ibn Taymiyya's remarks in the *Radd* provide no clue to the fact that the subject of this emotive response could be anything other than the individual. In ascribing this response to the collective here, he holds out the key for a different interpretation. The larger interpretive possibility this opens up is that in speaking of the pleasure and benefit that "we" derive from ethical norms—apparently deontological acts such as justice, truthfulness, or beneficence—Ibn Taymiyya has in mind not so much the benefit of the individual as the benefit derived by the community from the adherence to such norms. It is at this level that the question we have been asking—"Why benefit?"—can best be answered.[108]

The division between the individual and the community, of course, need not be drawn too sharply. Many of the best-known philosophical theories that have proposed to root ethical norms in social contracts, from Hobbes onward, have grounded them in the self-interest of individuals. Hume once again provokes the most interesting comparison, having claimed that "there is no passion . . . capable of controlling the interested affection, but the very affection itself" (*T* 492), and having made this central to his account of justice and injustice. For the convention instituted to bestow stable possession of external goods, thereby generating notions of justice, was based on a consideration that our own interests and the interests of our friends are better served by such a convention. It is thus "from the selfishness and the confin'd generosity of men . . . that justice derives its origin" (*T* 495). This original motivation, Hume suggests, shifted as society grew, and it is now our sympathy with the pain or pleasure that certain actions cause other people and indeed human society as a whole—"a sympathy with public interest" (*T* 499–500)—that underlies our emotional responses to those actions. Hume's aesthetic characterization of our response to fine actions, to which Ibn Taymiyya's remarks earlier recalled us, is in fact linked with our ability to command this more disinterested viewpoint.

Unlike Hume, however, Ibn Taymiyya does not offer us the material for constructing a clearer story about how the self-interested viewpoint of the individual and the viewpoint of the community are to be related—leaving it uncertain, for example, whether the interests of the two should be seen as perfectly coinciding.[109] This may well reflect the fact that his thoughts are implicitly focused on the first-person plural rather than the first-person singular in the discussions we have seen. And it is perhaps this interpretation of Ibn Taymiyya's hypnotic if unstated focus that can best explain an otherwise extraordinary fact that I left out of view in my discussion of the different ways "happiness" and "virtue" may coincide for the first person. For Ibn Taymiyya himself, as I mentioned earlier, does not volunteer the distinction between the different possible perspectives from which the question "Why joy (and pleasure and benefit)?" can be asked. This is tied to another remarkable omission. For having drawn our attention so emphatically to the pleasure we derive from morally good actions such as justice in the passages of the *Radd* quoted earlier, Ibn Taymiyya falls silent when it comes to counting their costs. We hear next to nothing about the reasons we have for *hating* justice apart from *loving* it.

These costs, as I have suggested, were brought to the limelight by the Muʿtazilites through the limiting notion of *ḥaqq*, which figured centrally in their notion of justice and justice. Facing its holder, *ḥaqq* may register in terms of its utility. When it faces others, it faces them as a limit and a source of obligation. What is then striking is that in these discussions of ethics, as in many others, both the notion of *haqq* and the evaluative concept of obligation (*wujūb*)—that concept to which the Muʿtazilites themselves ascribed the "highest rank" among the actions subsumed in the broader category of "goodness" (*ḥusn*)—remain conspicuously absent.[110] Even though Ibn Taymiyya, like any good Muslim jurist and theologian, elsewhere gives ample recognition to both notions, he never integrates them in his formal remarks about ethical value. To adapt a helpful terminology used by Henry Sidgwick, he focuses on an evaluative vocabulary that carries "attractive" rather than "imperative" force. Similarly, even though he gives abundant recognition elsewhere to the darker elements of our nature that draw us toward evil rather than good—human beings do evil, we hear elsewhere, either out of ignorance or because "they crave for it and take pleasure in it" (*yashtahīhi wa-yaltadhdhu bi-wujūdihi*)—this insight is never integrated into his discussion of our nature in these positioning remarks.[111]

This raises a question about Ibn Taymiyya's conception of human nature; it also raises a question about the character and above all the analytical depth of his ethical writing which I previewed at the start of this chapter. It may also provoke a question about the broader context of his discussion in the *Radd* and a greater curiosity to situate the excerpted remarks against his specific aims there—a task I will undertake in the next chapter. Putting such questions aside for the moment, what matters more for our immediate purposes is to take stock of where the discussion has brought us relative to the main thread we have been pursuing.

The Ethical Primacy of Welfare

Beginning from a stage-setting exposition of Ibn Taymiyya's *via media*, we were quickly brought up against a surprise: Ibn Taymiyya avowed an objectivist view of ethical value that was prima facie reminiscent of the view traditionally adopted by Muʿtazilite thinkers; yet in specifying this he made sole reference to considerations of utility, sidelining the deontological components that had been central to the Muʿtazilite view. How might we understand this? His programmatic remarks about the nature of value seemed to support the conclusion that utility forms the sole ground of value, just as it forms the paradigmatic object of human motivation. We turned to the *Radd* for further insight on how the relationship between utility and deontology could be construed. Analyzing Ibn Taymiyya's claim about the pleasure and benefit we derive from seemingly deontological actions such as justice and truthfulness—and digging beneath yet another surface resemblance with a characteristically Muʿtazilite view of moral motivation—we explored a number of ways in which the utility of such acts might be understood. One of the most significant, I suggested, is the one that recognizes the welfare of the community as the ontological ground, no less, of the value of these acts. With this in sight, we can finally join our ends to our beginnings. For it is precisely this notion of communal interest, we may now observe, that was marked out in the stage-setting exposition of Ibn Taymiyya's *via media*, when he had isolated the first ("objective") type of value as "the case in which an act contains benefit or harm . . . the way it is known that justice serves the good of the world [*maṣlaḥat al-ʿālam*] and injustice tends to its harm."[112]

Our answer to the positive question from which we began—How does Ibn Taymiyya understand the real form or nature of ethical value?—is relatively plain. There is little in the discussions we have seen that suggests that Ibn Taymiyya recognized the existence of intrinsic deontological features. The claim that human beings are intrinsically attracted to deontological acts such as justice, which was one of the interpretations of the *Radd* we considered and which might have supported the view that such features are defined independently of utility, seems to give way upon closer consideration. Ibn Taymiyya nowhere deploys the Muʿtazilite notion of *wujūh*, has nothing to say about *ḥuqūq* in his main ethical remarks, and maintains a stony silence with regard to the notion of desert, although its vocabulary makes unglossed appearances.[113] What of his talk of the rightness and wrongness of things "in themselves" (*fī nafs al-amr*) in our stage-setting exposition? Objectivist markers are profusely in evidence in this text—recall, for that matter, the vocabulary of "attributes" or *ṣifāt* that also appears in the same exposition. Yet the Muʿtazilites, drawing a distinction between those values that depend on the intrinsic features of actions and those that depend on their consequences, had reserved this objectivist vocabulary notably for the former class. Here and elsewhere, by contrast, Ibn Taymiyya deploys the vocabulary of *ṣifāt* to speak of consequences or utility.[114]

These objectivist markers may here be relevantly said to raise a question that remained in the margins in the above discussion, which focused on the human relationship to morally good actions and the description under which human beings desire them. Our stage-setting exposition of Ibn Taymiyya's *via media*, by contrast, had far more to say about God's relation to such acts and was organized by an insistence that God's command is not merely arbitrary but is grounded in the features of acts in themselves. The natural question to pose at this juncture would thus be the counterpart of the one we have asked at the human level, asking under what description certain classes of actions become the object of God's command and indeed—as the conclusion of that passage suggested: the Ashʿarites denied that "God loves what is right and hates what is wrong"—of God's love. The order of our narrative is best served by deferring the discussion of this point until chapter 4, where the theological dimensions of Ibn Taymiyya's position will be explored more directly. All I would do is preview its conclusions, namely that there too—and despite, once again, certain tensions—it is the contribution that particular classes of actions make to human welfare that forms the most relevant description under which God's love and command attaches to them.

This conclusion leaves much to be unpacked; yet it is already embodied in a view that Ibn Taymiyya takes about the nature of the divine Law that it is important to foreground at this juncture as further evidence for the primacy of welfare in his thought. As Ibn Taymiyya puts it in an epitomic statement, God sent prophets to people in order to "communicate to them what benefits them and harms them [*mā yanfaʿuhum wa-yaḍurruhum*], and to perfect their good [*mā yuṣliḥuhum*] in the present world and the next." And again: "The Law came to realize and perfect [human] interests [*maṣāliḥ*]."[115]

However unambiguously such statements fall, the evidence they offer may once again not appear to be beyond contest. For it might be observed that the notion of welfare that takes the stage so prominently in such statements elsewhere finds its complement in a different set of statements, in which it is justice (*ʿadl*) that is rather made the central term among the aims of the divine Law. "All that [God] commanded," we hear, "reduces to justice." The borders between the two types of statements often seem to be open, resulting in an easy slippage reminiscent of the one we witnessed in our stage-setting exposition. "The Law distinguishes between the acts that benefit [people] and the acts that harm them, and this is the justice of God in His creation."[116] This equivocation is also reflected in Ibn Taymiyya's discussion of specific legal prescriptions, such as the Law's prohibition of usury or gambling, which he refers to the demands of justice in some locations and to the demands of utility in others.[117] The question imposes itself again: Which of the two types of demand should be considered more basic?

It might be useful in answering this question to say something more about the more complex range of meanings that the notion of justice bears within Ibn Taymiyya's thought. Following well-established precedents, one of the ways he occasionally specifies justice and injustice is by reference to the notion of rights or claims: injustice is thus "wrongfully taking what rightfully belongs to another [*akhdh ḥaqq al-ghayr bi-ghayr ḥaqq*]."[118] Elsewhere this specification is joined by another, which ties justice more directly to the notion of parity or equality—an understanding that will not seem entirely unfamiliar to us. Justice, in these terms, means observing the principle of parity and treating like things alike. This is a principle, as we will later see, that Ibn Taymiyya deploys not merely as a concept of morality but equally so of rationality, connecting it to the notion of legal analogy (*qiyās*) and giving it a central place in his claims regarding the rationality of God and of His Law.[119]

This double significance is worth keeping in mind in considering the relationship of priority that holds between justice and welfare. The nature of this relationship then appears to be signaled clearly in a series of statements that directly bridge the two types of statements (justice-parsed and welfare-parsed) recorded above. Justice in human transactions, Ibn Taymiyya remarks in *al-Siyāsa al-sharʿiyya*, is the mainstay of human life, and "both the present world and the next depend on it in order to come to good [*lā taṣluḥu al-dunyā wa'l-ākhira illā bihi*]."[120] Discussing commutative transactions (*muʿāwaḍāt*) elsewhere—transactions that notably include buying and selling, renting and leasing, and in which the principle of just exchange plays a governing role—Ibn Taymiyya states: such transactions constitute "a worldly and religious necessity, for human beings cannot achieve their welfare in isolation, and need the help of their conspecifics.... Their welfare can only be achieved through commutative transactions, and *it is the justice for the sake of which God sent down His books and dispatched His messengers that puts these in good working order* [*ṣalāḥuhā bi'l-ʿadl*]."[121] The causal *bi* in both statements leaves no doubt that *ʿadl* and *ṣalāḥ/maṣlaḥa* are here placed in a relationship of means to end.

In many respects, these statements merely rehearse a view of the relationship between deontological norms and welfare that we have already seen. Indeed, they find a direct echo in the *Qāʿida fī ʾl-maḥabba* in the same vicinity in which Ibn Taymiyya articulates the social-contract model that grounds these norms in communal welfare more specifically.[122] Yet if we wished to anchor this view in a deeper context, and one closer to the heart of the Islamic religious sciences as against the philosophical tradition from which the notion of the social contract appears to derive, we would do well to look toward the fascinating discussion that Ibn Taymiyya offers us in one of his Qur'anic commentaries regarding a principle that belongs not to civil but to criminal justice, namely the principle of retaliation (*qiṣāṣ*).

Taking its religious foundation from a key verse in *al-Baqara*—"O believers, prescribed for you is retaliation, touching the slain; freeman for freeman, slave for slave, female for female" (2:178)—this is a principle that presents itself as a demand of justice in two separate ways. It is a form of punishment administered for bodily injury or homicide. It thus responds to offenses that represent breaches of what the Muʿtazilites would not have been alone in calling considerations of "justice," and more specifically of persons' rights (*ḥuqūq*). An act of unjustified harm breaches my right to physical integrity and, in the limit case, my right to life. In breaching an order of rights, the offense creates a new one. This act of punishment in fact belongs to the victim or their surviving family unit as their peculiar right or claim (*ḥaqq*). The act of punishment thus becomes constitutive of justice. Yet the notion of *ḥuqūq* foregrounded here finds its complement in the crucial role played by the notion of parity, as immediately evident in the verse itself, which demands that retaliation be practiced with due regard for the characteristics of the victims and offenders. The term "retaliation" (*qiṣāṣ*), Ibn Taymiyya explains, denotes parity and equality (*al-muʿādala wa ʾl-musāwā*) and it indicates that God prescribed justice and fairness (*ʿadl, inṣāf*) with regard to those killed.[123]

Yet this prima facie deontological norm, as Ibn Taymiyya approaches it, turns out to be embedded within a framework dominated by powerful teleological elements. For human beings, he states in opening his own interpretation of the verse, the practice of retaliation belongs to those things they "know they cannot live without," and their need for it is comparable to "their need for food and drink and shelter."[124] This teleological comparison will strike a strong chord, reminding us of a similar comparison we saw in the *Radd* only recently. The teleological good to which the practice of retaliation is more narrowly tied, however, is even more basic than food and drink, and it is indicated in the Qur'anic verse itself when it offers the explanatory-sounding continuation, "In retaliation there is life for you [*wa-lakum fī ʾl-qiṣāṣ ḥayā*]" (2:179). The explanation may seem paradoxical, for retaliation immediately results in the *taking* of life, not in its preservation. Yet the verse can be naturally taken as referring to the life of both the perpetrator and his victim protected through the deterring effect of this punitive norm.

Such explanations in fact formed the linchpin of an understanding of the divine Law that had entrenched itself firmly within Islamic legal theory by Ibn Taymiyya's time, one that gave a prominent place to the aims that organized the Law (*maqāṣid al-sharīʿa*) in accounting for its workings. Studied carefully, many of the prescriptions of the Sharīʿa could be seen to be anchored in a set of relatively consistent aims—a set of consistent goods or human interests. The Law's prohibition of consuming intoxicants, for example, and its related imposition of punishment for doing so can be linked to its concern to preserve human reason; its prohibition of adultery and its imposition of punishment for adultery to its concern to preserve the integrity of family lines. Something similar could be said about the prohibition of theft and the Law's concern with the protection of property, and—closing in on the case we just met—the prohibition of unlawful killing and the prescription of retaliation as punishment for it and the Law's concern to preserve human life. There will be more to say about this conception of the Law in chapters 4 and 5. Yet here it is crucial to recognize that it is this theoretical understanding that shadows Ibn Taymiyya's own view of the centrality of welfare in the law;[125] and it is then no less crucial to notice what this theoretical understanding imports. For one of its distinctive features is the programmatic reading of deontological norms that could be parsed in terms of *ḥuqūq* and identified as forms of justice—the prohibition of killing and the promulgation of punishment for its violation, the prohibition of theft and adultery and their respective punishments, and so on—as means for attaining particular goods: the protection of life, property, or family lines.

It is the presuppositions of this theoretical understanding, and more specifically the programmatic translation of deontological notions into instrumental terms, that appear to be reflected in Ibn Taymiyya's thinking and to govern the way he conceptualizes the relationship between justice and welfare. Taken as the general claim that the Law aims at the human good, this was a conception of the Law that Muʿtazilite theologians themselves had not only subscribed to, but indeed for which they had served as prime architects—though the theory of *maqāṣid* would achieve its archetypal formulations among Sunni jurists only after the lifetime of the theologians we have been considering. These theologians had likewise recognized, as already mentioned, the teleological significance of deontological notions such as *ḥaqq*-claims. Yet as we have seen, the Muʿtazilites had made efforts to safeguard the distinction, however fragile, between the deontological and the consequentialist components of their ethical theory. Ibn Taymiyya, by contrast, seems to enshrine the notion of utility as the basic term of his ethical thinking in a way that wholeheartedly succumbs to the logic of the legal discourse of *maqāṣid*.

In trying to balance Ibn Taymiyya's emphasis on considerations of welfare and his countervailing emphasis on considerations of justice, I have been suggesting, we have strong reasons to take the former as basic, reinforcing the conclusions of our earlier discussion and the positive response we give to the question regarding Ibn Taymiyya's understanding of the nature of ethical value. The answer to our positive question is interesting in its own right, but it also has far-reaching repercussions for the way we respond to our other question, regarding the story this tells about Ibn Taymiyya's relationship to the theological topography in which he is operating and to the traditional layout of the debate about "the determination of good and bad."

For what this shows is that Ibn Taymiyya's understanding of the nature of value departs from the Muʿtazilites' in some of its most fundamental features. What will then seem perplexing is that Ibn Taymiyya does not signal this himself. The only one of these departures that he comes close to signaling in his enumeration of his differences from the Muʿtazilites is his disavowal of desert. This disavowal may be said to be implicit in his insistence that God will punish only after He has sent prophetic revelation, and is made rather more explicit elsewhere, as we will see in chapter 4. These unlabeled departures—particularly his unlabeled exclusion of deontology—may make us wonder about his familiarity with Muʿtazilite works and about the identity of the Muʿtazilite thinkers that he thought himself as engaging in conversation. His stylized and spare exposition of the debate—a sparseness well poised, after all, to serve the rhetorical imperatives of a *via media* carved between two stark extremes—often seems too elliptical to supply evidence that would help with such questions. Abuʾl-Ḥusayn al-Baṣrī (d. 1044) is one of the few later Muʿtazilites whom Ibn Taymiyya quotes directly, though not in his ethical discussions. And while Ibn Taymiyya waged important polemical confrontations with Shīʿite theologians (such as al-Ḥillī in his *Minhāj al-sunna*) whose Muʿtazilite sympathies ought to have given him numerous opportunities for direct engagement with Muʿtazilite ethical ideas, his distance from the detail of these ideas may tempt us to extend Kevin Reinhart's observation that the Muʿtazilism critiqued by opponents "is often a straw man" to suggest that the same may hold true even of its partial and prima facie admirers.[126] Yet Ibn Taymiyya's neglect of the theory of *wujūh* and the deontological-consequentialist distinction may still surprise us given the relative clarity with which they had been brought up by several of the Muʿtazilites' opponents, including those, such as al-Rāzī, whose works Ibn Taymiyya had read with close attention.[127] It may thus make us wonder, more critically, whether this neglect should be described as a matter of deliberate choice or unintended oversight.

This somewhat invidious question is one to which I will be returning in chapter 3, as I believe it carries nonnegligible narrative consequences. Yet here it is more relevant to pull into view the beginnings of an alternative telling of the complex story of Ibn Taymiyya's relationship to the classical debates about ethics. The denouement to which we drove Ibn Taymiyya's conception of moral motivation in the previous section has already suggested one area where his views, initially calling attention to their Muʿtazilite affinities, turn out to resemble views characteristic of the Ashʿarites. Yet the more critical resemblance that has not yet stepped into the light concerns our central question regarding the nature of value itself. For the Ashʿarites had rejected the notion of inherent deontological grounds; they had rejected the view (we may recall al-Anṣārī's words) that a thing is "good on account of itself [*li-nafsihi*] or its class or an intrinsic attribute that is inseparably attached to it [*ṣifa nafsiyya lāzima lahu*]." Discounting objective features, they had focused on relative ones: the relationship to God's command; the relationship to contingent human purposes (*mā yuwāfiqu al-gharaḍ*).

The latter had presented itself as a naturalistic account of the way people use evaluative vocabulary, an account whose relativistic implications connect it to the similar-sounding formulation that Hobbes would offer when writing that "whatsoever is the object of any man's appetite or desire; that is it, which he for his part calleth *good*."[128] Yet later Ashʿarite writers would slough off these relativistic and linguistic trappings and give this proposal a more positive—or, let us say with Ayman Shihadeh, normative—expression, and no one more limpidly than al-Rāzī, who would state in his late work *al-Maṭālib al-ʿāliya*: "Everything that leads to preponderant benefit [*manfaʿa*] is good [*ḥasan*] and there is no other meaning to its being good than that fact, and everything that leads to preponderant harm [*maḍarra*] is bad [*qabīḥ*] and there is no other meaning to its being bad than that." Thus, there is "no meaning to good or bad than the fact of conducing to what serves and impairs one's welfare [*al-maṣāliḥ wa 'l-mafāsid*]."[129]

Fresh from Ibn Taymiyya's discussion of value, these words can only give us a start of anagnorisis. It is far from the sole start of recognition one experiences in holding up Ibn Taymiyya's ethical views against those that find voice in Ashʿarite writings. Similar responses could be provoked by leaning more closely over his notion of a social contract or the notion of communal welfare to which this is linked. To the more complex story of Ibn Taymiyya's relation to Ashʿarism that such threads promise, I will be returning in chapter 3.

OUR DISCUSSION TOOK its starting point from an exposition of Ibn Taymiyya's stance on the topic of the "determination of good and bad" that promised to illuminate the nature of his *via media*. Our initial impression of this *via media* was that it conceded so much to the type of rationalism and objectivism we associate with Muʿtazilite theology that it was tempting to call this a revised Muʿtazilism and close the subject. Yet a closer scrutiny of the evidence brought surprises, revealing that the objectivism Ibn Taymiyya adopts is in fact framed, seemingly exclusively, in terms of utility or benefit. These are terms that had formed only one moiety of the ethical theory developed by Muʿtazilite thinkers, in which deontological notions had occupied a prominent place. The consequences of this move have crucial repercussions not only for the way we understand the shape of Ibn Taymiyya's ethical thought but also for the way we write his relationship to his theological surroundings. Similarly, the fact that the nature of this move, and the distance it places between Ibn Taymiyya and the Muʿtazilites despite first impressions, should be an insight acquirable only by close scrutiny—by raising questions that Ibn Taymiyya does not himself pose, by working through conflicts and tensions that he does not call attention to, by the assiduous pursuit of interpretive inferences and textual juxtapositions—has much to tell us about the character of Ibn Taymiyya's thought and writing. This assiduous interpretive work may not always be able to find the threads it needs or seamlessly weave into the overall pattern every thread it finds, but it is rewarded by the discovery of sufficiently convincing patterns to make the case for its relevance.

We have taken one walk around Ibn Taymiyya's ethical understanding, but we are far from having yet surveyed it in full, just as we are far from having unraveled the entire range of messages present in the stage-setting exposition of his *via media*. To follow his *via media* further, we now need to splice back together two elements of the subject that were forcibly kept apart in the above discussion, finally reuniting questions of ontology to the questions of epistemology that formed their natural concomitant in classical discussions. A *via media* that acknowledges the objectivity of value—yet also a *via media* that acknowledges their accessibility to human reason. Human reason or, in that new idiom that has already come into view, human nature. Let us turn to Ibn Taymiyya's ethical epistemology.

2

Ethical Knowledge between Human Self-guidance and the Revealed Law

IT IS A claim that Ibn Taymiyya would repeat across his works with varying degrees of emphasis and depth. Opening his discussion in *al-Radd ʿala ʾl-manṭiqiyyīn* he would write: when people say "acts of justice are good and fine and their agents deserve praise and honor, and acts of injustice are evil and blameworthy and their agents deserve blame and dishonor," these judgments belong to "the greatest certainties known by human reason [*min aʿẓam al-yaqīniyyāt al-maʿlūma bi ʾl-ʿaql*]."[1] The claim is enunciated so clearly that there is no mistaking it: the knowledge of what is right and wrong is accessible to us by reason. Couched in the language of reason, elsewhere this claim is couched in the language of human nature or *fiṭra*.

My aim in this chapter will be to probe these claims more closely. Just what do people know about right and wrong through reason? How do the two ways of framing these claims—in terms of reason and in terms of nature—stand to be related? In doing so, my discussion will be guided by the same double aim that organized the previous chapter: to offer an insight into Ibn Taymiyya's positive view and an insight into how this view situates Ibn Taymiyya within his intellectual topography. As we will see in this chapter, on rather different terms than the last, these two insights cannot be so easily disengaged. What Ibn Taymiyya thinks is often made available to us only through what he says about what *others* think, frequently in a polemical context. Beginning with his thinking-*in-bello* in the *Radd*, I will plot the contours of the polemical exchange that provides the occasion for his ethical remarks and consider what we can take away about his positive understanding of ethical epistemology. I will then consider the notion of nature that comes together in this and other writings in order to address its status as a normative principle and epistemological source, before turning to the notion of reason—that more familiar focal term of classical Islamic debates about ethics—to assess the strength of the ethical appeal that Ibn Taymiyya makes to it.

For philosophical readers, the appearance of the notion of "nature" at this juncture—indeed a notion conjoined to that of reason—may provoke a sense of instant recognition. The notion of nature, as we know, has waged a long and fruitful partnership with ethical reflection in the Western intellectual tradition. The roots of this partnership can be found in ancient ethics and have sometimes been said to be already evident in Aristotle's appeal to the natural function of human beings when specifying the human good in the *Nicomachean Ethics* and tying this function to virtuous activity.[2] The ethical appeal to nature appears forcefully among Hellenistic writers, notably the Stoics, who develop it as the claim that living virtuously (and happily) is living according to nature. It is the Stoics who have been taken as the intellectual godfathers of what forms the best known ethical deployment of the concept of nature, linked, however, not to the perfectionist notion of virtue but to the more deontological notion of law—the tradition of natural law. The Roman writer Cicero offers a famous characterization of natural law when in the *Republic* he defines it as "right reason corresponding to nature, diffused in all . . . which commanding, calls to duty, and forbidding, deters from wrongdoing."[3] Taken over by Christian writers, this ethical appeal to nature was brought into dialogue with scriptural bases of the faith that included the well-known passage from Paul's epistle to the Romans: "For when Gentiles, who do not have the law, by nature do the things in the law, these, although not having the law, are a law to themselves, who show the work of the law written in their hearts" (*Romans* 2.14–15). Having led a vibrant life among the medieval scholastics, the notion of natural law achieved one of its most celebrated forms in the works of early modern writers such as Hugo Grotius and Samuel von Pufendorf. The connection between nature and reason evidenced in Cicero's statement constitutes a hallmark of this long tradition, tying the notion of natural law—as one writer epitomically puts it—to the idea of "a universal morality, accessible to all rational persons whatever their particular metaphysical or religious commitments."[4] In our day, ethical naturalism has continued to be revived in different forms among theorists who focus on natural law as well as among theorists preoccupied with virtue, and it has acquired new meanings outside these contexts that nevertheless continue to press the claim of its ethical relevance.[5]

Readers who think to align Ibn Taymiyya's ethical appeal to nature with the tradition just evoked may find much to surprise them. Yet this swift encapsulation of the ethical appeal to nature should after all not mislead us with false pretences of unity. The historical articulations of this appeal have been multifarious, and core notions, including the notion of nature itself, have not survived unchanged. Instructively calling up this history to read Ibn Taymiyya's ethical appeal against it will partly be a matter of choosing the episodes of this history on which to focus, keeping in mind that the documentation of difference can sometimes be more instructive than that of similarity. Before such broader comparisons can be possible, however, we need to lean closer to consider Ibn Taymiyya's view on its own terms and against its sources—and this includes its formative argumentative contexts.

Imagining Moral Judgments Away: A Philosophical Thought Experiment

The story of the ethical argument of the *Radd* can be told at least twice. Told from one perspective, it is the story of Ibn Taymiyya's engagement with the *falāsifa* and his fierce contestation of their epistemological claims. The broader aim of this work is to respond to and defeat the glorified view of philosophical logic as a tool for the attainment of true knowledge. Logic, Ibn Taymiyya will argue, is more a hindrance than a help, and human understanding can proceed no less, if not more, successfully without the benefit of its technical tools, such as those privileged stocks-in-trade, the definition and the syllogism. In the backdrop lies the larger story of what Michot has termed the "Avicennan pandemic," which swept through Islamic intellectual culture from the twelfth century onward, and of the confident march of logic on strongholds of the religious sciences such as theology and law.[6] Told from another perspective, the ethical argument of the *Radd* is the story of Ibn Taymiyya's engagement with Ashʿarite theologians, who had been among the most enthusiastic victims of this intellectual pandemic. The polemical encounter over ethics in the *Radd* thus takes shape as an encounter with the master practitioner of Islamic philosophy, Avicenna, and with the luminary of late Ashʿarism, al-Rāzī, in his capacity as a commentator on Avicenna's work. And it is a specific view of ethical propositions expressed by Avicenna and appropriated with little change by al-Rāzī that Ibn Taymiyya takes as his immediate target and as the foil for articulating his own position.

What had been that view? It was a claim that had appeared in several places of Avicenna's logical writings, in those sections where the class of "widely accepted propositions" had come up for discussion. Having identified the demonstrative syllogism (*qiyās burhānī*) as the type of syllogism uniquely capable of producing the highest degree of certainty (*yaqīn*), Avicenna had proposed to isolate the types of propositions that partook of the quality of certainty (*yaqīniyyāt*) and could be used as premises for such syllogisms. In this privileged list, he had included primary propositions (*awwaliyyāt*), sensory propositions (*maḥsūsāt*), experiential or empirical propositions (*mujarrabāt*), intuited propositions (*ḥadsiyyāt*), propositions transmitted by universal report (*mutawātirāt*), and propositions that contain their syllogisms (*qaḍāyā qiyāsatuhā maʿahā*).[7] Among the propositions pointedly excluded from this privileged category was the class of "widely accepted" propositions (*mashhūrāt* or *dhaʾiʿāt*) or "praiseworthy opinions" (*ārāʾ maḥmūda*), as he also termed them, which comprise familiar moral judgments such as that "justice is good" and "causing pain is bad." Such propositions "have no basis other than the fact of their wide dissemination" (*la ʿumdata lahā illā al-shuhra*) and are usable only for dialectical arguments.[8]

As an opening to one of the most interesting ethical discussions in Islamic intellectual history, this dry classificational claim may seem rather uncompelling, and it may not rouse us to an immediate response or capture our imagination. The next move to which Avicenna had coupled it, on the other hand, is not only calculated to provoke our imagination but is comprehensible only as a calculated appeal to it. For the claim that people do not know ethical propositions with certainty had to be maintained in the teeth of the fact that people often think they do. It was then a radical appeal to the imagination that Avicenna would offer his readers to help them mark the distinction between what they *think* they know and what they really *do* know. These propositions, he tells us in *al-Ishārāt wa ʾl-tanbīhāt*, are such that

> were a human being to be left with his bare intellect [*ʿaql mujarrad*], estimative power [*wahm*], and sense perception [*ḥiss*], were he not educated to accept and acknowledge their judgments, were induction [*istiqrāʾ*] not to incline his strong opinion to make a judgment due to the multiplicity of particular cases, and were one not provoked to them by the mercy, abashment, pride, zeal, and other [sentiments] that are found in human nature [*ṭabīʿa*], then his intellect, his estimative power, or his senses would not compel him to assert them [*lam yaqḍi bihā al-insān tāʿatan li-ʿaqlihi aw-wahmihi aw-ḥissihi*]. Examples are our judgment that it is wrong [*qabīḥ*] to despoil people of their property and that it is wrong to lie . . . [or] that it is wrong to slaughter animals, which flows from the instinctual response of sympathy. . . . Nothing of this is required by the pure intellect [*ʿaql sādhij*]. If a human being were to imagine himself [*law tawahhama*] as created at once with a complete intellect, having received no education and not being under the power of psychological and moral sentiments [*lam yuṭiʿinfiʿālan nafsāniyyan aw-khuluqiyyan*], he would not assert any such propositions. It is not the same with his judgment that the whole is greater than the part.[9]

The basic thrust of this remarkable passage can be summed up in a few words: Take human nature as you know it, peel away certain key features, and you will find that you can no longer make moral judgments as you used to. Your moral consciousness will suffer collapse. What are the features whose removal can have such a dramatic effect? Avicenna speaks of the education we receive, the inductive reasoning we practice, and the sentiments that move us.

This list may strike us as an odd one, in need of a commentary to help us see how its elements mesh. Elsewhere, Avicenna provides us with a partial but important interpretive key. For this passage, crucially, does not make clear that what you discover once you scratch the palimpsest clean and arrive at the deepest layer is something you can call your "nature." The term "nature," it will be noticed, does not appear in this passage, yet it does so in another passage of Avicenna's *Najā* in the context of his discussion of estimative propositions (*wahmiyyāt*). There, the notion of nature is brought up to be defined precisely in the terms of the imaginative vantage point conjured in the *Ishārāt*: "The meaning of nature [*fiṭra*] is for one to imagine oneself having come into the world in a single stroke as an adult possessed of reason [*bāligh ʿāqil*], yet having heard no opinions, espoused no doctrines, associated with no nation and come to know no government, but having observed perceptible things and derived images from them. One then presents something to one's mind and tries to doubt it, and if one succeeds in doubting it, one's nature does not testify to it. If it impossible for one to doubt it, it is necessitated [*tūjibuhu*] by nature."[10]

The character of this moment as an active appeal to the imagination—as an active thought experiment, to put it more recognizably for modern readers—that can serve as a practical tool for testing different types of judgments stands out far more clearly in this passage. And so will the lineaments of the insight at which it aims. For with the term "nature" now before us, one of the most potent yet also most familiar ways this thought experiment invites to be construed is in terms of a contrast between nature and what, using several varying terms across different texts (*ʿāda, iṣṭilāḥ, muwāḍaʿāt ittifāqiyya*), Avicenna suggests we think of as "convention."[11] Seasoned readers of Avicenna's work will notice a similarity between this thought experiment and others performed to even greater effect elsewhere in his work, such as the "flying man argument," designed to press an insight about the immateriality of the soul.[12] This particular thought experiment seems different in several respects, not least in the negativity of the insight at which it aims, serving not as an instrument for producing certainty but for engineering doubt.

The central contrast, and its creative doubt, will remind us of a perspective on morality that has carved long tracks in our intellectual history. We may think of that distinctive antithesis between *nomos* and *physis* that traversed ancient Greek thought, and whose relativistic implications when applied to morality were clearly drawn by the sophists. Closer to our own times, we may think of the skepticism different thinkers have expressed about the moral intuitions to which philosophers and laymen often appeal, querying their trustworthiness by reading them back to problematic and highly contingent origins—to "discarded religious systems," "warped views of sex and bodily functions," "customs necessary for the survival of the group in social and economic circumstances that now lie in the distant past."[13] Beliefs that seem to us intellectually basic may not always wear their real foundations on their sleeve.

The contrast between nature and convention may thus offer us the most intuitive way of reading the terms of Avicenna's thought experiment. In this capacity, we may recognize in it an imaginary that would later receive its most vivid dramatization in Ibn Ṭufayl's (d. 1185) philosophical novel *Ḥayy ibn Yaqẓān*, in which Avicenna's thought experiment would be converted into the tale of a lone human being growing up in isolation and developing an understanding of the world deriving solely from the data of his unspoiled nature.[14] Yet it will be clear that Avicenna's terms are not exhausted by this simple contrast. Moving too rapidly toward this intuitive reading, in fact, is liable to blind us to this experiment's peculiar features and to those of its features that are likely to provoke puzzlement rather than recognition. So what—to consider more closely—is the epistemic vantage point that this thought experiment isolates?

It is constructed, at the simplest level, by an act of exclusion and an act of inclusion. Included in the vantage point, the *Ishārāt* passage suggests, are three main features: estimation (*wahm*), sense perception (*ḥiss*), and reason or the intellect (*ʿaql*). Excluded are the features already mentioned: reactions that have been acquired through social education; emotional responses such as sympathy, zeal, and shame; and inductive judgments. To this list, the version of the thought experiment found in the logical section of Avicenna's *Shifāʾ* adds another: utility or welfare (*maṣlaḥa*), which al-Rāzī, reprising the experiment, parses using the more cognitive-sounding "*judgments* of utility" (*qaḍāyā maṣlaḥiyya*).[15] And considered this closely, Avicenna's terms may now seem perplexing. To ask one obvious question: there appear to be no fewer than *two* notions of nature at work here—one, indicated by the term *ṭabīʿa*, connected to features that we are asked to exclude (psychological and moral sentiments); another, indicated by the term *fiṭra*, connected to the vantage point we isolate by this exclusion. Why does Avicenna invite us to detach ourselves from nature in one sense and not in another?

The answer to this particular question is not too hard to piece together, and Avicenna offers us the resources for doing so in a seminal passage in the psychological section of his *Shifāʾ* that provides a crucial interpretive foil against which to read his remarks about ethical judgments. What we find fleshed out there is precisely the social genealogy of these judgments gnomically alluded to in his logical remarks. Human beings, we hear, need association (*mushāraka*) in order not merely to survive but indeed to flourish. One of the special features of human association is that "utility [*maṣlaḥa*] demands that among the acts [human beings] would ordinarily perform, there should be certain acts they must not perform. They come to learn this while young and they are brought up on it, and from the time of childhood they grow accustomed [*taʿawwada*] to hearing that they must not perform those acts, so that this belief comes to be ingrained in them like an instinctive response [*kaʾl-gharīzī*]."[16] These acts are called "bad" (*qabīḥ*), while the acts one should perform are called "good" or "fine" (*jamīla*). It is this conception of the social genealogy of ethical judgments that shadows Avicenna's reference, only moments later, to the peculiarly human emotion (*infiʿāl nafsānī*) of shame (*khajal*). Shame is a response that results from "a person's awareness that another is aware that he has done one of the things that it has been commonly agreed [*ujmiʿa ʿalā*] one should not do."[17] The evaluative standards built into our reflective self-assessment, this suggests, depend on socially acquired and—no less relevantly, as the reference to "common agreement" tersely indicates—socially *produced* beliefs about right and wrong. It is the educability of our emotions and their permeability to social influence that makes it necessary to exclude them from a thought experiment whose aim is to isolate a vantage point that is epistemically prior to social influence.

Acquired custom, as Avicenna's contemporary, the philosopher Miskawayh (d. 1030), would suggest more clearly, cuts in two ways, educating us into new emotional responses and rewiring the emotional responses and value judgments to which we are already disposed on a more instinctive, nonrational level. Thus, the instinctive sense of sympathy that derives from our animal nature (*ḥayawāniyya*) may lead us to judge the slaughter of animals abhorrent; this is a value judgment that is also mentioned by Avicenna and that often served as a flashpoint in debates about the relation between reason and revelation in light of the Law's prescription of the slaughter of animals. Yet why is it that butchers or veterans of war experience no such abhorrence? It is due to a difference in custom or habituation (*ʿāda*), for with repeated exposure, "the sense of revulsion falls away, and the act of slaughtering and butchering comes to seem no different . . . than that of sharpening a pencil or carving wood." The notion of custom is here deployed more widely to refer to formative processes that may introduce variations in the ethical responses of members of even a single social community. Yet it calls attention to the environmental modifiability of our responses that also seems critical for the way we receive Avicenna's discussion.[18]

In clarifying Avicenna's exclusion of sentiments from this vantage point, importantly, the above passage from the *Shifāʾ* also obliquely sheds light on another exclusion, that of utility or welfare. For to the extent that utility is interpreted through the notion of association (*mushāraka*) and refers us to the social community, which propagates those principles that are serviceable for communal life, the reason for its exclusion would seem to lie, once again, in the fact that it is posterior to the vantage point of the individual inquirer who, as the *Najā* put it, has "heard no opinions, espoused no doctrines, associated with no nation, and come to know no government."[19] Avicenna's emphasis on the inescapable necessity of association, at the same time, calls attention to a point that we may otherwise overlook. For in saying that ethical propositions are "merely" conventional, we may be tempted to hear the "merely" so loudly that we end up forgetting that such norms are vitally necessary for our social existence, and hence for our existence as such.

Yet while Avicenna was not denying the practical value of such principles, it is nevertheless evident that he intended to deny their epistemic value. And it is precisely at this point that a further and rather more pressing puzzle would seem to attach itself to the thought experiment he draws up in order to press that claim. If this thought experiment is intended to isolate a vantage point that carries a certain epistemic privilege, why does it include features that do not carry such privilege? For in the list of components included within this vantage point we see reason; but we also see estimation and sense perception. And what we know about the estimative faculty as Avicenna understands it is that it plays important roles in the mental life of human beings and indeed other animals, but also that its deliverances must often be treated with distrust. Estimation follows the senses, and it leads us astray when it oversteps its limits and tries to account for non-sensible things in sensible terms. Estimation, for example, would have us believe that every existent must be spatially located. It is the intellect that must correct for such errors and others—though even when it does so, estimation will often refuse to surrender its sense of conviction.[20]

It is for this very reason that the notion of *fiṭra* as Avicenna employs it cannot itself be considered epistemically privileged. In the *Najā*, Avicenna makes clear that both the deliverances of our estimative faculty *and* those of our rational faculty are included in the "testimony of our nature" (*shahādat al-fiṭra*). Hence it is that "not everything that is necessitated by human nature is true, but indeed much of it is false."[21] Deborah Black draws the obvious conclusion when she states that "any appeal to something's being in accordance with *fiṭrah* must of necessity be epistemologically irrelevant: it can tell us nothing in itself about whether or not we can trust our cognitive instincts."[22] It is only one *subset* of what is demanded by our natural cognitive instincts, in fact, that we can trust—and this is the subset of our nature that corresponds to the operation of reason. In Avicenna's own words: *innamā al-ṣādiq fiṭrat al-quwwa allatī tusammā ʿaqlan*.[23] So to ask again, why does the epistemic vantage point isolated by the thought experiment include features that speak to an epistemically unprivileged notion of nature?

The inclusion of the estimation, it should be said, seems puzzling for an additional set of reasons. For what Avicenna has to say about this faculty elsewhere is calculated to highlight how *closely* connected it is to the ethical domain. When he discusses the faculty of practical reason (*al-ʿaql al-ʿamalī*), which operates on the basis of the kind of ethical propositions under discussion here, he makes estimation a tributary to its work.[24] Even more crucially, in elucidating the functions of the faculty of estimation and identifying its peculiar objects, Avicenna explicitly links it with the notions of benefit and harm and their more sensory correlates, pleasure and pain, with what is agreeable and disagreeable (*muwāfaqa, mukhālafa*), and (in a stronger ethical register) with the notions of good and evil (*khayr, sharr*). These ligaments are brought out crisply in the paradigm case through which Avicenna exemplifies the operations of the estimative faculty: the sheep that "sees" the wolf's hostility. The sheep sees the wolf "as" hostile, as harmful, as *bad* for it—an act of seeing-as that is achieved through the estimation. These ligaments are also brought out in another example Avicenna uses to illustrate this type of instinctive response, one that our later discussion will place in a particularly evocative light, namely the manner in which infants attach themselves to their mother's breast. This is the product of an instinctive reflex that Avicenna speaks of as "implanted by God" (*gharīza fi 'l-nafs ja'alaha fīhi al-ilhām al-ilāhī*) and that show the infant as unwittingly orienting itself toward what serves its good.[25]

The interpretive skein that these puzzles roll out is too complex to untangle in full. Leaving this task to some of Avicenna's more dedicated readers, here I will have to flatten the skein into a simple proposal that I will posit rather than defend in detail. For this thought experiment, as I suggested, can be read as an attempt to help us mark the distinction between what we *think* we know and what we really *do* know. Its aim can most readily be seen as an attempt to provide a criterion for distinguishing between two types of propositions that carry a similar sense of self-evidence yet command unequal degrees of trust—namely widely accepted and primary propositions (*awwaliyyāt*).[26] The proposition often invoked to exemplify the latter class is the judgment that the whole is greater than the part. It is against this context, in fact, that the aims of the thought experiment, and the particular privilege its viewpoint carries, can be grasped more precisely. For taken on its own, Avicenna's claim about ethical propositions is not immediately a claim about their truth. "These widely accepted propositions," he writes in the continuation of the *Ishārāt* passage we have seen, "may be true, and may be false."[27] But if they are true, this will have to form the end rather than the starting point of an argument—and more specifically the conclusion of a demonstrative syllogism. In this, they are unlike primary propositions, which are epistemically sufficiently robust to serve as premises for demonstrative syllogisms.[28]

Primary propositions, crucially, are counted among the deliverances of reason: they are judgments "necessitated by pure reason through its essence [*yūjibuhā al-'aql al-ṣarīḥ li-dhātihi*]."[29] Despite the more inclusive reference to estimation and sense perception in the passage of the *Ishārāt* we heard, the more restricted reference to reason registers strongly in Avicenna's remarks—we will recall his assertion that "nothing of this is required by the pure intellect ['*aql sādhij*]." No less striking, in the variant of the thought experiment that is presented in the *Shifā'*, it is reason that is *exclusively* referred to as the constituent of the epistemic vantage point it seeks to isolate. Excluding all the factors mentioned in the *Ishārāt*, Avicenna asks us to refer to reason as the only arbiter (*lam yaltafit ilā ḥākim ghayr al-'aql*), and when he comes to state his conclusion—under such conditions, we will be brought to doubt judgments like "justice is good" and "injustice is bad"—he crucially parses this by referring once again to the more privileged perspective of natural reason (*ṣidquhā laysa mimmā yatabayyanu bi-fiṭrat al-ʿaql*).[30] This more restrictive parsing of the experiment, finally, is also the one we find reflected in al-Rāzī's reformulation in his commentary.

The most coherent way of understanding Avicenna's thought experiment is thus the one that takes it to be isolating an epistemic vantage point identified with the privileged term of reason, leaving open how the presence of the other faculties (*ḥiss* and *wahm*) should be construed.[31] Thus distilled, the terms we are left with return us to the governing contrast from which we began. Strip away the contingent accretions of social learning, strip yourself down to your original nature as a rational being, and you will find that your moral consciousness rolls up and disappears. With this disappearing act in sight, we are ready to turn to Ibn Taymiyya's reception of it.

Reclaiming Certainty: Moral Judgments between Natural Desire and Empirical Reason

It will be clear from the discussion above that Avicenna's thought experiment raises more questions than it answers. And one question it never addresses is just how we should consider its own probative status. Exactly what have you done when you have imagined what Avicenna has invited you to? Given the explicit concern of this experiment, particularly, to help us mark the difference between what we think we know and what we really do know, it is worth asking: How do you tell the difference between whether you have *really* imagined or whether you merely think you did? How would you respond to someone who said "I have imagined this, but my moral consciousness has not turned a hair"?

This kind of question may dispose us to lend a more attentive ear to the proposal articulated by Meryem Sebti regarding that seeming confrère of our own thought experiment, the "flying man argument," namely that it should be understood as carrying the probative force of an appeal to direct experience or *mushāhada*. Either you have that experience (this suggests) or you don't—and whether you do may depend on whether your intellectual gifts permit you.[32] The differences between the two thought experiments may prevent an easy transfer of this insight to our own case. But we can already see the grounds of the skepticism that some of Avicenna's readers would later direct to this type of experiment; as we can see the grounds of the complaint that Ibn Taymiyya lodges against it: it is nothing but a mere assertion (*daʿwā mujarrada*).[33]

In discussing the vantage point Avicenna seeks to isolate, I raised a question about the privilege attaching to it. Ibn Taymiyya's polemical campaign against Avicenna's view of ethical judgments is premised on a clear perception of the epistemic privilege Avicenna meant to deny them. His counterassertion has already come before us, but now we can hear it again: when people say "acts of justice are good and fine, and their agents deserve praise and honor, and acts of injustice are evil and blameworthy, and their agents deserve blame and dishonor," these judgments belong to "the greatest certainties known by human reason [*min aʿẓam al-yaqīniyyāt al-maʿlūma biʾl-ʿaql*]." A deeper probing of this counterclaim would seem to hold the promise of a better understanding of Ibn Taymiyya's ethical epistemology. Yet given that Ibn Taymiyya's claims are offered as counterclaims, in approaching them there will be two separate questions to consider, one regarding Ibn Taymiyya's positive view of ethical epistemology and one about how the terms of this view speak to the terms of his interlocutors as we have outlined them. And as we will see, there will be a further question to ask as to whether the two perspectives can be entirely disengaged.

Ibn Taymiyya's discussion leaves no doubt that part of it must be read in straightforwardly dialectical terms. Large segments of his discussion are devoted to uncovering the internal inconsistencies produced by Avicenna's ethical position. I have spoken of the questions provoked by Avicenna's thought experiment as "puzzles," yet what the interpreter receives as a puzzle, the polemicist will more naturally receive as a weakness. Even if the best interpretation of Avicenna's thought experiment might lie in excluding the estimation and sense perception from its terms, Ibn Taymiyya does not grant him the benefit of charitable interpretation and, taking him at his word, brandishes a long list of contradictions that result from their inclusion. You say the estimation has nothing of ethical significance to tell us—yet you acknowledge it allows animals and human beings to perceive other beings *as* hostile or friendly, attractive or repulsive. You say the senses are blind to ethical meaning—yet elsewhere you speak about the pleasure arising from virtuous actions, and this pleasure corresponds to an internal sense (*ḥiss bāṭinī*). You dismiss ethical propositions as epistemic chaff—yet you then build your view of the soul's afterlife and of posthumous intellectual pleasures on their foundation.[34]

It is this polemical intent that partly accounts for the dizzying plurality of epistemological registers with which Ibn Taymiyya's discussion is packed. Ibn Taymiyya has been walking around Avicenna's philosophy and taking notes, and he returns to the *Radd* and begins to work his way down his shopping list of cross-references. In doing so, he crucially takes on epistemological terms that speak to two moves that Avicenna's account had not wholly fused: his exclusion of ethical judgments from the class of certain premises suitable for demonstrative arguments (a larger class that included primary, empirical, and universally transmitted propositions, among others) and his exclusion of them from the class of premises known through the "original position" of nature (a class that, as I argued, was intended to isolate primary propositions). We thus see ethical propositions connected to reason, to sense perception, to the estimation—the privileged epistemic faculties included prima facie in the thought experiment. We also see ethical propositions connected to experience (*tajribiyyāt*)—one of the privileged propositions included in the class of *yaqīniyyāt*. The sheer luxuriance of epistemological terms in which this results is made evident when, in the space of a few lines, Ibn Taymiyya refers to "people's knowledge of these propositions through nature and through experience [*bi'l-fiṭra wa-bi'l-tajriba*]" and then again as propositions "known by the senses and by reason [*al-ḥiss wa'l-'aql*]."[35]

Yet in this fluid welter of polemically deployed terms, it is clear that Ibn Taymiyya is not merely arguing *ex concessis* but also arguing independently and speaking in his own voice. Thus, having taken Avicenna to task for giving contradictory accounts of the role of the estimation in ethics—"*you say* it has nothing ethically significant to tell us—yet *you also say* it allows animals and human beings to perceive other beings as hostile or friendly, attractive or repulsive"—Ibn Taymiyya continues:

> This faculty that he [i.e., Avicenna] calls "estimation" is the one through which human beings perceive the friendliness [*ṣadāqa*] of the friend and the hostility of the enemy, through which each of two spouses perceives the beloved quality of the other, and through which one human being inclines to or is repulsed by another.... And *it is known* that this faculty inclines toward the type of person who it knows to be just, honest [*ṣādiq*], and beneficent, and is repulsed by the type of person who it knows to be mendacious, unjust, and a wrongdoer—indeed, it inclines to this person even if it has not been benefited or harmed by him. People are naturally formed to love justice and those party to it, and to hate injustice and those party to it. And it is this love which is in human nature [*hādhihi al-maḥabba allatī fi'l-fiṭra*] that gives the meaning of [the former's] being good and it is this hatred that gives the meaning of [the latter's] being bad.[36]

Ibn Taymiyya appears to leave it open whether he is ready to follow Avicenna in calling this faculty *wahm*; but he leaves no doubt that he accepts that human beings perceive the specific qualities Avicenna had made the province of this faculty. What is central for our present question is that it is then in terms of this type of perception that Ibn Taymiyya signals—positively and in his own voice—that ethical perception must partly be understood.

This understanding will not be entirely new to us, having already stepped into our view in the previous chapter in the context of a question about the place of utility within Ibn Taymiyya's thinking. It is now a matter of turning it around to face toward the questions of epistemology that concern us more immediately—and this includes: toward the notion of *fiṭra* that we want to get in clear sight. The statement that concludes the above passage appears to press a more narrowly semantic claim: "good" and "bad," respectively, mean "provoking love" and "provoking hatred." As noted in chapter 1, this semantic claim locks onto an empirical claim: human beings in fact love certain types of actions and hate others. What we may now bring out more strongly is the fact that Ibn Taymiyya's epistemological view—both his contention that, *pace* Avicenna and his retinue, we know ethical propositions with certainty and his contention that we know them by nature—involves a crucial move away from a more cognitive vocabulary to the noncognitive vocabulary of love or desire. The claim that we know right and wrong by reason is partly given as a claim that we desire right and hate wrong. And the notion of human nature or *fiṭra* is in great part given through the notion of love or desire (*ḥubb, maḥabba*).

In chapter 1 I debated whether the emotional responses that people have to actions—or, as the passage above indicates, to the qualities of those who perform them—can be understood as a response to their intrinsic value or to the interests they serve, whether the individual agent's or the community's. My suggestion was that it is the latter interpretation that best harmonizes with Ibn Taymiyya's pervasive emphasis on utility; in this respect, the use of "love" as a translation for Ibn Taymiyya's linchpin terms may obscure interpretive possibilities that the use of "desire" makes it possible to pick out more clearly. The same emphasis on interest and indeed self-interest stands out in a seminal passage in the *Radd* that elicits Ibn Taymiyya's translation of cognitive claims about ethics into noncognitive terms with particular starkness:

> The foundations of these [i.e., ethical] judgments are necessarily known by people, for they are formed by nature to love what is agreeable to them and to hate what harms them [*al-nufūs . . . maftūra ʿalā ḥubb mā yulāʾimuhā wa-bughḍ mā yaḍurruhā*], and what is signified by the term "good" is what is agreeable to them and by "bad" what harms them. So if they are formed by nature to love the one [*maftūra ʿalā ḥubb*] and to hate the other . . . it is evident that people know these widespread propositions by their inborn nature [*bi-fiṭarihim*].[37]

It is *qua* beneficial and harmful, Ibn Taymiyya here makes clear, that we desire acts, and the qualities of acts *qua* beneficial and harmful that ground the meaning of evaluative terms. Ibn Taymiyya speaks of the meaning of terms, and I have accordingly described this as a "semantic claim." Yet what he seems to have in mind is not so much the question how "good" and "bad" are defined, but to which actions they are applied, and thus which features make actions good and bad. Nature, in turn, is the ground of ethical knowledge taken as the principle through which we desire what is beneficial to us and are averse to what is harmful.

Having brought this out, we stand face to face with what I believe lies at the heart of Ibn Taymiyya's understanding of the concept of *fiṭra* in the ethical context. It is as a principle of desire, and more specifically as a desire that has benefit as its primary object, that the notion of *fiṭra* is repeatedly characterized in Ibn Taymiyya's ethical remarks across a number of different writings. "People are naturally constituted to love what benefits them and hate what harms them," as Ibn Taymiyya encapsulates it in one of his epistles (*al-ʿabd maftūr ʿalā ḥubb mā yanfaʿuhu wa-bughḍ mā yaḍurruhu*).[38] It is a characterization that invites important questions, and one of the main questions I will be exploring later in this chapter is what it has to tell us about the status of nature as a normative principle and epistemological source within Ibn Taymiyya's scheme. Yet his understanding of *fiṭra* has been deployed in the context of a very specific argument. It is thus important to begin by considering how this conception engages its terms.

One of the reasons this argumentative exchange has seemed to me worth documenting in some detail is that I take it to have provided a key formative context for Ibn Taymiyya's ethical development of the notion of *fiṭra*. "Ethical propositions are not known from the perspective of human nature."—"On the contrary, they are."[39] Yet in subverting Avicenna's position and articulating his own counterclaim, it is clear that Ibn Taymiyya has done far more than remove the sign of negation over Avicenna's central claim. There are in fact a lot of questions to be raised concerning how Ibn Taymiyya speaks to the terms of the specific argument—if we allow ourselves to call this thought experiment "an argument"—with which Avicenna had supported it. It is undoubtable, on the one hand, that Ibn Taymiyya does not *wish* to wholly speak to its terms—and that is because he rejects many of them. He rejects Avicenna's category of "primary propositions," against which the thought experiment had been framed. He also rejects, crucially, the distinction between the "privileged" and "unprivileged" aspects of our nature, *wahm* and *ʿaql*, and rejects Avicenna's view about the inferior epistemic status of the estimation.[40] Yet the most important difference lies in the way he treats the notion of *fiṭra* itself. For even a superficial reading will reveal that the notion of *fiṭra* that Ibn Taymiyya deploys in asserting the claim "we know ethical propositions by nature" has little to connect it with the notion of *fiṭra* that Avicenna had deployed in denying it.

The emotional responses through which Ibn Taymiyya specifies our nature in this context—we naturally love and rejoice over the ethically good, and we naturally hate and are aggrieved by the ethically bad—invite us to consider them under what Avicenna had called "psychological and moral sentiments," though they can also be linked to the estimation, as we have seen.[41] The attraction and repulsion we respectively feel toward benefit and harm, through which he also specifies our nature here and elsewhere, seem to directly evoke what Avicenna and al-Rāzī had referred to as utility (*maṣlaḥa*). If I am right in thinking that the first type of emotional response is ultimately grounded in the natural attraction and repulsion we feel toward benefit and harm, it is our natural attraction to what serves our welfare that forms the core of Ibn Taymiyya's conception of *fiṭra* in the ethical context. Yet the key point is that both types of responses correspond to elements that Avicenna, and al-Rāzī after him, had excluded from the vantage point of the thought experiment, which picked out the contours of *fiṭra*, and more specifically, as I have suggested, of *fiṭrat al-ʿaql*—of the natural operation of reason.

The most radical criticism one can offer an argument, of course, is to interrogate its presuppositions. Yet while my main aim here is not to evaluate this argument on its own merits, a closer evaluation would have to raise a question as to whether this particular interrogation is accomplished without loss. For to the extent that Avicenna's reasons for excluding emotional responses from the vantage point of the thought experiment had rested on the insight that ethical sentiments are acquired precisely through a process of social enculturation reflecting the interests of the community, to simply appeal to the existence of such sentiments and ascribe them to human nature without argument would seem to beg the question as this had been put.[42] Ibn Taymiyya himself, we will recall from chapter 1, acknowledges this communal perspective elsewhere in his work, but this acknowledgment remains occluded in the *Radd* itself, where the different perspectives from which the benefit of actions and the emotional responses they provoke can be considered—first-person and third-person, first-person singular and first-person plural—are passed over without comment.

There will be something more to say in the next chapter about how these moments of Ibn Taymiyya's thinking connect. Here we should instead resume our main track of questioning. What can we say positively, I asked, about Ibn Taymiyya's ethical epistemology? Central to his epistemology, the above suggests, is a proposal to ground our knowledge of ethical propositions in human nature understood in desiderative terms. Yet Ibn Taymiyya's epistemological register in this discussion, as I noted earlier, is a rather more composite one. At places he speaks of our knowing ethical propositions "through nature and through experience" (*bi'l-fiṭra wa-bi'l-tajriba*); elsewhere he speaks of them as "known by the senses and by reason" (*al-ḥiss wa'l-ʿaql*). And it is indeed the emphasis on reason that rings out early in his discussion when he describes them as "the greatest certainties known by human reason" (*min aʿẓam al-yaqīniyyāt al-maʿlūma bi'l-ʿaql*).[43]

The emphasis on reason is doubly significant here. For apart from aligning Ibn Taymiyya's epistemological concern more directly with the cognitivist term that defined Avicenna's and al-Rāzī's vantage point, it even more crucially aligns his concern with the focal term that had stood at the heart of the classical *kalām* debates about the epistemology of value. For the polarizing topic of these debates had been parsed precisely as a question about the role of reason as the source of our epistemic access to the ethical value of actions. The claim that it does, as I have already mentioned, typified the viewpoint of Muʿtazilite theologians. "It belongs to mature reason [*kamāl al-ʿaql*] to know that injustice is something we deserve blame for," as we heard from ʿAbd al-Jabbār in chapter 1.[44] Once we know the ground or act-description that a given action instantiates, we have an immediate knowledge (*ʿilm ḍarūrī*) of its value (though extra reflection may be required in some cases). In making God's command the ontological cause of value, Ashʿarites, by contrast, had also made revelation its epistemic source. There is a more complex story, in fact, to be told about the Ashʿarite ethical viewpoint at this juncture, which will come into view in the next chapter. Yet the familiar Ashʿarite opposition to a rationalist epistemology of value makes it easier to explain why Avicenna's denial of such an epistemology would have found an eager audience among Ashʿarite theologians, and also easier—on the surface at least—to explain why one of Ibn Taymiyya's interlocutors in the *Radd* should have been an Ashʿarite.

It will not surprise us, then, to find that Ibn Taymiyya, opening his discussion in the *Radd*, quickly makes the link between this philosophical debate and the classical theological debates about value. The claim he frames in this vicinity, couched in terms of utility—what we identified as the primary good-making feature in his scheme in the previous chapter—is also couched in the epistemological term central to those debates, and registers as a clear claim of reason. "The goodness and badness that pertains to the actions of human beings is a matter of whether actions are beneficial or harmful to them [i.e., human beings]. And there is no doubt that this can be known by reason." Similar claims recur later in the *Radd*. "The most distinctive trait of human reason," we hear, "is that one knows what benefits one and does it, and knows what harms one and avoids it."[45]

Fresh from our discussion of Ibn Taymiyya's notion of human nature, however, our first response may be bafflement. Ibn Taymiyya has spoken of human nature as the source of our desire for what is beneficial, and thus as a source of knowledge: people are "formed by nature to love [*mafṭūra ʿalā ḥubb*] what is agreeable to them and to hate what harms them"—*therefore* "people know these widespread propositions by their inborn nature [*bi-fiṭarihim yaʿlamūna hādhihi al-qaḍāyā al-mashhūra*]." Now we hear that reason forms the source of that knowledge. What are we to make of this equivocation between nature and reason, and reason and desire? Ibn Taymiyya does not comment on this himself, and once again leaves it to his readers to speculate how his fluid transitions between these elements might be explained. These fluid seams, I would argue, point to an aspect of this exchange that has not yet come into view—to that second and more complex storytelling filter that concerns the Ashʿarite contribution to this exchange and Ibn Taymiyya's relationship to it. Deferring this part of our story to the next chapter, here I will consider the most fruitful way Ibn Taymiyya's welter of epistemological registers can be unified and his invocation of reason filled out.

We find the material for this unifying story by turning back to a passage we saw in part in the previous chapter, which it is now worth quoting more fully. When people say "justice is good," we heard, this means that people find joy in justice and derive benefit from it. When they say "injustice is bad," this means that people are aggrieved and harmed by it. And it is a fact, Ibn Taymiyya continues,

> that people's knowledge of these propositions through nature and through experience [*bi 'l-fiṭra wa-bi 'l-tajriba*] is greater than it is with respect to most medical judgments, such as that scammony purges bile. Why then are empirical propositions [*tajribiyyāt*] reckoned as certainties [*yaqīniyyāt*] while these ones, though more widespread among people and more widely tested by experience, are not reckoned as certainties? And this, even though those testing them through experience [*al-mujarribīn lahā*] are greater in number and have better knowledge and credibility, and even though the worldly particulars that relate to them exceed the particulars of the former in number . . .?

Covering old ground yet also breaking new:

> One naturally finds in justice, truthfulness, knowledge, and beneficence a pleasure and happiness which one does not find in injustice, lying, and ignorance. . . . That is why [people] experience love for those who do these things and a desire to praise them and wish them well, and they are naturally formed [*mafṭūrūn*] to love and take pleasure in this . . . just as they have been naturally formed to take pleasure in food and drink and to experience pain upon hunger or thirst. Why then should *those* propositions belong to the certainties known by the senses and by reason, such as by experience among other things, whereas *these* ones should not be considered rational propositions that are also known by the senses and by reason [*al-ḥiss wa 'l-ʿaql*], even though matters stand more strongly with respect to them?[46]

The lavish array of epistemological terms with which this passage is splashed may immediately confuse us. Yet out of this array, it is worth fastening on one key element that appears in the above passage: the notion of experience, or *tajriba*. This was a notion that had been explored most systematically by the *falāsifa* against a background of Greek philosophical sources, and it had been used to describe a form of knowledge produced by the regular conjunction of events. The example that served as a paradigm illustration for this type of knowledge was the one that Ibn Taymiyya invokes in the lines we just heard. "Experience," as Avicenna had explained in the *Shifāʾ*, is "e.g., our judgment [*ḥukmunā*] that scammony purges the gall-bladder. Since this (fact) recurs many times, it ceases to belong to what occurs by chance [*bi 'l-ittifāq*]."[47] Empirical judgments, more specifically, rest on the repetition of a sensation that is then preserved in the memory, and an implicit reasoning—effectively a latent syllogism—that this connection is not merely incidental. As the focal example betrays, the notion of *tajriba* as developed by the *falāsifa* had come to be virtually synonymous with medical knowledge.[48]

In his discussion of ethical propositions, Ibn Taymiyya does not address the notion of experience directly, yet he has done so earlier in the *Radd*. Drawing heavily on the resources of the philosophers, he characterizes empirical judgments (*mujarrabāt* or *tajribiyyāt*) as the product of a repeatedly perceived conjunction between events (*takarrur iqtirān aḥad al-amrayn bi'l-ākhar*). Thus "when people do something, they find that a certain effect follows from it, then this is repeated until one comes to know that this is the cause of that effect." Empirical judgments, as the last formulation suggests, are more specifically concerned with relations of cause and effect. The causal relation established by experience is to be understood in universal terms ("*whenever* a given thing is done to *anyone, such a thing* happens to him": *kull man fuʿila bihi dhālika yaḥṣulu lahu mithlu dhālika*). And crucially for the thread we are pursuing, the resulting judgment is a universal proposition that Ibn Taymiyya qualifies as the mixed product of sense perception and reason (*al-ḥiss wa'l-ʿaql*). For our senses tell us about particulars, and it is reason that then commutes these particular perceptions into general judgments.[49]

There will already be much in the above to indicate why empirical knowledge would offer an especially hospitable framework for locating Ibn Taymiyya's understanding of ethical judgments. Several of the statements we just heard point to the special connection that empirical judgments bear to human action and to events initiated by human beings ("when people *do* something," when people have something "*done* to them").[50] The association of empirical judgments with medicine—forged by the philosophers and appropriated by Ibn Taymiyya in his own discussion—is also significant, as it shows empirical judgments to be connected not merely with human action but also with human suffering, and with the effects of action on human well-being. Yet it is the peculiar concern that empirical judgments have with causal relations that speaks with particular directness to the terms of Ibn Taymiyya's ethical understanding.

For having noted Ibn Taymiyya's claim that the primary ground of value is utility, we may now note that this claim can in turn be intuitively construed in two separate ways—ways that Ibn Taymiyya himself does not entirely help to regiment clearly. An act can be beneficial by being immediately pleasurable, and it can be beneficial by serving as the causal means for later pleasure. This distinction is present if unmarked in Ibn Taymiyya's statement, which we have already heard, that the ethical distinction between good and bad "reduces to the difference between pleasure and pain *and their respective causes* [*asbab*]."[51] The consequences of actions, as we saw in chapter 1, play a critical role in explaining why, on Ibn Taymiyya's scheme, an agent might agree to act in a way that is not immediately pleasurable. These consequences reflect God's creative decision to assign specific causal powers to human actions as to other entities in the created world.[52] Some of them, as we also saw in chapter 1, extend over the mundane realm, and others over the otherworldly realm. The former includes a wide range of effects that relate to the intellectual, physical, and moral well-being of the agent. It also notably includes the social consequences densely referred to throughout the *Radd*—the fact that by acting ethically, we are rewarded with the intrinsically pleasurable esteem and love of other people.

And leaving the otherworldly realm out of view for the time being, empirical knowledge would seem to present itself as a natural paradigm on which to map Ibn Taymiyya's positive view of the way human beings come to know the causal effects of actions that determine their ethical value in the mundane realm by determining the overall balance of pleasure over pain. The passage of the *Radd* cited above that highlights this connection, it must be admitted, does not make for unequivocal reading.[53] Yet its interest in bringing moral judgments into close connection with the notion of experience appears to be sufficiently conclusive. This is patent in the first remark ("people's knowledge of these propositions through nature and through experience") and even clearer in the continuation (those propositions are "tested by experience," through contact with "particulars"). This understanding of Ibn Taymiyya's ethical epistemology, crucially, would permit us to unify the luxuriance of epistemological registers in the *Radd*, above all providing a way of accounting for the composite reference to sense perception (*ḥiss*) and reason (*ʿaql*) in many of the passages we have heard.[54] For empirical judgments are produced by the combined work of sense perception and reason, taking "sense perception" in an inclusive sense that might range over both the physical and the emotional domain and might thus incorporate both physical pleasures and emotional ones, such as the pleasures produced by social esteem.[55]

What about *fiṭra*? My understanding here will have to be simply stated. Allowing for the unstable boundaries of the concept and its fluid relationship to more cognitive elements—a relationship about which there will be more to say—the notion of *fiṭra*, as deployed in Ibn Taymiyya's ethical discussions, is primarily constructed as a principle of desire. Our natural disposition provides us with desires for certain kinds of pleasures and for our overall welfare, construed as a longer-term balance of pleasure over pain. Throughout Ibn Taymiyya's works, in fact, the types of pleasures and desires with which the notion of *fiṭra* is repeatedly drawn into the strongest connection are physical ones, such as the natural desire for food and drink, to which sexual desire is occasionally added.[56] *Fiṭra*, thus qualified, represents our nature as physical beings endowed with a characteristic set of physical needs and desires. As such, it forms the ground of the core values toward which we strive. It is in this modified sense that we might say it "tells us" what is good. With these motivational ends in place, the epistemological task is to discover how we can achieve them. The quality of actions *qua* immediately pleasurable is immediately (phenomenologically) available to us, falling under what Ibn Taymiyya in the *Radd* and elsewhere refers to as "sense perception."[57] The quality of actions *qua* instrumentally pleasurable, on the other hand, is not available to us in the same manner and requires a more complex epistemology like the one provided by empirical reason. It is significant that, having stated that reason tells us what benefits and harms us, elsewhere Ibn Taymiyya specifies that what reason informs us of more narrowly are the *consequences* of actions that constitute them as beneficial and harmful: "Acting on the basis of knowledge, which consists in pursuing what is beneficial to human beings and repelling what harms them through consideration of the consequences [of actions] [*bi 'l-naẓar fi 'l-'awāqib*], is the meaning of the term 'reason' [*al-'aql*] that predominates in the words of the pious forebears and imams [*al-salaf wa 'l-a'imma*]."[58]

It is a proposal whose virtue, I have suggested, lies in the way it allows us to unify many of the phenomena Ibn Taymiyya presents us with in his ethical discussions, as well as (albeit more glancingly) in other parts of his work. In his *Sharḥ al-Iṣbahāniyya*, for example, he uses a term with clear empirical resonance, induction (*istiqrā'*), to couch a point that can be essentially heard as an orotund claim that virtue and happiness coincide in the present world, and we know this by experience. An inductive consideration of human life reveals that "everyone who acts with gross injustice to people and causes great injury to them comes to an ugly end . . . and everyone who greatly serves people's welfare and acts with great beneficence toward them comes to good."[59] Yet what cannot but stand out, on the one hand, is the fact that having provided a few pregnant allusions to the connection between ethical and empirical judgments in the *Radd*, Ibn Taymiyya himself fails to fill in this skeletal frame in any detail. Similarly, while the conception of acts as causes (*asbāb*) and of ethical knowledge as consequential in form pervades his other writings, outside the *Radd* the terminology of "empirical judgments" virtually disappears into thin air. Even in the *Radd*, moreover, his analysis of empirical propositions, far from straightforwardly arguing for their relevance as a framework for ethical knowledge, often seems pointedly calculated to *undermine* it.

To see why, all we need to do is consider more attentively some of the examples with which Ibn Taymiyya proposes to illustrate the class of empirical judgments. "The generality of people," he writes when first introducing these judgments, "have established through experience [*jarrabū*] that drinking water is accompanied by [*yaḥṣulu ma'ahu*] the quenching of thirst, that severing the head is accompanied by death, and that severe beating necessarily causes [*yūjibu*] pain." Similar examples occur later in the work: thus "the fact that satiation and quenching arise after ['*aqība*] eating and drinking belongs to the class of empirical judgments . . . likewise with the fact that pleasure is experienced in/through those things [*bi-dhālika*], as through sexual intercourse and the like."[60] All these cases have an immediate bearing on human well-being, and as such appear to send their nerves into the heartland of Ibn Taymiyya's evaluative scheme. Yet on second glance, one cannot help being struck by the exceptional brevity of the causal sequence they place on display. This is already clear in the first set of examples, which refer us to the causal connection between eating and satiation, and drinking and the quenching of thirst. It is more visible still in the second, where the same set of actions (eating and drinking) is addressed, yet this time with pleasure and pain nominated as their causal effects. Ibn Taymiyya's uneasy linguistic turns and shifting choice of prepositions—"after" is replaced with "in" or "through" as he moves between examples—is here revealing; and what it reveals is the difficulty of separating the two "events" at stake and relating them in causal terms. Even if one accepts that satiation occurs *after* eating—and one might query the point: Do I feel satisfied *after* I finish eating or *while* I am engaged in the act? (everything would seem to hang on our conceptual grip on the notion of "satiation")—it is harder to grant that the pleasure produced by eating or drinking or sex can be described in causal terms that present it as temporally posterior to the respective actions.

Ibn Taymiyya's continuation suggests one reason such a conceptual representation—in terms of two separate events relating as prior to posterior in a temporal and causal sequence—might have appeared compelling. Drawing once more on epistemological notions current among the *falāsifa*, he goes on to refer to a distinction between "external" and "internal" perception that would seem to correspond to the precise distinction between "events" we have just seen, placing the sensory experience of smelling, eating, and so on on one side and the pleasure thereby experienced on another. One's external senses first "perceive a given thing; they see something, hear something, taste something, touch something; and then the fact that pleasure arises in the soul belongs to the experiences known through the internal senses [*al-ḥiss al-bāṭin*]."[61] Given this scheme, one can see why the act of eating and the pleasure derived might have presented themselves as distinct events. Given this scheme—and perhaps even without it. For later in philosophical history, Schopenhauer would collapse the distance between these "two" events and identify them in *The World as Will and Representation* as different ways of relating to a single thing.[62] Yet the fact that the distinction should need collapsing is a token of its intuitive hold, to the extent that we can intuitively distinguish between the act publicly available for representation and the internal experience that is not.

Even if we agree to distinguish these events and relate them in causal terms, however, it is clear that the causal sequence at stake is a singularly short one. And it is noteworthy, and not a little paradoxical, that the cases under consideration correspond not so much to the specification of utility that demands a real epistemic achievement—namely the future consequences of actions that determine the overall balance of pleasure and pain they involve—as to the specification of utility that consists in immediate pleasure and pain and that is immediately available in experience. While actions involving longer causal chains do come into view in Ibn Taymiyya's discussion,[63] the resources in his discussion of empirical judgments are overwhelmingly set up with a bias toward the short term or indeed the immediate present, as against the longer-term future in which the consequences of actions unfold. If we were looking for an explanation of why an action that is pleasant in the short term, like adultery or theft, might nevertheless not be in our interests due to its long-term consequences, we would not find it here. In writing about empirical judgments or *mujarrabāt*, Ibn Taymiyya does not appear to have the future consequences of actions in mind.

What this suggests is that Ibn Taymiyya does not fully develop the promise that the epistemology of *tajriba* would seem to hold as a framework for evaluative knowledge. Taken together with the poverty of his references to empirical judgments in other writings, this might make us wonder just how seriously to take his commitment to it. More narrowly, it may make us wonder whether his invocation of this epistemology should be construed in dialectical rather than positive terms—as a heuristic proposal developed in sufficient detail to question Avicenna's exclusion of ethical propositions from the privileged class of premises usable in demonstrative syllogisms (a class that notably included *tajribiyyāt*) but not intended as a positive proposal postulated in his own voice. Ibn Taymiyya's explicit references to this epistemology in the *Radd*, its coherence with other elements of his intellectual scheme, and its ability to lend coherence to his ethical remarks seem to me strong grounds for reading this proposal in positive terms. Yet it remains a fact—a fact worth keeping in view in the discussion that follows—that Ibn Taymiyya's remarks about ethical epistemology often bear a fragmentary and spartan character. Even though there is a more unified story that can be told to tie such phenomena together, it is instructive that this story should require a concerted interpretive exercise to be achieved.

Ibn Taymiyya's Appeal to Nature in Context: Nature as a Foundation for Ethics?

The above has offered a snapshot of the ethical epistemology that emerges from one of the key documents for Ibn Taymiyya's ethical views. In doing so, it has furnished many of the resources we need in order to turn to face our guiding questions more directly. How to understand Ibn Taymiyya's notion of nature as a normative principle and epistemological source? How far is Ibn Taymiyya prepared to push the claim that ethical norms are accessible to what we may more inclusively refer to as the epistemological resources internal to human beings? A more inclusive mode of reference is helpful here in allowing us to accommodate all of the central epistemological terms that have come up in our discussion. Earlier theological writers, as mentioned, had focused on one particular internal resource, reason, and questioned whether we have access to ethical norms by reason or require the external output of revelation. Ibn Taymiyya speaks of reason, yet he also speaks of *fiṭra*. It is time to consider how this understanding speaks to our starting questions. In this section my narrower concern will be with the notion of *fiṭra* and its status as a normative principle and epistemological source.

We have seen that Ibn Taymiyya's claim that ethical norms are known by nature is developed as a counterclaim to the view expressed by Avicenna: "Ethical propositions are not known from the perspective of human nature."—"On the contrary, they are." In pressing this claim, as I have suggested, Ibn Taymiyya has done far more than remove the sign of negation over Avicenna's, rewriting the notion of *fiṭra* in the process. Unlike Avicenna, Ibn Taymiyya thinks of *fiṭra* in desiderative terms; unlike Avicenna, he rejects the view that privilege attaches to our rational as against our estimative nature. Yet putting these more careful distinctions aside, at this juncture someone will want to ask the obvious question: Why all the fuss? Why care so much about whether this claim falls or stands?

There are many types of responses this question could invite—responses that open out to important insights into Ibn Taymiyya's motivations and the broader intellectual scheme in which his ethical understanding must be anchored. For our context, the most relevant way of reading this question is as an invitation to finally take a long-awaited step away from the context of the *Radd* to situate Ibn Taymiyya's deployment of the notion of *fiṭra* within a larger perspective. I suggested earlier that the story of Ibn Taymiyya's argumentative exchange about ethics in the *Radd* is worth following to the extent that it provided the formative context for his development of the notion of *fiṭra* in ethical terms. Yet this is by no means to say that his preoccupation with this notion was confined to this context or that it could be simply understood as its immediate product. Shadowing his discussion in the *Radd* is a larger preoccupation with the notion of *fiṭra* that runs through his work like an ever-present frieze.

In Avicenna's own writings, in those (far from numerous) passages where the notion of *fiṭra* emerges, it appears without ceremony and with little to mark it out as a concept invested with special significance or a broader place in the intellectual life of his time. Yet the notion of *fiṭra* had led a vivacious if somewhat unruly life in the Islamic religious tradition, and this richer intellectual presence forms the backdrop of Ibn Taymiyya's own engagement with it. In this engagement the ethical deployment of *fiṭra* does not in fact constitute the sole or even the most prominent strand. The more salient deployment—one might even say its master usage—is one that lies closer to the heart of the tradition and concerns not the knowledge of ethical value but the knowledge of God. The two types of deployment are far from hermetically sealed from each other, and are in fact bound together by important links. It is thus worth pausing to bring Ibn Taymiyya's theological usage of *fiṭra* into view and hold it up against his ethical usage, bolstering our understanding of the latter and shedding new light on its context.

The concept of *fiṭra* derived its centrality from its scriptural appearances, prime among them the appearance it makes in the Qur'an itself: "So set your face to the religion, a man of pure faith [*ḥanīfan*]—the nature (framed) of God, in which He has created man [*fiṭrat Allāh allatī faṭara al-nās ʿalayhā*]. There is no altering God's creation. That is the right religion, but most men know not" (Q 30:30). This verse was paired to several prophetic traditions, including the seminal hadith: "Every child is born with the natural constitution, and it is its parents that render it a Jew, or a Christian, or a Magean [*kull mawlūd yūladu ʿala ʾl-fiṭra, fa-abawāhu yuhawwidānihi aw-yunaṣṣirānihi aw-yumajissānihi*]."[64] In both scriptural passages, a certain connection is drawn between the notion of *fiṭra* and a religious state that seems to carry positive status. The Qur'an more specifically links the notion of *fiṭra* to that of *ḥanīfiyya*—a monotheistic belief in God taken to antedate revealed religions and finding its paradigmatic embodiment in Abraham.[65] Yet just how should this inborn religious state be characterized more precisely? Should one, for example, connect the notion of *fiṭra* to the primordial testimony given by humans acknowledging God as their Lord in the "Covenant of Alast" (Q 7:172) and see this as a universal pact uniting the whole of humanity to a primordial acknowledgment of God? Should one then say, more guardedly though not noncommittally, that all human beings are born believing in God? Or should one go so far as to say that all human beings are born Muslim?

These were some of the interpretations proposed by those approaching these scriptural bases with the aim of clarifying their meaning. The way one answered such questions had important practical repercussions, particularly with regard to conduct in war. Jurists thus debated the meaning of *fiṭra* with a view to answering practical legal questions such as whether the children of unbelievers should be killed, whether a child who has not yet come of age and is taken captive without its parents should be treated as an unbeliever, whether the children of non-Muslims who die in captivity should be buried as Muslims, or whether the children of non-Muslims whose parents die are capable of inheriting from them.[66] Far more divisive than these legal questions, however, were the theological questions to which these interpretive debates came to be harnessed, generating firewood for long-standing controversies about God's justice and human responsibility. The use to which Muʿtazilite theologians had put these scriptural traditions is indicative. Capitalizing on the interpretation that human beings are born in a religious state with positive valence, Muʿtazilites had employed it to press their distinctive defense of God's justice. For if children are born in a positively qualified religious state, this must mean that God does not punish the children of unbelievers and thus does not inflict pain on the innocent (an oft-debated topos). By the same train of reasoning, it must mean that God does not create or will unbelief or intentionally lead anyone astray (another key Muʿtazilite claim). For God's will must be reflected in the positive state in which human beings are born; and then subsequent unbelief might be ascribed to environmental factors or indeed, more optimistically and closer to the core of Muʿtazilite theological sentiment, to one's own free choice.[67]

These kinds of arguments Ibn Taymiyya would declare so full of holes as to make them unwearable, and his own stance on this debate would rest on a reworking of theological possibilities that may not seem unfamiliar given what we heard in the previous chapter. Rejecting the Muʿtazilite view of human freedom, his stance would reflect the conviction that two facets which the Muʿtazilites had represented as indetachable were in fact eminently capable of separation. Happy beginnings, more specifically, can be very amicably reconciled with unhappy ends. The state in which human beings are initially created and begin their lives is one of belief, yet the state in which they end their lives may yet be one of unbelief—or whatever fate God has determined for them. This position would on the one hand involve taking a stance on a refractory theological tradition, including apparently contradictory traditions received from Ibn Ḥanbal—a state of affairs that has prompted Geneviève Gobillot to comment almost despairingly, in her study of *fiṭra*, that "in the domain of theology as much as that of jurisprudence, there was a genuine awkwardness and profound confusion surrounding the tradition of *kull mawlūd*, which gave rise, among a number of thinkers, to choices that it would be extremely difficult and even impossible . . . to take on in their entirety."[68] Yet it would also, and more crucially, involve adopting a firmer stance on the central question of how the "positive" state at issue should be construed, forcefully embracing the claim that this should be dignified with the term "Islam." "One's nature itself," we hear, "requires that one acknowledge one's Creator [*nafs al-fiṭra tastalzimu al-iqrār bi-khāliqihi*]"; even more thickly: "One's nature entails and necessitates the Islamic faith [*fiṭratuhu muqtaḍiya mūjiba li-dīn al-Islām*]."[69]

Human beings, Ibn Taymiyya thus claims, are born with a knowledge—or, more accurately, with a *disposition* to know—God. One speaks of "knowing" God; yet in many of Ibn Taymiyya's works where this claim is expressed, particularly in his monumental *Darʾ taʿāruḍ al-ʿaql waʾl-naql*, where it is developed at greatest length, this cognitive-sounding claim is in fact articulated in a rather more complex set of terms. And here we find the beginning of the ligaments tying the theological deployment of *fiṭra* to the ethical deployment that forms our peculiar concern. For the disposition to acknowledge God that is enfolded within human nature is not merely a disposition to apprehend God as an object of representation or neutral existent. It is a tendency to respond to God in certain ways—ways specified in strongly emotive or affective terms. "One's nature itself requires that one acknowledge one's Creator"; yet what it also requires, as the continuation of this line makes clear, is that one "love Him and sincerely devote oneself to His service [*maḥabbatahu wa-ikhlāṣ al-dīn lahu*]."[70] Human nature here registers as a notion that looks to two separate directions: one cognitive, one affective or desiderative. It exacts a cognitive state, but it also exacts an affective state, which Ibn Taymiyya significantly parses using the same vocabulary that animates his discussion of *fiṭra* in the ethical context, namely "love."[71]

Yet this is not where the similarities stop. This becomes obvious when, at a particularly pregnant juncture of the *Darʾ taʿāruḍ*, Ibn Taymiyya turns to offer a rational argument for the scripturally grounded claim that we are naturally disposed to know and love God. I will run through the argument very swiftly because it is primarily its conclusion that interests us. All human beings, we are told, form beliefs (*iʿtiqādāt*), and all human beings, necessarily, have desires (*irādāt*). Beliefs sometimes correspond to the truth and sometimes they do not, and desires sometimes correspond to what is in our interests (*maṣlaḥa*) and sometimes they do not; and in the former case our desires and beliefs are good, in the latter bad (*ḥasana maḥmūda/sayyiʾa madhmūma*). Now *either* good beliefs and good desires, as against bad beliefs and desires, are equal with respect to our nature, *or* there is a special relationship between our nature and the good set, something in our nature that renders this set preponderant (*murajjaḥ*). But (and here I condense several steps in a single leap) if a person is faced with two options—"to tell the truth and be benefited, and to lie and be harmed"—his nature disposes him to choose the former. One conclusion that follows from this, according to Ibn Taymiyya, is that there is some power in our nature that leans toward good desires and good beliefs. Another conclusion is that our nature leans toward the belief and love of God, for the belief in God is true and the desire for God (*ḥubb* here replaces *irāda*) is beneficial.[72]

The historical fascination of this argument lies in the fact that Ibn Taymiyya is here seen adapting an argument that Muʿtazilite theologians had earlier used to ground their ethical claims, in particular the claim that people may act for moral reasons. Faced with the option of lying and telling the truth, the Muʿtazilites had argued, and supposing that each action produces equal results in terms of benefit and harm, people will always choose to tell the truth. In Ibn Taymiyya's recrafting, the argument seems highly problematic; yet the logical robustness of this argument is less relevant than the main point it helps to bring out.[73] For what it clarifies is that the telltale appearance of the vocabulary of "love" is not the only bridge between the ethical and the theological deployment of *fiṭra*. Soldering the two contexts even more strongly together is the basic premise that we are naturally disposed to love what benefits us and to hate what harms us. Our love for God and for the religion to which He holds us is, at least in part, a love organized by their description *qua* beneficial to us.[74] If what is objectively good, and what naturally attracts us, is what serves our welfare, as we hear in the ethical context, it is the relationship to God to which we are naturally disposed, as Ibn Taymiyya clarifies elsewhere, that achieves our truest welfare (*ṣalāḥ*) and thereby constitutes the highest fulfillment of the good.[75]

There will be more to say about this point later; yet here it is important to notice that this basic continuity is also reflected in the paradigm that Ibn Taymiyya appeals to pervasively in characterizing the natural disposition to know and love God—namely the child's instinctual desire for its mother's breast. "A child is formed by nature [*mafṭūr*] to drink milk through a drive of its own, so that given access to the breast, it will certainly suckle," he writes in the *Darʾ taʿāruḍ*; "it is in similar manner that one is born [*mawlūd*] to know God."[76] Or again our natural acknowledgment of God mirrors the way "every child is born with a disposition to love the foods and drinks that agree with [*yulāʾimu*] its body, so that it craves [*yashtahī*] the milk that suits it [*yunāsibuhu*]."[77] The term *mulāʾama* lays down a direct linguistic bridge to the terms of Ibn Taymiyya's discussion of ethics and to an expression of his view that we only recently left behind in the *Radd*: "The foundations of [ethical] judgments are necessarily known by people, for they are formed by nature to love what is agreeable to them and to hate what harms them [*al-nufūs . . . mafṭūra ʿalā ḥubb mā yulāʾimuhā wa-bughḍ mā yaḍurruhā*]." Throughout Ibn Taymiyya's works, as mentioned earlier, the notion of *fiṭra* is often linked to physical desires, such as the natural desire for food and drink and sex. These kinds of desires are used as the main frame of reference for talking about other human drives, such as religious and ethical ones. We may recall the crucial reference to these kinds of desires in a passage of the *Radd* we considered in chapter 1, where Ibn Taymiyya had compared our natural love for morally good actions to our natural disposition "to take pleasure in food and drink and to experience pain upon hunger or thirst." It is the identification of the good with the beneficial, we may say, and of the beneficial as the object of natural desire, that animates this analogy most intuitively; it is the same identification that stands out as the connecting ligament between Ibn Taymiyya's ethical and theological deployments of *fiṭra*.

In the theological context, as I have suggested, the notion of *fiṭra* is additionally given a cognitive turn, tying it to the disposition to form a substantive belief.[78] This substantive specification joins itself to a broader understanding of the cognitive dimensions of *fiṭra* that finds voice elsewhere in Ibn Taymiyya's work, as we will see, associating *fiṭra* very closely with the human faculties of reasoning. In many places the notion of "natural" knowledge is used in ways that render it virtually coextensive with that more specific subsection of reason that theologians typically referred to as "immediate" or "necessary" knowledge (*ʿilm ḍarūrī/ḍarūrat al-ʿaql*). In discussing our native knowledge of God, thus, Ibn Taymiyya often employs the two terms in a parataxis implying synonymity (*ʿulūm fiṭriyya ḍarūriyya*, or *uṣūl fiṭriyya ḍarūriyya*, or again of *al-ṭuruq al-fiṭriyya al-ʿaqliyya al-yaqīniyya*) and in certain locations explicitly identifies necessary knowledge with the knowledge of *fiṭra*.[79] In the ethical context, by contrast, this cognitive aspect falls away from view, and human nature is specified not so much in terms of a disposition to *know* what has value as to *desire* what has value—and this means, most immediately: what is beneficial.

Why care about whether Avicenna's claim falls or stands? I asked. The discussion above sought to provide further background for this question by locating Ibn Taymiyya's ethical appeal to nature against an even more fundamental appeal to nature in the theological domain. In doing so, it has given more substance to the ethical deployment we saw in the *Radd* and the terms in which Ibn Taymiyya specified it. It has also crucially bared to view what I take to form a core reason for Ibn Taymiyya's alacrity to defend the claim that ethical norms are accessible to us through the resources internal to our nature. For this is a tenet that feeds into a broader conception of the religious life as the highest fulfillment of the good. To the extent that this conception deploys a notion of "good" that is intuitively available to us—"good" is what serves our welfare—it supports a theological vision whose basic thrust, as previewed in chapter 1, is to argue for the convergence between the demands of the faith and the demands of our being.[80]

We will be returning to this notion of convergence shortly. Yet what I want to hold on to is the crucial fact that the notion of "nature" that figures in this thinking is vested with a far from neutral significance. This significance looks back to the scriptural bases of the notion, which connect it to a religious state understood in positive terms—to an original faith that represents the "right religion" (*al-dīn al-qayyim*), to a purer state in which God purposefully created people yet which may be corrupted. When such corruption takes place, it will mark a departure from God's own purposes.[81] There will be far more to say about this notion of divine purposefulness in chapter 4. Here it is important to note that it is a positive vision of God's character that is simultaneously at work in Ibn Taymiyya's own appropriation of the positive significance harbored by the scriptural appearances of *fiṭra*, expressing itself in the insistence that God vested human beings with natural resources carrying positive qualification. Spelling out the cognitive dimensions of human nature elsewhere in the *Radd*, Ibn Taymiyya refers to the natural human ability to form basic rational judgments about entities and writes that such judgments "belong to the *real* natural matters [*al-umūr al-ḥaqīqiyya al-fiṭriyya*] to which God naturally disposed people, just as He naturally disposed them to the different kinds of *wholesome* desires and *sound* motions [*al-irādāt al-ṣaḥīḥa wa'l-ḥarakāt al-mustaqīma*]."[82] The emphasis on the positive character of our natural endowments ("real," "wholesome," "sound") can be partly understood by reference to the positive conception of God's creative activity it parses.

It is this positive representation of human nature that appears to organize Ibn Taymiyya's engagement of *fiṭra* in both the theological and the ethical domain and his effort to connect it to positively valued content. The way we interpret the theological content of *fiṭra*, he indicates in the *Darʾ taʿāruḍ* when discussing the knowledge of God, should safeguard the premise that there is something "praiseworthy" (*yastaḥiqqu madḥan*) in it.[83] The concern to vouchsafe the praiseworthiness of human nature, similarly, was plainly attested in an argument about *fiṭra* we heard moments ago, which was designed to press the double conclusion that we are naturally inclined toward positively valorized or good beliefs but also, crucially for the ethical context, good desires (*irādāt ḥasana maḥmūda*).[84] The same concern is in turn reflected in Ibn Taymiyya's eagerness to contest Avicenna's position and to restore to human nature the privilege Avicenna was denying it. The positive valence carried by human nature then appears to be splashed in fluorescent colors across the pages of the *Radd*, with its effusive descriptions of the joy people naturally derive from the good.

Yet of course we have already had much to say about this natural joy and about the deeper sources of its derivation. In many ways the present discussion can be taken as a way of deepening and extending the insights of that earlier analysis. What that analysis had indicated and can now be spelled out more fully is that despite this patina of impressions, human nature cannot be understood as a straightforwardly privileged notion in the ethical context. More specifically, and despite the positive terms in which Ibn Taymiyya appears to inscribe it, natural desire does not provide a normative criterion for ethical value. The reasons for this may have already suggested themselves, and it is merely a matter of bringing them out.

For we have seen that in his ethical remarks, Ibn Taymiyya specifies human nature as a principle of desire. A desire for what? For "utility" or "benefit," we said, drawing on a number of his statements. Commenting on his ethical concern with the long-term consequences of actions, I drew a distinction between two ways in which the notion of utility could be construed: in terms of immediate pleasure and in terms of the overall future balance of pleasure over pain. This is a distinction that had been clearly signposted by earlier theologians, such as ʿAbd al-Jabbār, who had defined benefit (*nafʿ*) as pleasure and joy (*ladhdha, surūr*) and what leads to them. Distinguishing pleasure from benefit, such writers had used the term "benefit" (*nafʿ, manfaʿa, maṣlaḥa*) to refer inclusively to what is intrinsically good (generally identified as pleasure and joy) and what is instrumentally good, while tying it more closely to a judgment on the overall balance of pleasure and pain that actions involve.[85] With this distinction freshly in mind, we can now consider with sharper attention how Ibn Taymiyya's remarks about the natural human constitution speak to its terms.

Turning back to one of the passages we considered, we will recall Ibn Taymiyya's claim that "the foundations [*mabādi'*] of [ethical] judgments are necessarily known by people, for they are formed by nature to love what is agreeable to them and to hate what harms them [*mafṭūra ʿalā ḥubb mā yulā'imuhā wa-bughḍ mā yaḍurruhā*]." And again: "human beings are naturally formed [*mafṭūr*] to love what *benefits* them and hate what *harms* them."[86] Our natural desires, to do no more than rehearse, take our benefit or welfare as their object. Yet this specification of our natural constitution takes its place next to a number of other statements that give us something different, and that call attention this time not to the more inclusive notion of benefit, but to the more exclusive notion of pleasure. People, we heard, "experience [*yajidūna fī anfusihim*] a sense of pleasure, joy and happiness at the just man's justice," and they are naturally disposed to such experiences as they are disposed to "take pleasure in food and drink and experience pain upon hunger or thirst [*fuṭirū ʿalā wujūd al-ladhdha bi'l-akl wa'l-shurb wa'l-alam bi'l-jūʿ wa'l-ʿaṭash*]."[87] The psychological experience of joy and happiness provoked by ethically good actions here finds its counterpart in the physical experience of enjoyment provoked by physical goods. In both cases it is an immediate experience of pleasure (*wajada*: to perceive, to experience) that is made the correlate of our natural constitution. It is an emphasis on our natural susceptibility to certain types of pleasures and, as I suggested above, paradigmatically for physical pleasures that repeatedly surfaces in Ibn Taymiyya's remarks about our natural constitution.

Ibn Taymiyya's remarks about *fiṭra* thus speak to competing sides of this distinction. He himself does not mark the transition between these specifications of our natural disposition and in many places glides between them without anything to mark that there is a transition at stake or that anything hangs on it.[88] Despite the centrality of utility in his ethical thought, in fact, he never draws the distinction between the two construals of utility with comparable clarity. More than that: much of what he says in different contexts seems calculated to obscure it, and there are contexts where his thinking is premised on the programmatic suppression of the insight that evaluative criteria are constituted by anything other than immediate pleasure, and more specifically by pleasure of a sensory kind.

A good example is provided by an exchange that forms one of Ibn Taymiyya's best-known confrontations with the intellectual schools of his time: his polemics against the monistic theosophy of Ibn ʿArabī (d. 1240). This is a confrontation that Ibn Taymiyya wages across innumerable locations in his writings, and readers following the thread of his ethical views will quickly discover it is a context where this thread can be reliably sought out, for reasons that are not hard to come by. At the heart of Ibn Taymiyya's critical response to Ibn ʿArabī's brand of philosophical mysticism lies a concern about its pernicious impact on the religious life, and more specifically about the antinomian tendencies it harbors. It is a suspicion of the mystical path that had certainly been voiced before in the Islamic tradition, but Ibn Taymiyya formulates it in terms that speak more narrowly to the distinctive views of Ibn ʿArabī and his acolytes. In the brilliance of ecstatic states, Ibn Taymiyya complains, these mystics claim that the very distinction between good and evil burns up and falls away, a mere phenomenal distinction that collapses back into the primal ontological unity constituted by the divine reality. Such claims, he declares, mark a failure to maintain God's power and God's command in the necessary equilibrium and drastically undermine the divine Law—a parsing of his complaint that significantly locates it against a programmatic concern to calibrate this tension that we are already familiar with.[89]

Yet the etherealization of this distinction, Ibn Taymiyya argues—a distinction between good and evil, or what God loves and what He hates—flies in the face not only of scriptural evidence but indeed of all rational self-evidence. This distinction, he tells us in *al-ʿAqīda al-Tadmuriyya*, simply *cannot* disappear—not unless one proposes to leave one's bodily existence behind altogether. Whatever their visionary engrossment, it is humanly impossible that these mystics should fail to "find certain things pleasurable and other things painful, and distinguish between what can be eaten or drunk and what cannot be eaten or drunk, between the heat and cold that causes them discomfort and that which does not, and this distinction between what benefits them and what harms them is what religious legislative reality [*al-ḥaqīqa al-sharʿiyya al-dīniyya*] consists in."[90] Reprising the topic in another epistle: so long as these visionaries "feel hunger and thirst" and "can tell the difference between bread and drink" and between "what's bitter and brackish and what's sweet to the taste," their claim that good and evil fall away in these privileged states is shown to be hollow, whether by way of deceit or self-deceit. For the distinction between good and evil comes down to "the difference between pleasure and pain and their respective causes"; thus the difference between "good actions, which bring pleasure to their agent, and evil actions, which bring him pain, is a matter of sense perception known alike by all the beasts in the field [*amr ḥissī yaʿrifuhu jamīʿ al-ḥayawān*]."[91]

In these remarkable statements, Ibn Taymiyya can be seeing tying ethical notions exclusively to the immediate experience of pleasure, and indeed to pleasure of a sensory kind, as the startling last remark makes clear. While the notion of longer-term consequences is not wholly absent—it is present in the telltale reference to "pleasure and pain *and their respective causes*" and immediately evoked by the reference to "religious legislative reality," hardly intelligible in isolation from the otherworldly context—Ibn Taymiyya largely leaves it out of the picture. The notion of "benefit," while also terminologically present, seems to be narrowly interpreted through the notion of pleasure. And what is important is that the restricted attention to immediate experience as the ground of ethical value is central to the architecture of Ibn Taymiyya's argument for the ineliminability of ethical distinctions. For the distinction between immediate pain and pleasure is ineliminably present to us; that between painful and pleasant consequences is not.

This argumentative context thus exemplifies a notable tendency, in Ibn Taymiyya's writings, to blur the distinction between the narrower and broader specifications of utility. Yet of course one of the most important illustrations of this tendency we met in chapter 1 when studying the exuberant connection in which Ibn Taymiyya draws ethical action and positive phenomenological responses such as pleasure and joy in the *Radd*. This is a connection, as we saw, that obscures the costs that ethical action often involves—costs that, once brought out, require a reference to the pleasures anticipated in the future (and thus to utility in the broader sense) in order not to count against it. Ibn Taymiyya's silence with regard to these costs, we said earlier, is striking. This silence feeds into a positive representation of human nature and the motivational drives that constitute it. Having brought out the conflicts that Ibn Taymiyya suppresses and the normative perspective of long-term consequences that accounts for their resolution and that provides the full criterion of ethical value, we already have reason to think that this positive representation cannot provide the full picture. This becomes plainer once we take into account Ibn Taymiyya's composite specification of our natural disposition in terms of an orientation toward pleasures—particularly pleasures of a sensory kind—and an orientation to benefit. For to the extent that our natural desires attach to objects under their description as pleasant, natural desire cannot carry normative status. Not every natural desire we experience will be good; our desires will require further ordering. By the same token, and contrary to what Ibn Taymiyya invites us to think in the *Radd* by invoking *fiṭra* and the notion of epistemic certainty in the same breath, an empirical survey of our actual desires—a turn inward to what is subjectively available to us—cannot provide us with a "moral compass" that tells us how we ought to act.[92] The "natural" is neither a normative category nor a self-sufficient epistemological source.

That our desires require ordering, of course, is a thesis that would seem wholly unsurprising coming from the perspective of the divine Law, which openly proclaims it in stating, "It is possible that you dislike a thing which is good for you, and that you love a thing which is bad for you" (Q 2:216). Many of the desires subsumed in the scope of our natural constitution or *fiṭra* in fact form the object of explicit religious legislation that places limits on their fulfillment and provides a normative framework for their pursuit—a framework in which the notion of *ḥaqq* often serves as an illuminating joint. Thus, the natural desire for food and drink is one whose satisfaction is bounded by the ritual demands of the Law, such as the obligation to fast or to avoid certain food types like pork and carrion—obligations that represent rights of God (*ḥuqūq Allāh*)—just as it is bounded by the normative limits posed by human rights (*ḥuqūq al-ʿibād*), which accord individuals exclusive rights over particular goods and make it wrong for others to avail themselves of them for the satisfaction of their desires. Similarly with sexual desire, included by Ibn Taymiyya in the scope of our natural constitution, whose value clearly depends on its pursuit within the bounds of a lawful relationship generated through the right (contractual) forms and in turn generating rightful claims and obligations among the parties involved. Here and elsewhere, a firm line of norms—norms naturally specified through the notion of *ḥuqūq* that Ibn Taymiyya shuns in his main ethical remarks—provides the domain of natural desire with its frontiers.

The positively valorized way in which the notion of *fiṭra* and that of natural pleasure appear in Ibn Taymiyya's ethical remarks calls attention away from the need for frontiers. In other locations of his writings, however, these positive terms are revealed to have been only partial in reach, and the human inclination toward negatively valued desires is explicitly held out as the core of a more distrustful view of human nature. This distrust is succinctly expressed in Ibn Taymiyya's reference to the human "proclivity to evil desires" (*mayluhu ilā mā yahwāhu min al-sharr*).[93] The need in which our natural desires stand for normative ordering is similarly made plain when, speaking in the *Qāʿida fi ʾl-maḥabba* of those who "love food and drink and women"—archetypal desires of our *fiṭra*, we may recall—Ibn Taymiyya writes that, while such desires are "commendable and human welfare is vested in them," they must be pursued with "right measure and moderation [*al-ʿadl wa'l-qaṣad*]." This point is encapsulated again in an apophthegmatic remark in the same work, which now reveals the grounds for such normative ordering: "Many an immediate desire [*shahwa*] has had enduring grief as its bequest."[94] This is a remark all the more significant for its context, emphasizing the deleterious effects of natural pleasures, which include not only the ones derived from the illegitimate satisfaction of natural sexual desire (by adultery) but also the pleasures derived from injustice. Yet it was the natural love of justice that had been highlighted in the long passage of the *Radd* that gave us our starting point.

Here and elsewhere, Ibn Taymiyya openly acknowledges that wrongdoing is something toward which human nature inclines, and perhaps nowhere more clearly than in a statement from the *Fatāwā* that we already heard in the previous chapter: human beings "commit evil acts that have been forbidden to them due to their ignorance [of their evilness] or their need for [these acts], in the sense that they crave them and take pleasure in them." This statement brings into the open what the *Radd* entirely occluded: wrongdoing can also be a source of pleasure and object of desire. The distinction between good and bad desires arrives as its obvious concomitant.[95] This open admission is particularly striking seen against the thread of discussion from which it emerges, which presses a familiar message about the concordance between the demands of our nature and the demands of the religious faith. "For everything that God commanded," Ibn Taymiyya had written only a few lines above, "God created in the nature of human beings that which serves as its cause and necessitates it, and He set it up as an object of their need and as a basis of their welfare and perfection." The command to faith is one such example, for "every child is born with the natural constitution" according to the well-thumbed hadith. The command to knowledge, justice, and truth is another, for these are things that people "know and love, hence the fact that they are called 'right'" (*maʿrūf*: literally "what is known"), as is the divine prohibition of lying and injustice, actions that human beings naturally find repugnant (*tunkiruhā al-qulūb*).[96] The continuation just cited seems to arrive as a subversion and serious qualification of this view, bringing to the fore the way what is ethically good (and what is commanded by God) may *conflict* with our desires, and thus raising a question about how the message of concordance should be received.

What the above shows is that the notion of the "natural" has a more ambivalent status in Ibn Taymiyya's thinking than he lets on and that the conception of human nature at work in his thinking is likewise far from uniformly positive. If these ambivalent aspects fall away from view, especially when the discussion is parsed in the language of *fiṭra*, that is linked to the kind of intellectual investments outlined earlier—to Ibn Taymiyya's investment in appropriating the positive representation of *fiṭra* harbored by the scriptural texts in support of a certain vision of God's character and a particular message about the harmony between human nature and the demands of religious faith. It is not that this claim of concordance cannot be made. But if it is, this can only be by isolating one of the two aspects of our nature that Ibn Taymiyya picks out in his discussion, its responsiveness not to the subjective and fallible drive for pleasure but to the more objective and normative notion of long-term welfare. It is, after all, this objective notion, it could be observed, that figures more prominently in some of Ibn Taymiyya's most direct statements about natural desire. The term *fiṭra* might perhaps be definitionally reserved for that higher-order desire directed to the true good—a move that would of course leave the acknowledgment of lower-order natural desires untouched and thus leave it clear that faith will often demand things that are in conflict and not in harmony with one's natural desires in another sense of the "natural." Yet it is important that this is not a reservation that Ibn Taymiyya himself signals clearly, and the fluidity of his transitions between the notions of pleasure and benefit and the drives they correspond to makes it harder to argue for that as an explicit intention.

Ibn Taymiyya does, it may be said, offer a reflective viewpoint elsewhere in his writings that would show these two aspects of human nature to fall together and allow the positive value of natural desire as such to be preserved. "When a person's soul or temper becomes corrupt [*fasidat*]," we hear elsewhere in his *Fatāwā*, "one craves and takes pleasure in things that harm one."[97] Implied in this remark is a distinction between sound (*salīm*/*ṣaḥīḥ*) and corrupt (*fāsida*) nature that constitutes a recurring theme in Ibn Taymiyya's writings, and indeed flows immediately from the seminal prophetic tradition at work in them. For while every child may have been "born with the original disposition," as that tradition would have it, this disposition was subsequently exposed to fateful corruption through external factors ("it is its parents that render it a Jew, or a Christian, or a Magean").[98] The possibility of corruption is a presumption necessary for explaining how something can be innate yet fail to be universally manifested. Deployed in this context, it suggests that only desires flowing from corrupted natural constitutions may require normative ordering. Our natural desires might form a trustworthy guide to action so long as our natural constitution has not been impaired.[99]

The normative character of natural desire could thus be secured by introducing a normative filter at the level of human nature itself—a move that would mirror the effects of the definitional reservation just considered. This would not be the first time that a normative conception of nature would have turned out to form the heart of an ethical appeal to human nature. Heirs as we are to a long history of intellectual developments that saw the notion of nature transformed in the process, this is a point we have sometimes found it easy to miss in looking back to some of the most celebrated appeals of this kind, from ancient ethics onward. The notion of nature that animates this type of appeal in the ancient context is not, as Julia Annas points out, that of a "neutral" or "brute" scientific fact, as modern philosophers have presumed. Nature in fact forms an "ethical ideal" and an "ideal concept." One central way it is used in ancient ethics is thus as "the goal or end of human development; the natural life is the life led by humans who have developed in a natural way, this being understood as a way in which the potentialities which for us are given develop without interference from other, external factors." This presupposes, among other things, "that we can distinguish between what forms an expression of a person's nature and what forms a corruption of it." And it makes clear that we cannot "find out about human nature just by observing people."[100]

Something similar has been remarked about the appeal to nature at other stages of its history, as among the medieval scholastics, whose view of natural law, as Jean Porter notes, rests on a strongly teleological view of nature, presupposing "the overall goodness or value of a specific kind of life, the form of life appropriate to a given creature when it is flourishing in accordance with the intrinsic principles of its existence."[101] Porter is in fact prepared to make the case more broadly, suggesting that the concept of a human being simply cannot be detached from the concept of what it is to do *well* as a human being. Even more than among ancient philosophers, Christian reflection on natural law was tightly bound up with a consideration of the ways human nature has been corrupted or obscured. Later theologians, such as Martin Luther, would acknowledge the presence of natural law in human conscience yet consider the corrupting influence of sin a barrier to using it as a foundation for ethics.[102]

Yet even if Ibn Taymiyya's appeal to nature can be interpreted in normative terms that align it with this longer tradition—and his failure to call attention to this more openly in his ethical discussions leaves this interpretation unstable—the evocation of this historical foil seems designed to throw into relief what divides him from it rather than what unites him with it. For within this tradition, the appeal to nature had been brought into relation with a number of thick ethical concepts—a number of concepts reflecting modes of ethical thinking that we today are disposed to tell rather more sharply apart. We may recall Cicero's opening encapsulation, which identified natural law as "right reason corresponding to nature, diffused in all . . . which commanding, calls to duty, and forbidding, deters from wrongdoing" (*De Republica*, III, 33). The appeal to nature is here connected to a use of reason that is notably prescriptive and serves as a source of duty or obligation. This prescriptive law-like aspect would be strongly reflected in later articulations of the Stoic appeal to nature, in which natural law would come to be thought of as an idealized version of the actual law that governs political communities. It would likewise mark the reception of this notion among Christian writers, and would be reflected in the fact that Christian theologians from Augustine onward would connect natural law to the Golden Rule ("Whatever you want men to do to you, do also to them") and to the commandments included in the Decalogue ("Thou shalt not kill"; "Thou shalt not commit adultery"; "Thou shalt not steal"). At the same time, this prescriptive or law-like aspect, in several contexts—certainly in ancient ethics and among some of the best-known scholastic contributors to the natural law tradition, such as Thomas Aquinas—worked in synergy with thicker conceptions of human flourishing parsed in the vocabulary of the virtues.

Ibn Taymiyya's ethical invocation of nature seems starkly different. As I have already noted, his focal term in his ethical discussions, including those in which he deploys the notion of *fiṭra*, is not the "imperative" concept of obligation but the "attractive" concept of goodness. *Fiṭra*, by the same token, issues not a call of duty but a call of desire. Unlike the above types of appeal to nature, where nature is associated with reason—"the natural law," Albert the Great would characteristically write, "is nothing other than the law of reason or obligation, insofar as nature is reason"—the emphasis falls on the desiderative rather than the rational dimensions of human nature.[103] And the higher good that is made the object of natural desire has none of the thick texture that characterizes conceptions of the flourishing life among ancient and medieval thinkers. It is simply what "benefits" us—a notion of utility that ultimately reduces to pleasure and pain.

If we were trying to bring Ibn Taymiyya's appeal to nature into conversation with philosophical history, in fact, it is not the ancient appeal or its medieval and later resumptions that would provide us with the most ready term of comparison. It is rather some of the more recent architects of an ethical appeal to nature who defined themselves in opposition to earlier modulations of this appeal by calling attention away from reason and toward desire, away from rational intuition and toward empirical observation. This includes Hume, whose claim that morals are "founded entirely on the particular fabric and constitution of the human species" was executed as a project to ground ethical ideas in the passionate as against rational aspects of human nature ("morality . . . is more properly felt than judged of," *T* 470)—in emotions of approval and disapproval, love and hate, that are themselves forms of pleasure and pain and in turn respond to the pleasure and pain that actions cause.[104] It also includes some of the utilitarian philosophers who would see themselves as treading in Hume's footsteps, such as Bentham, who identified the good with pleasure and then made nature the source of ethics in the well-known statement that opens his *Introduction to the Principles of Morals and Legislation*: "Nature has placed mankind under the governance of two sovereign masters, *pain* and *pleasure*. It is for them alone to point out what we ought to do, as well as to determine what we shall do."[105]

Ibn Taymiyya does not frame his ethical claim in the universalizing terms in which utilitarians like Bentham and Mill parse it, as a pursuit of the happiness of the greatest number. His principle, in this respect, invites to be read in egoistic terms. For the purposes of our own narrative, however, the more interesting point of comparison—and the more relevant angle of questioning—lies elsewhere. For among both the earlier and particularly the later advocates of an ethical appeal to nature, this appeal had been twinned to a strong claim regarding the access human beings have to standards of right and wrong and the self-sufficiency of human ethical reflection. This had stood out with particular crispness among some of the later humanist exponents of this idea. Writing in his *Philosophical Dictionary*, Voltaire had expressed the point epitomically: "When Nature created our species and gave us instincts . . . after giving us our portion, she said to us: 'Now do the best you can.'" Jerome Schneewind glosses: "God created nature, and nature created us with the ability to guide our own affairs."[106]

This finally allows us to pull into focus an epistemological question that has been with us from the beginning of this chapter and that we can now face more directly. I have suggested that Ibn Taymiyya includes in his conception of nature desires that require further normative ordering, and as such nature cannot be taken to constitute a privileged category. That normative ordering, as I have explained, derives from a consideration of the longer-term consequences of these desires (or the actions they motivate). What is the epistemic source of that ordering? And what does this have to tell us about Ibn Taymiyya's understanding of our ability to "guide our own affairs" on the basis of epistemological resources internal to us as human beings? Or again: just how substantive is the capacity for ethical self-guidance that Ibn Taymiyya is prepared to concede human beings? It is to this question that I now turn.

Reason and Its Ethical Content

It is a question that, parsed in the language of reason, had stood at the heart of the classical *kalām* debates about ethics, as I have already said. "Reason tells us what is right and wrong."—"On the contrary, revelation forms our source." Yet this sharply distinguished pair of strident dichotomies, which may seem like a tempting way of schematizing the conflict between Muʿtazilite and Ashʿarite theological views, is liable to mislead us. In encouraging an exclusively yes/no construction of the debate, it may lead us to overlook that a lot of interesting things—if not indeed most of them—took place not at the level of *either/or* or *whether*, but on the level of *how* and *how much*.

Linda Zagzebski's observation must surely be allowed to stand: however different religious thinkers have configured the controversial relationship between morality and religion, all religions teach that "the ultimate goal of moral living is unattainable without the practice of that religion" and that "morality is incapable of standing alone."[107] Having evoked some of the more recent manifestations of the ethical appeal to nature, it is also salutary to keep in mind that the kind of capacity for independent ethical reflection that humanists like Voltaire and Hume or their utilitarian successors claimed for human beings was the product of a long history of intellectual developments in which ethical reasoning was gradually disengaged from religious and other cultural frameworks. The idea of the moral agent capable of reasoning autonomously about ethics—a construction of the everyman best known to us from Kant's depiction of him—is a modern invention that would have surprised many earlier natural law theorists.[108] The point has been relevantly made by Porter regarding the medieval scholastics' articulation of natural law. In linking natural law to reason, the scholastics had not attempted to derive "a system of natural law thinking out of purely natural data or rationally self-evident intuitions." Hence their otherwise surprising appeal to "Scripture to establish specific points of natural law morality—for example, the wrongfulness of fornication, which they cheerfully admit could not easily be determined by reason alone." Not *either/or* but *and*: "Human reason and Scripture are complementary and mutually interpreting."[109]

It is in the spirit of this inclusive *and* and in the light of the more open *how much* that the Muʿtazilites' own ethical understanding needs to be read—a reading that will provide a helpful backdrop for considering Ibn Taymiyya's stance. Islamic theological discussions regularly featured polemical jousts with iconoclastic figures—figures enjoying varying degrees of historical reality—who interrogated the need for prophecy building on claims about the innate human grasp of ethical truths. Given that ethical standards are accessible to human reason, why is revealed guidance needed at all? Looking more closely at the standards of action that revelation prescribes, it was additionally complained, we find they grate against the standards we know innately. The ritual prescriptions of the Law—prescriptions like praying and fasting or like slaughtering animals and circumambulating the Ka'ba during the hajj—formed a particularly tenacious topic in this connection.[110] Like many theological participants in these discussions, the Muʿtazilites agreed that revelation did not conflict with reason and that revelation had an important role to play in guiding human action. The task was then to explain just why and how, against the context of their affirmation that ethical standards are intuitively known.[111]

Central to the solution of the Baṣran Muʿtazilites, who will once again be my focus, was a distinction between two levels on which we may know what makes actions good or bad. We may know, on a general level (*ʿala 'l-jumla*), that injustice is bad or repelling harm from oneself is good. Yet if we want to evaluate acts, a second judgment will be required on the particular level (*ʿala 'l-tafṣīl*), which relates these specific cases to the general act-descriptions and recognizes them as instances of the latter. We need to recognize that *this* act is an act of injustice, and this will usually mean settling the facts about it, for example determining that it produces harm undeservedly or without countervailing benefit.[112] The case then made by the Baṣran Muʿtazilites was that the standards of action prescribed by revelation could be seen to relate to the standards of action indicated by reason as the particular to the general. "What the prophets convey," Mānkdīm would write in his *Sharḥ al-Uṣūl al-khamsa*, "can only constitute the particularization [*tafṣīl*] of a general knowledge [*jumla*] already established by reason."[113]

In talking about particularization in this context, these Muʿtazilites primarily had in mind a very specific type of evaluative standard belonging not to the deontological but to the consequentialist side of their ethical theory: the principle that we must seek what serves our welfare and repel what harms us. For we may know *that* pursuing what serves our welfare is good; but we may not know *what* serves our welfare. With the general evaluative principle firmly established in our reason, revelation comes to offer us the latter, particularizing (factual) knowledge. In doing so, the role of the prophets is "akin to that of physicians when they say, 'This herb is beneficial' and 'This herb is harmful,' " against the background assumption that it is good to seek what is beneficial and obligatory to repel what is harmful. Revelation, in Ibn Mattawayh's phrasing, comes to "reveal the presence of benefit or goodness in one act [and] the presence of harm or injuriousness in another."[114] A paradigmatic example is the prescription to perform ritual prayer. Left to our own devices, we would not know that, as this world is contingently and in fact at present organized, prayer can be instrumental to our ability to lead upright lives, a point indicated by the Qur'an when stating that "prayer restrains from shameful and unjust deeds" (Q 29:45). And while sometimes, as in this case, God may explicitly indicate to us the reasons behind His commands, in many other cases these reasons remain opaque to us. Any conflict we perceive between the demands of reason and the demands of revelation is to be ascribed to this position of ignorance. Having seen this, we may rest in the confidence that "all prescribed ordinances are in accord with reason [*muṭābiqa li'l-'uqūl*]."[115]

This is an important foil to keep in place in turning back to Ibn Taymiyya. For like the Mu'tazilites, Ibn Taymiyya offers a vigorous affirmation of the thesis that ethical truths are intuitively available to human beings, and he couples it to a similar message regarding the necessary concord between the dictates of our epistemic nature and the dictates of the Law. The right question to ask is thus not on the level of *whether* but of *how much*. My main conclusion can be put simply before offering the evidence that supports it: the independence that Ibn Taymiyya seems interested in securing for human judgments about ethical matters is in fact rather more limited than his affirmation of ethical rationalism may lead us to expect. Just how substantive are the terms in which we take him to be thinking of ethical knowledge, however, once again partly depends on the view we take of the relationship between deontological and consequentialist grounds within his ethical thinking.

The best wedge into the topic is afforded by considering an insight that Ibn Taymiyya has already offered us in explaining why people may do wrong. It is a question that exponents of a rationalistic ethics come under a relatively more pressing demand to respond to. For if we know what is good, why do we not do it? The answers given to this question across the history of philosophy have been many, and have included hopeful bids to reserve the term "knowledge" solely for those judgments that successfully express themselves in the way we act (we *really know* what is good only if we act on it). The answers Ibn Taymiyya offers us are two: people "commit evil acts ... due to their ignorance of [their quality] or their need [*ḥāja*] for them, in the sense that they crave them and take pleasure in them." As he phrases it in other passages, it is always one of two things, either "ignorance" (*ghafla*) or "desire" (*shahwa*).[116] Yet it is in fact the former that Ibn Taymiyya elsewhere names as the primary cause of wrongful action: "In reality, all bad deeds have their ground in ignorance." We will already have more than an inkling as to the relevant type of ignorance, yet even if we did not, Ibn Taymiyya himself makes it perfectly clear in his continuation: "If one knew ... that performing a given act would cause one preponderant harm, one would not do it; because that is the hallmark of rational beings [*khāṣṣiyyat al-'āqil*]."[117]

I suggested that in Ibn Taymiyya's ethical remarks, *fiṭra* is approached mainly as a principle of desire and includes desires that require further normative ordering. It is these kinds of desires that we may naturally see as the correlate of the second factor he names. What the last-cited statement now reminds us is that it is precisely the faculty of reason that Ibn Taymiyya has elsewhere invoked as the source of that knowledge of future consequences that provides a way of normatively ordering such desires and deciding which ones to overrule. In the *Radd*, Ibn Taymiyya had offered a number of statements that lent themselves to a rationalistic epistemology specified in terms of experience (*tajriba*), a kind of knowledge combining sense perception (*ḥiss*) and reason (*ʿaql*) and responding to the recurrent conjunction between types of events. His remarks there, I suggested, seem fragmentary and spartan, leaving it to his readers to connect the dots in order to elicit the possible lineaments of his positive epistemology. The coherence of this epistemology with other elements of his intellectual scheme—particularly his consequentialist understanding of value and his emphasis on reason—offer strong arguments for reading this proposal in positive terms. Yet even if we agree to see in empirical reasoning a source of evaluative knowledge, this is still to say nothing about its scope or extent.

And it is now the question of scope—not the question of *whether* but of *how much*—that is explicitly broached in a number of other remarks that we find widely dispersed across Ibn Taymiyya's works and that propose to tell us just how the knowledge of what benefits and harms us is to be attained. Conditioning these remarks is a message about the complementarity of our natural resources and the resources of revelation invoking a distinction between the "general" and the "particular" that will immediately seem familiar. Couched in the idiom of *fiṭra*, we hear this message in Ibn Taymiyya's *Kitāb Mufaṣṣal al-iʿtiqād* as a claim that our "natural constitution is perfected by the natural constitution that is revealed by God [*al-fiṭra mukammala bi ʾl-fiṭra al-munazzala*]; for the natural constitution knows a given thing in general form [*mujmalan*], and the Sharīʿa particularizes and clarifies it [*tufaṣṣiluhu wa-tubayyinuhu*] and attests what the natural constitution has no independent access to."[118]

About this paradoxical-sounding notion of a "revealed natural constitution" there will be something more to say in chapter 5. More important for our context is the fact that this message of complementarity elsewhere appears to give way to a rather less balanced view of the relationship between naturally available and divinely communicated resources. In Ibn Taymiyya's targeted remarks about ethics, this is a relationship on which he largely preserves a gnomic silence. This silence is broken in other locations, and nowhere more starkly than in his *al-ʿAqīda al-Tadmuriyya*. "Human beings," he writes there, "stand in need of a Law [*sharʿ*] in their earthly life, for they inevitably need to act in order to realize what benefits them and repel what harms them." And the crucial continuation: "And it is the Law that distinguishes between the actions that benefit them and the actions that harm them. This is the justice of God for His creatures, and His light among His servants; and so people cannot live without a Law through which they discern what they should do and what they should avoid."

It is a statement that Ibn Taymiyya continues to nuance in the ensuing passages, and the very next breath appears to bring mitigation, restoring the emphasis on the complementarity of different epistemic sources: "*Part of* this [i.e., what is beneficial or not] people *may* know through their natural constitution [*fiṭra*] just as they know they derive benefit from food and drink, and just as they know the things which they know necessarily through their natural constitution; *another part* of it they know only through a process of proof to which their reason guides them, while *yet another part* they only know through being informed by messengers and through the clarification and guidance [these messengers] provide them with." The first part named gives us the familiar link between *fiṭra* and physical needs, with *fiṭra* "informing" us of what we need on a physical level. The second part refers us to the role of reason in ways that might be heard as evoking the rationalist epistemology of experience explored earlier. Yet this emphasis on complementarity is in tension with the neighborhood in which it appears—not only what precedes it, but also what follows. For yet another breath arrives after it to restore more decisively the restrictiveness of the first, now bringing an added emphasis on the otherworldly domain. Speaking of what is agreeable and disagreeable (*mulāʾim/munāfir*): "The detailed knowledge of that [*maʿrifat dhālika ʿalā wajh al-tafṣīl*], and the knowledge of the end [*ghāya*] which will be the resulting consequence of actions—whether bliss or misery in the afterlife—is only known through revelation. For the details of the other world which the messengers have informed us about and the details of the laws they commanded us to obey cannot be known by people through reason."[119]

At another location in the *Fatāwā*, this claim is framed in ways that deliver with a clean single stroke all the distinctions that Ibn Taymiyya's ethical remarks elsewhere occlude:

> Just as one is always in need of God to help one . . . and meet one's needs, one is need of Him in order to know what brings one to good [or "what is in one's interest": *mā yuṣliḥuhu*] . . . and this is what command and prohibition and the Sharīʿa are about. Otherwise, should one satisfy the need one sought after and desired and it was not in one's interest, one would be brought to harm, even if one found it pleasurable and beneficial at the time. For what should be taken into account is the net or preponderant benefit, and this is something that God has informed His servants about through His messengers and His books.[120]

The distinction between what is immediately pleasurable and what is in our long-term interests appears here in scintillating terms, with the knowledge of the latter ascribed to revelation as its product. In yet another passage, this evaluative distinction is coupled even more revealingly to its epistemological counterpart. It is "the Law that is the light that distinguishes between what benefits and harms one [*al-sharʿ huwa al-nūr alladhī yubayyinu mā yanfaʿuhu wa-mā yaḍurruhu*]," Ibn Taymiyya writes in a set of concentrated remarks addressing the human need for the Law. But what is thereby meant is not the Law's "distinguishing between what is harmful and beneficial on the level of the senses [*al-ḍārr wa'l-nāfiʿ bi'l-ḥiss*], as this is something that even brute animals can do; for donkeys and camels distinguish between barley and dirt. Rather [what is meant is] the distinction between acts that harm their agents in this life and the next [*maʿāshihi wa-maʿādihi*]." A long list of actions follows—actions subsumable under the heading of beneficial actions—which includes faith and the acknowledgment of divine unity, justice and piety, beneficence and the discharging of obligations (*adāʾ al-ḥuqūq*), and virtues such as courage, chastity, and honesty. This is a list that is significant in containing many of the actions that recur in Ibn Taymiyya's targeted remarks about ethics, as well as in again reducing them to utilitarian terms. Were it not for revelation, Ibn Taymiyya concludes, people would have remained "in the status of cattle and beasts of the field" (*bi-manzilat al-anʿām wa'l-bahāʾim*).[121]

We may recall that it is precisely as a knowledge accessible to the beasts of the field that Ibn Taymiyya has spoken of moral distinctions elsewhere, notably in his polemics against monistic Sufis, comparing our grasp of them to our ability to discern "what's bitter and brackish and what's sweet to the taste" in a way that seems to have little to divide it from the distinction "between barley and dirt" just referred to. This open contradiction of a claim we will have already recognized as misleadingly partial is important, on the one hand, in placing on display the mercurial character of Ibn Taymiyya's terms. *Nāfiʿ* is used to refer both to what is immediately pleasurable—dubbed *nāfiʿ bi'l-ḥiss*—as well as what is beneficial in a longer-term sense. Yet more important for our purposes is the crucial fact that it recasts the distinction between the senses and reason, which elsewhere appears as the epistemological counterpart of the evaluative distinction between the immediately pleasurable and the beneficial, as one between the senses and revelation. It is revelation here, not reason, that tells us what our senses do not.

What the above suggests is that in some of Ibn Taymiyya's most direct positioning remarks about the consequences of actions—consequences, as I have said, that constitute the real criterion for their value—his vision of the complementarity of different epistemic resources yields to a way of scripting this balance that skews it heavily toward one of its terms, assigning to revelation the central role. If the value of actions lies in their utility, it is the Law that primarily informs us of this. The directness with which this message is pressed will make us wonder just how its force should be calibrated against the force of the message held out in the *Radd* and the empiricist picture of ethical epistemology it appeared to encourage. And the confidence of the former, weighed against the relatively threadbare development of the latter, may fan our doubts as to how seriously Ibn Taymiyya intended to claim this empiricist understanding as his own. This epistemology, I suggested earlier, harmonizes with several elements of Ibn Taymiyya's ethical discussion, including his emphasis on reason and his consequentialist view of value. Yet it will be noticed that it is at odds with an overwhelming emphasis on human dependence that stamps Ibn Taymiyya's work throughout and that is enshrined as a spiritual imperative that Sufi writers before him described as the virtue of *tawakkul* or trust in God.[122] It is also at odds with an understanding of the sheer reach of the Law that Ibn Taymiyya was far from alone within the Islamic tradition in embracing. The Sharīʿa makes a comprehensive claim on every aspect of our daily lives that must in each instance be identified through careful study. The "straight path" (*al-ṣirāṭ al-mustaqīm*), Ibn Taymiyya writes, "consists in one's doing at every moment whatever one has been commanded to do at that particular moment, whether by way of action or knowledge, and in not doing what one has been forbidden to do, and this requires that one know and do at every moment in time what one has been commanded to do at that particular time and what one has been forbidden." Having been created in a state of ignorance and injustice, we need particular knowledge (*ʿilm mufaṣṣal*) to counteract our ignorance and particular moderation or justice (*ʿadl*) to counteract our injustice and govern all our actions—our sleeping and our waking, our eating and our drinking. And "if God did not graciously give [*in lam yamunna*] [human beings] the particular knowledge they need and the particular justice they need," they would stray from the straight path.[123]

There are real interpretive tensions here, and no less relevant than resolving them will be to consider what they have to tell us about the nature of Ibn Taymiyya's engagement with ethical questions and about the motivations that ground it, an issue to which I will return in chapter 5. Here I will confine myself to spelling out one particular insight about the nature of this engagement that is relevant to the present context. For the construal of the relationship between reason and revelation in terms of the particularization of intuitively available ethical standards—a construal distinctly invoked in Ibn Taymiyya's remarks quoted above—was not, as I have said, a new move in the classical debates, and had been notably made by Muʿtazilite writers before. Yet this comparative foil now allows us to consider more clearly why this move should seem to yield a less substantive view of ethical reason in Ibn Taymiyya's case than it had done at the hands of the Muʿtazilites.

For the Muʿtazilites, as we saw in chapter 1, had stocked reason with a number of ethical requirements, only some of which had consequentialist form. "Pursue what is in your welfare" (and avoid what undermines it) was only one of these requirements, and it took its place next to a number of more substantive requirements such as "Do not lie under any circumstances," "Show gratitude to benefactors," and "Do not cause harm without just cause." It is also crucial to record that the Baṣran Muʿtazilite claim that divinely prescribed norms are instrumental to human welfare—thereby forming an instance of *lutf* or divine assistance—had involved a very particular understanding of the means and ends at stake. The end that revelation was instrumental in achieving was the fulfillment of the moral requirements available through reason (*ʿaqliyyāt* or *wājibāt wa-qabāʾiḥ ʿaqliyya*); and these were of course requirements that included commitments of a deontological kind. Put more clearly, they were instrumental not merely or primarily to the good but to the right. This was a relationship of priority implicit in the Qur'anic statement "Prayer restrains from shameful and unjust deeds" (Q 29:45) and unpacked more fully by Muʿtazilite thinkers. The fulfillment of what is right might resolve to utility in the long term, given the deserved consequences one's actions attract posthumously, yet the norms at stake as they present themselves to human reason were not parsed directly in utilitarian terms.

In all these respects, the Muʿtazilites had vested reason with an ethical content that seems decidedly substantive. In approaching the nature of value, Ibn Taymiyya, as we saw in the previous chapter, silently elides the deontological component of Muʿtazilite ethical theory, even though he continues to refer to deontological types of actions across his writings. Everything we have heard since will have served to cement that impression, accentuating Ibn Taymiyya's preoccupation with the notions of benefit or utility. Yet of course the imperative "Pursue what is in your welfare" is far thinner than requirements like "Do not lie" and "Do not harm without just cause"—a largely formal principle that carries little action-guiding significance prior to a thicker identification of what counts as one's (genuine) welfare and the means through which one's welfare can be achieved.

In the previous chapter, it may be pointed out, our story had followed Ibn Taymiyya's account with a question that bore a chiefly ontological inflection: What *makes* actions good? Our conclusion that deontological-sounding types of acts like justice and injustice ultimately "reduce" to utility was articulated expressly against this background, as a claim about what *makes* justice and injustice good. And the narrower proposal I outlined was that it is the utility of such actions for the social community—their public interest—that undergirds Ibn Taymiyya's conversion of justice and injustice into consequentialist notions. It may thus be wondered whether this ontological claim should be unquestioningly taken to translate into epistemological terms and, more precisely, whether it offers us an account of the descriptions under which ordinary moral agents *know* such actions to be good. Just how substantive ethical reason emerges out of Ibn Taymiyya's hands would partly depend on the way we answer this question.

Yet it will be remembered that the seams between the ontology of value and the human perception of value were not hermetically sealed in the previous chapter, which drew heavily on Ibn Taymiyya's discussion of the human attraction to ethically good acts. All I can do here is thus to rehearse the key facts that have already provided this question with a response. For as we have seen, Ibn Taymiyya indeed speaks of people as attracted to justice, beneficence, and truthfulness and repulsed by their contraries. More often than not, he uses the desiderative idiom of "desire" or "love" rather than the more cognitive idiom of "knowledge" to speak of the human relationship to deontological-sounding acts. What we hear is not so much "human beings know that justice is good" as "human beings desire justice." Yet the utilitarian timbre that dominates Ibn Taymiyya's characterization of the nature of value and the nature of human motivation means that the most intuitive way of receiving these statements is by taking them to signify that the *description* under which human beings ordinarily desire such actions—the description under which they consider them *good*—is precisely *qua* beneficial.

In the previous chapter, at the same time, I suggested that it is public interest rather than individual self-interest that Ibn Taymiyya isolates as the ultimate foundation of ethical norms. One of the most relevant questions to raise here, thus, might be just how *that* description should be taken to figure within the ordinary epistemic and motivational states of human beings. Taken as an object of motivation, it has often been queried whether what we know about the natural self-concern of human beings makes it plausible to envisage that the common good could figure among their motivating drives. "Experience," as Hume put it, "sufficiently proves, that men, in the ordinary conduct of life, look not so far as the public interest, when they pay their creditors, perform their promises, and abstain from theft, and robbery, and injustice of every kind. That is a motive too remote and too sublime to affect the generality of mankind" (*T* 481). Yet Hume himself, like other thinkers dissatisfied with deontological approaches to morality, would consider a broader concern with the good of others—an ability to command a more general viewpoint constituted by sympathy with the "good of mankind" and the "interest of society" (*T* 578–79)—the truest paradigm of the moral point of view.

Ibn Taymiyya, I noted in chapter 1, has little to say about how the motivational gap between self-interest and public interest might be bridged. Yet what is striking is that he issues unambiguous statements to the effect that public interest not only *makes* justice good but forms the description under which it is *known* to be such. No clearer statement of this kind can be found than the one appearing in the stage-setting exposition of Ibn Taymiyya's *via media* that opened the previous chapter. Outlining his threefold division of acts, Ibn Taymiyya had begun with the one that represented his most significant ethical positioning, namely "the case in which an act contains benefit or harm, [and it would do so] even if the Law had not come to report that," and he had significantly continued, "the way *it is known* that justice serves the good of the world [*maṣlaḥat al-ʿālam*] and injustice tends to its harm." [124] Yet this remarkable claim, it will be instantly noticed, is far from transparent. Digging beneath the ambiguous passivity of Ibn Taymiyya's "it is known," we would like to ask more openly: Exactly who is the grammatical subject implied here? Ibn Taymiyya nowhere seems to clarify how that statement should be received. Left with such meager interpretive aids, the most natural way of interpreting it will be by connecting it to the analysis offered in the previous chapter, where we had entertained a similar question about how the subject of our conversation should be identified—and more specifically, how the "we" that derives benefit from ethical norms should be construed. One of the most compelling ways of construing this, I had suggested, is not as a first-person singular but as the first-person plural of the community. It is on the same level that the subject of Ibn Taymiyya's present epistemic statement invites us to parse it. The communal "we" who knows injustice is bad is the same communal "we" whose welfare is impaired by it.

Taken together, the above suggests that Ibn Taymiyya's conception of ethical reason is far thinner than that of his Muʿtazilite predecessors whose position his own ostensibly resembles. Yet the last observation also helps bring another point more clearly into the open. For if the "we" buried in Ibn Taymiyya's passive "it is known" is not the first-person singular, what this calls attention to is just how little we seem to hear about the moral consciousness of the ordinary human agent in Ibn Taymiyya's ethical discussions and how overall grainy he leaves our picture of the processes of ethical reasoning.

The comparative robustness of the picture emerging from Muʿtazilite writings had to do, on the one hand, with the far more detailed table of contents they had provided in specifying the notion of moral reason. Yet it had then been reinforced in a multiplicity of other ways. In the intramural debates between Baṣran and Baghdādī Muʿtazilites, for example, each side made substantive appeals to what we would nowadays call "moral intuitions." In arguing against the Baghdādī view that God is obliged to optimize human welfare in the mundane realm (*wujūb al-aṣlaḥ fī 'l-dunyā*), the Baṣrans drew attention to what this moral principle would entail if it were brought to bear on ordinary human life: that a poor man would be entitled to avail himself of a rich man's property without the latter's permission, or that we would all be under an unlimited obligation to help the needy. And their case would rest on the claim that this conclusion conflicts with our ordinary moral intuitions about what is right or morally required of us. The strategy was a two-way street, and thus we also see Baghdādīs arguing for their position on the basis of the contrary intuition, that we would morally disapprove of an extremely wealthy person (not unlike God, for that matter) who sees another in dire need and begrudges him the simple means of stilling his hunger or thirst.[125]

The fact that these intuitions might internally conflict, as intuitions after all do—or indeed that this appeal to moral intuitions was motivated by a theological agenda, reflecting the distinctive Muʿtazilite understanding that human beings and God share a single set of ethical standards—is immaterial to the point. The Muʿtazilites, similarly, had elaborated at some length on the different senses in which one might speak of ethical knowledge as being rationally "available" to people. For to say that ethical norms are known by reason is not to say that the value of actions is always known immediately and that ethical judgment may not require an achievement. People will often need to take an extra step of reflection in determining the value of particular actions. This includes not merely the kind of reflection indicated earlier, using the distinction between "general" and "particular" judgments (I know injustice is bad, but do I know *this* is an instance of injustice?), but also a kind of reflection that Ibn Mattawayh designates in particularly pregnant terms as the "method of analogy" (*ṭarīqat al-qiyās*). We may thus know the moral judgment attracted by one type of act, for example lying that brings no benefit, but we may then require an extra cognitive move in order to transfer its qualification to a subsidiary case (*farʿ*) in which lying does bring some benefit by recognizing that the cause (*ʿilla*) of the qualification has remained the same.[126] The comparative robustness of ethical reason as portrayed by Muʿtazilite writers had also been reinforced by the programmatic interest shown within certain Muʿtazilite works in marking the boundaries between where our rational ethical knowledge ends and the ethical knowledge provided by the Law begins.[127]

I speak of a "comparative" robustness because, as I have pointed out elsewhere, the ethical theories of the Muʿtazilites always need to be read against the theological agenda that motivates them—above all, to affirm that God is just in all He does—and they do not float free from this agenda. Despite Ibn Mattawayh's intriguing invocation of the notion of "analogy," which in the domain of Islamic law that forms its foremost habitat was a *generative* tool for new evaluative decisions, reason is not approached as an action-guiding resource that indeed enjoys such independent and substantive status it might allow us (in Schneewind's expression) to "guide our own affairs." As already mentioned, there were hardly any theologians who would have wished to advocate such a self-sufficient role, rendering revealed guidance otiose, though it is not unimportant to record that Muʿtazilites like Ibn Mattawayh had avowed in principle that prophetic guidance might, under certain circumstances, be otiose and the ethical truths known by reason sufficient for guidance.[128]

It is an avowal that, even taken as a purely theoretical possibility, it is hard to envisage Ibn Taymiyya offering; in talking about ethics, he never quite imagines revelation away. And even if "robustness" is here a matter of degree, it is clear that, set against the Muʿtazilite example, Ibn Taymiyya's articulation of a claim that seems to share in the Muʿtazilite emphasis on reason as a source of ethical norms has none of the depth and detail typifying the Muʿtazilites' reflections. The ordinary moral subject uninformed by religious teachings might always have been a semifictional figure in theological debates about value. In Ibn Taymiyya's writings he is less than a ghost. I noted above that Ibn Taymiyya's discussions of ethical epistemology confront the reader with important tensions, demanding a decision, notably, about how to balance Ibn Taymiyya's allusive interest in an empiricist epistemology against his powerful emphasis on revelation as an epistemic source for the utility of actions. No less important than these tensions are the features of Ibn Taymiyya's writing they call attention to, above all the thinness and fragmentariness of his discussions of ethical epistemology and the rudimentary characterization of moral awareness they hold up. Ethical reason, I have suggested, looks back at us from Ibn Taymiyya's writings in gossamer terms. Yet this reflects not merely the content of Ibn Taymiyya's remarks about ethics, but also their form.

The comparison just struck between Ibn Taymiyya and the Muʿtazilites will seem to call for something further. For having invoked the motivations that underlie the ethical theories developed by Muʿtazilite writers, this will naturally invite a question about Ibn Taymiyya's motivations in advancing his own—motivations that may provide a helpful interpretive filter for approaching both the content and the form of his engagement. One description of these motivations has already come to the fore: Ibn Taymiyya's concern to press a message of harmony between reason (or nature) and the divine Law. There is more to be said about this message, and more specifically about the conception of God to which it is tied. We will be returning to this question in chapter 5 once Ibn Taymiyya's broader theological vision has stepped into view.

HAVING FOCUSED ON the question "What makes actions good?" in chapter 1, my main focus in this chapter was on the question "How do we know what actions are good?" Ibn Taymiyya claimed we know ethical norms by reason. He also, more distinctively, asserted we know these by our natural constitution or *fiṭra*. My aim was to clarify these two claims, shedding light on Ibn Taymiyya's positive ethical epistemology and situating it within its context, particularly his engagement of Avicenna in the *Radd*. We have seen that isolating Ibn Taymiyya's positive epistemology is no mean task, and is hampered by the nature of the textual bases he makes available to it. To the extent that we can prise out his epistemological view from its dialectical environment, we can say that he calls attention to empirical reasoning as an important paradigm for our knowledge of the long-term consequences of actions that form the main criterion for evaluating them. Yet elsewhere he brings this epistemology into question by delivering a vigorous emphasis on the Law as a source of this knowledge. Ethical reason, overall, is limned in very thin terms within Ibn Taymiyya's work. Human nature, as he deploys it in his ethical discussions, is conceptualized chiefly as a principle of desire. And to the extent that it ranges over natural desires that require further normative ordering, nature cannot be understood to carry the privilege or positive valence it prima facie appears to.

This is not the last word we have had on Ibn Taymiyya's evaluative epistemology. We will be revisiting it from another direction in chapter 5, when we turn to consider whether the epistemological views he articulates in the legal context have something new to contribute to our picture. But here there is a different part of the story we are pursuing that must more immediately claim our attention. One of my objectives in the foregoing was to elicit Ibn Taymiyya's positive views while situating them against their topography—the composite topography constituted both by *kalām* debates about ethics and by the philosophical writings of Avicenna which I suggested provided a formative context for Ibn Taymiyya's elaboration of some of his ethical views. In situating Ibn Taymiyya against the *kalām* debates, several of my comparative juxtapositions focused on the Muʿtazilites, whose emphasis on reason Ibn Taymiyya would most readily seem to be reprising. It is high time for the fuller topography to step into the light. For the story of the *Radd* itself, as I have said, needs to be told twice to account for the double life that the ideas it targets would lead in Avicenna's own writings and in those of his Ashʿarite readers. It is this richer telling of the story, as I hope to show, that we must look to for a deeper understanding of the formative context of Ibn Taymiyya's ethical views. It is an understanding that may lead us to reappraise the significance and indeed the accomplishment of Ibn Taymiyya's ethical approach, revealing his multiple affinities with—and plural debts to—Ashʿarite thought, including a crucial debt for the very claim of reason and the very arrogation of "nature" as a vocabulary for his ethical stance. Gaining these insights, however, will once again require working through certain misleading first impressions, as it will require becoming clearer on the contours of Ashʿarite ethical thought. To this task I turn.

3

Ibn Taymiyya's Ethics and Its Ashʿarite Antecedents

LOOKING OVER IBN Taymiyya's intellectual trajectory, it would not take much to conclude that Ibn Taymiyya and the Ashʿarites had never enjoyed an easy peace. It had been the Ashʿarites, as we know, that had been responsible for one of his earliest public trials after the publication of his *al-ʿAqīda al-Ḥamawiyya*, adding a new episode to an old history of hostile relations between Ashʿarite and Ḥanbalite thinkers and launching Ibn Taymiyya on a career of high-pitched polemical confrontations with Ashʿarism waged with both word and pen. Many of Ibn Taymiyya's best-known works are directed against targets that are either exclusively composed of Ashʿarites or include Ashʿarites as prominent mouthpieces. His famed *Darʾ taʿāruḍ al-ʿaql waʾl-naql* is pitted against a view of the relationship between reason and revelation notably developed by Ashʿarite theologians. His *Bayān talbīs al-jahmiyya* attacks a view of the divine attributes pressed by Ashʿarite theologians, and most particularly by al-Rāzī. His *al-Radd ʿalaʾl-manṭiqiyyīn* finds its stimulus in the insidious infiltration of logic into the religious sciences, which Ashʿarite thinkers like al-Ghazālī had spearheaded, and in his discussion of ethical propositions, it is characteristically an Ashʿarite thinker, al-Rāzī, that Ibn Taymiyya confronts along with Avicenna.

There is much truth in this appearance of conflict, and there is much in the Ashʿarite transactions with reason in theological matters that Ibn Taymiyya would trenchantly and unambiguously oppose. Yet turning to the topic of ethics, we will find that the relationship between Ibn Taymiyya and the Ashʿarites cannot be written in such straightforwardly conflictual terms. As with Ibn Taymiyya's engagement with the philosophers, which gave rise to al-Dhahabī's accusation that Ibn Taymiyya "repeatedly swallowed the poison of the philosophers and their works," in engaging the Ashʿarites what Ibn Taymiyya ingested turns out to have been greater than what he expelled. This is an insight, however, to be gained by working through several appearances that train the spotlight more sharply on what divides Ibn Taymiyya from the Ash'arites than what unites them.

In this chapter my aim will be to take the first major step in limning the relationship between Ibn Taymiyya and the Ash'arites on ethical questions. My emphasis will fall on key convergences that relate to the way these thinkers approach the nature of ethical value and the nature of human beings' epistemic access to it. Having documented what unites these viewpoints, it will then be the task of the next chapter to locate Ibn Taymiyya even more firmly within his theological topography by documenting what divides them and what constitutes the heart of Ibn Taymiyya's more distinctive contribution.

Schematizing Ash'arite Ethics: Reason, Natural Desire, Social Convention

It is an emphasis on what divides that emerged strongly in the stage-setting exposition of Ibn Taymiyya's *via media* considered in the first chapter, whose themes we are far from having depleted. Ibn Taymiyya had significantly objected to the Ash'arites for denying that "what is right [*ma'rūf*] is . . . right in itself [*fī nafsihi*]" and "what is wrong [*munkar*] in itself wrong" and that actions have objective qualities that provide grounds for God's command. He had remonstrated with them for making out ethical qualities to be a mere matter of "relation and association [*nisba wa-iḍāfa*]" and for not acknowledging any other meaning to such qualities besides "that which agrees with people's appetites [*mā yulā'imu al-ṭibā'*]."[1]

Yet looking back over the ground we have covered in the previous chapters, it will not be difficult now to pick out several features of Ibn Taymiyya's perspective that throw unmistakable bridges into the terrain typical of Ash'arite ethical thought. Ibn Taymiyya's sidelining of the deontological perspective was the first important bridge. This was an aspect of Mu'tazilite ethics that Ash'arite writers had also rejected in claiming, as we heard from al-Ghazālī, that evaluative judgments reflect the subjective desires of human agents. They had paired this to an egoistic view of human nature epitomized in al-Ghazālī's words in the *Mustaṣfā*: "Every person is formed by nature to love himself." These were words Ibn Taymiyya at first appeared to be exposing to vertical bouleversement with his counterclaim in the *Radd*: "People are naturally formed to love justice and those party to it." Yet his view turned out to be merely a new investiture of al-Ghazālī's under a different guise, and it was al-Ghazālī whom he elsewhere directly echoed. For the Ash'arites, as for Ibn Taymiyya, this was naturally paired with the claim that God is not subject to the ethical standards of human behavior.

This last claim, as we will recall from chapter 1, was one of the key objections Ibn Taymiyya had brought against Mu'tazilite ethics. We may notice that the other objections on his list had also met with vocal endorsement among Ashʿarite authors. The Ashʿarites had also claimed that God determines human actions. And they had similarly made the divine punishment of actions conditional on the arrival of revelation—God's word, after all, *created* the relationship between actions and their otherworldly consequences—rejecting the notion of desert that the Muʿtazilites had made the cornerstone of their account of this relationship. The notion of desert is likewise absent from Ibn Taymiyya's thinking, an absence that reflects a deliberate act of exclusion, as we will see more fully in chapter 4. No less relevant, Ibn Taymiyya's privileging of revelation as a source of our knowledge of the consequences (and thus the overall utility) of actions directly echoes a view adopted by Ashʿarite theologians. For having asserted that revelation institutes the consequences of actions, the Ashʿarites had asserted the natural corollary, namely that these consequences are epistemically accessible to people only by revelation. As al-Ghazālī had pithily written in *al-Iqtiṣād fi'l-iʿtiqād*: "The one who creates obligation is God, the one who informs is the prophet [*al-mūjib huwa Allāh taʿālā, al-mukhbir huwa al-rasūl*]."[2] God makes actions obligatory or prohibited by attaching reward or punishment to actions as their consequences; it then falls to the prophets to inform us of this.

In this light, Ibn Taymiyya's advertised objections to Ashʿarite ethics as expressed in the stage-setting passage of chapter 1 and as widely rehearsed elsewhere may in fact strike us as deeply perplexing.[3] For Ibn Taymiyya himself has referred ethical value to human desires and to what is "agreeable" to human beings. "Agreeability"—the very term he uses in dissociating himself from the Ashʿarite view that value is merely a matter of what "agrees with people's appetites" (*mā yulāʾimu al-ṭibāʿ*)—appears in several of his own remarks about value, including a seminal passage of the *Radd* we have already heard: "The foundations of [ethical] judgments are necessarily known by people, for they are formed by nature to love what is agreeable to them and to hate what harms them [*al-nufūs . . . mafṭūra ʿalā ḥubb mā yulāʾimuhā wa-bughḍ mā yaḍurruhā*], and what is signified by the term 'good' is what is agreeable to them and by 'bad' what harms them. So if they are formed by nature to love the one [*mafṭūra ʿalā ḥubb*] and to hate the other . . . it is evident that people know these widespread propositions by their inborn nature [*bi-fiṭarihim*]."[4] This passage will immediately put us in mind of the kind of analysis that al-Ghazālī had put forward in his *Mustaṣfā* in discussing the meaning of moral terms. Focusing on the term "good" (*ḥasan*), as we have seen, al-Ghazālī had proposed a naturalistic account of ordinary usage of this term, arguing that what we call "good" is whatever agrees with our purposes (*mā yuwāfiqu gharaḍ al-fāʿil*).[5] These self-interested purposes are grounded in our passionate or appetitive nature (*ṭabʿ*) and reveal evaluative terms to be fundamentally relative (*iḍāfī*) in nature. Every agent calls "good" whatever agrees with *his* purposes, and his purposes may not agree with another's; indeed they will often conflict. Given these dramatic resemblances, one must wonder how Ibn Taymiyya could possibly have meant to distinguish his ethical view from the one Ash'arites like al-Ghazālī had espoused. No less crucially, one must wonder how Ibn Taymiyya could have taken his view to be capable of securing the kind of ethical objectivism he made central to his quarrel with the Ash'arites. There must be something in the actions themselves (*fī nafs al-amr*) that makes them good, we heard. Yet what *is* that something if all there is to the value of actions is "what is agreeable"?

Juxtaposing Ibn Taymiyya's words to al-Ghazālī's, our eye will naturally first be caught by the similarities that connect them. A closer reading, however, may also call attention to certain palpable differences between the ways they couch their respective views—differences that may hold critical clues for answering such questions and that it is therefore worth bringing out. For the accent on desire (what a person "loves," in Ibn Taymiyya's idiom; what an agent takes as his "purpose," in al-Ghazālī's) may be shared, as may some notion of "agreeability" (whether *mulā'ama* or *muwāfaqa*). Yet is there nothing to be made of the fact that al-Ghazālī speaks of "purpose" where Ibn Taymiyya—both here and even more clearly elsewhere—speaks of the pair "benefit" and "harm"? "What I want" as against "what is good for me" or what in fact benefits me and serves my interests. We may put this difference most relevantly by using a notion not unlike that of "objectivity" we just queried. Ibn Taymiyya is referring evaluative concepts to the desire individuals have for their real welfare; al-Ghazālī is referring them to the contingent desires individuals happen to have for one thing or another—desires that may or may not serve their real welfare. What I "subjectively" consider good may not always coincide with what is "objectively" good for me. Having marked this distinction, we might connect it to another, this time more interestingly relating to the notion of "nature" with which each desire is associated. For where al-Ghazālī speaks of *ṭab'*, Ibn Taymiyya speaks of *fiṭra*. Al-Ghazālī connects the term *ṭab'* to the egoistic desires of particular individuals which he makes foundational to our ordinary usage of "good" and "bad." Ibn Taymiyya, by contrast, has connected the term *fiṭra* to natural (paradigmatically physical) desires that are universal to human beings and to a desire for objective good. In this respect, human nature as *fiṭra* would seem capable of serving as a foundation for ethical norms in a way that human nature as *ṭab'* could not. Taken as the seat of the egoistic desires of individuals, *ṭab'* supports a merely relative usage of the term "good." *Fiṭra*, by contrast, can serve as a basis of a more objective usage.

These differences in turn help propel to the foreground something else that might have otherwise passed unnoticed, namely the diverging ways al-Ghazālī and Ibn Taymiyya invite us to construe the nature of their accounts. Al-Ghazālī highlights the fact that this is *what people call* "good"; he emphasizes what people say, and in doing so emphasizes the subjectivity and fallibility of such "sayings" and "callings." Ibn Taymiyya's remarks are not free from such emphasis: *al-murād bi-qawlinā* ("what is signified by the term"), he says here; *al-nāsa idhā qālu … yaʿnūna* ("when people say … they mean"), he captions his concern elsewhere.[6] Yet his voice falls with a different accent, most visible in his concluding statement, which speaks not of "calling" or of "saying" but of *knowing*: "People *know* these judgments by their inborn nature." Not linguistics, but epistemology. Ibn Taymiyya's parsing thus appears objectivist twice over, in focusing on what *really* benefits or harms us and on what we *know* is good and bad—thus what is *really* good and bad. Emerging from his pen, the last statement seems less like the kind of statement one might have encountered in the work of a lexicographer documenting with descriptive neutrality the usage of language and more like what we might find in the work of a moralist, setting out in clear normative tones what *is* or *is not* right and wrong. "The goodness and badness of human actions is a matter of the benefit and harm acts involve," we heard earlier. And again: "The only kind of good that exists is in the sense of what is agreeable, and the only kind of bad that exists is in the sense of what is disagreeable."[7]

This way of indexing the differences between Ibn Taymiyya's view and the view expressed by al-Ghazālī will seem particularly interesting, and all the more compelling, for allocating a central place to the notion of *fiṭra* that we have recognized as a salient element of Ibn Taymiyya's ethical viewpoint and indeed of his theological vision as a whole. Setting out the context of Ibn Taymiyya's discussion in the *Radd* and his appeal to *fiṭra* as a foundation of ethical judgments, we earlier saw that he had pitted himself against a set of ideas that had found their home in the writings of Avicenna. Yet what is now important to bring out is that this is a home that had brought the Ashʿarites and Avicenna under the same roof, uniting them in a common ethical perspective.

The reasons why Ashʿarite thinkers came to find in Avicenna's approach to ethical judgments a particularly fertile resource for bolstering their own position are not hard to come by. Avicenna's discussion, we may recall, had found its purchase in the basic contention that not everything we consider self-evident may in fact constitute a primary rational truth. We may *think* we know certain truths, but we may be mistaken. Yet it was just such a claim of unassailable self-evidence that had typified the Muʿtazilite ethical viewpoint, set down as a nonnegotiable premise that Muʿtazilites stubbornly barricaded themselves behind and refused to converse with those who denied it. Everyone knows ethical truths; you do too—all you need to do is look inside you. A simple turn inward (*al-rujūʿ ila'l-nafs*), as ʿAbd al-Jabbār had said, was all that was needed to set the facts straight on certain questions, including questions about moral knowledge.[8] The turn inward to reason, as we also saw in the previous chapter, was coupled to an outward turn to the empirical world to harvest examples of ordinary people acting in disinterested ways that reflect the influence of purely ethical principles. In trying to secure the purest possible conditions for such case studies, this empirical turn outward, it is true, sometimes appeared to inch closer to something rather less real than ideal. Mānkdīm would thus use the telltale language of a "hypothesis" in rehearsing the point in his own voice: "We are hypothesizing" (or stipulating: *nafriḍu al-kalām*) that the person in question is hard-hearted, indifferent to praise or blame (or acting on a desert island where social praise cannot reach him), an unbeliever who does not believe in posthumous reward or punishment.[9]

Avicenna's discussion of ethical judgments would upstage the real-yet-ideal hypothesis of the Muʿtazilites by a more radical thought experiment designed to transport one to a perspective not merely materially outside the reach of human society, but intellectually prior to its epistemic influence. Seen from this perspective, the phenomenal surface of our ordinary moral consciousness can be plowed up to reveal our sense of self-evidence as the product of a longer genealogy built on the bedrock of self-interested desire as it makes its way upward through the social world. You think you know objective ethical truths, but you are mistaken. What you "know" are merely conventional ideas that have been etched into you in the social world that shaped you by harnessing your natural desires. Avicenna's account would thus allow the Ashʿarites to grant the Muʿtazilites their precious claims while emptying them of their significance, boring beneath them to displace the notion of "reason" no less than the notion of "disinterested action," and to replace them with a typically Ashʿarite view of desire and self-interested action as the heart of the ethical life.

The notion of a social genealogy had not been wholly absent from the brew of Ashʿarite theological ideas even prior to the more forceful engagement of Avicenna's philosophical resources from al-Ghazālī's time onward. Al-Ghazālī, certainly, was far from the first to propose an egoistic deconstruction of disinterested motivation. This was a proposal already at work in the thinking of earlier Ashʿarites, as attested by al-Juwaynī's (d. 1085) dense reference to people's "natural inclination to pleasures and their aversion to pains [*mayl al-ṭibāʿ ila 'l-ladhdhāt wa-nufūrihā ʿan al-ālām*]" in this context, and even earlier by the remark of al-Ashʿarī relayed by Ibn Fūrak (d. 1015): "For both good and bad, in the domain of the present world, the same thing holds: bad acts are avoided due to the deficiency and harm that redounds to one who commits them, and good and wise acts are chosen due to the benefit and perfection[10] that redounds to the one who performs them."[11] The pain and pleasure or benefit and harm at stake had often in turn been concretized in terms of the praise and blame attracted by actions. Yet to focus on praise is immediately to invite attention to the identity of those directing praise to certain actions over others. It is also to invite attention to the formative processes that effect the link between "morally good" actions and egoistic drives—and more specifically to the processes of education or habituation through which practices of praise cement that link.

The notion of habituation, and the implicit reference to the social community as its administrator, had already glimmered into the open in the works of earlier Ashʿarites, as in al-Juwaynī's anticipatory remarks in the *Niẓāmiyya*. Referring to people's drive toward noble behavior, he had stated that this "is caused by the strong influence praise usually exerts; for if one keeps at something and grows accustomed to it [*yataʿawwaduhu*], there comes a point where it becomes difficult for him to oppose it."[12] Yet it is a generation later, with al-Ghazālī, that it stands out more distinctly, in ways that betray the influence of Avicenna more clearly and also lay its deconstructive potential plain. The connection between ethical actions and praise, al-Ghazālī clarifies, cannot be done away with merely by temporarily removing ourselves from the physical reach of society, as the Muʿtazilites had fancied in postulating their semifictional "moral informants." Even if in a given instance an action is unlikely to be praised *in fact*, this connection is indelibly imprinted within us. "For one sees praise attaching to [*maqrūn bi*] this form [i.e., the action] and one supposes that praise attaches to it under all circumstances alike," just as when a person of healthy constitution (*ṭabʿ salīm*) who has been bitten by a snake sees a mottled rope and flinches from it in fear. And "what is conjoined to the pleasurable is pleasurable, and what is conjoined to the repugnant is repugnant."[13] Al-Ghazālī does not explicitly stress the notion of education or the role of the social environment in effecting this connection here, yet it must clearly be presupposed. As this remark suggests, it is our passionate nature or *ṭabʿ*—that aspect of ourselves that experiences pleasure and pain, desire and fear, and is capable of learning from them—that gives us our educability and also the dark core of our irrationality, a core that must therefore belong equally to our ethical responses.[14]

This is the genealogy that could be used to explain how universal moral judgments like "lying is bad" come to acquire the absolute airs that the Muʿtazilites had ascribed to them. For there are certainly cases, as al-Ghazālī writes in the *Mustaṣfā*, where lying is the right course of action, for example when it is a matter of saving a prophet's life. Yet in those cases, "one finds oneself shrinking from it, given how long he has been brought up thinking that this is bad. For it has been inculcated in him ever since he was a child, by way of disciplining and instruction [*al-taʾdīb waʾl-irshād*], that lying is bad and nobody should engage in it . . . and when one hears something at a young age, you might as well be carving it into stone."[15] Avicenna's thought experiment, in which the claim that ethical judgments are produced by social enculturation achieved a potent expression, would be reprised by al-Ghazālī directly in his discussion of widely accepted propositions in *Miʿyār al-ʿilm fī fann al-manṭiq*, as also in the logical introduction to the *Mustaṣfā*, and its motifs would then recur in his account of the ethical question of the "determination of good and bad."[16]

Many Ashʿarites after him would follow his example, injecting Avicenna's ideas forcefully into the bloodstream of Ashʿarite polemics against Muʿtazilite moral rationalism and developing them in ever-finer nuance. The key idea that society *teaches* us ethical standards, crisply set out in al-Ghazālī's last statement, would thus be reformulated by other Ash'arites more pointedly as a claim that society *produces* these standards. Writing in his *Nihāyat al-iqdām fī 'ilm al-kalām*, al-Shahrastānī (d. 1153) would deny, in true Ash'arite style, that good and bad constitute intrinsic qualities of acts, and would then offer the following alternative construal. Since these qualities have no real epistemic foundation, they must instead be founded on "people's custom [*'ādāt al-nās*] of calling what harms them bad and what benefits them good. For our part we do not deny these kinds of designations, but they vary from one people to another depending on their custom, they vary from place to place and from time to time ... and anything that varies depending on these [kinds of] relations and parameters [*al-nisab wa 'l-iḍāfāt*] has no intrinsic reality of its own [*ḥaqīqa ... fī 'l-dhāt*]."[17]

This statement is significant not only in offering an illustration of the notion of custom or convention as Ash'arite writers would deploy it but also in revealing the idea that would be taken as its logical adjunct, namely the relativity and variability of moral norms. In this respect, this understanding would align itself with a motif that formed one of the defining features of the Ash'arite approach. For the relativity of norms generated by social means, and their variability from one social milieu to another, mirrors the relativity of norms founded on self-interest and their variability from person to person. Al-Ghazālī had emphasized the latter point in the *Mustaṣfā* when speaking of the relative (*iḍāfī*) meaning of moral terms: people call things "good" when they agree with their personal purposes, and one man's purposes are not another's. To this view, al-Shahrastānī's claim now appears as the precise counterpart, yet with a telling shift from the individual to the community. Different societies call acts "good" when they benefit them, and what one society thinks beneficial and harmful may not be shared by another. Importantly, thus, moral norms may be explained by reference to the social whole taken as a suprapersonal unit with interests that can be harmed or served.

All that is left is to add the name of al-Rāzī to the list of Ash'arites imbibing this particular element of Avicenna's resources. It is indeed, as already mentioned, in his capacity as commentator to the relevant passage of Avicenna's *Ishārāt* that al-Rāzī appears as one of Ibn Taymiyya's chief interlocutors in that location of his *Radd* that provides the stage for a concerted treatment of ethical ideas. The cradle out of which Ibn Taymiyya's ethical deployment of *fiṭra* emerges, thus, is one in which his opposition to Ash'arism seems to be directly flagged. If in fact one was looking for a formulation of the precise statement that Ibn Taymiyya's entire discussion in the *Radd* would seek to overturn, one need not look beyond al-Ghazālī's discussion of widely accepted propositions in his *Mustaṣfā*. "The original nature," he had written about moral propositions, "does not entail them [*al-fiṭra al-ūlā lā taqḍī bihā*]."[18] Indeed it does, Ibn Taymiyya would counter. Given all the above, it would be only natural to conclude that the notion of *fiṭra* has a pivotal role to play in guarding the borders between Ibn Taymiyya's ethical viewpoint and the Ashʿarites'. The opposition seems simple and profound. The Ashʿarites had claimed ethical norms are mere matters of convention; Ibn Taymiyya claimed they have their basis in nature.

Yet this way of limning the relationship between Ibn Taymiyya and the Ashʿarites, as I hope to show, is not as straightforward as it appears, and the self-evidence it carries belies some deeper surprises that tell a rather different story about this relationship once probed more fully. To piece this story together, however, we need to bring more of the landscape of Ashʿarite ethical thought into view. And this means, among other things, training a sharper light on some of the central distinctions drawn above in juxtaposing Ibn Taymiyya and al-Ghazālī—between epistemology and linguistics, or the merely descriptive and normative perspective, or again between subjective and objective notions of the good—to ascertain their significance and place in the Ashʿarite understanding.

It is al-Ghazālī who once again offers us the edge of the wedge we need for turning to the first distinction, to assess the importance of the distance between "calling" and "knowing," or the "descriptive" and the "normative." And he does so by voicing a view to which he stands not as architect but simply as representative exponent. "Whoever seeks for meanings through words, loses his way and is led to ruin," al-Ghazālī writes in his *Mustaṣfā*; one should rather "first establish the meanings in one's mind" and language will follow. As long as we agree on the meaning, he continues, there is no need to quarrel about the words (*lā mushāḥḥa fi ʾl-alfāẓ baʿda maʿrifat al-maʿānī*).[19] In stating this, al-Ghazālī would be expressing a view about the relationship of mind and language that many of his fellow theologians would have recognized and endorsed. Language follows the mind; we apply words to realities after we have grasped their intelligible characteristics through the mind. In this respect, to frame something as a demand of our language is already to tie it umbilically to the demands of our thought. A gap between what is said and what is thought, however, would seem to arise to the extent that it would then be a further step to recognize "what is thought" as a product of *reason*, or indeed, as its *demand*. To put it in al-Ghazālī's language: it might be questioned whether, having discovered that people call something good when it agrees with their purposes, they are right to do so, so that this claim can be stated positively in one's own voice, not merely as a statement of semantics, but as an evaluative or normative claim.

I talk about a claim of "semantics" here, taking my cue from the terms of al-Ghazālī's and his fellow-Ashʿarites' discussions. Al-Ghazālī in the *Mustaṣfā* indicatively parses his question as one about the "meaning of good and bad" (*maʿnā al-ḥusn wa ʾl-qubḥ*). But the central focus of his discussion, in fact, seems to be less a question about what terms like "good" or "bad" mean than a question about what kinds of things "good" and "bad" are applied to—what kinds of things are therefore thought to *make* actions good or bad. Having noted this ambiguity (an ambiguity reflected, as we saw earlier, in Ibn Taymiyya's own remarks), it becomes easier to see why it would not have taken much for the door of semantics to open out to a more positive engagement of these evaluative judgments, and indeed to a more normative appropriation of them.

In the works of earlier Ash'arites, the normative cadence does not yet seem to have emerged strongly, though streaks of it already appear in Ibn Fūrak's account of al-Ash'arī's views.[20] The same might be said of al-Bāqillānī (d. 1013), one of the earliest Ash'arites to relate evaluative notions to human desires, who does not seem to have transcended the neutral tones of a semantic claim when, in his legal work *al-Taqrīb wa'l-irshād*, he accepted the definition of good and bad in terms of "what people's natures [*ṭibā'*] incline to and what attracts and repels their souls through instinctual dispositions [*gharīzat al-jibillāt*]—whether pleasures . . . or pains and different kinds of harm."[21] Yet if this cadence is not fully audible in al-Bāqillānī, it can be heard distinctly in the tones of his successor, al-Juwaynī, who would articulate a view fated to percolate widely through the writings of the later Ash'arite school. The new tones are perceptible still modestly in his theological work *Kitāb al-Irshād*; they assert themselves more openly in his late *al-'Aqīda al-Niẓāmiyya*; but it is in his work of legal theory, *al-Burhān fī uṣūl al-fiqh*, that this view unveils itself with the greatest clarity.

Resuming the traditional debate about the value of actions, al-Juwaynī announces his own preference for the following position as the one closest to the truth: "We do not deny that reason demands [*al-'uqūl taqtaḍī*] from its bearer to steer clear from dangers and hasten toward possible benefits [*ijtināb al-mahālik wa-ibtidār al-manāfi'*]. . . . To deny this would be to part ways with the deliverances of reason [*al-ma'qūl*]." This, al-Juwaynī clarifies, only "concerns the domain of human beings"—drawing a distinction between the application of evaluative standards to God and to human beings that will be familiar to our ears and that will instantly fall in place. Because if utility forms the main criterion for the application of evaluative terms, God is inaccessible to such considerations. Al-Juwaynī continues: it is only this preexisting rational judgment or demand that explains how the notion of "obligation" (*wujūb*) could have any meaning for human beings when they find themselves confronted with the revealed Law. For it is the harm that God threatens to visit upon us—the threat (*wa'īd*) of punishment for failing to perform the acts commanded in the Law—that gives the notion of obligation its purchase. Thus "were we to imagine that a categorical command should be issued by God without any threat attaching to its omission, to qualify this as 'obligatory' would have no rationally intelligible meaning [*ma'nan ma'qūl*] with respect to us."[22] Yet such a rationally intelligible meaning the notion of obligation indeed possesses.

To rephrase and clarify: it is only because, prior to revelation and thus "rationally," we exhibit certain evaluative responses to benefit and harm, seeking the one and avoiding the other, that the Law acquires its normative hold over us. It is our ability to experience punishment as an evil—what al-Juwaynī in the *Niẓāmiyya* calls an undesirable *ḥaẓẓ* or "stake"—that underwrites the notion of "obligation" and the obligating ability of the Law.[23]

To the extent that this view grounds the normative force of the Law in our existing motivations and desires, it involves an important modification of the one often associated with Ashʿarite ethics, according to which "good" and "bad" receive their definition from the Law itself. "Good," in this familiar view, means whatever agrees with God's command, and "bad" means whatever contravenes it. This is a view that would seem to leave a yawning chasm between the legal definitions of evaluative terms and actual human motivations, or between the value assigned by God to actions and any value assigned by human beings. The demand that human beings should respond to God's commands and prohibitions would then have to appear as inexplicable or dizzyingly high-minded as any Kantian motive of duty. Given the egoistic emphasis that shapes the Ashʿarite understanding of human nature, motives of self-interest would a priori offer themselves as the best if not the sole way of bridging this heady divide. With al-Juwaynī's remarks, this bridge is openly laid down, and the demand of the Law is decisively grounded in a claim of reason framed explicitly (*al-ʿuqūl taqtaḍī*) as a demand.

Looking forward to later legal theory, one can discover the implicit presence of this demand in the definitions of "obligation" that would be expounded by theorists of different stripes, where the threat of punishment for omission would be isolated as a central component. Looking backward, and with the benefit of some hindsight, one can also follow the thread of this view to the works of earlier Ashʿarites, including (however discreetly) al-Ashʿarī himself.[24] At the same time, were we to seek the beginning of this thread more widely, we would have to connect it with a view taken by the Muʿtazilites, and more narrowly the Baṣrans, which has already come before us. For Baṣran Muʿtazilites, as we saw in chapter 2, had not only spoken of the pursuit of benefit and avoidance of harm as moral demands of reason, but they had indeed made these demands the principal paradigm for relating the normative demands of reason to the normative demands of the revealed Law, casting the latter as a particularization of the former. Already knowing through reason that we must seek what benefits us and repel what harms us—"It has been established in reason," Mānkdīm would write, "that it is obligatory to repel harm from oneself"—we discover through revelation which particular acts serve our welfare and which impair it.[25]

Many later Ashʿarites would take up al-Juwaynī's normative claim, modulating it in different ways and with varying points of emphasis. Given the context of our own argument, it is worth observing that this rational demand was framed using terms that speak to a very specific side of the distinction we carved earlier between "what we want" and "what is good for us," and thus between "subjective" views of the good and "objective" good. What reason bids us is the avoidance, not of what we contingently happen to dislike, but of what objectively harms us. These terms reappear among later Ashʿarites rehearsing this claim, including, significantly for our story, al-Ghazālī. There is thus an interesting contrast—a contrast that al-Ghazālī himself does not mark or gloss for his readers—between al-Ghazālī's discussion in both the *Iqtiṣād* and the *Mustaṣfā* of the terms "good" and "bad" (*ḥasan/qabīḥ*) and of the term "obligation" (*wājib*). His emphasis on the subjective and relative nature of the former—each of us *calls* good what he desires—is strikingly absent from his discussion of the latter, which is defined through the notion of harmful consequences (*yastaʿqibu tarkahu ḍarar*).[26] And it is with reference to the latter, in addressing the controversial obligation to undertake religious inquiry (*wujūb al-naẓar*), which the Muʿtazilites had claimed is known by reason, that al-Ghazālī, openly rejecting this specific Muʿtazilite claim, concedes its partner—now already seen to have been conceded by al-Juwaynī—that reason bids us to avoid what harms us. Reason, or, indeed, nature; for talk of reason here should not obscure the fact that this is a knowledge grounded in natural desire. To call this *rational* is then simply to indicate its availability independently of revelation against the context of a familiar antithesis between "reason" and "revelation" as competing epistemic possibilities. "We do not deny," al-Ghazālī thus writes in this connection in the *Iqtiṣād*, that "a rational being is incited by his natural disposition [*al-ʿāqil yastaḥiththuhu ṭabʿuhu*] to protect himself from harm . . . and there is nothing objectionable in applying the term 'obligation' to this incitement." He continues, striking a note that we have already heard: "for one need not quarrel about the use of terms [*al-iṣṭilāḥāt lā mushāḥḥa fīhā*]."[27]

Certainly, with words one need not quarrel. Yet in al-Ghazālī's case one wonders whether this high-minded attitude toward language may not have concealed a certain hesitation about the normative claim at issue and may not indeed have served as a way of avoiding the awkward acknowledgment of any gap between the "semantic" and "normative" ways of inflecting this claim—and of perhaps using the back door of semantics to quietly let the normative into the house. For al-Ghazālī at times appears rather too eager to call attention to the linguistic character of his observations, speaking of what language "permits" or "prevents" and sequestering the empire of language in ways that seem to leave reason uninvolved.[28] This linguistic emphasis is visible, for example, in his naturalistic account of people's usage of moral terms in the *Mustaṣfā*. Yet it is an emphasis that is not uniformly sustained, as indicated by the last-quoted remarks in the *Iqtiṣād*, where the point is clearly put not as a claim of semantics but a demand of reason or nature. And it is likewise a less descriptive kind of emphasis that we see expressed in the remarks on obligation in the *Mustaṣfā*. "One cannot describe as 'obligatory,' " al-Ghazālī writes there, "something whose commission and omission are equal in our respect, for the only sense in which we can conceive of obligation is in terms of an act's performance having a preponderant claim over its omission relative to our purposes [*lā naʿqilu wujūban illā bi-an yatarajjaḥa fiʿluhu ʿalā tarkihi biʾl-iḍāfa ilā aghrāḍinā*]." The relationship between language and thought is here brought into plain view: what we grasp (*naʿqilu*) is seen to provide the basis for what we say about an action or how we describe it (*naṣifu*). Yet the normative note rings out distinctly: it is not only that our words mirror our contingent conceptions; it is that *we cannot* conceive of obligation except in these terms.[29]

The emphasis on reason as against language, and on a normative as against a semantic perspective, appears in different combinations and degrees among later writers. Al-Āmidī (d. 1233), who follows al-Ghazālī's lead particularly closely, issues a rather hybrid and uncertain sound, rehearsing the main elements of al-Ghazālī's account about people's linguistic usage yet redubbing this in several places as a judgment of reason. ("One may call 'good' ... what agrees with one's purpose from the perspective of reason": *mā wāfaqa al-gharaḍ min jihat al-maʿqūl*; and more clearly: *taqbīḥ al-ʿaql lahu bi-iʿtibār umūr khārijiyya ... min al-aghrāḍ*.)[30] But it is al-Rāzī who perhaps strikes the normative note most decisively, and he does so in the context of a sharp distinction—earlier introduced by al-Juwaynī—between the ability of reason to deliver ethical judgments with regard to the human domain and the relevance of these judgments for the divine one. The nub of these judgments is expressed in a set of statements from the *Maṭālib* that we already heard at the end of chapter 1: "Everything that leads to preponderant benefit [*manfaʿa*] is good [*ḥasan*], and there is no other meaning to its being good than that fact, and everything that leads to preponderant harm [*maḍarra*] is bad [*qabīḥ*], and there is no other meaning to its being bad than that." Thus there is "no meaning to good or bad than the fact of conducing to what serves and impairs one's welfare [*al-maṣāliḥ waʾl-mafāsid*]."[31]

A knowledge of reason, or indeed a knowledge of desire—so that our desire for certain things (our desire for them by nature) is implicitly commuted into a judgment of value that we may not object to dignifying with the term "knowledge." Several writers evince an endemic slippage between the notion of reason and that of desire in their remarks on the subject. Yet underlying this slippage seems to be a clear understanding that the language of reason, to the extent that it is used, takes desire—the biddings of our *ṭabʿ*—as its core and foundation. As such, this claim stands to be distinguished from the claim that had typified the Muʿtazilite brand of ethical rationalism. The concern to mark such distinctions is palpable in al-Ghazālī's remark in the *Mustaṣfā* that "it is our *appetitive nature* [*ṭabʿ*], naturally disposed to experience pain at punishment and pleasure at reward, that incites one to guard against harm," a remark that registers as a direct counter to Mānkdīm's formulation: "It has been established in *reason* that it is obligatory to repel harm from oneself." ("You have erred," al-Ghazālī continues, "in saying that reason motivates.")[32] In the *Iqtiṣād*, al-Ghazālī qualifies the relations between reason and desire in terms that hold up a picture essentially Humean in outline. Through reason we grasp the relevant facts and form the beliefs that inform our actions—most important, beliefs concerning the consequences of actions, formed on the basis of the facts revelation transmits to us. But it is our appetitive nature that sets the ends to which our actions are directed and that provides us with the motivation to pursue or avoid particular actions by finding itself in agreement or disagreement with their consequences.[33]

This schematic overview of the evolving Ashʿarite approach to ethics could be fine-tuned further. But for our purposes, we have enough before us to finally be able to rejoin the main trunk of our investigation.

Ibn Taymiyya's Ethics: New Wineskins, (Mostly) Old Wine

How, I began by asking, might we understand the relationship between Ibn Taymiyya's ethical viewpoint and the one expressed by Ashʿarite authors? In his exposition of his *via media*, Ibn Taymiyya advertised points of friction. The architecture of the *Radd* appeared to second the advertisement of conflict. A survey of his ethical positions, however, called attention to fundamental points of unison. Juxtaposing the statements of al-Ghazālī and Ibn Taymiyya, we looked more closely for the seams, and we seemed to find a promise of seams in certain perceptible differences of register. These included a difference between calling and knowing, or the linguistic against the normative perspective; between a subjective notion of "what I want" as against an objective notion of "what is good for me"; and between a related notion of nature: *ṭabʿ* as against *fiṭra*. What the above survey suggests is that these apparent differences collapse upon a more attentive consideration of Ashʿarite ethical thought in its evolution. For all of the facets that initially appear distinctive about Ibn Taymiyya's viewpoint turn out to have been critical components of the Ashʿarite ethical approach. By the same token, in collapsing these apparent differences, this discovery allows us to recognize the profound similarities that tie Ibn Taymiyya's viewpoint to the Ashʿarites', and suggests that here we may indeed need to speak less neutrally of "similarities" and more thickly of "debts."

We have seen, thus, that evaluative judgments were drawn into connection not only with fallible contingent desires but also with objective welfare in Ashʿarite works from at least as early as al-Juwaynī. Similarly, from at least al-Juwaynī's time prominent Ashʿarite thinkers embraced the view that reason delivers normative judgments concerning matters that affect our interests. What reason tells us is that it is obligatory to repel harm and good to pursue benefit. This admission was perfectly compatible with holding that reason does not tell us *what* repels harm and benefit, a point that al-Ghazālī drew attention to in discussing the obligation to undertake religious inquiry. Al-Juwaynī would put the point even more plainly and in more pregnant terms in his *Niẓāmiyya*: "Human reason may command a view of what is in our interests on a general level, yet it cannot arrive at its details [*wa-la-in tashawwafat al-ʿuqūl ilā kulliyyāt al-maṣāliḥ lam taqif ʿalā tafāṣīlihā*]."[34] Put this way of course, and using the language of general and particular, this statement will again evoke the scheme developed by the Baṣran Muʿtazilites for relating rational and revealed norms—a scheme that Ibn Taymiyya's resembles, as I noted in chapter 2, while excluding the deontological elements implicit in the Baṣran view. As such, it suggests a different and more compelling way of drafting this resemblance, one that also accommodates Ibn Taymiyya's exclusions.

No less seminal here is another resemblance that will have cried out for remark in the foregoing survey. In considering Ibn Taymiyya's ethical remarks in the *Radd*, we earlier recorded the notable slippage between his talk of *knowing* what is good and his talk of *desiring* what is good, and between the more cognitive notion of "reason" and the noncognitive notion of "desire" as an epistemic foundation of ethical norms. This slippage now turns out to reflect one that had been endemic in Ashʿarite writings. And this observation prepares us to pick up another point, and another seminal resemblance, this time linked to the critical notion of "nature" at stake in Ibn Taymiyya's and the Ashʿarites' thinking and shadowing their respective notions of "desire." Al-Ghazālī's *ṭabʿ* and Ibn Taymiyya's *fiṭra*, I heuristically suggested at the outset of this discussion, appear to be divided by important differences that relate to the types of desire to which each is coded. The first refers us to the egoistic desires of particular individuals; the latter to natural (paradigmatically physical) desires universal to human beings, and to a desire for objective good. Human nature as *fiṭra* thus seems eligible as a foundation of ethical norms in a way that human nature as *ṭabʿ* does not.

Yet on the one hand, we have seen that the notion of *ṭabʿ* was also tied by Ashʿarites to the desire for a more "objective" kind of good—for what *really* benefits and harms us. Similarly, physical desires like the ones Ibn Taymiyya connects to *fiṭra* must certainly be understood as forming part of the appetites constituting the Ashʿarite *ṭabʿ*. And if we wanted to seal the distance between the two notions of nature even further, all we would need to do is turn back to the discussion of the previous chapter to recapitulate one of its conclusions. For the domain of *fiṭra*, as we saw, includes natural desires whose satisfaction may not be in our interests. It thus includes desires that are not objectively good for us and that need to be ordered normatively by an external criterion not provided by our nature. To the extent that *ṭabʿ* refers us to a set of desires (and capacities for pleasure and pain) that provide the corrigible *material* for value but not its normative *criterion*, *fiṭra* and *ṭabʿ* hardly lie far apart. In the evaluative domain, at any rate, the notion of *fiṭra*—for all its resonance and all the rhetorical force deriving from its scriptural roots and its role in other significant contexts, such as the knowledge of God—would not seem to have traveled far from the notion of *ṭabʿ*.

Just how little it may have traveled, in fact, is a question that some of our Ashʿarite authors give us tantalizing occasions for asking, in doing so inviting a more pointed change of register from talk of "similarities" to talk of "debts." Particularly tantalizing here will be the otherwise unobtrusive remark with which al-Rāzī opens his discussion of benefit and harm and their relationship to our nature in the *Maṭālib*. For if *ṭabʿ* was the term we had grown accustomed to meeting among the works of our Ashʿarite authors—not only al-Ghazālī but also many of his predecessors speaking in the same context—here we find a rather delicate shift of diction. "There is no doubt," al-Rāzī writes, "that there is something which our nature [*ṭabʿ*] inclines to and which the original natural disposition [*aṣl al-fiṭra*] ordains that we desire to realize, and that there is something else which our pure natural disposition [*ṣarīḥ al-fiṭra*] ordains that we cringe from and flee."[35] What we incline to, of course, are pleasure and joy (*ladhdha, surūr*), and what we flee from are pain and grief (*alam, ghamm*). These represent respectively what we desire intrinsically and what we are intrinsically averse to, and they form the foundations, in turn, for the notions of benefit (*maṣlaḥa* or *khayr*) and harm (*mafsada* or *sharr*), which include both intrinsic and instrumental goods. None of these distinctions will seem surprising, having already made extensive rounds in theological and philosophical works. Nor is there anything to excite our surprise in the general point itself, which chimes in with the by now familiar Ashʿarite endorsement of normative judgments grounded in our nature (or reason). Yet it is the unobtrusive appearance of the vocabulary of *fiṭra* that lends this passage its special interest. For it appears at a juncture we will recognize: as the referent for our desire for benefit and our aversion to harm. And if this already provokes recognition, juxtaposed to al-Rāzī's definition of good and bad (which we saw moments ago) it will make our sense of familiarity instantly deepen. If the meaning of good comes down to benefit, and bad to harm, the claim that *fiṭra* forms the foundation of evaluative judgments lies but an ever so slight logical step away.

Al-Rāzī himself does not seem to take that particular step. Moreover, the language of *fiṭra*, appearing here so tantalizingly, flashes through the sky like a one-time comet and fails to return, and it is rather *ṭabʿ* that figures prominently throughout his discussion in the relevant contexts.[36] Even so, it will be difficult to dismiss the observation that it has already fulfilled the function that Ibn Taymiyya would later call upon it more openly and extensively to perform. Should we take this observation at face value and permit ourselves to read al-Rāzī's suggestive usage as a tributary to Ibn Taymiyya's development of this term in his moral epistemology—albeit not the sole one, and if only by way of seeding the latter—then we should be led to a surprising conclusion. For while it is one Ashʿarite (al-Ghazālī) who had provided the formulation from which Ibn Taymiyya would remove the sign of negation ("not by *fiṭra*") in order to frame his own view of ethical judgments, it is another Ashʿarite who had performed the same move before him and formulated the very positive claim that Ibn Taymiyya would defend.

The conclusion flowing from the above is that the distance dividing the Ashʿarite notion of *ṭabʿ* and Ibn Taymiyya's seemingly distinctive idiom may be nugatory indeed. On this reading, the distance between Ibn Taymiyya and the Ashʿarites would narrow down even further; the distance between Ibn Taymiyya and al-Rāzī even more. Having attuned ourselves to this point, we will find it easy to pick up on important similarities between these two theologians that attest to Ibn Taymiyya's fundamental indebtedness to al-Rāzī's work. Some of the greatest similarities—as in the claim that the meaning of ethical terms comes down to benefit and harm or that the latter are grounded in our nature, whether we call it *ṭabʿ* or *fiṭra*—we have already seen. But we may now note other similarities in more specific positions and formulations, revealing several of Ibn Taymiyya's characteristic turns of thought to have their anticipating counterparts in al-Rāzī. It will thus be hard not to hear echoes of the salient passage in the *Radd*, where Ibn Taymiyya had connected our love of justice and hatred of injustice to the meaning of moral terms, in the following remark from al-Rāzī's *Maṭālib*, addressed to Muʿtazilite theologians:

> If, in claiming that beneficence is good, you mean that it is beloved to our nature [*maḥbūb al-ṭabʿ*] and desired by the self [*marghūb al-nafs*] as a means for obtaining benefits, that is true and correct. Taken on this interpretation, we do not dispute your claim that our knowledge of its [i.e., beneficence] goodness is necessary [*ḍarūrī*]. Similarly, if what you mean in claiming that injustice is bad is that it is hated by our nature [*makrūh al-ṭabʿ*] and despised by the heart [*mabghūḍ al-qalb*] insofar as it is a cause of pains, griefs, and sorrows, there is no dispute concerning the fact that the knowledge that it [i.e., injustice] is bad is necessary, taken on this interpretation.

Using the term *ṭabʿ* instead of *fiṭra* and stating explicitly what Ibn Taymiyya had left it to his readers to deduce—namely that acts such as justice and beneficence are desired (or "loved") due to their impact on one's self-interest—this would seem to be the spitting image of the view we had heard in *Radd*.[37]

The kernel of this view does not seem to have been originated by al-Rāzī, as it had appeared earlier in al-Ghazālī's *Iḥyāʾ ʿulūm al-dīn* in the context of a set of remarks in which he had connected our love of others' beneficence to our natural self-interest. "Human hearts," he had written there, "have been naturally formed to love [*jubilat al-qulūb ʿalā ḥubb*] those who do well by them and those who do them harm"—a mere corollary of their fundamental self-love. Only moments later he had restated the point using the more telling vocabulary of *fiṭra*.[38] This is one of several moments in the *Iḥyā'* that directly prefigure Ibn Taymiyya's terminological usage, so that nothing but the simple linguistic transfiguration of *ṭab'* into *fiṭra* would seem to be missing to obtain Ibn Taymiyya's characteristic formulations. Perhaps the most evocative of these moments, in fact, are those that relate not to the ethical but to the theological context, and to the love of God. Al-Ghazālī's discussion of the human love of God is heavily laced with references to our natural *ṭab'*. This is the term he notably invokes to explain the very notion of love: to love a given thing means to have an inclination for it in one's nature (*ṭab'*). Yet it is al-Ghazālī's deployment of the notion of *sound* nature—reminding us of Ibn Taymiyya's emphasis on *fiṭra salīma* in his theological epistemology—that provokes the strongest echo with Ibn Taymiyya's understanding of our natural disposition to love God, when he refers the spiritual pleasure experienced in the divine to the "inclination of sound nature and right reason" (*mayl al-ṭab' al-salīm wa'l-'aql al-ṣaḥīḥ*).[39] This, of course, reveals a deployment of *ṭab'* in al-Ghazālī's writings in which it carries positive connotations that mirror those adhering to Ibn Taymiyya's deployment of *fiṭra*, even as, for al-Ghazālī's *ṭab'* no less than Ibn Taymiyya's *fiṭra*, nature remains material in need of discipline and education in order to be harnessed to its salutary bent.

Ibn Taymiyya himself often does little to signal the affinities that connect his ethical views to those of the Ash'arite school, though there are isolated occasions when he not only invites us to remark them but indeed openly advertises his indebtedness. One of the most significant of these occasions, in fact, concerns the very characterization of his ethical *via media* itself. In the *Minhāj al-sunna*, having reiterated the traditional debate about ethics and outlined its two extremes—two extremes that serve to identify his own approach as a middle road and third possibility—Ibn Taymiyya crucially adds that "there is a third view concerning this question which al-Rāzī opted for in his later works, and this is the view that good and bad are determined by reason as regards the actions of human beings but not as regards the actions of God."[40] For the basis of this remark, we need look no further than al-Rāzī's affirmation of this position in his *Maṭālib*. The qualification that al-Rāzī may not have been the originator of this position (this position having been earlier expressed by al-Juwaynī) leaves the substance untouched.[41]

Taken together, this serves to confirm the appearance of unison suggested by our initial tabulation of the convergences between Ibn Taymiyya's ethical views and those of the Ash'arite school, reinforcing the insight that these convergences run deep. Yet even if this insight is accepted, it may now be said, the appearance of conflict cannot be wholly cleared away. And there is one particular point where the conflict would seem to stand before us with particular obstinacy. This is the conflict that formed the heart of the argumentative exchange of the *Radd*, bringing

Ibn Taymiyya into unambiguous collision with the Ashʿarite viewpoint. For where the Ashʿarites had claimed that ethical norms have their basis (both epistemically and indeed ontologically) in social convention, Ibn Taymiyya claimed they have their basis in (human) nature. Yet once again, one only needs to scratch the surface of the facts to uncover a more complex story that calls the appearance of unambiguous collision into question and in doing so again deepens our understanding of Ibn Taymiyya's debts, while also providing the traction for addressing some of the consequences of his unmarked borrowing of Ashʿarite resources.

The best wedge into this more complex story can be found by turning back to that tantalizing deployment of the notion of *fiṭra* that al-Rāzī had made in the *Maṭālib* to confront the obvious paradox this deployment would appear to generate. For al-Rāzī, commenting on the *Ishārāt*, had not used the notion of *fiṭra* at that juncture; this was a notion, as we saw in chapter 2, that was after all not present in the relevant passage of the *Ishārāt*. Yet it was present in the counterpart of the thought experiment in Avicenna's *Shifāʾ*, and its connection to the topic was cemented by Avicenna's discussion of *fiṭra* in the *Najā*. Other Ashʿarites taking over these resources, such as al-Ghazālī, had incorporated it clearly in their discussion of ethical judgments. To the extent that the notion of *fiṭra* is implicit in the context of al-Rāzī's discussion, it might then seem paradoxical that al-Rāzī should be seen connecting the notion of *fiṭra* to ethical judgments in one context, while disconnecting it in another.

In the *Maṭālib*, of course, al-Rāzī had couched his point using both terms, *fiṭra* and *ṭabʿ*. This observation suggests one obvious way of making the paradox disappear, namely by interrogating the significance we attach to the terminological shift at stake. *Fiṭra* was, after all, a term that had long formed a living part of Islamic religious vocabulary given its scriptural origins, and had infiltrated ordinary usage in ways that may open to question the wisdom of hearing it as an exclusively technical term. The linguistic seams between the terms *fiṭra* and *ṭabʿ*, in fact, long appear to have been fluid in kind, as Gobillot brings out in her study of the former notion. In earlier phases of their linguistic history, thus, the terms *ṭabʿ* or *ṭabīʿa* and the term *fiṭra* had both been employed by different writers to designate the four humors or elements. This fluidity finds a particularly intriguing illustration in the work of al-Jāḥiẓ (d. 869) that directly anticipates the use later theologians would make of both terms in their ethical writings. God created animate beings, he writes in one of his epistles, and then "naturally disposed them to seek out benefits and avoid harms. . . . This is an inbuilt natural disposition and innate formation [*ṭabaʿahum ʿalā ijtirār al-manāfiʿ wa-dafʿ al-maḍārr . . . hādhā fīhim ṭabʿ murakkab wa-jibilla maftūra*]." We will instantly recognize this as the claim that Ibn Taymiyya would parse in terms of *fiṭra* and Ashʿarites in terms of *ṭabʿ*.[42]

Al-Rāzī's fluid transition from one mode of designation to the other should thus be taken to signal the light semantic weight this transition carries. The same weight, I would argue, is exhibited by several of the appearances of the term *fiṭra* in Avicenna's works, where it displays a loosely linguistic meaning that often lacks the technical force that, reading his works backward—especially backward from Ibn Taymiyya—one is tempted to hear.[43] In other locations, particularly in the context of the thought experiment that defines it, the notion of *fiṭra* indeed seems to carry a stronger meaning. Al-Rāzī's own attunement to the semantic force of the notion of *fiṭra*, this additionally suggests, might be modulated by the different contexts of its appearance. His simultaneous affirmation of *fiṭra* in one and (implicit) denial of *fiṭra* in the other then become easier to comprehend.

The more obvious resolution of the paradox, however, lies elsewhere. For on the one hand, it will be clear that the notion of *fiṭra* as deployed in the *Maṭālib* does not coincide with the notion deployed by Avicenna, where, as I have argued, it is most intuitively taken as referring to our intellectual nature. In the *Maṭālib*, by contrast, al-Rāzī uses it to refer to our nature as beings susceptible to certain characteristic forms of pleasure and pain, susceptibilities that determine what constitutes our welfare. The notion of *fiṭra* that figures in al-Rāzī's claim that "ethical judgments are grounded in our *fiṭra*" in the *Maṭālib* and in his implicit denial of this same claim in his Avicenna-related remarks is simply not the same. With this in view, we will now recall that al-Rāzī had explicitly excluded considerations of welfare from the perspective of the thought experiment. Once such considerations were included, ethical judgments would indeed be possible. To the extent, in fact, that our nature in the second sense (the sense of the *Maṭālib*) determines the kinds of things that we can count as goods, notably with respect to physical pleasures and pains, al-Rāzī could not have meant to deny that ethical judgments have a natural foundation. In this respect, the Ash'arite claim that ethical judgments are grounded in convention was perfectly compatible with the Ash'arite claim that ethical judgments, in another sense, are grounded in human nature taken as *ṭab'*.

Yet of course the crucial point that Avicenna had brought out is an insight that contemporary writers have often highlighted: what our nature "determines" is far more limited than we might suppose. Our biological nature may constrain cultural possibility, yet, as Alasdair MacIntyre notes, "man who has nothing but a biological nature is a creature of whom we know nothing."[44] It is precisely the educability of human nature and its permeability to cultural influence, I argued in chapter 2, that accounted for Avicenna's exclusion of moral and psychological sentiments from the thought experiment. Ash'arite writers assimilating Avicenna's insights had heard that point well, accentuating the central role of the community in shaping the ethical responses of individuals by harnessing the material of their nature. With this facet of the Ash'arite ethical approach freshly in our sights, in fact, the notion of "welfare" that al-Rāzī deploys in his reprise of Avicenna's thought experiment can be read more insightfully. For it will be noticed that al-Rāzī refers us to "*judgments* of utility" (*qaḍāyā maṣlaḥiyya*), a cognitive parsing that will seem surprising if we are thinking mainly of individuals' instinctive responses to pleasure and pain. Yet the fact that al-Rāzī is not thinking in these narrow terms becomes clear when in the immediate vicinity he refers more specifically to "public interest" (*maṣlaḥa ʿāmma*). This is a notion we may recall meeting earlier when surveying the Ashʿarite appropriation of Avicenna's conventionalism, which had fed into a view of the social community as both teacher and producer of ethical norms that was twinned to a conception of the community as a subject of benefit and harm. Different societies, al-Shahrastānī had suggested, call acts "good" when they benefit them and "bad" when they harm them.

These kinds of ideas similarly find an important expression in al-Rāzī's work. The idea that ethical standards are grounded in a social contract or convention is one that al-Rāzī develops more fully outside his commentary on the *Ishārāt*, claiming, as Shihadeh puts it, that "an implicit social agreement lies at the background of widely-accepted moral conventions, which is then, as it were, 'forgotten.'"[45] In responding to the Muʿtazilites in the *Maṭālib*, he refers to the general interests (*maṣlaḥat al-ʿālam*) that are served by the moral disapproval of lying and the approval of beneficence and that might lead people to adopt the convention (*iṣṭalaḥa ʿalā*) that lying is bad and beneficence good.[46] It is this notion of public interest, thus, that should be taken to interpret al-Rāzī's gloss on Avicenna's discussion of widely accepted propositions and the specific terms in which he frames the notion of utility. What is to be excluded from the "privileged" perspective of the thought experiment are "judgments of utility that have become habitual and familiar to oneself" (*mā taʿawwadtahu wa-aliftahu min al-qaḍāyā al-maṣlaḥiyya*), and that is to say: that have been taught to one by the community to which one belongs because of the way they service its interests (*al-maṣlaḥa al-ʿāmma, al-niẓām al-kullī*).[47]

To the extent that the community is involved in the inculcation and production of such moral principles, one has little difficulty seeing why they should appear on the conventional side of the divide at stake in Avicenna's thought experiment. Thus, to repeat, the Ashʿarite claim that ethical judgments are a matter of convention was not inconsistent with the claim that ethical judgments are grounded in human nature, taken in the sense of those instinctive responses that provide social convention with the educable material for its operation. If we thought that the essential distinction between Ibn Taymiyya's and the Ashʿarites' ethical views could be captured in the contrast between two diametrically opposed claims—"ethical judgments are founded on convention," yet "ethical judgments are founded on nature"—it is clear we need to think again. A more nuanced reading of the issue shows that the notion of nature itself admits of different interpretations, and that the relations between nature and convention are too complex to be accommodated by a simple disjunction that would place these terms on opposite sides of a sharp divide. And a less simplistic interpretation of the Ashʿarite position accordingly shows that they had inhabited both sides of this divide.

Having weakened this antithesis, in fact, we will be more prepared to bring to the fore something that readers who have followed the argument so far may already have found perplexing. For I noted in chapter 1 that in certain writings Ibn Taymiyya himself *also* employs the notion of a social contract or convention to talk about the origin of ethical norms. Through a mutual pledge and contractual agreement (*al-taʿāhud wa'l-taʿāqud*), we heard in *Qāʿida fi'l-maḥabba*, human beings have bound themselves to ethical norms that allow them to collaboratively pursue what benefits the community as a whole and to repel what harms it. These ethical norms include deontological-sounding principles such as telling the truth, keeping promises, and generally conforming to the demands of justice. The discovery, in chapter 2, that Ibn Taymiyya made a special point of grounding ethical norms *not* in convention but in nature cannot but have left readers bemused.

How could Ibn Taymiyya have intended us to understand the relationship between these claims? Ibn Taymiyya, once again, offers to shed no light on the question, never placing his remarks about *fiṭra* into conversation with his remarks about the social contract. Is this a case where we are simply forced, on account of the sheer dissonance of the intellectual phenomena, to postulate intellectual change and to hypothesize about diverging textual chronologies? The notion of the social contract, it will thus be noticed, makes isolated appearances in his work, even if the notion of public interest to which it is linked appears pervasively. And, measured against the centrality of *fiṭra* certainly, the notion of the social contract seems far less prominent in his ethical remarks. Guarding against strong claims about the status of the latter notion within Ibn Taymiyya's thought, all I would note here is that the need for complex hypotheses disappears once we see that this apparent dissonance can be dispelled even without sacrificing the interpretive heuristic of an unchanged intellectual viewpoint. Just how the two claims can be reconciled had after all been clearly demonstrated before Ibn Taymiyya by Ashʿarite thinkers, whose conception of a social convention and the related idea of communal welfare his writing reflects. While there is undoubtedly a more composite story one could tell about the infiltration of these ideas into Ibn Taymiyya's thought—particularly the idea of public welfare, which also found a salient home in Islamic legal writing—for the most intuitive pedigree we need not look past the writings of Ashʿarite theologians.

A closer analysis of the nature-convention antithesis thus suggests that *neither* party under consideration stood for a single term of this antithesis. As such, this antithesis seems useless as a tool for approaching the relationship between Ibn Taymiyya and the Ashʿarites, and more specifically for identifying the issues that divide them. The result of this analysis, in fact, is once again to reinforce our perception of what unites Ibn Taymiyya's ethical viewpoint with that of Ashʿarite theologians and to point us in the direction of his intellectual debts. Ibn Taymiyya's view of the nature of ethical value and his view of the human knowledge of ethical value appear to coincide with the Ashʿarites' in their essentials.

Yet looking back at our discussion in earlier chapters, it might now seem that it had brought to light a feature of Ibn Taymiyya's understanding where he had proposed to push things further, and showed a readiness to broach terrain where the Ashʿarites had been unwilling to tread. For in many locations, as we have seen, Ibn Taymiyya takes deontological types of actions such as justice or truth-telling as central foci in his discussion of our evaluative grasp. Human beings know such actions to be good—in Ibn Taymiyya's characteristic parsing, they love such actions. Hence the fact that such acts are called "right" or *maʿrūf*, literally "what is known." When the Qur'an thus says that the Prophet "commands [people] that which is right [*maʿrūf*] and forbids them that which is wrong" (Q 7:157), it implicitly refers us to an ethical grasp that predates its own advent and that is presupposed in understanding it. Something similar could be said about the statement that "God bids to justice and good-doing [*yaʾmuru biʾl-ʿadl waʾl-iḥsān*]" (Q 16:90). Such passages call attention to our extrarevelational ethical grasp in ways that undercut the Ashʿarite denial that ethical norms are known by reason, and resist the Ashʿarite definitional disemboweling of evaluative terms by referring them to God's command and prohibition. "God commands what He commands" is simply an empty statement.[48] Ibn Taymiyya's willingness to highlight such passages aligns him with a typically Muʿtazilite practice and, significantly for our context, gives evidence of his willingness to foreground deontological types of acts in specifying our ethical grasp.

In his seminal discussion of the proof of prophecy in *Sharḥ al-Iṣbahāniyya*, Ibn Taymiyya goes so far as to make the ordinary human knowledge of the value of such actions a *criterion* for evaluating the veracity of prophets. Everyone who has falsely claimed to be a prophet, he writes there, "has exhibited ignorance, lying, and turpitude ... that are plain to even the most undiscriminating, and everyone who has truthfully claimed to be a prophet has exhibited knowledge, truthfulness, uprightness, and varieties of good that are plain to even the most undiscriminating." It is our ability to ethically judge a prophet's actions and his character, conscripting an extrarevelational horizon of moral understanding that notably includes an evaluative response to deontological categories such as "lying" and "truth-telling," that underpins our ability to determine the truthfulness of a given prophet. The same point emerges even more forcefully in Ibn Taymiyya's additional claim that our assessment of a prophet's veracity is supported by an assessment of the content of his prophetic message itself. "Were we to suppose," thus, that someone came along and "commanded polytheism and idolatry and permitted foul deeds, injustice, and lying, and did not command the worship of God or belief in the hereafter—would this person need to be asked for a miracle [before his claims could be doubted]?"[49] The implication is clear: it is our ability to judge acts like injustice and lying bad independently of prophetic revelation that gives us a criterion for judging the soundness of any supposed revelation. These commands, we are in a position to say, are *all wrong*.

What we see in such passages is a powerful appeal to our independent moral intuitions that is notably couched in terms of deontological types of actions. It is an appeal that brings out Ibn Taymiyya's readiness to talk about the content of ethical awareness in ways that the Ashʿarites rejected, and as such it would seem to provide an important check on our picture of the near-exceptionless concordance between the ethical views of these parties. Yet this check in fact turns out to be far weaker than it appears; a closer examination of the reasons why offers a more judicious perspective on Ibn Taymiyya's ethical approach and on some of the consequences of his unlabeled borrowing of Ashʿarite resources.

For on the one hand, as we will see in greater detail in chapter 5, the prerevelational moral horizon Ibn Taymiyya evokes in discussing the ethical judgments that allow us to appraise prophetic veracity cannot be taken as a straightforward reference to the resources of reason. The backdrop for our appraisal of *one* prophetic revelation is often the pattern set by another and the divine signature these prophetic incidents collectively spell out. More relevant for our present context, however, is another point, one that formed a central theme of previous chapters and that we can now revisit for a more insightful consideration. One of the recurring motifs of our discussion from the very beginning has been a question about the ambiguous relationship between deontological and consequentialist considerations within Ibn Taymiyya's ethical outlook. If the argument in chapter 1 was correct, Ibn Taymiyya gives little sign of being invested in an ethical approach that gives a robust place to deontological considerations. On the ontological front, his embrace of a view that appears to resemble Muʿtazilite moral objectivism turns out to be sharply differentiated from the Muʿtazilite view by construing ethical value seemingly exclusively in consequentialist terms. On the epistemological front, as I argued in chapter 2, the most plausible way of construing the description under which people desire certain kinds of actions is their description *qua* beneficial—whether to themselves or whether to the community, recalling Ibn Taymiyya's enigmatic statement that "*it is known* that justice serves the good of the world [*maṣlaḥat al-ʿālam*] and injustice tends to its harm." And it is as objects of desire, I emphasized, that Ibn Taymiyya typically presents ethically good actions. In this respect he once again differs starkly from the Muʿtazilites, who had spoken of ethical actions as objects of knowledge. "There is no rational person [*ʿāqil*]," as Ibn Mattawayh had characteristically put it, "who does not know [*yaʿlamu*] that injustice is bad and justice is good, and that it is obligatory to return deposits . . . and give thanks for benefaction."[50]

Ibn Taymiyya's adoption of a noncognitivist idiom to talk about ethical epistemology, as I have shown, reflects his assimilation of a typically Ashʿarite approach. The same thing would have to be said about his adoption of an exclusively consequentialist understanding of ethical ontology. All this seems clear; yet what I particularly wish to call attention to here is the fact that in both cases, Ibn Taymiyya is adopting views that served a *reductive* function at the hands of Ashʿarite thinkers. They were views that had been developed as a counter to that more ambitious conception of ethical rationalism and ethical objectivism that had been articulated by Muʿtazilite theologians. The Ashʿarite claim that natural desire tells us what is good was designed as a deconstruction of the Muʿtazilite thesis that reason is our informant. The Ashʿarite claim that utility is what makes acts good was designed as a deconstruction of the Muʿtazilite thesis that deontological grounds (at least in part) make acts good. The notion of public interest, in turn, featured in an argument with a reductive function, aiming to show that the way ethical truths *appear* to us may not be a reliable indication of the way things are in themselves. Underlying the phenomena of ordinary moral consciousness is a longer social genealogy which reveals that judgments whose surface form is deontological and indeed absolutist in kind—"it is always bad to lie" or "it is always good to act justly"—are watered by consequentialist roots that are not transparent to ordinary consciousness.[51] Appearance and reality, surface and depth, come apart. In each case, the thesis the Ashʿarites asserted could not be understood independently from the counterthesis it served to disprove.

In taking over the Ashʿarite view, Ibn Taymiyya severs the umbilical cord between thesis and counterthesis. What are essentially Ashʿarite positions are presented to us as stand-alone assertions with little to betray their Ashʿarite origin and nothing to betray their original context and motivation. Ibn Taymiyya uses the noncognitivist language of desire without making clear to his readers whether this is a deliberate rejection of the language of reason or indeed a reinterpretation of it along Ashʿarite lines. He talks exclusively of utility as a ground of value and does not make clear to his readers what alternative view of its ground this excludes. It is not that the Muʿtazilite notion of deontological act-descriptions (*wujūh*) is brought up for explicit discussion and rejected. The theory of *wujūh* is simply never mentioned. While Ibn Taymiyya continues to refer to these kinds of act-descriptions, such as justice and truth-telling or injustice and lying, his silence on this front means that there is nothing to make such references register as a claim that such act-descriptions are ontologically and/or epistemologically basic. Taken on its own—to finally make contact with the beginning of this argument—the mere fact that Ibn Taymiyya refers to these act-descriptions is not a feature that fundamentally sets his ethical approach apart from the Ashʿarites'. Ashʿarites, after all, had also accepted that "deontological" types of acts could have value—because of their utility. They had also accepted that deontological types of judgments could figure in the content of our surface moral consciousness—itself the product of a consequentialist communal mindset. The more interesting distinctions turned out to center not on the level of *whether* but of *why*. Most intellectual systems, Arthur Lovejoy has observed, "are original or distinctive rather in their patterns than in their components," so that the "seeming novelty of many a system is due solely to the novelty of the application or arrangement of the old elements which enter into it."[52] This holds as true for Ibn Taymiyya as for any other thinker. Yet in Ibn Taymiyya's case, one cannot help but wonder whether, in the re-presentation of intellectual ingredients, something of the original pattern that gave these ingredients their meaning has fallen away from view.

Noting Ibn Taymiyya's neglect of the deontological side of Muʿtazilite moral theory in chapter 1, I suggested there is an invidious question to raise as to whether this neglect should be taken as the result of a deliberate choice or an unintended oversight, perhaps reflecting Ibn Taymiyya's limited familiarity with Muʿtazilite texts. Yet even if we eschew more invidious talk of oversight and confine ourselves to more neutral talk of silence, the thematization of his silences, we now see, is something to which we are inescapably driven when we seek to consider his ethical thought against its context and indeed its formative influences. Probed attentively, these silences hold the key for locating Ibn Taymiyya within his theological topography and situating his specific view of ethics against preexisting possibilities. Our story took its departure, in chapter 1, from a sense that Ibn Taymiyya's *via media* conceded so much to Muʿtazilite rationalism and objectivism that it was tempting to simply close the subject and conclude that his ethical approach was a *via media* that leans heavily toward one of its extremes. Its current denouement shows that such an impression could not be further from the truth, and masks Ibn Taymiyya's profound debts to Ashʿarite thought. Yet it is highly significant that there should be a discrepancy between what Ibn Taymiyya's remarks initially invite us to conclude and what a closer analysis reveals, and that the real contours of his ethical understanding should need to be elicited by an act of excavation that digs beneath his own representation of the debate to which he is contributing.

It is an act of excavation that has made for many of the turning points of our narrative thus far. It made for the discovery of Ibn Taymiyya's silence on deontological considerations in chapter 1, or his silence on nonimperative concepts of value. It made for the unearthing of the distinction between first-person and third-person perspectives that gave us one of the plots of the same chapter, and the distinction between individual and communal interest there and elsewhere. Many of these suppressions carry important consequences for the way we locate Ibn Taymiyya on the map of classical debates about ethics, as I have just said. They also carry important consequences for the cogency of his arguments, just as they carry consequences for the substantiveness of his ethical views. Having brought to light Ibn Taymiyya's Ashʿarite debts in founding ethical norms on communal welfare, we have been given additional grounds for adopting the suggestion outlined in chapter 2 regarding how the epistemological subject implicit in his gnomic statement "*it is known* that justice serves the good of the world [*maṣlaḥat al-ʿālam*] and injustice tends to its harm" should be construed—not as the first-person singular but as the first-person plural of the community. For in the Ashʿarite analysis that trails this statement, the perspective from which ethical judgments are shown to be grounded in communal welfare is not the perspective of ordinary ethical experience, but of a higher-order reflective (and indeed reductive) analysis of it. Yet to accept this conclusion is to be confirmed in the sense that the ordinary moral subject as this looks back at us from Ibn Taymiyya's writings is made of gossamer material indeed.

Such suppressions, to resume a theme that closed chapter 2, offer a testament to the theoretical thinness of Ibn Taymiyya's ethical remarks and provide us with telling indications regarding the character and also the limitations of his account. I hope the discussion pursued in the previous chapters will have given abundant reasons for thinking that a close analysis of Ibn Taymiyya's ethical remarks is worth undertaking *despite* these limitations. So long as our interest does not lie in narrowly engaging his views for their philosophical cogency or substantiveness, there are robust insights such analysis can offer regarding both the contours of his ethical understanding and his place within his theological topography. Yet no less central are the insights it affords us into the form of his ethical remarks and indeed of his writing more broadly. Appreciating the form of Ibn Taymiyya's writing, in this respect—including those features that throw obstacles before the effort to understand its content and that invite partial interpretations—is a part of the task equally crucial as appreciating its content.

What about Objectivity?

I have shown that Ibn Taymiyya's view of the nature of value and the human knowledge of value, scrutinized more carefully, turns out to share many of its distinctive features with the Ashʿarite view. In that case, it may be asked in closing, what of the points of conflict that Ibn Taymiyya called attention to in outlining his *via media*? For he may share far less with Muʿtazilite ethical rationalism and ethical objectivism than may be initially evident. Yet we will recall that it was a vigorous claim of ethical objectivity that had shaped his remarks in the stage-setting exposition we heard in chapter 1 and that formed the backbone of the disagreement he had expressed with the Ashʿarite perspective. He had objected to the Ashʿarites' denial that the value of actions is a matter of objective reality—that "what is right [*maʿrūf*] is . . . right in itself [*fī nafsihi*]" and "what is wrong [*munkar*] in itself wrong." Similarly, he had objected to their reduction of value to a mere matter of "relation and association" (*nisba wa-iḍāfa*), such as the relative value deriving from agreement with people's natural appetites (*mā yulā'imu al-ṭibā'*). Ibn Taymiyya's objection to the latter point will seem very puzzling, as signaled earlier, given the paramount role he also allocates to natural desires in his ethical account. What purchase, one may ask more broadly, could a notion of objectivity have within such an understanding?

The analogy with Hume that picked its way through earlier parts of our narrative is worth reviving at this juncture. In chapter 1, I compared Ibn Taymiyya's way of grounding morality in emotional responses to the sentimentalist view of morality articulated by Hume. Ibn Taymiyya's comparison of ethical reactions to aesthetic responses carried a similar resonance. The analogy seems illuminating, among other reasons, because it allows us to observe the ways certain ideas naturally organize themselves into similar neighborhoods and conjunctions in sharply diverging intellectual contexts. No less noteworthy than the common concern with the emotions and with utility or indeed the shared empiricist temper, in this respect, is the larger theological aim that shadows the projects of both thinkers. For the context of Hume's ethical project, as Schneewind has shown, was a long-standing conflict between rationalist and voluntarist views of God's relation to morality. Hume's own concern was to discredit the former by denying that "there are eternal fitnesses and unfitnesses of things, which are the same to every rational being," and that "the immutable measures of right and wrong impose an obligation, not only on human creatures, but also on the Deity himself" (*T* 456).[53]

Whatever their other differences (and there are many), it is an interest in driving a wedge between the human and the divine domain that Hume shares with Ibn Taymiyya. Yet Hume, on his side, made it clearer than Ibn Taymiyya had before him that this involved denying that morality is a matter of "conformity with reason," and that his proposal to ground morality in the passions was a proposal to ground morality in feeling *in contradistinction* to reason. He also made clear that the decision to ground morals, just "like the perception of beauty and deformity," in human nature—in "the particular fabric and constitution of the human species" with its particular emotional capacities and susceptibilities to pleasure and pain—was a decision to embrace a very different conception of what it means to talk about the objectivity of morality. You discover the moral quality of an action when you "turn your reflexion into your own breast, and find a sentiment of [approbation or] disapprobation, which arises in you"—a sentiment in turn reflecting the way this action impacts on human beings' dispositions to pleasure and pain. Hence this quality "lies in yourself, not in the object" (*T* 468–69).

Hume's choice of expression will seem highly evocative in considering the Islamic context. For it was a phrase just like this one, as we saw—inviting a simple turn inward (*al-rujū' ila'l-nafs*)—that 'Abd al-Jabbār had used in affirming the ethical testimony that our inner resources afford us. Yet 'Abd al-Jabbār, of course, had had an inward turn to the resources of reason more specifically in mind. And reason provides us with a window to real truths that are not merely a product of our own minds and that are not applicable to us alone by virtue of our specific features as subjects. This is a point that ʿAbd al-Jabbār and his fellow Muʿtazilites would dwell on at length in their works, often in response to a peculiarly Ashʿarite claim regarding those features of human subjects that made all the difference to the moral standards that applied to them. It is the fact that human beings are owned by God as chattels (*mamlūk*) and that God is the proprietor and lord (*mālik*) of created beings, Ashʿarites had suggested, that makes the former subject to ethical constraints and the latter immune to them. God's actions cannot be limited by moral standards, for they themselves serve as their source. Al-Ashʿarī had put the point clearly early on when writing that God "is the all-powerful Master, who is under the mastery of none, and has none above Him to issue sanctions, none to command or restrain or proscribe, and none to draw lines and trace out boundaries for Him [*man rasama lahu al-rusūm wa-ḥadda lahu al-ḥudūd*]; this being so, nothing He does can be evil." In this, God is entirely unlike human beings, who can overstep the boundaries set by their Master.[54]

The Muʿtazilite emphasis on the real features of acts that provide the grounds of their value came as a counter to this type of "theistic subjectivism" (in George Hourani's phrase). Acts have value because of something that relates to the acts themselves (*amr yarjiʿu ilayhā*) and that indeed operates as a necessitating cause (*ʿilla mūjiba*). This is the respect, as ʿAbd al-Jabbār would significantly comment elsewhere, in which ethical judgments diverge most sharply from aesthetic judgments, such as our response to pretty or ugly pictures, which vary from person to person and indeed from time to time. A picture is called ugly (*qabīḥ*) "to the extent that one dislikes looking at it [*min ḥaythu tanfuru al-nafs min al-naẓar ilayhā*]." As such, this disapproving response is grounded in something that relates to us rather than to the picture itself (*amr yarjiʿu ilaynā lā ilayhā*). The disvalue of lying or of injustice, by contrast, in no wise depends on the features of the agent contemplating such acts, whether human beings or God.[55]

Ibn Taymiyya's ethical claims, as we have seen, are often couched in terms that carry strong objectivist commitments. We have heard him speak of what an act is "in itself" (*fī nafsihi* or *fī nafs al-amr*) in our stage-setting text; we have heard him speak of the "attributes" (*ṣifāt*) of actions. Elsewhere he speaks more emphatically of *intrinsic* or *essential* attributes (*ṣifāt dhātiyya*), though in other locations he retreats from this strong specification. Yet in many of these instances, it is clear from the context that he is thinking, once again, of benefit and harm, which ultimately refer us to the material of human pleasure and pain.[56] Now it is not, to recapitulate an earlier observation, that the Muʿtazilites made no room for such notions within their framework. It is thus important to recall that within Muʿtazilite theory, deontological act-descriptions took their place next to a number of consequentialist considerations. What is crucial, however, is that the Muʿtazilites had reserved their strongest objectivist language for the former class as against the latter, for reasons that can be easily summed up.

Acts like lying or injustice, as Ibn Mattawayh explains, owe their value to unchanging characteristics (*ṣifa lāzima lā tazūlu ʿan al-mawṣūf bi-ḥāl*). Where the value depends on the consequences (the utility) of actions, by contrast, the same action can be good in some circumstances and bad in others. Ask yourself, "Is it good to travel for trade purposes?" or "Is it good to run?", and you will find that you cannot give absolute answers. Traveling may be good if there is a realistic chance of financial gain but bad in other circumstances. Running may be wrong in some circumstances—it seemed undignified to those critics of Muslim practice who lampooned many of the rituals, including running, comprised in the hajj—but it may be right if you are fleeing a beast of prey, if you are coming to greet your father, if the doctor has prescribed it for health, or if it has been prescribed by a caring Creator who has discerned other benefits that are hidden from your limited view. The context-dependence of such acts finds its complement in their dependence on features of agents, to the extent that they presuppose a disposition to benefit and harm.[57] Ibn Taymiyya thus applies the language of "objectivity" to actions that the Muʿtazilites had handled in distinctly relative terms. In the axis extending between "what relates to us" and "what relates to acts themselves," Ibn Taymiyya leans strongly to the former, just like the Ashʿarites before him. What makes acts good is very much a matter of the kinds of creatures we are and our natural disposition to characteristic pleasures and pains: its quality, to return to Hume's phrase, "lies in yourself, not in the object."[58]

Could we still speak of objectivity on these terms? Writing in a related connection, James Rachels has suggested that ethical naturalism can be seen as a "compromise between objective and subjective views of ethics. It is objective in that it identifies good and evil with something that is really 'there' in the world outside us, but at the same time, what is there is the power to produce feelings inside us."[59] Hume himself, while setting aside the notion of "conformity with reason" and instructing us to look for the passions moving within our breast, spoke of what this inward look discovers as a "matter of fact." The responses of pleasure and pain we find within our breast or wired into our body—responses that reflect our characteristic dispositions as the natural creatures we are—after all constitute some of the hardest facts in the world, and thinkers in the past have often judged them far more robust than alternative facts constituted by so-called rational intuitions. That certain kinds of actions and events produce certain effects or result in certain experiences that we find pleasurable or painful is another hard fact, which places our nature into conversation with the natural world we live in, though for Ibn Taymiyya this conversation also extends to the supernatural world that follows. Even if the "stuff" of value is human pleasure and pain, against such facts we can still draw distinctions, as suggested earlier, between pleasures that serve our overall interests and ones that do not—between a "subjective" sense of the good that reflects our fallible likes and dislikes ("what I want") and a more "objective" sense of the good that represents our true welfare in the long term ("what is good for me"). These distinctions become sharper still if, with Ibn Taymiyya, we believe there are objective facts of the matter as to what constitutes our true welfare and as to the means for achieving it.

A place for the language of "objectivity," this schematization suggests, could still be argued within this framework. Yet to the extent that we are considering Ibn Taymiyya against his theological topography, it will be crucial to be clear how far, once again, this would be from the place the Muʿtazilites had prepared for it and how much nearer to a kind of place Ashʿarite theologians would also have been prepared to concede.[60]

MY MAIN CONCERN in this chapter has been to document the fundamental convergences that unite Ibn Taymiyya's ethical positions to those articulated by Ashʿarite theologians, revealing Ibn Taymiyya's profound debts to the latter for his understanding of the nature of value and the mode of human beings' epistemic access to it. Any appearance of conflict on these issues gives way to a picture of deeper concord.

Yet this, in fact, is not to say that genuine conflict is not at stake between the outlooks of these thinkers. If we wish to identify the real location of Ibn Taymiyya's conflict with Ashʿarite ethical thought, however, it is not among the topics we have considered in this chapter that we should primarily seek it. These topics, it may now be observed, lie on one particular side of a boundary that we met early in our inquiry yet that has remained quietly in the background in these three chapters, namely the boundary between the human domain and the divine. To talk about what human beings can and cannot do, we earlier heard Ibn Taymiyya declare, is still to say nothing about God. The analogy between the human domain and the divine (*qiyās al-ghāʾib ʿalā al-shāhid*) that the Muʿtazilites practiced has to be categorically rejected. To say that the morality of human beings is not the morality of God, at the same time, is not to say that there is no sense whatsoever in which one can speak of a divine "morality." Having focused on the human domain thus far, it is to the divine domain that we need to make the leap in order to bring into view not merely the real grounds of Ibn Taymiyya's quarrel with the Ashʿarites, but indeed the larger theological vision in which his ethical views about human morality find their deepest roots and his *via media* achieves a further—and perhaps its most critical—articulation. If what we say about God is not what we say about ourselves, what *can* we say about God?

4

The Aims of the Law and the Morality of God

WHAT MAKES ACTIONS good, and how do we know it? These were the questions that focused the discussion of the preceding three chapters. Yet from the earliest history of *kalām* debates about ethics, these questions had never stood alone or been investigated purely for their intrinsic significance. Providing them with their deepest roots had been issues of far-reaching theological importance.

ʿAbd al-Jabbār was one of many Muʿtazilites who signaled that clearly when, opening his volume on "The Determination of Justice and Injustice" in the *Mughnī*, he had simply stated his aim: to prove that "God only does what is good, and cannot but do what is obligatory."[1] This theological focus is evident in the way Ibn Taymiyya himself characterizes the conflict that gave the classical debates their distinctive contours and generated the different theological stances. This was a conflict between God's justice and God's power, or again between God's title to absolute praise (*ḥamd*) and His title to absolute sovereignty (*mulk*). Different schools had seized upon a single one of those terms to the exclusion of the other: Muʿtazilites had run away with justice and deprived God of absolute power; Ashʿarites had run away with absolute power and deprived God of His entitlement to praise. The first had conceded so much to human freedom that it placed limits on God's, and made so much of objective morality that God appeared as the subject of a Law above Him. The latter had denied human freedom so flatly as to make the ethical life seem absurd and denied the existence of constraints on God's possible action so blatantly as to make God seem like a tyrant. The God we can love, or the God who can make things happen?

It is an impossible choice that thinkers have often come up against throughout our intellectual history in different forms. It is the question Socrates calmly debated with Euthyphro when asking whether that which is holy is "loved by the gods because it is holy, or is . . . holy because it is loved by the gods" (*Euthyphro* 10a), which continues to weave its way through discussions of the relation between God's goodness and omnipotence down to present times. It is the question that philosophers and theologians have debated in more impassioned tones when asking why evil happens, and how—particularly in a world that still counts God as a member—this can be explained. This of course is a concern that is far from academic, raising vital questions, as Susan Neiman writes, about "what the structure of the world must be like for us to think and act within it" and thematizing our ability to trust in the world we inhabit. Such questions have formed a driving force of inquiry for long swaths of our intellectual history, unsurprisingly given their deep-seated psychological roots.[2]

This broader history of tensions is worth keeping in the background; and so is the close enmeshment of these types of questions with more living human concerns. My aim in this chapter will be to bring into view one of the central components of Ibn Taymiyya's proposal for resolving the conflict that had riven classical Islamic debates. It is a conflict, we have already heard him say, that cries out for a *via media*. And this *via media*, he will state, is "the doctrine of the *salaf*," which sacrifices neither term and affirms that God "has both sovereignty and entitlement to praise in full measure."[3] My narrower concern in this chapter will be with Ibn Taymiyya's articulation of the second term of this nodal statement. For even as he announces the dissociation of human from divine morality, his distinctive claim is that the notion of divine morality cannot be surrendered altogether. God's justice—or, in Ibn Taymiyya's preferred focal term, God's wisdom—has to be upheld. These notions must be upheld as an imperative of God's entitlement to praise, yet they also respond to powerful imperatives belonging to the perspective of a more vital human experience.

Ibn Taymiyya's claims are developed in opposition to the view adopted by Ashʿarite theologians, and thus my discussion will once again pursue the double task of locating Ibn Taymiyya against his interlocutors and weaving together a positive understanding of his own claims. A positive exploration of God's morality will also open the space for raising afresh some of the questions about the nature of value that we have already posed. In previous chapters the aspects of Ibn Taymiyya's view we explored engaged the ethical debates of *kalām* and the conversation these had struck up with the writings of the *falāsifa*. In this chapter our discussion is set to relay us to a different conversation between *kalām* debates and legal discourse. The place where God's justice and God's power meet for an adjudicating contest is the very body of the divine Law.

After an initial characterization of Ibn Taymiyya's critical stance against the Ashʿarites—which targets their denial that God is wise and that He legislates for the sake of human welfare—I will devote the first part of my discussion to a closer investigation of the Ashʿarite understanding of the place of welfare in the Law, focusing on the conflict often said to subsist between Ashʿarite utterances in the theological and legal contexts. The second part of my discussion will address Ibn Taymiyya's positive understanding of God's wisdom and God's justice, focusing on two main reason-giving contexts: the reasons for God's commands and the reasons for God's punishment.

The Wisdom of God's Law: A Theological Rift and Its Internal Ashʿarite Tensions

There can be no better starting point than the stage-setting exposition of Ibn Taymiyya's *via media* that provided us with a foothold in chapter 1. It is an exposition that we have already engaged at length on several levels, yet in returning to it we will see that we have far from exhausted its orienting themes. Critically adumbrating the Ashʿarite view, Ibn Taymiyya had berated the Ashʿarites for their failure to acknowledge the objectivity of ethical values and for reducing them to a matter of mere relations—a criticism we found puzzling in light of Ibn Taymiyya's affinities with the Ashʿarite view. Yet if we return to that anchor passage to rehearse it once more, we will now find that the way he had parsed that point was rather more specific. On the topic of "the determination of good and bad," he had said, such theologians

> say that actions do not contain attributes that constitute [evaluative] qualifications [*aḥkām*] nor attributes that constitute the causes [*ʿilal*] of qualifications. Rather, [God] issued a command for one of two [equally possible] similar actions [*mutamāthilayn*] out of sheer arbitrary will, not due to any wise purpose, and not in order to promote any welfare [*maṣlaḥa*] in either the realm of creation [*khalq*] or command [*amr*]. And they say that it is possible that God might command one to polytheism, or forbid one from worshipping Him alone, and it is possible that He command injustice and foul deeds, and forbid righteousness and piety, and that the qualifications that attach to acts are only a [contingent or extrinsic] relation and association [*nisba wa-iḍāfa*]. And what is right [*maʿrūf*] is not right in itself [*fī nafsihi*], in their view, nor is what is wrong [*munkar*] in itself wrong. . . . Command and prohibition, making lawful and prohibiting, are in their view not [about] what is right or wrong, good or foul in itself [*fī nafs al-amr*], unless this is taken to refer to that which agrees with people's natural appetites [*mā yulāʾimu al-ṭibāʿ*], and this does not entail, according to them, that God loves what is right and hates what is wrong.[4]

Combing this passage for its linchpin critical terms, there are a number of notions we should allow to stand out: the reference to the qualifications and causes of actions; the reference to God's wise purpose; the reference to what God loves and hates. Yet what must be immediately noticed is something even more basic, namely the emphasis on the nature and grounds of God's commands that holds the entire passage together. With this emphasis in view, Ibn Taymiyya's criticism of the Ashʿarites' anti-objectivism can be read with fresh nuance. Probed more carefully, the offending view is not simply that actions do not have real ethical qualities; it is that God's command is not grounded in the real ethical qualities of acts.

It is the contention just isolated that forms the focus of some of Ibn Taymiyya's more truculent engagements with Ashʿarite ethical thought. In trying to reconcile God's praiseworthiness and God's power, Ibn Taymiyya will argue, the Ashʿarites failed to give the former its due. Bent on preserving God's sovereignty from the encroachment of limiting standards foreign to His will, they left His will brute and dark to reasons. There is no "Why?" to be asked of God's will; God's will is not responsive to anything outside it, to the real features of actions, of the world. When God chooses to do one thing or another—when He commands human beings to perform one action over another or when He creates one thing rather than another—He does so arbitrarily, preferring one of two equally possible actions without a ground (*takhṣīṣ/tarjīḥ al-mutamāthilayn bilā sabab*). Yet to take that position, in Ibn Taymiyya's view, is to deprive God of His praiseworthy description as "wise" (*ḥakīm*). The term "justice" (*ʿadl*), which formed the chief focus of Muʿtazilite theology, is not absent from Ibn Taymiyya's discussion. Yet it is the term "wisdom" (*ḥikma*) that forms the principal lodestone for his theological reflections in this context and the perfection whose ascription to God he is most anxious to secure. To secure this, as he writes in his *Minhāj al-sunna*, is to acknowledge that God's actions and commands are directed to "praiseworthy consequences" (*ʿawāqib maḥmūda*) and "beloved ends" (*ghāyāt maḥbūba*).[5] In commanding specific acts, more especially, God does not randomly choose between indifferent things. Far from commanding for no purpose, it may be said that God commands out of love: God *loves* (*yuḥibbu*) the actions He commands.

There will be further detail to add to these views as this chapter progresses. Yet for the grounds of Ibn Taymiyya's reproach against the Ashʿarites, one does not need to look far. We have already seen that Ashʿarites denied that actions have intrinsic attributes that account for the evaluative qualifications the Law distributes on them; such qualifications, in al-Anṣārī's already cited locution, rather "stem from God's word" (*āyila ilā qawl Allāh*). The implication that God could have commanded other actions than He in fact has was cheerfully drawn by several Ashʿarites. In his *Niẓāmiyya*, al-Juwaynī would be simply expressing this point on another level when stating that "from the perspective of divinity, all acts are equal [*biʾl-iḍāfa ilā ḥukm al-ilāhiyya fa-inna al-afʿāl mutasāwiya*]," as would al-Ghazālī in the *Iqtiṣād*, when he would put the point with an incendiary specificity in which the grounds of Ibn Taymiyya's accusations can be even more plainly seen: "Disbelief and faith, obedience and disobedience, are all equal as far as God is concerned [*Allāhu ta'ālā yastawī fī ḥaqqihi al-kufr wa'l-īmān wa'l-tā'āt wa'l-'iṣyān*]."[6] Yet few would express the spirit of arbitrariness that Ibn Taymiyya would take as his target more clearly than the Mālikite jurist al-Qarāfī (d. 1285), when he would assert: God "renders preponderant one of two [equally] possible things through His sheer will, which is such that it intrinsically renders preponderant without requiring a preponderating factor [*bal yurajjiḥu ta'ālā aḥad al-jā'izayn 'ala'l-ākhar bi-mujarrad irādatihi allatī sha'nuhā an turajjiḥa li-dhātihā min ghayr iḥtiyājihā li-murajjiḥ*]."[7]

All acts are equal to God; there is nothing in their inherent qualities to explain why God should attach positive value to one and not the other. And even if one still felt the need to ask "Why?" at this juncture, the space for doing so was sealed up even more programmatically by Ash'arites through their distinctive understanding of God's wisdom. For like most other theologians taking their point of departure from scripture in deciding what could and could not be said of God, the Ash'arites had affirmed that the notion of "wisdom" can indeed be predicated of God. Yet they had construed it in explicitly nonmoral terms, referring it chiefly to knowledge and to well-wrought (*muḥkam*) action on the basis of knowledge and will.[8] Excluded from the antecedents of such action, significantly, was anything that could be described as a "purpose" or "motive" (*'illa, bā'ith, dā'ī*). Such notions, Ash'arites contended, imply imperfection and need. An agent who aims at certain ends is an agent who is incomplete without them. God's wisdom thus had to be construed in terms that did not involve ascribing to Him intentional concepts.[9] A fortiori, what must also be excluded from the antecedents of divine action are ethically charged aims such as those with which the Mu'tazilites had proposed to stock the notion of wisdom, naming beneficence (*iḥsān*) as God's principal motivation.

Ibn Taymiyya himself, as we have seen, repudiates the Mu'tazilite claim that the ethical standards that constrain the actions of human beings are the same as those that constrain God's. Yet what is crucial is that it is the same notion deployed by Mu'tazilites to talk about God's motivation that Ibn Taymiyya places at the heart of his conception of God's wisdom. The problem with the Ash'arite denial of God's wisdom, Ibn Taymiyya elsewhere makes clear, is not simply the claim that God "renders preponderant one of two [equally] possible things through His sheer will." It is its specific exclusion of beneficence (*al-iḥsān ila'l-khalq*) as the factor that gives God's will its rational ground and makes it lean (*tarajjaḥa*) in one direction as against another.[10] And that is to say that the teleological notion of "praiseworthy consequences" to which God's will is directed must be understood, at least in part, in terms of a notion that has already emerged as the governing concept of Ibn Taymiyya's ethical thought in the human context, namely welfare (*maṣlaḥa*). To claim that God is wise is thus in part to claim that God directs His actions and commands to the achievement of human welfare. Both a closer consideration of the document of God's speech, the Qur'an, and a closer empirical consideration of the natural world that surrounds us reveal the purposefulness of God's actions and the concern with creaturely welfare that guides them.[11]

The connection between God's wisdom and human welfare, we will recognize in hindsight, was plainly visible in the stage-setting exposition of Ibn Taymiyya's *via media* that came before us. "God is knowing and wise [*ḥakīm*]," we heard Ibn Taymiyya say, "and knowing the benefits that qualifications comprise [*ma tataḍammanuhu al-aḥkām min al-maṣāliḥ*], He issued commands and prohibitions based on His knowledge of the benefits and harms that commands and prohibitions ... involve for His servants." Far from being the preserve of Muʿtazilites or their like-minded Shīʿite colleagues, Ibn Taymiyya explains in the *Minhāj*, the claim that God is wise in this sense is rather "the view of the majority of Muslim factions, including the scriptural exegetes, the jurists, the traditionists, the Sufis, the *mutakallimūn*, and others."[12] This proclamation of consensus will remind us of a similar proclamation that came into view in chapter 1, tied more narrowly to the thesis that acts are good or bad in themselves. Parsed now as the thesis that God commands for the human good, this proclamation takes on new meaning.[13]

It is in fact only a small fraction of the Muslim community that opposes this claim; and these are precisely theologians of Ashʿarite persuasion. The location of one of Ibn Taymiyya's main rifts with Ashʿarite theology, we can now say more clearly, lies in a question about the place of human welfare within God's creative and especially legislative activity. That this question is at the forefront of Ibn Taymiyya's concerns in articulating his position on "the determination of good and bad" is made evident in several passages, including a key passage in his *Qāʿida fi'l-muʿjizāt wa'l-karāmāt* where he revisits the topic. His overall proposal will be familiar to us: good and bad may constitute a "quality of our actions," and reason may perceive part of this, taken as a matter of benefit and harm;[14] the Law's commands and prohibitions may sometimes reflect the qualities of actions and sometimes be the source of new qualifications. Whoever denies that acts may bear intrinsic qualities (*ṣifāt dhātiyya*), he continues, "has denied the fact that revealed laws come to indicate [*jāʾat bi*] what serves our welfare and what works to our detriment [*al-maṣāliḥ wa'l-mafāsid*] and what is right and wrong, and [has denied] the relations of suitability [*munāsaba*] that hold between qualifications [*aḥkām*] and their causes [*ʿilal*] in the Law, and he has denied the proper task of legal science [*fiqh*] in religion, which is to know the wisdom behind the Law, its aims [*maqāṣid*] and its excellences."[15] The claim that acts have real ethical qualities and that these qualities are constituted by their beneficial tendency, this remark makes plain, is intimately tied to the claim that benefit or welfare forms the aim of God's laws.

Yet with the last-quoted passage before us, Ibn Taymiyya's reproach against the Ashʿarites may at the same time strike us as curious. Because several of the terms of this passage, it will be noticed, point us to one particular discourse among the Islamic sciences where such terms had achieved their critical articulation, namely legal theory (*uṣūl al-fiqh*). Jurists discussing God's commands and seeking to elaborate on the qualifications or rulings (*aḥkām*) God had assigned to specific actions, thus, had taken a special interest in the *ratio* or cause (*ʿilla*) that could be identified as the basis for these qualifications, with a view to extending the Law to new actions through analogical reasoning (*qiyās*). The notion of "convenience" or "suitability" (*munāsaba*) just invoked by Ibn Taymiyya appeared at this juncture, as a way of identifying the legal cause that was based on discerning the interests that particular rulings served to promote. Studying the behavioral norms that God had prescribed, it was possible to discern that many of them tended to the protection of certain key interests. In his landmark discussion in the *Mustaṣfā*, al-Ghazālī had identified these interests as religion (*dīn*), human reason (*ʿaql*), human life (*nafs*), property (*māl*), and "progeny" or the integrity of family lines (*nasal*). Thus, he would write, the Law's prescription of killing infidels could be put down to the preservation of religion. The Law's prescription of retaliation (*qiṣāṣ*) could be connected to the preservation of human life (*bihi hifẓ al-nufūs*); the imposition of punishment for drinking intoxicants to the preservation of reason (*bihi hifẓ al-ʿuqūl*), which is the foundation of legal responsibility; the imposition of punishment for adultery to the preservation of the integrity of family lines (*bihi hifẓ al-nasal wa ʾl-ansāb*); the punishment for usurpation and theft to the protection of property.[16] Al-Ghazālī had described these five interests as "necessities" (*ḍarūriyyāt*) and placed them on the highest rung of a tripartite scheme that included "needs" (*ḥājiyyāt*) and "improvements" (*taḥsīniyyat*). Many theorists in the legal tradition would come to speak of these interests as constituting the "aims of the Law" (*maqāṣid al-sharīʿa*).

It was a juncture within legal theory, as will be plain, in which the notion of welfare or human interests (*maṣlaḥa*) made a powerful appearance. And what is crucial for our context is that Ashʿarite thinkers had not only endorsed the developments that promoted welfare to a central place in the Law, but indeed played a seminal role in spearheading them. Al-Ghazālī is a case in point, having been, as Wael Hallaq remarks, "among the foremost theorists to elaborate a detailed doctrine of *munāsaba* and, thus, of public interest" or *maṣlaḥa*. In developing his views, al-Ghazālī looked back to earlier Ashʿarites, notably al-Juwaynī, and even further back to a period of Shāfiʿite history that had been deeply saturated in Muʿtazilite theological ideas. He also looked forward to a number of later Ashʿarite legal theorists, including al-Rāzī and al-Qarāfī, who would take the emphasis on welfare further and articulate it in ever more sophisticated ways.[17]

Considering the positions formulated by Ashʿarite thinkers in the context of legal theory, Ibn Taymiyya's complaint that the Ashʿarites denied the place of welfare in the Law may in this light seem highly peculiar. Yet having made this point, our attention may be drawn to a different observation. For these legal positions themselves, on closer consideration, may seem to be no less peculiar read against the light of the positions the Ashʿarites had expressed within the *theological* context. The tensions begin to appear the moment one scratches the surface of the legal discussions, and are already harbored by the very language that imposes itself in this context. We may notice the relatively harmless instrumental "through" (*bi*) that al-Ghazālī uses to frame the remarks cited above regarding the relationship between specific laws and the interests they serve: *bihi hifẓ al-nufūs* (talking about the prescription of retaliation), *bihi hifẓ al-ʿuqūl* (about the punishment for consuming intoxicants), *bihi hifẓ al-nasal wa'l-ansāb* (about the punishment for adultery). Yet al-Ghazālī himself, like many others, would elsewhere have to yield to the openly explanatory tones of a "because" (*li*), characteristically stating that wine was prohibited "*because of* the harm it leads to [*ḥurrima limā fīhi min al-ifḍāʾ ila'l-mafsada*]."[18]

In the scriptural texts themselves, the notion of causation was more often implied than explicit. "Satan's plan is (but) to excite enmity and hatred between you, with intoxicants and gambling, and hinder you from the remembrance of God, and from prayer," the Qur'an said in issuing the final prohibition of wine in *al-Māʾida* (Q 5:91), implicitly referring this prohibition to both social and religious goods and to the rational self-possession presupposed for the latter. "In retaliation there is life for you" (Q 2:179), the Qur'an said, implicitly referring the prescription of retaliation to its deterring effect. Yet theorists searching for legal causes under the aspect of their "suitability" were inescapably invested in bringing this purpose-rich subtext out into the open and in elaborating on the linguistic structures—"in order to," "because of," and so on (*li, kay, min ajl*)—through which causation was expressed in scripture. Such intentional language, however, distinctly enshrined in the concept of *maqāṣid al-sharīʿa*, seemed to place the Ashʿarites at loggerheads with their own theological views as conveyed in works of *kalām*. For there, as we have seen, they had categorically rejected the applicability of notions of intention and purpose to God. Reasons cannot be sought for God's actions; a fortiori human welfare cannot be ascribed to God as His legislative aim.

It was not the only point of tension to be found between the messages voiced by Ashʿarites in the theological and legal contexts. If this tension derived from the view the Ashʿarites had taken of the mind of God, another derived from the view they had taken of the nature of value, pointing to a further difficulty relating to their view of the mind of human beings. Ashʿarite writers, thus, frequently opened works of legal theory with an account of legal qualifications (*aḥkām*) that re-expressed an understanding of value also elaborated in works of *kalām*. Legal qualifications, as al-Bāqillānī would characteristically rehearse the Ashʿarite position in his *Taqrīb*, do not constitute attributes of the actions in question. His continuation, which registers in the tones of an explanation, will also sound familiar: for "what is forbidden by the Law may resemble what is obligatory in all of its features, yet the Law may judge these two [actions] differently even though reason pronounces them equal and alike [*yaftariqāni fī qaḍiyyat al-samʿ maʿa istiwāʾihimā wa-tamāthulihimā fī ḥukm al-ʿaql*]."[19] The focus of the latter part of this statement is epistemological, denying that a difference is *known* rather than *realized*, but the ontological focus of the first part serves as its interpreter. And it was an ontological point, as we have seen, that was carried by the traditional Ashʿarite claim that good and bad are merely a matter of command or prohibition coming to "attach" (*taʿalluq*) to particular actions, contrasting external attachment to intrinsic (*dhātī*) attribute.

The same point would be expressed by al-Juwaynī at the opening of his *Burhān*, yet now with a concreteness that made plain not only its meaning but also its difficulties. The legal qualification is not a real characteristic of the action; thus "if we say: the drinking of wine is forbidden, prohibition is not an intrinsic quality [*ṣifa dhātiyya*] of the drinking"; rather "what is meant by its being forbidden is that prohibition attaches to it."[20] "Not an intrinsic quality," "prohibition merely attaches"—yet all we need to do here is to recall the position taken on the topic of wine by legal theorists, who drew on scriptural evidence to explain the relevant rulings (the prohibition of consuming wine and the prescription of punishment for violating this prohibition) by reference to the deleterious effects of intoxicants on human reason. What this amounted to was a combination of positions that could not but seem paradoxical: affirming that the qualification "prohibited" attaches merely contingently to the drinking of wine, yet insisting that this qualification can in turn be explained by reference to the real consequences of the act. Ibn Taymiyya himself, as we saw in chapter 3, was prepared to speak of such consequences (and the value deriving from them) as "real" attributes or features. The Ashʿarites, as far as I am aware, had not embraced this usage. Yet to the extent that such consequences represent cause-and-effect relations that are sufficiently stable features of the world to be taken into account by the Lawgiver in prescribing one set of actions and proscribing another, this language could not be entirely shrugged off.

This point of tension calls attention to another, one that Ashʿarite thinkers may have been especially exposed to, but that reflects a worry that jurists belonging to a broader spectrum of opinion also labored under. For if the aim of jurists' interpretive activity was to discover a Law whose comprehensive embodiment resided in the "mind of God," in Bernard Weiss's phrase, there was a natural concern about the risk that this activity might obscure its object and that the mind of man might impose its own patterns on the apprehension of the divine ideal.[21] The reliability of human reason as a means for understanding the Law had been explicitly thematized in the use of analogy (*qiyās*) as a tool of legal reasoning. For analogy—that special method that involved identifying the cause of a ruling in a given case and transferring this ruling from the primary case (*aṣl*) to a subsidiary one (*farʿ*) on the basis of the shared cause—was nothing if not an exercise of reason. Different writers would thus openly characterize it as a form of "rational" proof (*ḥujaj/dalāʾil al-ʿuqūl*).[22]

It was this understanding of its character that underpinned the suspicion with which certain jurists within the Islamic tradition had treated the use of analogy in legal reasoning. These include not only jurists of a more traditionalist mindset, such as the Ẓāhirites, but also thinkers who otherwise seemed enthusiastic about engaging in rational inquiry in other domains. The early Muʿtazilite theologian al-Naẓẓām (d. ca. 836) is a case in point, offering an expression of this suspicion that would reverberate through many later discussions and defenses of analogy and that is all the more arresting for echoing a vocabulary that Ashʿarite thinkers would later use in framing their objections to ethical rationalism. "If we examine the precepts of the Law," he would state, "we find they form a disparate and variegated lot. There are some cases in which the Law has treated different things identically, and there are others where the Law has treated similar things as contraries [*minhā mā sawwā al-sharʿ fīhā bayna al-mukhtalifāt wa-minhā mā khālafa al-sharʿ fīhā bayna al-mutamāthilāt*]." Consider, for example, the way the Law made it off-bounds for a free woman to show her hair, but made it permissible for a slave woman to do the same. Or consider the way it demands a ritual washing of the entire body for certain kinds of impurities (such as sexual intercourse or menstruation) and only a limited ablution for others (such as urination or defecation). Such examples show that the Law follows a logic utterly inaccessible to human understanding.[23]

In formulating this point, it is significant that al-Naẓẓām would focus on types of acts that already in his time were grouped together under the heading of "ritual observances" or "acts of worship" (*ʿibādāt*) and were contrasted with "practical transactions" (*muʿāmalāt*), which included commercial and civil transactions between human beings such as buying or selling, lending or borrowing, and matters of marriage or inheritance. Later jurists endorsing the use of analogy would draw a sharp distinction—though its sharpness would vary among different schools—between the two categories in terms of their accessibility to rational understanding and thus to the operation of analogical reasoning. Whereas the former category resisted such reasoning, the latter was far more hospitable to it and likewise extended a stronger invitation to reflect on the human interests served by it. This kind of invitation would seem calculated to rouse even more powerfully the worry that the human mind might end up projecting its patterns on the ideal contained in the mind of God. It is this fear, as Aron Zysow writes, a fear of "the tendency of men to remake the law in their own image," that underpinned Ḥanafite lawyers' conservative stance on considerations of suitability (*munāsaba*), which engaged the notion of human welfare.[24]

Yet for Ashʿarite lawyers, this invitation would appear to generate an extra difficulty, seen against their other ethicotheological commitments. For if the effort to determine the cause of a given ruling involves, in al-Āmidī's striking phrase, making judgments as to what is "eligible" or "capable" of forming the Lawgiver's motivation or aim (*al-ashyāʾ allatī taṣluḥu an takūna bawāʿith, mā yaṣluḥu an yakūna maqṣūdan*), such judgments seem particularly problematic where considerations of human welfare are concerned.[25] For the claim that human reason can be relied upon to identify the interests that motivate legal rulings and that underlie the Law as its larger purposes—"suitability," al-Ghazālī tells us, refers to "an intelligible feature that is plain to reason and that can be readily established . . . through rational reflection"—would seem to conflict with the Ashʿarite view of the limited powers of human reason as a means of accessing evaluative truths.[26] The claim that human beings can recognize the goods that the Law reasonably aims to promote reflects a presumption that human beings can recognize these goods *as* goods, *worthy* of figuring among the concerns of the Law. In this respect, the assertion we heard from al-Bāqillānī, that actions attract different legal qualifications even as they are judged "equal and alike in the perspective of reason," would be belied by the fact that other Ashʿarite theorists had deemed reason supremely capable of marking certain distinctions between the acts God had forbidden and the acts He had made obligatory.[27]

In chapter 3, to be sure, we saw that many Ashʿarites after al-Bāqillānī voiced support for the idea that human beings can make certain basic evaluative judgments relative to their interests. These were judgments of natural appetite that Ashʿarites often referred to as judgments of reason and that could be summed up by saying "it is obligatory to avoid harm" and "it is good to pursue benefit." Yet of course these propositions, as they stand, carry little substantive content; they are purely formal. To concede them is thus perfectly compatible with holding that only the Law tells us *what* constitutes benefit and *what* constitutes harm, as al-Ashʿarī had early on suggested is the case. Reason, in the words reported by Ibn Fūrak, "contains no indication of the harms and benefits that form the outcome" of actions (*lā dalīla fīhi ʿalā mā yakūnu fi'l-ʿawāqib min al-maḍārr wa'l-manāfiʿ*) and that constitute them as overall beneficial or harmful.[28] The ability to recognize the interests served by the Law as good(s), by contrast, seems to presuppose something far more substantive, reflecting not only the formal knowledge *that* the pursuit of what is in our interests is good, but indeed a more substantive knowledge of the *what*.

There are several tensions, thus, that seem to arise when considering the positions adopted by Ashʿarites in legal theory from the perspective of their theological positions. It is at this precise juncture, as Zysow has noted, that Ashʿarite theologians had often been accused of a failure to harmonize the messages flowing from their different discourses, and more specifically of a failure to resolve the conflicts produced in the transition from the discourse of theology to that of legal theory.[29] Ibn Taymiyya himself would pick up on this tension in several locations of his work, remarking on the diverging views voiced by different groups in different contexts regarding the explanation (*ta ʿlīl*) of God's actions and commands and the status of legal causes, with one view appearing in the context of law (*fiqh*) and another in the context of theology (*uṣūl*).[30]

Given the central significance of this conflict both for the way we understand Ashʿarite ethical thought and the way we reconstruct Ibn Taymiyya's location within his intellectual topography, it is worth pausing to consider it more closely. In the next section, I will focus on two core elements of this apparent conflict: the tensions generated for Ashʿarite jurists by their view of the mind of human beings (their untutored evaluative grasp) and by their view of the mind of God (His inaccessibility to concepts of purpose). My argument will be that prominent Ashʿarites showed a notable willingness to acknowledge the thicker evaluative grasp involved in knowing the interests promoted by the Law, and I will raise a question as to how deeply this acknowledgment after all conflicted with their ethical viewpoint. It is with regard to the second, theological concern that a more genuine conflict would seem to arise, but Ashʿarites developed specific strategies for resolving it. It is against this context, and particularly against the Ashʿarite theological position, that Ibn Taymiyya's own conflict with the Ashʿarites and his distinctive position can best be addressed.

The Human Mind, the Mind of God: Ashʿarite Views of Welfare between Theology and Law

Turning to the first point, it will be important to notice the special care al-Ghazālī had taken in articulating his account of the five objectives of the Law in the *Mustaṣfā* and the distinct emphasis he had placed on one key fact: these objectives are to be understood as objects not of human desire, but of divine intention. In its "original" sense (*fī 'l-aṣl*), al-Ghazālī would note in introducing the notion of *maṣlaḥa*, this notion refers to the pursuit of benefit and the avoidance of harm (*jalb manfaʿa aw-dafʿ maḍarra*). Used in the context of the Law and as a potential legislative ground, however, "this is not what we mean by it; for the pursuit of benefit and repulsion of harm constitute objects of *human* intentions." Rather, *maṣlaḥa* here refers to "the preservation of the intention of the *Law*; and what the Law intends for people is fivefold: to preserve their religion, their life, their reason, their progeny, and their property for them."[31] What the *Law* intends; to preserve these things *for them*—markers of an external perspective that would bypass the traps of ordinary language by purging the term *maṣlaḥa* of the meaning that ordinarily attaches to it and annexing it to a separate corpus of technical speech. Not what *we* consider our good but what the Law intends.

The same focus on the intention of the Law, as against human conceptions of the good, registers in another key contention within al-Ghazālī's discussion, namely that it is scriptural evidence that constitutes the source for our knowledge of welfare (or "welfare"): "The aims of the Law are known through the Qur'an, the Sunna, and consensus."[32] This contention would seem to form but a natural continuation of the Ash'arite view that the Law is the sole source for our knowledge of value, as affirmed by Ash'arites within *kalām* debates. As Zysow has suggested, it was precisely a textual account of how the aims of the Law are established that presented itself to Ash'arite thinkers as the readiest means of avoiding the claim that the human mind provides us with epistemic access to them. If the Law itself informs us about its aims, the services of human reason are plainly not required.[33] The way the Law does so, Ash'arite jurists from al-Ghazālī through al-Rāzī to al-Qarāfī would argue, is by placing before us recurrent examples of a connection between particular rulings and particular purposes, which lead us inductively (through *istiqrā'*) to an understanding of its general purposes. It is by observing what al-Ghazālī in the *Shifā' al-ghalīl* would refer to as "the behavior of the Law" (*taṣarrufāt al-shar'*)—by observing God's textual behavior—that we acquire a sense of the Law's habit or custom (*da'b al-shar', 'ādat al-shar'*). This is similar to the way we acquire a sense of a person's character through a close observation that enables us to notice patterns and regular conjunctions between action and occasion.[34]

And yet if that is the overall import of al-Ghazālī's discussion in the *Mustaṣfā*, what are we to make of the remarks he offers on the very same topic elsewhere? For in his earlier work on legal theory, *Shifā' al-ghalīl*, the dominant accent had seemed to fall differently. Introducing the different classes of considerations of suitability (*munāsaba*), he had delivered an orienting statement that is worth quoting at some length:

> The highest among these are those that occupy the rank of necessities [*ḍarūrāt*], such as preserving human life, for it is the aim of the Lawgiver, and it is a necessity for people [*min ḍarūrat al-khalq*], and our reason indicates and affirms it ... and in the view of those who assert that reason determines what is good and bad [*taḥsīn al-'aql wa-taqbīḥihi*], it is such that no Law may ever fail to be without it. And even though we say that God may act as He wills toward His servants and that He is not obliged to promote what is in their interests, we do not deny that reason points to what constitutes our welfare and what impairs it, and that it warns against dangers and incites to the pursuit of benefits [*lā nunkiru ishārat al-'uqūl ilā jihat al-maṣāliḥ wa'l-mafāsid wa-taḥdhīrahā al-mahālik wa-targhībahā fī jalb al-manāfi'*] ... nor do we deny that messengers, peace be upon them, were sent for the benefit of people in both this world and the next, by way

> of God's mercy and grace [*faḍlan*] upon people, not by way of necessity and obligation [*wujūban*] upon Him.[35]

There are many messages to mine within this statement, but here we may simply register the most immediate one. For even allowing for some of the conservative qualifications that clothe the point (like the interpolation of the more hesitant *jiha* in *ishārat al-ʿuqūl ilā jihat al-maṣāliḥ*), in this passage al-Ghazālī appears to ascribe to reason precisely the kind of epistemic role vis-à-vis the interests promoted by the Law which in the *Mustasfā* he had disavowed. And he does so while self-consciously locating himself in the "we" of Ashʿarite theologians, defined by a denial that good and bad can be rationally determined. A rounder affirmation of the thesis that human beings rationally know the interests promoted by the Law could hardly have been desired. To the question just raised—"What to make of this fact?"—the only answer would seem to be: a flagrant contradiction.

It is a contradiction that has been remarked more broadly in the past by readers of al-Ghazālī's legal output, who have noted the palpably different spirit in which he approaches the notion of *maṣlaḥa* between these two works. The difference between al-Ghazālī's attitudes, some readers have suggested—between the "liberal pragmatism" of the *Shifāʾ al-ghalīl* and the "uncompromising literalism" of the *Mustaṣfā*—can be explained by reference to the different chronologies of each work. Thus, the *Shifāʾ al-ghalīl* was written at an earlier point in al-Ghazālī's career marked by a pedagogical and practical preoccupation with positive law as well as an engagement with the rational sciences. The *Mustaṣfā*, by contrast, is the product of a time postdating his spiritual crisis marked by a retreat from mundane affairs into an attitude of "fearsome piety," which was linked with a concern to present the "minimum doctrine" in a conservative manner without risking innovation or controversy.[36]

However we may seek to account for it, it is a kind of contradiction that would provide fodder for the view that the Ashʿarites confronted serious challenges in trying to harmonize different regions of their theory with one another, and that seems symptomatic of a type of entropy inherent in Ashʿarite theory that made a stable viewpoint hard to achieve. Yet I would argue that what should be underscored in this connection are less the discontinuities to be observed across al-Ghazālī's writings, than the continuities. These are continuities that pull the knowledge of value in the direction of reason; and they do so precisely through the usage of language, and with greater complicity than suggested by earlier talk of its "traps."

For al-Ghazālī's remark here that the preservation of human life is "the aim of the Lawgiver, and it is a necessity for people [*min ḍarūrat al-khalq*]" was echoed in the *Mustaṣfā* by the remark, apropos the need to preserve people's possessions, that these "constitute people's livelihood, and they stand in need of them [*hiya ma ʿāsh al-khalq wa-hum muḍṭarrūna ilayhā*]."[37] That the language of *ḍarūra* should appear in this context should come as no surprise, given that al-Ghazālī is illustrating the category of interests he has identified as "necessities" or *ḍarūrāt*. Yet if he had earlier invited us to purify words like *maṣāliḥ* from their habitual meanings and to hear them in a technical sense divorced from ordinary experience, such mental feats seem harder to pull off in this context in a way that would allow us to understand the language of needs, not in terms of anything we know from human experience—so that what is a need is what we *know* and *experience* as a need, referring us to a judgment made from within the human condition—but in terms of what the Law enjoins us to *call* a "need" from its external perspective outside the human world. To propose this, after all, would be to fly in the face of the most self-evident facts, which we only need to tune into another semantic shade of the term *ḍarūra* to state plainly: our life, and the means to our livelihood, are things that we are *compelled* (*muḍṭarr*) to treasure and seek out.

Having tuned ourselves into these semantics, it will be hard not to hear them again in the works of other Ashʿarites. In his *Burhān*, for example, al-Juwaynī would refer the legal validation of selling (*bayʿ*) to the fact that "if people could not barter what they have in hand, this would entail evident hardship [*la-jarra dhālika ḍarūra ẓāhira*]," as he would refer the validation of renting (*ijāra*) to the "urgent need for shelter [*masīs al-ḥāja ila ʾl-masākin*] combined with the inability to establish ownership," which constitutes an "evident need" (*ḥāja ẓāhira*). Yet "evident," here, demands to be taken at its epistemological face value, leaving the terms "need" and "necessity" untouched in their linguistic meanings and affirming the simple fact that shelter—like the means to our livelihood, and our very lives—is an object of experienced need and desire. Al-Juwaynī's references to our "natural motives" (*al-dawāʿī al-jibilliyya*) and to the concordance between the Law and our natural dispositions—"it is as if the Law harnesses the entailments of our nature as its support [*ka-anna al-sharīʿa tataʾayyadu bi-mūjib al-jibilla wa ʾl-ṭabīʿa*]"—may then have to be read precisely in the way that they immediately encourage us.[38]

The above suggests that a willingness to recognize the interests promoted by the Law as objects of rational knowledge—taken in the sense identified in the previous chapter, namely a knowledge of need or desire—was etched in the very notions that Ashʿarites took as their vernacular in discussing and explaining the provisions of the Law. And if, in certain of these cases, this presupposition remains buried among the instruments of speech, in other writers, and in other works of the same writers, it steps more plainly into the light. Al-Ghazālī himself provides us with the most brilliant illustration of the latter point, though it is not insignificant that he does so in the pages, not of a work of legal theory, but of his spiritual summa, *Iḥyāʾ ʿulūm al-din*. This is a work, we may recall, that, like the *Mustaṣfā*, was written in the period postdating his spiritual crisis. The purposes that guide this work, to be sure, differ sharply from those that organize his writings on legal theory; this is also one of several works that have sometimes been thought to sit uneasily within the corpus of al-Ghazālī's writings in terms of their development of certain key themes. A case in point is his treatment of the notion of causality, which appears to gravitate equivocally between Ashʿarite occasionalism and an Avicennan embrace of secondary causation across different works, including the *Iḥyāʾ*.[39] These are certainly important tensions; yet it is then all the more significant to be able to once again record those elements that make for the continuity of al-Ghazālī's understanding in the specific question we are considering, even as these elements are transposed into a more complex intellectual vision.

It is with a combination of recognition and surprise, in fact, that we will greet certain passages of the *Iḥyāʾ* that bring up for discussion several types of goods that, looking out from the vantage point of *uṣūl al-fiqh*, we may recognize as belonging to the gamut of the human interests identified as objectives of the Law. The sense of recognition has to be sought out, for these goods are approached through very different categories of interest in the *Iḥyāʾ*, and the intersection of its concerns with those of legal discourse remains unmarked by al-Ghazālī himself, who leaves the perspective of *fiqh* behind at the opening of the work, consigning it to the domain of the *dunyā* as against the *ākhira* and to the realm of the outer as against the inner—the qualities of the heart and the traits of character from which external actions spring and which alone give them value, yet over which legal science has no dominion.[40] When we thus meet some of the goods the jurists had discussed, we meet them modulated by a concern with the inner and located against the larger spiritual perspective for which the *Iḥyāʾ* strives. The mundane world, in this perspective, certainly forms the means by which human beings arrive at the next (*lā yatimmu al-dīn illā bi'l-dunyā*), yet our attachment to it must assume precisely an instrumental character, and our relationship to the mundane region must be examined in terms of the intentions and spiritual attitudes it incorporates, in ways calculated to transform the way we engage and evaluate the mundane goods addressed by the jurists. Within this broader context, we meet the jurists' "property" (*māl*), for example, under the rubric of the "etiquette" of earning a livelihood (*ādāb al-kasb wa'l-maʿāsh*). We meet it again, more negatively this time, in discussions impugning the value of the mundane world (*dhamm al-dunyā*) or discussions of spiritual traits like the love of wealth and miserliness, poverty and abstinence. Similarly, we meet the jurists' concern with "progeny" or offspring (*nasal* or *nasab*) in the section of the *Iḥyāʾ* devoted to the customs of daily life (*ʿādāt*) under the etiquette of marriage (*ādāb al-nikāḥ*). And it is this latter discussion that I will here focus on as a source of some of the most illuminating insights for our question.

The intersection with legal discourse, as I have suggested, has to be sought out, yet this is an effort that in many locations is facilitated by al-Ghazālī's own language. This is particularly so in the evocative remarks with which he opens his discussion of marriage and family life. "Praise be to God," he writes, who

> created human beings from water . . . and delivered people to the power of an appetite through which He compelled them [*shahwa iḍṭarrahum bihā*] to plow the land by a force beyond resistance, and preserved their progeny [*nasalahum*] by coercion and duress, and then attached high esteem to lines of kinship and assigned great value to them [*ʿaẓẓama amr al-ansāb wa-jaʿala lahā qadran*], and on their account [*bi-sababihā*] prohibited fornication and went to great lengths in declaring it evil [*taqbīḥihi*] by way of deterrence and reprimand, and made its commission a vile criminal deed . . . and commended marriage and exhorted people to it.[41]

It is a text remarkable for the depth of its resonance, and one need only scratch lightly over its surface to pick up a wealth of terms that throw down bridges to the concerns familiar to us from both the theological and legal domains. *Nasal* and *nasab* are terms that instantly recall us to legal theory and its enumeration of the five objectives, as does the term *iḍṭarra* to speak of the sexual desire that compels us to reproduction, which recalls us to legal talk of *ḍarūrāt*. Something similar will be said about the reference to adultery (*sifāḥ*) and the familiar instrumental connection drawn between the prohibition of adultery and the preservation of family lines. What will be especially striking given our questions is the emphasis al-Ghazālī appears to lay on God's evaluative activity in these remarks. "*Attached* esteem," "*assigned* value" (notice also the telltale *kalām* term: *taqbīḥ*): with these remarks, the value attaching to the good in question—reproductive activity and family life—appears to be starkly proclaimed as the product of God's willful assignment. Translated into the terms of legal theory, the message foreshadowed by these introductory remarks seems clear: the value of this good has to be sought in God's intentions. God installs sexual desire, God assigns value to its effects, God assigns disvalue to actions that undermine the good in question.

Indeed the term *maqṣūd*, when it makes its first notable appearance in the body of the discussion, seems to have God as its subject of predication. Listing the benefits of marriage, al-Ghazālī begins with the first, reproduction, and states: "This is the foundation, and the reason for which marriage was instituted; the purpose [*maqṣūd*] is propagation [*ibqāʾ al-nasal*], and that the world should not be free from the human species; and [sexual] appetite was created as a motive force that incites [*innamā al-shahwa khuliqat bāʿitha mustaḥiththa*]."[42] Yet the objective notion of divinely intended benefit (*fāʾida*) is certainly not the only level on which the notion of intention registers within al-Ghazālī's discussion. This emerges clearly when he turns to compare some of the benefits of marriage he has enumerated, and he refers to its advantage as a means of gaining rest, especially from intellectual and spiritual labors, through the lightening effect of female company. "Few people," he remarks, "seek marriage on its account"; by contrast, "the desire for children and the desire to manage [sexual] appetite and the like are widely in evidence [*ammā qaṣdu al-walad wa-qaṣdu dafʿ al-shahwa wa-amthāluhā fa-huwa mimmā yakthuru*]."[43] At work beside divine intention, this signals, is also the subjective experience of human desire.

And how, one may ask, could it have been otherwise? For even if we had worked through these statements with perfect scholarly neutrality, as ordinary readers we could not have accepted any other conclusion without abandoning common sense and without flouting the basic facts of our own experience. That people need shelter; that people need to earn a living and desire the possession of goods; that people, now, seek marriage out of a desire for children—none could have denied the status of these needs and desires as belonging to the content of experience and declared them to be prescriptions externally imposed on human beings from the otherworldly vantage point of the mind of God.

Elsewhere in his discussion, al-Ghazālī points to a crucial modification in the way we understand this choice, suggesting that there are many ways of reading the mind of God and that our own mind (our own desires) can serve as the vehicle through which God's mind receives its expression. To the extent that our desires derive from our body as this has been fashioned by God—*musabbib al-asbāb*, Disposer of causes—they offer themselves as yet another form of divine script from which God's purposes may be read off. In this respect, we hardly needed God's verbal command (through the intermediary of His Prophet) "Marry and beget children!" to learn of God's intentions. We can read this command no less imperiously off His human works and the language of their natural construction. Our own desire is then a sign, and points beyond itself.[44] To register this point fully would be to raise finer-grained questions about what it means to be the proper subject of a need or a desire and what it is for a desire or an intention to be distinguished as "human" as against "divine." All we need to retain of this more complex message at present—a message, notably, that, in heavily invoking the language of God's wisdom and purpose, brings al-Ghazālī into special tension with the Ashʿarite viewpoint—is its entailment: a coincidence between the intentions of human beings and those of God and an explicit acknowledgment that the goods promoted by the Law form objects of our own natural desire. And this, as I have suggested, is an acknowledgment that would find its echo, albeit more implicitly, in al-Ghazālī's other works and the works of those using the language of *ḍarūra* and sharing in its presuppositions.

If we were looking for another and perhaps less contentious avowal of this view, we could find it by turning to the work of the later Ashʿarite jurist and theologian al-Āmidī. Opening his discussion of "suitability" in *al-Iḥkām fī uṣūl al-aḥkām*, he begins by addressing the notion of the aim or objective (*maqṣūd*) of legal norms, and there he offers the following statement: "The intended object of instituting a given ruling is either the promotion of welfare, or the repulsion of harm, or the combination of the above, with respect to human beings—God being far above the reach of harm or benefit. And this may form the object of human intention insofar as it suits one and agrees with one [*rubbamā kāna dhālika maqṣūdan li'l-'abd li-annahu mulā'im lahu wa-muwāfiq li-nafsihi*]. Thus, if [*idhā*] a being endowed with reason [*al-'āqil*] is given a choice between its existence and its nonexistence, he chooses its existence over its nonexistence."[45] The ambiguity of this strategic *rubbamā* may hold us up for a moment: should we hear this as a *sometimes* or a *possibly*? Yet whichever way we hear it, and combined with the reference to reason (*al-'āqil*) that points us to an epistemic state of being prior to or independent of the Law—one further buttressed by the implications of the real conditional *idhā*—the concession to human intention seems to stand out plainly.

Should we remain unconvinced, several other moments in al-Āmidī's discussion ply us with additional evidence. Particularly significant here is an invocation of the notion of *'āda* (custom, habit) that shows this notion to have undergone a subtle but telling displacement from the meaning we earlier documented in the legal work of al-Ghazālī.[46] The reference to the human domain is no longer a paradigm used to illustrate the way we understand God's textual behavior and read the Law's objectives off the latter ("as we observe human behavior, so we observe the behavior of the Law"). Human behavior or "custom" serves as an object of observation in its own right, and the objectives promoted by the Law appear to coincide with the objectives of human beings as we can read them from their natural behavior. Speaking about the highest level of the five *ḍarūriyyāt*: "The restriction to these five classes *arises from consideration of the facts* [or reality: *naẓaran ila'l-wāqi'*], and from the knowledge that there is no necessary aim that lies outside these in the ordinary course of things [*fi'l-'āda*]." Even more clearly, speaking about "improvements" (*taḥsīniyyāt*), exemplified by the Law's denying slaves the right to provide testimony: given the lowly position of a slave and the dignity of testimony, "the office of testimony does not befit him . . . *in accordance with what people are accustomed to and the customs they deem commendable* [*jaryan li'l-nās 'alā mā alifūhu wa-mā 'addūhu min maḥāsin al-'ādāt*]."[47] With this background to frame it, the experiential notion of need embedded in al-Āmidī's language (*mā tad'ū ḥājat al-nās ilayhi*, we hear), as in that of his predecessors, can be heard more openly, its implicit message now explicit before us.

It is this view of custom that Weiss, commenting on this dimension of al-Āmidī's legal thought, put pithily in the following summation:

> As we reflect upon the human part of the created order, that is to say, upon human life, we discover patterns of need and aspiration that are as much a part of the divine custom as patterns visible in the nonhuman part of

> the created order, such as the daily rising and setting of the sun. We discover that there are recurring human conditions that constitute well-being (*maṣlaḥa, manfaʿa*) and that there are other such conditions that constitute affliction (*maḍarra*); and we also discover that certain things are conducive to well-being and certain others to affliction. We discover, for example, that security of life, rationality, lineage, property, and even worship of God are constitutive of well-being and that certain concrete measures or social arrangements are conducive to their realization. These discoveries in no way depend upon revelation as mediated through prophets.[48]

The analogy struck by Weiss between the human and the nonhuman domain is instructive. It reminds us, on the one hand, that whatever we might make of the epistemological question we have been asking—How do we know the interests promoted by the Law?—it is God's creative arrangement of the world that determines that human beings experience certain things as goods or that certain courses of action lead to the realization of certain goods, and thus God's imparting of ontological structure that determines what can constitute an "interest" in both its intrinsic and instrumental senses. (Compare al-Ghazālī's remarks in the *Iḥyā*ʾ above.) By the same token, it calls attention to the fact that to affirm that the interests promoted by the Law are known by reason does not entail an abandonment of the hermeneutical stance, or indeed of the divine text (custom) as the hermeneutical object. It is only a matter of one divine text being replaced with another, for both the regularities of human life and the regularities of the scriptural texts share their character as a divinely composed script.

In emphasizing the Ashʿarite acceptance of a "rational," that is to say prerevelational, knowledge of the interests served by the Law, Weiss's voice joins that of several other readers of Ashʿarite legal texts converging on the thought that, whatever the prejudices of Ashʿarite ethics may have groomed us to expect, this position enjoyed an appeal among prominent Ashʿarite jurists.[49] It is a position, I observed earlier, that would seem to be in conflict with the more limited view of the intuitive evaluative grasp of human beings that Ashʿarite thinkers had taken elsewhere. And yet I would argue that the conflict here does not run as deep as may appear.

For on the one hand, Ashʿarite thinkers had indeed often emphasized the fact that only the Law informs us of the value of actions—a mere corollary of the fact that it *creates* it. It does so, as al-Ghazālī had put it in the *Iqtiṣād*, when God freely chooses to attach (*rabaṭa, anāṭa*) consequences to actions that "tip" them (*rajjaḥa*) into the domain of obligation or into the domain of prohibition.[50] Yet the emphasis in this picture had fallen primarily on the consequences of actions in the *otherworldly* domain, that is, reward and punishment. There is nothing "in" actions that makes them naturally attract reward or punishment; it is merely an artificial act of attachment or *ta ʿalluq* on the part of God. The corresponding emphasis, epistemologically, was on the human inability to know the posthumous consequences of actions. This is evident, for example, in al-Ghazālī's remark in the *Iḥyāʾ* that reason cannot gain insight into "harm after death" (*al-ḍarar baʿda al-mawt*). It is also implicit in many of the juridical definitions of legal qualifications, which are framed in terms of consequences in the otherworldly domain. Here is al-Ghazālī again, defining "prohibition" in the *Mustaṣfā*: that act is prohibited "whose commission one has been given to understand will be punished *in the hereafter* [*mā ushʿira bi-ʿiqāb fiʾl-ākhira ʿalā fiʿlihi*]."[51] The interests served by the Law, by contrast, take the worldly domain as their immediate frame of reference. The five objectives, several jurists including al-Rāzī and al-Qarāfī explicitly state, represent "mundane interests" (*maṣāliḥ al-dunyā*).[52]

This observation must be complemented by an even more fundamental one, which helps put in perspective the epistemological concession Ashʿarite jurists were offering in acknowledging that human beings independently recognize the value of the goods the Law aims to promote. For this concession, as the foregoing discussion suggests, needs to be located against the same epistemological horizon that Ashʿarites had described in their theological works. The evaluative "knowledge" at issue is a knowledge grounded in desire, indeed knowledge *of* desire. We know that property, offspring, and the integrity of our life are goods in the sense that we are compelled (*muḍṭarr*) to seek them—we experience a visceral need for them. This continuity is at times lit up by clear linguistic markers. Discussing the natural desire for reproduction in the *Iḥyāʾ*, thus, al-Ghazālī had spoken of God's creation of sexual desire (*shahwa*) as a motive force (*bāʿitha mustaḥiththa*) that incites people to procreation. These terms (*bāʿith, mustaḥithth*) were ones he elsewhere linked with the notion of *ṭabʿ*—a notion in turn appearing copiously in the *Iḥyāʾ* to refer to our natural inclinations—when addressing the question of ethics.[53] The evaluative vision deriving from natural needs and desires, it is worth recalling here, was a vision indexed to the first-person singular: what each person naturally desires is what is good for himself. (Al-Ghazālī: "Every person is formed by nature to love himself").

Seen from this perspective, al-Ghazālī's concession that we rationally recognize an interest promoted by the Law—that of *nasal*—as a good may appear in a different light. For if all that means is that we naturally desire to reproduce, it does not immediately follow from that desire that its satisfaction outside marriage is wrong—as the Law, in proscribing adultery for the protection of this good, declares. The desire for reproduction would seem indifferent to the means used to achieve it. Similarly, from the fact that we desire certain goods for our sustenance, it does not follow that the satisfaction of this desire using goods that belong to other people is wrong—as the Law, in proscribing theft for the protection of property, declares. This suggests that the object of human desire (what our desire "sees" as good) and the object of the Law (what the Law promotes as a good) do not coincide. And they fail to do so for reasons that directly evoke the reasons put forward in an earlier chapter in proposing that the evaluative knowledge provided by the human *fiṭra*, within Ibn Taymiyya's framework, must be more limited than initially apparent. Natural desire needs to be ordered normatively by the Law. Or again, what is subjectively held to be good needs to be modified by more objective conceptions of the good.

If one wished to plot the distance between the surface of our preexisting evaluative comprehension and the surface of the evaluative comprehension introduced by the Law—between human *maqāṣid* and *maqāṣid al-sharīʿa*—one might hazard the following schematization. On the one hand, the Law introduces a new, "deontological" element of normativity into our relationship with the goods at stake. The interest or good of human life, to take one example, is vouchsafed by God's institution of a prohibition against its removal (*al-qaḍāʾ bi-taḥrīm al-qatl*), which finds its counterpart in the institution of a worldly punishment for its violation (*ījāb al-qiṣāṣ*).[54] A good that we already valued from our subjective perspective is thereby provided with normative scaffolding by becoming the object of a command that faces in two directions. With the first, the good of human life acquires a normative character: it is obligatory to protect it and forbidden to violate it. The second supports this character by setting up sanctions in this world, which are complemented by sanctions in the next—the ultimate court in which the normative claims of mundane life are settled. In this way God provides our sense of what is valuable with normative force and places it under normative limits. Reaching for a vocabulary that formed the lingua franca of the legal tradition, we might say that what the Law does is to set up a normative structure of *ḥuqūq*-claims that enshrines and promotes our interests or *maṣāliḥ*, reminding us again of the intimate relationship between these two concepts. (*Ḥaqq al-ʿabd maṣāliḥuhu*, in the already-cited words of al-Qarāfī). This conversion of the teleological into the deontological, of *maṣlaḥa* into *ḥaqq*, also marks the entry of this good into the social world. For the integrity of human life, the possession of property, or the integrity of family lines are goods that constitute *maṣāliḥ* for the individual enjoying them. But when this *maṣlaḥa* confronts other human beings, it faces them as a *ḥaqq*—as something that limits their free action.[55]

The Law provides goods with normative force, partly by supporting them with sanctions. Put in a more consequentialist idiom, on the other hand, what the Law does is to show us the means through which these goods can best be achieved. The prohibition of adultery and the punishment instituted for its commission, to take one example, are related to the interest of *nasab/nasal* or progeny as means to end. Adultery causally undermines this interest for reasons that al-Ghazālī would indicate in his *Shifāʾ al-ghalīl* and al-Rāzī would repeat almost verbatim in his *Maḥṣūl*. Unchecked sexual relations, al-Ghazālī would write, lead to competition, to confused genealogical lines and uncertain paternity and thus to neglect of one's responsibility to care (*taʿahhud*) for one's children, as well as to violence and aggression. Punishment for adultery, on the other side, promotes this interest through its deterring effect (*zajr*).[56] It is this consequentialist vantage point that would unsurprisingly dominate legal writings addressing the place of interests in the Law, in which specific rulings would be related to their intended purposes as means to ends or causes to effects. Much of the finer print of the Law—its detailed provisions for the application of particular rulings, or what al-Juwaynī would refer to in his *Burhān* as particular "cases and degrees" (*al-ḥālāt waʾl-darajāt*)—would seem to fall under this same logic. Having extended its protection to the good of human life by punishing homicide with retaliation, for example, the Law also clarifies that this good is safeguarded most efficiently if retaliation is exacted without regard for the nature of the weapon employed by the perpetrator, punishing equally acts carried out with a sharp or a blunt weapon. Or again, it clarifies that it is safeguarded best by modifying the principle of equal requital that operates in ordinary circumstances so that where a group of individuals commit an act of homicide in concert, many may be killed in retaliation for one.[57]

Thus, while we might "recognize" the goods the Law promotes in the sense that we possess needs and desires broadly directed to these goods—and might thus be said to have a general command of the "what" of value—the Law comes to provide us with a normative framework for the pursuit of these desires. It likewise comes to inform us of the principles by means of which these goods can be achieved (the "how"). The fact that we need the Law to provide us with this knowledge does not preclude that we should be able to discern the underlying rationale in hindsight, when it is a matter of cause-and-effect relations—for example, the deleterious effects of adultery on family lines, or the deterring effect of punishment—in the mundane sphere, with whose workings we are to a great extent familiar. "Though human reason may command a view of what is in our interests on a general level [*kulliyyāt*]," we heard al-Juwaynī say in his *Niẓāmiyya* earlier, "it cannot arrive at its details [*tafāṣīl*]." These words, and the same contrast between general and particular, would be echoed again in his legal work *Burhān* (*al-kullī mā yataṭarraqu ilayhi al-ʿaql maʿa nisyān al-tafāṣīl*). Some such understanding of the relationship between the general and the particular as we have outlined it would offer an intuitive way of interpreting these statements and of reconstructing the relationship between the evaluative knowledge of reason (or natural desire) and the evaluative knowledge of revelation.[58]

The Ashʿarite concession that human beings know the goods promoted by the Law *as* goods, the above suggests, need not be understood to involve the acknowledgment of an especially substantive ethical grasp. There is one perspective from which this acknowledgment might come to seem more substantive; and that is if this grasp was taken to be indexed not to the first-person singular but to the first-person plural, and the interests promoted by the Law were taken to be known by ordinary people not in their status as objects of self-interested natural desire but as goods serving the interests of the community as a whole. The interests promoted by the Law have, after all, often been understood to carry a communal dimension, as attested by the frequent translation of *maṣlaḥa* in this context not merely as "interest" but indeed "*public* interest."[59] This reflects the intimate connection in which they stand to the crucial legal concept of the rights or claims of God (*ḥuqūq Allāh*), as distinct from the rights or claims of human beings (*ḥuqūq al-ʿibād*).

Ranging the contents of the Law under these two headings, jurists would often include in the latter most economic transactions, matters of family law, as well as parts of penal law, notably the right to exact retaliation (*qiṣāṣ*); in the former they would include acts of worship, many of the so-called *ḥudūd* punishments, and taxes like *kharāj* and *zakāt*. To hold a right or claim, in the dominant analysis of this concept, is to enjoy the right to waive this claim. Thus the distinction between these two kinds of claims registers as the fact that human beings can freely decide to drop the claims that belong to them—as by waiving a debt or the right to retaliate—yet they cannot decide to waive the claims of God, and God's claims must be unconditionally enforced.[60] Yet this differential ability in turn reflects a point of broader significance about the distinction as articulated by classical jurists, and more specifically a critical dichotomy between the private and the public domain that it maps on to. The notion of *ḥaqq al-ʿibād*, as Baber Johansen has illuminatingly characterized the point in connection with the Ḥanafites, refers us to a network of contractual relationships initiated between isolated individuals and private proprietors, governed by a principle of just exchange whose "relativist" or nonabsolute character Johansen stresses. With the notion of *ḥaqq Allāh*, by contrast, the free exchanges between individual subjects are transcended to the larger community, and the notion of the public sphere and public interest comes into view, bringing with it a claim more absolute in nature. "The term *ḥaqq Allāh*," Johansen writes, "is used to denote those one-sided public demands upon the individual that are legitimized by the *sharīʿa* in the interest of the public"—an interest "free from all individual and selfish demands." The public sphere is "the realm of the absolute, the realm of God."[61] It is the link between God's rights and public interest that in turn forges the link with the state, in charge of the public sphere and responsible for implementing divine rights. While the link between *ḥuqūq Allāh* and *maṣāliḥ ʿāmma* would come to special prominence in the works of Ḥanafite jurists, it is an understanding that enjoyed wider appeal. Ibn Taymiyya himself provides an instance of this in *al-Siyāsa al-sharʿiyya* and elsewhere, when he connects the claims of God with a utility that redounds to the community as a whole (*al-maṣāliḥ al-ʿāmma/ manfaʿatuhā li-muṭlaq al-muslimīn*).[62]

While the objectives of the Law would not seem to be coextensive with God's claims,[63] the two are closely linked to the extent that several of the interests included in these objectives were protected by means of punishments classed as *ḥudūd*—notably, the punishment of apostasy, theft, adultery, false slander, and the consumption of intoxicants—and as such entered the scope of claims of God. This reflects the importance of the interests in question for the community as a whole: it is the entire community that has a stake in upholding religion or safeguarding the rational behavior of individuals, in safeguarding people's enjoyment of their rightful possessions against theft, in maintaining the purity of sexual mores and the order of family life, and in safeguarding individuals' reputation against wrongful damage.[64] It is this communal dimension that Zysow had in mind in addressing the tension between the ethical positions Ashʿarites expressed in their *kalām* writings and the positions they adopted in the context of *uṣūl al-fiqh*. Zysow's conclusion was that "the demands of legal practice produced a considerable mitigation of their anti-objectivism," leading them to acknowledge that God's purposes "could be recognized by the human mind" and recognizing "larger common purposes" alongside "purely personal ends."[65]

Yet if the above account is correct, what the human mind offers us is a knowledge of desire indexed to the first-person singular, which the Law then places under normative limits and brings into contact with the social community. What we possess beforehand is necessity (*ḍarūra*); need (*ḥāja*); desire (al-Ghazālī: *shahwa*). And we may here recall al-Āmidī's pointed phrase about the objective of the Law: "This may form the object of human intention insofar as it suits one and agrees *with oneself* [*mulāʾim lahu wa-muwāfiq li-nafsihi*]." The interests promoted by the Law would seem to be accessible to the human mind not under their description as "common purposes" or "common standards" of action, but under their description as objects of desire, indeed self-interested desire, or precisely what Zysow refers to as "personal ends."[66]

No doubt there is more that could be done to refine our understanding of how the Ashʿarites' conception of the human mind and its ethical capacities unfolded between the competing demands of theology and Law. But for our own argument, it is more important that we should finally turn to the second point identified earlier as a source of tension or competition—and this is where Ashʿarite views touched not on the mind of human beings, but on the mind of God. "God does not have aims or purposes."—"Yet God's Law aims at human welfare." How could such a conflict be resolved? The overall evidence in fact indicates that it is this conflict—the one generated by the use of the language of "purpose" in legal discourse and its programmatic denial in theological discourse—that Ashʿarite jurists perceived as a more pressing source of intellectual instability and that figured as the object of more intense preoccupation. Yet the conflict, they would suggest, was not irremovable. There were definite strategies by which it could be addressed without sacrifice of theological conviction.

Even those like al-Ghazālī who were prepared (at least in their more liberal moments, as in the *Shifāʾ al-ghalīl*) to accord an important role to reason in the knowledge of the interests promoted by the Law would in the same context draw the line at the implication that purpose should be attributed to God. Yet they would do so in ways immediately calculated to fuel afresh the accusations of their adversaries. Al-Ghazālī would thus write: God "intended [*arāda*] the welfare of people in both their religious and mundane affairs." Yet he would continue in the next breath: "God is above being affected by purposes and being altered by motivating incentives or disincentives." And then again: "Yet [laws] were legislated for the interests of people [*shurriʿat li-maṣāliḥ al-khalq*]."[67] Both intending and above intention; both an open statement denying divine purpose and an ascription of purpose through the prepositional structures (*shurriʿat li*) registering in the next moment—flagrant contradiction, the Ashʿarites' critics might say, if there ever was one.

Such apparent contradictions would be found in the work of other Ashʿarite jurists, and to the extent that one wished to speak about the aims of the Law and the interests that explained its rulings, they would seem ineradicable. The solution could not be to abandon this language—a language that, as we have seen, the Ashʿarites themselves had a large hand in cementing within legal discourse. It was not about avoiding the forms of language, but rather about renegotiating the commitments such use of language was understood to involve, and more specifically about reconceptualizing the meaning of one's words in ways that made it possible to bring the commitments of theology and law into fuller harmony. As al-Qarāfī would succinctly put the Ashʿarite solution in his *Nafāʾis al-uṣūl: al-ittifāq fiʾl-iṭlāq waʾl-ikhtilāf fiʾl-maʿnā*. We all agree on the words to be spoken; what is in dispute is how these words should be understood.[68]

The words, and their truer meaning; the language, and its interpretation. The kind of renegotiation that was possible here was already adumbrated by al-Ghazālī in his *Shifāʾ al-ghalīl*, when, right on the heels of the remarks we just heard, he had written: the Law is promoted for the sake of human interests, yet "we understand this through the Law, and not through reason." This statement may remind us of his earlier remarks about how we discover *which* specific interests are promoted by the Law, namely through a detailed observation of the textual "behavior" of the Law (*taṣarrufāt al-sharʿ*). The present statement, addressing itself more directly to the question of how we discover *that* the Law is promoted for human interests, registers as the broader counterpart of that point. This "quasi-empiricist," "bottom-up" method of establishing the Law's concern with human welfare, as Ahmed El Shamsy has recently suggested, was in fact central to post-Ghazālian Ashʿarites' response to the "rationalist," "top-down" method associated with the Mu'tazilites, who deduced this thesis from a priori assumptions about God's moral character.[69]

Yet how, al-Ghazālī's readers will wonder, could the means by which we discover the truth of this proposition affect its substance—that God acts and commands with purposes—and thereby remove its thorn? Almost a century later, it is al-Rāzī who would offer the clearest Ash'arite answer to this question by comparing the relationship between legal norms and human interests to the relationship between events in the natural world. Consider the way satiation occurs after (*'aqība*) eating, burning upon (*'inda*) contact with fire, and so on with familiar natural phenomena. These natural connections are not necessary (*wājib*); they only represent the way God has made it His custom (*ajrā al-'āda*), albeit a reliable custom, that events should be arranged, regularly following one another without real causal bonds subsisting between them. This is how we should understand the connections between legal rulings and human interests, *aḥkām* and *maṣāliḥ*. There is correlation but not causation; and this is a correlation, significantly, that is known through the Law—through a reading of God's scriptural custom modeled on the reading of God's custom as expressed in the text of the natural world and sharing the same principled denial of real causation.[70]

Many of the linchpin terms employed by al-Rāzī point back to al-Ghazālī's discussion. And they would travel down the works of ensuing generations of Ash'arite thinkers, with whom the key distinctions would become progressively clearer and the claim would step into sharper light. At its heart lay a denial of necessity parsed in different yet closely related forms. Ontologically, it involved a denial that the conjunction between legal rulings and human interests was necessary in the sense that this conjunction was not upheld by the causal force of divine intention. This was paired to a denial that the conjunction was upheld by the normative force of a moral obligation, which was what the Mu'tazilites had argued, claiming that God was *obliged* to promote human interests in the religious domain (at least once He had placed them under the moral Law). The conjunction in question, Ash'arites maintained, was not a matter of necessity but a matter of contingent fact (not *wujūb* but *ittifāq*).[71] The denial of causal and normative force on the ontological level had an immediate corollary on the epistemological level. For if the connection between legal provisions and human interests is known only through an inductive reading of scripture (*istiqrā'*), and not as the entailment of a rationally self-evident moral principle to which God's behavior is necessarily subject, what results is not certainty but probability (*ẓann*).

What this renegotiation of "language as against its interpretation" seemed to amount to was epistemology without ontology; a justification of our usage of certain notions while denying them ontological foundation. Al-Āmidī would put the point with particular suggestiveness in his own discussion of the question in the *Iḥkām* when he would write: even if God's acting purposefully is not necessary (*wājib*), as the Ashʿarites hold, "His acting with an intention is more congenial to rational understanding than His acting without an intention; so an intention follows from His action by way of probability [*fiʿluhu liʾl-maqṣūd yakūnu aqrab ilā muwāfaqat al-maʿqūl min fiʿlihi bi-ghayr maqṣūd; fa-kāna al-maqṣūd lāziman min fiʿlihi ẓannan*]."[72] This remark invites us to turn our attention away from the reality of God's action and to focus on the way human beings perceive this reality. On that level, we may see that the ascription of purpose to divine action is in greater agreement with our forms of thought and the forms (customs) of human life, given the deep-rooted presence of notions of purpose and intention within them. (Contemporary thinkers might have said: human beings just can't help adopting the "intentional stance.") As such, we may continue to discuss divine action in these terms—we may call this a kind of license or *rukhṣa*, granted in recognition of our characteristic epistemic needs as human beings. Yet our use of such notions, it should not be forgotten on a higher-order level, represents merely the human way of rationalizing the Sharīʿa, and the notion of purpose is but a projection of the human mind without claim on divine reality.

With these distinctions and qualifications in place, however, many Ashʿarite jurists would affirm that God's rulings were instituted for the sake of human interests. In his theological work *al-Arbaʿīn fī uṣūl al-dīn*, al-Rāzī would describe the Muʿtazilite view that "God's actions and rulings are explained [*muʿallala*] in terms of the promotion of human welfare" as "the preferred view of most later jurists" and declare his own refusal to join this chorus.[73] Yet it is important to note that this was a refusal to join a chorus singing not the language of purposefulness—this was etched far too deeply into the existing vision of the Law to disclaim it—but a substantial interpretation of this language in more robust ontological terms, through a more realist concept of causation that al-Rāzī and many of his Ashʿarite colleagues rejected. It is a view, admittedly, that would be maintained with a sense of tension and accompanied by phenomena suggestive of open contradiction—between the statements of different thinkers, between the statements of single thinkers across different works, or even the statements of single thinkers within single works (as exemplified above by al-Ghazālī).[74] In demanding the displacement of words from their ordinary meanings and indeed the suspension of basic forms of the human mind, the wedge between language and its interpretation required special exertions to be held in place.

Thematizing Wisdom: Why Does God Command?

I began this chapter by suggesting that neither the relative nor the positive aspects of Ibn Taymiyya's *via media*—neither his relationship to his topography nor the content of his distinctive contribution—could be appreciated without making the move to the theological context. I then drew into focus Ibn Taymiyya's oft-voiced criticism of the Ashʿarites for their failure to acknowledge that God's legislative activity is governed by His wisdom, and more specifically by human interests. God's will is not brute, but tempered by a concern with human welfare. Having sifted more carefully through the tensions in the Ashʿarite view of the mind of human beings and the mind of God between theology and law, it is on the second of these two issues that we must concentrate as the most relevant context for our present concern. Having brought Ibn Taymiyya's conflict with the Ashʿarites into sharper view, we will then have the leverage we need for addressing his understanding on more positive terms.

In their theological writings, as we have seen, the Ashʿarites had provided sufficient material for Ibn Taymiyya's accusations, denying that the notion of purpose could be predicated of God in any fashion. In their legal writings, by contrast, they had integrated the thesis that the Law promotes human welfare deeply into the methods of legal reasoning. They had done so, however, by offering an interpretation of this thesis that defanged it from its ontological implications. To that extent, the justice of Ibn Taymiyya's criticism of the Ashʿarites would seem to hang on the delicate divide separating an affirmation from its interpretation. In many of his critical remarks about the Ashʿarite view, Ibn Taymiyya does not appear to mark this divide. Yet elsewhere, he offers clear signals that it is the affirmation as modified by this interpretation that gives him cause for concern, as when in *Sharḥ al-Iṣbahāniyya* he critically rehearses the Ashʿarite view as the claim that when something appears to serve human welfare, "this is nothing but a conjunction [*mujarrad iqtirān*] that forms part of [God's] custom without His effecting this through causes [*bi-sabab*] in any way and without His acting for the sake of a wise purpose [*li-ḥikma*] in any way." The claim that the Law's aim to promote human interests is known only through an inductive reading of scripture (*istiqrāʾ*) is also isolated for explicit critique.[75]

The divide between affirmation and interpretation may at first sight strike us as a gossamer one; yet closer consideration will suggest otherwise. For taken as a divide between the way things *seem* and the way things *are*, it surely makes all the difference as to whether we can think of God as having what I earlier called a "morality," as against the mere appearance of one. If the Ashʿarites had proposed epistemological appearance without ontological reality, in fact—things may *look* purposeful, but they really *are not*—it will be telling to observe that Ibn Taymiyya elsewhere proposed a precise reversal of this order of priority: even if things do *not* look purposeful, they nevertheless in themselves are. Bringing up the question of God's wisdom in *Bayān talbīs al-jahmiyya*, Ibn Taymiyya raised a doubt about our ability to ask "Why?" of God's actions and expect to uncover definite answers. Yet "to deny the existence of a thing is not the same as to deny one's knowledge of it"; thus to deny that "Why?" can be asked of God's actions is "not to deny the existence of a wise purpose [*ḥikma*] which forms His intended end in the reality of things [*fī nafs al-amr*]."[76]

No less interesting than this resounding embrace of objectivist language to speak of God's wisdom will be the ligaments such language forges with a view that once again formed the characteristic preserve of Muʿtazilite thinkers. It is a point Muʿtazilite theologians had notably emphasized in the context of their analysis of scriptural prescriptions and prohibitions, which, as we have seen, they grounded primarily in their utility. Yet to know in general—by way of *jumla—that* these provisions serve our welfare is not to say that we will invariably know *why* or *how* do they do so. More broadly, "it is not necessary," in the words of ʿAbd al-Jabbār, "that one should know the specific ground of wisdom [*wajh al-ḥikma*] in every single one of [God's] acts." So long as we have a firm belief that God is good and always acts wisely, we will know that every one of His acts conforms to the same principle and that there is a hidden wisdom at work in them.[77] This is a view that had achieved a wider appeal among thinkers who acknowledged that the Law promotes human interests. A noteworthy case here is Ibn ʿAqīl, who had expressed a similar view in his legal work *al-Wāḍiḥ fī uṣūl al-fiqh*, and to whom Ibn Taymiyya himself attributes a position very close to the one we just heard in *Bayān talbīs*. He "affirmed God's wisdom in general but declared himself incapable of giving an account of its particulars [*yuthbitu al-ḥikma wa'l-taʿlīl min ḥayth al-jumla wa-yuqirru bi'l-ʿajz ʿan al-tafṣīl*]."[78]

Not merely an appearance of wisdom but a reality—a reality robust enough to survive our ignorance of it. It is in this strong claim that we could locate one of the most fundamental rifts between Ibn Taymiyya's and the Ashʿarites' ethical-theological understanding. And it is a deeper examination of this claim, by the same token, that would seem to hold the key to a more positive understanding of Ibn Taymiyya's distinctive theological viewpoint. The morality of God may not be the morality of human beings; yet God's acts are not free from governing standards. God acts according to standards and out of reasons that allow us to speak of His wisdom and justice in more substantive ways.

My aim for the remainder of this chapter will be to probe this view more closely and to unpack the notion of "reasons" or "standards" to the greatest extent that it allows. In doing so, I will not be attempting an exhaustive overview of Ibn Taymiyya's understanding of divine wisdom. I will not, for example, be offering a comprehensive reading of Ibn Taymiyya's response to the burning question of theodicy: How to explain the existence of suffering? (Though this is a question that will come into view.) Instead, I will focus on two main topics: God's reasons for commanding human actions (the topic of this section) and God's reasons for punishing human actions (the topic of the next). Underpinning my train of investigation will be a question about how the standards that govern God's actions relate to the standards that govern those of human beings as we earlier saw them—two sets of standards that Ibn Taymiyya himself has carved steeply apart—and how the kinds of considerations we examined in earlier chapters, consequentialist and deontological, figure within the content of God's distinctive morality. And although my task will be to elicit Ibn Taymiyya's positive understanding, once again this task cannot be pursued without a parallel engagement of the ways Ibn Taymiyya's understanding relates to his theological interlocutors'.

WHY DOES GOD command the actions He does? The insistence that the question "Why?" can be asked at this juncture shapes Ibn Taymiyya's remarks about divine wisdom throughout his work. Both in the domain of God's creative activity (*khalq*) and the domain of His legislative activity (*amr*), God's choices are not the result of mere arbitrary will. There is something "in the reality of things" that weights (*yurajjiḥu*) God's will toward commanding one action as against another. We heard Ibn Taymiyya frame this point clearly in the stage-setting exposition of his *via media* that reopened this chapter.

Yet for readers familiar with the Western philosophical tradition, Ibn Taymiyya nowhere opens up the space for asking "Why?" more evocatively than when he restates his claim that God *commands* acts wisely as a claim that God *loves* the acts He commands. The Ashʿarite view of God's command, we hear in *Sharḥ al-Iṣbahāniyya*, is flawed insofar as it is "premised on the notion that all entities and acts are equal in actual reality [*sawāʾ fī nafs al-amr*], and that some of these do not contain an attribute that necessitates [*tūjibu*] their being preferred over others, so that God might love [*yuḥibbu*] the one and command it, and hate the other and forbid it." Love, we hear even more distinctly elsewhere, "must be grounded in a quality [*maʿnā*] in the object of love that is beloved to the one who loves it [*inna al-maḥabba lā takūnu illā li-maʿnan fiʾl-maḥbūb yuḥibbuhu al-muḥibb*]."[79] The terms of Socrates's question—"Is that which is holy loved by the gods because it is holy, or is it holy because it is loved by the gods?"—would seem to stand reembodied before us. And so would a vigorous avowal of the view that the order of priority is the one reflected in the first of these options. God's will does not create value: it responds to it.

The responsiveness of God's attitudes is highlighted with unusual force in the following passage from the *Fatāwā*, which focuses more directly on God's creative rather than legislative activity:

> God is knowing and wise, so He knows things as they are in themselves, and He is wise in what He loves and wills, what He speaks, what He commands and what He does. So if He knows that a given act and a given thing is characterized by that which renders it worthy of blame [*madhmūm*] and deserving [*mustaḥiqq*] of hatred and repugnance, it is part of His wisdom that He should hate it and find it repugnant. And if He knows that

> by coming into existence it will help realize a praiseworthy and beloved wise purpose [*ḥikma maḥbūba maḥmūda*], it is part of His wisdom that He should create it and will it on account of [*li-ajl*] this beloved wise purpose which it serves to realize.[80]

God's responses follow the intrinsic merit of things in themselves: when He loves something, it is because that thing *deserves* to be loved. His responses are based on His knowledge of the way things are in themselves. This last point will remind us of a peculiar affirmation the Muʿtazilites had made when describing God's relationship to ethical qualities.[81]

There will be something more to say about the status of the notion of "love" within Ibn Taymiyya's thinking shortly. Yet our immediate task must be to turn our attention to the notion of "the reality of things" or "the way things are in themselves" that Ibn Taymiyya has deployed to consider it more closely. It is a reality that Ibn Taymiyya has called up as a ground for God's actions, and more specifically for His commands. What is that ground? Put more relevantly, the question we must ask here is: What *are* those aspects of actions that provide grounds for God's commands? Turning back now to our stage-setting exposition, we may recall Ibn Taymiyya's complaint against the Ashʿarites: they had claimed that "what is right [*maʿrūf*] is not right in itself [*fī nafsihi*] . . . nor is what is wrong [*munkar*] in itself wrong." And we will recall his positive view: "God is knowing and wise [*ḥakīm*], and knowing the benefits that qualifications comprise [*mā tataḍammanuhu al-aḥkām min al-maṣāliḥ*], He issued commands and prohibitions based on His knowledge of the benefits and harms that commands and prohibitions . . . involve for His servants." The implication of the second statement is obvious, and it extends a simple answer to the question we have just asked that ties in naturally with everything we have heard so far about Ibn Taymiyya's ethical understanding. The reason God commands human beings to undertake certain actions as against others is because these actions serve their welfare. It is the beneficial tendency of actions that forms the aspect of their "actual reality" which makes God love them and hate them.

This answer presents itself so naturally that there might appear to be little space for even considering alternatives. Yet the earlier thread of our inquiry brought us up against an important alternative when, engaging Ibn Taymiyya's ethical discussion at a similar juncture, we asked just how the notions of "right" and "wrong," and indeed specific acts such as justice or truth-telling which Ibn Taymiyya mentions in the same vicinity, relate to the emphasis on welfare that dominates the context. My argument in previous chapters was that Ibn Taymiyya reduces such deontological-sounding types of acts to their utility: both what *makes* such acts good, and the description under which people *know* them to be good (or *desire* them as good), is their utility. Given the wedge that he has driven between the ethical domain and the divine, however, what holds true of the latter is a case that would have to be made separately. Concretized into a focus question, we may ask: Does God command justice because it is beneficial to people, or does He command it because it is intrinsically good?

There are certainly places in Ibn Taymiyya's work where he gives signs of being invested in a claim of the latter kind. A case in point is his articulation of an idea that marks yet another confrontation with a typically Ashʿarite viewpoint, the idea of God's "self-binding." It is an idea that is best read as a response to the question: Can God do evil? This is a question that leans upon the answer one gives to the prior question: What *is* evil? Ashʿarites, as we have briefly seen, had placed God beyond the definitional reach of "evil" by specifying this concept in terms of conformity with God's command and (later on) conformity with natural desires. And they had then drawn the natural conclusion: God can do anything He pleases. All that *we* can rely on in order to predict His behavior—to know, for example, that He will not consign pious believers to hellfire—is His self-report (*khabar*) that He will not in fact do a given thing, which corresponds to His knowledge that He will not do it. Reporting this view in his commentary on a well-known hadith by Abū Dharr, Ibn Taymiyya would reject it on two grounds. The Ashʿarite view fails to tell us *why* God will act the way He does—only *that* he will do so (*lā yubayyinu wajh fiʿlihi wa-tarkihi/ mā yadʿū ilaʾl-fiʿl wa-lā ilaʾl-tark*); and it fails to provide an account of God's action that presents it as *praiseworthy* (*bayān li-kawnihi maḥmūdan mamdūḥan ʿalā fiʿl hādhā wa-tark hādhā*).[82] The hadith reported by Abū Dharr provides us with an account that satisfies both criteria. "Oh my servants," it begins, "I have forbidden injustice to myself and rendered it forbidden amongst you." This hadith clarifies that God will not do injustice because He took a free decision to forbid Himself injustice, promising for example to honor people's good deeds by rewarding them.

Ibn Taymiyya's focus, in discussing this topos, falls on God's act of self-binding as a response to the question "Why does God act the way He does?," and he seems peculiarly tight-lipped when it comes to saying anything about the inherent quality of the act of injustice itself which could also figure as a response to this question. He has, after all, prefaced His discussion with a stern reproof against the Muʿtazilites for placing God under a moral "Law" (*sharīʿa*)—a Law they had spelled out precisely in terms of such inherent qualities—and the model of God's self-binding notably serves to emphasize His freedom vis-à-vis the norms of justice. Yet his discussion would appear to rest precisely on some recognition that justice is an ethical norm with antecedent existence and indeed an antecedent positive value from *our* perspective: *hence* the praiseworthiness we see in God's decision to forbid Himself this act.[83]

Yet taking everything together, Ibn Taymiyya gives us limited grounds for thinking that when he speaks of the "reality" of actions he has the independent status of such deontological values in mind. Instead, it is once again the notion of welfare that seems to underpin his understanding of God's reasons for commanding. I said above that the wedge Ibn Taymiyya drives between the human and divine domains means that any argument about the relationship between deontological and consequentialist considerations has to be made separately. But of course many of the evidential bases I examined in chapter 1 when making the case for the reduction of the former to the latter were statements that concerned the role of such considerations *in the Law* and thus in God's legislative activity. "The Law came to realize and perfect [human] interests [*maṣāliḥ*]," we heard. Yet "all that God commanded," we also heard, "reduces to justice."[84] A closer scrutiny suggested that the notion of justice (*ʿadl*) primarily relates to that of welfare (*ṣalāḥ*/*maṣlaḥa*) as means to an end. And this reflects a programmatic conversion of deontological concepts into teleological ones—of *ḥuqūq* into *maṣlaḥa*—that had been enshrined in legal theory in its discourse on the aims of the Law. The aspect under which God safeguards human *ḥuqūq*-claims would seem to be precisely their description as means to human well-being.

In Ibn Taymiyya's ethical remarks, the insistence that acts possess real evaluative features had been intimately linked with an insistence that God's will does not give preference to one of two similar things (*turajjiḥu mithlan ʿalā mithl*) arbitrarily and that there is a factor that "weights" God's will in one direction as against another.[85] Yet we will now recall that it is beneficence that Ibn Taymiyya elsewhere explicitly names as that factor. The objectivist vocabulary he employs in this connection—referring us to how things are "in actual reality" (*fī nafs al-amr*) or to actions' attributes (*ṣifāt*)—is likewise one we saw to be associated with benefit and harm. In *Sharḥ al-Iṣbahāniyya*, Ibn Taymiyya contributes another element to this vocabulary when he stipulates the existence of "something that pertains to [the action]" (*maʿnan yaʿūdu ilayhi*) as the only way of avoiding the unacceptable conclusion that the Lawgiver prefers one of two similar things without a real factor to weight His decision. This explanatory locution will instantly remind us of the terms Ibn Taymiyya used in framing his epitomic consequentialist claim that "the goodness and badness of human actions pertain to [*yarjiʿu ilā*] the benefit and harm acts involve."[86]

It is the axiological notion of *khayr* (good) and *maṣlaḥa* that organize Ibn Taymiyya's understanding of God's wisdom. "God is wise and merciful": "He only does good" (*lā yafʿalu illā khayran*).[87] Yet the primacy of utility in Ibn Taymiyya's conception of God's wisdom is laid bare even more starkly in a specific understanding of the view just framed that achieves pervasive expression in his work and that goes to the heart of some of the questions of theodicy that had held Muslim theologians in thrall for centuries before him. For the claim that God only does good must after all be held in the teeth of the fact that the world we inhabit is not free from evil. There is what has often been called "natural" evil—the pain and suffering that people experience as a result of events in the natural world and as a result of their natural constitution as beings that belong to that world. And there is what we call "moral" evil"—the evil people themselves perpetrate, often causing other people to suffer. In religious schemes, moral evil is typically understood as in turn commuting again to the evil of suffering by way of redress. Both kinds of evil make us ask "Why?" in agonized tones. And the religious commutation of wrongdoing into suffering—indeed of ceaseless suffering in an otherworldly domain in which human beings harvest the consequences of their actions in the present life—often leads to deeper questions about the freedom of human beings to act otherwise.

This is the context in which we must read Ibn Taymiyya's narrower claim that acting wisely is often a matter, not simply of choosing what is absolutely good (*khayr*), but of choosing what is comparatively better. "Wisdom demands giving precedence to the best of two goods by sacrificing the lesser one [*tarjīḥ khayr al-khayrayn bi-tafwīt adnāhumā*]." And again: it is good on the part of a wise agent (*fā ʿil ḥakīm*) to allow the existence of evil (*sharr*) for the sake of a preponderant good (*al-khayr al-arjaḥ*).[88] God acts wisely, this suggests, when He weighs different goods against each other and against the evils they involve and prefers what realizes the greatest amount of good. The terms *khayr* and *sharr* elsewhere give way to the more openly utilitarian language of *maṣāliḥ* and *mafāsid*, and Ibn Taymiyya makes the quantificational character of this act of weighing clear when he refers to the general good that is secured as being "many times the amount" (*aḍ ʿāf*) of the partial evil allowed. This comparative aspect is reflected again in his characterization of the Law's task as that of "giving preponderance to the best of two goods . . . realizing the greatest of two benefits [*a ʿẓam al-maṣlaḥatayn*] by sacrificing the lesser one, and repelling the greatest of two harms [*a ʿẓam al-mafsadatayn*] by tolerating the lesser one."[89]

This last statement may remind us of the kind of weighing of goods against evils indicated by the Qur'an itself as the backdrop of the evaluative qualifications it assigns to particular actions, for example in connection with its prohibition of games of chance and the consumption of wine: "In both is great sin, and (some) utility [*manāfi ʿ*] for men; but the sin of them is greater than their usefulness" (Q 2:219). And while the less teleological notion of "sin" (*ithm*) appears here, we have seen that elsewhere the Qur'an refers the prohibition of intoxicants, in a more strongly teleological register, to their tendency to "excite enmity and hatred" and to "hinder [people] from the remembrance of God, and from prayer" (Q 5:91)—a proof-text that would in turn shadow the jurists' consequentialist analysis of this prohibition.

There will be something more to say in the next chapter about the weighing of conflictual utility considerations just noted. Here it is worth focusing on the different types of questions that Ibn Taymiyya calls attention to in framing his more specific claim regarding the quantitative supremacy of good over evil in God's decisions ("the general good promoted is 'many times the amount' (*aḍʿāf*) of the partial evil allowed"). The context of this remark refers us precisely to those vexed questions of theodicy that had preoccupied earlier theologians when considering the otherworldly destinies of different individuals. Why do some people believe in God and reap the rewards of paradise, while others disbelieve and wind up in the fires of hell? Is this a matter of people making different choices out of their own free will, or is it a matter of God providing special guidance to good-doers or indeed determining their actions? Muʿtazilite theologians had adopted the first view, ascribing to people a strong moral responsibility for their acts. Ashʿarites had countered this proposal with a deterministic view of human action. Ibn Taymiyya himself, as we have seen, highlights God's determining activity in self-conscious opposition to Muʿtazilite thought.[90] It is the presumption that God determines who believes and who fails to that shadows the examples Ibn Taymiyya uses to illustrate his quantitative construal of God's wisdom. Consider the case of Pharaoh and his rejection of Moses's message. Had Pharaoh accepted the message and thereby escaped divine chastisement, there would have been no occasion for the divine signs that have brought untold benefit to humanity and served as an enduring source of spiritual edification. Thus, "those who benefited from this were many many times [*aḍʿāf aḍʿāf*] the amount of those who were harmed by it." Or consider Muhammad's prophetic message. Had many people—including the grandees of Quraysh—not rejected it, there would have been none of the great miracles and signs or the noble war effort (*jihād*) waged by believers. And the saved once again vastly outnumber the damned.[91]

Such cases suggest that any moral evil God allows in the world—evil that translates into suffering for its perpetrators in the next—is outweighed by the moral good and thus the otherworldly happiness this makes possible for others. We may restate this by saying: the happiness of the few is outweighed by the happiness of the many. This is a criterion that prominent thinkers in our intellectual history, particularly our recent history, have considered a perfectly adequate conception of morality. Ibn Taymiyya's account of God's morality echoes nothing if not the axiom of utilitarianism articulated by Bentham: "It is the greatest happiness of the greatest number that is the measure of right and wrong." This, of course, is an axiom that has often been thought challenged to accommodate our ordinary intuitions about justice, bidding us to promote universal welfare with a single-mindedness that is liable to conflict with constraints of a deontological kind we would normally place on actions. Our ordinary intuitions, for example, would suggest that the distinction between persons has real moral weight. In this light, one could not sacrifice the happiness of one person—all the more when what is in question is the ultimate and eternal happiness of that person—for the sake of the happiness of another without moral loss.[92] They would similarly suggest that punishing those who were not free to do otherwise also entails grave moral loss.

Ibn Taymiyya, on the other hand, has made it clear that our ordinary moral intuitions cannot be used as a guide to the ethical standards that are applicable to God. God's morality is not the morality of human beings. God's morality, the above suggests, is framed overwhelmingly in terms of the axiological notions of "good" and "welfare." That much seems plain; nevertheless, it will be important for gaining a fuller insight both into the answers Ibn Taymiyya gives to questions about God's wisdom and also into the questions he does not answer even though they go to the heart of the relationship between God's "praiseworthiness" and sovereignty he wishes to recalibrate, to observe that the kinds of considerations that figure in our intuitions are not entirely excluded from view. Such considerations—or something like them—indeed show up in God's decision making as Ibn Taymiyya reconstructs this, and they come up, crucially, as a negative: as a reason that counts against acting, but that is overridden in favor of a higher good. Ibn Taymiyya makes this clear in a limpid passage:

> God created things for a wise purpose, and He loves that wise purpose and is well pleased with it [*yarḍāhā*]. When He creates what He hates, it is for the sake of what He loves. Those who differentiate between love [*maḥabba*] and will [*irāda*] have said: a sick man wants [*yurīdu*] medicine but does not love it; he loves what it results in, namely restored vigor and elimination of ill health. God created all things according to His will, and He wills everything He has created and the wise purpose that He loves. And even if He does not love certain entities or actions among the things He has created, He loves the wise purpose on account of which [*li-ajlihā*] He created them.

Thus, God may hate acts such as unbelief (*kufr*), wickedness (*fusūq*), and disobedience (*ʿiṣyān*) with regard to their intrinsic features (*bi-iʿtibār mā ittaṣafa bihi min al-ṣifāt al-madhmūma*), but He may love them as a means for achieving something that He loves as an end in itself (*bi-iʿtibār annahu wasīla ilā maḥbūb li-dhātihi*). Do we not, he repeats—reprising the medical metaphor—recognize from experience that we can love something from one perspective and hate it from another?[93]

This remarkable passage is important for several reasons. On the one hand, it brings out a distinction that plays a momentous role within Ibn Taymiyya's articulation of God's wisdom, one that once again takes its context in the competing choices that confronted earlier thinkers approaching the relationship between God's justice and God's sovereignty. The more particular question here was: When human beings act in ways that contravene God's command, how should we qualify the relationship of such acts to God's will? Should we say God *willed* them—and accept the corollary that God might will evil things? Or should we say God *did not will* them—and accept the corollary that things may take place that God would have preferred not to? Ibn Taymiyya's special business would again be with the position adopted by Ashʿarite theologians, whose fervor for God's sovereignty had made them seize the first horn in a dogmatic spirit of either/or without regard for the consequences. For everything indeed happens according to God's will (this Ibn Taymiyya granted); but one may still distinguish between what God wills and what God loves. The Qur'an itself does not collapse these two terms but applies them distinctly to God. The acts God loves are those He commanded, and to thus deny that God loves particular types of acts and hates others is to undermine the religious Law. However far one pushes the recognition of God's sovereignty, one has to make sure one preserves the authority of God's command. Criticizing Ashʿarites like al-Juwaynī for collapsing God's love into His will, Ibn Taymiyya would make central to his own account a distinction between two types of will: God's "ontological" or "determinative" will (*irāda kawniyya/qadariyya*) and God's "legislative" or "religious" will (*irāda sharʿiyya/dīniyya*). The latter he would in turn identify with God's love or good pleasure (*riḍā*), to then claim that God may will all actions *ontologically*, yet He wills *legislatively* the actions He has commanded—and that is equivalent to saying He loves those actions.[94]

This distinction is at the foreground of the passage just cited: God may will things that He does not love, such as wicked deeds and unbelief. What this brings out, of course, is that to the extent that the latter show up as a "negative" in God's decision making, it is not so much by way of nodding to human moral intuitions about what is right as of bowing to God's own express statements about what is commanded. We will be returning to this point from another direction shortly. For our purposes, however, more interesting in the above passage will be the remarkable comparison that drives it. The sick person who shuts his eyes and holds his nose as he washes down a draft of unpleasant medication is a familiar figure in discussions of prudential motivation and was also a fixture in classical Islamic texts. Accept that you must do something unpleasant now, so you can enjoy something more pleasant later. There will be a loss, but you will see that it is dwarfed by the benefits. This mode of reasoning, of course, makes perfect sense for a finite being confronting limited options shaped by the hard facts of the world she inhabits. If you want to get well, the only way of doing so is to tolerate something else you do not want; you can obtain *x* only if you do *y*. Yet how can the application of such reasoning be understood in the context of an unlimited being who shapes the world itself and *makes* the hard facts what they are? Why *must* God suffer a loss?[95] If God's wise purpose can be achieved only on condition that certain bad things happen, this appears to imply that God is limited by certain features of reality that are not amenable to His will. Why couldn't there be a world in which *both* goods could be simultaneously achieved?

This is a question that will seem deeply familiar to students of that long history of philosophical and theological inquiry devoted to asking "Why?" questions about the world and seeking to account for its nature in light of its originating source, often against a sense of discontent with the world as we find it. Why is the world as it is? Could it have been crafted differently? The negative response to this question has been associated with Plato, whose work provided the resources for a philosophical optimism that would travel the length of Western history and find its best-known expression in Leibniz's claim that this is the best of all possible worlds. In the Islamic tradition this view received a powerful articulation in the work of al-Ghazālī. Yet throughout its history, not only among the medieval scholastics but also among philosophers closer to our own time, it is a view that has provoked controversy by appearing to place limitations on God's will, implying that God's choices are dictated by a certain rational order—by a certain sequence or economy of Forms, in one salient understanding—that is independent of His will. It is with reference to the demands of this rational order that we can understand why certain imperfections or evils simply *must* be included in the world God creates.[96] All God can do, at best, is choose among limited possibilities. "Before God decided which of all possible worlds He should choose to make real," Susan Neiman glosses Leibniz's account, "He looked at all the forms, calculated which ones would fit together, and chose the best of all possible combinations." It is as if we see "God comparing essences in a ghostly supermarket"—an uncanny picture that brings to the fore the way that Leibniz has "put reason above God himself." Al-Ghazālī's formulation of this view, in the Islamic context, courted controversy for reasons that resonate with this broader history.[97]

A similar sense of optimism runs through Ibn Taymiyya's remarks and emerges clearly in the oft-made expression that God does not only what is good or what is better, but indeed what is best (*al-aḥsan*). Yet what is striking is that Ibn Taymiyya never appears to squarely confront the implications of this view, namely that there is something in the nature or reality of things that is independent of God's will and that places certain constraints on His options. Having widely emphasized the responsiveness of God's will to real features of the world—the "real" (utility-based) features of actions that *necessitate* (*tūjibu*) that God love and command them, the real cause-effect relations that mean that God *must* accept some amount of evil in order to achieve a greater balance of good—Ibn Taymiyya falls silent when it comes to explaining how this acknowledgment still preserves God from the peculiar impiety the Muʿtazilites had committed in placing God "under a Sharīʿa" and thus presuming the existence of something foreign to His will.[98]

I suggested that Ibn Taymiyya's understanding of God's reasons for commanding, and of God's wisdom more broadly, is chiefly specified in terms of the concept of welfare; then I paused to consider an important implication of his model of God's decision making—an implication that brings to view the critical questions he leaves unanswered in developing it, and that in doing so provides telling indications regarding the depth to which he pushes his account. There will be more to say about the depth of Ibn Taymiyya's development of these theological ideas in the next section. Here we need to move on to a different point that is crucial for providing the main question we have been pursuing with a fuller response. For the capacity of certain actions to promote human welfare indeed forms a central answer to the question "Why does God command particular actions?" or "Why does He love them?"—an answer that Ibn Taymiyya propels to the fore throughout his work. Yet from Ibn Taymiyya's perspective, this response remains incomplete, for reasons that call into sharp focus his relationship to the theological topography that frames his stance.

In making the promotion of human welfare central to God's commands, Ibn Taymiyya, as we have seen, adopts a position that has often been associated with Muʿtazilite theologians. The principal ground for God's actions is the motive of beneficence (*iḥsān*). Yet it would be one of Ibn Taymiyya's complaints against the Muʿtazilites that in confining God's motives to this sole basis, they left us with a God who is wise to the point of foolishness—an agent that could seem only incomprehensible or mad. For rational or wise agents do not act out of pure beneficence without expecting to get back from their action *anything whatsoever*. God himself, when He acts, cannot act for a wise purpose that exhausts itself on the human level. There is also, there must also be, a wise purpose that redounds to God himself (*ḥikma taʿūdu ilayhi*).[99] It is tempting here to ask: What might that purpose be? I feel the terms of this question are liable to mislead us, triggering complex efforts to uncover deep explanations that answer to the grammar of the statement "The purpose is—" when the facts lie closer to the surface. For what Ibn Taymiyya seems to have in mind relates to a seminal distinction between two fundamentally different ways of considering God.

The first standpoint is the basic human standpoint: it is the standpoint we occupy as we look out from our own human lives as shaped by our multiple needs and desires. Looking out to the world from the perspective of our neediness, we see everything under its description as useful or beneficial *for us*. We see God as the provider, as the one who determines whether we fulfill our needs, achieve our welfare or fail to. It is a standpoint, as we have seen, that carries strong normative force, and it is a perfectly legitimate one. Yet there is also, besides this one, the standpoint of God himself. And God certainly looks at human beings under the aspect of what they need. But He also looks at them under the aspect of what they owe to Him. God looks out to the world through the demands generated by His own intrinsic majesty and the self-love with which He relates to His intrinsic being. From this higher-order standpoint, God created human beings not merely to benefit them, as the Muʿtazilites had highlighted;[100] He created them to worship Him, as stated in the Qur'an (Q 51:56). And to worship, simply, is to obey.

It is a distinction between standpoints that Ibn Taymiyya develops in at least two different contexts. It emerges as a distinction between two types of praise: "praise in the sense of thankfulness" (*ḥamd shukr*) and "praise in the unrestricted sense" (*ḥamd muṭlaq*). The first is the kind of praise we give to God for His beneficence (*li-iḥsānihi*), and it is relative to our needs; the second is the praise we give to God for His own intrinsic features (*li-dhātihi*). This corresponds to two different ways of loving God: as a fulfiller of human needs, and as an intrinsic object of love and admiration.[101] The distinction between these standpoints is also at stake in a distinction between two ways of affirming the unity of God that plays a foundational role in Ibn Taymiyya's thinking, namely *tawḥīd al-rubūbiyya/al-rabbāniya* (affirming God's unity under the aspect of His lordship) and *tawḥīd al-ilāhiyya/al-ulūhiyya* (affirming His unity under the aspect of His divinity). The first involves an acknowledgment of God in His creative capacity and as the exclusive source of power, yielding the invocation found in *al-Fātiḥa* (Q 1:5): "You [alone] we ask for help" (*iyyāka nastaʿīnu*). The second involves the acknowledgment of God in His lawgiving capacity and as the exclusive object of worship and obedience, yielding the other moiety of *al-Fātiḥa*: "You [alone] we worship" (*iyyāka naʿbudu*).[102]

The two standpoints are not hermetically sealed from each other; it is indeed by honoring the demands of God's divinity that human beings realize their highest good. ("Obedience and worship constitute the *welfare* of human beings.")[103] Yet the distinction between them is nevertheless a seminal one, and allows us to flag the position of paramount importance that the concept of worship (*ʿibāda*) occupies within Ibn Taymiyya's theological vision. When Ibn Taymiyya speaks of the "wise purpose that redounds to God," I would suggest, it is simply the second standpoint—the one constituted by God's status as an object of intrinsic praise and love and an object of worship—that he means to affirm. What God "gets back" from the actions He commands is the fulfillment of the demands of His divinity through human worship and obedience.

This affirmation is one that Ibn Taymiyya does not take to mark a breach with the Muʿtazilite viewpoint alone. Turning back to his earlier criticism of Ashʿarite theologians, we will recall our puzzlement at his accusation that these theologians analyze command and prohibition only in terms of "that which agrees with people's appetites [*mā yulāʾimu al-ṭibāʿ*]," which "does not entail, according to them, that God loves what is right and hates what is wrong." Ibn Taymiyya's accusation becomes more intelligible, however, if we connect it to this distinction. For in failing to distinguish between God's will and God's love and thereby to acknowledge that God loves actions in a sense separate from their description as agreeing with human appetite or need, the Ashʿarites had failed to uphold a fundamental perspective representing the demands of God's divinity. This failure was linked to a larger Ashʿarite failure to acknowledge the status of God not only as a subject of love, but also as an object of intrinsic love.[104] Ibn Taymiyya's criticism of this failure would thus be part of a more wide-ranging venture to recalibrate the emphasis placed on the notion of love (*maḥabba*) in approaching the relationship between man and God and to give it its proper due. And the notion of love, here, comes up twice, as just indicated. It is a concept, on the one hand, that we must predicate of God, upholding God's own self-description in scripture. For God spoke of himself as *loving* people (e.g., Q 3:31, 5:54) and more specifically of loving good-doers, the just, the God-fearing (e.g., Q 2:195, 49:9, 9:7). But it is also a concept that we must make integral to our understanding of the response that we as human beings owe to God, forming a core element of the spiritual relationship we seek to establish with Him. Both aspects come together in the Qur'anic reference to a "people He loves, and who love Him" (Q 5:54).

The emphasis on the spiritual significance of love is one we will recognize as a key constituent of Sufi spirituality, and as such must figure prominently in the way we seek to reconstruct Ibn Taymiyya's elusive relationship to Sufism.[105] Yet what is important for our present purposes is to consider how the above bears on the question about God's reasons for loving or commanding particular actions that we have been tracking, and more specifically what it has to tell us about how these reasons relate to actions' intrinsic characteristics. And here, the simple answer would seem to be: for the most part, they do not. From this God-centered perspective, everything is seen under its aspect as an expression of love and obedience, and ultimately reflects back to God's self-love. God's own love for human beings, as one telling passage reveals, attaches to human beings insofar as they do what He loves and fulfill the demands of His self-love: "God's love for his servant is in accordance with the servant's doing what God loves. And what God loves, in terms of being worshipped and obeyed, is a corollary of His love of Himself, and this love is the cause of [His] love of His faithful servants; so His love of the believers is a corollary of His love of Himself."[106] From this perspective, actions are simply tokens of worship and obedience: they are loved by God precisely in their relative character *qua* commanded. This point cannot be made meaningfully regarding those actions that already incorporate a relation to God, such as faith (*īmān*) and obedience (*ṭāʿa*) or disbelief (*kufr*) and disobedience (*ʿiṣyān*)—actions that form the centerpiece of Ibn Taymiyya's concern in many of his discussions. These are actions that can be directly counted as forms of honoring or dishonoring the demands of God's divinity. It is thus with respect to these actions that Ibn Taymiyya can be seen as offering the sharpest counter to al-Ghazālī's (as al-Juwaynī's) earlier claim that "disbelief and faith, obedience and disobedience, are all equal as far as God is concerned." Actions that do not bear such an internal relation, however, such as justice or injustice, truth-telling or lying, will be good or bad in this context not so much because of their intrinsic features but insofar as God has made them objects of command and prohibition. It may already have been the case that truthfulness is good and injustice bad. But it is only once God commands us to be truthful and forbids us to be unjust that the demands of His divinity—His rights or claims (*ḥuqūq*) as God—become entangled with these acts, thereby investing these acts with the capacity to serve as signifiers of worship and obedience.[107]

In the above, I have sought to piece together a fuller picture of Ibn Taymiyya's conception of divine wisdom by focusing on a topic of sweeping significance for his theological vision: God's reasons for commanding. Faced with God's commands, it must be possible to ask "Why?," refusing to succumb to the grim notion of divine arbitrariness that Ashʿarites had pressed. Inverting the Ashʿarite emphasis on the *appearance* of wisdom and their denial of its *reality*, Ibn Taymiyya staked a claim for a real wise purpose that can be understood on two general levels: one that redounds to human beings, and the other to God. The former, I suggested, revolves around the ability of actions to serve human welfare, the latter around the ability of actions to serve as tokens of submission and love. On this second level, the value of actions is merely relative, and Ibn Taymiyya's frequent references to the "reality" of actions or their intrinsic "attributes" would seem to be intelligible mainly with regard to the first. With this picture in place, we can now turn to a question that is intimately linked to the one we have just pursued and that promises to shed new light on Ibn Taymiyya's understanding of the standards to which God's actions respond. "Why does God command particular actions?" The question "Why does He punish the performance of particular actions?" forms its natural counterpart.

Thematizing Justice: Why Does God Punish?

It is a question that Ibn Taymiyya foregrounds in several locations in his work and invites us to bring into connection with the first. And nowhere more so than when he inscribes it at the heart of the dispute about "the determination of good and bad." Writing in his *Nubuwwāt*, he would state: all parties accept that acts may be good or bad taken in the sense of what is pleasant and painful, suitable and unsuitable. The *real* "dispute concerns whether [acts] are objects of praise and reward" or blame and punishment.[108] Traveling back to our discussion in chapter 1, we will now remember a crucial point that Ibn Taymiyya had made when enumerating his divergences from the Muʿtazilite viewpoint. The Muʿtazilites had claimed that punishment is incurred for actions even prior to the arrival of the revealed Law. Yet the Qur'an, Ibn Taymiyya countered, clearly states, "We never chastise, until We send forth a Messenger" (17:15). Ibn Taymiyya's charge would seem to reflect a salient aspect of Muʿtazilite analysis, to the extent that the Muʿtazilites included the desert incurred by actions—not only praise and blame, which are after all integral to the definition of ethical concepts, but also reward and punishment—within the dictates of our rational ethical grasp.[109]

Readers approaching Ibn Taymiyya's reflections on this subject, however, will find that it is his disagreement with the Ashʿarite rather than the Muʿtazilite viewpoint that often occupies center stage. This is a disagreement, crucially, that is organized not merely by the question *whether* (whether acts are objects of praise and reward) but *why*, and by a firm demand for reasons in the face of Ashʿarite opposition that ties his concern directly to the one we have just studied. While the notion of wisdom also figures prominently in this concern, it is the notion of justice that is more strongly highlighted. Leaning closer to Ibn Taymiyya's view of the posthumous consequences of actions, my aim will be to scrutinize his demand for reasons in order to consider how deeply he articulates his response to it. This is a question, as we will see, that will return us again to the motifs of our preceding narrative by thematizing anew—and indeed by problematizing—the repercussions of Ibn Taymiyya's circumscription of value in consequentialist terms.

The charge recurs throughout Ibn Taymiyya's work: Ashʿarite theologians failed to supply the otherworldly consequences of actions, namely reward and punishment, with adequate explanatory force. We might put Ibn Taymiyya's charge more revealingly by saying: the Ashʿarites had not only denied that people are punished *before* the arrival of the Law; they had also denied that, strictly speaking, people are punished for their actions even *after* its arrival. For they had refused to allow that actions and their otherworldly consequences are connected as causes to effects—*asbāb* to *musabbabāt*—and had repudiated the causal language that would allow one to openly state that a person is punished *for* or *through* or *because of* (*bi*) his actions.[110] Once again, Ibn Taymiyya traces this back to a failure to properly balance the imperative of upholding God's power and the imperative of upholding God's Law—the domains, respectively, of *qadar* and *sharʿ*, *mulk* and *ḥamd*. Out of excessive zeal to preserve God's sovereignty, the Ashʿarites had severed any link between human actions and otherworldly consequences that might register dangerously as a human claim and a divine obligation. This had led them to claim that God in His absolute liberty might commit madmen and innocent babes to the Fire and treat arch-sinners to the delights of eternal reward. In doing so, they had drastically undermined the divine Law, a great part of whose normative and motivational force derives from the connection taken to subsist between actions and their consequences.

Looking at Ashʿarite works, one will hear the grounds of Ibn Taymiyya's complaint, for example, in al-Juwaynī's bald statement in the *Burhān* that God "metes out torment to whom He wills, and bestows felicity upon whom He wills."[111] These words find their immediate echo in al-Ghazālī's *Iqtiṣād* and appear even more rebarbatively in his *Iḥyāʾ* when he states, "God may inflict pain upon people and torment them with no prior offense [*min ghayr jirm sābiq*], and with no subsequent reward, contrary to what the Muʿtazilites hold; for [in so doing] God disposes over His property [*mutaṣarrif fī milkihi*] . . . and injustice consists of disposing of others' property without their permission."[112] As the last phrase suggests, this point was linked to the basic stance Ashʿarite theologians had taken regarding the nature of evaluative standards, invoking God's status as proprietor and lord (*mālik*) of created beings and to human beings' status as owned vassals (*mamlūk*), and claiming that God's status lifted His actions to a value-free domain and foreclosed the possibility that human beings might have any entitlement He is obligated to honor.

The Ashʿarites, of course, had averred that we know that God *will* in fact reward and punish along certain lines on the basis of His explicit statements to that effect in His revealed message, as we saw in the previous section. Several Ashʿarites, including al-Ashʿarī himself, had in this respect drawn a distinction between God's absolute freedom rationally considered and the way this freedom may be exercised in the postrevelational order.[113] The language of "causes," similarly, made crucial appearances in legal works, including the works of Ashʿarite jurists, where it was made integral to the definitions of legal values. Thus, obligatory acts (*wājib*), in al-Ghazālī's words in the *Mustasfā*, are those that serve as a "cause of punishment in the hereafter" (*sabab al-ʿiqāb fi 'l-ākhira*).[114] Even outside the legal context, there were instances in which prominent Ashʿarites had made lavish use of the language of *asbāb* to talk about the connection between actions and their consequences. Al-Ghazālī's extensive deployment of this language in the *Iḥyāʾ ʿulūm al-dīn* is a case in point.[115] What both contexts—legal and spiritual—share, to be sure, is a more practical concern with action. And there have been serious questions about how the commitments of this practical perspective stand to be harmonized with the commitments articulated in more theoretical contexts, where Ashʿarites have often been understood as adopting an occasionalist view of causality according to which God is the sole cause of events and any apparent causes in the world are not real causes but merely occasions. As al-Ashʿarī had epitomically expressed it: "Everything that is created in time is created spontaneously and new by God, without a reason [*sabab*] that makes it necessary or a cause [*ʿilla*] that generates it."[116]

Putting aside the finer print of the Ashʿarite message and taking the Ashʿarites to have interrogated the relevance of the notion of causality at this juncture sufficiently loudly to justify Ibn Taymiyya's preoccupation, we will then be interested to hear how Ibn Taymiyya articulates his own response. "God may torment without a sin [*bilā dhanb*]," the Ashʿarites had said; yet "God does not torment or punish save for/through/because of one's sins [*lā yuʿadhdhibuhu wa-yuʿāqibuhu illā bi-dhunūbihi*]," Ibn Taymiyya would counter.[117] Yet just how should we understand the reason-giving "because" that figures in this statement? And more to the point: how strongly? This is a question that Ibn Taymiyya provides resources for answering when, in one of his *Fatāwā*, he is challenged to explain a point that may seem puzzling coming from the direction of what he has told us regarding the nature of ethical value. How does the claim that actions are *really* good or bad, it may be asked, hang together with the claim that people are not always punished for committing bad actions? Not everyone would see the space for a wedge between these two claims; Ibn Taymiyya does. Challenged to explain his position, he offers the following reply: actions "are causes [*asbāb*] for punishment, yet they depend on a condition [*sharṭ*]"—namely the arrival of a revealed message to serve as proof against one.[118]

If this remark suggests one limitation—cause *y* requires certain conditions *x* to effect *z*—the wedge is driven deeper in a short epistle that Ibn Taymiyya devotes to the topic of reward. "Does anyone enter paradise through their works?" reads the title. It is false, Ibn Taymiyya states in the conclusion of his discussion, to think that "what occurs through a cause [*bi-sabab*] cannot occur without it"; death, for example, may come about through another's action or through other means. Thus "the cause does not necessitate the effect [*al-sabab lā yūjib al-musabbab*]," and indeed God "may create the effect without the cause."[119] Thus, effect *z* can be brought about without cause *y* altogether; and as Ibn Taymiyya makes clear in this context, it is God's mercy and beneficence that provides the ultimate way of filling the prepositional "through" or "because" that carries one across heaven's door. The entire dramatic performance is nothing but a refraction of divine bounty: God in His bounty creates people; God in His bounty creates their good works; God in His bounty creates their requital. Everything good that people experience both in this world and the next is a "pure bounty from Him, without a prior cause which necessarily confers a right [*ḥaqq*] upon them."[120] These remarks give us more than a glimpse into the grounds of Jon Hoover's strongly worded conclusion concerning Ibn Taymiyya's understanding of secondary causality. "God's perspective," he writes, "appears to be that of a real but inert world of tools and raw materials that is wholly dependent upon God's will for its every movement. God creates by means of these instruments in accord with his wise purpose. The human perspective is that of a world of naturalistic cause and effect and reward and punishment into which God can intervene at any point."[121]

The operation of *asbāb*, the above already suggests, is subject to important limitations. Yet if we wish to probe the justificatory or explanatory nature of this causal relation more deeply, there will be a more relevant question to ask at this juncture. We may put this as follows: If actions may not *always* lead to certain consequences, what is it about actions that makes them lead to such consequences when they *do*? Thinking about the operation of causes in the natural world, for example, to affirm that a real causal connection holds between natural events—and that they are not, as occasionalists would have it, produced through the direct action of God—would typically involve making some kind of statement about the properties of the interacting elements. As Ibn Taymiyya himself rehearses the point in the *Radd*, if fire burns, or if water has a cooling effect, if the eye sees, or if eating causes satiation, this is because "there is a force [or potentiality: *quwwa*] in fire that necessarily produces a heating effect, there is a force in water that necessarily produces a cooling effect," and so on.[122] Mutatis mutandis, when we affirm that "God does not torment or punish save for [through, because] of one's sins," we need to ask: What is it about the *nature* of these actions that renders them a fit object of God's punishment in the first place? Why do *these* actions attract punishment and not others?

It is a question that the Muʿtazilites had answered earlier by pointing to the various act-descriptions (*wujūh*) that ground the value of actions and to the desert entailments or judgments (*aḥkām*) of praise and blame that are realized when an act corresponding to a given act-description is performed. The desert of reward and punishment attracted by actions forms merely a natural extension of the desert of praise and blame these actions attract. To ask "Why punish?" (and "Why reward?") within this scheme is on one level simply to call attention to these act-descriptions and via these to their entailed deserts. As ʿAbd al-Jabbār had indicatively stated in the *Mughnī*, writing about the moral norms known by reason (*ʿaqliyyāt*): "One deserves reward and is preserved from punishment through them because of the qualities [*awṣāf*] they possess; indeed it is because of these attributes that desert is realized."[123] The explanatory power of these act-descriptions indeed emerges more clearly once we recall how these descriptions had been specifically understood. For they included considerations that went beyond utility to span a number of deontological grounds, such as lying, ingratitude, and injustice and their contraries. As I observed earlier, the deontological notion of *ḥaqq* (right, claim) played an organizing role in several of these grounds, notably injustice. Injustice, thus, is a matter of violating the rights of other persons, and it is the violation of such rights that translates into the right of punishment (*ḥaqq fiʾl-ʿiqāb*) that God possesses in the afterlife.[124] Reward and compensation, similarly, form human claims that God is charged with faithfully administering.

Ashʿarite theologians had flatly rejected this view, denying that deserts were generated by actions themselves in a manner that would place God under moral obligation to respond to them. With this in mind, it will be interesting to observe that the remark that gave us our starting point in this section—the real dispute concerns whether acts are objects of (*yataʿallaqu bihi*) praise and blame, punishment and reward—was in fact a mirror image of one al-Rāzī had earlier delivered in his *Arbaʿīn*. Yet al-Rāzī's own remark had been rather more nuanced. The *real* dispute, he had written, concerns "whether the fact that certain acts are objects of blame in the present world and punishment in the hereafter [*mutaʿallaq al-dhamm ... waʾl-ʿiqāb*], and certain others objects of praise in the present world and reward in the hereafter, is because of a quality of the action [*li-ajl ṣifa ʿāʾida ilaʾl-fiʿl*] or whether ... it is rather because of the sheer fact that the Law has thus determined it [*ḥukm al-sharʿ bi-dhālika*]."[125] It was the latter position that represented the Ashʿarite view—a view that Ashʿarites had then qualified further by claiming that actions serve not as causes (*ʿilla*) of reward and punishment, but only as signs (*amāra*) of one's future fate.[126]

Crucially, thus, it was as a question about the deeper *why* of otherworldly consequences that al-Rāzī's remark had parsed the backbone of the debate—a *why*, moreover, that explicitly thematized the Muʿtazilites' deontological commitments. In his *Nubuwwāt*, Ibn Taymiyya mentions the Ashʿarite view of acts as "signs" only to reject it, objecting to the idea that acts should be "only a sign of [otherworldly] bliss or misery without there being anything in the respective actions that is suited to reward or punishment [*min ghayr an yakūna fī aḥad al-fiʿlayn maʿnan yunāsibu al-thawāb aw-al-ʿiqāb*]."[127] It is a remark that seems tantalizing in openly conveying a demand for an explanation of otherworldly consequences that would tie them to something inherent in the actions themselves. Yet what, now, might that "something" be? For Ibn Taymiyya, as we have seen, has offered an account of the value of actions that is articulated exclusively in consequentialist terms. "Good" actions are those that are beneficial and "bad" actions those that are harmful, and benefit and harm depend on the consequences that actions lead to, including their consequences in the otherworldly domain. To ask "Why punish?," however, is to ask *why* certain kinds of actions lead to benefit and others to harm. And such a question this evaluative account would seem greatly challenged to answer without falling into circularity—a kind of circularity Ibn Taymiyya himself exemplifies when he writes: "Since, in the present world, one hasn't lived the beneficial life for which one was created . . . one will also not do so in the hereafter."[128]

Probed more closely, attempts to answer this question on purely consequentialist terms would seem doomed to end up in tangles, leading to logical absurdity at best and blatant injustice at worst. Al-Rāzī had picked up on both of these unwelcome repercussions when addressing the topic of punishment in his *Maṭālib*. For if we take the value of actions to be grounded in their otherworldly consequences as these impact on the agent's self-interest, the hapless sinner might well ask, "You punish me, God, for not doing actions that serve my own interests?" If instead we appeal to the benefit accruing to third parties from the punishment of given individuals, especially in terms of its deterring or edifying effect, this, al-Rāzī notes, would appear to be the "essence of injustice" (*maḥḍ al-ẓulm*).[129] From the perspective of our ordinary moral intuitions, it seems indefensible that one should sacrifice the good of one person for the good of another or indeed of a far greater number of others. As regards the justification of deterrence, moreover, the mere *belief* that punishment will be incurred—as against its actual realization—suffices for the effect. Al-Rāzī's discussion, of course, was built on the assumption that the otherworldly consequences of actions attach to them on no other ground than the decree of the Law, there being nothing in actions themselves that serves to ground their value. As al-Ghazālī had earlier put it: God freely attaches (*rabaṭa, anāṭa*) consequences to actions that "tip" them (*rajjaḥa*) into the domain of obligation or into the domain of prohibition.

Now the notion of *ḥuqūq*-claims that the Muʿtazilites had deployed widely in their ethical theory, as I mentioned in chapter 1, is not entirely absent from Ibn Taymiyya's writings. And there are places where Ibn Taymiyya brings the concept into play in discussing the posthumous domain, reflecting the important scriptural foundations of this turn of thinking.[130] Yet overall, these appearances remain isolated and circumstantial and do not appear to be integrated more programmatically within his viewpoint. Here as elsewhere, deontological notions are not given the kind of robustness that would allow them to carry real explanatory weight. No less crucially, Ibn Taymiyya leaves his readers in no doubt that the Muʿtazilite view of otherworldly consequences stands to be rejected for reasons that mirror those voiced by Ashʿarite theologians. "Human beings," he writes in *Minhāj al-sunna*, "have no claim over God by themselves and cannot make anything obligatory on their Lord [*inna al-ʿabd lā yastaḥiqqu bi-nafsihi ʿalā Allāh shayʾan wa-laysa lahu an yūjiba ʿalā rabbihi shayʾan*]."[131] We will recognize the same stance in his earlier remark that everything good that people experience both in this world and the next is a "pure bounty from [God], without a prior cause which necessarily confers a right [*ḥaqq*] upon them."

Affirming a *causal* "through" (*bāʾ al-sababiyya*), he elsewhere clarifies, is not the same as affirming a *commutative* "through" (*bāʾ al-muqābala*)—the way we say, "I bought such-and-such a thing *in exchange for* [*bi*] this amount," or the way we think of a laborer as working in return for a wage "which he is entitled to [*yastaḥiqquhā*] just as the seller is entitled to the price [of a product]."[132] Unlike the employer, God stands to gain nothing from us and we work for our own benefit, so the model familiar to us from the domain of human commutative transactions (*muʿāwaḍa* or *muqābala*) fails to transfer. Similarly—and echoing a reasoning that had found a home not only within Ashʿarite polemics but also within Baghdādī Muʿtazilite thinking about reward—the benefits we receive from God are so prodigious that no order of commutation and compensatory parity could ever make it reasonable to speak of human desert, given the indebtedness that precedes and underwrites it.[133]

Ultimately, it is precisely in the extrinsic manner al-Ghazālī had indicated that Ibn Taymiyya also appears to think of the relationship between actions and their otherworldly consequences. It is not insignificant that his own vocabulary directly echoes al-Ghazālī's when, in a highly telling passage, he compares the connection between actions and their otherworldly consequences to the causal connection between natural events such as eating and satiation or drinking and the quenching of thirst, which God firmly bound together (*rabaṭa . . . rabṭan muḥkaman*) in an exercise of absolute freedom unconstrained by the inherent nature of the events or acts themselves. Reward (*thawāb*), Ibn Taymiyya explains, receives its name from the fact that it comes back to (*yathūbu*) an agent from his action; punishment (*ʿiqāb*) from the fact that it occurs after (*yuʿqibu*) his act. What this simple picture of temporal succession, of neutral before and after, pointedly excludes is the stronger normative and explanatory force that Muʿtazilites had packed into the relation between acts and their consequences.[134]

Responding to an Ashʿarite view, I began by saying, Ibn Taymiyya voices a demand for a more robust understanding of the connection between acts and consequences than the Ashʿarites had established. But in framing this point, I have been suggesting, he qualifies this connection in critical ways and does not provide it with a deep explanatory foundation—a fact that reflects not only his unmarked occlusion of deontological concepts, but also his deliberate exclusion of desert from his ethical outlook. It is significant, in this respect, that in echoing al-Rāzī's formulation of the true focus of the dispute, Ibn Taymiyya does not seem to register the explanatory level at which al-Rāzī had parsed it. I will come back to the question of how, if not in such terms, punishment *can* receive a justification at all from Ibn Taymiyya's viewpoint. Yet before doing so, it will be important to place Ibn Taymiyya's reason-giving demand in clearer perspective and to consider how this demand may be most instructively construed.

For all its causal tones, I would argue, the emphasis that Ibn Taymiyya places on reasons in the context of his critique of the Ashʿarites needs to be read as a demand for something far less deep, and far thinner, than what we might be prepared to count as an "explanation" or an explanatory ground. As Hoover has insightfully pointed out, what piqued Ibn Taymiyya about the Ashʿarite position was the arbitrariness it appeared to carry. "God may punish whom He wills, may reward whom He pleases," the Ashʿarites had said. On the contrary: "God only punishes *those who* have sinned." It is this last formulation that offers us a more judicious way of hearing Ibn Taymiyya's central claim, reading it in its concern to affirm, not so much a "because," as a stable identifying "who" or "what"; and a correlative concern, not with explanation, but with regularity. What this delivers is an assurance of a very particular kind: that there is a regular conjunction between the characteristics of human beings and God's actions toward them, and that God does not act arbitrarily but always treats cases with the same relevant characteristics in identical ways.[135]

The wise and indeed rational person is one who (also) acts for his own benefit, we heard above when considering Ibn Taymiyya's conception of God's wisdom and his stipulation of a wise purpose that "redounds to God." The same imbrication of standards of morality and standards of rationality is evident in Ibn Taymiyya's conception of God's justice (*ʿadl*), to the extent that justice is demarcated from wisdom. But here it is less the teleological concept of benefit than the more formal concept of regularity that constitutes the organizing element. The essential form of rationality, Ibn Taymiyya contends in several locations of his work, lies in the ability to join like to like and distinguish like from unlike (*al-jamʿ bayna al-mutamāthilayn wa ʾl-farq bayna al-mukhtalifayn*).[136] It is a conception of rationality that he often deploys in discussing the epistemological faculties of human beings. Yet it is plain that it also supplies the backbone of what he thinks we can say about the rationality exhibited by God.

To treat differently cases that share all their relevant features marks a failure of rationality that is also a failure of justice, as Ibn Taymiyya clarifies in setting out his view of God's justice. Once again this is a view Ibn Taymiyya invites us to read in its character as a *via media* and as an attempt to balance the Muʿtazilite understanding of justice, with its objectionable notion of divine obligation, against the Ashʿarite understanding, with its problematic refusal of the notion of injustice as inapplicable to God by definition.[137] Against these views Ibn Taymiyya foregrounds a third, which already boasted a long presence in the theological milieu. The notion of "justice" can be applied to God taking justice to mean "putting everything in its proper place" (*waḍʿ kull shayʾ fī mawḍiʿihi*). Putting things in their right place involves an exercise of precisely the form of rationality just outlined, as the following statement reveals: "Justice consists of putting everything in its proper place, and God is a just arbiter who puts things in their proper places and only puts a given thing in the place that suits it [*yunāsibuhu*] and that wisdom and justice demand. He does not differentiate between similar things nor does He place different things on an equal footing, and He only punishes those who deserve punishment, and thus puts [punishment] in its proper place."[138]

It is this understanding of rationality, then, that Ibn Taymiyya seems most anxious to defend in his polemics against the Ashʿarite view of punishment. Yet of course it will be noticed that the type of reason-giving demanded by this understanding is one fairly limited in kind. All that is needed to satisfy it is the existence of a regular conjunction between God's actions and the identifying descriptions of their human objects. As to *why* these specific descriptions are conjoined to these specific actions, that does not enter the equation. To restate: what this tells us is that people with identical qualities are treated in identical ways; the question why any of them *should* be treated in this way or another, on the other hand—why such a pairing is "suitable" or "proper"—belongs to a different story. The difference between these two stories, however, comes down to a difference between two diverging deployments or conceptions of reason: a formal or procedural notion of reason as against a more substantive notion of moral reason such as the one the Muʿtazilites had employed at this juncture. Bringing up this definition of justice in his *Sharḥ al-Uṣūl al-khamsa*, Mānkdīm would reject it precisely on the grounds of its failure to pick out distinctively ethical considerations.[139] The point can be put even more instructively by drawing on a distinction marked by John Rawls between two types of justificatory questions that can be asked about the practice of punishment (or any other practice), one at the level of justifying a particular action falling under this practice, another at the level of justifying the practice itself. The question "To whom may punishment be applied?" and the answer "Only to an offender for an offense" speak to the first level—and it is to this level that Ibn Taymiyya's preoccupation with fixing the identifying "who" corresponds. But this still leaves open how the practice of punishment could be justified at all.[140]

In focusing on regularity without normativity and conjunction without necessity, thus, Ibn Taymiyya appears to leave the justification of punishment in a state of abeyance. How *could* punishment then be justified on a deeper level within the terms of his scheme? One of the few locations where Ibn Taymiyya comes near to probing this "Why?" more substantively is in a brief discussion that appears in one of his Qur'anic commentaries. "The only beneficial place" for evil souls is "the one that is suitable to them,"[141] he opens by saying, promisingly resuming the terms of his definition of justice alongside the characteristic terms of his consequentialism. He then proceeds to place before us a series of concrete cases by way of comparison:

> One who wished to make snakes and scorpions live among people the way cats do would not be acting well [*lam yuṣliḥ*]. One who wished to make a liar a witness for people would not be acting well. The same goes for one who wished to appoint an ignoramus as a teacher or mufti over people, or to make a helpless coward a fighter for people. . . . Things like that necessarily spread corruption in the world, and they might [indeed] be impossible, as it would be to try to make a stone float on the surface of the water like a ship or ascend into the sky like the wind, and the like. So it is not fitting [*lā taṣluḥu*] for malignant souls to be in the wholesome paradise in which there is no malignancy to be found, for that would necessarily bring corruption, or be impossible.[142]

The invitation seems clear: we should use such cases as models for thinking about the unsuitability of lodging wrongdoers in paradise (building on a discernment of the "likeness" that joins them). Yet this argument, it is clear, rests on certain notions about what is advisable and inadvisable within the ordinary world as we know it; indeed, as the last line reveals, it more specifically rests on certain notions about what is possible and impossible that derive from an empirical reflection on the world we inhabit and the laws that happen to shape it. As with Ibn Taymiyya's earlier invocation of the "sick patient" metaphor to describe God's toleration of evils in pursuit of a preponderant good, we may therefore wonder how it can be used to justify the choice of action on the part of an agent who operates outside these limitations—or how it can do so without implying that He is subject to significant limitations.

To the extent that Ibn Taymiyya does offer us resources for answering the question "Why punish?" on a deeper level, in fact, it seems to me that these might be found by looking, not to the intrinsic features of particular actions themselves, but to their relative character as signifiers of worship and obedience, and thus ultimately as expressions of God's self-love. This is the explanatory level that we may read Ibn Taymiyya as calling attention to in *al-ʿAqīda al-Tadmuriyya* when he writes, "Reward and punishment are incurred for doing what the One rewarding and punishing [respectively] loves and is well pleased with, and is angered by and hates."[143] It is by reference to God's love for actions under their description as objects of command, this remark densely suggests—as objects carrying the claims (*ḥuqūq*) of His divinity, and thus as potential tokens of worship and love—that His response to the human failure to perform such acts can be understood.[144] God loves those who express their love for Him by honoring the demands of His divinity; God hates those who hate Him and who dishonor these demands.

The intention with which one performs acts, Ibn Taymiyya emphasizes throughout his writings, is what determines their character and their success, in line with a well-known prophetic tradition (*innamā al-aʿmāl biʾl-niyyāt*). Only those acts that we perform for the sake of God (*li-wajh Allāh*)—not for the sake of worldly goods, not even for the sake of otherworldly compensation, and not for the "intrinsic moral value" of the act—create value in the eyes of God. "Human beings are rewarded for performing good deeds," we hear elsewhere, "if they perform them . . . for the sake of God [*ibtighāʾ wajh rabbihi*] and in order to obey God and the Prophet."[145] This, indeed, ties in with what I take to form an important element of Ibn Taymiyya's criticism of the Muʿtazilite failure to uphold the claims of God's divinity. For one of the corollaries of the Muʿtazilites' larger failure to acknowledge that God created people not merely to benefit them but to be worshipped was their exaltation of a purely moral motivation that failed to "point" acts to God, and that similarly saw God in His merely instrumental role as dispenser of deserts as against an object of intrinsic love. If this is correct, acts derive their otherworldly value from the context of the relationship between man and God rather than from the nature of acts themselves. It is the normative conception of human motivation that emerges from this same context, I would also suggest, that provides Ibn Taymiyya's pervasive emphasis on self-interested motivation with its conditioning ideal. Ibn Taymiyya, like many of the Sufi writers whose teachings water his own thinking here, would call it an ideal of "sincerity" or *ikhlāṣ*.

Whether this is the understanding that Ibn Taymiyya elsewhere had in mind when describing punishment as something created by God for a wise purpose, "with regard to which it is an act of wisdom and mercy [*al-ʿadhāb . . . min makhlūqātihi, alladhī khalaqahu bi-ḥikma, huwa bi-iʿtibārihā ḥikma wa-raḥma*]," seems uncertain.[146] His reference to "mercy," in fact, would point us to the human rather than the divine level on which God's wisdom stands to be realized, and one cannot help wondering whether what Ibn Taymiyya was considering was precisely the deterring or edifying effect whose morally problematic character al-Rāzī had underscored. Overall, the attention Ibn Taymiyya devotes to the deeper justification of punishment seems exiguous. This striking reticence may return us to a distinction he had drawn in *Bayān talbīs* between the objective existence of a wise purpose and the human ability to know it. It is a doubt about the possibilities of human knowledge that he would voice throughout his work. "God does what He does for a wise purpose that He knows" and may sometimes choose to reveal this to people, or to some people—such as the prophets and the pious *salaf*—and other times He may not.[147]

This conservative view reflects the spirit of the Qur'anic dictum "He shall not be questioned as to what He does, but they shall be questioned" (Q 21:23). It is also reflects the spirit that breathes through Ibn Taymiyya's account of the divine attributes more broadly, and that governs his insistence that we should affirm all the attributes with which God has described Himself in scripture while recognizing that we may not know their modality (for "like Him there is naught," Q 42:11). As Hoover writes: "The modalities of the concrete realities to which the names of the unseen God refer are unknowable because they are completely unlike referents given the same names in the created world." Ultimately, these realities may be known to none other than God himself.[148] The point is expressed in *al-ʿAqīda al-Tadmuriyya* in a way that directly includes the notion of wisdom in its scope. "Human beings do not know the realities [*ḥaqāʾiq*] of His attributes, may He be exalted, and the attributes of the afterlife He informed them about, *nor do they know the realities of the wisdom He purposed in His creation and command*, or the realities of the will and power that proceed from Him."[149] Nothing, finally, could be more in keeping with the traditional Ḥanbalite stance embodied in Aḥmad ibn Ḥanbal's renowned *bilā kayf*: we affirm the divine attributes without asking how. Ibn Taymiyya's *bilā lima*—we affirm divine wisdom without asking why—would only form a natural extension of this basic stance.[150] Certain general answers to the question "Why?" can of course be given, allowing us for example to connect God's commands to His concern for human welfare or to the demands of His own divinity. A more detailed knowledge of God's reasons and designs, on the other hand, lies out of our reach. Applying this insight to our case, we might say: there must be a wise purpose in punishment, a real answer to the deeper "Why punish?" that would reveal its necessity. But if so, it may be something human beings cannot know.

A programmatic wariness about probing God's wisdom too closely may indeed be at work in Ibn Taymiyya's reticence regarding the deeper justification of punishment. Yet there is also a different and broader point that needs to be brought out at this juncture, one that concerns the organizing aims of Ibn Taymiyya's theological exercise and that it is crucial to consider if we wish to place its character as well as its limitations in clearer perspective. For what difference, one might ask, does it after all make whether we talk about God's wisdom or justice in one way or another? The simplest answer to this question would seem to be: it matters the same way it matters to hold true beliefs about any other subject in which there is scope for getting things right or wrong. And what is at stake in this instance is the greatest subject of all: the nature of God Himself. It is a purist conception of why truth "matters" that has often appealed to thinkers. As William James put it: "When you've got your true idea of anything, there's an end of the matter. You're in possession; you *know*; you have fulfilled your thinking destiny . . . you have obeyed your categorical imperative." Yet this lofty conception of our intellectual life seems to fall short as an account of the multiple and profound ways in which beliefs may matter to those who hold them. This is the point to which James himself would try reorient attention by the focusing pragmatist question: "What concrete difference will [an idea's] being true make in any one's actual life?" and again: "What experiences will be different from those which would obtain if the belief were false?"[151]

We might need a more complex train of reflection in order to determine how we could speak of "experiences" in connection with, say, mathematical truths. But we will not need much in order to see the relevance of this point for theological discussion. For on the one hand, in raising questions of theological truth and contesting others' versions of them, Ibn Taymiyya places a critical accent on the fact, as Hoover reformulates this, that "thinking and speaking well of God is part of the law (*sharīʿa*)" and that people are obligated to find a way of speaking "that ascribes to God the highest perfection or praise."[152] This is a normative demand, we might say, a "categorical imperative" in James's (Kantian) locution. The qualifier "well" in Hoover's formulation, it is important to clarify, does not refer us merely to thinking and speaking truthfully or correctly in an entirely neutral sense. Speaking well of God is speaking in a way that confers on God the praise that He is entitled to, the praise that does justice to His merits. Yet this is a justice—we may say, still in a categorical register—that we *owe* Him. Ibn Taymiyya's affirmation of God's wisdom and justice can be read in this light. As he puts it in one place, "To say that [God] creates evil that contains no good, brings no benefit to anyone and involves no wise purpose or mercy, and that He torments people without a sin, would not be a praiseworthy description of Him but the reverse."[153]

Yet our ability to confer the more detached response of "praise," Ibn Taymiyya makes clear elsewhere, is intimately linked to our ability to confer the rather less detached response of love. Even if we might, conceivably, be commanded to love a tyrannical or unjust God, a God who does not care about human well-being and exercises His power without limitations, establishing this kind of spiritual relationship would in practice seem highly problematic. No less imperiled would be our ability to commit ourselves to the obedience of the Law this God has invited us to submit to. What we believe about God's moral attributes is not, thus, immaterial to our own spiritual well-being. This spiritual concern registers visibly at several junctures of Ibn Taymiyya's polemical engagement with the Ashʿarite denial that God acts wisely, and more specifically that He has human welfare at heart. For "we know that if a person believes that obeying God and the Prophet's command may not be in his interests or to his advantage . . . but on the contrary may be harmful and disadvantageous to him . . . there can be few greater disincentives against his doing as God and His Prophet have commanded." Add to this the unqualified claim that God may act as He pleases without constraints, and your assurance that it pays to do what God and His Prophet command has been left even more deeply bruised. Soon you find yourself mouthing the terrible words "There is nothing more harmful to the creature than the Creator."[154] Don't just think of the consequences this belief has for the religious life. Think of the consequences it has for the desire to live life at all.

It is a sensitivity to the pragmatic consequences of theological beliefs that has often been foregrounded by Ibn Taymiyya's readers in the past. His theological practice, as Henri Laoust suggested early on, is best read in light of his governing preoccupation with what leads to a deeper worship of God and with evaluating doctrines "through their function and value for action." Yet "action" here seems too narrow, as it leaves out the attitudes of the heart that spell out the fuller meaning of worship as a "fullness of submission and love" (*kamāl al-dhull wa ʾl-ḥubb*).[155] Theological beliefs simply cannot be considered independently of the attitudes of the heart they enable—the spiritual stance or particular kind of piety they serve to constitute.

The intimate connection between theological belief and spiritual consequence emerges starkly, as I have just said, in the question of God's wisdom and justice. It emerges equally starkly in other theological contexts, in ways calculated to elicit more clearly the peculiar repercussions of this pragmatic concern for the character of Ibn Taymiyya's theological engagements. The pragmatic standpoint dominates, for example, several of Ibn Taymiyya's remarks on the question of divine determination (*qadar*), which isolate the notion of "livability" as a criterion of paramount importance in approaching the topic. There is a certain way of assenting to the thesis of divine determination that would subvert ordinary life altogether. To appeal to God's determination of human acts, thus, to justify one's own wrongdoing is a way of engaging this thesis that "cannot be lived" and through which human interests are not served (*lā yumkinu aḥadan minhum an yaʿīsha bihi wa-lā taqūmu bihi maṣlaḥat aḥad min al-khalq*). At the broadest level, a belief in divine determination cannot be allowed to jeopardize the commitment to obeying the religious Law, in which human interests find their highest fulfillment. To the extent that a belief in divine determination is part of the Law itself, this would make the Law self-defeating (*fa-qad adhhaba al-aṣl*).[156]

The view we take of God's determination, however, does not merely affect our commitment to a life of religious obedience taken in the sense of external conformity to the demands of the Law. It similarly affects the spiritual attitudes that shape our inner life and from which our actions also flow. And here, apparently competing views may each carry important spiritual ramifications. The belief that we determine our actions on some level, for example, has the salutary consequence that we experience contrition for our evil acts and take responsibility for changing. The belief that God determines our acts has the salutary consequence that we experience gratitude toward God for the good we do, avoiding the evils of spiritual pride, that we feel humbled by our limitations, and that we trust in God as the sole determiner of our weal or woe.[157] *Both* beliefs, thus, have far-reaching spiritual consequences, and it cannot be a matter of upholding one of them so unequivocally that we entirely leave the other out of view. They have to be sustained in a perpetual tension calibrated to the demands of the spiritual life. Ibn Taymiyya's "real" higher-order view of the matter, as noted in earlier chapters, is that God ultimately determines human acts; yet his concern with keeping spiritual consequences in balance means that this "real" view is not presented without ambiguity or tension across his work.

Something similar, it may now be said, holds about the connection between actions and their otherworldly consequences that has formed our focus. That it was not a question of merely *affirming* causes—and the status of acts as causes—*simpliciter* but also of correctly *calibrating* the way we affirm them is something that Ibn Taymiyya signals clearly in several places. There is such a thing as believing in causes too little, but there is also such a thing as believing in causes too much. To turn away from causes entirely is to impugn the Law (*al-iʿrāḍ ʿan al-asbāb kulliyyatan qadḥ fi ʾl-sharʿ*) for it leads to neglect of the acts God has commanded, declaring them the means for entering paradise. Yet to turn to causes entirely—to trust in the strength of one's works alone—is to impugn the unity of God (*al-iltifāt ila ʾl-asbāb shirk fi ʾl-tawḥīd*).[158] For nothing ultimately takes place without God's will, and no cause operates wholly independently in necessitating its effect. This is a tension that is mirrored in a number of the scriptural statements that serve as reference points within Ibn Taymiyya's discussion. On the one hand, the Qur'an has said: "Enter paradise for/because of what you used to do [*udkhulū al-janna bimā kuntum taʿmalūna*]" (Q 16:32). Yet from the Prophet we hear: "None shall enter paradise through their works [*lan yadkhula aḥadukum al-janna bi-ʿamalihi*]."[159]

The particular type of "through" that the Prophet meant to deny in this last statement, Ibn Taymiyya explains, is the commutative "through" (*bāʾ al-muqābala*) the Muʿtazilites had affirmed. We do not have *claims* (*ḥuqūq*) over God the way wage laborers do; we are not *entitled* to anything. The problem with this view of human action once again lies in its spiritual consequences: it makes people trust in their own works instead of trusting (*tawakkala*) in God, and it feeds spiritual pride.[160] At the same time, human beings need to have a sufficiently robust assurance that God *will*—a "will" in the experiential register of a "must"—reward them for their deeds in order to be motivated to undertake them. Bowing to that psychological necessity, Ibn Taymiyya does not therefore entirely exclude the stronger notion of *ḥaqq* from his description of the connection between human acts and otherworldly consequences. It appears distinctly, for example, in the context of the *topos* of God's self-binding we considered earlier, where we hear Ibn Taymiyya refer to the human right to be rewarded for good deeds and not to be unfairly punished. Yet it is crucial here that this is described as a right that "God imposed/took upon Himself through His words," that is, His vow to justice *(hādhā al-ḥaqq alladhī ʿalayhi huwa aḥaqqahu ʿalā nafsihi bi-qawlihi*). God's originary commitment, thus, must be constantly retained in awareness, ensuring that we always read our rights as products of God's free beneficence (*iḥsān*).[161]

One must not, thus, rest in perfect assurance of the connection between acts and consequences; yet too little assurance would be pernicious for the spiritual life. There is also a further distinction to be drawn depending on whether we are thinking of reward or punishment. Ibn Taymiyya repeatedly places a different emphasis on the force of the causal connection binding these two outcomes to human action, suggesting that this connection is weaker in the case of reward than in the case of punishment, and stressing God's free bounty in the former and human action in the latter.[162] This distinction once again derives its importance from the spiritual repercussions of believing that evil comes from oneself whereas good comes from God. Similarly, a powerful conviction of the reliability of the causal connection between acts and consequences may be motivationally useful prior to the act. But if we fail to act well, the same belief may lead us to despair of divine mercy and stray even further from the path.

I have been suggesting that Ibn Taymiyya's development of his theological positions takes place against the horizon of a distinct preoccupation with the impact these positions will have on the spiritual lives of those who entertain them. Looking back to the starting point of our discussion, the following reflection will suggest itself. For our discussion of Ibn Taymiyya's conception of God's morality took its point of departure from a critical distinction between the way Ashʿarite thinkers had approached God's wisdom and the way Ibn Taymiyya proposed to treat it. In the reality of things, Ashʿarites suggested, God does not act for reasons, and more specifically for reasons to do with human welfare. The practical demands of legal reasoning, however, compel us to make use of the notion of reasons and of a purposive "mind of God." That is merely a heuristic—a reflection of human epistemic limitations. Ibn Taymiyya, we saw, appeared to invert this position by claiming the mind-independent reality of God's reasons. There are, no doubt, fundamental differences that divide these two viewpoints. Yet it is also worth emphasizing what unites rather than what divides them. For the articulation of theological truth, as Ibn Taymiyya pursues this, does not present itself as a venture to make the mind's content conform to a mind-independent reality. It takes place in distinct relation to the vital needs and vulnerabilities—not narrowly epistemic but more broadly spiritual—of the human subject as it engages this reality.

Ibn Taymiyya's "pragmatic" concern in pursuing theological ideas is important to foreground if we are to appreciate the character of his pursuit, providing us with yet another insight into its special form as against its content. For these spiritual aims, as I have tried to show, affect the unity and cohesion that Ibn Taymiyya's theological views carry, to the extent that the interest in stating theological truths is conditioned by the need to maintain in balance competing beliefs with different experiential consequences. They would also seem to have a bearing on the depth to which Ibn Taymiyya is motivated to develop his theological views. It could be debated here whether the character of his concern with the justification of punishment and the depth to which he is prepared to push the question "Why?" could be read in this light, reflecting an assessment that a deeper response to this theological question, for the purposes of the spiritual life, is simply not required. *That* God will reliably visit punishment for some acts and not for others is all we need to lead upright lives; a more probing exploration of *why* that is the case can perhaps be left to the mysteries of divine wisdom that the human mind cannot plumb. However we engage this point, the above discussion will have made clear not only the outlines of Ibn Taymiyya's positive conception of God's morality, but also the limits of his articulation of these ideas.

I BEGAN THIS chapter with a bid to investigate the real grounds of Ibn Taymiyya's conflict with Ashʿarite theology. Making the move from the domain of human morality to that of divine morality, I suggested that these grounds can be located by considering the Ashʿarite stance on the role of human welfare within the Law. This was a point on which Ashʿarite authors had often been accused of failing to harmonize the contents of legal and theological discourse, and I outlined two principal sources of tension, one connected with their view of the human mind and its limited evaluative capacities, the other with their view of the mind of God and the inapplicability of concepts of purpose to Him. Addressing Ibn Taymiyya's positive articulation of God's morality, I focused on two questions: "Why does God command certain actions?" and "Why does God punish actions?" Ibn Taymiyya's response to the first question looks in two directions: God's concern with human welfare and God's concern with the demands of His own divinity. His response to the second question turns out to revolve around a thin demand for the regular conjunction between acts and consequences that speaks to his specific conception of God's justice but leaves the deeper question "Why?" in abeyance. This may, or may not, have to do with the pragmatic concerns that shape Ibn Taymiyya's exposition of his theological views on this and other subjects. Many of the distinctive features of his treatment of both theological questions—as well as some of their distinctive difficulties—reflect, once again, the primacy of welfare within his ethical thought.

With the above in place, we may push ahead to the final stage of our story. We have seen the stance taken by Ashʿarite authors on the ability of the human mind to engage the human interests that the Law aims to promote. Ibn Taymiyya's own stance on this type of question has not yet come into view, yet it provides a crucial additional setting in which his evaluative epistemology must be sought. Focusing back on the human domain, the task of the next chapter will be to consider what Ibn Taymiyya's legal epistemology has to contribute to our picture of human evaluative capacities as he understands them. This will position us for a final reflection on the place and significance of the claim of ethical rationalism within Ibn Taymiyya's vision, and also for a broader comment on the view of the relationship of reason and revelation against which this claim may be located.

5

Broader Perspectives on Ibn Taymiyya's Ethical Rationalism

ETHICAL JUDGMENTS, IBN TAYMIYYA had said in the *Radd*, are among the "greatest certainties of human reason." These are judgments that he appeared to construe in exclusively consequentialist terms: "good" and "bad" come down to benefit and harm. Probing his ethical epistemology more closely, I observed in chapter 2, one elicits messages that vary significantly in their emphasis. Here Ibn Taymiyya offers what sounds like a strong claim of reason and indicates that our judgments about what is beneficial and harmful may be the product of experience (*tajriba*). There he narrows down the field and tells us that the Law informs us of what benefits and harms us. It is "the Law that is the light that distinguishes between what benefits and harms one," we heard.

In the context of this particular remark, Ibn Taymiyya had added a crucial specification: the Law reveals what benefits and harms us *both* in "this life and the next" (*al-maʿāsh waʾl-maʿād*).[1] The domain of the present life and the next here appear together with nothing to distinguish between them, spelling out the span of the Law in the most comprehensive possible terms. Yet elsewhere Ibn Taymiyya seemed to draw a distinction between the human ability to make evaluative judgments in one domain as against the other. People can partly grasp what is beneficial and harmful "through their reason as concerns this-worldly matters [*umūr al-dunyā*]." It is rather the consequences of the afterlife (*al-dār al-ākhira*) that can be known only by revelation.[2] Jurists discussing the aims of the Law, as we saw in the previous chapter, qualified the human interests at stake as pertaining to the domain of the present life. To ask how Ibn Taymiyya approaches the notion of welfare within legal reasoning is thus to open a new question about the operation of ethical judgments in the realm of ordinary human experience.

In this chapter, my aims will be composite. The aim of the first part of the chapter will be to consider Ibn Taymiyya's engagement with the notion of welfare in the context of his legal epistemology, focusing on a set of key questions. To what extent, or in what sense, are the interests promoted by the Law accessible to human reason? How substantively does Ibn Taymiyya envisage human inquirers as engaging considerations of welfare in the legal context? And what does this have to tell us about the capacity of human reason to operate independently of revealed guidance? Ibn Taymiyya's remarks on the topic, as I will show, harbor conflicting tendencies and invite competing interpretations. To the extent that we can organize these tendencies into a more cohesive whole, I will argue that it is a conservative stance on the topic that dominates his remarks, underscoring the textual framework that bounds human reasoning. My aim in the second part of the chapter will be to provide an additional set of interpretive foils against which to read Ibn Taymiyya's emphasis on reason in the ethical domain. Thematizing the competing tendencies of his work, I will first offer a broader comment on the interpretive difficulties that hamper the reconstruction of his ethical views and use this to raise a question about his deeper aims in pressing the claim of ethical reason. I will then consider the larger understanding of the relationship between reason and revelation against which this claim naturally asks to be located, concluding with a final reflection on what it means to look for the ethical deliverances of "pure" reason against the complex background of preexisting religious but also social practices that frames these.

In order to find the beginning of this argument, we now need to make the leap from the theological to the legal context to consider the evidence.

Considerations of Welfare in Legal Reasoning: A Substantive Engagement?

It is a leap, our discussion in chapter 4 indicated, that may often be attended by important consequences. It was in effecting just such a transition between discourses, as we saw—a transition from their theological to their legal writings—that Ashʿarites were confronted with critical tensions in their viewpoint and came under pressure to produce new intellectual adjustments. In the case of Ashʿarite thinkers, the transition between discourses marked an identifiable shift in genre. For the thematic repertories of these two discourses, to be sure, interfaced at several points, and *uṣūl al-fiqh* sometimes provided a fresh stage for continuing debates that unfolded in *kalām*; the question of the value of actions was a case in point. Yet the theological treatise and the compendium of legal theory nevertheless represented distinct genres of writing with their own peculiar structures, topics, and aims.

The leap between discourses in Ibn Taymiyya's case confronts us on very different terms. For if we except the legal work *al-Musawwada fī uṣūl al-fiqh*, produced by accretion by three generations of scholars of the Taymiyyan family—its unusual method of composition and fractured authorial identity mirrored in its tentative title ("A Draft")—Ibn Taymiyya's output does not include an extended and systematic work of legal theory that might have allowed us to seek out his views in structured ways under familiar headings. For the topic that narrowly concerns us, namely the place of welfare in the Law, the discussion of "suitability" as a means of identifying the legal cause in the context of analogy and the discussion of unattested interests (*maṣāliḥ mursala*) as a source of Law formed two of the most important rubrics under which competing views had been articulated in major legal treatises. Ibn Taymiyya's remarks on legal theory take the form of short treatises or *fatwa*s on specific themes, many of them compiled in volumes 19 and 20 of his collected *Fatāwā*, and sometimes appear as excursions woven into other, often polemical contexts. His theoretical remarks, similarly, are not cleanly isolated from his more practical discussions of concrete legal rulings.[3] The leap in question is thus less a leap between genres than a leap between topics, and topics to be tracked down through a variety of topographies.

My account here will focus on three topics that are seminal for piecing together a clear understanding of Ibn Taymiyya's engagement with the notion of welfare in the legal context: his foregrounding of "pragmatic" considerations within his practical legal rulings; his emphasis on the role of preponderant utility as a determinant of legal rulings; and his theoretical remarks about the role of unattested interests as a source of Law. In each of these cases, he gives a prominent role to considerations of welfare in ways that appear to invest him in a substantive engagement with such considerations and in a robust claim about the human ability to confront evaluative grounds and undertake evaluative reasoning independently. Yet a finer-grained reading of the evidence offers crucial correctives to this picture, calling attention to the paramount importance of the scriptural texts in regulating and conditioning this evaluative engagement.

In the previous chapter, I invoked the notion of "pragmatism" as a means of characterizing Ibn Taymiyya's approach to theological truth. This same notion has been invoked by several of Ibn Taymiyya's readers on a different level as a means of characterizing his approach to legal decisions. We have already had much to say about the centrality of "welfare" in his vision of the divine Law. But in talking about his legal pragmatism, it has often been a more specific inflection of this concept that has taken the foreground, namely that of necessity or hardship. The positions advocated by Ibn Taymiyya on a variety of practical legal questions—many of them highly controversial positions that challenge preexisting legal practice—often turn out to be unified by one key feature: the cardinal emphasis they place on considerations of hardship.

Addressing Ibn Taymiyya's legal thought in a recent essay, Yossef Rapoport highlights the relevance of this point for approaching several of his distinctive legal rulings. His ruling against holding water to be impure when a minimal impure quantity has dissolved in it, or his ruling in favor of menstruating women performing the *ṭawāf* during the hajj, can be seen in this light. So can his contentious ruling permitting the use of all clauses other than those that have been expressly forbidden by scripture—as against those explicitly permitted—in drawing up different kinds of contracts, or his ruling in favor of using circumstantial evidence in courts. The same holds for another contentious ruling, in favor of leasing orchards, traditionally frowned upon by jurists due to the element of uncertainty it involves.[4] In many of these cases, Ibn Taymiyya issues legal rulings that antagonize what he sees as an excessively restrictive legal spirit—a restrictiveness whose absurdity becomes all the more plain when legal stratagems are then widely devised to enable people to evade it—on account of the hardship this causes. The Law, we are given to understand, cannot have prohibited something that produces great hardship. Rapoport here quotes one of the statements Ibn Taymiyya offers in defending the lease of orchards: "The point is this: the community could not abide by a prohibition like that [i.e., the lease of orchards], *as it brings about intolerable harm. It is therefore known that it is not prohibited.* . . . Whatever people need for their sustenance, and is not caused by sin . . . then it is not prohibited for them, because they are like the one who is in need."[5]

Considerations of hardship (*ḍarūra*), to be sure, had been far from foreign to Islamic legal practice. Such considerations had been enshrined in the widely endorsed principle of *rukhṣa* or "license," which stipulated that the strict demands of the Law could be relaxed when their observation involved special and unusual difficulty. Thus, fasting might be deferred or omitted by pregnant women or travelers, and ritual prayer might be performed in a less rigorous fashion during illness. The consumption of carrion, normally prohibited, was permitted when starvation threatened and human life was at risk. The principle of legal license, as these examples indicate, faced in two directions, justifying the relaxation or suspension of both obligations and prohibitions. It was a principle that rested on clear scriptural roots, including the Qur'anic verse that reads, "God desires ease for you, and desires not hardship for you" (Q 2:185).[6]

In treating hardship as a consideration vested with normative significance, Ibn Taymiyya thus leans his weight on a longer legal tradition. Yet his legal positions seem to take this significance further by calling upon it not merely as a negative principle for the mitigation of the strict letter of the Law, but also as a positive action-guiding principle that applies in the absence of contrary legal guidance and that indeed serves to discourage the gratuitous extension of the Law's reach, thereby broadening the sphere of its own application. This point was recently highlighted by Felicitas Opwis in the context of her larger study of *maṣlaḥa* in the classical legal tradition, where she distinguished between two principles at work in Ibn Taymiyya's substantive legal decisions that separately highlight the primacy of welfare in his thought. One is the principle of legal license, which recognizes hardship as the basis for temporarily permitting actions that the Law has prohibited or relaxing the performance of actions it has declared obligatory; the other is its positive counterpart, which recognizes human need as the basis for deeming permissible actions that the Law has not expressly prohibited.[7] The notion of welfare that forms the heart of this more positive application is a broad one, and notably includes economic interests, as the ruling on the lease of orchards suggests ("whatever people need for their sustenance" or livelihood [*ma'āsh*]). An equally broad notion of interests is thematized by the ruling on contractual clauses, given the wide range of transactions with a contractual basis, which include not only economic transactions such as buying and selling but also marital relations, among others.

What human beings need and what serves their most pressing welfare, such evidence suggests, carries a distinct normative force. The prohibition of leasing orchards "brings about intolerable harm," we just heard, and "*it is therefore known* that it is not prohibited." This normative force would seem to find its natural counterpart in an epistemological transparency which reflects the fact that these kinds of needs are not simply judged, but felt. "Such-and-such an activity is acutely needed [*inna hādhā mimmā tamissu al-ḥāja ilayhi*]," Ibn Taymiyya tirelessly repeats in this context. This expression will immediately remind us of a set of very similar locutions that we encountered in the previous chapter when considering the views of Ash'arite writers regarding the accessibility of the Law's objectives to the human mind. (Al-Juwaynī: *masīs al-ḥāja ila'l-masākin*; al-Ghazālī: *hiya ma'āsh al-khalq wa-hum muḍṭarrūn ilayhā*; al-Āmidī: *mā tad'ū ḥājat al-nās ilayhi.*) In throwing down bridges to these discussions, Ibn Taymiyya, on the one hand, invites us to redeploy the conclusions we had reached in that context to the present one. Here, as there, the notion of "need" and "welfare" at stake would demand to be read, not as one revealed through or defined by the external vantage point of the Law, but as one recognized through lived experience and grounded in a prerevelational grasp as basic as the need for physical survival and making a living.

Yet in laying down these bridges, Ibn Taymiyya also reminds us of another crucial context in which the notion of *ḍarūra* as well as that of *ḥāja* had appeared in the writings of jurists before him; and this was in reflecting more systematically on the objectives of the Law and on the human interests that underpinned legal rulings. Al-Ghazālī and those who followed in his footsteps, as we saw, had offered a three-tiered scheme for organizing the interests promoted by the Law, dividing them into "necessities" (*ḍarūriyyāt*), "needs" (*ḥājiyyāt*), and "improvements" (*taḥsīniyyāt*). With this scheme back in sight, another facet of Ibn Taymiyya's position can now stand out for attention, which brings into view not the similarities that unite him with al-Ghazālī, but rather an important point of division.

Talking about classical jurists' engagement with the notion of welfare in chapter 4, we saw that this engagement had been conditioned by a fear about the danger that in seeking to determine the divine Law, human beings would "remake the law in their own image." This sense of guard had been manifest in the way jurists had handled the notion of "suitability" as a method for identifying the legal cause with a view to extending the Law analogically. Yet it emerged even more sharply in connection with the hotly contested topic of what were known as "textually unregulated" or "unattested" interests (*maṣāliḥ mursala*). Writing in his *Mustaṣfā*, al-Ghazālī had provided a useful compass for situating the latter and for appreciating the special problems they raised. Human interests, he had written, fall in three different classes, representing three different ways of relating to the revealed texts. There are interests that the Law has distinctly testified should receive consideration; there are interests that the Law has distinctly testified should not; and finally there are interests regarding which the Law has offered no testimony.[8] The operation of analogy, which extended the Law through the prior identification of legal causes partly by means of "suitability," looked to the first class of interests, working on the basis of what the Law had said. Unattested interests, as their name betrays, represented the last class; they were interests on which the Law had been silent.

One has little difficulty seeing why this class would give grounds for special worry to jurists concerned with preserving the purity of the divine Law. For the human mind's engagement with the notion of welfare in the context of analogy was embedded in a textual framework and remained an exercise essentially interpretive in nature. To ask whether a certain interest on which the Law had been silent should form the basis for prescribing or proscribing a given action, by contrast, was to envisage a far more direct confrontation between the human mind and considerations of welfare. It was to invest human reason with the capacity to deliver more substantive evaluative judgments, and as such to entrust it with the performance of legislative offices that many jurists saw as rightfully belonging to God. Even those who were prepared to accord an important place to human interests in the context of analogy and to recognize the role of reason in apprehending these interests expressed greater misgiving when it came to textually unregulated benefits. Al-Ghazālī would convey his own misgivings in unambiguous tones when he would conclude his relevant discussion in the *Mustaṣfā* with the aphoristic admonition: "He who would judge [actions] on the basis of human welfare has engaged in legislation [*man istaṣlaḥa, fa-qad sharraʿa*]."[9]

It is within this context that we must situate al-Ghazālī's threefold classification of human interests into "necessities," "needs," and "improvements." This scheme, as Benjamin Jokisch points out, was articulated against a clear concern to find ways of safeguarding the juridical appeal to welfare against abuse.[10] For there are indeed cases where the human interests served by a given action seem so compelling that to deny their evaluative force, or the space for decision they open up, would be absurd. The example often brought up for discussion in this connection is one that modern readers will recognize as a textbook case of moral conflict. Suppose Muslims are at war with unbelievers, and the enemy seizes Muslims to use as shields. If Muslims hold fire, the enemy will overrun their land and slaughter them en masse without restraint, yet if they turn their fire on the enemy, they take innocent lives. What should be done? Or to restate this more relevantly, what should be taken to be the stance of the religious *Law* on this difficult situation?

Confronting such cases in the *Mustaṣfā*, al-Ghazālī would say: human interests must indeed dictate the course of action even without an explicit textual indicant, in this case ruling in favor of the permissibility of killing Muslim shields, which is the course of action that preserves the greatest amount of (innocent) life. This case in fact illustrates three major conditions that must be met if unattested interests are to form the basis of a ruling: they must be general (*kulliyya*), affecting the community as a whole; they must be epistemically certain (*qaṭʿiyya*), leaving no doubt that these interests are under threat and that the action taken will successfully protect them; and the choice must be unavoidable (*ḍarūriyya*). But also the interest or good at stake must belong to the highest rung of "necessities" in terms of the threefold scheme we have seen, in this case, the good of life.[11] What is important about necessities is not only that they represent the highest and most imperative class of human interests but also—and crucially for the concern with textual safeguarding—that they are confined to five very specific and clearly circumscribed goods: religion, reason, progeny, life, and property.

Given the explicit thematization of the role of human reason in confronting welfare considerations in the debate about unattested interests, Ibn Taymiyya's own stance on the topic will hold special interest for us. His most concentrated and oft-cited remarks on unattested interests emerge in an epistle entitled *Qāʿida fī ʾl-muʿjizāt wa ʾl-karāmāt* in a broader vicinity that hosts a number of other significant remarks regarding the evaluative role of human reason. And what is important is that the views he voices there appear to align him with a liberal stance on the topic, in doing so wedding his theoretical remarks about welfare to the understanding suggested by his practical legal decisions.

Opening his discussion with a reference to the fivefold tabulation of interests—which he lists as religion, reason, life, property, and honor (*al-nufūs wa ʾl-amwāl wa ʾl-aʿrāḍ wa ʾl-ʿuqūl wa ʾl-adyān*)—Ibn Taymiyya criticizes this scheme for its excessive restrictiveness. Part of this criticism seems to be linked to a perception that the fivefold scheme as traditionally articulated carries an overwhelmingly negative emphasis, having been articulated with a focus on punishments—punishments that serve to deflect harm from positive goods—and as such singling out only one moiety of welfare: the negative deflection of harm as against the positive pursuit of benefit.[12] Another part seems to reflect the concern that such punitive measures attend exclusively to what is external and not internal, to the acts of the body as against the inner state of the soul. Putting the latter point aside, it is then worth noting that when Ibn Taymiyya turns to specify the positive component sidelined by the traditional approach, he refers us to those worldly "transactions [*muʿāmalāt*] and acts which are said to serve the welfare of people in the absence of a legal prohibition."[13]

The echo with Ibn Taymiyya's practical legal discussions will be obvious. The last phrase ("in the absence of a legal prohibition"), more particularly, will remind us of what I described above as the positive counterpart of the principle of legal license: *maṣlaḥa* or need forms the ground for deeming permissible human actions and transactions (such as contractually based acts of sale, marriage, and so on) that the Law has not expressly prohibited. Yet with the debate about unattested interests in clearer view, it will also be obvious that this is a singularly vague gesture with which to fill the category of positive benefit that jurists like al-Ghazālī had stocked in more determinate terms in the interest of closing the door against a more direct engagement with human welfare. To reject the scheme of "five essentials" and to refer generally to "transactions and acts" and to the broad welfare they serve without qualifying this more determinately—in Ibn Taymiyya's usage, as Rapoport notes, the "definition of *maṣlaḥa* can potentially encompass all that is beneficial to human society"[14]—would seem to open that door in a way calculated to let in a decided draft. It will then be hard to avoid the conclusion Opwis thereby draws: by disarming the formal criteria and procedures that had constrained the juridical engagement with interests, and by additionally failing to give a clear account of the procedural rules regulating the interaction with the texts, Ibn Taymiyya has considerably weakened the textual safety valves and taken a big step toward a more substantive confrontation with human interests than al-Ghazālī and textualist-minded jurists after him sanctioned.[15] And it is a confrontation that would seem to bring with it a correlative reliance on the resources of reason.

Studying Ibn Taymiyya's engagement with considerations of welfare through his *fatwas*, Jokisch may seem to have offered a corrective to this picture, emphasizing the textualist character of Ibn Taymiyya's enterprise in observing that while Ibn Taymiyya recognizes *maṣlaḥa* as a source of Law, he consistently sets it in the context of analogy. In his hallmark ruling in favor of the lease of orchards, thus, Ibn Taymiyya does not argue directly on the basis of welfare but rather on the basis of analogy with other practices already invested with legal sanction, such as the *ʿarāyā* contract, which involves trading unripe dates on the palm tree against their projected value as edible dried dates. Despite the element of risk (*gharar*) this contract involves, jurists had permitted it by way of legal license on grounds of need (*ḥāja*). Yet Jokisch immediately places this textualist commitment in a very different light when he observes that it is nothing more determinate than the broad notion of need that Ibn Taymiyya invokes as the basis of this analogical transfer.[16]

In contrasting a "textualist" with a "substantive" approach to human welfare, of course, everything will hang on the way we understand the notion of a "textual indicant" at work. The broad notion of need or pressing welfare that Ibn Taymiyya invokes, as we have seen, looks back to distinct Qur'anic dictums such as "God desires ease for you, and desires not hardship for you" (Q 2:185). To the extent that considerations of hardship have received the Law's imprimatur through statements of this sort, any decision made on the basis of such considerations, it could be said, in some sense "derives" from an indicant contained in the revealed Law. With a sufficiently enlarged conception of what it means for *maṣlaḥa* to "appear" in the texts, little need remain outside it. Enlarged this way, however, the notion of a textual indicant would seem to be in danger of losing its meaning and arbitrative role. What to call "derivation" or "support," as Malcolm Kerr observes, was a central question in debating the place of human interests in the Law and in distinguishing between the different types of relationships in which interests can stand to the revealed texts. For "to the extent that there is convincing support for a given consideration in the revealed sources, *whether in a general or particular way*, of course such a consideration is not *mursala*." Yet to open the notion of "support" too much in the direction of generality, as certain liberal-minded exponents of *maṣlaḥa* proposed to do, would dissolve the relevant distinctions, making it "appear questionable that in its absolute and literal sense a conception of *maṣlaḥa mursala* really existed at all."[17] And in doing so, it would lead straight into the open sea of an unregulated confrontation with unattested interests that most jurists shrank from. The controversial case of Ibn Taymiyya's contemporary and one-time student Najm al-Dīn al-Ṭūfī (d. 1316) provides the most instructive illustration of this danger. Drawing on the broad message expressed in the solitary hadith "Do not inflict injury or repay one injury with another [*lā ḍarar wa-lā ḍirār*]," al-Ṭūfī advocated one of the most substantive confrontations with the notion of welfare that the classical legal tradition would play host to, raising *maṣlaḥa* to the status of a supreme law-making principle capable of overriding the very letter of the Law, and thereby illustrating the possibility that a textual foundation could launch one out of the orbit of the textual system altogether. Ibn Taymiyya, as Jokisch notes, does not go as far as al-Ṭūfī in the legislative status he accords to welfare.[18] Yet in opening up the notion of need so widely—a move that, to the extent that it is grounded in the texts, would have to reflect a highly general construal of what counts as a textual indicant—his approach pulls strongly in that direction.

The evidence carried by Ibn Taymiyya's theoretical remarks about unattested interests and by his practical legal decisions thus appears to press an understanding of his viewpoint that underscores the ability of the human mind to confront considerations of welfare directly and evaluate them independently of textual guidance. The same picture receives support from another central feature of his legal discussions. Studying the notion of divine wisdom in chapter 4, we will recall that one of the most important characterizations of wisdom that Ibn Taymiyya had offered was comparative in kind. The wise person is not simply the one who chooses what is good; it is the one who knows to choose what is best in situations where good and evil, or different kinds of goods and different kinds of evils, have to be weighed against each other: "Wisdom demands giving precedence to the best of two goods by sacrificing the lesser one." This view was reflected in Ibn Taymiyya's characterization of the Law, which does not simply promote what is beneficial but rather "gives preponderance to the best of two goods ... realizing the greatest of two benefits [*aʿẓam al-maṣlaḥatayn*] through sacrificing the lesser one, and repelling the greatest of two harms [*aʿẓam al-mafsadatayn*] by tolerating the lesser one."[19]

It is a point, I noted in the previous chapter, that will remind us of the cost-benefit comparisons alluded to by the Qur'an itself as the underlying rationale of its rulings, for example in relation to the prohibition against the consumption of wine and gambling. ("In both is great sin, and [some] utility [*manāfiʿ*] for men; but the sin of them is greater than their usefulness" (Q 2:219).) Situations of conflict, Ibn Taymiyya suggests on numerous occasions across his writings, are pervasive in human life. There are cases where one good cannot be achieved without sacrificing another, and other cases where evil cannot be avoided and it is simply a matter of preferring the lesser one; there are cases where good cannot be achieved without allowing some evil to be realized, and other cases where evil cannot be avoided without some good being sacrificed.[20] In the case of wine and games of chance, God Himself executes the task of comparing benefits and harms and making the call as to which side preponderates, translating this wise judgment into a clear prohibition of these acts. In several locations, however, this is a comparative judgment that Ibn Taymiyya signals that human inquirers must undertake, actively using it as a decision-making tool to determine what should and should not be done.

We will all be familiar with this decision-making tool as it operates in ordinary human life: we use it every time we take a draft of bitter medicine in the interest of preserving or producing health. It is this basic judgment, as Ibn ʿAqīl suggests in the *Wāḍiḥ*, that is exercised by the thirsty person who turns away from a source of water the moment he sees the footprint of a lion on approach.[21] Yet what will be more interesting for our argument is the way this decision-making tool expresses itself in the religious life and in the application of divinely prescribed precepts. One of the most important contexts in which Ibn Taymiyya discusses it is the performance of the well-known duty of commanding right and forbidding wrong (*al-amr biʾl-maʿrūf waʾl-nahy ʿan al-munkar*). For to accept *that* this precept must generally be obeyed is still to leave much room open for questions about *how* it should be applied in particular cases—and even, at times, *whether*. This is a room that demands of individuals a highly delicate exercise of judgment regarding the balance of benefits over costs. There are times when, weighing up these consequences, we may decide that it is best to abandon the duty altogether—for example, when those committing wrong are persons in power or when forbidding a certain wrong will lead to the breach of a graver right.[22]

It is in the context of discussing the duty of commanding right and forbidding wrong that Ibn Taymiyya offers the following remarkable methodological statement in his treatise *al-Ḥisba*: "If benefits and harms conflict ... one must give precedence to that which preponderates.... So even if commanding [right] and forbidding [wrong] involves the realization of benefit and the repulsion of harm, one must examine that which conflicts with it. If the benefit that is forgone or the harm that is repelled is greater, it [i.e., commanding right and forbidding wrong] has not been commanded; it has rather been forbidden if the harm it involves is greater than the benefit."[23] The balance of utility, this suggests, forms a ground, no less, for concluding that a particular act exemplifying a category that has been commanded or forbidden by the Law in general terms should be deemed to be "commanded" as against "forbidden" in that particular instance. This is a balance that individuals confronted with a choice of acting will have to establish through their own judgment, using the above methodological principle (*qāʿida*) as a rule of proceeding.

Textualism: The Engagement of Welfare in Its Scriptural Framework

I have been suggesting that there is a considerable body of evidence that appears to press a liberal understanding of Ibn Taymiyya's transactions with the notion of welfare, in doing so highlighting the role of human reason in making substantive independent judgments about the consequential tendencies of actions. Yet the evidence in fact does not speak so unambiguously; probed more closely, these liberal messages turn out to be interlocked with a rather different set of messages that repeatedly serve to ground them within a more conservative conditioning frame.

Working our way backward through each of the three topics we have surveyed, we can see this clearly in connection with Ibn Taymiyya's emphasis on the importance of establishing the overall balance of benefits and costs. For a closer reading of some of his most concentrated remarks regarding situations of conflict shows that the majority of examples he uses to illustrate this thesis are ones in which the preferred action has been established on scriptural grounds. A person who must choose between the good of making expenditure for one's family and the good of devoting funds to religious war should choose the former—a prophetic tradition makes this order of priority plain. A woman faced with the evil of performing the *hijra* without an accompanying male family member and the evil of remaining in the domain of war should opt for the former—an incident recounted in the Qur'an (Q 60:10) provides clear grounds for this choice. Killing is an evil, but so is unbelief, and scripture has clarified that the latter evil outweighs the former so that it is acceptable to kill when the faith comes under threat (Q 2:217). Stoning the adulterer and amputating the hand of the thief may be evils, but they prevent even greater evils from occurring, hence the Law's prescription of these and other punishments.[24]

In all these cases the conflict between the beneficial and harmful tendencies of particular actions is mentioned only to be immediately referred to scriptural grounds that arbitrate between these tendencies and deliver a verdict on what should be done. It is not incidental that the cases Ibn Taymiyya discusses in this context include the type of conflict that jurists considered under the rubric of legal license, where it is a matter of choosing between the good of conforming to the Law and the evil of great visceral harm—for example, when starvation can be staved off only by eating carrion. Yet the choice of action in these kinds of cases had once again been elaborated by jurists on the basis of clear scriptural texts (such as Q 2:173 with regard to carrion).

The duty of commanding right and prohibiting wrong, where the utilitarian calculus seems to register especially strongly as a decision-making tool, forms a more complex case, given its deeper links to Ibn Taymiyya's political morality. These links are evidenced in his special concern with constraining the practice of this duty vis-à-vis persons in power, and his cautious stance here points to his disagreement with the aggressive view of this duty taken by other Muslim factions, such as the Khārijites and the Muʿtazilites, who considered that fulfilling the duty might even sanction rebellion against the ruling power. In deciding which side of the equation to privilege and in ruling that the harm may outweigh the benefit in this case, Ibn Taymiyya invokes an understanding of the proper attitude toward political rulers that leans on distinct scriptural bases. There is a default duty of obedience we owe to rulers that is indicated by the Qur'an itself when stating, "O believers, obey God, and obey the Messenger and those in authority among you" (Q 4:59), and even more pointedly by the Prophet when advising people, "Give rulers their due, and ask God for your [own] dues," thereby driving a wedge between rulers' rectitude and the allegiance we owe them.[25] Yet this political stance, some commentators have emphasized, ultimately leans on a pragmatic concern with the deleterious consequences of rebellion and the way it undermines the public good.[26]

In analyzing Ibn Taymiyya's view of this duty, however, it will be important to attend to the terms in which he himself invites us to construe the cost-benefit analysis that underpins his approach in some of the most direct remarks he devotes to the topic. It is in connection with the duty of commanding right and forbidding wrong, as we saw above, that he offers a stark methodological statement suggesting that the overall utility of actions must be evaluated substantively through independent human judgment (even if it "involves the realization of benefit and the repulsion of harm, one must examine that which conflicts with it"). Yet another reading of the context of this statement places it in a more ambivalent light. Ibn Taymiyya immediately continues: "Harms and benefits, however, must be considered using the measuring scales of the Sharīʿa [*mīzān al-sharīʿa*]." The notion of the "measuring scales," as we will see later in this chapter, is one that Ibn Taymiyya elsewhere connects with a scripturally circumscribed mode of reasoning and indeed with legal analogy, betraying that the confrontation with utility he has in mind is not as substantive as appears but should rather be understood as taking place on interpretive terms within the regulating framework of scripture. The ambivalence is not entirely expunged in the ensuing lines: "So *when* a person can follow texts," Ibn Taymiyya continues, "he should not veer from them." Scriptural texts may sometimes be unavailable, this suggests, reopening the door to the prospect of a more substantive evaluative judgment. The door swings more decisively shut, however, in Ibn Taymiyya's final sentence: "Yet it is rare that one who is well acquainted with the texts and with their way of indicating qualifications [*aḥkām*] should be lacking in textual indicants."[27]

Having uncovered the deeper ambivalence present in Ibn Taymiyya's discussion of the criterion of preponderant utility and the more conservative textualist emphasis that ultimately seems to underpin it, we will then be more prepared to notice a similar pattern when we turn to one of the other topics we considered above—the question of unattested interests. Here, too, the liberal note that we heard turns out to be far from representative of the overall acoustic pitch of Ibn Taymiyya's discussion in his seminal epistle *Qāʿida fi 'l-muʿjizāt wa 'l-karāmāt*. People have erred both ways, he points out: by refusing to consider something a benefit (*maṣlaḥa*) unless it has been mentioned in the texts; and by deeming a benefit something that is not, on the assumption that religion supports benefits in general. The latter diagnosis signals a restrictive attitude that marks a departure from the more liberal standpoint he appears to express elsewhere. It is the same attitude that shapes a linchpin statement that commentators have often picked up on as a crucial token of his view of the place of interests in the Law and the role of reason in accessing them:[28]

> The inclusive view is that the Law never neglects matters of welfare [*maṣlaḥa*] . . . and when reason considers something to be in one's interests even though it has not appeared in the revealed texts, one of two things must hold: either revelation has somehow indicated it even though this particular inquirer has not grasped that, or it is not in one's interests . . . for welfare consists in the total or preponderant benefit, and people often fancy

> that a given thing is beneficial in religious and worldly matters [*fi 'l-dīn wa 'l-dunyā*] when it involves benefit that is [in fact] outweighed by harm.

This statement carries its meaning on its sleeve, and Opwis spells it out plainly when she writes: "A legal ruling that is based on other than textual indication is invalid. Unattested *maṣlaḥas*, by definition, fall outside the scope of religious law."[29] With this passage, Ibn Taymiyya thus appears to align himself with the more textualist view of welfare commonly identified with al-Ghazālī. Interests have to be read out of the Law; any interest that the Law does not indicate falls out of consideration. In this light, the first prong of Ibn Taymiyya's diagnosis of common error—the refusal to consider as a benefit something that has not been mentioned in the scriptural texts—turns out to be erroneous on account of its presupposition: for in fact nothing that constitutes a true benefit can fail to be mentioned in the texts. Our confrontation with interests is not substantive but bounded by textual evidence.

It is in fact the chary tones of al-Ghazālī's discussion of unattested interests—*man istaṣlaḥa, fa-qad sharra'a*—that Ibn Taymiyya echoes almost verbatim in yet another seminal if somewhat diffuse remark, which is worth listening to in full for reasons that will become evident:

> To affirm unattested interests is to legislate in religion [*yusharri'u*] matters for which God did not give His sanction. This resembles in certain respects the question of *istiḥsān* and *al-taḥsīn al-'aqlī* and arbitrary opinion [*ra'y*] and the like, for *istiḥsān* is to seek what is good and what is best [*al-ḥasan wa 'l-aḥsan*] . . . and it is to consider [*ru'yat*] something to be good, just as *istiqbāḥ* is to consider it to be bad. What is good [*ḥasan*] is what serves one's welfare [*maṣlaḥa*], so *istiḥsān* and *istiṣlāḥ* are close in meaning. And *al-taḥsīn al-'aqlī* is the claim that reason perceives what is good.[30]

I have left several terms of this passage untranslated in order to avoid marking the seams between two different semantic directions, and two separate discursive habitats, in which these terms can be understood as facing. Taken as a technical term proper to legal theory, we normally translate the term *istiḥsān* as "juristic preference," often understood as a jurist's decision to favor a ruling that deviates from the one derivable from strict analogy.[31] Yet it is important not to hear this term in an exclusively technical register in a way that might mask its etymological ligaments to the terms *ḥasan* and *taḥsīn* appearing in the same vicinity. The latter pair of terms forges a link with a broader question about the nature of evaluative judgments and about the "determination of good and bad" (*al-taḥsīn wa 'l-taqbīḥ*) that had unfolded principally within the theological context. Ibn Taymiyya himself, we will notice, draws our attention to this link at the end of this passage.

The sudden confrontation of these two discursive habitats in the space of a single paragraph will seem highly suggestive. For the position Ibn Taymiyya assumed in this theological debate, we will recall, took the form of a strong claim that people know what is good by reason and that what is good comes down to what constitutes welfare. Leaping to the legal context with this conception of ethical knowledge in place, we would anticipate that the ascription of a confident role to reason in the apprehension of welfare would provide the best fulfillment of Ibn Taymiyya's ethical claims. In this respect, Opwis's comment that "Ibn Taymiyya backs his *rejection* of using unattested *maṣlaḥa*s in the legal process with an analysis of the intellect's ability to grasp that something is good (*taḥsīn ʿaqlī*)," appears paradoxical and ultimately misguided. His analysis of the latter would rather offer, prima facie, the best support for his *acceptance* of the former.[32] Yet Ibn Taymiyya's ethical view, as we saw it in that theological context, turned out to be subject to important qualifications. Similar qualifications, crucially, appear to be in force in the present context. In both passages cited above, Ibn Taymiyya highlights the fallibility of reason taken as a means of identifying what serves our interests, and the possibility of error recurs in both sets of remarks as a guiding theme. The analysis of *istiḥsān* in the second passage in terms of "consider[ing] something to be good" might, thus, be heard as nothing but a purely linguistic explanation of this term. Yet in light of the emphasis placed on people's proclivity to misjudge what constitutes true benefit in the first passage ("people often fancy that a given thing is beneficial" when it is not)—an emphasis that recurs throughout the epistle and is here significantly extended to both the secular and religious domain (*fī ʾl-dīn wa ʾl-dunyā*)—this will register not so much as a linguistic observation as a pointed wedge between what we *consider* to be the case and what *really is* so.

The dominant thrust of these passages thus lies in diminishing the role of reason and accentuating our epistemic dependence on the Law in engaging considerations of welfare. With the above in place, we can finally turn to the topic that opened our discussion: Ibn Taymiyya's wide-ranging invocation of the notion of "need" or "hardship" in his practical legal judgments. In invoking this notion, Ibn Taymiyya appears to go beyond the negative principle of legal license to embrace human need more positively as an action-guiding principle. Human need is not only the basis for exceptionally suspending or relaxing the demands of the Law; it is also the basis for permitting actions that the Law has not expressly prohibited, telling us how to act in the face of the Law's silence. As such it carries a normative force that finds its counterpart in an epistemological immediacy. Yet here too, I would argue, Ibn Taymiyya's position cannot be read as simply as it initially invites. Shadowing his positive invocation of human need, in fact, is a broader theological context that has to be brought into view if the significance of this move is to be fully appreciated, and that serves to drastically modify the normative force and epistemological immediacy we understand the notion of need to carry.

It will take little to uncover this broader theological context, as it is implicit in the very language one reaches for in characterizing Ibn Taymiyya's viewpoint. Human need is the ground for permitting what the Law has not prohibited, I just suggested, telling us how to act in the face of the Law's silence. Readers familiar with the register of classical debates will not need much encouragement to hear in this last formulation the tones of a theological controversy that had formed one of the satellite battlegrounds of the debate concerning the value of actions. Unfolding in works of legal theory, this was a controversy that was dubbed *ḥukm al-afʿāl qabla wurūd al-sharʿ*. Its focusing question, as its terms betray, was: What was the normative status of actions prior to the advent of the Law?[33] This is a question bearing a natural relation to the kinds of questions discussed under the topic of "the determination of good and bad," and in many ways it can be viewed as a continuation of the puzzles that organized the latter. Ashʿarite theologians, as we have seen, had suggested that God constitutes the value of acts by commanding or prohibiting them. Yet the arrival of God's command and prohibition was a historical event: there was a time when God had not yet spoken, and then there was a time when He had. There was a *before* revelation and an *after*, a world before the event of God's word. How should we understand the way human life unfolded in that antediluvian "before"? For even in that antediluvian horizon, people would have acted; and more specifically, they would have moved to avail themselves of goods present in the world around them. They would have reached out to eat the fruit of the earth and drink what their environment offered. Would that have been *okay*? Would it have been permitted, taking into account that God is the proprietor of the created world and as such everything in the world rightfully belongs to Him? Or would it have been forbidden?

The responses given to this question by different theologians traveled the whole length of the spectrum, with some asserting that such actions were "permitted," others that they were "prohibited," and still others declaring that neither qualification rightly applied and judgment had to be suspended. The close relations between this question and the questions about ethical value made certain combinations more natural—if not ineluctable—than others. Ruling that such acts were permitted meshed more naturally with the affirmation that there are objective evaluative standards accessible to human reason prior to the revealed message. Ruling that acts were prohibited or that judgment should be suspended could both be taken as natural corollaries of the voluntarist claim that God was the sole author of value. Many Muʿtazilites, thus, had taken the first view, while prominent Ashʿarites had defended the view that no assessment was possible. Among the Ḥanbalites opinion had been mixed, yet there were a number of notable school members who had adopted the first position, including al-Tamīmī and al-Kalwadhānī. Ibn Taymiyya would thus have important Ḥanbalite precedents in staking his claim for this very position, asserting that prior to the advent of the Law, the default status of actions was "permitted" (*al-aṣl al-ibāḥa/ al-ʿafw/ al-jawāz*).[34]

The question animating this debate might seem academic, the product of an idle hypothesis that may remind us of those other exuberant imaginaries that pervaded classical theological reflection about ethics. We will recall Avicenna's "Imagine yourself into a world before society and you will question what you think you know about ethical values," or the Muʿtazilites' "Imagine yourself into a desert island and you will be certain of what you know about ethical values." Yet this particular imaginary would appear to be rather more idle, as it did to several jurist-theologians who questioned the wisdom of engaging in this debate. For there have in fact been cases where people have found themselves on desert islands or grown up in isolation from society. Yet the world, such thinkers pointed out, has never been without revelation: the very first human being, Adam, was subjected to commands and prohibitions from the moment of his creation. This question remains a live one, some would propose, to the extent that it is conceivable that "God should create [a person] in the desert knowing nothing about matters of the Law," or that one might be born on an island in the middle of the ocean and might then wonder whether the fruit or plants one finds are there to be freely enjoyed. More plausibly, it is possible that even in the present time people may fail to come into contact with the divine message.[35]

Yet an even more cogent defense for the usefulness of such inquiries was available elsewhere, which al-Kalwadhānī would spell out in a key statement quoted by Ibn Taymiyya in the *Musawwada*. For "supposing the Law[36] did not contain a ruling" regarding certain actions, such as our use of certain goods, there will be a question to ask as to "what the ruling should be" with respect to these actions. Yet if one declares the original status of acts to be prohibited or permitted, one may then say, "I searched for an indicant [*dalīl*] regarding that [act] in the Law and I did not find one, and I therefore remain with the original ruling [*ḥukm al-aṣl*]." The notion that al-Kalwadhānī invokes in this remark is one that would receive wide articulation within the legal tradition as the principle of "presumption of continuity" (*istiṣḥab al-ḥāl*). "A legal state of affairs," as Wael Hallaq sums it up, "is presumed to continue to be valid until there is reason to change this presumption."[37] In this case, the original status of acts, whether permitted or prohibited, is presumed to be valid until a textual indicant dislodges it. It is this backdrop that lends the question "What was the original status of acts prior to revelation?" a more tangible significance for legal practice, translating it from a speculative question concerning a state of nature in the distant historical past to a practically relevant question concerning the normative force of actions in the living present. Not so much the historical "Actions were once permitted before the Law declared their values" as the normative "We are to judge that actions are permitted so long as the Law has not declared opposite values."

There will be something more to say about the principle of "presumption of continuity" shortly. What is important here is that it is the same understanding of the normative significance of this question that is reflected in Ibn Taymiyya's own writings and more particularly his substantive legal decisions, which are governed precisely by the normative principle just formulated and now traced to its broader theological context. Acts like selling, renting, and making gifts, we hear in a telling passage, are "customary acts" (*ʿādāt*) that "people need for their livelihood [*maʿāsh*], as they do food, and drink, and clothing." Within these actions, Ibn Taymiyya continues, the Law came to "prohibit those that lead to harm, to make obligatory those that are necessary, to declare reprehensible those that should be avoided, and to commend those that contain preponderant advantage." Hence "people [may] go on buying and renting among themselves as they please so long as the Law has not issued a prohibition [*yatabāyaʿūna wa-yastaʾjirūna kayfa shāʾū mā lam tuḥarrim al-sharīʿa*], just as they [may] go on eating and drinking as they please so long as the Law has not issued a prohibition. . . . And so long as the Law does not set any bounds in the matter, they remain within the original state of liberty [*ʿalaʾl-iṭlāq al-aṣlī*]."[38]

"One may do as one pleases so long as the Law has not set any bounds": it is a message that is revisited repeatedly in Ibn Taymiyya's legal discussions and that comes into play with special clarity in his ruling concerning the use of contractual formulations. Any formulations may be legitimately used so long as they have not been expressly prohibited by the Law. This contrasts with the view—a view that would seem to be naturally affianced to the opposite side of the theological debate outlined above—that the use of such formulations is contingent on express legal permission. Putting the point more generally, one might say: people are free to undertake the contracts they wish on the terms they wish so long as they do not collide with any limits set by the Sharīʿa, whether to their form or their content. To take an example brought up by Ibn Taymiyya that speaks to the second kind of restriction: slaves may constitute personal property, yet should a person wish to lend his slave girl to another for sex, the Sharīʿa would intervene to prevent this mode of disposing of one's property, as this is not a form of sexual relationship that it recognizes as legitimate. The content of one's transaction, and one's freedom to transact with one's property as desired, would here be circumscribed by the Law.[39]

This way of relating human actions to the divine Law may remind us of a characterization of Islamic Law offered by Johansen that came before us in the previous chapter: the domain of free contractual exchanges between private individuals contrasted with the domain of the divine Law represented by the public sphere and the eschatological sphere of God's promise and threat; a domain of freely undertaken obligations bounded by, and upheld through, God's commands and prohibitions. Yet for the thread we are pursuing, the focus must fall on the fact that the freedom to initiate transactions and contract obligations, as Ibn Taymiyya presents it, is a freedom governed by practical necessity, which takes its content from the pursuit and satisfaction of needs and derives its normative status from the selfsame source. Acts are not permitted on merely negative grounds—namely the absence of the Law's statement. Acts are permitted on positive grounds, consisting in the human needs they serve. This normative relation is laid bare with special distinctness in the following remark, in which Ibn Taymiyya recapitulates a familiar point regarding the permissibility of contractual terms. Unless a set of terms is self-defeating or contravenes a legal prohibition, he writes, "there is no ground for prohibiting it, and *it is necessary that it be ruled licit, because it is an action people desire and need*; for were it not for their need, they would not do it [*al-wājib ḥilluhu, li-annahu ʿamal maqṣūd li ʾl-nās yaḥtājūna ilayhi idh law lā ḥājatuhum ilayhi lamā faʿalūhu*]."[40]

Because it is an action people need: the justificatory force peals out here in unmistakable terms; and in doing so it prepares our ears to pick out more distinctly a related message on the epistemic level. For there are all the telltale terms lined up before us: there is the vocabulary of "need" (*ḥāja*); there, too, is the notion of "intention" (*maqṣūd*); and the term "custom" (*ʿāda*) was only recently in our sights. These terms will instantly recall us to the discussion that unfolded in the previous chapter when considering the stance of Ashʿarite theologians on the apprehension of the human interests promoted by the Law. Yet this ensemble of evocative terms delivers its fruit more directly in a broad positioning statement that Ibn Taymiyya offers us elsewhere. Human actions, he writes, fall in two categories: ritual observances (*ʿibādāt*) that carry benefit in religious matters and customary or conventional acts that people need in their mundane affairs (*ʿādāt yaḥtājūna ilayhā fī dunyāhum*): "And through an inductive reading [*bi-istiqrāʾ*] of the sources of the Law, we know that it is only through revelation that acts of worship . . . are established as having been commanded [*lā yathbutu al-amr bihā illā bi ʾl-sharʿ*]. As for customary acts, they are [those acts] people need and customarily pursue in their worldly affairs, and with respect to them the original condition is the absence of prohibition [*wa ʾl-aṣl fīhi ʿadam al-ḥaẓar*], so that nothing is prohibited among them save what God has prohibited."[41]

We will recognize many of the themes of earlier remarks, and certainly the concluding keynote. We may also recognize a distinction that jurists often foregrounded in discussing the place of welfare in the Law, connecting rationally apprehensible welfare with mundane acts and dissociating it from ritual acts.[42] More interesting for our immediate purposes will be the notion of "inductive reading" that opens this statement. The notions of need (*ḥāja* and *ḍarūra*) invoked by Ibn Taymiyya at this juncture of his writings, I suggested earlier, demand to be read just like the Ashʿarites' before him, pointing to a sense of need that is recognized from the vantage point of experience. One of the ways this prerevelational recognition had been parsed among Ashʿarite writers, as we saw in the previous chapter, was as a question about the "custom" out of which the interests promoted by the Law can be read. Is it through an inductive reading of the behavior of the Law and its special textual custom (*daʾb al-sharʿ, ʿādat al-sharʿ*)? Or is it rather through a reading of human life and its customs, and thus through the unaided faculties of human reason? This is the question that Ibn Taymiyya's invocation of "induction" appears to flag. And while he does not make his answer explicit, his governing contrast seems suggestive enough: the imperative for performing ritual acts may be delivered by the Law; for those acts that serve our mundane interests, by contrast, we stand in need of no command to experience their imperative and discover their value.

It is a substantive specification of human welfare that will once again strike us with the singular openness of its texture. A starker expression of this openness could scarcely be conceived than the one found in the statement we heard moments ago: unless a contract contravenes a prohibition it should be deemed licit, "because it is an action people desire and need, for were it not for their need, they would not do it." Ibn Taymiyya continues: "For in the undertaking of an action lies the presumption of one's need for it [*al-iqdām ʿala'l-fiʿl maẓinnat al-ḥāja ilayhi*]."[43] Restating this cumbersome last point, we might say: if we act, it is because we need. Yet were we to hear this as an attempt to isolate a *criterion* for identifying needs worthy of consideration, it is hard to see how any action could fail to qualify. All we seem to have here is the truism: action is motivated by desire. We couldn't be further away from the finer-grained distinctions between types of desire or need—such as those reflected in the three-tiered scheme of *ḍarūriyyāt, ḥājiyyāt, taḥsīniyyāt* or in the fivefold enumeration of *ḍarūriyyāt*—that other jurists had offered at this same juncture.

The sheer openness of Ibn Taymiyya's notion of desire or need, I would suggest, already foretokens that the above understanding of the normative force attaching to need, and the epistemic commitment involved in affirming it, requires serious qualification. It is a closer scrutiny of the theological postulate underpinning Ibn Taymiyya's views, and of the juridical context of this postulate, that allows the qualifications to emerge more plainly. For I have spoken of the normative character of need, and of its force as a "because" that provides positive good-making grounds. Yet this justificatory force cannot be entirely appreciated without locating it against the governing logic of the postulate that frames it. This logic, as we have seen, bears a distinctly conditional aspect. Acts are permitted *as long as* no express prohibition has arisen. People may go on buying and selling "as they please, *so long as* [*mā lam*] the Law has not issued a prohibition," and "*so long as* the Law does not set any bounds in the matter, they remain within the original state of liberty." Or again, using a different grammatical construction to identical effect: "Anything that people need for their livelihood *and* that is not a cause of sin . . .

is not forbidden to them."[44] It is this conditional structure that was similarly reflected in the schema invoked earlier to qualify Ibn Taymiyya's view: a domain of freedom bounded by the Law. The implications of this limiting condition on the normative level are so clear as to hardly require stating. Need or desire is only a ground of value on condition that no opposing ground happens to be realized by an action. The value of an action that is grounded in the satisfaction of need is a defeasible one.[45]

This conclusion may seem less surprising once we recall that the particular value that we have been referring to as "grounded" in need is the relatively weak value of permissibility (*jawāz, ḥill, ibāḥa*). Ibn Taymiyya himself brings out the conditional character of this value even more plainly when he elsewhere rephrases it using a purely negative set of terms, speaking of the "absence of prohibition" (*ʿadam al-ḥaẓar/al-taḥrīm*). It is a conceptual turn that may remind us of a point that has been framed more broadly with regard to the notion of "good" by recent thinkers. Peter Geach thus observes that "there is a logical asymmetry between good and bad acts: an act is good only if everything about it is good, but may be bad if *anything* about it is bad; so it might be risky to say we knew an act to be good *sans phrase*, rather than to have some good features."[46] Yet it will also remind us of a turn more indigenous to the Islamic tradition, in which the insight stated by Geach had received an even more direct articulation.

For readers of Muʿtazilite texts may recognize an intriguing affinity between the analysis that implicitly governs Ibn Taymiyya's thinking in this context and the analysis that Baṣran Muʿtazilite theologians had developed more explicitly to account for the evaluative qualification *mubāḥ* (permissible) or *ḥasan* ("plain" good).[47] It was an evaluative category that had reposed with some tension within the Baṣrans' overall scheme and their analysis of other core values, such as "obligatory" and "bad," for reasons immediately connected with its conditional character. Other values appeared to be necessarily entailed by their respective grounds (*wujūh*). The instantiation of the act-description "injustice" by a given act, for example, necessarily entailed (*iqtaḍā*) its qualification as "bad"; the instantiation of "gratitude for benefaction" necessarily entailed its qualification as "obligatory." The grounds that gave rise to the quality of "plain good," by contrast, seemed to be defeasible in ways that the causal model applied to the other evaluative categories was ill equipped to accommodate. An act of truth-telling thus might ordinarily be *ḥasan*; yet add the discovery that it leads to harm, and it ceases to be so. Similarly, and more resonantly for our own context: an act that redounds to one's benefit might ordinarily be *ḥasan*; yet enter the fact that this benefit was unjustly obtained, and it ceases to be so.

Successive generations of Baṣran theologians would advance different proposals for ironing out the perplexities of this evaluative category. One of the most important among these would identify the quality of goodness as the product of two considerations, one positive and one negative in nature: the act serves some kind of purpose (*gharaḍ*), *and* the grounds of badness are absent. This conjunctive proposal will instantly remind us of one of the formulations we heard from Ibn Taymiyya above: an act is licit if it is needed for people's livelihood *and* not a cause (*sabab*) of sin. A similar sense of recognition will be carried by the terms in which the Muʿtazilites had construed the positive consideration at stake. For on the one hand, and despite the connotations of the word *gharaḍ*, it would be misleading to understand this consideration in exclusively consequentialist terms; the example of truth-telling already indicates that clearly.[48] Yet the benefit an act brings to its agent indeed provided one of the most salient ways in which this consideration was specified. This is a specification that we will have no difficulty recognizing as the counterpart of Ibn Taymiyya's broad notion of need or welfare. Ibn Taymiyya himself does not connect his view of the original status of actions to the Muʿtazilite analysis, yet it is noteworthy that this connection had been flagged in the same context by his Muʿtazilite-minded predecessor al-Kalwadhānī. So long as the benefit one derives from certain goods "contains no ground of badness" (*wajh min wujūh al-qubḥ*), he had written in his *Tamhīd,* reason endorses our enjoyment of these goods as permissible.[49]

The Muʿtazilites' analysis of the concept of "permissibility" thus allows the conditional logic of this concept to stand out with special clarity; yet at the same time, it drives a sharp wedge into the epistemic implications of this logic. For if the qualification of "goodness" or "permissibility" is ontologically dependent on the absence of bad-making grounds, it follows that our knowledge that a given act is good or permissible will be contingent on our knowledge that these bad-making grounds are absent. ʿAbd al-Jabbār had spelled this out clearly in the *Mughnī* when he had written: "It is not possible, in our view, that we should know that a given act is good unless we know that the grounds of badness are absent from it [*illā maʿa al-ʿilm bi-intifāʾ wujūh al-qubḥ ʿanhu*]."[50] The problems this would pose for Baṣran Muʿtazilite moral epistemology form the topic of another story, but it already points to the denouement for our own. It is Ibn Taymiyya himself, however, who moves the plot forward in that direction when he offers a key statement couched in a juridical term that we encountered at the outset of our discussion, "presumption of continuity," and whose relevance for our topic we can now consider more attentively. The context is again the discussion of contracts, and the talk is again of the postulate—*al-aṣl ʿadam al-taḥrīm*—underpinning Ibn Taymiyya's stance. Contracts and their terms, he writes, belong to customary acts, and as such "the original status is the absence of prohibition; so there is a presumption of continuity for 'lack of prohibition' with regard to them [*fa-yustaṣḥabu ʿadam al-taḥrīm*] until a [textual] indicant establishes prohibition." A few lines down, reconfirming: "Lack of prohibition is established through rational presumption of continuity [*al-istiṣḥāb al-ʿaqlī*], and through the absence of a legal indicant [*intifāʾ al-dalīl al-sharʿī*]."[51]

The phrasing is awkward in places, yet the meaning can be summed up simply as follows. The default status ("permissibility"/"no prohibition") does not suffice for establishing permissibility; what is additionally required is the assurance that no prohibition has come to counteract it. Central to this point is the notion of "presumption of continuity," which it is thus worth pausing over for a brief additional comment. This principle, as we have heard Hallaq express it, stipulates that "a legal state of affairs is presumed to continue to be valid until there is reason to change this presumption." The presumption that there are only five prayers, for example, comes to be firmly established once the sources have been examined and all textual evidence has been taken into account. Once this presumption has been set in place, if anyone should think there is a sixth mandatory prayer, the burden of proof rests on him to establish it. Any existing presumption may be dislodged only on the basis of evidence. Crucially, the presumption of continuity "must be sustained by reliable knowledge of the *absence* of evidence that might otherwise change this presumption." And "knowledge of the absence of evidence," Hallaq adds, "is to be distinguished from the absence of knowledge of any evidence."[52] Evidence must be *shown* to be absent; and this, of course, is a demonstration to be undertaken in conformity with familiar methods of proof and epistemological criteria as these were articulated in the legal tradition.

The legal example (the five prayers) with which Hallaq illustrates this principle should not distract us.[53] In Ibn Taymiyya's discussion, the presumption of continuity relates to the status of the kinds of customary actions that stand at the heart of his concern—buying, selling, renting, and generally contractual activity of a paradigmatically economic character—as this attaches to them prior to the Law. The default evaluation for these actions: permissible. Yet to call this a "default" position may be misleading if what this suggests to us is an epistemic equilibrium only to be disturbed once sufficient evidence arrives from the outside to query it. For this equilibrium, Ibn Taymiyya's last-quoted statements signal, has to be earned before it is allowed to stabilize, and one may not rest in it until *after* one has actively established that no evidence exists to oppose it. Ibn Taymiyya puts the point with felicitous clarity in a remark that appears later in the same discussion. One may affirm the absence of prohibition "only *after* one has undertaken independent reasoning [*ijtihād*] with regard to a given class or question [to establish]: have any legal indicants appeared that entail prohibition or not?" One may not rule on the basis of the presumption of continuity and the absence of legal indicants "until after one has looked into the specific [textual] indicants, assuming one belongs to those duly qualified to do so. For everything that God and His Prophet have made obligatory, and that God and His Prophet have forbidden, alters[54] this presumption [*mughayyir li-hādhā al-istiṣḥāb*], so *one may not place assurance in it until after one has inquired into the indicants of the Law [fa-lā yūthaqu bihi illā ba'da al-naẓar fī adillat al-shar'].*"[55]

One may thus place assurance in the "default status" only after a textual indicant has arisen; one may trust in the normative force of need or desire only after the Law has had its say—and after one has striven to make the Law speak, trusting in its ability and intention to make its voice heard. ("He has explained to you in detail what is forbidden to you," Q 6:119).[56] It is only after obtaining the sanction of the Law that need or desire can attract its normative status *qua* desire. To restate the point again, so that the nucleus of the position can stand before us unobscured: desire is good only if the Law has informed us of this fact, though it should do so by means of its meaningful demonstrated silence. Or again: it is the Law that normatively orders our desires and discriminates between good and bad ones. As Ibn Taymiyya tellingly puts it elsewhere, invoking the notion of "permissibility" and a familiar notion of normative ordering in the same breath: "That one should obtain a desired advantage [*ḥuṣūl al-gharaḍ*] from certain things does not entail that they are permissible [*ibāḥa*], even though this advantage should [in itself] be permissible; for that action might contain harm that outweighs its benefit, and the Law came to realize and perfect what is beneficial."[57]

Peeled down to its skeletal elements, this position will remind us of the view that emerged from a closer scrutiny of Ibn Taymiyya's theoretical remarks about welfare in the *Qā'ida fī 'l-mu'jizāt wa 'l-karāmāt*, where I suggested that the dominant accent was a conservative one: any interest that the Law does not indicate falls out of consideration; for a knowledge of our true interests, we must wait upon the Law. Whether we speak of the *absence of an opposing indicant*, as in the context of Ibn Taymiyya's practical legal writings, or the *presence of an affirming indicant*, as in the context of his theoretical remarks ("either revelation has somehow indicated it even though this particular inquirer has not grasped that, or it is not in one's interests"), and whether we think of the indicant in terms of the substantiated and thus pregnant silence of the Law or in terms of the full substantiality of the Lawgiver's speech, the bottom line appears to be the same: the demand for a textual indicant. In both cases, we must look to the Law in order to discover what lies in our true interest, and from the open field of desire, to sift out those desires that are in our interest or at least not to our harm.[58]

Studied against the logic of the theological postulate that underpins it and the juridical concept of "presumption of continuity" with which it is linked, Ibn Taymiyya's invocation of human need turns out to be subject to serious qualifications. Both the normative force and the epistemological immediacy this notion carries are weaker than initially apparent, and point us to deeper relations of dependence to the scriptural text. In doing so, they contribute material toward a conservative picture of Ibn Taymiyya's transactions with the notion of welfare that is painted with several brushes across his work.

Ibn Taymiyya's Claim of Ethical Reason against Its Theological Aims

Our discussion in this chapter began with a question about Ibn Taymiyya's engagement with the notion of welfare in the legal context. To what extent, I asked, are the interests promoted by the Law accessible to human reason? How substantively does Ibn Taymiyya envisage that human inquirers may confront considerations of welfare in the legal context? And what does this reveal about the ability of human reason to operate independently of scriptural guidance? On at least three separate counts—in his emphasis on the criterion of preponderant utility, in his theoretical remarks about unattested interests, and in his foregrounding of "pragmatic" considerations within his practical legal rulings—Ibn Taymiyya appears to support a substantive engagement with welfare that gives a strong role to the capacities for evaluative response that human beings possess independently of revelation. Yet a closer reading of each topic paints a different picture, bringing out the textualist commitments that undergird his approach and accentuating the limitations of our native epistemic resources—of reason, or of that desiderative conception of our prerevelational perspective that has surfaced in our discussion throughout.

The picture that emerges from this rereading, particularly in its most recent statement, will provoke in us a critical sense of anagnorisis. For in its essentials, it coincides with the understanding of Ibn Taymiyya's ethical view that emerged from the earlier stages of our inquiry, which had focused on his position relative to the familiar theological debate about "the determination of good and bad." There too, one of his central messages had been that our desires must await the letter of the Law for a decisive pronouncement on their value, which is vested in long-term consequences and a broader balance of utility that the Law comes to reveal. Our leap to the legal context, in this respect, does not appear to have led us far from our initial conclusions.

In re-adopting this conclusion, it will be important not to lose sight of a point that had emerged in our earlier discussion, namely that the characterization of the relationship between native human resources and the resources of revelation was not a matter of sharply disjunctive *either/or*s. The most interesting questions about this relationship did not revolve on the level of *whether* (whether the former should be allocated a role) but of *how much* or *how* (how extensive or of what kind this role should be). Many of the prominent participants in this debate, as we saw in previous chapters, embraced an understanding of this relationship that saw revelation as serving to particularize, and thus complement, our natural resources. "Human reason may command a view of what is in our interests on a general level [*kulliyyāt*]," we heard al-Juwaynī say when considering the Ashʿarite view of evaluative knowledge, yet "it cannot arrive at its details [*tafāṣīl*]." "Were it not for the prophetic message," as Ibn Taymiyya himself puts it, "reason would not arrive at the details [*tafāṣīl*] of what is beneficial and harmful in this life and the next [*fi 'l-ma'āsh wa 'l-ma'ād*]."[59] Left to our own devices, thus, we naturally perceive our own needs and pressing desires, on Ibn Taymiyya's terms as much as the Ash'arites'. We can also sometimes order our needs and desires through an appreciation of their longer-term consequences—the way we know to drink the bitter physic in the interests of health or to turn away from the water source upon noticing the footprint of a beast of prey. Yet much of what Ibn Taymiyya says serves to highlight the limitations of the evaluative knowledge such responses carve out and to underscore their fallibility and need for substantial supplementation. In balancing the evaluative assessments we can perform independently against the evaluative assessments for which we must lean on revelation, Ibn Taymiyya attaches heavy weights to the latter.

Even with this qualification, however, the above conclusion inevitably brings us up against another and more important point. For this conclusion, as the train of our discussion has made clear, rests on an interpretive decision as to how to order the competing tendencies with which Ibn Taymiyya confronts his reader in his legal remarks, privileging certain of these tendencies over others. Certain features of his writings suggest a liberal stance on the engagement of considerations of welfare and a more independent use of our evaluative resources; other features press a more strongly conservative view. I have outlined what seems to me the most cogent way of determining the balance between these features, and I am aware that this is a balancing act that may not persuade those of Ibn Taymiyya's readers who, looking to his political morality, have seen him as "more of a moralist, and less of a jurist," or who, looking to his legal decisions, have emphasized the priority of his pragmatic concern to "make Islamic law relevant to everyday life" over his commitment to a more formally stringent exegetical stance.[60] I have not sought to bury the grounds for these alternative interpretations, and my discussion may do more to open rather than close a debate about how the competing messages within Ibn Taymiyya's work could be reconciled. It might be debated, for example, whether such a reconciliation would require drawing distinctions of a deeper and finer-grained kind than those I developed above—as between the concerns that in fact fundamentally animate Ibn Taymiyya's stances, and the way Ibn Taymiyya himself understands the basis of his stances or wishes their basis to be understood.

However we write this particular balance, for our present purposes it is important to highlight the characteristics of Ibn Taymiyya's writing that problematize it and in doing so to join them to a larger picture that emerged over the preceding chapters. For a similar picture of competing tendencies, we will now recall, had emerged when considering Ibn Taymiyya's ethical remarks in the theological context, and more specifically when approaching the role of reason in the knowledge of the long-term consequences that constitute the fuller criterion for evaluating actions. In certain locations, as in the *Radd*, Ibn Taymiyya seems prepared to acknowledge this role more strongly, cuing us to map ethical judgments onto the operation of empirical reasoning. Elsewhere, it is revelation that appears to be enthroned as our chief informant of long-term consequences and of the fuller value of actions.

In both cases—Ibn Taymiyya's evaluative epistemology in the legal context and his evaluative epistemology in a more theological context—these interpretive competitions reflect something important about the nature of the texts that confront us. We meet Ibn Taymiyya's views about welfare not through concerted discussions of the relevant topics in systematic legal works but through isolated remarks or through practical applications whose relation to his more theoretical positionings is not immediately transparent and has to be sought out. We meet Ibn Taymiyya's views about ethical knowledge not under the relevant headings of systematic theological treatises but in a clutch of engagements of a polemical nature and in a number of recurrent yet limited reprises in different contexts united by common themes, whose dispersion means that what Ibn Taymiyya thinks often has to be elicited by stretching unusually long interpretive lines between what he says in one place and another. Having avowed the rationality of ethical knowledge in many of his ethical remarks, for example, Ibn Taymiyya himself does not limit its scope in that context. It is only in conjunction with evidence gleaned in heterogeneous contexts that this claim emerges significantly diminished in scope, and it does so in ways that depend on interpretive activity and logical argument at every juncture. *Given* Ibn Taymiyya's claim in location *x* that long-term or overall benefit determines the value of actions, and *given* his claim in location *y* that overall benefit is revealed by the Law, ethical knowledge cannot be accessible through reason. Indeed, Ibn Taymiyya himself not only does not help this argument, but in obscuring the boundaries between some of its central concepts—such as the narrower and broader evaluative perspectives of pleasure and benefit—he sets obstacles to its course. In the legal context, the epistemological implications of his view of the original status of actions demanded a similar exercise of interpretive reasoning to be brought out. These are among many moments in which his writing forces the interpreter's activity to self-consciousness; for while all interpretive activity constructs, some constructs more than others.

Such interpretive tensions thus pick out an aspect of the form of Ibn Taymiyya's ethical remarks that complicates the effort to determine their content and to provide a unifying account of his ethical thought. Like the complexities brought into view in earlier chapters when studying the elusive identity of Ibn Taymiyya's *via media* against its theological topography, this is an aspect that it is crucial to foreground in engaging his work, as I have already suggested, viewing it not as an obstacle to the interpretive task but as an education as to its nature, and as a positive tool for understanding the character of his thought. The graininess and fragmentariness of the interpretable evidence, the multiple directions in which it pulls, its many moments of elusiveness, may be especially instructive in considering Ibn Taymiyya's influence and intellectual legacy, allowing us to see why his work might provide a breeding ground for plural interpretations and permit itself to be appropriated in competing ways.

These kinds of features will remind us of the characterizations of Ibn Taymiyya's writing that have often been offered by commentators considering his output more broadly, who have spoken of the "explosive quality," "digressive" and "rambling" style, and overwhelmingly negative character of his writing.[61] There are no doubt different ways, carrying varying degrees of depth, with which these aspects could be understood. Commentators have sometimes read them as a diagnostic of intellectual weakness and sometimes of intellectual strength, and have sometimes referred them to Ibn Taymiyya's specific intellectual identity (Michot: "the opinions of a theologian-mufti cannot be expected to constitute a comprehensive, integrated system of thought") and sometimes, in a deeper register, to his aims (Hallaq: Ibn Taymiyya gave "priority to ... showing the weaknesses of one doctrine or another, not to the elaboration and development of a doctrine of his own").[62] However these features of Ibn Taymiyya's writing are understood on a broader level, I would suggest that when it comes to his ethical writings, they have something more to tell us about the nature of his engagement with ethical questions which touches on the deeper and more positive notion of his aims. My objective in the remainder of this chapter will be to situate his ethical engagement against two contexts that speak to his larger intellectual aims: the theological vision that frames his ethical engagement (to be discussed in this section) and the larger vision of the relationship of reason and revelation that governs his work and also shadows his ethical engagement (to be discussed in the next section). Both contexts provide important interpretive filters for receiving Ibn Taymiyya's ethical rationalism and, more specifically, for reading the substantiveness with which he is invested in developing it.

Calling attention to the interpretive tensions that adhere to Ibn Taymiyya's views in chapter 2, I had suggested that these tensions reveal something about the fragmentariness of his discussions of ethical epistemology, which is reflected in turn in the remarkable thinness that his characterization of ethical reason carries. At the same time, I had suggested, the thinness of this characterization reflects the particular terms in which he specifies ethical reason, and his overwhelming focus on utility to the exclusion of deontological considerations. Compared with deontological requirements such as those that had figured in the Muʿtazilites' moral tables—"Do not lie under any circumstances," "Do not harm without just cause," "Practice gratitude toward benefactors"—the imperative "Pursue what is in your welfare" is a thin and indeed merely formal principle, one that carries little action-guiding significance prior to identifying more thickly how one's welfare is best achieved. Add to this Ibn Taymiyya's emphasis on revelation as the source for our understanding of how our welfare is to be achieved, and the picture of ethical reason becomes thinner still. Thus, while Ibn Taymiyya stakes a claim for the rational accessibility of evaluative standards, he leaves the moral consciousness of ordinary agents singularly underdeveloped.

This conclusion stands out starkly when one compares Ibn Taymiyya's ethical remarks with the writings of the Muʿtazilites whose position his own initially appears to resemble, and with the rather more robust picture of ordinary moral consciousness they had presented. The comparison is instructive on many levels. On the one hand, as I already observed in chapter 1, it reminds us that the kinds of interpretive challenges that Ibn Taymiyya's works pose are far from unexampled, and should not take us by surprise even when the comparison is with those theologians known for their copious output on moral questions. The dialectical character (and thus expository thinness) of Muʿtazilite writing, the sheer sprawl of the textual output that potentially harbors significant interpretive resources, the serendipity required for alighting in disputational contexts on unique *responsa* that provide new interpretive keys to the Muʿtazilites' views—all features that find their more or less direct counterparts in Ibn Taymiyya's writing—are only a few of the factors that complicate the task of reconstructing what the interpreter then goes on to call "the Muʿtazilite ethical view."[63] With the Muʿtazilites as with Ibn Taymiyya, such factors make the interpreter self-conscious about her interpretive activity and bring home its creative character as a construction.

The comparison with the Muʿtazilites, however, is also instructive in training the light on those features of their writing that facilitate rather than impede the interpreter's task. For even allowing for the historical transformations that Muʿtazilite theology underwent and the multiple factional divisions that fractured it internally, Muʿtazilite theologians developed their views against a set of general commitments—notably their commitment to the defense of God's unity and justice—that picked out their rough boundaries as a school. Even if the boundaries of theological commitment might shift with time or vary among different Muʿtazilite factions (as between the Baṣrans and the Baghdādīs), the school context in which they developed their views meant that positions were articulated and rearticulated, rehearsed and clarified and refined, in numerous texts and at the hands of a number of different thinkers, often across generations. Their overarching theological commitments, similarly, meant that specific views were often developed in architectural relation to other known views, and usually in relation to a clear set of opponents. These features provide strong interpretive facilitators that constitute a far more hospitable environment for readers seeking to piece together the Muʿtazilites' ethical views. All these facilitators are lacking for Ibn Taymiyya, whose Ḥanbalite affiliation provides no interpretive key to his engagement of ethical questions, who raises his voice to contribute to intellectual debates in *kalām*—as indeed *falsafa* and *uṣūl al-fiqh*—without adopting their genres or distinctive forms, and who distances himself altogether from the affiliations that organized classical debates about ethics with his headline of a *via media* and leaves the identity of his *via media* to be established case by case. It is little wonder, in this light, that some of his positions should be hard to read and some of his claims hard to decide whether to take at face value. His apparent avowal of the intrinsic human love for morally good actions, which we probed in chapter 1, is a particularly good example here. In the works of the Muʿtazilites, this thesis had been architecturally linked to the defense of a specific view of God's moral character—a view that Ibn Taymiyya, however, rejected, thus compelling one to search from scratch for the reasons why this thesis is one he might have been motivated to affirm, despite indeed his overwhelming though unadvertised affinities with Ashʿarite views that worked against it.

Yet if the comparison between Ibn Taymiyya's and the Muʿtazilites' ethical engagement is instructive on these levels, it is even more illuminating on another. Because for all its comparative robustness, Muʿtazilite ethical theory, as I indicated in chapter 2, had developed in relation to a distinct set of theological aims. In articulating the ethical standards accessible to ordinary moral consciousness and staking a claim for their objectivity, Muʿtazilite theologians had been primarily concerned with establishing that these same standards governed the action of God. ʿAbd al-Jabbār made the point plain when opening one of the ethical volumes of the *Mughnī* with a simple asseveration of his aim: to demonstrate that "God only does what is good, and cannot but do what is obligatory."[64] It was this programmatic aim that determined the character of the Muʿtazilites' ethical preoccupations. Their interest in documenting the content of ordinary moral consciousness in close detail, in particular, seems highly intelligible in light of the basic assumption that the moral standards known to human beings are also standards that apply to God.

There is thus an immediate question to raise about Ibn Taymiyya's own aims in pressing the claim of ethical reason and about the relationship of these aims to the character of his preoccupation and the interest he takes, or fails to take, in a closer documentation of ordinary moral consciousness. An avowal of ethical rationalism and ethical objectivism recurring throughout his works—why might Ibn Taymiyya have cared to make it? This understanding of value, he signals in several locations, is one that is suggested by scripture itself. The view that actions have intrinsic moral qualities, we hear in one place, "is indicated by the Qur'an and the Sunna," for "God spoke of the actions of unbelievers in ways that entail that they were bad, evil, and blameworthy before the Prophet had come to them"—for example, in demanding that they repent of them and ask for forgiveness.[65] Pointing elsewhere to Lot's condemnation of his people with the words "What, do you commit such indecency as never any being in all the world committed before you?" (Q 7:80), Ibn Taymiyya draws the conclusion that "this was an act of indecency [or wicked deed: *fāḥisha*] among them before [God] had forbidden them [to commit it]."[66]

This will remind us of the use that Muʿtazilite theologians had earlier made of Qur'anic passages in the service of a similar argument. Seeking to defend the claim that moral truths are known by reason and not generated by revelation, Muʿtazilites had often revisited the Qur'anic verse "God commands justice, the doing of good . . . and He forbids all shameful deeds, and injustice" (Q 16:90, *inna Allāha yaʾmuru biʾl-ʿadl waʾl-iḥsān . . . wa-yanhā ʿan al-faḥshāʾ waʾl-munkar*).[67] In employing the notions of justice and injustice, this verse would appear to invoke a preexisting understanding of their content, and thus a preexisting set of moral norms. It is the same semantic tunnel that would seem to open up under the feet of another Qur'anic idiom embodied in the terminological pair *maʿrūf* and *munkar*. *Maʿrūf* literally means "what is known"; and this, as Michael Cook points out, refers us to "specific standards of behaviour already known and established."[68] Ibn Taymiyya himself often visits this pair of terms in his ethical remarks in ways that suggest he is building on the reference to the prerevelational evaluative horizon encoded within them.

Yet of course the resources of scripture had always seemed amenable to different interpretations, and different theologians had frequently claimed scriptural support for their competing positions. It is thus Ibn Taymiyya's deeper theological commitments, just like the Muʿtazilites' before him, that must interest us at this juncture. And here, all we need to do is to turn back to consider the larger theological perspective summoned in the previous chapter to finally situate Ibn Taymiyya's ethical concern against it. For like the Muʿtazilites, he insists that something positive needs to be said about God's morality: we must affirm that God is just, and indeed wise. It is the notion of divine wisdom (*ḥikma*), as we saw in the previous chapter, that forms the linchpin of Ibn Taymiyya's theological vision and the ground of one his most telling disagreements with the Ashʿarite viewpoint. God's creative and legislative activity is governed everywhere by wise purposes that God loves. In the legislative domain, this means that God's commands are grounded—at least in part, given Ibn Taymiyya's additional emphasis on a wise purpose that redounds to God himself—in the aim of promoting human welfare.

To say that God is wise is to "speak well" of God, to speak of Him with the highest praise. Yet in this case, to secure God as an object of praise is also to secure ourselves in a belief that is necessary for our own spiritual well-being. If we are to submit ourselves wholeheartedly to the divine Law and to establish a relationship of love with its Promulgator—seeing Him as the sole object of love and the sole object of trust, the sole end and the sole means of our action, as the *tawḥīd al-ilāhiyya* and *tawḥīd al-rubūbiyya* respectively demand—we need to believe that God's will is not arbitrary and that God has our welfare at heart. The perspective we bring to the Law, in one respect, is remarkably simple: we arrive with a prior set of natural desires and a natural concern for our own welfare. In submitting ourselves to the religious life, our most basic requirement is that we should be able to believe that our natural desires and the evaluative standpoint they constitute coincides with the aims the Lawgiver Himself is pursuing. To restate the point: we should be able to believe that *our* sense of the good and the *Lawgiver's* sense of the good coincide. "This is the religion that God naturally disposed people to accept [*faṭara Allāhu ʿalayhi khalqahu*]; it is beloved [*maḥbūb*] to everyone," Ibn Taymiyya writes elsewhere, reframing a claim of coincidence or concordance that we already heard in chapter 2 in slightly different terms. And the reason for this is that "it commands the right actions [*maʿrūf*] that are beloved to human hearts, and forbids the wrongful actions [*munkar*] that are hateful to them, and it permits what is useful and wholesome [*ṭayyibāt*] and forbids what is harmful and malignant."[69] The actions in question, on the one hand, include prima facie deontological types of acts such as justice and injustice, truth-telling and lying. But they also include, even more crucially and fundamentally, actions whose value is understood teleologically, in terms of their promotion of welfare, to which, as I suggested in earlier chapters, the value of deontological acts—and the reason why such acts are "beloved to human hearts"—ultimately reduces.

It is the concern with affirming this rudimentary concordance, I would suggest, that underpins Ibn Taymiyya's ethical engagement and his avowal of the rational accessibility (and objectivity) of ethical norms on an important level. Yet this claim can be upheld through a far thinner and more limited understanding of the ethical content of reason than the Muʿtazilites, for their part, had deemed necessary. So long as some broad agreement can be posited between what the Law commands us and our ordinary evaluative judgments as just described, the aim will have been achieved, allowing us to then take on trust the existence of such an agreement in those cases where it cannot be readily discerned. Taking the basic content of our ethical reason to be the judgment that the pursuit of benefit is good, and taking on board the theological affirmation that God intends human benefit, the coincidence between our sense of value and the one expressed in the revealed Law will be secure. To the extent that spiritual imperatives here shape Ibn Taymiyya's concern, indeed, it may be said that if the imperative of love does not require an especially substantive specification of ethical knowledge, the imperative of trust in God and the appreciation of the extent of our dependence—the need for prophetic guidance, we hear elsewhere, is even greater than the eye's need for light and the body's need for food and drink or indeed our need for our very life—positively requires the reverse.[70] As we have also seen, moreover, Ibn Taymiyya rejects the Muʿtazilite view of divine morality and severs the morality of human beings from the morality of God. Yet it was the bridge the Muʿtazilites had erected between these two domains that in great part motivated their more substantive documentation of the moral consciousness of ordinary human beings. Ibn Taymiyya's relative indifference to this task will thus appear doubly unsurprising.

In the case of the Muʿtazilites, the theological aims structuring their ethical theory have sometimes seemed easy or tempting to miss, given the prodigious output of ethical arguments and analyses in which they issued, which carry an air of self-sufficiency suggestive of an intellectual task that contains its ends within itself.[71] Ibn Taymiyya's discussions of moral knowledge, by contrast, bring no such temptation. It will be clear from the account of the foregoing chapters that Ibn Taymiyya's remarks are often limited in length and elliptic in character—a set of reflections that do not add up to anything we might be prepared to call a full theory of moral value or a systematic epistemological scheme. His ethical remarks, in this respect, tell no lies, and deliver more direct testimony to their theological ends than the Muʿtazilites' before him, whose painstakingly erected edifice of moral knowledge would be left standing with all the absurd grandeur of a monument that had extravagantly outbuilt its genetic aims. For the task of theology once complete, the prescriptions of revelation take over to leave such edifices without use. With Ibn Taymiyya, this takeover comes more swiftly and the edifice of moral knowledge only has the modest dimensions of the basic rational assurance our relationship with these prescriptions requires for its support.

Reason and Revelation in Broader View

The theological vision in which Ibn Taymiyya's ethical positions are anchored, I have been arguing, forms a critical foil for considering the character of his ethical remarks and for appreciating their limitations, providing us with additional ways of explaining why—besides the reasons that reflect the broader features of his writing as a whole—his ethical epistemology receives only an allusive development and also why a more substantive avowal of reason may not have been a great concern to him. Having connected Ibn Taymiyya's ethical claims with this theological vision, it will now be easier to make the link with another aspect of his intellectual program that can be summoned as an even more embracing context for his ethical engagement, namely his view of the relationship between reason and revelation. This is an aspect of his outlook, as we will see, that is exposed to interpretive tensions not unlike those we have already witnessed in approaching his ethical views. Yet once again, it is a more conservative view of reason that ultimately seems to shape his understanding of this relationship, providing yet another situating filter for the conservative view of reason he adopts in the ethical context.

Ibn Taymiyya's ethical motivations, I just suggested, are partly given in an insistence that the surface of our evaluative comprehension and of the evaluative comprehension carried by the Law—what we rationally or prerevelationally consider good and what the Law enjoins us—coincide. Readers familiar with Ibn Taymiyya's writings may have recognized in this formulation the echo of a headline that runs through his work as a defining frieze. Reason and revelation, put simply, can never be in conflict. Sound or pure reason (*ṣarīḥ al-maʿqūl*) and authentic revelation (*ṣaḥīḥ al-manqūl*) must always be in agreement. It is a frieze whose very persistence provides an eloquent token of the reasons why the difficulties of chronology that cling to Ibn Taymiyya's works are so easy in practice to shrug aside, for it belongs to a large number of intellectual motifs that recur in, and thereby exert a unifying influence over, many of his writings. This particular motif is one whose development we associate most strongly with the period immediately postdating his imprisonments in Cairo and Alexandria, and more specifically with his monumental work *Darʾ taʿāruḍ al-ʿaql waʾl-naql*.

The aim of this work, as its title suggests, is precisely to advance a claim about the harmony of reason and revelation. What is especially significant for our context is that this claim emerges as a polemical response to an alternative view of this relationship implicit in an approach to scriptural interpretation that had received a number of different expressions among different thinkers, both *mutakallimūn* and *falāsifa*, but that was organized by one basic tendency: to promote reason to a troubling position of primacy in relation to the revealed texts. It is the articulation of this view by practitioners of *kalām*, particularly by Ashʿarite theologians such as al-Ghazālī and al-Rāzī, that preoccupies Ibn Taymiyya in the *Darʾ* with particular intensity. Using the incendiary language of a "law," such theologians had proclaimed the "general law" (*qānūn kullī*) of scriptural interpretation to be: when reason and revelation conflict, it must be the latter that cedes, not the former, because reason forms the foundation of revelation. When the meaning of scripture is at stake, thus, it is reason that possesses the role of arbiter and the claim to priority.[72]

Ibn Taymiyya categorically rejects the view that human reason can constitute a "criterion" (*miʿyār*) for scripture.[73] Yet integral to his response is a denial of its very presupposition: reason and revelation, in fact, can never be conflict. It is a claim, to be sure, that had not been made for the first time. The drive to establish this relation of harmony had been shared by theologians of many stripes, and what had often divided them was not the end, but the means. Despite their other disagreements, Muʿtazilites and many later Ashʿarites had to a great extent converged in their view of both the end and the means with regard to one of the key theological topics that appear in the crosshairs of Ibn Taymiyya's discussion, namely the attributes of God. Their common point of departure was a prima facie sense of conflict between what scripture sometimes said and what human reason demanded. Scripture, for example, described God as having hands and sitting on the throne; reason disclaimed this as unacceptably anthropomorphic and sought for subtler ways of interpreting the surface meaning, in doing so restoring harmony between divine revelation and the human mind.

In repudiating such approaches, Ibn Taymiyya takes a clear step away from the strong rationalism they stand for and appears to distance himself from the claims of reason as such. Much of his discussion in the *Darʾ taʿāruḍ* seems to reinforce this picture by displaying a series of wide-ranging polemical assaults on the different arguments offered by rationalist-minded theologians on a variety of topics, including arguments for the existence of God and arguments about the nature of God's attributes, such as His speech and His spatial location. A closer examination of these arguments reveals that the much-vaunted "reason" theologians like al-Ghazālī and al-Rāzī appointed as their highest arbiter cannot hold its weight. Reason, as it emerges from Ibn Taymiyya's critique, appears to be deeply flawed. Witness, in a similar vein, the disagreements that tear rationalist-minded factions apart even on the most basic questions, such as the content of the foundational epistemic notion of necessary or self-evident knowledge (*ʿilm ḍarūrī*). Putting our ear to what different theologians have to say about it, we find a welter of contradictory claims. *A* claims *x* is known necessarily by reason; *B* denies it. It is a pattern we see repeated all over theological writings:

> Most people endowed with mature reason [*ʿuqalāʾ*] say: we know that it is impossible for a contingent thing [*ḥādith*] to originate without a contingent cause, yet a group of them say: that is possible. Most people endowed with mature reason say: it is known through the immediate necessity of reason [*ḍarūrat al-ʿaql*] that it is impossible that an entity should be characterized as "knowing" without knowledge, "powerful" without power, "living" without life, yet others dispute that. Most people endowed with mature reason say: it is known through the immediate necessity of reason that a single thing cannot simultaneously be a command and a prohibition and a statement, while others dispute that.

Thus "every person endowed with mature reason says that reason affirms or necessitates or provides warrant for what his neighbor says that reason denies or deems impossible or disallows." These kinds of disputes reveal that "reason is not a single thing that is clear in itself," but "rather exhibits such manner of fractiousness and disorder."[74] The most immediate conclusion that Ibn Taymiyya draws from this observation locks onto his main concern in the *Darʾ*. For reason is affected by this kind of disorder precisely in those cases in which it has often been accorded priority over revelation.

This large-scale critique of the uses of reason will seem fundamentally negative in kind—an exercise in deconstruction. As such, it will remind us of Yahya Michot's suggestive commentary on the *Darʾ taʿāruḍ*, which he proposes that we consider in the light of George Saliba's reading of Arabic astronomy at the end of the thirteenth century. This was a period marked by an unprecedented level of intellectual critique of the Ptolemaic system and by a growing sense that the limits of traditional scientific rationality were being reached—a period that may thus need to be recognized as a still unresearched "golden age" of philosophy. It is as a document for a parallel development that the *Darʾ taʿāruḍ* might be read, argues Michot, this time concerning the state of religious rationality. What the *Darʾ taʿāruḍ* reveals is religious rationality, like its scientific counterpart, beginning to knock against its limits and questioning its foundations as never before. It is a work that delivers a diagnosis of "the flagrant state of exhaustion and petrification" affecting the principal vehicles of religious rationality—*kalām*, philosophy, and mystical theosophy—of the time. This state stands on display in the cacophony of contradictions and disputes, controversies and divergences agitating these discourses, as just adumbrated, a pandemonium of voices that makes it possible and indeed necessary to speak of "rationalities" in the plural rather than of a single shared rationality. ("Reason is not a single thing that is clear in itself," we just heard Ibn Taymiyya say.)[75]

Yet having called attention to Ibn Taymiyya's critical aim—a negative diagnostic of the uses of reason that appears to distance him from the claims of reason altogether—Michot then goes on to highlight something more positive: a more positive aim, and more positive view of reason, to which it is linked. Implicit in Ibn Taymiyya's program is not merely a diagnosis but the intimations of a cure. "Philosophico-theologico-mystical reason, in Sunni Islam," Michot writes, may "yet have known at the time the turn conducive to its renewal." This is a turn that he suggests we may find in the notion of *fiṭra*, which figures in the *Darʾ taʿāruḍ* as a prominent epistemological theme, and in Ibn Taymiyya's invitation to return to our "sound natural constitutions" (*fiṭar salīma*) to ground ourselves in them anew.[76] Cast in these terms, *fiṭra* would offer itself as a foundation for thinking that would replace the exhausted forms of rational thought: as the promise, no less, of a new (or newly recovered) Islamic reason.

We may recall hearing something about the connection between the notion of *fiṭra* and that of reason at an earlier juncture of our narrative (chapter 2), when considering Ibn Taymiyya's double specification of *fiṭra* in cognitive and desiderative terms. This specification comes into the fullest fruition in his discussion of theological knowledge—a key theme of the *Darʾ taʿāruḍ*—and in his claim that we know and love God by our natural disposition. It is a positive claim that he notably develops in response to the popular *kalām* view that such knowledge must be acquired through rational inquiry (*naẓar*) and that is accompanied by a detailed deconstructive criticism of the rational arguments *mutakallimūn* had advanced for the purpose. In their technicality and dogmatism, he maintains, such arguments bar ordinary people from the simpler access to theological truth already naturally available to them.[77] The notion of ordinary or natural rationality is developed even more directly in the *Radd*, written in the same period as the *Darʾ*, this time in opposition to the technical conception of human reasoning proposed by the logicians, who form Ibn Taymiyya's immediate target in this work. Such specialized approaches offer abstruse "unnatural means" to arrive at "natural matters" (*al-umūr al-fiṭriyya . . . juʿila lahā ṭuruq ghayr fiṭriyya*) and blind us to the fact that we already have God-given natural abilities to reason about the world.[78] The notion of *fiṭra* is in turn often deployed by Ibn Taymiyya to frame his hallmark claim regarding the harmony between reason and revelation. "The sound, clear and indubitable proofs of reason—nay, those things we know necessarily through our natural constitution [*al-ʿulūm al-fiṭriyya al-ḍarūriyya*]—are in accord with what the prophets have informed us of and do not conflict with it," we hear in one place, registering a message that traverses the *Darʾ taʿāruḍ* like a red thread and reappears as an equally incarnadine theme in others.[79]

It is a positive embrace of reason that has often been picked up by Ibn Taymiyya's readers in the past. Yet given his disavowal of the strong conception of a "criterial" reason, it has been a matter of some debate just how strongly or positively to understand the appeal to reason he endorses and incorporates in his practice. This was the question that Binyamin Abrahamov proposed to broach in an essay considering the relationship between reason and revelation in Ibn Taymiyya's thought, parsing it as a question concerning the extent of reason's epistemic independence. His own view was plainly expressed in his concluding words: Ibn Taymiyya "rejects any rational external doctrine or term and confines the process of reasoning to the contents and methods of revelation as he understands them. Reason, according to him, has no independent status as is the case in Ibn Rushd. His general law is that the basis of reason is revelation, and that hence there can be no disagreement between the two elements."[80] Yet Abrahamov would later reject this view, affirming that reason indeed serves in an independent role.[81] In doing so, he would express a view that Michot would also appear to extend support to, and that Jon Hoover, in his book-length study of Ibn Taymiyya's theology, would similarly describe as his own. "Revelation embodies true rationality," Hoover writes in this context. "Once one has access to revelation, one identifies it as identical to whatever truth one knew previously through reason."[82]

These statements seem to me suggestive, and they do so in ways that point to the difficulties involved in seeking to determine Ibn Taymiyya's position with full assurance. For on the one hand, in several locations, Ibn Taymiyya suggests that rational considerations, while intimately enmeshed with scriptural grounds, form a distinct epistemic route that can independently lead us to the truth. As he writes in the *Darʾ taʿāruḍ*, "Since the pathway to the truth comprises revelation [*samʿ*] and reason and these two are inseparably connected [*mutalāzimān*], whenever one follows the path of reason it points one to the path of revelation—namely [by pointing to] the truthfulness of the prophets—and whenever one follows the path of revelation, it clarifies for one the proofs of reason."[83] This epistemic independence is most readily illustrated by his claim concerning the knowledge of God. The preexisting acknowledgment of God, as Ibn Taymiyya presents it, is robust enough to form the basis of human accountability, making people liable to blame and punishment when a prophet is sent bringing the monotheistic message. For "if a rational proof affirming the Creator was not given in the natural constitution [*fiṭra*]," the prophet's message could never serve as a proof of people's guilt and be used to condemn them. It is only the testimony of their own reason that can serve in this role. "The very faculty of reason through which they know the oneness of God is a proof against polytheism—this *stands in no need for a prophet* [to inform them of it]."[84]

Ibn Taymiyya's reference to the role of reason in demonstrating the truthfulness of the prophets in the above passage can be understood in different ways, but one of these we have already come across. For as we saw in chapter 3, Ibn Taymiyya invites us to consider our rational knowledge of right and wrong as nothing less than a criterion for assessing the content of a given prophetic message and evaluating the veracity of its bearer. This prerevelational perception of ethical facts elsewhere appears to work in tandem with a prerevelational perception of the ethical character of God himself. In Ibn Taymiyya's *Kitāb al-Nubuwwāt,* as Hoover observes, the rational affirmation of God's wisdom is invoked to play a cardinal role in supporting our belief in the truthfulness of the prophets. God, in His wisdom, marks the similarities between like and like just as He marks the necessary distinctions between like and unlike, and therefore does not equate the good and the bad, the just and the unjust, or indeed the truthful and the lying. It is as a consequence of these demarcations—demarcations demanded by God's wisdom—that God lends His support to the truthful prophets as against the mendacious.[85] Our own belief in the truthfulness of the prophets thus requires our rational belief in God's wisdom as its epistemic presupposition.

This, in fact, links to a broader and no less important moment within Ibn Taymiyya's work where a vigorous emphasis appears to be placed on the ability of reason to function independently and deliver substantive truths, and this is in providing access to the attributes of God. For on the one hand, Ibn Taymiyya's theological outlook is shaped by the insistence that the way we speak of God must be grounded in the traditional sources, and that God's attributes must be affirmed as scripture affirms them. In a recurring formulation, "God must be described as He has described Himself, and as His messengers have described Him."[86] Yet having made this point, Ibn Taymiyya goes on to outline an additional epistemic possibility. This is a possibility, crucially, that invokes reason as its foundation, suggesting, in Hoover's words, that "much of the same information concerning God's attributes is known by reason independently of revelation."[87] The centerpiece of this strategy is the so-called a fortiori argument (*qiyās al-awlā*), which stipulates that where a perfection is ascribed to human beings, it should a fortiori be ascribed to their Creator. On the basis of this reasoning, one may establish, for example, that God must be speaking, hearing, powerful, knowing, and living, for we consider such attributes perfections for created beings, and to deny them of God would be to ascribe imperfection to Him. How should the exercise of reason be understood in this connection? In a manner we might dignify with the notion of a "natural theology," Hoover suggests at the end of his analysis. Ibn Taymiyya, he writes, "employs *a fortiori* argumentation to build a kind of natural theology that takes human perfection as its point of departure for defining God's perfection while exonerating God of neediness and creaturely modalities."[88]

In addition to these appeals to reason, there is another, which is indeed what best illuminates Hoover's above-quoted remark about the rationality "embodied" in revelation. For the metaphor of embodiment refers us most immediately to a position that occupies a salient place in Ibn Taymiyya's understanding of the relationship between reason and revelation and in his response to the competing view of this relationship targeted in the *Darʾ taʿāruḍ*. In rejecting this view, central to Ibn Taymiyya's strategy is an effort to dismantle the rigid polarity of "reason" and "revelation" on which it was premised. Reason is not like a ladder—the *mutakallimūn*'s much-vaunted ladder of "rational inquiry" (*naẓar*)—that leads us into the universe of revelation by convincing us of certain foundational facts, such as the existence of God or the truth of revelation, and is then simply thrown away as we come face-to-face with the majestic nonrational discourse of the Law. Reason does not solely appear *outside* revelation, but is also alive inside the universe of God's speech. Revelation is not in fact a collection of mere assertions or reports to be accepted purely on the basis of say-so—mere *khabar* sustained by *fiat*. On the contrary, scripture teems with appeals to our rational judgment and in many places clearly draws on rational considerations—what might be called arguments or, with the Qur'an, "similitudes" (*amthāl*)—to produce conviction.[89]

Take the way in which God addressed the question of resurrection. This was not simply handed down to us as a brute fact, but rather was recommended to our reason through a prior clarification of its possibility—possibility forming the prerequisite for actuality—by comparing it to the first act of creation and identifying re-creation as a lesser and thus even more eminently possible achievement. Thus: "Have they not seen that God, who created the heavens and earth, is powerful to create the like of them?" (Q 17:99). And again: "And he has struck for Us a similitude [*mathal*] and forgotten his creation; he says, 'Who shall quicken the bones when they are decayed?' Say: 'He shall quicken them, who originated them the first time.... Is not He, who created the heavens and earth, able to create the like of them?' " (Q 36:78–81). Or take the way the Qur'an establishes the fact of divine unity. Appealing to our native judgments, it compels us to admit that to ascribe to God associates would be to ascribe to Him something we would consider a blemish and weakness for ourselves—that what we own should be taken as our equal. Thus: "He has struck for you a similitude from yourselves; do you have, among that your right hands own, associates in what We have provided for you so that you are equal in regard to it, you fearing them as you fear each other?" (Q 30:28).[90] In these and other ways, revelation can be seen to encompass reason. In seeking to secure conviction, importantly, these rational proofs would seem to involve a substantive appeal to our capacities for rational judgment, and to be expected to work on us not only after, but as a means to, accepting the truth of the revelation in which they appear.[91]

Taken together, the above would suggest that Ibn Taymiyya ascribes a substantive and independent role to reason in several areas of his thinking. Yet I would argue that the picture is more complex, and that Ibn Taymiyya's invocation of reason is rather less substantive than it appears, and in fact turns out to rest on deeper scriptural foundations. Hoover's evocative statement—"*Once* one has access to revelation, one identifies it as identical to whatever truth one knew previously through reason"—already provides a token of this complexity in calling attention to the responsive character of reason. Ibn Taymiyya directly highlights this point in an explanatory gloss he offers on the term "rational" (*ʿaqliyya*) in connection with the rational proofs contained in the Qur'an. "Those proofs are rational," he writes, "in the sense that reason knows [or: recognizes] their soundness when alerted to them [*bi-iʿtibār anna al-ʿaql yaʿlamu ṣiḥḥatahā idhā nubbiha ʿalayhā*]."[92] Yet the milder element of responsiveness elsewhere gives way to something stronger. For in several locations Ibn Taymiyya signals that revelation does not merely appeal to our reason, but indeed *constitutes* reason, and is vested with the power to arbitrate what rationality—what *true* or *sound* rationality—consists in.

One may consider here the crucial discussion of reason that Ibn Taymiyya offers us in the *Radd*. In previous chapters we engaged this work as a key stage for his development of the notion of *fiṭra* as an element of his moral epistemology—a development in which, as I suggested, *fiṭra* is understood mainly in desiderative terms. Yet this work also serves as the stage for a broader development in which the notion of *fiṭra* is given a sharply cognitive inflection, and is associated with a set of basic cognitive operations that bring it into connection with the notion of reason. The most basic function of natural reason is specified by Ibn Taymiyya in terms that we may recall from our earlier account of divine rationality and indeed divine morality (God's justice, though also His wisdom). As with God, so with human beings, the essential feature and truest form of natural rationality consists in the ability to tell similarity and difference, to join like to like and separate like from unlike. "The capacity to discern similarity and difference," Ibn Taymiyya writes in a series of passages liberally peppered with the vocabulary of both *fiṭra* and *ʿaql*, is "one of the greatest characteristics of reason [*min aʿẓam ṣifāt al-ʿaql maʿrifat al-tamāthul wa ʾl-ikhtilāf*]."[93] This is a form of rationality that he takes to be paradigmatically exemplified in legal analogy, which aims to discern the features that unite different actions (*al-waṣf al-jāmiʿ al-mushtarak*) and to thereby enable the transfer of legal qualifications from one set of actions to another. In reflecting the natural pattern-seeking abilities of reason, legal analogy thus presents itself as a quintessential expression of natural rationality.

Talk of our "*natural* rationality," as just indicated, is encouraged by Ibn Taymiyya's fluid transitions between the vocabulary of reason and nature in his discussion, which invite us to think of the mode of cognition he is picking out as an untutored form of intelligence. Yet this characterization is called into question in the same discussion when Ibn Taymiyya suddenly introduces a new concept—that of the "balance" or "scales" (or "measure": *mīzān*). This is a concept that derives from the Qur'an, which describes it as revealed by God, and Ibn Taymiyya notes that it has been interpreted by commentators as a reference to God's justice (*ʿadl*). He goes on to connect this concept to the means of measurement that human beings use for determining similarity and difference: "The means by which we come to know the similarity between similar things, and likewise the difference between different things . . . derives from [or: "forms part of"] the scales [*min al-mīzān*]. Thus, the knowledge that these dirhams or other heavy bodies weigh the same as those ones is obtained through their means of measurement [*mawāzīn*] . . . similarly with the knowledge that this thing is as long as that one, which is obtained through its standard, namely the cubit."[94] The slippage between "scales," "standard," and again "means of measurement" in this translation is symptomatic of a certain difficulty in disentangling the meaning of Ibn Taymiyya's remarks, one likewise reflected in the uncertain translation of the first statement. "Derives" *or* "forms part of"? Which term might best convey the way Ibn Taymiyya is interested to cast the connection at stake? Both terms seem to make for an awkward semantic fit. For what might it mean to say that these familiar ("natural") ways of measuring weight and size are either *generated by* or *subsumed in* the Qur'anic scales to which the first occurrence of the term *mīzān* appears to refer us?

What is clear is that even as Ibn Taymiyya continues to speak of this pattern-seeking capacity as an aspect of our natural reason, a new claim has emerged that holds down the note of "derivation" struck above and ascribes this capacity to revelation as its product. This is expressed plainly in the following remark in ways calculated to add fuel to the questions just posed:

> The scales that God revealed with the Book—where He said: "God it is who has sent down the Book with the truth, and also the Balance" (Q 42:17), and said: "Indeed, We sent Our Messengers with the clear signs, and We sent down with them the Book and the Balance" (Q 57:25)—is a just scales

> which involves considering a given thing in terms of what it is like and unlike to, so that it treats similar things alike and discriminates between different things, through the knowledge of likeness and unlikeness that God installed in people's natural constitutions and their rational faculties [*yusawwī bayna al-mutamāthilayn wa-yufarriqu bayna al-mukhtalifayn bimā ja'alahu Allāhu fī fiṭar 'ibādihi wa-'uqūlihim*].[95]

The seams between these two modes or kinds of measuring—natural and revealed—merge in this passage without distinction. Both revealed and naturally installed in our reason, both taught and untaught: how could these two go together? It is this very question that Ibn Taymiyya is called upon to respond to in the next breath, and in doing so he introduces a distinction that will instantly seem familiar. Referring to the rational elements contained by revelation, he writes: it is through such use of rational elements—through similes, arguments, and examples—that the prophets "showed people the way and guided them to the means by which they might come to know justice [*al-'adl*] and by which they might know the sound rational arguments [*al-aqyisa al-'aqliyya al-ṣaḥīḥa*]" or standards for establishing religious truths. "Thus they perfected the natural constitution [*kammalat al-fiṭra*] by alerting and guiding it [*bimā nabbahathā 'alayhi*: notice the echo from our earlier passage] to things the natural constitution was set against; or the natural constitution had been corrupted [*kānat al-fiṭra qad fasidat*] through the corrupt beliefs and desires that had arisen in it, and they removed this corruption and set out plainly what the natural constitution was set against, so that the natural constitution came to know the scales which God revealed and his prophets set out plainly."[96]

It is thus in terms of that pivotal relationship we saw in chapter 2 in connection with evaluative knowledge—by way of perfecting or completing our imperfect *fiṭra*—that the relationship between our natural reasoning and the reasoning revealed by God might be understood. As in the evaluative context the desires stemming from our natural disposition turned out to be fallible and to stand in need of correctives from the revealed Law, so the modes of reasoning that stem from our natural disposition stand in need of scriptural correctives. Yet it will be important to observe that in providing such cognitive correctives, the Law would appear to be providing nothing less than the means of identifying what constitutes our true nature and the true forms of rational thought. Indeed, it would be providing nothing less than a constitution and authoritative definition of rational thought.

With this in view, we should notice another crucial element that this account has introduced, namely a normative distinction between perfect and imperfect, or sound (*ṣaḥīḥ, salīm*) as against corrupt (*fāsid*) dispositions. "*If the natural constitution is sound*," as Ibn Taymiyya puts it more explicitly elsewhere, "it measures things through the rational scales."[97] A normative distinction between true and untrue, sound and unsound, had in fact already been clearly signposted in the *Darʾ taʿāruḍ*. In framing his characteristic claim of harmony, Ibn Taymiyya's more specific view was that *sound* reason (*ṣarīḥ al-maʿqūl*) and *authentic* revelation (*ṣaḥīḥ al-manqūl*) could never be found in conflict. It is against this differentiation indeed that we may partly understand the prodigious energy he expends in this work to the negative task of criticizing his rationalist opponents' particular arguments or the interest he takes in documenting the disagreements that reign between different theological factions. For this critical effort shows that such thinkers rely on modes of reasoning that do not represent the sound reason that forms the real partner to revelation in the relationship of harmony. The proofs contained in the Qur'an are far superior (*akmal*), Ibn Taymiyya tells us, to the ones offered by such thinkers in both *kalām* and *falsalfa*, which are replete with contradictions and errors and burdened with unnecessary complexity.[98] Yet scripture does not merely indicate the modes of reasoning that are superior in the sense of being more likely to secure conviction, but that are indeed to be judged fundamentally acceptable or sound, particularly when it comes to God. It is thus important to note that the a fortiori argument that was isolated as the linchpin of Ibn Taymiyya's strategy for a "rational" apprehension of God's attributes is endorsed precisely because it is employed in scripture itself and by the pious *salaf*, ultimately reflecting the Qur'anic dictum that "God's is the loftiest likeness" (Q 16:60).[99] It is the scriptural endorsement of this mode of reasoning, to restate, that imparts to it its legitimacy and underpins its status as a "sound" method.

The above has focused on the role of scripture in picking out the methods by which truths may be rationally established. Yet there is much to suggest that this role, like the normative distinction between "sound" and "unsound" that supports it, also extends, no less crucially, to the very substance of the truths themselves. For turning back to one of the main topics we considered as evidence for Ibn Taymiyya's readiness to acknowledge the role of reason in more substantive terms—his treatment of God's attributes—it ultimately seems misleading, as Hoover himself suggests, to take the notion of independent rational discovery, or indeed of a "natural theology," too far: "Although Ibn Taymiyya claims that independent reason or the natural constitution, exercised without corrupting influences, will arrive at correct theological doctrine, it is perhaps going too far . . . to speak of the shaykh as building a natural theology. Rather, it seems clear enough that he is devising his rational arguments so as to arrive safely at theological doctrines held *a priori* on the basis of the authoritative tradition."[100] Reason does not confront the realm of intellectual possibility naïvely and carve its way independently through open epistemic space to arrive at a concrete vision of God. It begins from the way in which God describes Himself in scripture and works backward. This seems nowhere more evident than in Ibn Taymiyya's treatment of those attributes that other rationalist-minded theologians had made the focus of their effort to provide allegorical interpretations of the surface meaning of scripture in order to obviate its conflict with reason. It had been debated, for example, whether the notion of "love" can be intelligibly predicated of God, and several theologians who saw a difficulty in attributing a passion to God had sought to interpret it in other terms, such as by semantically reducing the notion of "loving" to that of "willing." Raising this point in *Sharḥ al-Iṣbahāniyya*, Ibn Taymiyya simply refers us to the fact that "the obligation every Muslim is under to assent to everything that God and His Messenger have reported regarding His attributes does not depend on the possibility of producing a rational proof for a given attribute." Since scripture speaks of God as "loving," we must also speak of God in these terms. A few lines down he continues: "The prophetic route generates the faith that is beneficial for the hereafter without [the theologians' analogical arguments (*qiyās*) or the mystics' revelations (*kashf*)], and *then* [*thumma*] if an analogical argument or a revelation should arise which is in agreement with what the Messenger has said, well and good."[101]

Yet it is perhaps Ibn Taymiyya's discussion of one of the most hotly contested qualifications of God—the topic of God's "aboveness" or "elevation" (*fawqiyya, ʿuluww*)—that provides the most telling token of the direction of his own rational argumentation and of the normative distinctions that underlie it. For this is one of several attributes whose knowledge Ibn Taymiyya in various places refers to our natural disposition, in doing so claiming the concordance between the requirements of our nature and the requirements of scripture. God's "elevation above the world is known through the natural disposition and reason, and through the Law and revealed report."[102] A prime scriptural reference point for this view is the Qur'anic verse "The All-compassionate sat Himself upon the Throne" (Q 20:5), which finds its complement in a well-known hadith that describes God as descending to the lowest heaven (*al-samāʾ al-dunyā*) in the last part of the night. Yet these kinds of scriptural descriptions had formed a pivot of rationalist-minded theologians' concerns given the anthropomorphic implications they appear to carry. God, such theologians had insisted, cannot be "above" anything because spatial terms are fundamentally inapplicable to Him, a reflection of His inaccessibility to material or bodily terms tout court. Reason, which lays down these basic postulates, here demands a different interpretation of the surface meaning of scripture.

"Reason affirms God's aboveness," we hear Ibn Taymiyya say. Yet "reason denies it," his opponents had asserted. How could such disagreement—a strident disagreement that resembles the symptoms of the intellectual malaise Ibn Taymiyya himself targeted in the *Darʾ taʿāruḍ*—be resolved? There is, no doubt, a more complex story one could tell about this particular resolution. Yet Ibn Taymiyya provides us with one of the most important keys to it when at one point he states: "This premise is ingrained in the natural dispositions of all people *whose natural dispositions have not been altered through suppositions or willfully adopted views.*"[103] The deliverances of a *sound* natural disposition—one that has not been corrupted by external factors—will constitute that sound reason whose hallmark is its agreement with what revelation tells us. It is thus by introducing a normative distinction at this juncture that Ibn Taymiyya ring-fences the notion of reason's deliverances and secures their conformity to the revealed word. In doing so, however, he gives more than a clue as to the ultimate derivation of the deliverances he aims to hold down.

It is in fact the theologians' distance from the revealed texts, Ibn Taymiyya repeatedly emphasizes in the *Darʾ taʿāruḍ*, that is responsible for their chronic disputes. Such disputes can be resolved only by a renewed turn toward the texts. It is no accident that Ibn Taymiyya's cataloguing of the contestations of necessary knowledge by different factions—*A* claims *x* is known necessarily by reason; *B* denies it—should culminate in the following words, which arrive as balm and antidote to this disorder:

> As for the revealed Law, it is in itself the utterance of the Truthful one, and this forms its abiding attribute, which does not vary with the varying circumstances of people; and it is possible to gain knowledge of it, just as it is possible to refer people to its authority, and this is why revelation bade us refer people to the authority of the Book and the Sunna should conflict arise . . . for were they to turn to anything else—to the minds of men, and their views and measurements and proofs—they would only reap even greater disagreement and disorder.[104]

It is the steady certainty of the unchanging divine speech that stands to still and replace the clamor of disputing human voices.

Before Revelation: Ethical Reason and Its Socioreligious Sediments

I have been arguing that Ibn Taymiyya's invocation of reason turns out to be far less substantive that it initially strikes us, and is grounded in deeper scriptural foundations in many of the junctures at which its independence seems to be particularly loudly advertised. In this respect, the dominant picture we form of Ibn Taymiyya's broader view of the relationship of reason and revelation dovetails with the dominant picture that emerges from a reading of this relationship in the ethical domain more narrowly. In neither case does reason play a criterial role. Bringing these two pictures together for one last conversation, I will end this chapter by addressing one of the more narrowly ethical points enumerated above as suggestive of a substantive approach to reason—the appeal to ethical judgments for the confirmation of prophetic truth—in order to once again bring out its implicit scriptural backing, using this to raise a larger question about what it means to look for the ethical voice of "pure" reason and to train a final light on the criterial role of revelation in the ethical domain.

Ibn Taymiyya, I noted above, invites us to regard our rational knowledge of right and wrong as nothing less than a criterion for assessing the content of a given prophetic message and judging its veracity. We consider the actions a given would-be prophet commands us against the ethical judgments we make independently of revelation, and we ask ourselves: Do these commands conform to our ethical expectations—to what we know by our "natural disposition and pure reason" (*al-fiṭra wa 'l-ʿaql al-ṣarīḥ*)?[105] "Were we to suppose," as Ibn Taymiyya put it in a passage of *Sharḥ al-Iṣbahāniyya* quoted in chapter 3, that someone came along and "commanded polytheism and idolatry and permitted foul deeds, injustice, and lying, and did not command the worship of God or belief in the hereafter," we would need to look no further for disproof of his prophetic pretensions. Yet elsewhere Ibn Taymiyya offers several reasons for thinking that the basis for this assessment—and the source of the expectations against which we scrutinize a given set of divine commands—may not be quite what his reference to "pure reason" immediately suggests. After all, as he observes a few pages later, "the prophetic office has subsisted among human beings since the time of Adam," and people have come to be familiar with "the kinds of things that prophetic messengers enjoin." Often the veracity of a prophet is known through "the fact that he brings a similar message" to the one brought by previous prophets. For there are certain general principles (*uṣūl kulliyya, maqāṣid kulliyya*), including certain views of human action, which all prophets converge on.[106]

There will be a delicate balance to be drawn here between continuity and novelty, recognition and surprise. If continuity with earlier prophetic revelations serves to confirm the authenticity of a message, an excess of continuity will render it otiose, as it will raise questions about the source of Muhammad's own access to this message. (Did he receive it through divine inspiration, or did he merely acquire it from the historical environment he inhabited?)[107] These types of concerns would shape the way other Muslim writers would approach the relationship between the Islamic message and previous prophetic messages. This was a topic that was thematized at several junctures within legal works, as in debates about whether the content of different messages could coincide, what it took for a given revelation to be abrogated, and whether Muhammad himself was subject to the laws of earlier revelations prior to his own mission. What is important for our context is that such debates reflected and cultivated a distinct awareness that human life prior to the Islamic message was already long embedded within the universe of God's speech. Hence, as we saw earlier in this chapter, the question raised by some writers regarding the futility of asking: What was the status of acts prior to the advent of revelation? "Before *this* revelation" is always after *another*, sufficiently to place in question whether "before revelation" as a category exists at all. In this light, the appeal to what is before revelation, far from being an appeal to "pure" reason, is an appeal to the human mind as already informed by the divine speech.

This prior embeddedness will be relevant for approaching Ibn Taymiyya's invocation of reason in connection with the veracity of prophets. Yet given that this invocation centers on types of actions that figure prominently in his discussion of ethical judgments elsewhere—justice, truthfulness, the keeping of oaths—it will also be relevant for approaching his claim of ethical reason more broadly. Looking away from these familiar categories of action, here it will be particularly instructive to consider one rather narrower ethical precept in connection to which Ibn Taymiyya frames his characteristic claim of reason, the principle of retaliation (*qiṣāṣ*). This principle already came into view in chapter 1 in the context of an argument about Ibn Taymiyya's teleological construal of deontological norms. Some of his most concentrated remarks on the topic, unsurprisingly, appear in his commentary on the Qur'anic verse *al-Baqara*—unsurprisingly, given that this is the primary scriptural locus where this principle receives religious sanction. "O believers, prescribed for you is retaliation, touching the slain; freeman for freeman, slave for slave, female for female"; for "in retaliation there is life for you" (Q 2:178–79).

While the principle of retaliation finds scriptural support in this verse, it will be interesting to note that Ibn Taymiyya himself, in these remarks, does not simply present it as deriving its normative force and its epistemic availability from a divine prescription. Once again, he claims a rational or natural ground for it. Taken in the sense that a murderer must be put to death—a precept that exercises a deterrent effect on potential murderers and thus spares the life of both offender and victim—this is an evaluative knowledge available to everyone and "deeply embedded in their nature" (*maghrūz fī gharīzatihim*):

> No human being deems it acceptable that a person should be killed and the murderer not be put to death, but in fact all of them without exception allow that the murderer be put to death. . . . So if this meaning belongs to the fundaments of human understanding, which human beings know they cannot live without, it is of a piece with their need for food and drink and shelter, and it is beneath the dignity of the Qur'an to propose to inform people of these self-evident things.

What the Qur'an came to inform us of more particularly, Ibn Taymiyya's special argument will be, is not so much *that* it is right to retaliate against murderers, but rather *how* this principle should be practiced. It should be

> a free man killed for a free man, a slave for a slave, a woman for a woman; and making the blood money [*diya*] the same for both, and the blood of one as the blood of the other, involves rendering them equal in terms of their blood and the blood-money. Through this even requital [*muqāṣṣa*] their life was preserved [*kāna lahum ḥayā*] from strife, which would otherwise lead ineluctably to their ruin, as is well known.... For the term "retaliation" [*qiṣāṣ*] denotes parity and equality [*al-muʿādala wa ʾl-musāwā*] and it indicates that God prescribed justice and fairness with regard to those killed.[108]

What revelation thus came to demand was the observation of parity in the administration of punishment. This, Ibn Taymiyya explains more fully in the vicinity of these remarks, notably involves disregarding the social station, importance, or power of the individual concerned. To observe parity in this manner grants people life inasmuch as retaliation exacted without fair measure leads to endless blood feuds.[109] We will recall Ibn Taymiyya's earlier description of the Law as coming to particularize the evaluative knowledge that is already available to us. Before us we would seem to have one brilliant example of how this office might be executed. Through our natural resources—the term *gharīza* is replaced by the term *fiṭra* later in this discussion[110]—we know that retaliation must take place, and indeed that it must take place because it serves our vital interests. What revelation tells us is that observing parity in the practice of this principle is the best means by which this vital end can be attained. Knowing the *that* and the *why*, we are given insight into the *how*.

Yet what I would like to call attention to now is the interesting and not a little paradoxical relationship in which Ibn Taymiyya's specification of our intuitive ethical grasp would appear to place him to a discussion that the Ashʿarite theologian al-Shahrastānī had earlier offered in his *Nihāyat al-iqdām*. Reprising the debate about the value of actions in this work and bringing down the weight of his own argument against the Muʿtazilite position, it was precisely the case of retaliation that al-Shahrastānī had also made the subject of special focus. He had done so, however, with a striking difference: for he had taken this to provide a strong argument *against* the view that reason can secure ethical conviction. Left to its devices, he had written, human reason finds itself overwhelmed by dilemmatic choices and incapable of determining what constitutes the right ethical response to a given situation. The response to murder is a case in point. When a person takes the life of another, and

> we present this case to pure reason [*al-ʿaql al-ṣarīḥ*], we find there are different views [about how to deal with the case], all of them in conflict with each other. One of these is that the person should be killed in retaliation [*qiṣāṣan*] to deter aggressors from acts they would otherwise dare to undertake; and

> in doing so one also preserves the human species, satisfies the need for revenge . . . and appeases human feelings. Yet this thought is opposed by another—that this is destruction in return for destruction, and violence in exchange for violence, and that the first person will not come back to life by killing the other; and while deterrence might preserve [life] through future anticipation and imagination, retaliation involves the destruction of a person in the present and in actual fact.

Faced with such conflicting considerations, reason finds itself at a loss. This ambivalence, for al-Shahrastānī, was an unequivocal sign of our need for a divinely promulgated Law to serve as a moral arbiter and source of normative direction. It is only through the action of a divine legislator (*shāriʿ*) and by way of revelation (*waḥyan wa-tanzīlan*) that such moral dilemmas can achieve their resolution.[111]

Yet what is singular is that, with these remarks, al-Shahrastānī had expressed a doubt directed against the precise moral proposition that Ibn Taymiyya proclaims as a certainty of reason: the very *that* of the deontological principle of retaliation. This doubt, the passage above suggests, might be understood as the result of different considerations. It may be a doubt as to whether the punishment of retaliation indeed offers the best means to the valued end of protecting human life (for while it *potentially* preserves life, it *actually* destroys it); or it might be a doubt as to whether it is a means that serves our total interests, which include life but also other goods (such as a rejection of violence). Whatever its underlying rationale, it would seem to stand in an orthogonal relation to Ibn Taymiyya's own claim; and in doing so it would reproduce a disagreement that both readers of Ibn Taymiyya's *Darʾ taʿāruḍ* but also readers of the broader history of Islamic theological ethics will find intimately familiar.

"Reason tells us."—"Yet reason does not." This confrontation of a thesis and its antithesis had often featured in the pages of theological disputes about the nature of moral value and the human knowledge of it. The Muʿtazilites had said: reason necessarily speaks *thus and so*; the Ashʿarites had denied this. This debate had often seemed doomed to descend into a collision of mere say-so. To your claim "that certain things are necessarily known to be good or bad," al-Juwaynī had written in his *Irshād*, we simply retort: "your claim is contested and rebuffed." For "those who disagree with your claims have covered the face of the earth," and it contradicts the very essence of necessary knowledge that "one faction of rational beings should be the sole to possess" part of its content.[112] It is a collision that led one to wonder to what extent reason could be invoked as a trustworthy epistemic arbiter instead of being a witness in the pay of whatever party called it to court. Was it possible to confront the contents of reason naïvely and let the oracle speak in a voice other than that of its tendentious interrogators? How to arbitrate between competing accounts of reason's true voice?

It is a question that would revive itself at this juncture. And for those disposed to feel that al-Shahrastānī's argument derives its power from the way it captures their own experience of moral ambivalence, its immediate effect might be to provoke a question about Ibn Taymiyya's notable lack of it. Yet this lack of doubt—and the implicit ground of Ibn Taymiyya's arbitration of this dispute—becomes easier to comprehend once we locate this particular ethical precept against a more composite understanding of the prerevelational or extrarevelational "reason" it invokes. For on the one hand, the broad prescription of retaliation had its counterpart in previous prophetic messages, including the Jewish Law. This is a continuity that the Qur'an calls attention to (Q 5:45) and that writers discussing the relationship between the Islamic and earlier divine revelations had in turn frequently picked up on. Ibn Taymiyya himself explicitly brings out this broader horizon in his own remarks on the principle.[113]

The horizon prior to the Islamic revelation that Ibn Taymiyya makes contact with here may in fact have to be understood in even thicker terms, as a horizon constituted not only by an awareness of earlier religious practices, but indeed by an awareness of the concrete social practices that provided the historical backdrop for the genesis of Islamic Law. Modern commentators have sometimes voiced strongly worded views regarding the ahistorical manner in which medieval Muslim jurists approached the divine Law. "Law, in classical Islamic theory," Noel Coulson remarked in his *History of Islamic Law*, "is the revealed will of God, a divinely ordained system preceding and not preceded by the Muslim state, controlling and not controlled by Muslim society. There can thus be no notion of the law itself evolving as an historical phenomenon closely tied with the progress of society." One recalls the distinction often drawn between *fiqh* and *sharīʿa*, taking *fiqh* to represent the fallible human activity directed toward the discovery of the ideal eternal Law signified by the term *sharīʿa*, which ultimately resides in the "mind of God." Given this conception of the Sharīʿa that would have it "floating above Muslim society as a disembodied soul, freed from the currents and vicissitudes of time," it would appear only natural that classical Islamic jurisprudence should resist notions of historical process and take little interest in the evolution of the Law—or, to take a step closer to our own concern, to the relationship between the postrevelational world and the pre-Islamic world it superseded.[114]

The rich matrix of connections between these two domains has seemed obvious to those considering Islamic Law from a more historical perspective, who have highlighted multiple continuities between Islamic norms and pre-Islamic Arab practices. It is the Sunna of the Prophet that provided the most immediate conduit through which pre-Islamic practices entered the postrevelational world of the Sharīʿa, which they did, as Hallaq observes, by undergoing a purifying "transformation ... from the 'heretical' Jāhilī environment to the realm of the divine ...

through the agency of the Prophet."[115] With the exception of explicit Qur'anic legal reforms, Hallaq notes, the Prophet followed many of the preexisting Arab practices. These reforms spanned several fronts and included legislation intended to improve the position of women and the weak, to reduce sexual laxity and limit private vengeance, as well as more specific prohibitions like those of wine, usury, and gambling.[116]

Hallaq himself suggests that, transformed in this manner, this relationship is one that jurists were prepared to acknowledge. And indeed Coulson's thesis, as it stands, seems rather too rough-hewn for approaching the complex ways in which Muslim thinkers engaged notions of the past in the legal context. The past, certainly, was directly thematized in one of the debates we considered earlier, the status of actions prior to the advent of revelation. Like other writers before him, Ibn Taymiyya develops his position with an emphasis on its normative relevance for the living present, yet the historical dimension of the debate shadows his discussion throughout. Given the focus of this debate on the relationship between the "original" status of actions and the effect of legal rulings on this status, an attention to the element of change introduced by the Law naturally went hand in hand with an attention to the preexisting realities it dislodged or preserved.[117] It is clearly an awareness of the human transactions and economic activities taking place prior to the arrival of the Islamic message—an awareness that people bought and sold, rented and married, and generally engaged in activities of a contractual kind that involved determinate notions of what made a contract binding and what constituted its fulfillment—that informs Ibn Taymiyya's legal discussions and his view of the normative status of such activities.

Such an awareness of the pre-Islamic horizon providing the divine Law with its historical antecedents may also be said to be reflected in Ibn Taymiyya's account of the principle of retaliation. For retaliation, as we know, was widely practiced in pre-Islamic Arab society. The reforming aim of Islamic Law with regard to this principle, as Joseph Schacht points out, lay in limiting its practice and eliminating blood feuds. Yet the most helpful characterization of this reform comes from Coulson, who observes that many of the structural features of this principle remain unchanged between its pre-Islamic and Islamic embodiment. The key innovation lies in "the moral standard of just and exact reparation" introduced by Islamic Law.[118] This of course corresponds precisely to Ibn Taymiyya's proposal for relating our prerevelational evaluative grasp to the evaluative contribution of revelation. We know the normative *that* and the *why*; Arabs of pre-Islamic times also knew these things, as attested by the pre-Islamic maxim that Ibn Taymiyya's student Ibn Qayyim al-Jawziyya (d. 1350) tellingly cites at this juncture: "Killing is a surer means to eliminate killing [*al-qatl anfā li 'l-qatl*]." What revelation tells us is the *how* that best realizes the ends the principle serves, namely the preservation of life.[119]

Whether we read the prior horizon in which the principle of retaliation is anchored as one constituted by prior acts of divine speech or by preceding historical practices, however, both readings will heavily modify the way we receive Ibn Taymiyya's claim of ethical reason and the way we understand what it means to speak of this horizon as one of "reason." "Reason" here turns out to be conditioned by revelation on at least two separate levels. On the first reading, this will be a reason whose perception of value already stands informed by God's speech. The conditioning effect exercised by the second reading may not be as immediately obvious, but it will take only a moment's reflection to make it plain. For even if social views and evaluative judgments support a given practice, as in the case of retaliation, there is after all a natural question to raise as to whether this suffices to secure its normative force. Why should the contingent fact that people happen to hold certain evaluative beliefs—beliefs expressed in their actual practices—serve as a warrant for their soundness? Concerning any given social practice, one may always ask: Can it be justified? To do so, of course, involves taking a step away from these practices to examine them from a critical viewpoint.

This is a critical viewpoint that is also implicit in Ibn Taymiyya's discussion, and one that is construed in highly specific terms. As we have seen in considering Ibn Taymiyya's view of the original status of acts, all acts and practices, including those grounded in need—in which class the unqualified principle of retaliation falls, as Ibn Taymiyya signals: "People cannot live without it"—must receive the imprimatur of the Law, if only by its pointed silence, before their preexisting status can be allowed to stand. The principle of retaliation stands justified not as an actual practice expressive of the rational evaluative judgments of human beings, but as a practice endorsed and corroborated by the Law, which has permitted it to cross over from the world-before-Islamic-revelation to the postrevelational universe and thereby confirmed its legitimacy. If, disregarding the sediment that earlier prophetic guidance has already deposited in human reason, we were still to speak of "reason" here, this would be a reason sifted and certified for soundness—a reason rendered pure or *ṣarīḥ*—by the revealed Law. The normative voice against which one puts one's ear is the voice of reason as this reaches one filtered by God's speech.[120]

The conflict introduced by al-Shahrastānī thus mirrors the conflict discussed in the previous section in connection with the theological question of God's "aboveness" by similarly yielding a more accurate diagnosis of the direction in which reason moves. Ibn Taymiyya's immunity to the ambivalence conveyed by al-Shahrastānī may be taken as a sign that reason is confronted not naïvely, but under conditions calculated to protect it against the doubts produced by the pull of competing intuitions in the face of complex moral realities. Dwelling in a world already governed by the revealed Law, the hurly burly of moral realities is simply one to which one need not remain attuned.[121]

Al-Shahrastānī's own words, it may now be pointed out, had suggested a rather different construction of the critical viewpoint that might be summoned on ethical possibilities. His choice of term had also been *ṣarīḥ* when he had written: "We present this case to pure reason [*yuʿraḍu liʾl-ʿaql al-ṣarīḥ*]" and "we find there are different views." These words may make our memory stir. For it was that telltale term *ʿaraḍa*, with its theatrical connotations—conjuring the image of a judge surveying, from his lofty position, the data paraded before him for his authoritative verdict—that Avicenna and several of his commentators had employed to frame that potent thought experiment that came into view at an earlier point of our discussion. If you wish to know the difference between what is merely widely accepted (*dhāʾiʿ*) and what is natural (*fiṭrī*), Avicenna had stated, then simply "present your statement 'justice is fine' and 'lying is evil' to the natural disposition [*iʿraḍ qawlak* . . . *ʿala ʾl-fiṭra*]."[122] From the lofty viewpoint of pure reason constituted by this thought experiment, it is not merely that the right decision in particular cases is uncertain. Even more relevant, it is that all ethical judgments, however certain they might have appeared, are called into doubt, revealed as contingent products of convention that come to condition the mind so profoundly through the educative practices of the social world we grow up in that their underlying roots rarely rise up to conscious awareness.

It is a viewpoint that would thus come to pit itself against Ibn Taymiyya's yet again, claiming an ability to tap into the lofty oracle of reason with a purity outshining Ibn Taymiyya's own claim and undercutting that notion of reason—so heavily layered with social and religious accretions—he invokes, just as it had undercut the Muʿtazilites' before him. It is not my intention here to arbitrate between these two perspectives and to ascribe to Avicenna's or al-Shahrastānī's vantage point the higher ground it would claim for itself. For from what position could *that* arbitration be undertaken? Al-Shahrastānī's perspective may speak to our own experience of moral ambivalence and our sense of uncertainty about the existence of hard moral facts anchored in the "fabric of reality" that could resolve it. The more positive counterpart of Avicenna's programmatic doubt—its claim to have secured a rational perspective purified from the influences that have shaped us, taking us to a vantage point before revelation, prior to the social world, digging beneath evaluative judgments to discover the genealogy that produced them—will speak to us no less deeply. The possibility of isolating this kind of higher perspective has exercised a magnetic appeal over us ever since Plato's experiments in a radical transformation of vision that would leave the ordinary human perspective behind and see reality with the transcending objectivity of the gods. Yet this drive is after all one we should know better than to trust. Approaching Islamic theological debates about ethics and the constructions and deconstructions of reason—the constructions of reason and its other—that organize it, it is an insight well worth keeping in mind.

LEAPING FROM THE THEOLOGICAL to the legal context, in this chapter I proposed to examine Ibn Taymiyya's approach to considerations of welfare or utility (*maṣlaḥa*) in his legal discussions. Certain elements in these discussions—notably his pervasive invocation of "pragmatic" grounds of need in his practical legal rulings, his reference to preponderant utility as a criterion for evaluating actions, and his more theoretical remarks about unattested interests—appear to provide evidence for his endorsement of a more substantive manipulation of such considerations. Yet a closer reading of these same topics brings a different picture to light, suggesting that the revealed text provides a strong limiting framework for this engagement. Human reason does not confront utility with a significant degree of independence. In this respect, what Ibn Taymiyya tells us about the mind's transactions with value in his legal writings dovetails with what we hear about these transactions in the theological writings examined in previous chapters.

In both cases, Ibn Taymiyya's writing compels us to thematize its character, particularly the interpretive tensions and ambiguities that define it, and that contribute to the notable thinness that adheres to his evaluative remarks. Developing a long-running comparison with the evaluative writings of the Muʿtazilites, I suggested that some of these features—more broadly, Ibn Taymiyya's relative indifference to pressing a substantial *and* substantive account of ethical reason—can be illuminated by situating his ethical project against its theological aims, and against the concern with pressing a vision of the wisdom of God that speaks to human beings' spiritual needs. Having conjured this interpretive foil, I sought to situate his project in an even larger one, namely the seminal avowal of a concord between reason and revelation that shapes his thought. In advancing this claim of concord, just how independently, I asked, does Ibn Taymiyya think that reason can be consulted? The answer to this question, I argued, mirrors the one that emerges from considering the operations of reason in the ethical context. It is revelation that constitutes, and arbitrates on the identity of, sound reason; and it is revelation that, to a great extent, provides the intellectual ends that, working backward, reason seeks to defend. Returning to Ibn Taymiyya's invocation of reason in ethics, we may recognize the conditioning effect of God's speech on ethical reason on fresh levels.

6

Return to the Present

THIS BOOK, AS I explained at the outset, found its original impetus in a response of surprise provoked by a notion that appears pervasively in contemporary Muslim discourse and that receives its archetypal expression in the ubiquitous catchphrase, "Islam is the religion of our original nature." Leading away from the present, this surprise led back to the past, and there to a story that took a different turn, stimulating a more direct engagement with Ibn Taymiyya's thought. With that story in place, it is now possible to briefly return to the present to reflect on the ground covered and to consider the new roads that might open out from this position. My aim here will not be to undertake the full transition between past and present, but to build a few tentative bridges that may supply a more ambitious venture to narrate this transition with some of its galvanizing beginnings.

The contemporary use of the notion of *fiṭra,* I suggested at the opening of the book, appears to carry a set of important commitments—commitments that, once spelled out, point to a twofold relationship or pattern of correspondences: a correspondence between the commands of the Islamic faith and the demands of human nature, on the one hand; and a related correspondence between God's commands and the nature of actions, on the other. In carrying this freight, the notion of *fiṭra* evokes a spirit of moral rationalism familiar to us from the form in which the Muʿtazilites had cast it, yet in which Sunni theological tradition had overwhelmingly rejected it. These elements, it can be confirmed, find an immediate parallel in the works of Ibn Taymiyya. There is the notion of *fiṭra*—absent from familiar *kalām* debates on the value of actions. There too, emblazoned in brilliant form, is the vision of a concordance between the commands of the Islamic faith and the demands of human nature; and, with it, a rationalistic approach to ethics redolent of Muʿtazilite affinities.

Yet it has been a key proposal in this study that Ibn Taymiyya's rationalism needs to be read less in its innovativeness—in its discontinuities—than in its continuities, and more specifically in its continuities with an understanding of reason and its evaluative content that owes far more to the intellectual standpoint of Ashʿarism than might be readily apparent. Human beings know by reason that it is good to pursue what serves their welfare and best interests. Our very nature (*fiṭra*) as embodied beings opens us to characteristic forms of well-being and ill-being which determine that certain things are good for us and others bad. But as to what constitutes our truest well-being from a long-term perspective that takes into account the overall balance of benefit and harm, that is a thicker evaluative knowledge that we look to revealed religion to provide. Even so, we know that the commands of God have our welfare as their aim. In this respect, our sense of value and the sense of value manifested in God's Law coincide.

The understanding of moral knowledge just outlined, which expresses the commitments of Ibn Taymiyya's ethical thought as we saw them, found direct parallels in Ashʿarite theology. From al-Juwaynī onward, Ashʿarites had also affirmed that human reason gives its assent to a basic evaluative judgment regarding the self-interested pursuit of welfare. They had also spelled out their position in ways that grounded this "judgment" in desire and in the imperatives of our appetitive nature. The Ashʿarites, it is true, had emphasized God's freedom from motivating purposes, a fortiori from purposes connected to human welfare, and they had showed little interest in the moralized conception of God's justice and wisdom that Ibn Taymiyya was concerned to press, securing God as a worthy object of praise and love. Ibn Taymiyya's emphatic message of evaluative concordance, likewise, was one that they had been more reluctant to sound. Yet it was a message that they too had been compelled to sound in making the notion of welfare (*maṣlaḥa*) central to legal discourse and to their account of the aims of the Law, as we may recognize from earlier moments in our discussion.

We may thus recall al-Juwaynī's affirmation, falling on our ears with the air of a sudden (yet still struggling) intuition: "It is as if the Law harnesses the entailments of our nature as its support." We may recall al-Ghazālī's bolder spiritual conjunction, in the discussion of marriage in the *Iḥyāʾ ʿulūm al-dīn*, between the demands posed by our natural drives—themselves a script of divine intentions—and the demands expressed in the Law—themselves a more explicit script of the same. More broadly, this message of concordance was implicit in the experiential vantage point flagged by the notions of "need" and "necessity" (*ḥāja, ḍarūra*) deployed lavishly in the discourse of *maqāṣid al-sharīʿa*. To recall these moments of the foregoing account, of course, is to recall the moment that offered itself as yet another denouement, namely the conclusion that Ibn Taymiyya's specific epistemological vocabulary—that of *fiṭra*, injected into this debate with such salience seemingly for the first time and vested with positive connotations owed in great part to its Qur'anic roots—and the Ashʿarite vocabulary of *ṭabʿ* were divided by only a slender conceptual distance. Most important, both converged in a view of natural desire as requiring normative ordering to be provided by the Law.

Thus, Ibn Taymiyya's ethical understanding had much to connect it with that of the Ashʿarites'. But to read Ibn Taymiyya's outlook in its continuities with these of his predecessors is also to read the present in its continuities with its past. "Islam does not conflict with human nature or innate desires," we heard the Syrian jurist Wahba al-Zuḥaylī say, "because it is the religion of our original nature [*fiṭra*] and the religion of moderation."[1] The first concordance, here expressed, would appear to find its counterpart in the second concordance captured by al-Qaraḍāwī's remark: "God has made permissibility and prohibition dependent upon intelligible grounds [*ʿilal maʿqūla*], which relate to the interests of human beings themselves. . . . It thus became known in Islam that the prohibition of something depends on its malignancy and harmfulness."[2] Both types of concordance conveyed in these remarks can now be situated clearly against a longer intellectual pedigree and related to forms of thought that Ashʿarite theology had also achieved in its increasingly sophisticated development. The language of *ʿilal* itself points us to the legal context in which some of the most significant of these developments had taken place, and to the questions about legal analogy and legal causation that had provided a crucial setting for Muslim jurists in general for engaging notions of welfare—and the role of human evaluative judgments—in the Law. The notion of welfare, occupying a central place in classical Islamic legal thought, has seen its star rise even more sharply in modern Islamic thinking about the Law, and its pervasive presence in the contemporary context on its own should hardly surprise us.

What remains of the divisions between Ibn Taymiyya and the Ashʿarites, as just noted, is a more decisive emphasis on the message of concordance than the Ashʿarites had delivered, and a stronger affirmation of God's wisdom and of the rationality of the divine Law. Some of what *appears* to divide them, on the other hand—such as Ibn Taymiyya's seemingly louder emphasis on the objectivity of moral value and the rationality of moral knowledge—gives way on closer examination. It is an emphasis that exercises an important influence on expectations in ways that give the eventual discovery of its truer significance the character of a surprised unveiling. For Ibn Taymiyya's understanding of moral reality and of the content of unaided reason turn out to be thinner than his discussion encourages one to presume, particularly in light of his sidelining of the deontological considerations that shaped Muʿtazilite ethics. Ibn Taymiyya's embrace of reason turns out to be more limited in scope, and the rationalism he immediately conveys is one whose large print is belied by its detail. In this respect and in others, reason takes revelation as its point of departure, and looks to revelation for its more substantive specification.

It is important to take this conclusion on board in considering how the fuller story of the transition between past and present might be told. Given the far-reaching influence Ibn Taymiyya has exercised on the Muslim theological scene in the contemporary period, it is highly likely that the diffusion of this vigorous message of concordance may owe part of its impetus to his influence. To that extent, the analysis of his views I have offered might do well to resurface as an open question: Just how seriously should one take the commitment to reason that this message appears to carry?

A detailed response to this question lies beyond my scope, and all I hope to do here is trace out some heuristic comparisons. A particularly suggestive comparison in this connection is provided by considering the case of Sayyid Quṭb. A key protagonist of the modern Islamist movement, Quṭb is a figure who has cast a long shadow on the contemporary Muslim world, and who in turn labored strongly under the shadow cast by Ibn Taymiyya. It may thus come as no surprise that several motifs of Ibn Taymiyya's thought register their presence equally in Quṭb's writings. These include, notably, the language of *fiṭra* and a claim of moral rationalism tightly linked with this language. In attending to these more closely, I take my lights from the illuminating recent discussion by Frank Griffel.

It is a discussion that takes its context in a larger interpretive exchange, as it emerges as a response to an earlier set of remarks by Emilio Platti, who noted an apparent paradox, or contradiction, characterizing the Muslim fundamentalist concept of the Sharīʿa. Discussing the Islamist writer Abuʾl-Aʿlā Maudūdī—another prominent figure in the formation of the Islamist movement—Platti suggested that Maudūdī appeared to hold two conflicting views on the relationship between Sharīʿa and natural law. Although in one of his works, *The Islamic Way of Life*, Maudūdī "had praised the perfect compatibility of the Islamic moral system with the universal values expressed through the Qur'anic term *'al-Ma'ruf,'*" in another work, *The Islamic Law and Constitution*, he had rejected the conflation of "the positive, moral and social Law of God" with any notion of "natural law." Islam, in this latter work, is defined as submission to the positive divine Law.[3] *Both* harmony with universal moral values *and* Islam as complete submission to the revealed Law—how could these two be reconciled?

In taking up this question, Griffel turned his attention to Quṭb—who was heavily influenced by Maudūdī—to consider the place of this notion of harmony in his thought. It is a notion that leaps out of many of Quṭb's most important works as a recurring leitmotif. It leaps out in his seminal *Maʿālim fiʾl-ṭarīq*; it leaps out again, and more predictably, in his commentary on the Qur'an, *Fī Ẓilāl al-Qur'ān*. Commenting on the verse that had served as a linchpin for the traditional articulation of *fiṭra* (Q 30:30), Quṭb writes: with these words, "the natural disposition [*fiṭra*] of the human soul is connected to the nature [*ṭabīʿa*] of this religion; both are created by God; both are in agreement with the law of existence [*nāmūs al-wujūd*]; both are in harmony with each other in their nature and direction."[4] A harmony, then, involving at least three separate terms: a harmony between human nature and revealed religion; and between these two and a broader natural order. This vision finds its counterpart in Quṭb's *Maʿālim fiʾl-ṭarīq*, where the Sharīʿa is cast, as Griffel notes, "as the foundation of a holistic normative order that mirrors the order of the natural world."[5]

This claim is in turn interestingly combined with a related claim concerning the nature of moral knowledge and with an outright affirmation of the rational accessibility of moral truths. Human beings, writes Quṭb in his commentary, are "capable of distinguishing between what is good [*khayr*] and what is evil [*sharr*], just as they are equally capable of directing themselves toward good and toward evil. . . . This capacity lies within their being, and the Qur'an sometimes refers to it through the term 'inspiration' [*ilhām*]."[6] Quṭb's statement is couched in terms in which the classical theological tradition may not have recognized its concerns, as in the vocabulary of "inspiration" used to refer to the source of our evaluative knowledge, or "the faculty of (moral) awareness" (*al-quwwa al-wāʿiyya*). The well-worn vocabulary of *ḥusn* and *qubḥ* has likewise given way to an idiom less reminiscent of the classical discussions. Much has happened here in the transition from the traditional theology still taught at al-Azhar in Quṭb's time to the new theological discourse produced by writers like Quṭb who had not received their formation through traditional structures of learning. Similarly, several things also seem to have happened between Quṭb and Ibn Taymiyya, with whom Griffel aligns Quṭb's interpretation of *fiṭra* in its essential features. Quṭb's embrace of a belief in the human liberty to choose, for example, is one that Ibn Taymiyya would not have accepted quite as it stands; Quṭb's analysis of the opposing tendencies of human nature (toward both good and evil) would recognize a kind of conflict that Ibn Taymiyya, in his discussion of *fiṭra*, tended to occlude.

More important in this context, however, is to note what unites the two thinkers rather than what divides them; and it is precisely this aspect that Griffel next provides the material for remarking when he goes on to raise the question of how Islamists like Maudūdī and Quṭb propose to establish the proposed harmony between the religious law and our moral judgments. It is not, it seems clear, a matter of holding up the contents of one against the contents of the other to confirm their concord. Islamist theologians, he suggests, "make no attempts to establish the harmony of Sharīʿa and natural law from a detailed comparison of the two. When faced with the question, what is the normative law of nature? Islamists answer that it is represented by the rulings of the Sharīʿa. This response is not descriptive but normative. It is based on the prior claim of the harmony between Sharīʿa and natural law. . . . Sharīʿa is the only point of reference for knowledge of what natural law is. . . . Reason can never by the judge (*ḥākim*) of the truths of revelation." Thus, he concludes, the apparent contradiction Platti identified is not so much a contradiction as a vicious circle: "The claim that Sharīʿa is in harmony with natural law is verified with the assertion that natural law follows Sharīʿa."[7]

This, as Griffel observes, is a view that brings telling difficulties, which emerge when competing claims are made about the contents of reason that bring reason into conflict with the stipulations of the Sharī'a. One of the examples considered by Quṭb in illustrating the thesis of harmony provides a case in point. Discussing the Islamic provision of polygamy, he suggests that this follows a natural ratio in sexual relations that is not equal between the sexes, in a way that "reflects the reality of the human *fiṭra* and the reality of life." Quṭb's brother Muhammad refers to the natural division of labor between the sexes in a similar context, explaining the relatively restricted rights of women in the Sharī'a compared to men by pointing to their natural role in caring for the family.[8]

In these rulings as in others—the ruling on apostasy, often taken to conflict with the universal right to freedom of thought and religion, forms one of the most salient examples—the pronouncements of the Sharī'a as traditionally understood would appear to be in tension with scruples arising from different quarters and bearing a moral character. In such cases, the claim of harmony between what reason says and what revelation commands could be supported only by discounting the epistemic status of these contradictory intuitions. And this involves excluding them from the domain of reason, in a move that serves as a normative arbitration of reason's content and, while taking its traction from the presumed harmony between reason and the Law, expresses a particular understanding of which of the two terms carries the privilege. Thus: "If Sharī'a is truly rational, rationality must follow Sharī'a."[9]

The parallel with Ibn Taymiyya's account may already be plain. For whether we call it *ḥākim* or *mi'yār*, it is the same function that Ibn Taymiyya denied to reason, even while maintaining as an axiom that reason and revelation must necessarily be in concord. Over revelation, reason cannot act as arbiter. If the two appear to be in conflict, it is reason that needs to realign itself with revelation anew—and in doing so discover its truer nature. The confrontation of reason itself takes place not naïvely, we concluded, but in terms seasoned by the givens of revelation. On the ethical plane, this relationship of priority was not immediately evident in Ibn Taymiyya's annunciation of the natural constitution as the ground of ethical knowledge, yet a closer probing brought it into clear view. For *fiṭra*, as we saw, was associated mainly with desire in the ethical context, yet natural desire does not carry normative force and requires to be ordered normatively through an awareness of its consequences and of the overall balance of benefit and harm—and this is an awareness that only revelation can fully provide. What this entails is that our actual desires may indeed often conflict rather than accord with the dictates of the Law; and thus the accord between our nature and the Law is not to be found in experience but to be realized by aligning our desires with the evaluative vantage point of the Law and its vision of our truer good.

In neither case, thus, does the claim to harmony involve a comparison between the actual deliverances of our nature and the commands of the faith that would support it; and in both cases, the message of rationalism initially evoked by the language of *fiṭra* seems to be belied by a closer consideration of the detail. Also worth remarking is that in both cases it is a conflict with opposing intuitions that reveals the direction in which reason moves. The sense of moral dissonance provoked by the stipulations of the Law on apostasy or gender relations, as we saw it in Quṭb, in this respect mirrors the dissonance—or ambivalence—discussed in chapter 5 in connection with the principle of retaliation, on which moral reactions would appear to be more divided than Ibn Taymiyya was prepared to concede. And if in this last case reason is read backward with the data of revelation already giving it form, other examples can be cited that parallel more closely the ones mentioned by Griffel, to the extent that they reflect not merely scriptural facts but social realities, prejudices, and norms. A good illustration is Ibn Taymiyya's proposed explanation of the legal provision that forbids women to marry their slaves, which he accounts for by pointing to the natural hierarchy that gives men the status of masters and lords over women, since "everyone knows by *fiṭra* that males are superior to females."[10]

It is equally worth observing that in both cases just addressed—in the modern context as much as in Ibn Taymiyya's—these conflicting reactions arise with reference to that area of the religious law in which the deontological notion of rights and obligations (*ḥaqq*) comes into play. This was an aspect that, as I suggested earlier, received second place in Ibn Taymiyya's account, which focused predominantly on considerations of welfare and on the character of the Sharīʿa as promoting the latter. These deontological considerations, of course, were not so much absent as indirectly present through the assumption that they too ultimately reduce to teleological terms, in keeping with the conceptual architecture of the legal discourse of *maqāṣid al-sharīʿa* and its view of the place of interests in the Law.

This relationship of subordination—of deontological to consequentialist notions—is interesting, on the one hand, because it points to ways of responding to the sense of conflict just described that would build on that relationship to open up avenues for legal revision, for those at least prepared to embrace a more substantive view of the place of welfare in the Law. And while in the classical period many jurists treated such an approach with great distrust—the boldest articulation of this view, by the Ḥanbalite jurist Najm al-Dīn al-Ṭūfī, never achieved wide appeal—and gravitated toward the more cautious textualist approach represented by al-Ghazālī, in the modern context this approach has come to the foreground as a more attractive even if still hotly contested possibility.[11]

At the same time, this would seem to mark a certain difference between Ibn Taymiyya's usage of *fiṭra* and that of modern writers, who show themselves more willing to specify the content of *fiṭra* in deontological terms without directly placing these in contact with considerations of welfare. The short tract by al-ʿUthaymīn referred to at the opening of this book—enumerating the varieties of rights and obligations, ascribed directly to *fiṭra* in the title—provides a good example of this tendency. The writings of the Moroccan thinker ʿAllāl al-Fāsī provide another, though an example of a more finely textured and reflective kind. In al-Fāsī's best-known work, *Maqāṣid al-sharīʿa al-Islāmiyya wa-makārimuhā*, the notion of *fiṭra* appears as a salient motif. Early in the work he addresses it by offering a distinction between the notions of *ṭabīʿa* and *fiṭra*, taking the former to designate the animal side of human nature and the latter to signify the side in which our truer humanity is vested, which is both spiritual and, importantly, social in character. Al-Fāsī then connects *fiṭra* to the primordial covenant between human beings and God indicated in the Qur'an (Q 7:172) and to the freedom and responsibility acquired by human beings in entering it.[12] The connection between *fiṭra* and the so-called covenant of Alast had been made before in the Islamic tradition. In al-Fāsī's appropriation, however, the effect is to draw the notion of *fiṭra* into a more palpably deontological field and toward the language of rights and obligations (*ḥuqūq wa-wājibāt*) used to specify the notion of covenant (*ʿaqd* or *mīthāq*). This is a move that reflects a deeper concern to bring the notion of *fiṭra* into relationship with the evaluative concepts organizing contemporary moral discourse.

Welfare, to be sure, plays a central role in al-Fāsī's conception of the Law and retains a strong presence in the backdrop of his understanding of *fiṭra*—as it did in the classical legal scheme, where the notion of *ḥaqq* was throughout shadowed by that of *maṣlaḥa*. As such, the difference in question might be said to represent merely a difference between what is spoken and left unspoken, or what takes the foreground and shapes the gestalt, drawing on a fund of preexisting intellectual possibilities. A similarly delicate yet not inconsequential reorganization of preexisting possibilities would seem to be in evidence in the way al-Fāsī approaches the status of *fiṭra*. For having distinguished between the two notions of human nature, lower and higher, and having reserved *fiṭra* for the latter, al-Fāsī's continuing discussion brings out more plainly what this distinction already implied, namely that *fiṭra* is to be understood in normative terms, as a higher ideal, and hence not as something all people actually and effortlessly possess but as something that may require achievement. Al-Fāsī thus talks of *fiṭra* as something that we may lack (*tanquṣuhu al-fiṭra*), whose principles (*qawāʿid*) we may fail to realize, which we may need to "discover" or be "reminded of"—precisely by the prompting of the revealed Law.[13] The normative character of *fiṭra* is directly conveyed in the statement al-Fāsī offers to clarify the harmony at stake between the Law and our nature: "What is meant by the fact that Islam is the religion of our original nature is that it is the religion which *makes* the acts of human beings natural [*fiṭriyya*], thereby rendering them worthy to be considered human beings and not animals."[14] If *fiṭra* is an achievement, it is through obedience to the revealed Law that it stands to be achieved.

Ibn Taymiyya's paradoxical-sounding notion of "a revealed natural disposition" (*fiṭra munazzala*), discussed in chapter 5, seems to be in the offing at several points in this discussion; and it is worth remarking the prominent presence of the works of Ibn Taymiyya and Ibn Qayyim al-Jawziyya in al-Fāsī's spare bibliography. It is similarly Ibn Taymiyya's tones we can hear in the telling view of reason voiced by al-Fāsī, which is synopsized in one of two possibilities: reason may agree with revelation; or reason may serve in an auxiliary and thus subordinate role.[15] Yet in Ibn Taymiyya's own discussion, the normative status of *fiṭra* stood out far less certainly, and the tension between the more negative view of nature (particularly natural desire) present in his work and the positive connotations carried by the notion of *fiṭra* were nowhere addressed. Al-Fāsī's terminological distinction between different concepts of nature provides an explicit tool for addressing this tension, though in doing so it highlights even more sharply that the claim of harmony between human nature and the Law is not one to be established on experiential grounds.

Such readjustments and reworkings of preexisting intellectual possibilities can have important effects, some of them more far-reaching than others. As such, they invite one to attend more closely to the continuities and discontinuities filling the distance between the modern and classical context and to seek a more finely tuned understanding of modern developments. If the differences noted above track some of the potential discontinuities separating modern writers from Ibn Taymiyya's context, another has already come into view. Discussing Quṭb's characterization of the harmony between our nature and the divine law, we saw that this harmony consisted of an agreement between not just two, but indeed three separate elements: the religious law; the nature of the human soul; and what Quṭb referred to as "the law that governs existence." The last two elements in fact point us to two different senses in which the term "natural law" can be taken. In the ethical context, as we saw in chapter 2, this term refers us to a multifaceted intellectual tradition in which it has been connected with the moral principles available to human beings through their inborn reason. In the second and the most familiar sense, "natural law" refers us not to the moral but to the scientific plane, and to the laws governing the phenomena of the natural world that form the object of scientific investigation.

It is the latter sense that Quṭb underscores in several parts of his account, as in the following statement from his *Maʿālim fi ʾl-ṭarīq*: "The Sharīʿa that God has ordained for the life of humanity is a universal Sharīʿa in the sense that it is connected to [*muttaṣil bi*] and in harmony with [*mutanāsiq maʿa*] the general law of the universe. Obedience to Sharīʿa is necessary for humans in order to bring their lives into harmony with the movements of the universe they live in."[16] This threefold harmony—between the religious law, our native moral judgments, and the laws of nature—plays a prominent role in Quṭb's account. But the inclusion of the last term bears a wider significance in pointing to a theme that has formed a key motif in the Muslim engagement with modernity, and that manifests as a concern to affirm the harmony between Islam and the modern viewpoint by effecting a rapprochement with natural science, while subordinating the latter to the perspective of the revealed Law.

This is a concern that we can also see reflected in the work by al-Qaraḍāwī referred to earlier, *al-Ḥalāl wa 'l-ḥarām*. For if al-Qaraḍāwī employs the traditional language of *maṣlaḥa* to assert that God's commands can be explained through their aim of promoting human welfare, the rationality of God's commands is illustrated more particularly with reference to consequences brought to light through a scientific process of investigation. Thus, the wisdom of God's prohibition of consuming pork or the Prophet's admonition against defecating in sources of water, on the open road, and in shadows has become more intelligible to us in the light of recent scientific discoveries concerning the dangers such actions pose to health.[17]

In this rationalistic approach to the relationship between divine command and human reason, then, it is more specifically "scientific reason" that comes to additionally fill the second term of the concordance. It is a naturalistic understanding of the Law that has been developing an increasing cultural reach, as Gregory Starrett has shown in his illuminating study of the teaching of religion in primary and secondary Egyptian schools in *Putting Islam to Work: Education, Politics, and Religious Transformation in Egypt*. Starrett introduces the notion of "functionalization" to describe the way Egyptian textbooks present religious teachings. Functionalization, as he puts it, consists of a set of "processes of translation in which intellectual objects from one discourse come to serve the strategic or utilitarian ends of another discourse," such that "traditions, customs, beliefs, institutions, and values that originally possessed their own evaluative criteria and their own rules of operation and mobilization become consciously subsumed by modern-educated elites to the evaluative criteria of social and political utility."[18]

Concretely, and most relevant for the present context, functionalization manifests itself as a trend of explaining religious observances and injunctions in overtly naturalistic terms. The performance of ritual ablution provides a stark illustration of this point. In the functionalized pedagogical discourse of Egyptian textbooks, ablution is presented to schoolchildren as an observance ordained for the purpose of promoting hygiene, health, and well-being—a view of its value supported not just by ordinary good sense but also by modern science.[19] Methodically pursued, the reason-giving cultivated in this pedagogical setting seems designed to cement a naturalistic understanding of the purposes the religious Law aims to serve. The message implicit in this strategy is that "Islamic practices are to be examined for their latent functions and their social effect" and that religious commands may be linked with "the observable world, both natural and social." One of the corollaries of this approach, as Starrett points out, is that "the ordinary educated Muslim need not master a complex body of legal or philosophical material in order to participate in functionalist discourse; the physician, the engineer, and the bureaucrat are equally well-equipped to bring their experiences of social, mechanical, and natural order into the discussion of God's nature"—or indeed His commands.

Such popular presentations serve to reinforce a naturalistic understanding of the Law, in doing so adding complexity to the twofold notion of "nature" and "natural law" as modern writers deploy it. This is a complexity, it may be noted, with important effects on how the concordance between nature and the religious Law is to be understood in epistemological terms. For this way of filling the notion of "natural law" would certainly register as publicly and independently available to human reason, taken in its scientific embodiment. Given the strong ligaments connecting divinely prescribed norms to human welfare—ligaments that scientific reason is called upon to illuminate—this suggests that the epistemological story of the concordance at stake would partly hinge on the true distance that separates the moral and the scientific specifications of "natural law."

To return to our starting question: How to understand the notion of *fiṭra* as employed by modern writers? And just how seriously to take the commitment to reason carried by its modern usage? The above discussion suggests that such questions stand to be illuminated by considering them in the light of Ibn Taymiyya's earlier development of this notion, and that his work can serve both as an index of the continuities binding the present to its past and as a foil allowing the discontinuities to be thrown into sharper relief. It is an index, as I have highlighted on several occasions in this study, that does not everywhere speak in a single voice, and that is fractured by interpretive disunities with important implications for the way we read Ibn Taymiyya's message. This, too, is crucial to keep in mind in effecting the leap from past to present and in reading Ibn Taymiyya's intellectual legacy in its full potency. For its greatest potency, and its greatest fertility, may lie precisely in the complex messages to which his work plays host and in its capacity to offer itself as a welcoming soil to competing appropriations and plural interpretive possibilities.

Notes

INTRODUCTION

1. Al-Zuḥaylī, *Akhlāq al-Muslim*, 21.
2. Al-Qaraḍāwī, *al-Ḥalāl wa 'l-ḥarām fi 'l-Islām*, 28.
3. Taken as a question about the contemporary recrudescence of specifically Muʿtazilite theological views, this would not be a new question to ask. Much has been said already about the presumed modern revival of such views and about the legitimacy of talk of a "neo-Muʿtazilite" movement. For an in-depth examination of this topic, see Hildebrandt, "Waren Ǧamāl ad-Dīn al-Afġānī und Muḥammad ʿAbduh Neo-Muʿtaziliten?" and his book-length study, *Neo-Muʿtazilismus?*
4. Fakhry, *Islamic Philosophy, Theology, and Mysticism*, 101, and see generally chapter 8, "The progress of anti-rationalism and the onset of decline." Cf. the remarks by Leaman and Rizvi in "The developed *kalām* tradition," 83, 84.

CHAPTER 1

1. The phrase (*khiyār al-umūr awsāṭuhā*) is from Ibn Taymiyya, "Sharḥ ḥadīth innī ḥarramtu al-ẓulm ʿalā nafsī," in *Majmūʿ Fatāwā shaykh al-Islām Aḥmad ibn Taymiyya*, 18: 137.
2. Little, "Religion under the Mamluks," 180.
3. Laoust, *Essai sur les doctrines sociales et politiques de Taḳī-d-Dīn Aḥmad b. Taymīya*, 221. See also the remarks in Laoust, "L'influence d'Ibn-Taymiyya," 15–33, esp. 20. The most direct textual anchor for Laoust's remarks can be found in Ibn Taymiyya's "Al-ʿAqīda al-Wāsiṭiyya," in *Majmūʿ Fatāwā*, 3: 141. This creed has been translated by Swartz in "A seventh-century (A.H.) Sunnī creed."
4. See Michot, *Against Extremisms*, xx–xi.
5. Ibn Qudāma, *Taḥrīm al-nazar fī kutub ahl al-kalām*.

6. Shams al-Dīn al-Dhahabī, *al-Naṣīḥa al-dhahabiyya li-ibn Taymiyya*, ed. by Muḥammad Zāhid al-Kawtharī (Damascus 1347/1928–29), 33, quoted by Kügelgen in a piece devoted to investigating Ibn Taymiyya's philosophical appropriations: "The poison of philosophy," 257–58. The significance of Ibn Taymiyya's engagement with philosophical resources and the rational sciences more broadly has been emphasized by a number of recent scholars, including Michot in studies such as "A Mamlūk theologian's commentary on Avicenna's *Risāla Aḍḥawiyya*"; cf. his explicit invitation in "Vanités intellectuelles" to find in Ibn Taymiyya "the most important reader of the *falāsifa* after Fakhr al-Dīn al-Rāzī in the Sunni world" (599). See also on this point Hoover, "Ibn Taymiyya as an Avicennan theologian." The emphasis on Ibn Taymiyya's rationalist commitments marks much of Hoover's work. It also finds expression, more recently, in Anjum's *Politics, Law, and Community in Islamic Thought*, esp. chapter 4.
7. "Fluctuating scepticism": the description is Bori's in "Ibn Taymiyya *wa-jamāʿatuhu*," 33. For the point regarding Ibn Taymiyya's influence, see El-Rouayheb, "From Ibn Ḥajar al-Haytamī (d. 1566) to Khayr al-Dīn al-Ālūsī (d. 1899)," 305 quoted.
8. Swartz, "A seventh-century (A.H.) Sunnī creed," 96–97.
9. Ibn Taymiyya, *Sharḥ al-Iṣbahāniyya*, 180.
10. Several of these familiar formulations will be fine-tuned in the chapters that follow. For an account of this larger debate, good starting points include Hourani, *Reason and Tradition in Islamic Ethics* and *Islamic Rationalism*; Vasalou, *Moral Agents and Their Deserts*; Fakhry, *Ethical Theories in Islam*, part 2; Frank, "Moral obligation in classical Muslim theology"; Shihadeh, "Theories of ethical value in kalām."
11. See Shihadeh, *The Teleological Ethics of Fakhr al-Dīn al-Rāzī*, 38–39, for the relevant remarks from al-Rāzī's *Tafsīr*.
12. Ibn Taymiyya's refusal of such a surrender to mystery is emphasized by Hoover in his account of Ibn Taymiyya's view of action; see *Ibn Taymiyya's Theodicy of Perpetual Optimism*, chapter 4.
13. Throughout the following discussion I will mostly use "good" as a translation for the term *ḥasan*; "right" carries a stronger normative or "imperative" force than *ḥasan* invites, and as such would obscure some of the issues I raise with regard to Ibn Taymiyya's focal evaluative concepts later in this chapter and elsewhere.
14. The quote is from al-Dhahabī's *Nubdha min sīrat shaykh al-Islām Taqī al-Dīn Aḥmad ibn Taymiyya*, edited and translated by Bori in "A new source for the biography of Ibn Taymiyya," 341; though al-Dhahabī himself, as we have already seen and this document also makes clear, did not have a solely eulogistic attitude to Ibn Taymiyya.
15. "Explosiveness" is Bori's term in "The collection and edition of Ibn Taymīyah's works," 55. Bori's discussion casts a very helpful light on both the form and the formation of Ibn Taymiyya's writings.
16. Ibn ʿAbd al-Hādī, *al-ʿUqūd al-durriyya min manāqib shaykh al-Islām ibn Taymiyya*, 72.

17. Michot, *Against Extremisms*, xxiv.
18. "What distinguishes fatwa literature," Weiss remarks, "is its basic character as a collection of discrete units. . . . Fatwa literature does not attain the degree of systematization that is found in the great treatises" ("Ibn Taymiyya on leadership in the ritual prayer," 64). The previous quote is from 63.
19. See Bori's remarks in "The collection and edition of Ibn Taymīyah's works," 56.
20. Michot, "A Mamlūk theologian's commentary," 161; and see the structural illustration from the *Dar᾿ ta῾āruḍ* that follows.
21. Anjum, *Politics, Law, and Community in Islamic Thought*, 183. His next remark falls more ambiguously: Ibn Taymiyya, he writes, "was far from being a system builder; in this lay his greatest strength as well as the limit of all his thought." For Hallaq's discussion, see *Ibn Taymiyya against the Greek Logicians*, l–lii.
22. Michot, *Against Extremisms*, xxiv.
23. See my *Moral Agents and Their Deserts*, 8–9. For the interpretive debates about al-Ghazālī referred to above, see Griffel, *Al-Ghazālī's Philosophical Theology*.
24. Based on a remark in the *Minhāj al-sunna*, Makdisi suggested that Ibn Taymiyya composed a separate work on the topic that failed to reach us ("Ethics in Islamic traditionalist doctrine," 56). The quoted remark, however, does not seem to me unambiguous. Many of the passages in which Ibn Taymiyya addresses the question of *taḥsīn* contain tantalizing references to a fuller discussion of the matter elsewhere; it is unclear to me which of the texts considered in this study Ibn Taymiyya might have had in mind.
25. Or more accurately: exponents of the view that human beings create their own acts (*qadariyya*), generally identified with the Mu῾tazilites. On Ibn Taymiyya's use of this term, see Hoover, *Ibn Taymiyya's Theodicy*, 105–8.
26. Correcting the text, which has *aḥkām*, not *af῾āl*.
27. The translation is Marmaduke Pickthall's, with a couple of revisions. Throughout this work, I have drawn selectively on three translations of the Qur'an—Pickthall's, Arthur John Arberry's and 'Abdullah Yusuf Ali's—using the one that has seemed to me the most helpful on each occasion, and occasionally introducing small modifications.
28. The phrase is *Allāhu ḥarrama al-muḥarramāt fa-ḥarumat, wa-awjaba al-wājibāt wa-wajabat*. Given Ibn Taymiyya's ensuing argument, the *fa* that serves as a syntactic connector cannot denote causation or consequence. My translation tries to make the best sense of these formulations in light of his argument.
29. The entire passage just translated can be found in Ibn Taymiyya, "Mas᾿alat taḥsīn al-῾aql wa-taqbīḥuhu," in *Majmū῾ Fatāwā*, 8: 428–36.
30. Ibid., 428.
31. See, for example, Abū Ya῾lā, *al-Mu῾tamad fī uṣūl al-dīn*, 21–22, 113; cf. 118: God is not subject to any moral standards known by reason. The quote is from Cook, *Commanding Right and Forbidding Wrong in Islamic Thought*, 130.

32. Ibn ʿAqīl, *al-Wāḍiḥ fī uṣūl al-fiqh*, 1: 12. Makdisi describes this work as a product of Ibn ʿAqīl's "mature years" (*Ibn ʿAqil*, xiv). Some of Makdisi's most concentrated remarks on Ibn ʿAqīl's view of ethical qualifications can be found at 124–30. On Ibn ʿAqīl, see also Makdisi's earlier work, *Ibn ʿAqîl et la résurgence de l'Islam traditionaliste au XI*[e] *siècle*. This also seems to have been Ibn Qudāma's view: *Rawḍat al-nāẓir wa-jannat al-munāẓir fī uṣūl al-fiqh ʿalā madhhab al-Imām Aḥmad ibn Ḥanbal*, 22: *al-ʿaql lā madkhala lahu fi ʾl-ḥaẓar wa ʾl-ibāḥa*.
33. See, for example, Ibn Taymiyya, *al-Radd ʿala ʾl-manṭiqiyyīn*, 420–21. Al-Kalwadhānī's view of ethical judgments is expressed in his *al-Tamhīd fī uṣūl al-fiqh*, 4: 294–306. Ibn Taymiyya's list in the *Radd* includes a number of traditionists, such as Abū Naṣr al-Sijzī (d. 1052) and Abuʾl-Qāsim al-Zanjānī (d. 1078/79). The former's rationalist view of ethical judgments is densely gestured at in his *Risālat al-Sijzī ilā ahl Zabīd fi ʾl-radd ʿalā man ankara al-ḥarf wa ʾl-ṣawt*, 95. I am grateful to Ahmed El Shamsy for directing my attention to this work. If we wished to build a more holistic view of the Ḥanbalite engagement with this subject, we would need to include into our scope a number of other thinkers, such as Ibn Taymiyya's one-time student Najm al-Dīn al-Ṭūfī (d. 1316), whose *Darʾ al-qawl al-qabīḥ bi ʾl-taḥsīn wa ʾl-taqbīḥ* was recently edited by Ayman Shihadeh.
34. The claim of majority appears widely in Ibn Taymiyya's discussion; see, for example, *Radd*, 421: *akthar al-ṭawāʾif ʿalā ithbāt al-ḥusn wa ʾl-qubḥ al-ʿaqliyyayn*; cf. Ibn Taymiyya, *Sharḥ al-Iṣbahāniyya*, 704: *jumhūr al-fuqahāʾ bal wa-jumhūr al-umma*. Yet this claim appears more guarded, and indeed apostrophized, elsewhere. Compare, for example, *Darʾ taʿāruḍ al-ʿaql wa ʾl-naql*, 7: 457, 9: 49–50.
35. Al-Kalwadhānī makes that claim of majority explicit: this is the view of "most [*ʿāmmat*] of the learned, jurists and theologians alike, and most of the philosophers" (*Tamhīd*, 4: 295), though this is not what he identifies as the prevailing view among Ḥanbalites (271); the editor of the text interestingly contests this claim. The competing claim is more implicit in Ibn ʿAqīl's remarks in *Wāḍiḥ*, 1: 12. Ibn Taymiyya might thus be said to be following al-Kalwadhānī in his own demographical remarks. A more intelligible parsing of Ibn Taymiyya's claim of consensus will come into view in chapter 4. To the extent that this claim of consensus or majority seems misleading, it will not be without parallel in Ibn Taymiyya's work. As Shahab Ahmed notes, for example, in "Ibn Taymiyyah and the Satanic verses," Ibn Taymiyya characterizes his position on the Satanic verses as the view of the majority and the *salaf* when it is in fact far from representative of the mainstream view.
36. Ibn Mattawayh, *al-Majmūʿ fi ʾl-Muḥīṭ bi ʾl-taklīf*, 1: 236. The text is problematic in this vicinity, but the basic point is rehearsed in many other passages of both Ibn Mattawayh's and other Baṣrans' writings. Ibn Mattawayh is more specifically drawing a distinction between deontological and consequentialist types of grounds that will come into view in the main text shortly.
37. ʿAbd al-Jabbār, *al-Taʿdīl wa ʾl-tajwīr*, 57.

38. Ibn Mattawayh, *Majmūʿ*, 1: 255–56.
39. Al-Ghazālī, *al-Mustaṣfā min ʿilm al-uṣūl*, 1: 56. For another representative statement of this claim, see al-Shahrastānī, *Nihāyat al-iqdām fī ʿilm al-kalām*, 370.
40. Al-Anṣārī, *al-Ghunya fi ʾl-kalām*, 2: 998.
41. See, for example, al-Ashʿarī's view (framed with reference to the value of lying) in *Kitāb al-Lumaʿ fi ʾl-radd ʿalā ahl al-zaygh wa ʾl-bidaʿ*, 117. Cf. al-Anṣārī, *Ghunya*, 2: 1002. And see more directly Ibn ʿAqīl, *Wāḍiḥ*, 1: 129–31, in the context of discussing the question of abrogation (*naskh*).
42. Al-Ghazālī, *Mustaṣfā*, 1: 56. The two proposals, it may be noticed, share the same basic structure and organizing terms: al-Ghazālī's *mā wāfaqa al-gharaḍ* comes as a counterpart to the earlier Ashʿarite *mā wāfaqa al-amr*. For the latter formulation, see, for example, al-Bāqillānī, *al-Inṣāf fīmā yajibu iʿtiqāduhu wa-lā yajūzu al-jahl bihi*, 49.
43. For example, Ibn Mattawayh, *Majmūʿ*, 3: 180: "*Every rational being* [or *every person who is compos mentis*] knows that injustice is bad and justice good [*lā ʿāqila illā wa-huwa yaʿlamu qubḥ al-ẓulm wa-ḥusn al-inṣāf*]."
44. Jackson, "The alchemy of domination?," 186–87.
45. Hoover, *Ibn Taymiyya's Theodicy*, 38.
46. See, for example, Ibn Taymiyya, *Minhāj al-sunna al-nabawiyya fī naqḍ kalām al-Shīʿa al-qadariyya*, 1: 447–48; "Qāʿida fiʾl-muʿjizāt waʾl-karāmāt wa-anwāʿ khawāriq al-ʿādāt wa-manāfiʿihā wa-maḍārrihā," in *Majmūʿ Fatāwā*, 11: 353–54; "Al-ʿAqīda al-Tadmuriyya," in *Majmūʿ Fatāwā*, 3: 116; "Aqwam mā qīla fiʾl-qaḍāʾ waʾl-qadar waʾl-ḥikma waʾl-taʿlīl," in *Majmūʿ Fatāwā*, 8: 98.
47. Again both points recur in Ibn Taymiyya's ethical remarks. For the affirmation of *qadar* in this context see, for example, "Qāʿida fiʾl-muʿjizāt waʾl-karāmāt," in *Majmūʿ Fatāwā*, 11: 354; for the issue of punishment: "Fī anna al-tawba waʾl-istighfār yakūnu min tark al-wājibāt wa-fiʿl al-muḥarramāt," in *Majmūʿ Fatāwā*, 11: 677; *Darʾ taʿāruḍ*, 8: 493.
48. These purely indicative phrases are drawn from Ibn Taymiyya, "Risāla fī maʿnā kawn al-rabb ʿādilan wa-fī tanazzuhihi ʿan al-ẓulm," in *Jāmiʿ al-rasāʾil*, 1: 129.
49. "The question of the determination of good and bad," he explicitly states, "is not necessarily connected to the question of *qadar*" ("Masʾalat taḥsīn al-ʿaql wa-taqbīḥuhu," in *Majmūʿ Fatāwā*, 8: 431).
50. Ibn Taymiyya, "Masʾalat taḥsīn al-ʿaql wa-taqbīḥuhu," in *Majmūʿ Fatāwā*, 8: 434–35.
51. A particularly instructive insight into this historical complexity with respect to later Muʿtazilism is provided by Schwarb in "Muʿtazilism in the age of Averroes."
52. See, for example, ʿAbd al-Jabbār, *Taʿdīl*, 122. "Ground" was Hourani's choice of term: see *Islamic Rationalism*, s.v. "ground."
53. Though there are certain qualifications that are generated by the case of lying with special relevance (if not exclusively). On this topic see Hourani, *Islamic Rationalism*, 76–81, and more broadly Marmura, "A medieval Islamic argument for the intrinsic value of the moral act" and Vasalou, "Equal before the Law."

54. McNaughton, "Intuitionism," 271.
55. For this point, see, for example, Ibn Mattawayh, *Majmūʿ*, 1: 22, 3: 184–85; and see my discussion in chapter 2. My main remarks about this "list-like spirit" can be found at Vasalou, *Moral Agents and Their Deserts*, 20–23. For the ends of rational persuasion, one may consider, for example, ʿAbd al-Jabbār's remarks in *Taʿdīl*, 18.
56. This distinction can be found in several places, including Ibn Mattawayh, *Majmūʿ*, 1: 236, 253, 3: 447; ʿAbd al-Jabbār, *Taʿdīl*, 58 (contrasting what is bad *li-amr yakhtaṣṣu bihi* versus *li-taʿalluqihi bimā yuʾaddī ilayhi*); ʿAbd al-Jabbār, *al-Taklīf*, 530–31. This distinction comes into special use in the Baṣran account of the relationship between rational and revealed standards of action (cf. Ibn Mattawayh, *Majmūʿ*, 3: 426: *laysa wujūb hādhihi al-sharāʾiʿ li-amr yarjiʿu ilā aʿyānihā wa-ṣuwarihā wa-wujūh lā tanfakku ʿanhā kamā naqūluhu fiʾl-ʿaqliyyāt*). What may seem to muddle this distinction is that in several places the second, "consequentialist" category is specified using a deontological conception of consequences. See the discussion in chapter 2.
57. Though, as I have noted elsewhere, there is a question as to whether the Baṣrans conceptualize desert as a consideration that can *trump* considerations of utility (*Moral Agents and Their Deserts*, 92–93).
58. Mānkdīm Shashdīw, *Sharḥ al-Uṣūl al-khamsa*, 301. And see Vasalou, *Moral Agents and Their Deserts*, 44–45, for the presence of the notion of *ḥaqq* in Baṣran act-descriptions, and chapter 4 more broadly for the notions of *ḥaqq/istiḥqāq* in the Baṣran scheme.
59. ʿAbd al-Jabbār, *Taʿdīl*, 18. And see my *Moral Agents and Their Deserts*, 72–76, for more on the notion of moral reality (and the relationship between words and meanings) just invoked, and also on the implicit conditions regulating desert entailments.
60. ʿAbd al-Jabbār, *Taklīf*, 503, reading *lahā* for *lahu* in the last phrase.
61. Ibn Mattawayh, *Majmūʿ*, 3: 301; cf. ʿAbd al-Jabbār, *Taklīf*, 513. "At least in part due to its intelligible moral ground": see Vasalou, *Moral Agents and Their Deserts*, 71–72, for some context on this rider.
62. On this topic, see my "Equal before the Law."
63. Ibn Mattawayh, *Majmūʿ*, 3: 299. The Baṣrans in fact put the point equivocally when they speak of acting *liʾl-wujūb* or *li-wajh al-wujūb*. What does it mean to act for the sake of *wujūb* if not to act for the sake of the desert entailments that constitute this moral quality? To the extent of course that the concern to avoid punishment will be a prudential motivation, one's motivation will not constitute "impulsive desire" or *shahwa*.
64. This point comes across clearly in Ibn Mattawayh, *Majmūʿ*, 1:253; cf. ʿAbd al-Jabbār, *Taklīf*, 531.
65. I partly draw here on Ibn Mattawayh's remarks in *Majmūʿ*, 1: 244–45. The one obvious exception to this rule (God acts out of beneficence) is God's act of punishment.

66. For more on this composite nature of injustice, see Vasalou, *Moral Agents and Their Deserts*, 59 ff., 92–93; Hourani, *Islamic Rationalism*, 70–75.
67. Ibn Taymiyya, *Radd*, 422.
68. Correcting *yaḥṣulu*.
69. Ibn Taymiyya, "Risāla fi'l-Iḥtijāj bi'l-qadar," in *Majmū' Fatāwā*, 8: 308–9.
70. These terms are obviously not coextensive; the distinctions between them, and their significance for Ibn Taymiyya's account, will come into view in the next chapter.
71. Ibn Taymiyya, *Qā'ida fi'l-maḥabba*, 112.
72. Ibid., 65 (the term is again *maqṣūd*). The last statement is from Ibn Taymiyya, "Al-Ḥasana wa'l-sayyi'a," in *Majmū' Fatāwā*, 14: 298.
73. Ibn Taymiyya, *Radd*, 436: *al-'adl ... ḥasan, ay taḥṣulu bihi al-manfa'a wa'l-maṣlaḥa; wa'l-ẓulm ... qabīḥ, ay taḥṣulu bihi al-maḍarra wa'l-fasād.*
74. My use of the term "deontological" to speak of such acts here and elsewhere may seem awkward. As we often use this term, "deontological" denotes not types of acts but rather higher-level views about what makes acts ultimately right (and on a related, albeit not necessarily related, level, about the descriptions under which we should choose them). In this sense many acts, including the acts named in the main text, could be approached in both deontological and consequentialist terms. But of course the types of acts named above have often figured centrally within properly "deontological" theories. And in the context we are considering, Mu'tazilite thinkers did regard such acts in the more familiar, higher-level sense of "deontological." My usage of this term can be taken as a shorthand reference to this understanding and to the questions it opens out for Ibn Taymiyya.
75. Ibn Taymiyya, *Radd*, 423.
76. Ibid.
77. Love and hate, but also pride and humility, their reflexive counterparts. Hume, *A Treatise of Human Nature*, 469, hereafter cited as *T.*
78. The terms cited are from Mānkdīm's discussion in *Sharḥ al-Uṣūl*, 308; cf. Ibn Mattawayh, *Majmū'*, 1: 263. Note that this argument is as much about empirically known value judgments as about empirically known behavior: the accent often falls on what people *approve of* (Mānkdīm: *kull 'āqil ... yastaḥsinu irshād al-ḍāll*) as against how people *act.* At the same time, one should be careful not to overstate the high-mindedness of the Mu'tazilite vision of human motivation. It is indicative that several arguments that attempt to establish the reality of moral motivation betray a striking reluctance to focus on cases where moral action is chosen *despite* conflict with self-interest and frame the point in far more conservative ways. This is the case with the most famous "truth-versus-lying" proof, in which one chooses the good (to tell the truth) only *after* competing considerations of utility have been neutralized. See Vasalou, "Equal before the Law," and the passages referred to there, particularly 'Abd al-Jabbār, *Ta'dīl*, 210 ff.

79. Al-Ghazālī, *Mustaṣfā*, 1: 61, 58.
80. This phrase is from Ibn Taymiyya, *Radd*, 429.
81. Cf. the third-person perspective marked in the following passages. Ibn Taymiyya, *Radd*, 429: "this faculty inclines toward the person it knows to be just, truthful, and beneficent"; 430: "human beings as a whole are drawn toward those characterized by fine qualities." Of course, the third-person perspective is not necessarily the perspective of the beneficiary—it can be the perspective of a party who personally gains nothing from such acts; and Ibn Taymiyya makes clear that one may be drawn to virtuous individuals even if one receives no benefit (e.g., 429).
82. Ibn Taymiyya, "Al-Tuḥfa al-ʿirāqiyya fiʾl-aʿmāl al-qalbiyya," in *Majmūʿ Fatāwā*, 10: 84.
83. Ibn Mattawayh, *Majmūʿ*, 3: 303. The need for desire (*shahwa*) as a source of hardship recurs in ʿAbd al-Jabbār's discussion of the conditions for reward in *Taklīf*, 511–19. See also briefly Vasalou, *Moral Agents and Their Deserts*, 79–80, and the references there. The connection between the notions of *kulfa* and *taklīf* was by no means a Muʿtazilite preserve and is found widely among other authors. See, for example, al-Baghdādī, *Kitāb Uṣūl al-dīn*, 207, using a turn of phrase very similar to the one just heard from Ibn Mattawayh.
84. Ibn Mattawayh, *Majmūʿ*, 3: 141.
85. ʿAbd al-Jabbār, *al-Aṣlaḥ/Istiḥqāq al-dhamm/al-Tawba*, 334; al-Qarāfī, *Kitāb al-Furūq*, 1: 312.
86. Cf. Ibn Mattawayh, *Majmūʿ*, 3: 411: "When we refer to something as a claim against someone [*ḥaqq ʿalayhi*], this means it is such that its exaction involves harm for him."
87. In Ashʿarite writings the discomfort we feel due to our inescapable sympathetic entry into others' suffering is often conscripted to support a self-interested account of human motivation. Al-Ghazālī's discussion in the *Mustaṣfā* is indicative in stressing the self-referential character of the sympathetic imagination, reducing the response of sympathy (*riqqa*) to a self-interested concern for one's own welfare (1: 59–60). This understanding is echoed by several other writers, such as Ibn Fūrak, *Mujarrad Maqālāt al-shaykh Abiʾl-Ḥasan al-Ashʿarī*, 142. Cf. Ibn Taymiyya's (apostrophized) remarks in "Aqwam mā qīla," in *Majmūʿ Fatāwā*, 8: 89–90.
88. Aristotle, *Nicomachean Ethics*, 1099a10–15.
89. Frede, "Pleasure and pain in Aristotle's ethics," 257, emphasis added. For al-Ghazālī's influential reworking of the virtues, see Sherif, *Ghazali's Theory of Virtue*. The end of habituation, al-Ghazālī writes, is that acts should become pleasurable (*ghāyatuhu an yaṣīra al-fiʿl al-ṣādir minhu ladhīdhan*): *Iḥyāʾ ʿulūm al-dīn*, 3: 50. There is a real question to be asked, though, as to whether the Islamic theological reworking of the virtues fully sustains the Aristotelian conception of pleasure, in light of the influence of a Platonic view of the soul (with its agonistic conception of the inner life), and of an instrumental view of the relation between action and pleasure and an emphasis on the arduousness of the ethical life that form pervasive elements of the Islamic intellectual tradition.

90. Ibn Taymiyya, "Masʾala fīmā idhā kāna fiʾl-ʿabd maḥabba limā huwa khayr wa-ḥaqq wa-maḥmūd fī nafsihi," 445. I am very grateful to Ahmed El Shamsy for calling my attention to this epistle. Ibn Taymiyya's remarks in the same vicinity seem to qualify his description of the dominance of such motivation: for example, "God *might* create" in people a love of truthfulness, justice, and so on (445).
91. See, for example, ʿAbd al-Jabbār's engagement of the aesthetic comparison in *Taʿdīl*, 19–20.
92. Ibn Taymiyya, "Masʾala fīmā idhā kāna fiʾl-ʿabd maḥabba," 446.
93. Ibn Taymiyya, *Qāʿida fiʾl-maḥabba*, 64. On the next page he relabels these, using a more distinctive philosophical terminology, as *ladhdhāt ḥissiyya, wahmiyya, ʿaqliyya*.
94. The phrase is from ibid., 115. Ibn Taymiyya's emphasis on sensory or physical goods will come into view in chapter 2 when we discuss the notion of *fiṭra*, but it surfaces clearly later in the epistle we have been considering: Ibn Taymiyya, "Masʾala fīmā idhā kāna fiʾl-ʿabd maḥabba," 447, last paragraph. As we will see in the next chapter, he also links ethical judgments to reason, which assesses the long-term consequences of immediate pleasures. A link with *wahm* also floats around in Ibn Taymiyya, *Radd* (e.g., 429), but there is a question to be asked as to whether this is a positive or a dialectical use of Avicenna's epistemological terms.
95. Ibn Taymiyya, "Qāʿida fiʾl-muʿjizāt waʾl-karāmāt," in *Majmūʿ Fatāwā*, 11: 358. The point often emerges in Ibn Taymiyya's criticism of the Muʿtazilite conception of disinterested action, which takes shape as a double claim that people neither *in fact* act disinterestedly nor *ought* to do so.
96. A more properly Aristotelian answer, of course, would have to make reference to the character of the agent, but I hope the purposes of the discussion are served by this rough and heuristic comparison.
97. Respectively, Ibn Taymiyya, *Radd*, 431; Ibn Taymiyya, *Qāʿida fiʾl-maḥabba*, 154.
98. The terms are from Ibn Taymiyya, *Qāʿida fiʾl-maḥabba*, 64.
99. Ibn Taymiyya, "Ḥaqīqat kasb al-ʿabd mā hiya," in *Majmūʿ Fatāwā*, 8: 396–98.
100. Ibn Taymiyya, *Qāʿida fiʾl-maḥabba*, 129. Both sets of consequences interpret Ibn Taymiyya's remark apropos evil consequences (*qubḥ ʿāqibatihi*) in *Radd*, 431.
101. See, for instance, Ibn Taymiyya, "Suʾila ʿan rajul ukhidha māluhu ẓulman bi-ghayr ḥaqq," in *Majmūʿ Fatāwā*, 30: 364–65.
102. Ibn Taymiyya, *Radd*, 423.
103. Ibn Taymiyya, "Al-Ḥisba," in *Majmūʿ Fatāwā*, 28: 100.
104. Reading *yafʿalūna* instead of *yanfūna*.
105. Ibn Taymiyya, *Majmūʿ Fatāwā*, 20: 67. Matters are rather more complex than my remarks suggest, given that Ibn Taymiyya does not employ the notion of agreement or convention in this context to isolate those norms that originate exclusively in the human community, but uses it as an overarching notion that includes human convention as one of its instances and *prophetic* agreement as another. Despite its recurrence, Ibn Taymiyya's deployment of the notion of a social convention strikes me as nebulous.

106. Human beings thus "must make obligatory upon themselves the things that they need, and prohibit to themselves the things that harm them . . . and this can only take place through their joint agreement, which is for them to mutually pledge and contract themselves [*al-taʿāhud wa ʾl-taʿāqud*]" (Ibn Taymiyya, *Qāʿida fī ʾl-maḥabba*, 47–48). Ibn Taymiyya refers to this collaborative project as the "common religion" (*dīn mushtarak*) of human beings. Just how seriously he intends this as a sociological genealogy of religion is a prickly question that may be sidestepped here.

107. Ibid., 103; cf. 47–48.

108. A similar analysis could be given for other instances in which Ibn Taymiyya connects human nature to a love of justice, as in the interestingly composite remark in *Bayān talbīs al-jahmiyya fī taʾsīs bidaʿihim al-kalāmiyya*, 2: 333, that one naturally desires justice and benefit (*bi-fiṭratihi yurīdu al-ʿadl wa ʾl-maṣlaḥa*). In the very next breath he refers us to "the natural association that [people] cannot live without [*al-ijtimāʿ al-fiṭrī al-ṭabīʿī alladhī lā yaʿīshūna bi-dūnihi*]," suggesting that it is once again the first-person plural, communal perspective on justice that underpins his thinking.

109. Among Ibn Taymiyya's immediate interlocutors, this is an assumption that underpins the thinking of al-Rāzī (Ibn Taymiyya's multiple debts to whom are explored in chapter 3), at least in his earlier work, though he would later renege on it when succumbing to pessimism on several fronts. See Shihadeh's discussion in *Teleological Ethics of Fakhr al-Dīn al-Rāzī*, 80–83, 170–81.

110. The characterization is Ibn Mattawayh's (*Majmūʿ*, 1: 242).

111. The phrase is from Ibn Taymiyya, "Qāʿida fī anna jins fiʿl al-maʾmūr bihi aʿẓam min jins tark al-manhiyy ʿanhu," in *Majmūʿ Fatāwā*, 20: 121. For Sidgwick's distinction, see *The Methods of Ethics*, 105.

112. Ibn Taymiyya, "Masʾalat taḥsīn al-ʿaql wa-taqbīḥuhu," in *Majmūʿ Fatāwā*, 8: 435–36.

113. Ibn Taymiyya does occasionally use the term *wajh*, but not in a robust sense: for example, "Masʾala fīmā idhā kāna fiʾl-ʿabd maḥabba," 447 (*wajh al-ḥusn*), "Tafsīr sūrat al-Fātiḥa," in *Majmūʿ Fatāwā*, 14: 21 (*wajh ḥusnihi wa-khayrihi*). And see chapter 4 for what he *does* say elsewhere about desert. The language of *ḥuqūq* of course makes numerous appearances in Ibn Taymiyya's practical legal writings.

114. See, for example, Ibn Taymiyya, "Qāʿida fiʾl-muʿjizāt waʾl-karāmāt," in *Majmūʿ Fatāwā*, 11: 354. See also the discussion of this point in chapter 3.

115. Ibn Taymiyya, "Qāʿida nāfiʿa fī wujūb al-iʿtiṣām biʾl-risāla," in *Majmūʿ Fatāwā*, 19: 95; Ibn Taymiyya, "Faṣl jāmiʿ fī taʿāruḍ al-ḥasanāt aw-al-sayyiʾāt," in *Majmūʿ Fatāwā*, 20: 48.

116. The statements are, respectively, from Ibn Taymiyya, "Ḥadīth innī ḥarramtu al-ẓulm ʿalā nafsī," in *Majmūʿ Fatāwā*, 18: 157 (cf. *al-Siyāsa al-sharʿiyya fī iṣlāḥ al-rāʿī wa ʾl-raʿiyya*, 134); and Ibn Taymiyya, "Al-ʿAqīda al-Tadmuriyya," in *Majmūʿ Fatāwā*, 3: 114. Cf. Anjum's emphasis on the centrality of justice in Ibn Taymiyya's thought in *Politics, Law, and Community in Islamic Thought*, 241–44.

117. The former kind of demand is highlighted, for example, in Ibn Taymiyya, *al-Siyāsa al-shar'iyya*, 134–35, discussing rulings that include the prohibition of usury and gambling. Yet it is the latter that is highlighted, with reference to much the same kinds of cases, in Ibn Taymiyya, *al-Qawā'id al-nūrāniyya al-fiqhiyya*, 171, 169, referring to the corruption or harm (*fasād/mafsada*) resulting from them. Cf. the remarks in Ibn Taymiyya, "Al-Qiyās fi'l-shar' al-Islāmī," in *Majmū' Fatāwā*, 20: 538–39. In raising the question which of these demands is basic, it is worth noting that this is once more a question Ibn Taymiyya himself does not wedge open; he often treats the relevant notions as if there is no distinction to be marked between them. Indeed in the *Qā'ida fi'l-maḥabba* (36–37), Ibn Taymiyya explicitly states that terms such as *nāfi'*, *ṣāliḥ*, *'adl*, and so on, signify the same thing (*asmā' mutakāfi'a musammāhā wāḥid bi'l-dhāt*).
118. Ibn Taymiyya, "Qā'ida fīmā yajibu min al-mu'āwaḍāt wa-naḥwa dhālika," in *Majmū' Fatāwā*, 29: 188. Cf. *Majmū' Fatāwā*, 28: 183–84; "Ḥadīth innī ḥarramtu al-ẓulm 'alā nafsī," in *Majmū' Fatāwā*, 18: 165 (tellingly lining up *ẓulm* next to the more teleological notion *fasād*).
119. See indicatively Ibn Taymiyya, "Al-Qiyās fi'l-shar' al-Islāmī," in *Majmū' Fatāwā*, 20: 504–5: sound analogy consists in "uniting similar things and distinguishing between dissimilar things . . . and it forms part of the justice [*'adl*] that God brought through His messengers." Cf. Ibn Taymiyya, *Qā'ida fi'l-maḥabba*, 36.
120. Ibn Taymiyya, *al-Siyāsa al-shar'iyya*, 134.
121. Ibn Taymiyya, "Qā'ida fīmā yajibu min al-mu'āwaḍāt wa-naḥwa dhālika," in *Majmū' Fatāwā*, 29: 189–90.
122. Ibn Taymiyya, *Qā'ida fi'l-maḥabba*, 103: justice in partnerships and commutative transactions (*al-mushārakāt wa'l-mu'āwaḍāt*) is necessary for social cooperation. Cf. 56 (the context is apostrophized, but this statement seems to be in Ibn Taymiyya's own voice): "justice, truthfulness, and the keeping of oaths" are "among the things without which the welfare of mundane life cannot be achieved."
123. Ibn Taymiyya, "Tafsīr sūrat al-Baqara," in *Majmū' Fatāwā*, 14: 80.
124. Ibid., 79.
125. Though, as we will see in chapter 5, Ibn Taymiyya himself is critical of this restrictive way of regimenting the aims of the Law.
126. Reinhart, *Before Revelation*, 161. Ibn Taymiyya refers to Abu'l-Ḥusayn al-Baṣrī in various locations, notably in the *Dar' ta'āruḍ*, e.g., 8: 17 ff., 8: 295–96, 9: 132 ff. His greater familiarity with al-Baṣrī's work probably reflects the latter's influence among some of the thinkers Ibn Taymiyya engages more directly, such as al-Rāzī. This picture of Ibn Taymiyya's limited engagement of Mu'tazilite texts is supported by the helpful list of his bibliographical references compiled by al-Shāmī in "Ibn Taymiyya." One of the few references to notable Mu'tazilite texts appearing in this list is to 'Abd al-Jabbār's works on prophethood (239).

127. The emphasis should be on "relative" here. See, for example, al-Rāzī, *al-Maṭālib al-ʿāliya min al-ʿilm al-ilāhī*, 3: 66, where al-Rāzī notes that in the Muʿtazilite view, "the question whether something is good or bad is distinct from the question whether it promotes welfare or undermines it [*iʿtibār al-ḥusn wa 'l-qubḥ mughāyir li-iʿtibār kawnihi maṣlaḥa wa-mafsada*]"—though this statement marks the distinction by overshooting the mark, given what was said earlier concerning the importance of considerations of utility in the (Baṣran) Muʿtazilite scheme. The notion of *wujūh* appears in several places in his discussion, e.g., 3: 338, 3: 285, in a passage very similar to one from al-Rāzī's *al-Arbaʿīn fī uṣūl al-dīn* cited by Ibn Taymiyya himself in his *Sharḥ al-Iṣbahāniyya*, 444. Cf. al-Anṣārī, *Ghunya*, 2: 1009 ff. There are places where Ibn Taymiyya gestures toward the distinction carried by al-Rāzī's first quote, for example, Ibn Taymiyya, "Al-ʿAqīda al-Tadmuriyya," in *Majmūʿ Fatāwā*, 3: 115; this distinction is also to an extent implicit in a related distinction drawn on the level of motivation, which Ibn Taymiyya discusses in several places, between interested and disinterested actions (between actions that "give something back to the agent" [*yaʿūdu ilayhi*] and actions that do not: see, for example, Ibn Taymiyya, "Aqwam mā qīla," in *Majmūʿ Fatāwā*, 8: 89–90). But such gestures do not seem to build up to a thick acknowledgment of the relevant distinctions on the level of ethical ontology.
128. Hobbes, *Leviathan*, 39.
129. Al-Rāzī, *Maṭālib*, 3: 66. "Normative" is a term Shihadeh employs in this context to speak of a stance he identifies already with al-Ghazālī (*Teleological Ethics of Fakhr al-Dīn al-Rāzī*, 55). There will be more to say about this in chapter 3, where the Ashʿarite position will come more fully into view.

CHAPTER 2

1. Ibn Taymiyya, *Radd*, 423.
2. Though, as Annas points out, Aristotle himself does not flag the notion of nature in that discussion and does not clearly present the argument as an appeal to nature; it is in his *Politics* that the notion of nature is put to work in a stronger ethical sense (*The Morality of Happiness*, chapter 2, section 4).
3. *De republica*, III, 33, as translated in Porter, *Nature as Reason*, 2.
4. Porter, *Nature as Reason*, 1; though part of Porter's aim in this work is to interrogate certain aspects of the understanding reflected in this formulation.
5. Many of these new meanings can be considered by looking up the entry on "ethical naturalism" in almost any recent handbook for ethical theory. Annas has insightful remarks about the connection between contemporary invocations of nature and the one at work in ancient ethics (*Morality of Happiness*, chapter 2, section 3).
6. Michot, "La pandémie avicennienne au VIe/XIIe siècle."

7. Avicenna, *al-Najā min al-gharq fī baḥr al-ḍalālāt*, 126, read in conjunction with *al-Ishārāt wa 'l-tanbīhāt, ma 'a sharḥ Naṣīr al-Dīn al-Ṭūsī*, 1: 391.
8. Avicenna, *Ishārāt*, 1: 399.
9. Ibid., 1: 400. My translation is very loosely inspired by Inati's: *Remarks and Admonitions*, 122.
10. Avicenna, *Najā*, 117, correcting *yūjibu* to *tūjibu*. Black translates this passage slightly differently, notably placing a weaker emphasis on the element of activity involved: "Then something occurs to his mind about which he is in doubt" ("Estimation (*wahm*) in Avicenna," 233). But this active note is brought out distinctly by Avicenna at various places, including his version of the thought experiment in the *Kitāb al-Shifā ': al-Manṭiq: al-Burhān*, 65–66: *idhā fa 'ala dhālika kullahu wa-rāma an yushakkika fīhi nafsahu amkanahu al-shakk*.
11. Avicenna, *Najā*, 119: *innahā ghayr fiṭriyya walakinnahā mutaqarrira 'inda al-anfus li-anna al- 'āda tastamirru* [correcting *yastamirru*] *'alayhā mundhu al-ṣibā wa-fī 'l-muwāḍa 'āt al-ittifāqiyya*. Cf. the reference to "conventional views" (*ārā '* ... *iṣṭilāḥiyya*) in Avicenna's remarks about practical reason in *Kitāb al-Shifā ': al-Ṭabī 'iyyāt: al-Nafs*, 37.
12. For more on the argument, see Black, "Avicenna on self-awareness and knowing that one knows," and references there. For a reading of its connection to the thought experiment concerning widely accepted premises, see Black, "Estimation (*wahm*) in Avicenna," esp. 236–39.
13. Singer, "Sidgwick and Reflective Equilibrium," 516.
14. The notion of *fiṭra* itself makes several appearances in this work; for more on this, see Gauthier's (rather polemical) remarks in his introduction to Ibn Ṭufayl, *Hayy ben Yaqdhân*, esp. xii–xvii.
15. Avicenna, *Burhān*, 65. Al-Rāzī's formulation can be found in Ibn Taymiyya, *Radd*, 397–99, and also in al-Rāzī, *Sharḥ al-Ishārāt wa 'l-tanbīhāt*, 1: 268–69.
16. Avicenna, *Nafs*, 183; the relevant discussion begins on 181.
17. Ibid., 183.
18. The quote is from al-Tawḥīdī and Miskawayh, *al-Hawāmil wa 'l-shawāmil*, 317, read against the preceding discussion. Miskawayh's conclusion, as I take it, is that this variability counts against considering such responses to constitute judgments of reason. Avicenna's phrasing, when he refers to the slaughter of animals and the response of *riqqa* (*Ishārāt*, 1: 400), leaves it more ambiguous whether he is calling attention to the variability of this particular response (*ittibā 'an limā fī 'l-gharīza min al-riqqa li-man takūnu gharīzatuhu kadhālika, wa-hum akthar al-nās*). If the proposal outlined later in the main text is correct, the fact that such emotions reflect our animal rather than our rational nature may also account for their exclusion. The case of animal slaughter was the subject of a familiar challenge to the revealed Law and indeed to the value of prophecy as such on the part of the "Barāhima." See indicatively al-Anṣārī, *Ghunya*, 2: 1003, and for some extra context, see Crone, "Barāhima." Miskawayh's

argument is interestingly reprised by other participants in the *kalām* debate about ethics: see, for example, Ibn ʿAqīl, *Wāḍiḥ*, 1: 112.

19. Al-Rāzī makes the connection to the social whole plain when he refers to *al-niẓām al-kullī wa'l-maṣlaḥa al-ʿāmma*. Ibn Taymiyya, *Radd*, 398; al-Rāzī, *Sharḥ al-Ishārāt*, 1: 268.
20. Many of these points can be found gathered in Avicenna's discussion of estimative propositions in *Najā*, 115–18.
21. Ibid., 117.
22. Black, "Estimation (*wahm*) in Avicenna," 254n77.
23. Avicenna, *Najā*, 117 (cf. his reference to *fiṭra fāsida* in connection with the estimation on 118). It is tempting to speak of two conflicting uses of nature here, but we should keep in mind Gutas's broad point that *fiṭra* refers us to nothing thicker than the "natural operation of the mind," the "natural mode of operation of each faculty" ("The empiricism of Avicenna," 408, 409). The positive aspect of *fiṭra* is also highlighted in the connection between *fiṭra* and the notion of intuition (*ḥads*) remarked by Gutas in *Avicenna and the Aristotelian Tradition*; see his discussion of intuition 159–76. For a more focused discussion of Avicenna's notion of *fiṭra*, see Griffel, "Al-Ghazālī's use of 'original human disposition' (*fiṭra*) and its background in the teachings of al-Fārābī and Avicenna," though Griffel's claim that Avicenna "has a much more precise notion of *fiṭra* [than Fārābī] that he fully integrates in his epistemological theories" (11) does not entirely convince me. I owe many moments in my understanding of this complex paper trail to extensive exchanges with Frank Griffel, who gave me generously of his time and his superior knowledge of the sources.
24. Avicenna, *Nafs*, 37.
25. Ibid., 163. These remarks mainly draw on 147–48, 162–64, and Avicenna, *Najā*, 347. Helpful accounts of Avicenna's view of estimation that offer a more holistic view of its operations include Black, "Estimation (*wahm*) in Avicenna"; Hasse, *Avicenna's* De Anima *in the Latin West*, 127–41. Another feature of Avicenna's notion of the estimation that generates tensions in this context is the fact that in certain passages he connects the estimation to the emotions (e.g., *Nafs*, 162, 166). This will seem puzzling in part given that Avicenna elsewhere associates the emotions with the appetitive side of our animal nature (the emotions of shame and embarrassment, notably, are referred to as *al-quwwa al-ḥayawāniyya al-nuzūʿiyya* in *Najā*, 330–31). More relevant for us, it makes the inclusion of the estimation in the thought experiment doubly puzzling given Avicenna's exclusion of emotional response from this experiment. See Hasse, *Avicenna's* De Anima *in the Latin West*, 133–34, 139–40, for some pertinent remarks on the connection between the emotions and the estimation. I do not find Hasse's solution wholly satisfying, but this probably reflects the "sketchy" character of Avicenna's discussion and the problems created by his excessive ambition in

trying "to put too much into the scheme he developed," as pointed out by Hasse himself (136, 140).

26. Avicenna's interest in drawing that distinction is flagged at several moments in the passage from the *Ishārāt* cited in part earlier. Ibn Taymiyya himself also clearly takes this to be central to Avicenna's aims, as attested by the energy he devotes to the deconstruction of the class of primary propositions; see Ibn Taymiyya, *Radd*, 399 ff.
27. Avicenna, *Ishārāt*, 1: 401. Cf. Marmura, "Ghazālī on ethical premises," 263; Black, "Estimation (*wahm*) in Avicenna," 241.
28. Avicenna, *Nafs*, 37: "*if* [these propositions] are demonstrated, they also become part of the premises of reason"—a big *if*.
29. Avicenna, *Ishārāt*, 1: 392. Cf. Avicenna, *Najā*, 121: *muqaddimāt taḥduthu fi ʾl-insān min jihat quwwatihi al-ʿaqliyya*.
30. Avicenna, *Burhān*, 65–56. It is also noteworthy that when Avicenna elsewhere refers to widely accepted propositions, he refers to their difference from rational propositions (*al-muqaddimāt al-ʿaqliyya al-maḥḍa, al-awwaliyyāt al-ʿaqliyya al-maḥḍa*) as having been established "in the books of logic"; see, for example, Avicenna, *Nafs*, 37; Avicenna, *Najā*, 331.
31. The inclusion of sense perception will not seem hard to account for even if we take Avicenna's interest to lie in isolating primary intelligibles. Sense perception, as various commentators have emphasized, is a precondition for the formation of these intelligibles; in this sense they are not *a priori* or *innate*. See, for example, Gutas, "The empiricism of Avicenna," 406–7; cf. Black, "Certitude, justification, and the principles of knowledge in Avicenna's epistemology," 125–26. It is doubtful to me whether a similar story could be constructed for the estimation. Avicenna's explicit reference in the *Ishārāt* passage to sense perception and estimation as epistemic arbiters as against mere preconditions (*lam yaqḍi bihā al-insān tāʿatan li-ʿaqlihi aw-wahmihi aw-ḥissihi*) certainly creates tension for such interpretations.
32. Sebti, "Avicenna's 'flying man' argument as a proof of the immateriality of the soul."
33. Ibn Taymiyya, *Radd*, 428. I have in mind the skepticism al-Rāzī himself would express about the ability of this thought experiment to achieve the epistemological position it claims for itself. Confronting a Muʿtazilite response to this experiment ("I imagine myself free from all these conditions—and still I affirm this moral judgment"), al-Rāzī suggests that to *think* you have stepped outside the human condition and divested yourself from the social contingencies that shaped you is not the same as having succeeded. We are back to the willful disputation of necessary knowledge on which debates about ethics often foundered. See the instructive remarks in *al-Maḥṣul fī ʿilm uṣūl al-fiqh*, 1: 39; compare al-Ghazālī's confidence in proposing this experiment in *Mustaṣfā*, 1: 49.

34. For these arguments, see, respectively, Ibn Taymiyya, *Radd*, 428–29, 432, 424. Cf. Ibn Taymiyya's evocation of the ethical dimensions of the estimation in *Darʾ taʿāruḍ*, 6: 52–55, raising a question about the distinction between *wahm* and *ʿaql*.
35. Ibn Taymiyya, *Radd*, 423–24.
36. Ibid., 429.
37. Ibid., 430.
38. Ibn Taymiyya, "Sharḥ kalimāt min 'Futūḥ al-ghayb,'" in *Jāmiʿ al-rasāʾil*, 2: 85.
39. Given this context, as just mentioned, it may not seem surprising that it is in the *Radd* that the notion of *fiṭra* figures most prominently within Ibn Taymiyya's ethical remarks. It also makes important appearances in other texts, particularly the *Darʾ taʿāruḍ al-ʿaql waʾl-naql*, written in the same period. Yet there is certainly a question to be asked as to why the use of this notion is not sustained with unflagging consistency across Ibn Taymiyya's output. It is a question one asks, for example, faced with the *Qāʿida fiʾl-maḥabba*, whose subject matter would have naturally attracted the language of *fiṭra* in the *Radd* and elsewhere, yet in which this language remains curiously absent. One might ask similar questions apropos Ibn Taymiyya's remarks about ethics in works such as *al-ʿAqīda al-Tadmuriyya, Kitāb al-Nubuwwāt*, or *Sharḥ al-Iṣbahāniyya*, to mention but a few examples. A satisfying explanation of this fluctuating presence would unfortunately require a firmer chronology of Ibn Taymiyya's works than we possess.
40. This is linked to the controversial theological question regarding God's spatial location, particularly the possibility of describing God as being "above" the world, which philosophically minded thinkers dismissed as a faulty product of the estimation. Affirming this characterization of God, Ibn Taymiyya rejects the latter diagnosis. Some of his most direct discussions of this point can be found in the sixth volume of *Darʾ taʿāruḍ*. See also Marcotte, "Ibn Taymiyya et sa critique des produits de la faculté d'estimation (*Wahmiyyāt*) dans le *Darʾ Taʿāruḍ al-ʿaql waʾl-naql*."
41. Ibn Taymiyya does not make his position crystal clear. In one of his most direct remarks (*Radd*, 428), in fact, he connects Avicenna's psychological sentiments to the notion of "agreeability," which is tied more immediately to our response to benefit. We also heard Ibn Taymiyya dialectically suggest a link between our emotional responses and the "inner senses" (432).
42. Similarly, to the extent that the pleasure people take in morally good actions, as I suggested in chapter 1, ultimately comes down to the awareness of their consequences—such as the social consequences of people's hatred and the religious threat of punishment (Ibn Taymiyya, *Radd*, 431)—this pleasure clearly rests on prior processes of social and religious education.
43. Ibid., 423–24.
44. ʿAbd al-Jabbār, *Taʿdīl*, 18.

45. Ibn Taymiyya, *Radd*, 422, 429.
46. Ibid., 423–24.
47. Avicenna, *Burhān*, 95, drawing on Janssens's translation in "'Experience' (*tajriba*) in classical Arabic philosophy (al-Fārābī–Avicenna)," 55.
48. Or more specifically, Gutas suggests, with the practice of medicine ("Medical theory and scientific method in the age of Avicenna," 151–52). For more on Avicenna's notion of *tajriba* and its relation to his epistemological scheme (including the notion of induction or *istiqrā*ʾ), see Janssens, "'Experience' (*tajriba*) in classical Arabic philosophy (al-Fārābī–Avicenna)"; McGinnis, "Scientific methodologies in medieval Islam."
49. For these points, see in order Ibn Taymiyya, *Radd*, 95, 386, 92 (cf. 386: *hādhā al-jins taḥṣulu bihi al-ladhdha/al-alam*), 386. Many of Ibn Taymiyya's remarks on *mujarrabāt/tajribiyyāt* can be found in concentration in *Radd*, 92–95, 386–88. For further commentary on Ibn Taymiyya's treatment of this subject and the related subject of natural causation, see Kügelgen, "The poison of philosophy," 306–12.
50. Though whether they *necessarily* bear such a connection is an issue debated in the *Radd*, notably in discussing the relationship between the propositions designated as *ḥadsiyyāt* and empirical judgments. See, for example, *Radd*, 93–94.
51. Ibn Taymiyya, "Risāla fiʾl-Iḥtijāj biʾl-qadar," in *Majmūʿ Fatāwā*, 8: 308–9. Cf. the causal emphasis in Ibn Taymiyya's specification of what is "agreeable" (*mulāʾim*) and "disagreeable" (*munāfir*) in "Al-ʿAqīda al-Tadmuriyya," in *Majmūʿ Fatāwā*, 3: 114–15: "this is for an act to be the cause [*sabab*] of what the agent loves and takes pleasure in, and what he hates and suffers harm from."
52. See especially Ibn Taymiyya's suggestive remarks in "Ḥaqīqat kasb al-ʿabd mā hiya," in *Majmūʿ Fatāwā*, 8: 396–98; see also the discussion in chapter 4.
53. For example, the grammar of the sentence "why then are judgments of experience . . . while these ones . . ." seems to imply a contrast between the two that would count against taking the latter to constitute a subset of the former.
54. Note here Ibn Taymiyya's formulation at *Radd*, 423—"Why then should *those* propositions belong to the certainties known by the senses and by reason, such as by experience [*al-ʿaql kaʾl-tajriba*] . . .?"—which subsumes *tajriba* under reason.
55. Ibn Taymiyya refers the pleasure we derive from esteem to the "internal sense" (*ḥiss bāṭin*) in crafting his argument against Avicenna at *Radd*, 432. Once again, of course, it is not easy to disentangle Ibn Taymiyya's dialectical arguments from his positive views; plus, in the same vicinity he refers this pleasure to the estimation (*wahm*), a classification that is in greater accord with the threefold scheme of pleasures outlined in *Qāʿida fiʾl-maḥabba*, 64–65. However we classify this type of pleasure, it seems important to make room for it.
56. See, for example, Ibn Taymiyya, *Darʾ taʿāruḍ*, 8: 450 (where the desire for knowledge is also mentioned), 9: 374–75. For this specification of our *fiṭra*, cf.

in a different context Ibn Taymiyya, *Bayān talbīs*, 2: 335. Outside the ethical context, to the extent that such distinctions can be drawn at all sharply, *fiṭra* is defined by a desire or love for God; see the next section.

57. See the discussion in the next sections of this chapter for further documentation of this usage.
58. Ibn Taymiyya, *Darʾ taʿāruḍ*, 9: 22.
59. Ibn Taymiyya, *Sharḥ al-Iṣbahāniyya*, 700. This is a point that, raised in more narrowly religious terms (as a question about the relation between religious uprightness and worldly happiness: e.g., Ibn Taymiyya, *Qāʿida fi ʾl-maḥabba*, 113 ff.), takes its place within Ibn Taymiyya's broader polemical engagement with Ashʿarite theology, particularly the Ashʿarite interrogation of the link between God's Law and human welfare.
60. Ibn Taymiyya, *Radd*, 92, 386.
61. Ibid., 386.
62. Schopenhauer, *The World as Will and Representation*, 1: 95 ff.
63. An example is Ibn Taymiyya's reference to the connection between lethal poisons and illness or death (*Radd*, 386), a longer causal chain fully at home in the medical context with which experiential judgments are ranged.
64. For more on this tradition, helpful starting points are Ess, *Zwischen Hadith und Theologie*, 101–14, and for its later development, Adang, "Islam as the inborn religion of mankind," and references there. A more concentrated treatment of the notion of *fiṭra*, though not a uniformly methodical one, is provided by Gobillot in *La conception originelle*.
65. See Watt, "Ḥanīf."
66. For more on these legal dimensions, see Gobillot, *La conception originelle*, 18–31; Adang, "Islam as the inborn religion of mankind," 403–8. See also Macdonald, "Fiṭra." These dimensions surface in many places of Ibn Taymiyya's engagement with this tradition in volume 8 of *Darʾ taʿāruḍ*. It was in fact A. J. Wensick's view that this hadith found its origins in questions concerning conduct in war; for this view and Ess's alternative proposal, which stresses this tradition's exegetical nature, see Ess, *Zwischen Hadith und Theologie*, 101–3.
67. For more on the Muʿtazilite position, see Gobillot, *La conception originelle*, 32–45, *passim*. I speak more cautiously of a "positively qualified religious state" because it does not appear to me from Gobillot's discussion or from some of the texts she cites that the Muʿtazilite interpretation of this notion was a wholly unified one and that this state was predominantly characterized by the Muʿtazilites as "Islam," even though this has often been taken to represent the Muʿtazilite position (e.g., Macdonald, "Fiṭra," 932).
68. Gobillot, *La conception originelle*, 45. In taking Ibn Taymiyya to have combined an affirmation of our natural knowledge of God and a deterministic position, my view departs from the one defended by Holtzman in "Human choice, divine guidance and the *fiṭra* tradition." Holtzman ascribes to Ibn Taymiyya

the view that "faith and unbelief are not predetermined but are rather a matter for human choice" (175), suggesting that the *fiṭra* tradition "is used by Ibn Taymiyya to assert the existence of human free will when it comes to the matter of belief and unbelief" (165). There is much evidence in volume 8 of the *Darʾ taʿāruḍ* that contradicts this view, most succinctly 8: 361–62: *al-mawlūd yūladu ʿala ʾl-fiṭra salīman thumma yufsiduhu abawāhu wa-dhālika ayḍan bi-qaḍāʾ Allāh wa-qadarihi*; cf. 8: 389, 410; and see generally 359 ff. for a discussion of Ibn Ḥanbal's two interpretations and Ibn Taymiyya's commentary. For further discussion of Ibn Taymiyya's view of *fiṭra*, see Gobillot's brief remarks in *La conception originelle*, 64–65, as well as the introductory remarks to her translation of Ibn Taymiyya's *Risālat al-kalām ʿala-l-fiṭra* in "L'épître du discours sur la *fiṭra* (*Risāla fī-l-kalam ʿalā-l-fiṭra*) de Taqī-l-Din Aḥmad Ibn Taymīya (661/1262–728/1328)"; Hoover, *Ibn Taymiyya's Theodicy of Perpetual Optimism*, 39–44; Hallaq, "Ibn Taymiyya on the existence of God," focusing on the role of *fiṭra* in religious epistemology (a discussion limited by its textual bases, as noted by Hoover); and in the context of Ibn Taymiyya's critique of logic, Kügelgen's remarks in "Ibn Taymīyas Kritik an der aristotelischen Logik und sein Gegenentwurf," esp. 194–99. See also Anjum, *Politics, Law, and Community in Islamic Thought*, chapters 5 and 6, *passim*; Özervarli, "Divine wisdom, human agency and the *fiṭra* in Ibn Taymiyya's thought."

69. Ibn Taymiyya, *Darʾ taʿāruḍ*, 8: 383.
70. Ibid.
71. Besides the argument outlined next in the main text, other passages that mark the composite scope of *fiṭra* include ibid., 8: 463: *al-muqtaḍī fīhā [=al-fiṭra] li ʾl-ʿilm wa ʾl-irāda al-nāfiʿa qāʾim*; 7: 425: *al-nufūs fīhā irādāt fiṭriyya wa-ʿulūm fiṭriyya*.
72. See ibid., 8: 456–60 for this argument; the rational arguments for *fiṭra* extend from 8: 456 ff.
73. For more on the Muʿtazilite argument, see Vasalou, "Equal before the Law"; Marmura, "A medieval Islamic argument." Ibn Taymiyya, on the one hand, has recrafted the argument in a way that has shorn it of its distinctive edge. For the Muʿtazilites had framed this as a choice between telling the truth and lying where self-interest was neutralized, and it was then an interesting question what human beings would do faced with a choice in which only moral value remains to distinguish two actions. Ibn Taymiyya, by contrast, stacks *both* moral value *and* self-interest on the same side, tipping the scales so heavily that the conclusion becomes trivial, as trivial as the proposition—which he strangely treats as a matter for proof—that we desire what is in our interests. Similarly, it clearly does not follow from the fact that we desire what benefits us that we in fact desire everything that benefits us—for we may not know of a given thing (including God) that it does so. Mutatis mutandis about beliefs.

74. "At least in part": this description leaves out the "God-centered perspective," which sees God as an object of intrinsic love and worship, as against an agent for the fulfillment of human needs. See chapter 4.
75. This is clearly a theme, for example, in the discussion in Ibn Taymiyya, "Tafsīr sūrat al-Fātiḥa," in *Majmūʿ Fatāwā,* 14: 12–15.
76. Ibn Taymiyya, *Darʾ taʿāruḍ,* 8: 448.
77. Ibid., 8: 384.
78. In this context the cognitive and affective elements often seem to shade into each other without distinction, but the relationship between them is explicitly thematized in places. This relationship is most basically one of logical dependence, to the extent that a judgment of existence is logically implied by emotional responses that take God as their object. Thus attitudes of "love, humility, fear, hope, glorification . . . and so on, are conditional on [*mashrūṭ bi*] the awareness of the object of one's . . . love, hope, fear, worship," and thus "the experience of love, fear, desire and veneration for God is derivative from [or posterior to: *farʿ ʿalā*] the acknowledgment of God, and the latter entails [*mustalzim*] the former" (Ibn Taymiyya, *Darʾ taʿāruḍ,* 3: 136–37). Cf. 8: 450, where love and cognition are identified as separate forms of entailment (*iqtiḍāʾ*) of our *fiṭra: lā budda an yakūna fi ʾl-fiṭra muqtaḍin li ʾl-ʿilm wa-muqtaḍin li ʾl-maḥabba, wa ʾl-maḥabba mashrūṭa bi ʾl-ʿilm fa-inna mā lā yashʿuru al-insān bihi lā yuḥibbuhu.*
79. The quotes are from Ibn Taymiyya, *Darʾ taʿāruḍ,* 8: 489 (cf. 491: *al-fiṭra al-ṭabīʿiyya al-ʿaqliyya*); *Bayān talbīs,* 2: 18; *Darʾ taʿāruḍ,* 9: 171. For the last point, see *Darʾ taʿāruḍ,* 6: 105–6.
80. When earlier characterizing this convergence, of course, I had framed it in terms of reason and revelation. I will be returning to this characterization, as to Ibn Taymiyya's motivations in pressing his ethical claims, in chapter 5.
81. On one level at least, relating to God's legislative will, though not His ontological will. See chapter 4.
82. Ibn Taymiyya, *Radd,* 26.
83. Ibn Taymiyya, *Darʾ taʿāruḍ,* 8: 445. This requirement is closely involved in Ibn Taymiyya's analysis of what it means to say we are born "with" knowledge of God. He seems to understand this claim not in occurrent but in dispositional terms, so that its truth comes down to the truth of the conditional statement "if people are/were left to the devices of their sound nature and no obstructions or corrupting influences arise/arose, they will/would attain actual knowledge and belief." He thus frequently uses terms suggestive of capacity or receptivity (*quwwa/qubūl/istiʿdād/ṣalāḥiyya,* 8: 446). Yet there is a question as to whether this disposition requires external causes (*asbāb*) to be realized, partly parsed as a question about whether our nature necessitates this knowledge (*taqtaḍī/tūjibu/tastalzimu*) if left unimpeded or merely makes it possible (*mumkin*), and then external causes are required to actualize it (8. 447). I take it that the onus falls on the denial of the need for external causes, which Ibn Taymiyya argues would

nullify the very notion of a specific disposition to belief as against unbelief, for unbelief is also realized through external causes and belief/unbelief is then imputed to the cause (*uḍīfat ila ʾl-sabab*, 8: 448). For more on this, see Hoover, *Ibn Taymiyya's Theodicy of Perpetual Optimism*, 40–42; Hallaq, "Ibn Taymiyya on the existence of God"; Anjum, *Politics, Law, and Community in Islamic Thought*, 221–23. Central to Ibn Taymiyya's position is the idea that this is the position that best meshes with the ascription of a commendable or praiseworthy aspect to the human *fiṭra*.

84. Ibn Taymiyya, *Darʾ taʿāruḍ*, 8: 456–58.
85. See ʿAbd al-Jabbār, *Aṣlaḥ*, 34–35. This distinction is mirrored in al-Rāzī's remarks in *Maṭālib*, 3: 22. And see Ibn Mattawayh's remarks about the balance of overall pleasure/pain in relation to these notions in *Majmūʿ*, 3: 166–67 (*innamā yūṣafu bi-annahu nafʿ idhā lam yuʿqib ḍararan yūfī ʿalayhi*).
86. Ibn Taymiyya, *Radd*, 430; Ibn Taymiyya, "Sharḥ kalimat min 'Futūḥ al-ghayb,'" in *Jāmiʿ al-rasāʾil*, 2: 85.
87. Ibn Taymiyya, *Radd*, 423. Where does the notion of *mulāʾama* stand relative to this distinction? The passage from the *Radd* (430) quoted above contrasts it with the term *ḍarar*, aligning it with the more inclusive and less experiential notion of benefit. Yet elsewhere it appears to be construed in more experiential terms, as, for example, in the following parataxis from *Qāʿida fiʾl-maḥabba*, 64: "Love is the efficient cause for attaining that which is agreeable, beloved, desired [*al-mulāʾim al-maḥbūb al-mushtahā*]."
88. An example of this we have already seen: "When people say 'justice is good and injustice is bad,' what they mean by this is that justice is beloved to our nature, so that its realization causes [one's nature] *pleasure and joy*, and that it is *beneficial* for its bearer and for those other than its bearer" (Ibn Taymiyya, *Radd*, 423).
89. Cf. Meier, "The cleanest about predestination," 318–24; Bell, *Love Theory in Later Ḥanbalite Islam*, particularly 89–91. Bell picks up on the evident resemblance connecting Ibn Taymiyya's critique of the monists to his critique of the Ashʿarites, which will come into view in chapter 4; in both cases the charge is that of undermining the distinction between what God loves and what God hates. In Ibn Taymiyya's view, Bell suggests, the Sufis translated into practice what the Ashʿarites had expressed in dogmatic terms. For Ibn Taymiyya's broader critique of monistic Sufism, see Knysh, *Ibn ʿArabi in the Later Islamic Tradition*, chapter 4.
90. Ibn Taymiyya, "Al-ʿAqīda al-Tadmuriyya," in *Majmūʿ Fatāwā*, 3: 117.
91. Ibn Taymiyya, "Risāla fiʾl-Iḥtijāj biʾl-qadar," in *Majmūʿ Fatāwā*, 8: 309–10.
92. The phrase is Anjum's in *Politics, Law, and Community in Islamic Thought*, 224, speaking of *fiṭra*. The questions regarding the extent of ethical knowledge and the ethical status of *fiṭra* are key themes in Anjum's discussion, especially in chapters 5 and 6. While my view converges with Anjum's on a number of points—he also emphasizes, for example, the conative aspect of *fiṭra* (221:

"while intellect is a tool, *fiṭra* is an inclination") and the role of empirical reasoning in ethics (224)—my account also diverges from his in several others, for example in giving a stronger hearing to the ambivalent role of the natural in Ibn Taymiyya's understanding ("*fiṭra* is a divinely placed inclination in the human psyche toward all that is good," 223), as also in giving a stronger hearing to Ibn Taymiyya's objectivist emphasis (contrast Anjum's characterization of Ibn Taymiyya's *via media* on 225). And although Anjum also notes the limitations of reason in the ethical life (e.g., 201), it seems to me that the description of reason as "effective" in this domain (207) is too unnuanced.

93. Ibn Taymiyya, "Tafsīr sūrat al-Fātiḥa," in *Majmūʿ Fatāwā*, 14: 38.
94. Ibn Taymiyya, *Qāʿida fī ʾl-maḥabba*, 36, 130.
95. Ibn Taymiyya, "Qāʿida fī anna jins fiʿl al-maʾmūr bihi aʿẓam min jins tark al-manhiyy ʿanhu," in *Majmūʿ Fatāwā*, 20: 121. Cf. "Al-Ḥisba," in *Majmūʿ Fatāwā*, 28: 143: even if misdeeds such as adultery, theft, or injustice of different kinds are "disapproved of and considered blameworthy by reason and religion, they are also coveted [*mushtahā*]." The distinction between right and wrong desires sometimes seems to be enshrined in terminological choices, with good desires referred to using the term *maḥabba* and bad desires using the term *hawā* or *shahwa* (a negative association with strong Qur'anic roots). Yet this distinction is not uniformly sustained, as already indicated by Ibn Taymiyya's use of the term *ishtahā* to speak of the infant's positively valenced natural desire. The positive valence of *maḥabba* also disappears elsewhere, as in a passage from *Qāʿida fī ʾl-maḥabba* (30), where Ibn Taymiyya draws a distinction between desiring something as an end and desiring it as a means, which often means acting in ways that contradict one's immediate desire. Ibn Taymiyya at first appears to reserve the term *maḥabba* for the "higher" desire and the term *hawā* for the desire one must forgo, yet in a clear statement he employs the terms *hawā* and *maḥabba* to refer to both desires without distinction: *lā yatruku al-ḥayy mā yuḥibbihu wa-yahwāhu illā limā yuḥibbuhu wa-yahwāhu.*
96. Ibn Taymiyya, "Qāʿida fī anna jins fiʿl al-maʿmūr bihi," in *Majmūʿ Fatāwā*, 20: 121. "Nature" is *jibilla* in the first quote, but the term *fiṭra* appears straight after it.
97. *Al-insān idhā fasidat nafsuhu aw-mizājuhu yashtahī mā yaḍurruhu wa-yaltadhdhu bihi* (Ibn Taymiyya, *Majmūʿ Fatāwā*, 19: 34).
98. This is also the message of another prophetic tradition widely quoted by Ibn Taymiyya, which compares the original disposition of people before it is perverted with the original physical integrity of animals before they are mutilated. See, for example, Ibn Taymiyya, *Darʾ taʿāruḍ*, 8: 362, 445.
99. Cf. the point made in Ibn Taymiyya, *Majmūʿ Fatāwā*, 20: 44: "God naturally disposed people toward the truth, and if the natural disposition is not altered, it sees things as they really are, and knows [or declares] that which is wrong to be wrong, and that which is right to be right [*ankarat munkarahā wa-ʿarafat maʿrūfahā*]."

100. Annas, *Morality of Happiness*, 137, 177; see generally chapter 2, section 3.
101. Porter, *Nature as Reason*, 88.
102. As noted by Pope in "Natural law and Christian ethics," 82.
103. Quoted in Porter, *Nature as Reason*, 53, though Porter's aim in the chapter opened by this quote is in fact to tell a more complex story about the notion of nature that figures in the scholastic appeal, emphasizing the significance of "nature as nature" in ways that call attention to the continuities between human beings and other animals.
104. The first quote ("fabric") is from Hume's "Enquiry concerning the principles of morals," in *Enquiries Concerning Human Understanding and Concerning the Principles of Morals*, 170.
105. Schneewind, *Moral Philosophy from Montaigne to Kant*, 462.
106. Schneewind, "Voluntarism and the foundations of ethics," in *Essays on the History of Moral Philosophy*, 217.
107. Zagzebski, "Morality and religion," 344.
108. See on this point Schneewind's illuminating discussion in "Modern moral philosophy: from beginning to end?" in *Essays on the History of Moral Philosophy*.
109. Porter, *Nature as Reason*, 17.
110. For a good starting point on this type of debate, see Crone, "Barāhima," and references there.
111. Though note that Baṣran Muʿtazilites, crucially, acknowledged that revelation may not *always* be needed: see Ibn Mattawayh's discussion in *Majmūʿ*, 3: 425–30.
112. See, for example, ibid., 184–85.
113. Mānkdīm, *Sharḥ*, 565. Cf. ʿAbd al-Jabbār, *al-Tanabbuʾāt waʾl-muʿjizāt*, 45: "Revelation [*al-samʿ*] . . . reveals the particulars of qualities known by reason."
114. The quotes are from Mānkdīm, *Sharḥ*, 565; Ibn Mattawayh, *Majmūʿ*, 3: 446. For more on this, see Vasalou, *Moral Agents and Their Deserts*, chapter 3, esp. 48 ff.; my discussion there also brings to view a more deontological (*ḥaqq*-focused) level on which the Baṣran Muʿtazilites developed their account of the particularizing role of revelation. For the rather different Baghdādī account of the relationship between God's commands and the dictates of reason, see Zysow, "Two theories of the obligation to obey God's commands." I use the imperative language of obligation ("we must seek what serves our welfare"), following Mānkdīm's own reference to *wujūb al-maṣlaḥa wa-qubḥ al-mafsada*. A more accurate formulation of the Baṣran view, however, is that the repulsion of harm is obligatory, whereas the pursuit of benefit is normally only "plain good" (*ḥasan*)—a more guarded phrasing that Mānkdīm himself reverts to a few lines down.

115. Ibn Mattawayh, *Majmūʿ*, 1: 22. The idea that prayer is commanded due to its beneficial ability to "lead us to choose to do what is obligatory" (ʿAbd al-Jabbār, *Taʿdīl*, 64) clearly leans on the Qur'anic verse cited above. Cf. Ibn Mattawayh, *Majmūʿ*, 3: 434, for a broader proposal for unpacking this causal effect.
116. Ibn Taymiyya, "Qāʿida fī anna jins fiʿl al-maʾmūr bihi," in *Majmūʿ Fatāwā*, 20: 121. Another recurrent characterization of this conjunction is in terms of "ignorance and injustice" (*al-jahl waʾl-ẓulm*)—a characterization with strong Qur'anic resonance (Q 33:72). The view that wrongdoing is a result of ignorance and need, interestingly enough, had been articulated distinctly by Baṣran Muʿtazilites; see, for example, ʿAbd al-Jabbār, *Taʿdīl*, 185 ff. In Ibn Taymiyya's version, however, it has been sanitized through a reinterpretation of its epistemic component as a knowledge not of what is deontologically right and wrong, but of what is beneficial and harmful.
117. Ibn Taymiyya, "Al-Ḥasana waʾl-sayyiʾa," in *Majmūʿ Fatāwā*, 14: 287, reading *fa-lam yafʿal* instead of *wa-lam yafʿal*; cf. Ibn Taymiyya, *Kitāb al-Nubuwwāt*, 2: 925: one "mistakenly thinks . . . that a given act is in one's interest and [in fact] it is not."
118. Ibn Taymiyya, "Kitāb Mufaṣṣal al-iʿtiqād," in *Majmūʿ Fatāwā*, 4: 45. Compare Ibn Taymiyya's reference to the prophets' divine commission to "perfect our natural constitution" in "Risāla fiʾl-Iḥtijāj biʾl-qadar," in *Majmūʿ Fatāwā*, 8: 312; cf. Ibn Taymiyya, *Bayān talbīs*, 2: 18. The examples could be multiplied ad infinitum.
119. See Ibn Taymiyya, "Al-ʿAqīda al-Tadmuriyya," in *Majmūʿ Fatāwā*, 3: 114–15. The passage continues: "just as people do not know by reason the particulars concerning God's names and attributes which the prophets have informed us about, even though they might know their generalities [*jumal*] through reason." The comparison is an important one. Compare also the restrictive remark in his *Fatāwā*, that "were it not for the prophetic message, reason would not arrive at the details of what is beneficial and harmful in this life and the next [*fiʾl-maʿāsh waʾl-maʿād*]" ("Qāʿida nāfiʿa fī wujūb al-iʿtiṣām biʾl-risāla," in *Majmūʿ Fatāwā*, 19: 100).
120. Ibn Taymiyya, "Tafsīr sūrat al-Fātiḥa," in *Majmūʿ Fatāwā*, 14: 35.
121. For the above, see Ibn Taymiyya, "Qāʿida nāfiʿa fī wujūb al-iʿtiṣām biʾl-risāla," in *Majmūʿ Fatāwā*, 19: 99–100.
122. There will be something more to say about the place of such spiritual values in Ibn Taymiyya's theological work in chapter 4.
123. Ibn Taymiyya, "Tafsīr sūrat al-Fātiḥa," in *Majmūʿ Fatāwā*, 14: 37–39.
124. Ibn Taymiyya, "Masʾalat taḥsīn al-ʿaql wa-taqbīḥuhu," in *Majmūʿ Fatāwā*, 8: 434–35.
125. I draw on Ibn Mattawayh's discussion in *Majmūʿ*, 3: 130 ff.
126. Ibid., 184–85.
127. See my *Moral Agents and Their Deserts*, chapter 5.
128. See the discussion in Ibn Mattawayh, *Majmūʿ*, 3: 425–30.

CHAPTER 3

1. Ibn Taymiyya, "Masʾalat taḥsīn al-ʿaql wa-taqbīḥuhu," in *Majmūʿ Fatāwā*, 8: 433.
2. Al-Ghazālī, *al-Iqtiṣād fi ʾl-iʿtiqād*, 195; cf. Ibn Fūrak, *Mujarrad Maqālāt al-shaykh Abi ʾl-Ḥasan al-Ashʿarī*: "The reward and punishment that attach to acquired actions . . . attach to them by way of revealed report rather than reason" (99); discussing the notion of obligation: "There is no indicant in [reason] regarding the benefits and harms that form the consequences [*al-ʿawāqib*]" of actions (286).
3. Ibn Taymiyya's critical remarks about the Ashʿarites can be tracked in many of the locations cited in chapter 2. For further expressions of the objections that opened this section, see "Risāla fiʾl-Iḥtijāj biʾl-qadar," in *Majmūʿ Fatāwā*, 8: 343–44; *Sharḥ al-Iṣbahāniyya*, 448–49; *Nubuwwāt*, 1: 459.
4. Ibn Taymiyya, *Radd*, 430.
5. Al-Ghazālī, *Mustaṣfā*, 1: 56.
6. Ibn Taymiyya, *Radd*, 423.
7. Ibid., 422; Ibn Taymiyya, "Risāla fiʾl-Iḥtijāj biʾl-qadar," in *Majmūʿ Fatāwā*, 8: 309.
8. The phrase is from ʿAbd al-Jabbār, *Taʿdīl*, 185.
9. Mānkdīm, *Sharḥ*, 308. The unbelievers' moral awareness is frequently invoked by Muʿtazilites in support of their position: see, for example, Ibn Mattawayh, *Majmūʿ*, 1: 254; ʿAbd al-Jabbār, *Taʿdīl*, 109 (*yaʿrifūna dhālika wa-yukhbirūna bihi ʿan anfushim*). The "desert island" condition often turns up in anti-Muʿtazilite critiques; see, for example, al-Rāzī, *Maṭālib*, 3: 67.
10. The text has *jamāl* (a term that appears elsewhere in the same vicinity) but with Shihadeh (*Teleological Ethics of Fakhr al-Dīn al-Rāzī*, 51) I take the meaning of *kamāl* to offer a more natural counterpart to the preceding *naqṣ*.
11. Al-Juwaynī, *Kitāb al-Irshād ilā qawāṭiʿ al-adilla fī uṣūl al-iʿtiqād*, 265; Ibn Fūrak, *Mujarrad*, 141–42. In reading Ibn Fūrak's remarks as a psychological claim rather than a claim about the definition of ethical concepts, my view departs from the one expressed by Shihadeh in *Teleological Ethics of Fakhr al-Dīn al-Rāzī*, 51; cf. his "Theories of ethical value in kalām." See also, as part of this same longer lineage, al-Bāqillānī's *Kitāb al-Tamhīd*, remarking that everyone acts in order to obtain benefit or repel harm, and "the only kinds of agents one can conceive in the present realm [*al-shāhid*] are of this kind" (107).
12. Al-Juwaynī, *al-ʿAqīda al-Niẓāmiyya fi ʾl-arkān al-Islāmiyya*, 36; note the interesting continuation, juxtaposing custom and nature: *li ʾl-ʿādāt āthār ghayr mankūra fi ʾl-jibillāt*. The notion of custom or indeed convention is also present in al-Anṣārī's *Ghunya*—note for example his reference to right and wrong in the sense of "that which people agreed upon" (*tawāḍaʿ ʿalayhi*) or which is grounded "in their conventions and purposes" (*awḍāʿihim wa-aghrāḍihim*) (2: 1003)—but

it does not seem to me to be foregrounded. The term *ʿāda* itself is used to refer more broadly to the familiar or natural operation of the world, including human nature (e.g., 2: 998: *mā yaʾbāhu al-ṭabʿ . . . fī mustaqirr al-ʿāda*).

13. Al-Ghazālī, *Mustaṣfā*, 1: 60.
14. Our irrationality: al-Ghazālī speaks of the subservience of the soul to the imagination or "estimation": *khuliqat quwā al-nafs muṭīʿa liʾl-awhām* (ibid., 1: 59). The appearance of *wahm* at this juncture will certainly remind us of Avicenna, whose remarks on the educability of the estimation by "something like experience" (*shayʾ kaʾl-tajriba*) al-Ghazālī echoes: see *Nafs*, 163–64; cf. Black, "Estimation (*wahm*) in Avicenna," 226–27. Yet the key idea, as well as its defining vocabulary, had been in the intellectual bloodstream much longer. See the particularly suggestive remarks in this regard in al-Jāḥiẓ's epistle "Min Kitāb al-Masāʾil waʾl-jawābāt fiʾl-maʿrifa," 322–23. A new edition of this epistle is forthcoming by Professor James Montgomery, to whom I owe my closer reading of it.
15. Al-Ghazālī, *Mustaṣfā*, 1: 59; cf. al-Ghazālī, *Iqtiṣād*, 167: *al-ṭabʿ yunaffaru ʿanhu min awwal al-ṣibā bi-ṭarīq al-taʾdīb waʾl-istiṣlāḥ*.
16. See al-Ghazālī, *Miʿyār al-ʿilm fī fann al-manṭiq*, 193–97; al-Ghazālī, *Mustaṣfā*, 1: 48–49, and the discussion of *taḥsīn* from 55 ff. Compare the reprise of the terms of the thought experiment in al-Shahrastānī, *Nihāyat al-iqdām*, 371–72; also al-Āmidī, *Ghāyat al-marām fī ʿilm al-kalām*, 235.
17. Al-Shahrastānī, *Nihāyat al-iqdām*, 373, reading *lā ḥaqīqata lahu* instead of the present *lahā*.
18. Al-Ghazālī, *Mustaṣfā*, 1: 48.
19. Ibid., 21, 28.
20. This cadence certainly seems present, albeit discreetly, in the remark found in Ibn Fūrak's *Mujarrad* (142): unless an action brings benefit to a person, "there is no longer any motivation for him to perform the act, and one does not choose that act assuming he is wise/rational [*ḥakīm*]." In my view the notion of "wisdom" or "rationality" deployed in this manner clearly registers with normative tones. I would also hear al-Ashʿarī's remarks on the notion of obligation (285–86) in the same tones, as does Gimaret, *La doctrine d'al-Ashʿarī*, 213.
21. The remark is in al-Juwaynī's abridgment of the work, *Kitāb al-Talkhīṣ fī uṣūl al-fiqh*, 1: 159. Cf. the remark in *Tamhīd*, where, arguing against the view that we know what is good by reason, al-Bāqillānī distinguishes the possibility that by "good" one might be referring to no more than our "natural inclination toward pleasure and natural aversion to pain" (122–23). The text reads, *muyūl al-ṭibāʿ ilā fiʿl al-ladhdhāt wa-nufūruhā ʿan fiʿl al-ālām*—a phrase virtually identical with the one used by al-Juwaynī in the same context in his *Irshād*—but the notion of *fiʿl* must be read in context; the argument seems to refer us to the pleasure/pain caused by *others*.
22. Al-Juwaynī, *al-Burhān fī uṣūl al-fiqh*, 1: 91–92.

23. See the relevant remarks in al-Juwaynī, *Niẓāmiyya*, 58–59 (*fa-law lam yathbut ḥaẓẓ al-ʿabd fī tanakkub al-ʿiqāb, la-mā taqarrara fī ḥaqqihi al-wājib*). Al-Juwaynī's role in the adoption of this position has been remarked by Schmidtke in *The Theology of al-ʿAllāma al-Ḥillī*, 102–103; cf. ʿAbd al-Qādir, *al-Masāʾil al-mushtaraka bayna uṣūl al-fiqh wa-uṣūl al-dīn*, 78. It is thus a mistake to credit al-Ghazālī with the central role in this development, as Frank has suggested in a couple of works. See his remarks in *Creation and the Cosmic System*, 67, where he discusses al-Ghazālī's seemingly innovative transformation of "the juridically obligatory," which he associates with earlier Ashʿarism, into the "prudentially necessary." The argument for this thesis seems to me somewhat elliptical and obscure, but in any case the above clearly suggests that this transformation had already taken place. Part of Frank's argument—an argument that forms part of a broader reading of al-Ghazālī's ambivalent relationship with the Ashʿarite school and his tactic of effecting subtle subversions of traditional Ashʿarite positions—rests on al-Ghazālī's use of the notion of *ṭabʿ* in his discussion of obligation in the *Iqtiṣād*. Frank takes this to introduce the notion of secondary causation—unfashionable in Ashʿarite theology—into the discussion (*Al-Ghazālī and the Ashʿarite School*, 34). Yet this reading of the term *ṭabʿ* overlooks its longer pedigree in the ethical writings of earlier Ashʿarites, including al-Bāqillānī and al-Juwaynī.
24. See n20.
25. Mānkdīm, *Sharḥ al-Uṣūl*, 68.
26. Al-Ghazālī, *Iqtiṣād*, 161.
27. Ibid., 190.
28. See, for example, the remark in ibid., 162: *al-iṣṭilāḥāt mubāḥa lā ḥajra fīhā liʾl-sharʿ wa-lā liʾl-ʿaql wa-innamā tamnaʿu minhu al-lugha idhā lam yakun ʿalā wifq al-mawḍūʿ al-maʿrūf.*
29. Al-Ghazālī, *Mustaṣfā*, 1: 66. Here, interestingly, the more subjective notion of *aghrāḍ* takes the place of the objective notion of *ḍarar* that appears more frequently in *kalām/uṣūl al-fiqh* definitions of obligation. This should caution us against taking such distinctions too rigidly. In the works of certain Ashʿarites, such distinctions are indeed even harder to draw; a good example is al-Āmidī, who seems to use both in *Ghāyat al-marām* with little distinction.
30. Al-Āmidī, *Ghāyat al-marām*, 235, 234.
31. Al-Rāzī, *Maṭālib*, 3: 66.
32. Al-Ghazālī, *Mustaṣfā*, 1: 62, 61. See also al-Anṣārī's stark comments in *Ghunya*, 2: 1008.
33. Al-Ghazālī, *Iqtiṣād*, 194–95. This involves a revised understanding of the role of reason: not to provide us with knowledge independently of revelation but to serve as an instrument for understanding revelation. An indicative token of the slippage noted above, as well as the foundational role assigned to desire in this transition, is provided by al-Rāzī in his *Maṭālib* in the context of affirming the

existence of "rational" ethical knowledge: "Pleasure and joy are objects of intrinsic desire [*maṭlūbatāni bi'l-dhāt*], and pain and grief objects of intrinsic repugnance [*makrūhatāni bi'l-dhāt*]. . . . Our claim is thus established: namely, that reason judges [*al-ʿaql yaqḍī*] that certain things are good and that certain others are evil" (3: 290). See generally 289–90 for an interesting set of remarks that distinguish more clearly than has emerged in the above discussion between the judgments parsed in terms of "good" and those parsed in terms of "obligatory."

34. Al-Juwaynī, *Niẓāmiyya*, 61; a variant has *tasāwaqat* for *tashawwafat*.

35. Al-Rāzī, *Maṭālib*, 3: 21. I am indebted to Shihadeh's *Teleological Ethics of Fakhr al-Dīn al-Rāzī* for calling attention to al-Rāzī's usage of both terms—*fiṭra* and *ṭabʿ*—in several instances of his writings.

36. It is the notion of *ṭabʿ* likewise that Shihadeh foregrounds in his account of al-Rāzī, for example, *Teleological Ethics of Fakhr al-Dīn al-Rāzī*, 58–59. It is indicative that when al-Rāzī rephrases the same point elsewhere in the book—as in *Maṭālib*, 3: 348—the language of *ṭabʿ* alone appears. The vocabulary of *fiṭra* had certainly made earlier (though seemingly equally isolated) appearances in Ashʿarite ethical discussions before al-Rāzī's time. For example, in dismissing the Muʿtazilite view of ethical responses as judgments of reason, al-Anṣārī instead tied them to "the nature with which God vested human beings [*jibilla faṭara Allāh al-ʿibād ʿalayhā*]" (*Ghunya*, 2: 1008); cf. 2: 1030–31: *al-fāʿil minnā . . . fuṭira ʿalā bunya yajūzu ʿalayhi maʿahā jarr al-manāfiʿ wa-dafʿ al-maḍārr*. A longer study of this paper trail would be needed to trace the fuller trajectory of the notion of *fiṭra* in classical ethical discussions.

37. Al-Rāzī, *Maṭālib*, 3: 347. Elsewhere the conflict between the first- and third-person perspectives that Ibn Taymiyya obscured is also clearly picked out by al-Rāzī; see Shihadeh, *Teleological Ethics of Fakhr al-Dīn al-Rāzī*, 77. Cf. the remark quoted by Shihadeh from al-Rāzī's *Nihāyat al-ʿuqūl*, which makes the impact on self-interest even clearer while still using the key notions of love and hate: "If the wrongdoer declares [*aftā*] that wrongdoing is good, someone else will soon wrong him. Since, in his natural disposition [*ṭabʿ*], he hates that anticipated wrongdoing, and since all that leads to what is hated is itself hated in the natural disposition, wrongdoing will indeed be hated by the wrongdoer. The same applies to all other [commonly accepted moral norms]" (*Teleological Ethics of Fakhr al-Dīn al-Rāzī*, 81). My thanks to Ayman Shihadeh for providing me with additional textual detail.

38. Al-Ghazālī, *Iḥyāʾ*, 4: 255–56: *ḥubb al-qalb li'l-muḥsin . . . jibilla wa-fiṭra lā sabīla ilā taghyīrihā*—a continuation with Qur'anic echoes. Cf. al-Anṣārī's statement of this view in *Ghunya*, 2: 1004. Ibn Taymiyya's statement to the same effect ("Al-Tuḥfa al-ʿirāqiyya," in *Majmūʿ Fatāwā*, 10: 84), quoted in chapter 1, can now be heard as a direct echo of al-Ghazālī's view.

39. For the first remark, see al-Ghazālī, *Iḥyāʾ*, 4: 254: *kull ladhīdh maḥbūb ʿinda al-multadhdh bihi wa-maʿnā kawnihi maḥbūban anna fi'l-ṭabʿ maylan ilayhi. Al-ṭabʿ*

al-salīm: see 4: 255; cf. the typical Taymiyyan conjunctions: *huwa muqtaḍāhā bi 'l-ṭab' / muqtaḍā ṭab'ihā* (4: 264). The positive connotations carried by al-Ghazālī's *ṭab'* may not seem surprising given his reading of natural desire as a script of divine intentions, as we will see in the next chapter. The above debts provide further support for Michot's recent remarks about Ibn Taymiyya's extensive familiarity with (though also critical engagement of) al-Ghazālī's work: see his "An important reader of al-Ghāzalī."

40. Ibn Taymiyya, *Minhāj*, 1: 450.
41. Al-Rāzī, *Maṭālib*, 3: 289. Ash'arites were not the only ones to adopt the strategy of separating the claim that we know right and wrong by reason from the claim that right and wrong apply to God. This strategy, for example, seems to be at work in the spare remarks on the topic by one of the traditionalists that Ibn Taymiyya refers to, al-Sijzī, in his *Risālat al-Sijzī ilā ahl Zabīd*, 140.
42. See Gobillot, *La conception originelle*, 112–29; For al-Jāḥiẓ's remark, see "Risālat al-Ma'āsh wa'l-ma'ād," in *Rasā'il al-Jāḥiẓ*, 1: 102. Cf. Bernand, "La critique de la notion de nature (*ṭab'*) par le *kalām*," esp. 60–62.
43. As Gutas notes, the term *fiṭra* is not the only one that appears in Avicenna's relevant remarks; it neighbors on a number of synonymous terms, such as *jibilla, gharīza*, and indeed *ṭab'* ("The empiricism of Avicenna," 406–7).
44. MacIntyre, *After Virtue*, 161.
45. Shihadeh, *Teleological Ethics of Fakhr al-Dīn al-Rāzī*, 82. For the notion of a social contract, see 176–81.
46. See al-Rāzī, *Maṭālib*, 3: 68, 69, and the argument on 291. For further discussion of these passages, see Shihadeh, *Teleological Ethics of Fakhr al-Dīn al-Rāzī*, 77–83.
47. Ibn Taymiyya, *Radd*, 398; al-Rāzī, *Sharḥ al-Ishārāt*, 1: 269.
48. This point emerged clearly in the stage-setting passage cited in chapter 1: Ibn Taymiyya, "Mas'alat taḥsīn al-'aql wa-taqbīḥuhu," in *Majmū' Fatāwā*, 8: 433. See also the additional remarks about the Qur'anic foundations of Ibn Taymiyya's ethical rationalism in chapter 5.
49. Ibn Taymiyya, *Sharḥ al-Iṣbahāniyya*, 540, 544; it is a theme that surfaces in several places in this work, but see especially the discussion at 539–48. Cf. Anjum's remarks, discussing the *Nubuwwāt*, in *Politics, Law, and Community*, 204.
50. Ibn Mattawayh, *Majmū'*, 3: 180.
51. Though it is worth noting that some Ash'arites, such as al-Rāzī, considered that the content of individuals' motives may involve direct reference to the consequences of "deontological" acts like justice and injustice taken in the sense of their impact on one's self-interest. One acclaims the value of justice because one knows that to do otherwise would be to expose one's own person and property to threat (al-Rāzī, *Maṭālib*, 3: 68).
52. Lovejoy, *The Great Chain of Being*, 3–4.
53. See Schneewind, "Hume and the religious significance of moral rationalism," in *Essays on the History of Moral Philosophy*.

54. Al-Ashʿarī, *al-Lumaʿ*, 117; cf. al-Bāqillānī, *Inṣāf*, 50: *huwa al-mālik ʿala ʾl-ḥaqīqa, yataṣarrafu fī milkihi kamā yashāʾu, lā yusʾalu ʿammā yafʿalu wa-hum yusʾalūna.* The phrase can be found almost verbatim in other Ashʿarite works.
55. Quotes are from ʿAbd al-Jabbār, *Taʿdīl*, 20, 25. Cf. Ibn Mattawayh, *Majmūʿ*, 3: 140: "Just as if an act constitutes injustice, it is bad for any agent [to perform it], similarly if the ground of obligation is realized in an act, different agents should not stand in a different relation to it." Certain considerations about persons did of course matter in this context—for example, whether one acted intentionally or had reached the age of responsibility. See ʿAbd al-Jabbār's discussion in *Taʿdīl*, 87 ff., where his concern is precisely to mark off features about the agent that are relevant to the value of the action (93: they have a *taʿalluq* or connection to the action) and features that are not. As always, the picture becomes more complex the closer one looks; as I have emphasized elsewhere, the subject-independence of Muʿtazilite ethics finds an important qualification in the subject-dependence introduced by the foundational notion of *ḥaqq*. See *Moral Agents and Their Deserts*, chapter 4, and synoptically the remarks on 86.
56. In "Qāʿida fiʾl-muʿjizāt waʾl-karāmāt," in *Majmūʿ Fatāwā*, 11: 354, Ibn Taymiyya appears to embrace the language of essential (*dhātiyya*) attributes, whereas in *Radd*, 422, he rejects this language for reasons that flow naturally from his consequentialism: whether or not a given act is beneficial is not a fixed feature of that act but may vary according to circumstances. That the language of *ṣifāt* is deployed with a reference to utility is clear from the former passage and is also made clear in *Sharḥ al-Iṣbahāniyya*, 448. Compare also the remark interpreting "intrinsic attributes" in terms of utility by ʿAbd al-Qādir, whose discussion in many places reads as an unmarked rehearsal and clarification of Ibn Taymiyya's views (*al-Masāʾil al-mushtaraka*, 80–81). In this respect Anjum's characterization of Ibn Taymiyya's ethical *via media* as a rationalist epistemology combined with a voluntarist ontology (*Politics, Law, and Community*, 225) seems to me to overlook the complexity of Ibn Taymiyya's statements on both topics.
57. For Ibn Mattawayh's remarks, see *Majmūʿ*, 3: 447–48; compare Mānkdīm's discussion in *Sharḥ al-Uṣūl*, 564–67. Of course, not all acts whose value invokes the notion of benefit accrue to the agent and thus depend on his features—beneficence is a case in point. Cf. Ibn Mattawayh's distinction between self-regarding and other-regarding acts (*taʿalluq biʾl-fāʿil* versus *biʾl-ghayr*) in *Majmūʿ*, 1: 244–45, in the context of circumscribing God's possible modes of action.
58. It is not incidental that ʿAbd al-Jabbār's sentimentalist account of aesthetic judgments—we call a picture ugly because we are repelled by it—anticipates not only al-Ghazālī's claim that we call acts bad when they disagree with our purposes but also Ibn Taymiyya's own claim that we call acts bad because we

are repelled by them. Notice the pregnant occurrence of the term *ṭabʿ* in ʿAbd al-Jabbār's framing of the point in *Taʿdīl*, 55: *yanfuru al-ṭabʿ ʿanhā*.

59. Rachels, "Naturalism," 87.
60. Though, as we will see in chapter 4, the character of the causal relation invoked in these remarks was the topic of another important point of friction between Ibn Taymiyya and Ashʿarite theologians.

CHAPTER 4

1. ʿAbd al-Jabbār, *Taʿdīl*, 3.
2. Neiman, *Evil in Modern Thought*, 5.
3. Ibn Taymiyya, "Al-Ḥasana wa'l-sayyi'a," in *Majmūʿ Fatāwā*, 14: 309.
4. Ibn Taymiyya, "Mas'alat taḥsīn al-ʿaql wa-taqbīḥuhu," in *Majmūʿ Fatāwā*, 8: 433.
5. Ibn Taymiyya, *Minhāj al-sunna*, 1: 141. Cf. Ibn Taymiyya, "Al-ʿAqīda al-Tadmuriyya," in *Majmūʿ Fatāwā*, 3: 19. Justice, to be sure, did not form the only focus of Muʿtazilite reflection, and it is useful to keep in mind that in the Muʿtazilites' discussions, as in Ibn Taymiyya's, the boundaries between the notions of wisdom and justice are permeable. See indicatively ʿAbd al-Jabbār's discussion of these two terms in *Taʿdīl*, 48–51.
6. Al-Juwaynī, *Niẓāmiyya*, 36; al-Ghazālī, *Iqtiṣād*, 187.
7. Al-Qarāfī, *Nafā'is al-uṣūl fī sharḥ al-Maḥṣūl*, 7: 3450.
8. See, for example, al-Anṣārī, *Ghunya*, 2: 1032. Cf. Shihadeh, *Teleological Ethics of Fakhr al-Dīn al-Rāzī*, 51.
9. See the discussion of this theological point in al-Shahrastānī, *Nihayat al-iqdām*, 397–416; al-Rāzī, *al-Arbaʿīn fī uṣūl al-dīn*, 249–53; cf. Gimaret, *La doctrine d'al-Ashʿarī*, 447–51.
10. Ibn Taymiyya, "Al-Ḥasana wa'l-sayyi'a," in *Majmūʿ Fatāwā*, 14: 313, stating the objectionable view *wa-lā irādatuhu murajjaḥa li'l-iḥsān ila'l-khalq*.
11. Ibn Taymiyya outlines some of the evidence provided by the first kind of document in *Sharḥ al-Iṣbahāniyya*, 178–79, and some of the evidence provided by the second kind of document on 698, 700. Both methods of establishing God's wisdom can be read instructively against El Shamsy's distinction between "rationalist" and "empiricist" approaches to God's wisdom in "The wisdom of God's law."
12. Ibn Taymiyya, *Minhāj al-sunna*, 1: 141; cf. Ibn Taymiyya, "Tafsīr sūrat al-Baqara," in *Majmūʿ Fatāwā*, 14: 144, more broadly: *hādhā madhhab a'immat al-fuqahā' qāṭibatan wa-salaf al-umma wa-ʿāmmatihā*. For the stage-setting phrase, see again Ibn Taymiyya, "Mas'alat taḥsīn al-ʿaql wa-taqbīḥuhu," in *Majmūʿ Fatāwā*, 8: 434.
13. And indeed becomes more intelligible; cf. my discussion in "Ibn Taymiyya's ethics between Ashʿarite voluntarism and Muʿtazilite rationalism."

14. Ibn Taymiyya also refers to "perfection" and "imperfection" (to what is *mukammil/munaqqiṣ*), but I set this point aside to avoid complicating our story. Ibn Taymiyya is probably influenced by al-Rāzī here; see Shihadeh, *Teleological Ethics of Fakhr al-Dīn al-Rāzī*.
15. Ibn Taymiyya, "Qāʿida fiʾl-muʿjizāt waʾl-karāmāt," in *Majmūʿ Fatāwā*, 11: 354.
16. Al-Ghazālī, *Mustaṣfā*, 1: 286–88.
17. The quote is from Hallaq, *A History of Islamic Legal Theories*, 132. For more on the legal development of the notion of *maṣlaḥa*, see Opwis, Maṣlaḥa *and the Purpose of the Law*. And see El Shamsy, "The wisdom of God's law," for an illuminating discussion of the transformation of Muʿtazilite ideas on welfare among earlier Shāfiʿites by al-Ghazālī. Cf. Chaumont's remarks in "La notion de *wajh al-ḥikmah* dans les *uṣūl al-fiqh* d'Abū Isḥāq al-Shirāzī," with reference to al-Shirāzī: if Ashʿarism triumphs in theological history, it is Muʿtazilism that triumphs in legal history. This collection of articles appeared late in the preparation of the present study, and I have drawn selectively on its contents.
18. Al-Ghazālī, *Shifāʾ al-ghalīl fī bayān al-shabah wa ʾl-mukhīl wa-masālik al-taʿlīl*, 146.
19. Al-Juwaynī, *Talkhīṣ*, 1: 151. As al-Bāqillānī's ensuing remarks show (160), this point is linked to an oft-voiced objection to the Muʿtazilite position: certain acts to which the Muʿtazilites (say we rationally) assign different values—such as killing by way of retaliation and killing by way of intentional homicide—share the same intrinsic reality (*tamāthuluhumā fī ḥaqīqat al-fiʿl*), yet one is bad, the other good; hence the intrinsic attributes of actions do not ground their value. (Cf. al-Anṣārī, *Ghunya*, 2: 1006.) The objection seems weak, as it turns on what we consider the "reality" at stake; shouldn't the conditions (*asbāb*) of the act—for example, unjust violation of the right to life in the case of *qiṣāṣ*—be included in the description of that reality? As al-Rāzī would later point out, the Muʿtazilites incorporated such distinctions in their account of the act-descriptions (*wujūh*) grounding the value of actions, and as such this objection involves a misunderstanding of their views (*Maṭālib*, 3: 338–39).
20. Al-Juwaynī, *Burhān*, 1: 86.
21. The expression is from Weiss, *The Spirit of Islamic Law*, 171.
22. See, for example, Ibn ʿAqīl, *Wāḍiḥ*, 4b: 354; Āl Taymiyya, *al-Musawwada fī uṣūl al-fiqh*, 365.
23. Ibn Barhān, *al-Wuṣūl ila ʾl-uṣūl*, 2: 233–34. I read this next to Reinhart's essay "Ritual action and practical action," in which the rationality (or lack thereof) of ritual action in particular forms a key theme; see the concentrated remarks on al-Naẓẓām at 76–80.
24. Zysow, *The Economy of Certainty*, 398.
25. Al-Āmidī, *al-Iḥkām fī uṣūl al-aḥkām*, 3: 366, 388–89; cf. Ibn ʿAqīl's use of this very phrase in *Wāḍiḥ*, 4b: 363: as we sift through the properties of wine, the only feature we find that is "fit [*yaṣluḥu*] to be the cause of its prohibition" is its transporting effect.

26. Al-Ghazālī, *Shifā' al-ghalīl*, 143: *na'nī bi'l-munāsaba ma'nan ma'qūlan ẓāhiran fi'l-'aql yatayassaru ithbātuhu 'ala'l-khaṣm bi'l-naẓar al-'aqlī.*
27. In relation to al-Bāqillānī, of course, the above remarks carry a danger of anachronism, as the programmatic development of the discourse of *maqāṣid al-sharī'a* still lay in the future. Yet to the extent that al-Bāqillānī's statement reflects a typically Ash'arite view also expressed by later writers, the juxtaposition is not unwarranted.
28. Ibn Fūrak, *Mujarrad*, 286.
29. Zysow's illuminating discussion of this point in *The Economy of Certainty*, esp. 341–47, has formed one of my main starting points here.
30. See, for example, Ibn Taymiyya, *Sharḥ al-Iṣbahāniyya*, 705; Ibn Taymiyya, *Minhāj al-sunna*, 1: 455.
31. Al-Ghazālī, *Mustaṣfā*, 1: 286–87.
32. Ibid., 1: 310.
33. See the remarks in Zysow, *Economy of Certainty*, 343–47.
34. It is al-Ghazālī in his *Shifā' al-ghalīl* who seems to originate the analogy between the way we read the Law and the way we read human behavior; see especially 191 ff. The analogical role of the human paradigm is made clear on 191–92: *ka'l-wāḥid minnā . . . ka-dhālika ma'ānī al-aḥkām tu'qalu bi-mithl hādhā al-ṭarīq.* This idea is expressed again by al-Rāzī in *Maḥṣūl*, 2: 332; cf. al-Āmidī's reference to *al-naẓar ilā jary al-'āda al-ma'lūfa min shar' al-aḥkām* in *Iḥkām*, 3: 376; cf. al-Qarāfī, *Nafā'is al-uṣūl*, 7: 3454: *al-sharā'i' kulluhā maṣāliḥ li'l-khalq bi'l-istiqrā'*. See also the discussion that follows in the main text.
35. Al-Ghazālī, *Shifā' al-ghalīl*, 162.
36. See Hallaq, "*Uṣūl al-fiqh*," esp. 189–91.
37. Al-Ghazālī, *Mustaṣfā*, 1: 288.
38. Al-Juwaynī, *Burhān*, 2: 923, 924, 925, 938. A closer study of the *Burhān*, however, would be in order before this could be done with stronger certainty and greater assurance of their meaning.
39. See Griffel, *Al-Ghazālī's Philosophical Theology*, for a conspectus of this debate and the offer of an irenic solution.
40. Al-Ghazālī, *Iḥyā'*, 1: 15 ff.
41. Ibid., 2: 19.
42. Ibid., 2: 22.
43. Ibid., 2: 28.
44. This train of reflection can be followed in ibid., 2: 22 ff., where it is (significantly, given a Taymiyyan criticism of the Ash'arites that will shortly come into view) a notion of what God loves—of procreation as the wise purpose that God loves—that serves as a guiding thread, revealing God's love/God's wisdom as the ground of the command "Marry and beget!" God gave us the seeds, the plow, and the arable land, and to let our natural disposition go to waste would be to waste the instruments God wisely constructed for particular purposes.

The notion of *fiṭra* makes a pregnant appearance here: in allowing such waste, we would be offending against "the aim of our natural disposition": *maqṣūd al-fiṭra wa 'l-ḥikma al-mafhūma min shawāhid al-khilqa, al-maktūba ʿalā hādhihi al-aʿḍā' bi-khaṭṭ ilahī* (2: 23); cf. 2: 25: *al-walad huwa al-maqṣūd bi 'l-fiṭra wa 'l-ḥikma wa 'l-shahwa bāʿitha ʿalayhi*. This reading of the *Iḥyā'* finds its complement in El Shamsy's remarks in "The wisdom of God's law," 32–33, which focus on al-Ghazālī's discussion of God's wisdom in *al-Ḥikma fī makhlūqāt Allāh*. El Shamsy also comments on the bridges this discussion puts down to legal theory and offers an interesting proposal (relating to al-Ghazālī's engagement with Galen's work) for understanding the development of al-Ghazālī's "empiricist" approach to God's wisdom.

45. Al-Āmidī, *Iḥkām*, 3: 389. Weiss interprets this passage differently; he glosses it: "The Legislator's purpose may also *become* the purpose of the human creature in that it is especially pertinent to him and in that he, as a rational being, *will* embrace it" (*The Search for God's Law*, 609–10, emphasis added).
46. Though it is more continuous with the notion of "reading" the natural (including human) world found in the *Iḥyā'*, as my next remarks will suggest.
47. Al-Āmidī, *Iḥkām*, 3: 394, 396.
48. Weiss, *Search for God's Law*, 622.
49. See Zysow's discussion in *Economy of Certainty*, 343–47. Cf. Jackson's remarks in *Islamic Law and the State*: despite the reluctance of earlier Ashʿarites to admit "the practical good or utility of God's commands for the Here and Now . . . later Ashʿarites, particularly outside Baghdad, are much more explicit in admitting the practical utility of God's commands along with reason's ability to apprehend this" (28). This corrects a misperception that, as Jackson notes, has often clung to readings of the Ashʿarite approach and is notably expressed in Kerr's gloss on the implications of this approach: "There is really nothing for men to learn in the moral sphere except the revealed obligations, which have no foundation in a natural order in the world, nor in a natural order in the human personality, nor in a rational order of justice" (*Islamic Reform*, 59). Putting aside the third item on this list, the above discussion has suggested that Ashʿarite jurists had accepted both kinds of natural foundation: in the natural order and the order of the human personality (or nature: *ṭabʿ*). Kerr's next remarks (60) evoke a familiar point regarding the tension between Ashʿarite theology and the practical and legal sphere in this regard. Yet as we have seen, the acknowledgment of at least one of these foundations, human nature, had been expressed in theological no less than legal Ashʿarite discourse.
50. Obligation comes down to the preponderance (*tarjīḥ*) of harm, and it is God who creates this preponderance (He is the *murajjiḥ*): see the remarks in al-Ghazālī, *Iqtiṣād*, 192–93, and the discussion of obligation on 161–62.
51. Al-Ghazālī, *Iḥyā'*, 1: 100; al-Ghazālī, *Mustaṣfā*, 1: 28. The point would thus encompass all definitions of legal value that make reference to punishment—though

as Weiss notes, remarking al-Āmidī's exclusive reference to blame (*dhamm*), not all do (*Search for God's Law*, 105). Cf. al-Ashʿarī's reference to reward and punishment as what is established by scripture and not by reason (*mimmā taʿallaqa bihā khabaran lā ʿaqlan*): Ibn Fūrak, *Mujarrad*, 99.

52. Al-Rāzī, *Maḥṣūl*, 2: 320–21; cf. the remarks in al-Qarāfī, *Nafāʾis al-uṣūl*, 7: 3404–5. This characterization may seem paradoxical with regard to some of these objectives. If the protection of life, family lines, and property clearly pertain to the mundane domain, it is harder to think of the protection of religion—or indeed of reason, whose value is partly explained through its significance for the religious life—as worldly interests. In the most basic sense, these interests are "mundane" to the extent that they are upheld through specific social and political arrangements and through provisions enforced by secular powers.
53. See, for example, al-Ghazālī, *Mustaṣfā* 1: 62 (*al-ṭabʿ ... huwa al-bāʿith al-mustaḥiththh*); cf. al-Ghazālī, *Iqtiṣād*, 194.
54. Both elements appear in discussions of the aims of the Law; see, for example, al-Āmidī, *Iḥkām* 3: 390; cf. al-Ghazālī, *Shifāʾ al-ghalīl*, 160.
55. Which is not to say that one's interests need to be protected solely against the violations of others: consent is certainly not the only normative principle at work. Thus, one's interests may also need to be protected from oneself, as when the Law protects one's property by prohibiting one from borrowing money on interest or throwing one's own money into the sea. The example is al-Qarāfī's in *Furūq*, 1: 312.
56. Al-Ghazālī, *Shifāʾ al-ghalīl*, 160; cf. al-Rāzī, *Maḥṣūl*, 2: 320.
57. These examples receive discussion in several texts; see Opwis, Maṣlaḥa *and the Purpose of the Law*, 50–51, 106, and references there. The expression is from al-Juwaynī, *Burhān*, 2: 933.
58. Al-Juwaynī, *Burhān*, 937.
59. See Hallaq, *Islamic Legal Theories*, 112; Schacht, *An Introduction to Islamic Law*, 61.
60. Though in actual practice this was not so frequently the case. For a helpful overview of these notions, see Johansen, *Contingency in a Sacred Law*, chapter 4; "Ḥaqq."
61. Johansen, *Contingency in a Sacred Law*, 211–12.
62. See, for example, Ibn Taymiyya, *al-Siyāsa al-sharʿiyya fī iṣlāḥ al-rāʿī waʾl-raʿiyya*, 57, referring to God's rights: *al-ḥudūd waʾl-ḥuqūq allatī laysat li-qawm maʿniyyīn bal manfaʿatuhā li-muṭlaq al-muslimīn*. Cf. the reference to generalized harm (*al-fasād al-ʿāmm*) in speaking of brigandage (*muḥāraba*) (69); cf. Ibn Taymiyya, "Bāb al-qaṭʿ fiʾl-sariqa," in *Majmūʿ Fatāwā*, 34: 239.
63. Abd-allah's remark in "Theological dimensions of Islamic law," 243, that "in Islamic jurisprudence, the purpose of the rights of God is to uphold the ultimate objectives of the law" seems inaccurate in this respect.

64. The preservation of honor (*ʿirḍ*) was in fact listed as a sixth objective by some jurists. At the same time, the community has a stake in upholding goods that do not correspond to divine claims. The value of human life is a case in point: its preservation is included among the objectives of the Law, yet it is protected through a type of punishment (*qiṣāṣ*) that forms a private or human claim. There is in any case some artificiality in drawing the boundaries between these two kinds of claims too sharply, for reasons indicated in n144.
65. Zysow, *Economy of Certainty*, 346–47.
66. This would also question the view expressed by Weiss, quoted in the main text (*Search for God's Law*, 622), which seems to stress the status of these interests as goods that tend to the well-being of the human community—to the extent at least that this is intended as a characterization of the prerevelational or "rational" ethical viewpoint. Additional documentation of the textual grounds for this view would have been helpful for engaging it further. It is also worth recalling that the evaluative perspective of the social community was inscribed as a "higher-order" viewpoint normally inaccessible to the ordinary consciousness of individuals in the context of the Avicennan thought experiment appropriated by Ashʿarite theologians.
67. Al-Ghazālī, *Shifāʾ al-ghalīl*, 204.
68. Al-Qarāfī, *Nafāʾis al-uṣūl*, 7: 3450.
69. El Shamsy, "The wisdom of God's law."
70. See al-Rāzī, *Maḥṣūl*, 2: 332. Taking this to represent al-Rāzī's view involves taking a stance on the complex phenomena with which the *Maḥṣūl* presents one. Al-Rāzī's discussion of the causal nature of considerations of suitability is organized in two parts, representing two alternative explanations of this causality: one that presupposes that God acts to promote human welfare and one that does not (see, respectively, 2: 327–31, 332–44). The remarks on 2: 334 (with their reference to a *burhān qāṭiʿ*) and a comparison of his defense of the second position with the discussion of *taʿlīl afʿāl Allāh* in his *Arbaʿīn*—which includes an argument against God's purposefulness on the basis of God's creation of human acts, and thus of evil and disobedience (*Arbaʿīn*, 251), that is paralleled in the *Maḥṣūl*—argues strongly that al-Rāzī's sympathies lie with the latter view. See also on this topic Opwis, Maṣlaḥa *and the Purpose of the Law*, chapter 2.3, esp. 113–21; her discussion in "Attributing causality to God's Law" closely follows the book. Given the complexities of the evidence, Opwis's indecisive treatment of the topic—she opens by associating al-Rāzī with the first view ("Rāzī accepts that God's purpose in prescribing His rulings is the *maṣlaḥa* of humankind," 96) and concludes by hesitantly associating him with the second (120)—is not too helpful. Al-Raysuni attributes the first view to al-Rāzī in *Imam al-Shatibi's Theory of the Higher Objectives and Intents of Islamic Law*—he adopts a "firm, even enthusiastic position in defence of *taʿlīl* in relation to Islamic Law" (204; and see generally 197–205)—by apparently confining his attention exclusively to the

first part of al-Rāzī's discussion. My own understanding of al-Rāzī's position is aligned to Shihadeh's; see *Teleological Ethics of Fakhr al-Dīn al-Rāzī*, 98–101, where a translation of the central passage in al-Rāzī's discussion is offered.

71. See, for example, al-Āmidī, *Iḥkām*, 3: 411. Cf. the contrast between obligation and beneficence in al-Ghazālī, *Shifāʾ al-ghalīl*, 162; al-Qarāfī, *Sharḥ Tanqīḥ al-fuṣūl fī ikhtiṣār al-Maḥṣul fiʾl-uṣūl*, 92. Baghdādī Muʿtazilites construed God's obligations even more broadly, ascribing to God a more general obligation to promote human interests in the mundane domain as well.
72. Al-Āmidī, *Iḥkām*, 3: 411. The second part of this remark is awkward, yet it seems clear that the *lāzim minhu* refers us to our epistemological need to draw such a conclusion. Cf. Frank's distinction between the practical and absolute viewpoint in the legal usage of the notions of reason and purpose in "Moral obligation in classical Muslim theology," 214. Al-Āmidī's ensuing discussion in the *Iḥkām* is perplexing on a different level, though, as he goes on to offer a surprising affirmation—an affirmation indeed on rational grounds—of God's wisdom and purposefulness that would seem to conflict with the Ashʿarite position as he himself had expressed it in *Ghāyat al-marām*; see *Iḥkām*, 3: 411–23.
73. Al-Rāzī, *Arbaʿīn*, 249.
74. Al-Qarāfī provides an interesting example: having affirmed God's sheer will as the uncaused preponderating factor in his *Nafāʾis al-uṣūl*, as we saw, he appears to offer a direct disavowal of this view in *Sharḥ Tanqīḥ al-fuṣūl*, 92, where he accepts the role of interests in determining legal values.
75. The quote is from Ibn Taymiyya, *Sharḥ al-Iṣbahāniyya*, 406. For the point about *istiqrāʾ*, see Ibn Taymiyya, *Nubuwwāt*, 1: 465–66, and also the manuscript variant in *Sharḥ al-Iṣbahāniyya*, 705n6.
76. Ibn Taymiyya, *Bayān talbīs*, 2: 8, 7. The same point is rehearsed in Ibn Taymiyya, *Sharḥ al-Iṣbahāniyya*, 421.
77. ʿAbd al-Jabbār, *Taklīf*, 59. See also Ibn Mattawayh, *Majmūʿ*, 1: 265; cf. 1: 235. Given these strong expressions of epistemic limitation, I am unsure that Abū Isḥāq al-Shirāzī's expression of a similar point (we may not know the interests God's laws serve), noted by Chaumont in "La notion de *wajh al-ḥikmah* dans les *uṣūl al-fiqh* d'Abū Isḥāq al-Shīrāzī," 47–48, distances him from Muʿtazilism as much as Chaumont suggests.
78. Ibn ʿAqīl, *Wāḍiḥ*, 4b: 366, speaking more narrowly of ritual acts: once we know that God in His wisdom only institutes rulings for the sake of welfare (*maṣāliḥ*), we know for certain on the general level (*fiʾl-jumla*) that all prescribed acts serve our welfare even if we do not know the *wajh al-maṣlaḥa* in a given case. For Ibn Taymiyya's remark, see *Darʾ taʿāruḍ*, 8: 55–56; his appropriation of Ibn ʿAqīl's view may be placed in the context of a positive (and changed) attitude to this otherwise controversial Ḥanbalite thinker, as noted by Makdisi in *Ibn ʿAqil*, 48–49. In this light it will be interesting to note that in several places Ibn Taymiyya criticizes the Muʿtazilites—or *certain* Muʿtazilites—for undertaking

detailed accounts of God's wisdom (e.g., "Fī qudrat al-rabb ʿazza wa-jalla," in *Majmūʿ Fatāwā*, 8: 38). Perhaps he has in mind the type of proposal developed by the Muʿtazilite-minded legal theorist al-Qaffāl al-Shāshī, as described by Reinhart in "Ritual action and practical action," 74–76.

79. Ibn Taymiyya, *Sharḥ al-Iṣbahāniyya*, 449; Ibn Taymiyya, "Risāla fiʾl-Iḥtijāj biʾl-qadar," in *Majmūʿ Fatāwā*, 8: 345.
80. Ibn Taymiyya, "Risāla fiʾl-Iḥtijāj biʾl-qadar," in *Majmūʿ Fatāwā*, 8: 363.
81. See, for example, Mānkdīm, *Sharḥ al-Uṣūl*, 302: God is essentially knowing (*ʿālim bi-dhātihi*), and as such must know all things from the respect, or under the description, in which it is possible for them to be known; one of these descriptions (*wujūh*) is their ethical quality.
82. Ibn Taymiyya, "Ḥadīth innī ḥarramtu al-ẓulm ʿalā nafsī," in *Majmūʿ Fatāwā*, 18: 148–49; and see the discussion on the ensuing pages.
83. Note, for example, Ibn Taymiyya's insistence that God "deserves praise for that which He bound himself to" and his insistence that "this injustice which God forbade Himself is indeed *injustice* without a doubt" (ibid., 18: 151, 156).
84. Ibn Taymiyya, "Taʿāruḍ al-ḥasanāt aw-al-sayyiʾāt," in *Majmūʿ Fatāwā*, 20: 48; "Ḥadīth innī ḥarramtu al-ẓulm ʿalā nafsī," in *Majmūʿ Fatāwā*, 18: 157.
85. The particular expression is from Ibn Taymiyya, "Fī kawn al-rabb ʿādilan," in *Jāmiʿ al-rasāʾil*, 1: 141, but similar expressions appear widely, as we have seen.
86. Ibn Taymiyya, *Sharḥ al-Iṣbahāniyya*, 449; Ibn Taymiyya, *Radd*, 422.
87. Ibn Taymiyya, "Al-Ḥasana waʾl-sayyiʾa," in *Majmūʿ Fatāwā*, 14: 300.
88. Ibn Taymiyya, *Darʾ taʿāruḍ*, 8: 475; Ibn Taymiyya, "Suʾila ʿan abyāt fiʾl-jabr," in *Majmūʿ Fatāwā*, 8: 512.
89. Ibn Taymiyya, "Al-Ḥasana waʾl-sayyiʾa," in *Majmūʿ Fatāwā*, 14: 276; "Taʿāruḍ al-ḥasanāt aw-al-sayyiʾāt," in *Majmūʿ Fatāwā*, 20: 48.
90. Though there is a more complex story to be told at this juncture. For a finer-grained study of Ibn Taymiyya's view of human action, see Hoover, *Ibn Taymiyya's Theodicy of Perpetual Optimism*, chapter 4.
91. Ibn Taymiyya, "Al-Ḥasana waʾl-sayyiʾa," in *Majmūʿ Fatāwā*, 14: 276, read in conjunction with Ibn Taymiyya, *Darʾ taʿāruḍ*, 8: 476–77.
92. This is a moral intuition that is paradoxically often voiced by Ashʿarite theologians in polemics against Muʿtazilite views: see, for example, al-Anṣārī, *Ghunya*, 2: 1042; al-Rāzī, *Maṭālib*, 3: 325. This is not to say that problematic situations do not arise in ordinary human life in which we might rule that sacrificing the fewer for the many is the right choice—as indeed Muslim jurists debating the dilemmatic wartime situation of "human shields" frequently concluded (see chapter 5). What will partly make the ethical difference here is whether we experience this as a loss as against a choice without moral remainder; and part of the question, as will emerge in the main text shortly, is why God (Himself not prisoner to the contingencies of the human world that make such tragic conflicts unavoidable) should be compelled to suffer this loss.

93. Ibn Taymiyya, "Risāla fi'l-Iḥtijāj bi'l-qadar," in *Majmūʿ Fatāwā*, 8: 362–63.
94. For this distinction and some of Ibn Taymiyya's remarks on the topic of love versus will, see indicatively "Fī qawlihi taʿālā innamā qawlunā li-shay' idhā aradnāhu," in *Majmūʿ Fatāwā*, 8: 187–90; "Hal arāda Allāh taʿālā al-maʿṣiyya min khalqihi am lā?," in *Majmūʿ Fatāwā*, 8: 159–60; "Aqwam mā qila," in *Majmūʿ Fatāwā*, 8: 131; "Qāʿida fi'l-muʿjizāt wa'l-karāmāt," in *Majmūʿ Fatāwā*, 11: 355 ff. The accuracy of Ibn Taymiyya's representation of the Ashʿarite position could be questioned, as the conflation of will and love is associated more narrowly with al-Juwaynī, whose view, however, did not command uniform assent among later Ashʿarites. Al-Rāzī is a case in point, having not only distinguished between will and love but indeed proposed the very kind of distinction between prescriptive and creative wills that Ibn Taymiyya champions. Al-Ghazālī, similarly, clearly affirms the distinction between what God loves and what God hates; see, for example, *Iḥyā'*, 4: 78 ff. (cf. the distinction between *irāda* and *maḥabba* in 4: 77). This distinction also emerges in the discussion of marriage considered earlier in this chapter. On this point, see Hoover's survey at *Ibn Taymiyya's Theodicy of Perpetual Optimism*, 128–29, and Bell's discussion of the Ashʿarite position in *Love Theory in Later Ḥanbalite Islam*, chapter 3.
95. Cf. Ibn Taymiyya's phrasing in *Dar' taʿāruḍ*, 8: 476: God did not create something He had commanded because "it would *necessitate* [*yastalzimu*] forgoing something else He had commanded which He loved more."
96. On this topic, see Lovejoy's classic study, *The Great Chain of Being*.
97. See Ormsby, *Theodicy in Islamic Thought* and for Neiman's remark, *Evil in Modern Thought*, 27.
98. In one of the few locations where Ibn Taymiyya cites al-Ghazālī's view, he does so approvingly, with what seems like a perfunctory consideration of the challenge it poses to God's power and only a glancing proviso to secure the latter: "Fī kawn al-rabb ʿādilan," in *Jāmiʿ al-rasā'il*, 1: 141–42 (and see the foregoing discussion for several expressions of the view that God does what is best). Compare Hoover's remarks in *Ibn Taymiyya's Theodicy of Perpetual Optimism*, 224–27.
99. Ibn Taymiyya, "Aqwam mā qīla," in *Majmūʿ Fatāwā*, 8: 89–90, and more positively "Al-Ḥasana wa'l-sayyi'a," in *Majmūʿ Fatāwā*, 14: 309–10, and "Fī qudrat al-rabb ʿazza wa-jalla," in *Majmūʿ Fatāwā*, 8: 35–36, which is translated in Hoover, *Ibn Taymiyya's Theodicy of Perpetual Optimism*, 97.
100. See, for example, ʿAbd al-Jabbār, *Taklīf*, 134, for a paradigmatic statement of this point.
101. For the distinction between these types of praise (and love), see Ibn Taymiyya, "Al-Ḥasana wa'l-sayyi'a," in *Majmūʿ Fatāwā*, 14: 300 ff.; "Fi'l-furūq allatī yatabayyanu bihā kawn al-ḥasana min Allāh," in *Majmūʿ Fatāwā*, 8: 207 ff.; "Al-Tuḥfa al-ʿirāqiyya," in *Majmūʿ Fatāwā*, 10: 47–48, 84–85. The distinction between types of praise is certainly not original to Ibn Taymiyya. See, for example, al-Anṣārī's reference to this distinction in *Ghunya*, 2: 1027.

102. For the distinction between these types of *tawḥīd*, a good starting place is Ibn Taymiyya's commentary on *al-Fātiḥa* (in *Majmūʿ Fatāwā*, 14: 1–40); see also Hoover, *Ibn Taymiyya's Theodicy of Perpetual Optimism*, 26–29. The centrality of worship in Ibn Taymiyya's thought is likewise stressed by Laoust in *Essai sur les doctrines sociales et politiques de Takī-d-Dīn Aḥmad b. Taymīya*, 177–78.
103. Ibn Taymiyya, "Tafsīr sūrat al-Fātiḥa," in *Majmūʿ Fatāwā*, 14: 34.
104. Some of the bases for these remarks can be found concentrated in Ibn Taymiyya, "Risāla fiʾl-Iḥtijāj biʾl-qadar," in *Majmūʿ Fatāwā*, 8: 303 ff., in which the way we distinguish actions from our perspective as appetitive natural beings (*al-farq al-ṭabīʿī*) and the way God distinguishes them from *His* perspective (*al-farq min jihat al-ḥaqq taʿālā*) forms a key theme. A nodal point in Ibn Taymiyya's criticism of the Ashʿarites' failure to represent God as an object of intrinsic love is their treatment of the beatific vision (e.g., 8: 344–45). Again, there is a question to be asked about the justice of the above line of criticism. Al-Rāzī, for example, seems to have acknowledged God both as a subject and an object of love, as suggested by Shihadeh in *Teleological Ethics of Fakhr al-Dīn al-Rāzī*, 113–14. Al-Ghazālī provides the most obvious counterexample to Ibn Taymiyya's thesis in eloquently affirming the human love of God in the *Iḥyāʾ*. His view of *God's* love for human beings is more open to question, as across different works he presses an image of God's indifference; see, for example, *Iqtiṣād*, 194; *Iḥyāʾ*, 4: 76: human beings' "happiness lies in their nearness to [God]," yet "God has no need of them, whether they draw near or remain far." Ibn Taymiyya, of course, also affirms God's needlessness; just how this affirmation can be reconciled with the affirmation of God's love is a key question in reconstructing his account, as both Bell and Hoover show.
105. This relationship has sometimes been slow to be acknowledged due to Ibn Taymiyya's well-known polemics against particular Sufi tendencies and schools, notably Ibn ʿArabī's monism. The influence of Sufi spirituality on Ibn Taymiyya's thought was emphasized by Laoust in *Essai sur les doctrines sociales et politiques de Takī-d-Dīn Aḥmad b. Taymīya*, 89–93, and Ibn Taymiyya's Sufi credentials have been argued by Makdisi in "Ibn Taymiyya: A Ṣūfī of the Qādiriyya order,"; but see also here Meier, "The cleanest about predestination," 309–34, including the remarks on 317–18n9. See also more broadly Makdisi, "The Ḥanbalite school and Ṣūfism"; Michot, "Ibn Taymiyya's commentary on the *Creed* of al-Ḥallāj" and references there, as well as the commentary and translations in Michot's *Against Extremisms*; and Anjum, "Sufism without mysticism?"
106. Ibn Taymiyya, "Aqwam mā qīla," in *Majmūʿ Fatāwā*, 8: 144. Cf. Bell, *Love Theory in Later Ḥanbalite Islam*, 72: "God's love for himself is necessarily the greatest of all loves, and his love for certain men and their acts is subordinate to this first love."
107. See also in this connection n144.

108. Ibn Taymiyya does not mention blame and punishment explicitly, yet his ensuing reference to pleasure and pain signals that he naturally has both in mind (*Nubuwwāt*, 1: 453). Cf. the remark in Ibn Taymiyya, "Risāla fi'l-Iḥtijāj bi'l-qadar," in *Majmūʿ Fatāwā*, 8: 309.
109. This is visible at many junctures of Muʿtazilite discussions of reward and punishment, which are throughout grounded in arguments of a rational sort; for example, it is the hardship (*mashaqqa*) that obligations entail that makes reward necessary from a rational point of view, as briefly stated by al-Zamakhsharī in *A Muʿtazilite Creed of az-Zamakhšarî*, 73. Cf. Mānkdīm's succinct remark in *Sharḥ al-Uṣūl*, 619: *ammā istiḥqāq al-ʿiqāb, fa'lladhī yadullu ʿalayhi al-ʿaql wa'l-samʿ ayḍan.*
110. As the (Baṣran) Muʿtazilites, for example, had; see my *Moral Agents and Their Deserts*, 95–102.
111. Al-Juwaynī, *Burhān*, 1: 308.
112. Al-Ghazālī, *Iḥyā'*, 1: 99. Compare al-Ghazālī, *Iqtiṣād*, 185: "If God imposes obligations on people and they obey Him, He is not obliged to reward them—He will reward them if He so pleases, and He will punish them if He so pleases."
113. This is what I take away from the remarks relayed by Ibn Fūrak, *Mujarrad*, 163; note the description of believers' versus unbelievers' respective reward and punishment as "surely" or "inevitably" taking place (*kā'in lahum lā maḥāla*). Compare Abū Yaʿlā's remarks in the *Muʿtamad*, 213–15: *law ʿadhdhaba ahl samāwātihi wa-arḍihi ibtidā'an lā ʿalā dhanb sābiq minhum kāna ḥukman ʿadlan*—yet He has in fact made certain promises which it is *impossible* that He would renege on (cf. 120).
114. Al-Ghazālī, *Mustaṣfā*, 1: 28. Cf. al-Āmidī, *Iḥkām*, 1: 138: *al-wujūb al-sharʿī ʿibāra ʿan khiṭāb al-shāriʿ bimā yantahiḍu tarkuhu sababan li'l-dhamm sharʿan fī ḥāla mā.*
115. See, for example, the powerful passage in al-Ghazālī, *Iḥyā'*, 4: 77–78.
116. Ibn Fūrak, *Mujarrad*, 131, as translated in Griffel, *Al-Ghazālī's Philosophical Theology*, 126, with a small modification. As the above indicates, there are more probing questions one could ask regarding the relevance of Ibn Taymiyya's criticisms, which would require a far closer study of the complex and evolving Ashʿarite views on the topic. Griffel's book provides a good gateway to these: see, for example, the conspectus of pre-Ghazālian Ashʿarite views in chapter 5.
117. Ibn Taymiyya, "Al-Ḥasana wa'l-sayyi'a," in *Majmūʿ Fatāwā*, 14: 342. Cf. Ibn Taymiyya, "Fī kawn al-rabb ʿādilan," in *Jāmiʿ al-rasā'il*, 1: 126: *lā yajzī aḥadan illā bi-dhanbihi.*
118. Ibn Taymiyya, "Fī anna al-tawba wa'l-istighfār yakūnu min tark al-wājibat wa-fiʿl al-muḥarramāt," in *Majmūʿ Fatāwā*, 11: 686. While this condition affects the case of punishment, blame and praise are apparently taken to attach to actions even prior to the Law (686); to deny this would after all involve denying that people consider actions blameworthy and praiseworthy. Cf. *Dar' taʿāruḍ*,

8: 492, where Ibn Taymiyya uses stronger causal language in speaking of these consequences: *[al-afʿāl] muttaṣifa bi-ṣifāt ḥasana wa-sayyiʾa taqtaḍī al-ḥamd waʾl-dhamm.*

119. Ibn Taymiyya, "Risāla fī dukhūl al-janna, hal yadkhulu aḥad al-janna bi-ʿamalihi," in *Jāmiʿ al-rasāʾil*, 1: 152.
120. Ibn Taymiyya, "Al-Ḥasana waʾl-sayyiʾa," in *Majmūʿ Fatāwā*, 14: 261.
121. Hoover, *Ibn Taymiyya's Theodicy of Perpetual Optimism*, 164.
122. Ibn Taymiyya, *Radd*, 94.
123. ʿAbd al-Jabbār, *Tanabbuʾāt*, 65. Cf. Ibn Mattawayh, *Majmūʿ*, 3: 435: "the desert of reward is pursuant upon the intrinsic obligatoriness" of an act (*yatbaʿu wujūbahu fī nafsihi*). I say "on one level" because there were a number of more general explanations that Baṣran Muʿtazilites offered in this context, for example, tying the necessity of reward to the difficulty (*mashaqqa*) morally good acts involve.
124. For a slower unpacking of these claims, see my *Moral Agents and Their Deserts*, chapter 4.
125. Al-Rāzī, *Arbaʿīn*, 246. Cf. al-Qarāfī's transcription of the contentious Muʿtazilite view as the claim that evil acts "contain a quality *on account of* which their agent deserves blame [*al-qabīḥ huwa al-mushtamil ʿalā ṣifa li-ajlihā yastaḥiqqu ṣāḥibuhu al-dhamm*]" (*Sharḥ Tanqīḥ al-fuṣūl*, 90).
126. Al-Rāzī, *Arbaʿīn*, 389; cf. Ibn Fūrak, *Mujarrad*, 99.
127. Ibn Taymiyya, *Nubuwwāt*, 1: 464–65. Cf. Ibn Taymiyya, "Suʾila ʿan abyāt fiʾl-jabr," in *Majmūʿ Fatāwā*, 8: 468.
128. Ibn Taymiyya, "Al-Ḥasana waʾl-sayyiʾa," in *Majmūʿ Fatāwā*, 14: 297–98.
129. See the discussion in al-Rāzī, *Maṭālib*, 3: 323–36.
130. See Ibn Taymiyya, "Ḥadīth innī ḥarramtu al-ẓulm ʿalā nafsī," in *Majmūʿ Fatāwā*, 18: 187–89. Cf. Ibn Taymiyya, *Qāʿida fiʾl-maḥabba*, 152, speaking of victims of adultery: "Victims of justice may exact their rights [*lahu istīfāʾ ḥaqqihi*] either in this world or the next."
131. Ibn Taymiyya, *Minhāj al-sunna*, 1: 467.
132. Ibn Taymiyya, "Suʾila ʿan ḥadīth . . . inna Allāh qabaḍa qabḍatayn," in *Majmūʿ Fatāwā*, 8: 70; Ibn Taymiyya, "Hal yadkhulu aḥad al-janna bi-ʿamalihi," in *Jāmiʿ al-rasāʾil*, 1: 148.
133. See "Hal yadkhulu aḥad al-janna bi-ʿamalihi," in *Jāmiʿ al-rasāʾil*, 1: 145–52, for Ibn Taymiyya's fuller reason-giving. For this kind of Ashʿarite argument, see al-Juwaynī, *Irshād*, 382. The reasoning with which al-Juwaynī pairs it on the next page—our obedience to God is owed to Him by way of gratitude (*shukr al-niʿma*) and cannot generate further claims—reflects that of Baghdādī Muʿtazilites, who grounded the necessity of human obedience in the backward-looking obligation to gratitude, so that reward then appeared as an act of beneficence (*jūd*) rather than an obligation grounded in human desert. See briefly Mānkdīm, *Sharḥ al-Uṣūl*, 617–19. For more on the Baghdādī view, its

competitors, and its historical fate, see Zysow, "Two theories of the obligation to obey God's commands."

134. Ibn Taymiyya, "Ḥaqīqat kasb al-ʿabd mā hiya," in *Majmūʿ Fatāwā*, 8: 397. Ibn Taymiyya tantalizingly refers to God's enclosing in actions a "feature that *leads* to reward" (*khāṣṣa tufḍī ilaʾl-thawāb*), but this does not receive clarification. Cf. Hoover's conclusion in *Ibn Taymiyya's Theodicy of Perpetual Optimism*, 158 (emphasis added): "God has *made* deeds causes of reward and punishment just as He has made poison a cause of illness and illness a cause of death."
135. For Hoover's point, see *Ibn Taymiyya's Theodicy of Perpetual Optimism*, 219. This parsing of his concern is in places explicitly brought out by Ibn Taymiyya, as in the remark in "Ḥadīth innī ḥarramtu al-ẓulm ʿalā nafsī," in *Majmūʿ Fatāwā*, 18: 143–44: *min al-ẓulm al-manfiyy ʿuqūbat man lam yudhnib*. As a conception of divine justice, this has clear Qur'anic bases: see, for example, Q 68: 35 (*a-fa-najʿalu al-muslimīn kaʾl-mujrimīn*), Q 38: 28, Q 45: 21.
136. This phrase is from Ibn Taymiyya, "Al-Qiyās fiʾl-sharʿ al-Islāmī," in *Majmūʿ Fatāwā*, 20: 505–6, speaking of legal analogy (which exemplifies this form of rationality), but it is in the *Radd* that this view is developed with special directness. I would certainly argue that the notions of divine wisdom and justice often shade into each other; the concept of rationality discussed in the main text is sometimes associated with both.
137. That is, injustice involves trespassing against another's property or sovereign domain or transgressing against an order, and neither is conceivable in God's case. See briefly Gimaret, *La doctrine d'al-Ashʿarī*, 442–43 (though compare the qualification in Ibn Fūrak, *Mujarrad*, 148); cf. al-Ghazālī, *Iqtiṣād*, 183–84.
138. Ibn Taymiyya, "Fī kawn al-rabb ʿādilan," in *Jāmiʿ al-rasāʾil*, 1: 123–24. For further discussion of Ibn Taymiyya's view of justice, see Hoover, *Ibn Taymiyya's Theodicy of Perpetual Optimism*, 212–24.
139. Mānkdīm, *Sharḥ al-Uṣūl*, 348.
140. Rawls, "Two concepts of rules." My formulation in the main text also draws on Hart's reprise of this point in *Punishment and Responsibility*, chapter 1.
141. The phrase is awkward: *lam yakun maḥalluhā yanfaʿuhu illā mā yunāsibuhā*.
142. Ibn Taymiyya, "Al-Ḥasana waʾl-sayyiʾa," in *Majmūʿ Fatāwā*, 14: 343–44. Cf. "Kawn al-ḥasana min Allāh," in *Majmūʿ Fatāwā*, 8: 226.
143. Ibn Taymiyya, "Al-ʿAqīda al-Tadmuriyya," in *Majmūʿ Fatāwā*, 3: 27.
144. The transfiguration of actions into divine *ḥuqūq* through command and prohibition is after all the reason why the distinction between human and divine claims is a porous one. As al-Qarāfī points out, God has a claim over everything He commands and prohibits (*Furūq*, 1: 312: *ḥaqq Allāh amruhu wa-nahyuhu*); in this respect human claims derive their ultimate normative force by forming objects of God's command and prohibition: *mā min ḥaqq liʾl-ʿabd illā wa-fīhi ḥaqq li-llāh taʿālā wa-huwa amruhu bi-īṣāl dhālika al-ḥaqq ilā mustaḥiqqihi* (312).

Cf. Weiss's discussion of "higher-order" and "lower-order" obligation in *Search for God's Law*, 12–13.

145. Ibn Taymiyya, "Al-Ḥasana wa'l-sayyi'a," in *Majmū' Fatāwā*, 14: 278. This is also a central theme of the epistle "Mas'ala fīmā idhā kāna fi'l-'abd maḥabba"; see esp. the remark on 450: acting for the sake of the intrinsic value one perceives in certain actions, as against the sake of God, is insufficient to generate posthumous reward. Cf. Ibn Taymiyya, *Qā'ida fi'l-maḥabba*, 91: "Whoever loves or esteems something other than God for itself [*li-dhātihi*] commits idolatry."

146. Ibn Taymiyya, "Al-Ḥasana wa'l-sayyi'a," in *Majmū' Fatāwā*, 14: 273.

147. Ibn Taymiyya, "Aqwam mā qīla," in *Majmū' Fatāwā*, 8: 93. The specification of the prophets and the *salaf* is a brush stroke added in Ibn Taymiyya, *Dar' ta'āruḍ*, 8: 57.

148. Hoover, *Ibn Taymiyya's Theodicy of Perpetual Optimism*, 51, and see generally 48–52; cf. the remarks on justice on 219–20. Note also Hoover's remarks about Ibn Taymiyya's relative reticence (particularly when compared with Ibn Qayyim al-Jawziyya) regarding God's wisdom in "God's wise purposes in creating Iblis," 121.

149. Ibn Taymiyya, "Al-'Aqīda al-Tadmuriyya," in *Majmū' Fatāwā*, 3: 65.

150. Ibn Taymiyya explicitly brings together the "How?" and "Why?" questions in *Bayān talbīs*, 2: 3 ff., leading up to another statement of epistemic limitation: "Human minds are incapable of fathoming the intended end of [God's] actions" (8).

151. James, "Pragmatism's conception of truth," in *Pragmatism and Other Writings*, 88.

152. Hoover, *Ibn Taymiyya's Theodicy of Perpetual Optimism*, 25.

153. Ibn Taymiyya, "Kawn al-ḥasana min Allāh," in *Majmū' Fatāwā*, 8: 207; cf. 213.

154. Ibn Taymiyya, *Qā'ida fi'l-maḥabba*, 140, 114. This reflects the fact that the religious life often requires taking things on trust—trusting that its prescriptions will serve our good before we can see this fact for ourselves—as emphasized, among other places, in Ibn Taymiyya, *Sharḥ al-Iṣbahāniyya*, 683, using a familiar analogy with doctors.

155. The phrase is from Ibn Taymiyya, "Al-'Aqīda al-Tadmuriyya," in *Majmū' Fatāwā*, 3: 89–90. For Laoust's point, see *Essai sur les doctrines sociales et politiques de Taḳī-d-Dīn Aḥmad b. Taymīya*, 158.

156. Ibn Taymiyya, "Aqwam mā qīla," in *Majmū' Fatāwā*, 8: 106.

157. This pragmatic concern is strongly in evidence in Ibn Taymiyya's commentary on Q 4:78–79, much of it found in volume 14 of *Majmū' Fatāwā*. See, for example, 14: 223: "*If* you reflect on [the fact that your good deeds are the result of divine beneficence], you thank God and He gives you more; and if you know that evil only has its origin in you, you repent and it is removed." Cf. 319: one of the benefits (*fawā'id*) of believing that evil comes from oneself is that one does not trust in oneself (*al-'abd lā yarkunu ilā nafsihi*). As this suggests, the emphasis is placed differently depending on whether what is under consideration are good or bad deeds.

158. Ibn Taymiyya, "Suʾila ʿan ḥadīth . . . inna Allāh qabaḍa qabḍatayn," in *Majmūʿ Fatāwā*, 8: 70.
159. Both passages are cited in ibid.
160. Cf. the telling phrase in "Hal yadkhulu aḥad al-janna bi-ʿamalihi," in *Jāmiʿ al-rasaʾil*, 1: 151: *allā yuʿjaba al-ʿabd bi-ʿamalihi.*
161. The quote is from Ibn Taymiyya, "Ḥadīth innī ḥarramtu al-ẓulm ʿalā nafsī," in *Majmūʿ Fatāwā*, 18: 150. Ibn Taymiyya makes the conditioning role of beneficence clear on 202: *laysa wujūb dhālika ka-wujūb ḥuqūq al-nās baʿḍihim ʿalā baʿḍ, alladhī yakūnu ʿadlan lā faḍlan.* There is a real question to be asked as to how fundamentally this view diverges from the one expressed by Muʿtazilite theologians. Baṣran Muʿtazilites certainly applied the concept of obligation to God, but they also articulated this concept in conditional terms—as the product of a prior act of beneficence. See briefly Ibn Mattawayh, *Majmūʿ*, 1: 232: *ammā al-wājib fa-lan yathbuta fī fiʿlihi aṣlan ibtidāʾan . . .*; cf. 244: *al-wājib yatbaʿu mā qad tafaḍḍala bihi.* Compare also ʿAbd al-Jabbār's reference to "obligation" as being predicated of God "to the extent that God made [certain acts] obligatory upon Himself" (*Taʿdīl*, 34), which seems very close to Ibn Taymiyya's own wording. It is only after God imposes obligations on human beings that certain actions, such as providing them with assistance (*luṭf*) or rewarding them, become obligatory on Him. This view was at the forefront of the Baṣran quarrel with the Baghdādī view of God's obligation to do what is best, as Ibn Mattawayh makes clear in his reprise of the debate in *Majmūʿ*, 3: 130 ff.
162. See, for example, Ibn Taymiyya, "Al-Ḥasana waʾl-sayyiʾa," in *Majmūʿ Fatāwā*, 14: 260–61. God's beneficent action is often free and unconnected to humanly engendered antecedents (e.g., the benefits of life, health, livelihood enjoyed by the good and bad alike, God's merciful inclusion of the undeserving in paradise), whereas God's punitive action is always connected to the antecedent of human action.

CHAPTER 5

1. Ibn Taymiyya, "Qāʿida nāfiʿa fī wujūb al-iʿtiṣām biʾl-risāla," in *Majmūʿ Fatāwā*, 19: 99–100.
2. Ibn Taymiyya, "Risāla fiʾl-Iḥtijāj biʾl-qadar," in *Majmūʿ Fatāwā*, 8: 311; cf. "Al-ʿAqīda al-Tadmuriyya," in *Majmūʿ Fatāwā*, 3: 115: "The knowledge of the end [*ghāya*] which will be the resulting consequence of actions—whether bliss or misery *in the afterlife*—is only known through revelation."
3. For a conspectus of those of Ibn Taymiyya's writings with relevance to *uṣūl al-fiqh*, see Al-Matroudi, *The Ḥanbalī School of Law and Ibn Taymiyyah*, 27–30, and Krawietz, "Transgressive creativity in the making," 48–51 for an overview of Ibn Taymiyya's legal writings and of past research on his legal theory. Cf. the remarks by Opwis in Maṣlaḥa *and the Purpose of the Law*, 181–83; Opwis takes the nature of this textual basis as a reflection of a deliberate methodological positioning.

4. See Rapoport, "Ibn Taymiyya's radical legal thought," for further discussion of these cases.
5. Ibid., 217 (emphasis added).
6. For a brief overview of the principle, see Kamali, *Principles of Islamic Jurisprudence*, 436–38.
7. Opwis, Maṣlaḥa *and the Purpose of the Law*, 184–85. Opwis also refers to the broader legal precept that in cases where benefit and harm are both realized in an action, the ruling should be determined by the preponderant element. We will return to this shortly.
8. Al-Ghazālī, *Mustaṣfā*, 1: 284.
9. Ibid., 315. For brief discussions of unattested interests, see Zysow, *Economy of Certainty*, 394–99, and Kamali, *Principles of Islamic Jurisprudence*, chapter 13; in greater detail, see Opwis, Maṣlaḥa *and the Purpose of the Law*, s.v.
10. Jokisch, *Islamisches Recht in Theorie und Praxis*, 190.
11. See the discussion in al-Ghazālī, *Mustaṣfā*, 1: 294 ff. As will be evident, this case demands precisely the kind of weighing of costs and benefits (*tarjīḥ*) foregrounded by Ibn Taymiyya, as will emerge in the main text shortly. Unsurprisingly, Ibn Taymiyya brings it up in this very context in "Taʿāruḍ al-ḥasanāt aw-al-sayyiʾāt," in *Majmūʿ Fatāwā*, 20: 52–53, notably suggesting that the deciding interest at stake is religion rather than human life. Given the discussion to follow in the main text, it is interesting that al-Ghazālī himself indicates that the principle that the general takes precedence over the particular (which underpins his resolution of this conflict) is provided by the Law itself (*Mustaṣfā*, 1: 303).
12. Cf. Makari, *Ibn Taymiyyah's Ethics*, 103–4, in the context of a larger discussion of Ibn Taymiyya's jurisprudence; Makari tersely characterizes Ibn Taymiyya's stance on unattested interests as one of "less-than-enthusiastic acceptance."
13. See Ibn Taymiyya, "Qāʿida fiʾl-muʿjizāt waʾl-karāmāt," in *Majmūʿ Fatāwā*, 11: 342–43.
14. Rapoport, "Ibn Taymiyya's radical legal thought," 199.
15. See the remarks in Opwis, Maṣlaḥa *and the Purpose of the Law*, 198–99.
16. Jokisch, *Islamisches Recht in Theorie und Praxis*, 183 (Ibn Taymiyya's analogical use of the *ʿarāyā* contract, Jokisch notes, would have been a highly contestable one); see also his concentrated remarks on Ibn Taymiyya's view of *maṣlaḥa* at 187–95.
17. Kerr, *Islamic Reform*, 85 (emphasis added). See also Opwis's related remarks apropos al-Rāzī's approach, in Maṣlaḥa *and the Purpose of the Law*, 128–29.
18. Jokisch, *Islamisches Recht in Theorie und Praxis*, 193. For more on al-Ṭūfī's approach, see as a starting point Opwis, Maṣlaḥa *and the Purpose of the Law*, chapter 4.3 and references there.
19. Ibn Taymiyya, *Darʾ taʿāruḍ*, 8: 475; Ibn Taymiyya, "Taʿāruḍ al-ḥasanāt aw-al-sayyiʾāt," in *Majmūʿ Fatāwā*, 20: 48.

20. Ibn Taymiyya, "Taʿāruḍ al-ḥasanāt aw-al-sayyiʾāt," in *Majmūʿ Fatāwā*, 20: 51.
21. Ibn ʿAqīl, *Wāḍiḥ*, 4b: 355, using the expression *tarjīḥ aḥad al-ḍararayn ʿala ʾl-ākhar*. Cf. Ibn Taymiyya's remark ("Taʿāruḍ al-ḥasanāt aw-al-sayyiʾāt," in *Majmūʿ Fatāwā*, 20: 54): "The rational person [*ʿāqil*] is not the one who can tell what is good from what is bad; the rational person is the one who can tell what is the best of two goods and the worst of two evils." Ibn Taymiyya also invokes a medical example in the next paragraph, though it seems to refer us to the expert judgment of the doctor.
22. Ibn Taymiyya, "Taʿāruḍ al-ḥasanāt aw-al-sayyiʾāt," in *Majmūʿ Fatāwā*, 20: 58–59; cf. "Al-Ḥisba," in *Majmūʿ Fatāwā*, 28: 127 ff.
23. Ibn Taymiyya, "Al-Ḥisba," in *Majmūʿ Fatāwā*, 28: 129. Compare Baber Johansen's translation and discussion of this passage and the relevant duty in "A perfect Law in an imperfect society," 281–84. Johansen likewise places the accent on the importance of such active weighing of consequences, though it seems to me that his discussion otherwise calls stronger attention to the textualist aspects of Ibn Taymiyya's understanding (275: "In all questions concerning governance in the name of the sacred law, the Sultan uses his power in following the counsel of the scholar who bases his advice on a concept of . . . 'revealed law' as a complete and independent normative system that contains solutions to all problems"). Abou El Fadl also places the accent on this cost-benefit analysis in *Rebellion and Violence in Islamic Law*, 271–79, in the context of examining Ibn Taymiyya's view of rebellion. For further discussion of Ibn Taymiyya's view of this duty, see Cook, *Commanding Right and Forbidding Wrong in Islamic Thought*, chapter 7, esp. 151–57.
24. For all these examples (and the ones that follow in the main text), see Ibn Taymiyya, "Taʿāruḍ al-ḥasanāt aw-al-sayyiʾāt," in *Majmūʿ Fatāwā*, 20: 51–54.
25. This tradition is cited by Ibn Taymiyya in discussing the duty of commanding right and forbidding wrong in "Al-Ḥisba," in *Majmūʿ Fatāwā*, 28: 128.
26. See Abou El Fadl, *Rebellion and Violence in Islamic Law*, 271–79.
27. Ibn Taymiyya, "Al-Ḥisba," in *Majmūʿ Fatāwā*, 28: 129.
28. Opwis, Maṣlaḥa *and the Purpose of the Law*, 189; cf. Al-Matroudi, *The Ḥanbalī School of Law and Ibn Taymiyyah*, 80; Rapoport, "Ibn Taymiyya's radical legal thought," 199. The passage appears in "Qāʿida fiʾl-muʿjizāt waʾl-karāmāt," in *Majmūʿ Fatāwā*, 11: 344–45.
29. Opwis, Maṣlaḥa *and the Purpose of the Law*, 183. This is also the conclusion drawn by Meier, without an explicit yet with a transparent reference to this text, in "The cleanest about predestination," 312. Cf. Rapoport's gloss on this remark in "Ibn Taymiyya's radical legal thought," 199: "The definition of *maṣlaḥa* can potentially encompass all that is beneficial to human society, as long as it can be supported by an indicant from the revealed sources." A conservative stance is also reflected in the remarks on unattested interests in Ibn Taymiyya, *Qāʿida fi ʾl-maḥabba*, 37.
30. Ibn Taymiyya, "Qāʿida fiʾl-muʿjizāt waʾl-karāmāt," in *Majmūʿ Fatāwā*, 11: 344.

31. In this context it is worth noting that Opwis includes as an additional source of tension in Ibn Taymiyya's view his rejection of *maṣāliḥ mursala* and his approval of juristic preference (Maṣlaḥa *and the Purpose of the Law*, 182–83). For the latter, as Kerr notes, involves the preference of one analogy over another for reasons that amount to an appeal to *maṣlaḥa* (*Islamic Reform*, 89). See Opwis, "The construction of *madhhab* authority," for further discussion of Ibn Taymiyya's approach to *istiḥsān*.
32. Opwis, Maṣlaḥa *and the Purpose of the Law*, 190, emphasis added. Opwis's discussion of Ibn Taymiyya's ethical views is not the best guide to the topic, based as it is on a slender textual basis and hampered by a partial understanding of the Muʿtazilite position, which cannot be identified with the view that the value of actions depends on their consequences (192; see also 30). Opwis's conclusions are nevertheless close to (albeit more strongly worded than) my own: good and bad can be known by reason "though only in [the] form of the meaning given to them in the revelatory texts," and "independent from the law, the human intellect is unable to know what constitutes good in the eyes of God" (195, 196).
33. The terms used to parse the question shift between "actions" (*afʿāl*) and "things" (*ashyāʾ*, *aʿyān*). But the latter formulation should not obscure the fact that what was at issue was the human action of enjoying or using these things or goods. In the following I will simply refer to actions.
34. For more on this question and the relationship of different legal and theological schools to it, see Reinhart, *Before Revelation*. Ibn Taymiyya himself notes the close connection between questions about the status of actions prior to revelation and the role of reason in evaluative knowledge, so that taking a position on the former (a fortiori the position of permissibility) is intelligible only against a positive stance on the latter. See the remarks in Ibn Taymiyya, *Minhāj*, 1: 450–51.
35. Most of the points above draw on the discussion of the question in Āl Taymiyya, *Musawwada*, 474 ff. (esp. 485–87); Ibn ʿAqīl, *Wāḍiḥ*, 4b: 346 ff. Note Ibn ʿAqīl's highly evocative language in characterizing the question: *hādhā mafrūḍ mutawahham* (3: 195)—precisely the language used by those framing the other imaginaries referred to in the main text.
36. The edition of al-Kalwadhānī's *Tamhīd* has *sharʿ* without a definite article; Ibn Taymiyya uses *al-sharʿ*, though the editor also gives the indefinite form as a variant. My interpretation in the main text additionally draws on Ibn Taymiyya's reprise in drawing together two points that al-Kalwadhānī himself seems to present as separate ones. For this quote and the one that follows, see al-Kalwadhānī, *Tamhīd*, 4: 272; cf. Āl Taymiyya, *Musawwada*, 486.
37. Hallaq, *A History of Islamic Legal Theories*, 113.
38. Ibn Taymiyya, *Qawāʿid*, 165.
39. The example comes from ibid., 274.

40. Ibid., 281.
41. Ibid., 163.
42. Zysow, *Economy of Certainty*, 340; cf. Kamali, *Principles of Islamic Jurisprudence*, 351–52. Yet note al-Raysuni's relevant discussion in *Imam al-Shatibi's Theory of the Higher Objectives and Intents of Islamic Law*, 172 ff. And see now in greater detail Reinhart, "Ritual action and practical action."
43. Ibn Taymiyya, *Qawāʿid*, 281.
44. Ibid., 205.
45. There is a linguistic awkwardness here given that we often use the term "need," as against "desire," to pick out a subset of our desires that carries a more authoritative aspect. But it is of course possible to be mistaken as to whether one needs something, and thus to make fallible use of that vocabulary.
46. Geach, "The moral law and the law of God," 166.
47. For more on this, see Vasalou, *Moral Agents and Their Deserts*, 87–89. *Jāʾiz* and *ḥalāl* were terms also taken by the Baṣrans to refer to the same category; see, for example, ʿAbd al-Jabbār's discussion in *Taʿdīl*, 31–36.
48. For a fuller list of the relevant considerations, see Vasalou, *Moral Agents and Their Deserts*, 88.
49. Al-Kalwadhānī, *Tamhīd*, 4: 272.
50. ʿAbd al-Jabbār, *Taʿdīl*, 59.
51. Ibn Taymiyya, *Qawāʿid*, 276.
52. Hallaq, *A History of Islamic Legal Theories*, 113–15, emphasis in the penultimate remark added. Cf. Ibn Qudāma, *Rawḍat al-nāẓir*, 79: *hādhā ʿilm bi-ʿadam al-dalīl, lā ʿadam ʿilm al-dalīl.*
53. For a broader set of examples illustrating the operation of this principle, see Ibn ʿAqīl, *Wāḍiḥ*, 3: 190 ff. This principle was also invoked by some, including Ibn ʿAqīl himself, to argue for the default validity of previous divine laws.
54. On a variant: *mufassir.*
55. Ibn Taymiyya, *Qawāʿid*, 289. Compare al-Kalwadhānī's remarks on the need for (but also the limits to) such textual questing in *Tamhīd*, 4: 253; Ibn Qudāma, *Rawḍat al-nāẓir*, 79–80.
56. This is a verse with clear significance for this context; it is cited by Ibn Taymiyya in *Qawāʿid*, 276. It is worth keeping in mind that Ibn Taymiyya's view of the original status of actions is throughout grounded in considerations of a scriptural sort. The normative force of need is indicated in the Qur'an in several places, as we have seen, both in those verses that speak of the general concern of the Law to alleviate distress (*rafʿ al-ḥaraj*) (e.g., Q 22:78, Q 2:185, Q 4:28, cited in *Qawāʿid*, 204) and those that indicate the effect of necessity (*ḍarūra*) on legal strictures (e.g., Q 2:173, Q 5:3, cited in *Qawāʿid*, 205). The Qur'an also criticizes the introduction of unwarranted legislation that restricts people's enjoyment of licit goods—a criticism that Ibn Taymiyya's affirmation of the "permissibility" status was twinned with—for example, in the verse "O

believers, forbid not such good things as God has permitted you" (Q 5:87; cf. Q 10:59, Q 42:21, cited by Ibn Taymiyya in this context in *Qawāʿid*, 164). It is also worth noting that several writers took the status of *ibāḥa* to have been indicated by scripture, in statements such as "He it is Who created for you all that is in the earth" (Q 2:29) and "Who has forbidden the beautiful (gifts) of God which He brought forth for His servants, and the good things of His providing?" (Q 7:32). See al-Kalwadhānī, *Tamhīd*, 4: 281; Ibn Qudāma, *Rawḍat al-nāẓir*, 22. In this respect, as I take it, endorsing this qualification need not entail abandoning the view that revelation constitutes the qualifications of actions.

57. Ibn Taymiyya, "Al-Tawassul waʾl-wasīla," in *Majmūʿ Fatāwā*, 1: 264–65.
58. This account tries to unify tensions that find their reflection in the wavering readings that Ibn Taymiyya's commentators have offered on this aspect of his thought. A good example is provided by al-Badawī's *Maqāṣid al-sharīʿa ʿinda Ibn Taymiyya*; see esp. his discussion of the rational knowledge of interests at 291–98 and the discussion of unregulated interests at 351–59. On the one hand, al-Badawī takes Ibn Taymiyya (1) to affirm that reason provides us with an independent knowledge of certain interests, specifically where "customary" or "empirical" matters (*ʿādat, khibrāt, aʿrāf*) are concerned, and that it is permissible to take unattested interests into consideration in such matters. On the other hand, working with the well-thumbed passage of the "Qāʿida fiʾl-muʿjizāt waʾl-karāmāt," he takes Ibn Taymiyya (2) to deny that our rational understanding of welfare can serve as a legislative basis and to assert that reason must instead look to the Law to ascertain what the latter adjudges an interest. These readings seem to be in open tension; yet it is clear that al-Badawī's (1) rests heavily on some of the key passages of the *Qawāʿid* studied above, and as such is subject to the above reading of their epistemic limitations. Despite these ambivalent notes, al-Badawī's viewpoint falls in with the one I have outlined when he speaks of revelation as the foundation of reason (*al-naql huwa asās al-ʿaql*, 297).
59. Ibn Taymiyya, "Qāʿida nāfiʿa fī wujūb al-iʿtiṣām biʾl-risāla," in *Majmūʿ Fatāwā*, 19: 100.
60. The first remark is Abou El Fadl's in *Rebellion and Violence in Islamic Law*, 278; the second is Rapoport's in "Ibn Taymiyya's radical legal thought," 212.
61. For some expressions of this point, see chapter 1.
62. Michot, *Against Extremisms*, xxiv; Hallaq, *Ibn Taymiyya against the Greek Logicians*, li.
63. See my remarks on this point in *Moral Agents and Their Deserts*, 8–11.
64. ʿAbd al-Jabbār, *Taʿdīl*, 3.
65. Ibn Taymiyya, *Darʾ taʿāruḍ*, 8: 493; the explanation is from Ibn Taymiyya, "Al-Tawba waʾl-istighfār," in *Majmūʿ Fatāwā*, 11: 679.

66. Ibn Taymiyya, "Al-Tawba wa'l-istighfār," in *Majmū' Fatāwā*, 11: 680; see also the vicinity of this remark. Elsewhere Ibn Taymiyya ascribes this view to the "pious ancestors" or *salaf*, as we heard in chapter 1.
67. For an example of this kind of deployment, see 'Abd al-Jabbār, *Ta'dīl*, 113.
68. Cook, *Commanding Right and Forbidding Wrong in Islamic Thought*, 15; cf. Izutsu's discussion of these terms in *Ethico-Religious Concepts in the Qur'ān*, 213–17. See also here Hourani's discussion of the objectivist commitments of Qur'anic language in "Ethical presuppositions of the Qur'an," in *Reason and Tradition in Islamic Ethics*, 23–48.
69. Ibn Taymiyya, *Dar' ta'āruḍ*, 8: 456. The term *ma'rūf* is normally tied to actions, but note that elsewhere Ibn Taymiyya includes faith in God in its scope (e.g., 9: 375, *a'raf al- ma'rūf*).
70. Ibn Taymiyya, "Qā'ida nāfi'a fī wujūb al-i'tiṣām bi'l-risāla," in *Majmū' Fatāwā*, 19: 101.
71. For discussion of this, see Vasalou, *Moral Agents and Their Deserts*.
72. For a succinct presentation of this "law," see Ibn Taymiyya, *Dar' ta'āruḍ*, 1: 5; and see 8–13 for an exposition of the distinction between theological and philosophical interpretive approaches. For more on Ibn Taymiyya's key hermeneutical position in the *Dar'* (and the view of reason and revelation it involves), see Heer, "The priority of reason in the interpretation of scripture"; Abrahamov, "Ibn Taymiyya on the agreement of reason with tradition"; Anjum, *Politics, Law, and Community in Islamic Thought*, chapter 5. Several papers in the volume edited by Rapoport and Ahmed, *Ibn Taymiyya and His Times*, cast light on Ibn Taymiyya's polemics with the *mutakallimūn* on the question of hermeneutics. See particularly Özervarli, "The Qur'ānic rational theology of Ibn Taymiyya and his criticism of the *mutakallimūn*"; el Omari, "Ibn Taymiyya's 'theology of the Sunna' and his polemics with the Ash'arites." For a discussion of Ibn Taymiyya's own exegetical approach based on his *Muqaddima fī uṣūl al-tafsīr*, see Saleh, "Ibn Taymiyya and the rise of radical hermeneutics."
73. This term features in a statement that appears in the *Dar' ta'āruḍ* (9: 51) embedded in a characteristically thick wrapping of exegetical layers—as a commentary on a view of Ibn Ḥanbal's cited and commented on by al-Kalwadhānī, whose work Ibn Taymiyya is citing and commenting on—where Ibn Taymiyya distinguishes between "those who make out human reason to be a criterion [*mi'yār*] on the Sunna [*man ja'ala 'uqūl al-nās mi'yāran 'ala'l-sunna*]" and "those who make out reason to be in agreement with the Sunna [*man yaj'alu al-'uqūl muwāfiqa li'l-sunna*]," aligning Ibn Ḥanbal's view with the latter and implicitly claiming it as his own.
74. For all the above, see Ibn Taymiyya, *Dar' ta'āruḍ*, 1: 144–46; cf. 1: 156 ff., 1: 194 for a similar message.

75. Michot, "Vanités intellectuelles," 601, 600.
76. Ibid., 601. Cf. Anjum's similar reading of the significance of the epistemology of *fiṭra* in *Politics, Law, and Community in Islamic Thought,* chapter 5.
77. Ibn Taymiyya's discussion of this topic extends over volumes 7 (352 ff.) and 8 of the *Darʾ taʿāruḍ*. See 8: 17–18 for a quotation of Abuʾl-Ḥusayn al-Baṣrī that provides a particularly telling illustration of the dogmatic view of the progress of rational inquiry Ibn Taymiyya objects to.
78. Ibn Taymiyya, *Radd,* 249. For more on Ibn Taymiyya's project in the *Radd,* see Hallaq's introduction to *Ibn Taymiyya against the Greek Logicians*; Kügelgen, "Ibn Taymīyas Kritik an der aristotelischen Logik und sein Gegenentwurf," particularly the remarks on *fiṭra* at 192–99. Ibn Taymiyya's argument in the *Radd* reads like a direct response to the statement that appears early in Avicenna's *Najā* (9) regarding logic: "It is possible for sound human nature [*al-fiṭra al-salīma*] and sound taste to dispense with the need for learning grammar and prosody. Yet no human nature engaged in the employment of the reflective faculties can dispense with the effort to develop this instrument [*āla*]." The common denominator in both projects, theological and logical, is a strong drive against elitist approaches to human knowledge, an aspect of Ibn Taymiyya's program emphasized by several writers: see, for example, the expressions in Anjum, *Politics, Law, and Community in Islamic Thought,* 228–29; Michot, "A Mamlūk theologian's commentary on Avicenna's *Risāla Aḍḥawiyya,*" 171–72.
79. Ibn Taymiyya, *Darʾ taʿāruḍ,* 1: 133; cf. indicatively 1: 147, 1: 155.
80. Abrahamov, "Ibn Taymiyya on the agreement of reason with tradition," 272. A similar note seems to be struck by Heer in "The priority of reason in the interpretation of scripture," yet his categorical conclusion that "as a Ḥanbalite traditionalist Ibn Taymīyah held firmly to the position that scripture was in no way dependent on rational arguments, either for the establishment of its truth or for an explanation of its meaning" (191–92) is certainly too one-sided, for reasons to be set out shortly. Cf. Tamer's remarks in "The curse of philosophy," 370–74, in the context of an interesting discussion of contemporary presentations of Ibn Taymiyya as a philosopher.
81. See Abrahamov, *Islamic Theology,* 51.
82. Hoover, *Ibn Taymiyya's Theodicy of Perpetual Optimism,* 31. For Michot's remarks, see his introduction to *Lettre à Abû l-Fidâʾ*, 18. Michot describes the Qur'an and the prophetic Sunna as the peak "upon which the twin roads of reason and revelation meet again—and from which they depart." Talk of a "meeting place" suggests the independence of these roads, yet this seems to be immediately modified by talk of scripture as their common point of departure.
83. Ibn Taymiyya, *Darʾ taʿāruḍ,* 7: 394.
84. Ibid., 8: 491.

85. See Ibn Taymiyya, *Nubuwwāt*, 2: 904 ff., and also *Sharḥ al-Iṣbahāniyya*, 698–701; in both contexts he emphasizes the *empirical* basis of this knowledge. Cf. Hoover, *Ibn Taymiyya's Theodicy of Perpetual Optimism*, 219.
86. Ibn Taymiyya, "Al-ʿAqīda al-Tadmuriyya," in *Majmūʿ Fatāwā*, 3: 3.
87. Hoover, *Ibn Taymiyya's Theodicy of Perpetual Optimism*, 56; and see Ibn Taymiyya, "Al-ʿAqīda al-Tadmuriyya," in *Majmūʿ Fatāwā*, 3: 88 ff. for a clear development of this claim.
88. Hoover, *Ibn Taymiyya's Theodicy of Perpetual Optimism*, 68. For brief expositions of the a fortiori argument, see Ibn Taymiyya, *Bayān Talbīs*, 2: 345–50; *Darʾ taʿāruḍ*, 7: 322–24. The point is also cast more expressly in the vocabulary of *fiṭra*; it is by *fiṭra*, for example, that we know that God is truthful (*ṣādiq*) and that we know God's location above the world (His "aboveness"). See, respectively, Ibn Taymiyya, "Tafsīr sūrat Āl ʿImrān," in *Majmūʿ Fatāwā*, 14: 191–92; *Bayān talbīs*, 2: 454; *Darʾ taʿāruḍ*, 6: 12 (and ff.), to be read in its context.
89. Cf. Michot, *Lettre à Abû l-Fidâ'*, 17–19; Anjum, *Politics, Law, and Community in Islamic Thought*, 203–4.
90. A concentrated account of these kind of immanent Qur'anic proofs can be found, among other places, in Ibn Taymiyya, *Darʾ taʿāruḍ*, 1: 30–38.
91. This point registers with special directness in Ibn Taymiyya, "Tafsīr sūrat al-Nisāʾ," in *Majmūʿ Fatāwā*, 14: 437.
92. Ibn Taymiyya, *Darʾ taʿāruḍ*, 8: 37.
93. Ibn Taymiyya, *Radd*, 370.
94. Ibid., 371–72. Kügelgen discusses and translates some of the passages of the *Radd* relating to the notion of the "balance" or "scales" in "The poison of philosophy," 316–18; as she points out, Ibn Taymiyya's remarks on the topic are intended partly as a counter to the view that logic constitutes the scales for rational thought.
95. Ibn Taymiyya, *Radd*, 382.
96. Ibid. The term *qiyās* of course also refers us to legal analogy, which is elsewhere linked to the notion of justice, with the privileged (sound) analogy said to have been revealed by God. See, for example, Ibn Taymiyya, "Al-Qiyās fiʾl-sharʿ al-Islāmī," in *Majmūʿ Fatāwā*, 20: 504–505: *al-qiyās al-ṣaḥīḥ huwa alladhī waradat bihi al-sharīʿa . . . huwa min al-ʿadl alladhī baʿatha Allāh bihi rasūlahu*.
97. Ibn Taymiyya, *Radd*, 375. Cf. the remark that "the foundation of reason is sound nature [*mabnā al-ʿaql ʿalā ṣiḥḥat al-fiṭra*]" (323).
98. Ibn Taymiyya, *Sharḥ al-Iṣbahāniyya*, 180. Note Ibn Taymiyya's qualification of these proofs elsewhere as "known only through the Prophet," emphasizing our dependence on revelation for access to them (*Bayān Talbīs*, 2: 137).
99. See the Qur'anic evidence cited in Ibn Taymiyya, *Sharḥ al-Iṣbahāniyya*, 395. The embrace of this particular method, Ibn Taymiyya makes clear in this context and others, involves the rejection of the methods typically used by theologians and philosophers—what he here refers to, respectively, as *qiyās al-tamthīl* and *qiyās al-shumūl*.

100. Hoover, *Ibn Taymiyya's Theodicy of Perpetual Optimism*, 56, and see the continuation for Hoover's finer-grained view; his earlier discussion of Ibn Taymiyya's method in "Perpetual creativity in the perfection of God," as I understand it, also picked up on its responsive or apologetic character (see esp. 295). This conclusion seems to me to flow naturally from the opening passage of Ibn Taymiyya's relevant discussion in "Al-ʿAqīda al-Tadmuriyya" (in *Majmūʿ Fatāwā*, 3: 88): even though God's attributes can *also* be known by reason, it is the Qur'an that provides us with these rational arguments, and thus also with the facts they serve to establish. It is worth noting that the theological knowledge acquired by reason, whatever its direction or liberty, is one that Ibn Taymiyya construes in very limited terms given his view that only revelation provides a particularized knowledge of God's names and attributes (*maʿrifat Allāh bi-asmāʾihi wa-ṣifātihi ʿalā wajh al-tafṣīl*) (*Bayān talbīs*, 2: 137).
101. Ibn Taymiyya, *Sharḥ al-Iṣbahāniyya*, 39, 41.
102. Ibn Taymiyya, *Bayān Talbīs*, 2: 454. Note Ibn Taymiyya's qualification in this context that while God's elevation above the world is known by reason, God's sitting on the throne (*istiwāʾ*) is known by revelation. Cf. "Al-ʿAqīda al-Tadmuriyya," in *Majmūʿ Fatāwā*, 3: 49.
103. Ibn Taymiyya, *Darʾ taʿāruḍ*, 6: 14. The more complex story of Ibn Taymiyya's views would have to pass through a closer study of this particular volume of the *Darʾ taʿāruḍ* (and also of its counterpart discussions in the *Bayān Talbīis*), in which Ibn Taymiyya engages, among others, the philosophical deconstruction of this intuitive judgment as a false judgment of the estimation (*wahm*).
104. Ibn Taymiyya, *Darʾ taʿāruḍ*, 1: 146–47; cf. 166–68 (and circa), following another exposition of the disagreement and uncertainty reigning among philosophers and theologians: the cause of people's perception of conflict (*muʿāraḍa*) between reason and revelation lies in their willful distance (*iʿrāḍ*) from revelation—and the solution must lie in a return to it. Compare also the remarks in Ibn Taymiyya, *Sharḥ al-Iṣbahāniyya*, 431–32: the further away different groups are from prophetic guidance, the greater their internal disagreements.
105. The phrase is from Ibn Taymiyya, *Sharḥ al-Iṣbahāniyya*, 572.
106. Ibid., 548, 685, 687.
107. Hence the emphasis placed by Ibn Taymiyya and other writers on the pagan and corrupted forms of religion dominating the environment in which Muhammad grew up, and indeed on Muhammad's illiteracy (ibid., 687); cf. the emphasis on novelty at 550–51: "Has anyone said the same thing before him?"
108. Ibn Taymiyya, "Tafsīr sūrat al-Baqara," in *Majmūʿ Fatāwā*, 14: 79–80.
109. See, for example, ibid., 77–79; cf. Ibn Taymiyya's reprise of this account in *al-Siyāsa al-sharʿiyya*, 125–26. Compare al-Ghazālī's similar suggestion concerning the teleological purpose of the "parity" principle in the practice of *qiṣāṣ* in *Mustaṣfā*, 1: 288.
110. Ibn Taymiyya, "Tafsīr sūrat al-Baqara," in *Majmūʿ Fatāwā*, 14: 84.

111. Al-Shahrastānī, *Nihāyat al-iqdām*, 387–88.
112. Al-Juwaynī, *Irshād*, 260; cf. al-Bāqillānī's remarks in *Tamhīd*, 122, referring to the Muʿtazilite claim that it is known necessarily that it is obligatory to thank the benefactor: "What is the difference between you and those who say you know necessarily that this is not so?" Such doubts had surfaced much earlier; al-Jāḥiẓ's epistle "Min Kitāb al-Masāʾil waʾl-jawābāt fiʾl-maʿrifa" already provides a good document in this regard.
113. Ibn Taymiyya, "Tafsīr sūrat al-Baqara," in *Majmūʿ Fatāwā*, 14: 73, 84–85.
114. For Coulson's remarks, see *A History of Islamic Law*, 1–2. Cf. Weiss's remarks on the distinction between *fiqh* and *sharīʿa* in *The Search for God's Law*, 13–16.
115. Hallaq, *A History of Islamic Legal Theories*, 13. Two examples Hallaq considers are the pre-Islamic practice of *qasāma* and the charitable distribution of surplus money (*faḍl al-māl*), noting Ibn Ḥazm's acknowledgment of the Jāhilī origin of the former.
116. See the overview in Schacht, *Introduction to Islamic Law*, 13.
117. This attention is in evidence in many places in Ibn Taymiyya's discussion, which is peppered with references to pre-Islamic practices and the prerevelational horizon. See, for example, *Qawāʿid*, 277, referring to the pledges made in the Jāhiliyya period and which people were commanded to fulfill; 282, talking about the validity of contracts and acquisitions after the transition into Islam.
118. Coulson, *History of Islamic Law*, 17–18.
119. Ibn Qayyim al-Jawziyya, *Iʿlām al-muwaqqiʿīn ʿan rabb al-ʿālamīn*, 2: 103.
120. In this respect the simplest fact—that Ibn Taymiyya's discussion of retaliation takes the form of a Qur'anic commentary—is also the most revealing.
121. It is interesting in this connection to note the remarks Ibn Qayyim al-Jawziyya would later offer on the same topic, which emerge in the context of a broader discussion of the wise purposes underlying God's prescription of particular punishments—a discussion replete with Taymiyyan themes, including the emphasis on God's wisdom, on the human interests served by the Law, and on a concordance between what our reason or nature (*al-fiṭar waʾl-ʿuqūl*) indicates and what the Law commands. It is in this context that Ibn Qayyim is challenged to justify the practice of retaliation as an expression of divine wisdom—a wisdom, importantly, that we can *recognize* as such—given all the reasons that, rationally considered, seem to militate against it. In confronting this challenge, it is precisely the kind of ambivalence al-Shahrastānī earlier picked up on that Ibn Qayyim appears to engage directly. The crux of his reply is the following: in the balance of countervailing considerations—which are cast in terms of utility, as competing benefits and harms—there is greater benefit in the practice of retaliation than in its omission (*Iʿlām al-muwaqqiʿīn*, 2: 103: *al-mafsada allatī fī hādhihi al-ʿuqūba khāṣṣatan waʾl-maṣlaḥa al-ḥāṣila bihā aḍʿāf aḍʿāf tilka al-mafsada*). And here he refers to several of the considerations al-Shahrastānī discussed, such as deterrence, satisfaction of the desire for revenge, preservation of the human

species, the exacting of justice (2: 104; and see generally the discussion on 100 ff.). Ibn Qayyim's view amounts to a simple claim: the conflict between benefit-harm considerations that al-Shahrastānī had taken to be irresolvable *can* in fact be rationally resolved. Another juxtaposition of an assertion and its denial? All I would note are the commitments at work in both positions. Al-Shahrastānī: to claim that reason has no access to the value of actions, and revelation is required to inform us of the latter. Ibn Qayyim: to claim that reason does have such access and that what it informs us of agrees with what revelation prescribes.

122. Avicenna, *Najā*, 119. The same term appears in many other versions of the thought experiment, including al-Rāzī's (Ibn Taymiyya, *Radd*, 398; al-Rāzī, *Sharḥ al-Ishārāt*, 1: 269), as well as al-Shahrastānī's own reprisal in *Nihāyat al-iqdām*, 371–72.

CHAPTER 6

1. Al-Zuḥaylī, *Akhlāq al-Muslim*, 21.
2. Al-Qaraḍāwī, *al-Ḥalāl wa 'l-ḥarām*, 28.
3. Platti, "La théologie de Abū l-Aʿlā Mawdūdī,", 250.
4. Quṭb, *Fī Ẓilāl al-Qur'ān*, 5: 2767.
5. Griffel, "The harmony of natural law and Sharī'a in Islamist theology,", 55. See Quṭb, *Maʿālim fi 'l-ṭarīq*, particularly the chapter "Sharīʿa kawniyya," 93–104. One reproach to be registered against Griffel's otherwise illuminating essay is a habit of anachronistic reference, and more particularly of projecting the term *fiṭra* backward into the classical theological debates about value, for example, in his gloss of the Ashʿarite view as the claim that "Sharī'a cannot be part of *fitra*" (45) and his gloss of the Muʿtazilite and early Shī'ite view as the claim that "*fiṭra* . . . contain[s] the same rulings and laws that have been revealed by the divine law of Islam" (44). The term *fiṭra*, however, had been absent from the characteristic expressions of these views in the classical period.
6. Quṭb, *Fī Ẓilāl al-Qur'ān*, 6: 3917.
7. Griffel, "The harmony of natural law and Sharī'a in Islamist theology," 59–61.
8. Ibid., 53–54.
9. Ibid., 61.
10. Ibn Taymiyya, *Nubuwwāt*, 2: 890–91.
11. See Hallaq, *A History of Islamic Legal Theories*, chapter 6, particularly 214–31 ("Religious utilitarianism"), for an overview of such modern engagements. See also Opwis, "*Maṣlaḥa* in contemporary Islamic legal theory"; Johnston, "A turn in the epistemology and hermeneutics of twentieth century *uṣūl al-fiqh*," though his reading of the relationship of this "turn" to the classical theological field would benefit from a more nuanced view of the evaluative commitments of Ashʿarism as explored in this study.

12. See al-Fāsī, *Maqāṣid al-sharīʿa al-Islāmiyya wa-makārimuhā*, 8–9. The sharp distinction between *fiṭra* and *ṭabīʿa* will be interesting in light of our discussion in chapter 3, though al-Fāsī does not seem to sustain it with full consistency throughout the work. For further discussion of al-Fāsī's views, see Johnston, "ʿAllal al-Fāsī."
13. See, for example, al-Fāsī, *Maqāṣid al-sharīʿa*, 9: *mā kāna lahā an tastaqilla bi-nafsihā li-idrāk qawāʿid al-fiṭra*; cf. 19: *iktishāf al-fiṭra*. The distinction between actual and ideal is central to the distinction between *fiṭra* and *ṭabīʿa* al-Fāsī draws at the outset; the latter, he notes, consists of "what belongs to things intrinsically, and is not to be detached from them" (9).
14. Ibid., 74.
15. Ibid., 68. One is certainly reminded of Ibn Taymiyya's "revealed natural disposition" by a remark such as *jāʾat al-fiṭra taḥuddu min ghulawāʾ al-ṭabīʿa*, which casts *fiṭra* as an *event*. Cf. the telling phrase on 11–12: *al-khurūj ʿan al-ṭāʿa … khurūj ʿan al-fiṭra*. A more thorough study of al-Fāsī's account would be needed to read these tokens more confidently in their significance.
16. Quṭb, *Maʿālim fi ʾl-ṭarīq*, 99–100, as translated in Griffel, "The harmony of natural law and Sharīʿa in Islamist theology," 56.
17. Al-Qaraḍāwī, *al-Ḥalāl wa ʾl-ḥarām*, 29–30.
18. Starrett, *Putting Islam to Work*, chapter 1.
19. Ibid., chapter 3, section 5. See also the functionalized discussion of prayer and fasting in chapter 3, section 6.

Bibliography

WORKS IN ARABIC

ʿAbd al-Jabbār, Abuʾl-Ḥasan b. Aḥmad al-Hamadhānī al-Asadābādī. *Al-Mughnī fī abwāb al-tawḥīd waʾl-ʿadl.*

———. Vol. 6/1: *al-Taʿdīl waʾl-tajwīr*, ed. Aḥmad Fuʾād al-Ahwānī. Cairo: al-Muʾassasa al-Miṣriyya al-ʿĀmma liʾl-Taʾlīf waʾl-Tarjama waʾl-Ṭibāʿa waʾl-Nashr, 1962.

———. Vol. 11: *al-Taklīf*, ed. Muḥammad ʿAlī al-Najjār and ʿAbd al-Ḥalīm al-Najjār. Cairo: al-Dār al-Miṣriyya liʾl-Taʾlīf waʾl-Tarjama, 1965.

———. Vol. 14: *al-Aṣlaḥ/Istiḥqāq al-dhamm/al-Tawba*, ed. Muṣṭafā al-Saqā. Cairo: al-Muʾassasa al-Miṣriyya al-ʿĀmma liʾl-Taʾlīf waʾl-Anbāʾ waʾl-Nashr, al-Dār al-Miṣriyya liʾl-Taʾlīf waʾl-Tarjama, 1965.

———. Vol. 15: *al-Tanabbuʾāt waʾl-muʿjizāt*, ed. Maḥmūd al-Khuḍayrī and Maḥmūd Muḥammad Qāsim. Cairo: al-Muʾassasa al-Miṣriyya al-ʿĀmma liʾl-Taʾlīf waʾl-Anbāʾ waʾl-Nashr, al-Dār al-Miṣriyya liʾl-Taʾlīf waʾl-Tarjama, 1965.

ʿAbd al-Qādir, Muḥammad al-ʿArūsi. *Al-Masāʾil al-mushtaraka bayna uṣūl al-fiqh wa-uṣūl al-dīn*, 2nd ed. Mecca: Maktabat Rushd, n.d.

Al-Āmidī, Sayf al-Dīn Abuʾl-Ḥasan ʿAlī b. Abī ʿAlī. *Ghāyat al-marām fī ʿilm al-kalām*, ed. Ḥasan Maḥmūd ʿAbd al-Laṭīf. Cairo: al-Majlis al-Aʿlā liʾl-Shuʾūn al-Islāmiyya, Lajnat Iḥyāʾ al-Turāth al-Islāmī, 1971.

———. *Al-Iḥkām fī uṣūl al-aḥkām*. Beirut: Dār al-Kutub al-ʿIlmiyya, 1983. 4 vols.

Al-Anṣārī, Abuʾl-Qāsim Salmān b. Nāṣir. *Al-Ghunya fiʾl-kalām*, ed. Muṣṭafā Ḥasanayn ʿAbd al-Hādī. Cairo: Dār al-Salām, 2010. 2 vols.

Al-Ashʿarī, Abuʾl-Ḥasan ʿAlī b. Ismāʿīl. *Kitāb al-Lumaʿ fiʾl-radd ʿalā ahl al-zaygh waʾl-bidaʿ*, ed. Ḥammūda Ghurāba. Cairo: Maṭbaʿat Miṣr, 1955.

Avicenna. *See* Ibn Sīnā.

Al-Badawī, Yūsuf Aḥmad Muḥammad. *Maqāṣid al-sharīʿa ʿinda Ibn Taymiyya*. Amman: Dār al-Nafāʾis, 2000.

Al-Baghdādī, Abū Manṣūr ʿAbd al-Qāhir b. Ṭāhir. *Kitāb Uṣūl al-dīn*. Istanbul: Madrasat al-Ilāhiyyāt bi-Dār al-Funūn al-Turkiyya, 1928.

Al-Bāqillānī, Abū Bakr Muḥammad b. al-Ṭayyib. *Kitāb al-Tamhīd*, ed. Richard J. McCarthy. Beirut: al-Maktaba al-Sharqiyya, 1957.

———. *Al-Inṣāf fīmā yajibu iʿtiqāduhu wa-lā yajūzu al-jahl bihi*, ed. Muḥammad Zāhid bin al-Ḥasan al-Kawtharī. Cairo: Muʾassasat al-Khānjī, 1963.

Al-Fāsī, ʿAllāl. *Maqāṣid al-sharīʿa al-Islāmiyya wa-makārimuhā*. Beirut: Dār al-Gharb al-Islāmī, 1993.

Al-Ghazālī, Abū Ḥāmid Muḥammad b. Muḥammad. *Al-Mustaṣfā min ʿilm al-uṣūl*. Bulaq: al-Maṭbaʿa al-Amīriyya, 1322–24/1904–6. 2 vols.

———. *Iḥyāʾ ʿulūm al-dīn*. Cairo: Muṣṭafā al-Bābī al-Ḥalabī, 1346/1927. 4 vols. in 2.

———. *Miʿyār al-ʿilm fī fann al-manṭiq*, ed. Sulaymān Dunyā. Cairo: Dār al-Maʿārif, 1961.

———. *Al-Iqtiṣād fiʾl-iʿtiqād*, ed. Ibrahim Agâh Çubukçu and Hüseyin Atay. Ankara: Nur Matbaasi, 1962.

———. *Shifāʾ al-ghalīl fī bayān al-shabah waʾl-mukhīl wa-masālik al-taʿlīl*, ed. Ḥamad al-Kubaysī. Baghdad: Maṭbaʿat al-Irshād, 1971.

"Ḥaqq." *Al-Mawsūʿa al-fiqhiyya*, vol. 18. Kuwait: Wizārat al-Awqāf waʾl-Shuʾūn al-Islāmiyya, 1990.

Ibn ʿAbd al-Hādī, Abū ʿAbd Allāh Muḥammad b. Aḥmad. *Al-ʿUqūd al-durriyya min manāqib shaykh al-Islām ibn Taymiyya*, ed. Abū Muṣʿab Ṭalʿat ibn Fuʾād al-Ḥulwānī. Cairo: al-Fārūq al-Ḥadītha, 2002.

Ibn ʿAqīl, Abuʾl-Wafāʾ ʿAlī b. ʿAqīl. *Al-Wāḍiḥ fī uṣūl al-fiqh*, ed. George Makdisi. Beirut: Franz Steiner, 1996–2002. 4 vols. in 5 parts.

Ibn Barhān, Abuʾl-Fatḥ Aḥmad b. ʿAlī. *Al-Wuṣūl ilaʾl-uṣūl*, ed. ʿAbd al-Ḥamīd ʿAlī Abū Zunayd. Riyad: Maktabat al-Maʿārif, 1984. 2 vols.

Ibn al-Farrāʾ, Abū Yaʿlā Muḥammad b. al-Ḥusayn. *Al-Muʿtamad fī uṣūl al-dīn*, ed. Wadīʿ Zaydān Ḥaddād. Beirut: Dar al-Mashreq, 1974.

Ibn Fūrak, Abū Bakr Muḥammad b. al-Ḥasan. *Mujarrad Maqālāt al-shaykh Abiʾl-Ḥasan al-Ashʿarī*, ed. Daniel Gimaret. Beirut: Dar el-Machreq, 1987.

Ibn Mattawayh, Abū Muḥammad al-Ḥasan b. Aḥmad. *Al-Majmūʿ fiʾl-Muḥīṭ biʾl-taklīf*, ed. J. J. Houben, Daniel Gimaret, and Jan Peters. Beirut: al-Maṭbaʿa al-Kathūlīkiyya; Dar al-Machreq, 1965–99. 3 vols.

Ibn Qayyim al-Jawziyya, Shams al-Dīn Abū ʿAbd Allāh Muḥammad b. Abī Bakr. *Iʿlām al-muwaqqiʿīn ʿan rabb al-ʿālamīn*, ed. Muḥammad Muḥyī al-Dīn ʿAbd al-Ḥamīd. Cairo: al-Maktaba al-Tijāriyya al-Kubrā, 1955. 4 vols.

Ibn Qudāma, Muwaffaq al-Dīn ʿAbd Allāh b. Aḥmad. *Censure of Speculative Theology: An Edition and Translation of Ibn Qudama's Taḥrīm al-nazar fī kutub ahl al-kalām*, ed. and trans. George Makdisi. London: Luzac, 1962.

———. *Rawḍat al-nāẓir wa-jannat al-munāẓir fī uṣūl al-fiqh ʿalā madhhab al-Imām Aḥmad ibn Ḥanbal*. Beirut: Dār al-Kutub al-ʿIlmiyya, 1981.

Ibn Sīnā, Abū ʿAlī al-Ḥusayn b. ʿAbd Allāh. *Kitāb al-Shifāʾ: al-Manṭiq: al-Burhān*, ed. Abuʾl-ʿAlā ʿAfīfī. Cairo: Wizārat al-Tarbiyya waʾl-Taʿlīm, 1956.

———. *Al-Ishārāt waʾl-tanbīhāt, maʿa sharḥ Naṣīr al-Dīn al-Ṭūsī*, ed. Sulaymān Dunyā. Cairo: Dār al-Maʿārif, 1960. 3 vols.

———. *Kitāb al-Shifāʾ: al-Ṭabīʿiyyāt: al-Nafs*, ed. Georges Anawātī and Saʿīd Zāyid. Cairo: al-Hayʾa al-Miṣriyya al-ʿĀmma liʾl-Kitāb, 1965.

———. *Remarks and Admonitions, Part One: Logic*, trans. Shams Constantine Inati. Toronto: Pontifical Institute of Mediaeval Studies, 1984.

———. *Al-Najā min al-gharq fī baḥr al-ḍalālāt*, ed. Muḥammad Taqī Dānishpazhūh. Tehran: Intishārāt-i Dānishgāh-i Tehrān, 1364/1985.

Ibn Taymiyya, Taqī al-Dīn Abuʾl-ʿAbbās Aḥmad b. ʿAbd al-Ḥalīm. *Al-Radd ʿalaʾl-manṭiqiyyīn*, ed. ʿAbd al-Ṣamad Sharaf al-Dīn al-Kutubī. Bombay: al-Maṭbaʿa al-Qayyima, 1949.

———. "Masʾala fīmā idhā kāna fiʾl-ʿabd maḥabba limā huwa khayr wa-ḥaqq wa-maḥmūd fī nafsihi," ed. Muḥammad Rashād Sālim. In *Dirāsāt Islāmiyya wa-ʿArabiyya muhdā ilā adīb al-ʿArabiyya al-kabīr Abī Fihr Maḥmūd Muḥammad Shākir*, ed. Ayman Fuʾād Sayyīd, Aḥmad Ḥamdī Imām, al-Ḥassānī Ḥasan ʿAbd Allāh, 435–55. Cairo: Maṭbaʿat al-Madanī, 1982.

———. *Al-Siyāsa al-sharʿiyya fī iṣlāḥ al-rāʿī waʾl-raʿiyya*. Beirut: Dār al-Āfāq al-Jadīda, 1983.

———. *Jāmiʿ al-rasāʾil*, ed. Muḥammad Rashād Sālim, 2nd ed. Jeddah: Dār al-Madanī, 1984. 2 vols.

———. *Minhāj al-sunna al-nabawiyya fī naqḍ kalām al-Shīʿa al-qadariyya*, ed. Muḥammad Rashād Sālim. Riyad: Jāmiʿat al-Imām Muḥammad ibn Saʿūd al-Islāmiyya, 1986. 9 vols.

———. *Darʾ taʿāruḍ al-ʿaql waʾl-naql*, ed. Muḥammad Rashād Sālim, 2nd ed. Riyad: al-Mamlaka al-ʿArabiyya al-Saʿūdiyya, Wizārat al-Taʿlīm al-ʿĀlī, Jāmiʿat al-Imām Muḥammad ibn Saʿūd al-Islāmiyya, 1991. 11 vols.

———. *Majmūʿ Fatāwā shaykh al-Islām Aḥmad ibn Taymiyya*. Beirut: Muʾassasat al-Risāla, 1997; reprint of original 1381–86/1961–67 Riyad edition. 37 vols.

———. *Kitāb al-Nubuwwāt*, ed. ʿAbd al-ʿAzīz bin Ṣāliḥ al-Ṭawayān. Riyad: Maktabat Aḍwāʾ al-Salaf. 2000. 2 parts in 1.

———. *Al-Qawāʿid al-nūrāniyya al-fiqhiyya*, ed. Aḥmad ibn Muḥammad al-Khalīl. Dammam: Dār Ibn al-Jawzī, 1422/2001.

———. *Qāʿida fiʾl-maḥabba*, ed. Muḥammad ibn Riyāḍ al-Aḥmad al-Atharī. Beirut: ʿĀlam al-Kutub, 2005.

———. *Bayān talbīs al-jahmiyya fī taʾsīs bidaʿihim al-kalāmiyya*, ed. Yaḥyā b. Muḥammad al-Hunaydī, et al. Medina: Mujammaʿ al-Malik Fahd, 2005. 10 vols.

———. *Sharḥ al-Iṣbahāniyya*, ed. Muḥammad bin ʿAwda al-Saʿawī. Riyad: Dār al-Minhāj, 1430/2009.

Ibn Taymiyya, Āl (Majd al-Dīn, Shihāb al-Dīn, and Taqī al-Dīn). *Al-Musawwada fī uṣūl al-fiqh*, ed. Muḥammad Muḥyī al-Dīn ʿAbd al-Ḥamīd. Cairo: Maṭbaʿat al-Madanī, 1964.

Ibn Ṭufayl, Abū Bakr Muḥammad b. ʿAbd al-Malik. *Hayy ben Yaqdhân*, ed. Léon Gauthier. Beirut: Imprimerie Catholique, 1936.

Al-Jāḥiẓ, Abū ʿUthmān ʿAmr b. Baḥr b. Maḥbūb. *Rasāʾil al-Jāḥiẓ*, ed. ʿAbd al-Salām Muḥammad Hārūn. Cairo: Maktabat al-Khānjī, 1964–79. 4 vols in 2.

———. "Min Kitāb al-Masāʾil waʾl-jawābāt fiʾl-maʿrifa," ed. Charles Pellat. *Al-Machriq*, 63 (1969), 315–26.

Al-Juwaynī, Abuʾl-Maʿālī ʿAbd al-Malik b. ʿAbd Allāh. *Kitāb al-Irshād ilā qawāṭiʿ al-adilla fī uṣūl al-iʿtiqād*, ed. Muḥammad Yūsuf Mūsa and ʿAlī ʿAbd al-Munʿim ʿAbd al-Ḥamīd. Cairo: Maktabat al-Khānjī, 1950.

———. *Al-Burhān fī uṣūl al-fiqh*, ed. ʿAbd al-ʿAẓīm al-Dīb. Doha, 1399/1978 or 1979. 2 vols.

———. *Al-ʿAqīda al-Niẓāmiyya fiʾl-arkān al-Islāmiyya*, ed. Muḥammad Zāhid al-Kawtharī. Cairo: al-Maktaba al-Azhariyya, 1992.

———. *Kitāb al-Talkhīṣ fī uṣūl al-fiqh*, ed. ʿAbd Allāh Jawlam al-Nībālī and Shubbayr Aḥmad al-ʿUmarī, 2nd ed. Beirut: Dār al-Bashāʾir al-Islamiyya, 2007.

Al-Kalwadhānī, Abuʾl-Khaṭṭāb Maḥfūẓ b. Aḥmad. *Al-Tamhīd fī uṣūl al-fiqh*, ed. Mufīd Muḥammad Abū ʿAmsha and Muḥammad ibn ʿAlī ibn Ibrāhīm. Mecca: Jāmiʿat Umm al-Qurā, Markaz al-Baḥth al-ʿIlmī wa-Iḥyāʾ al-Turāth al-Islāmī, 1985. 4 vols.

Mānkdīm Shashdīw, Abuʾl-Ḥusayn Aḥmad b. Abī Hāshim. *[Taʿlīq] Sharḥ al-Uṣūl al-khamsa*, ed. ʿAbd al-Karīm ʿUthmān. Cairo: Maktabat Wahba, 1965.

Al-Qaraḍāwī, Yūsuf. *Al-Ḥalāl waʾl-ḥarām fiʾl-Islām*, 13th ed. Beirut: al-Maktab al-Islāmī, 1980.

Al-Qarāfī, Shihāb al-Dīn Abuʾl-ʿAbbās Aḥmad b. Idrīs. *Sharḥ Tanqīḥ al-fuṣūl fī ikhtiṣār al-Maḥṣul fiʾl-uṣūl*, ed. Ṭāhā ʿAbd al-Raʾūf Saʿd. Cairo: Maktabat al-Kulliyyāt al-Azhariyya and Dār al-Fikr, 1973.

———. *Nafāʾis al-uṣūl fī sharḥ al-Maḥṣūl*, ed. ʿĀdil Aḥmad ʿAbd al-Mawjūd and ʿAlī Muḥammad Muʿawwaḍ. Mecca: Maktabat Nazār Muṣṭafā al-Bāz, 1997. 9 vols.

———. *Kitāb al-Furūq: Anwār al-burūq fī anwāʾ al-furūq*, ed. Muḥammad ʿUthmān. Cairo: Maktabat al-Thaqāfa al-Dīniyya, 2009. 4 vols.

Quṭb, Sayyid. *Maʿālim fiʾl-ṭarīq*, 6th ed. Beirut: Dār al-Shurūq, 1979.

———. *Fī Ẓilāl al-Qurʾān*, 32nd ed. Beirut: Dār al-Shurūq, 2003. 30 vols. in 6.

Al-Rāzī, Fakhr al-Dīn Abū ʿAbd Allāh Muḥammad b. ʿUmar. *Al-Arbaʿīn fī uṣūl al-dīn*. Hyderabad: Dāʾirat al-Māʿarif al-ʿUthmāniyya, 1353/1934.

———. *Al-Maṭālib al-ʿāliya min al-ʿilm al-ilāhī*, ed. Aḥmad Ḥijāzī al-Saqā. Beirut: Dār al-Kitāb al-ʿArabī, 1987. 9 vols. in 5.

———. *Al-Maḥṣul fī ʿilm uṣūl al-fiqh*. Beirut: Dār al-Kutub al-ʿIlmiyya, 1988. 2 vols.

———. *Sharḥ al-Ishārāt waʾl-tanbīhāt*, ed. ʿAlī Riḍā Najafzādeh. Tehran: Anjuman-i Āthār va Mafākhir-i Farhangī, 2005. 2 vols.

Al-Shahrastānī, Tāj al-Dīn Abu'l-Fatḥ Muḥammad b. ʿAbd al-Karīm. *Nihāyat al-iqdām fī ʿilm al-kalām*, ed. Alfred Guillaume. London: Oxford University Press, 1934.

Al-Shāmī, Rizq Yūsuf. "Ibn Taymiyya: Maṣādiruhu wa-manhajuhu fī taḥlīlihā." *Majallat Maʿhad al-Makhṭūṭāt al-ʿArabiyya*, 38 (1994), 183–269.

Al-Sijzī, Abū Naṣr ʿUbayd Allāh ibn Saʿīd. *Risālat al-Sijzī ilā ahl Zabīd fi'l-radd ʿalā man ankara al-ḥarf wa'l-ṣawt*, ed. Muḥammad ibn Karīm ibn ʿAbd Allāh. Riyad: Dār al-Rāya, 1994.

Al-Tawḥīdī, Abū Ḥayyān, and Miskawayh, Abū ʿAlī. *Al-Hawāmil wa'l-shawāmil*, ed. Aḥmad Amīn and al-Sayyid Aḥmad Ṣaqr. Cairo: Lajnat al-Taʾlīf wa'l-Tarjama wa'l-Nashr, 1951.

Al-Ṭūfī, Najm al-Dīn Abu'l-Rabīʿ Sulaymān b. ʿAbd al-Qawī. *Darʾ al-qawl al-qabīḥ bi'l-taḥsīn wa'l-taqbīḥ*, ed. Ayman Shihadeh. Riyad: Markaz al-Malik Fayṣal li'l-Buḥūth wa'l-Dirāsāt al-Islāmiyya, 2005.

Al-Zamakhsharī, Jār Allāh Abu'l-Qāsim Maḥmūd b. ʿUmar. *A Muʿtazilite Creed of az-Zamakhšarî (d. 538/1144): Al-Minhağ fî uṣûl ad-dîn*, ed. and trans. Sabine Schmidtke. Stuttgart: Deutsche Morgendländische Gesellschaft, 1997.

Al-Zuḥaylī, Wahba. *Akhlāq al-Muslim*, vol. 2: *ʿAlāqatuhu bi'l-nafs wa'l-kawn*. Damascus: Dār al-Fikr, 2005.

WORKS IN EUROPEAN LANGUAGES

Abd-allah, Umar F. "Theological dimensions of Islamic law." In *The Cambridge Companion to Classical Islamic Theology*, ed. Tim Winter, 237–57. Cambridge: Cambridge University Press, 2008.

Abou El Fadl, Khaled. *Rebellion and Violence in Islamic Law*. Cambridge: Cambridge University Press, 2001.

Abrahamov, Binyamin. "Ibn Taymiyya on the agreement of reason with tradition." *Muslim World*, 82 (1992), 256–72.

———. *Islamic Theology: Traditionalism and Rationalism*. Edinburgh: Edinburgh University Press, 1998.

Adang, Camilla. "Islam as the inborn religion of mankind: the concept of *fiṭra* in the works of Ibn Ḥazm." *Al-Qanṭara*, 21 (2000), 391–410.

Ahmed, Shahab. "Ibn Taymiyyah and the Satanic verses." *Studia Islamica*, 87 (1998), 67–124.

Anjum, Ovamir. "Sufism without mysticism? Ibn Qayyim al-Ğawziyyah's objectives in *Madāriğ al-sālikīn*." In *A Scholar in the Shadow: Essays in the Legal and Theological Thought of Ibn Qayyim al-Ğawziyyah*, ed. Caterina Bori and Livnat Holtzman, *Oriente Moderno*, 90 (2010), 161–88.

———. *Politics, Law, and Community in Islamic Thought: The Taymiyyan Moment*. Cambridge: Cambridge University Press, 2012.

Annas, Julia. *The Morality of Happiness*. New York: Oxford University Press, 1993.

Aristotle. *Nicomachean Ethics*, trans. Robert C. Bartlett and Susan D. Collins. Chicago: University of Chicago Press, 2011.

Bell, Joseph Norment. *Love Theory in Later Ḥanbalite Islam*. Albany: State University of New York Press, 1979.

Bernand, Marie. "La critique de la notion de nature (*ṭabʿ*) par le *kalām*." *Studia Islamica*, 51 (1980), 59–101.

Black, Deborah L. "Estimation (*wahm*) in Avicenna: The logical and psychological dimensions." *Dialogue*, 32 (1993), 219–58.

———. "Avicenna on self-awareness and knowing that one knows." In *The Unity of Science in the Arabic Tradition*, ed. Shahid Rahman, Tony Street, and Hassan Tahiri, 63–87. Dordrecht: Springer, 2008.

———. "Certitude, justification, and the principles of knowledge in Avicenna's epistemology." In *Interpreting Avicenna: Critical Essays*, ed. Peter Adamson, 120–42. Cambridge: Cambridge University Press, 2013.

Bori, Caterina. "A new source for the biography of Ibn Taymiyya." *Bulletin of the School of Oriental and African Studies*, 67 (2004), 321–48.

———. "The collection and edition of Ibn Taymīyah's works: concerns of a disciple." *Mamlūk Studies Review*, 13.2 (2009), 47–67.

———. "Ibn Taymiyya *wa-jamāʿatuhu*: authority, conflict and consensus in Ibn Taymiyya's circle." In *Ibn Taymiyya and His Times*, ed. Yossef Rapoport and Shahab Ahmed, 23–52. Karachi: Oxford University Press, 2010.

Chaumont, Éric. "La notion de *wajh al-ḥikmah* dans les *uṣūl al-fiqh* d'Abū Isḥāq al-Shīrāzī (m. 476/1083)." In *Islamic Law in Theory: Studies in Jurisprudence in Honor of Bernard Weiss*, ed. Robert Gleave and Kevin Reinhart, 39–53. Leiden: Brill, 2014.

Cook, Michael. *Commanding Right and Forbidding Wrong in Islamic Thought*. Cambridge: Cambridge University Press, 2004.

Crone, Patricia. "Barāhima." *Encyclopaedia of Islam*. 3rd ed. Brill Online, 2014. Accessed 7.10.14.

Coulson, Noel. *A History of Islamic Law*. Edinburgh: Edinburgh University Press, 1964.

El Omari, Racha. "Ibn Taymiyya's 'theology of the Sunna' and his polemics with the Ashʿarites." In *Ibn Taymiyya and His Times*, ed. Yossef Rapoport and Shahab Ahmed, 101–19. Karachi: Oxford University Press, 2010.

El-Rouayheb, Khaled. "From Ibn Ḥajar al-Haytamī (d. 1566) to Khayr al-Dīn al-Ālūsī (d. 1899): changing views of Ibn Taymiyya among non-Ḥanbalī Sunni scholars." In *Ibn Taymiyya and His Times*, ed. Yossef Rapoport and Shahab Ahmed, 269–318. Karachi: Oxford University Press, 2010.

El Shamsy, Ahmed. "The wisdom of God's law: two theories." In *Islamic Law in Theory: Studies in Jurisprudence in Honor of Bernard Weiss*, ed. Robert Gleave and Kevin Reinhart, 19–37. Leiden: Brill, 2014.

Ess, Josef van. *Zwischen Hadith und Theologie*. Berlin: Walter de Gruyter, 1975.

Fakhry, Majid. *Ethical Theories in Islam*. Leiden: Brill, 1994.
———. *Islamic Philosophy, Theology, and Mysticism: A Short Introduction*. Oxford: Oneworld Publications, 1997.
Frank, Richard M. "Moral obligation in classical Muslim theology." *Journal of Religious Ethics*, 11 (1983), 204–23.
———. *Creation and the Cosmic System: al-Ghazâlî and Avicenna*. Heidelberg: Carl Winter, 1992.
———. *Al-Ghazālī and the Ashʿarite School*. Durham, NC: Duke University Press, 1994.
Frede, Dorothea. "Pleasure and pain in Aristotle's ethics." In *The Blackwell Guide to Aristotle's* Nicomachean Ethics, ed. Richard Kraut, 255–75. Malden, MA: Blackwell, 2006.
Geach, Peter. "The moral law and the law of God." Reprinted from *God and the Soul*, in *Divine Commands and Morality*, ed. Paul Helm, 165–74. Oxford: Oxford University Press, 1981.
Gimaret, Daniel. *La doctrine d'al-Ashʿarī*. Paris: Cerf, 1990.
Gobillot, Geneviève. "L'épître du discours sur la *fiṭra* (*Risāla fī-l-kalam ʿalā-l-fiṭra*) de Taqī-l-Din Aḥmad Ibn Taymīya (661/1262–728/1328): Présentation et traduction annotée." *Annales Islamologiques*, 20 (1984), 29–53.
———. *La conception originelle: ses interprétations et fonctions chez les penseurs musulmans*. Cairo: Institut Français d'Archéologie Orientale, 2000.
Griffel, Frank. "The harmony of natural law and Shari'a in Islamist theology." In *Shari'a: Islamic Law in the Contemporary Context*, ed. Abbas Amanat and Frank Griffel, 38–61. Stanford: Stanford University Press, 2007.
———. *Al-Ghazālī's Philosophical Theology*. Oxford: Oxford University Press, 2009.
———. "Al-Ghazālī's use of 'original human disposition' (*fiṭra*) and its background in the teachings of al-Fārābī and Avicenna." *Muslim World*, 102 (2012), 1–32.
Gutas, Dimitri. *Avicenna and the Aristotelian Tradition*. Leiden: Brill, 1988.
———. "Medical theory and scientific method in the age of Avicenna." In *Before and After Avicenna*, ed. David C. Reisman, 145–62. Leiden: Brill, 2003.
———. "The empiricism of Avicenna." *Oriens*, 40 (2012), 391–436.
Hallaq, Wael B. "Ibn Taymiyya on the existence of God." *Acta Orientalia*, 52 (1991), 49–69.
———. "*Uṣūl al-fiqh*: beyond tradition." *Journal of Islamic Studies*, 3 (1992), 172–202.
———. *Ibn Taymiyya against the Greek Logicians*. Oxford: Clarendon Press, 1993.
———. *A History of Islamic Legal Theories*. Cambridge: Cambridge University Press, 1997.
Hart, Herbert L. A. *Punishment and Responsibility: Essays in the Philosophy of Law*. 2nd ed. Oxford: Oxford University Press, 2008.
Hasse, Dag Nikolaus. *Avicenna's* De Anima *in the Latin West: The Formation of a Peripatetic Philosophy of the Soul, 1160-1300*. London: Warburg Institute, 2000.

Heer, Nicholas. "The priority of reason in the interpretation of scripture: Ibn Taymīyah and the *Mutakallimūn*." In *Literary Heritage of Classical Islam: Arabic and Islamic Studies in Honor of James Bellamy*, ed. Mustansir Mir, 181–95. Princeton, NJ: Darwin Press, 1993.

Hildebrandt, Thomas. "Waren Ǧamāl ad-Dīn al-Afġānī und Muḥammad ʿAbduh Neo-Muʿtaziliten?" *Die Welt der Islam*, 42 (2002), 207–62.

———. *Neo-Muʿtazilismus? Intention Und Kontext Im Modernen Arabischen Umgang Mit Dem Rationalistischen Erbe Des Islam*. Leiden: Brill, 2007.

Hobbes, Thomas. *Leviathan*, ed. Richard Tuck. Cambridge: Cambridge University Press, 1996.

Holtzman, Livnat. "Human choice, divine guidance and the *fiṭra* tradition." In *Ibn Taymiyya and His Times*, ed. Yossef Rapoport and Shahab Ahmed, 163–88. Karachi: Oxford University Press, 2010.

Hoover, Jon. "Perpetual creativity in the perfection of God: Ibn Taymiyya's hadith commentary on God's creation of this world." *Journal of Islamic Studies*, 15 (2004), 287–329.

———. "Ibn Taymiyya as an Avicennan theologian: a Muslim approach to God's self-sufficiency." *Theological Review*, 27 (2006), 34–46.

———. *Ibn Taymiyya's Theodicy of Perpetual Optimism*. Leiden: Brill, 2007.

———. "God's wise purposes in creating Iblis: Ibn Qayyim al-Ǧawziyyah's theodicy of God's names and attributes." In *A Scholar in the Shadow: Essays in the Legal and Theological Thought of Ibn Qayyim al-Ǧawziyyah*, ed. Caterina Bori and Livnat Holtzman, *Oriente Moderno*, 90 (2010), 113–34.

Hourani, George F. *Islamic Rationalism*. Oxford: Clarendon Press, 1971.

———. *Reason and Tradition in Islamic Ethics*. Cambridge: Cambridge University Press, 1985.

Hume, David. *Enquiries Concerning Human Understanding and Concerning the Principles of Morals*, ed. L. A. Selby-Bigge, rev. P. H. Nidditch. 3rd ed. Oxford: Clarendon Press, 1975.

———. *A Treatise of Human Nature*, ed. L. A. Selby-Bigge, rev. P. H. Nidditch. 2nd ed. Oxford: Clarendon Press, 1978.

Izutsu, Toshihiko. *Ethico-Religious Concepts in the Qurʾān*. Montreal: McGill-Queen's University Press, 2002.

Jackson, Sherman A. *Islamic Law and the State: The Constitutional Jurisprudence of Shihāb al-Dīn al-Qarāfī*. Leiden: Brill, 1996.

———. "The alchemy of domination? Some Ashʿarite responses to Muʿtazilite ethics." *International Journal of Middle East Studies*, 31 (1999), 185–201.

James, William. *Pragmatism and Other Writings*. New York: Penguin, 2000.

Janssens, Jules L. "'Experience' (*tajriba*) in classical Arabic philosophy (al-Fārābī–Avicenna)." *Quaestio*, 4 (2004), 45–62.

Jokisch, Benjamin. *Islamisches Recht in Theorie und Praxis: Analyse Einiger Kaufrechtlicher Fatwas von Taqī'd-Dīn Aḥmad b. Taymiyya*. Berlin: Klaus Schwarz, 1996.

Johansen, Baber. *Contingency in a Sacred Law: Legal and Ethical Norms in the Muslim* Fiqh. Leiden: Brill, 1999.

———. "A perfect Law in an imperfect society: Ibn Taymiyya's concept of 'governance in the name of the sacred Law.'" In *The Law Applied: Contextualizing the Islamic Shari'a,* ed. Peri Bearman, Wolfhart Heinrichs, and Bernard G. Weiss, 259–94. London: I. B. Tauris, 2008.

Johnston, David L. "A turn in the epistemology and hermeneutics of twentieth century *uṣūl al-fiqh." Islamic Law and Society,* 11.2 (2004), 233–82.

———. "ʿAllal al-Fāsī: Shari'a as blueprint for righteous global citizenship?" In *Shari'a: Islamic Law in the Contemporary Context,* ed. Abbas Amanat and Frank Griffel, 83–103. Stanford: Stanford University Press, 2007.

Kamali, Muhammad Hashim. *Principles of Islamic Jurisprudence.* Cambridge: Islamic Texts Society, 2003.

Kerr, Malcolm. *Islamic Reform: The Political and Legal Theories of Muḥammad ʿAbduh and Rashīd Riḍā.* Berkeley: University of California Press, 1966.

Knysh, Alexander D. *Ibn ʿArabi in the Later Islamic Tradition: The Making of a Polemical Image in Medieval Islam.* Albany: State University of New York Press, 1999.

Krawietz, Birgit. "Transgressive creativity in the making: Ibn Qayyim al-Ǧawziyyah's reframing within Ḥanbalī legal methodology." In *A Scholar in the Shadow: Essays in the Legal and Theological Thought of Ibn Qayyim al-Ǧawziyyah,* ed. Caterina Bori and Livnat Holtzman, *Oriente Moderno,* 90 (2010), 43–62.

Kügelgen, Anke von. "Ibn Taymīyas Kritik an der aristotelischen Logik und sein Gegenentwurf." In *Logik und Theologie: Das* Organon *im Arabischen und im Lateinischen Mittelalter,* ed. Dominik Perler and Ulrich Rudolph, 167–225. Leiden: Brill, 2005.

———. "The poison of philosophy: Ibn Taymiyya's struggle for and against reason." In *Islamic Theology, Philosophy and Law: Debating Ibn Taymiyya and Ibn Qayyim al-Jawziyya,* ed. Birgit Krawietz and Georges Tamer, 253–328. Berlin: De Gruyter, 2013.

Laoust, Henri. *Essai sur les doctrines sociales et politiques de Taḳī-d-Dīn Aḥmad b. Taymīya.* Cairo: Imprimerie de l'Institut Francais d'Archéologie Orientale, 1939.

———. "L'influence d'Ibn-Taymiyya." In *Islam: Past Influence and Present Challenge,* ed. Alford T. Welch and Pierre Cachia, 15–33. Edinburgh: Edinburgh University Press, 1979.

Leaman, Oliver, and Rizvi, Sajjad. "The developed *kalām* tradition." In *The Cambridge Companion to Classical Islamic Theology,* ed. Tim Winter, 77–96. Cambridge: Cambridge University Press, 2008.

Little, Donald P. "Religion under the Mamluks." *Muslim World,* 73 (1983), 165–81.

Lovejoy, Arthur O. *The Great Chain of Being.* Cambridge, MA: Harvard University Press, 1964.

Macdonald, D. B. "Fiṭra." *Encyclopaedia of Islam.* 2nd ed. Leiden: Brill, 1960–2004. Vol. 2, 931–32.

MacIntyre, Alasdair. *After Virtue*. 3rd ed. Notre Dame, IN: University of Notre Dame Press, 2007.

Makari, Victor E. *Ibn Taymiyyah's Ethics: The Social Factor.* Chico, CA: Scholars Press, 1983.

Makdisi, George. *Ibn 'Aqîl et la résurgence de l'Islam traditionaliste au XIe siècle.* Damascus: Institut Français de Damas, 1963.

———. "The Ḥanbalite school and Ṣūfism." In *Actas do IV Congresso de estudos árabes e islâmicos, 1968*, 71–84. Leiden: Brill, 1971.

———. "Ibn Taymiyya: A Ṣūfī of the Qādiriyya order." *American Journal of Arabic Studies*, 1 (1973), 118–29.

———. "Ethics in Islamic traditionalist doctrine." In *Ethics in Islam*, ed. Richard G. Hovannisian, 47–63. Malibu, CA: Undena, 1985.

———. *Ibn 'Aqil: Religion and Culture in Classical Islam.* Edinburgh: Edinburgh Press, 1997.

Marcotte, Roxanne D. "Ibn Taymiyya et sa critique des produits de la faculté d'estimation (*Wahmiyyāt*) dans le *Dar' Ta'āruḍ al-'aql wa'l-naql*." *Luqmān*, 18 (2002), 43–58.

Marmura, Michael E. "Ghazālī on ethical premises." *Philosophical Forum*, (NS) 1 (1969), 309–23. Reprinted in *Probing in Islamic Philosophy*, 261–65. Binghamton, NY: Global Academic Publishing, Binghamton University, 2005.

———. "A medieval Islamic argument for the intrinsic value of the moral act." In *Corolla Torontonensis: Studies in Honour of R. M. Smith*, ed. Emmet Robbins and Stella Sandahl, 113–31. Toronto: TSAR, 1994.

Al-Matroudi, Abdul Hakim I. *The Ḥanbalī School of Law and Ibn Taymiyyah: Conflict or Conciliation.* London: Routledge, 2006.

McGinnis, Jon. "Scientific methodologies in medieval Islam." *Journal of the History of Philosophy*, 41 (2003), 307–27.

McNaughton, David. "Intuitionism." In *The Blackwell Guide to Ethical Theory*, ed. Hugh LaFollette, 268–87. Malden, MA: Blackwell, 2000.

Meier, Fritz. "The cleanest about predestination: a bit of Ibn Taymiyya." In *Essays on Islamic Piety and Mysticism*, trans. J. O'Kane, 309–34. Leiden: Brill, 1999.

Michot, Yahya M. "La pandémie avicennienne au VIe/XIIe siècle: présentation, *editio princeps* et traduction de l'introduction du *Livre de l'advenue du monde* (*Kitāb ḥudūth al-'ālam*) d'Ibn Ghaylān al-Balkhī." *Arabica*, 40 (1993), 287–344.

———. *Lettre à Abû l-Fidâ'*. Louvain-la-Neuve: Institut Orientaliste, Université Catholique de Louvain, 1994.

———. "Vanités intellectuelles ... l'impasse des rationalismes selon *Le Rejet de la contradiction* d'Ibn Taymiyyah." *Oriente Moderno*, 19/80 (NS) (2000), 597–617.

———. "A Mamlūk theologian's commentary on Avicenna's *Risāla Aḍḥawiyya*." *Journal of Islamic Studies*, 14 (2003), 149–203, 309–63.

———. "Ibn Taymiyya's commentary on the *Creed* of al-Ḥallāj." In *Sufism and Theology*, ed. Ayman Shihadeh, 123–36. Edinburgh: Edinburgh University Press, 2007.

———. *Against Extremisms*. Paris: Albouraq Editions, 2012.

———. "An important reader of al-Ghazālī: Ibn Taymiyya." *Muslim World*, 103 (2013), 131–60.

Neiman, Susan. *Evil in Modern Thought: An Alternative History of Philosophy*. Princeton, NJ: Princeton University Press, 2004.

Opwis, Felicitas. "*Maṣlaḥa* in contemporary Islamic legal theory." *Islamic Law and Society*, 12 (2005), 182–223.

———. "The construction of *madhhab* authority: Ibn Taymiyya's interpretation of juristic preference (*istiḥsān*)." *Islamic Law and Society*, 15 (2008), 219–49.

———. Maṣlaḥa *and the Purpose of the Law: Islamic Discourse on Legal Change from the 4th/10th to 8th/10th Century*. Leiden: Brill, 2010.

———. "Attributing causality to God's Law: the solution of Faḫr ad-Dīn ar-Rāzī." In *Islamic Philosophy, Science, Culture, and Religion: Studies in Honor of Dimitri Gutas*, ed. Felicitas Opwis and David Reisman, 397–418. Leiden: Brill, 2012.

Ormsby, Eric L. *Theodicy in Islamic Thought: The Dispute over al-Ghazālī's "Best of All Possible Worlds."* Princeton, NJ: Princeton University Press, 1984.

Özervarli, Sait M. "The Qurʾānic rational theology of Ibn Taymiyya and his criticism of the *mutakallimūn*." In *Ibn Taymiyya and His Times*, ed. Yossef Rapoport and Shahab Ahmed, 78–100. Karachi: Oxford University Press, 2010.

———. "Divine wisdom, human agency and the *fiṭra* in Ibn Taymiyya's thought." In *Islamic Theology, Philosophy and Law: Debating Ibn Taymiyya and Ibn Qayyim al-Jawziyya*, ed. Birgit Krawietz and Georges Tamer, 37–60. Berlin: De Gruyter, 2013.

Platti, Emilio. "La théologie de Abū l-Aʿlā Mawdūdī." In *Philosophy and Arts in the Islamic World*, ed. U. Vermeulen and D. de Smet, 243–51. Leuven: Peeters, 1998.

Pope, Stephen J. "Natural law and Christian ethics." In *The Cambridge Companion to Christian Ethics*, ed. Robin Gill, 77–95. Cambridge: Cambridge University Press, 2001.

Porter, Jean. *Nature as Reason: A Thomistic Theory of the Natural Law*. Grand Rapids, MI: W. B. Eerdmans, 2005.

Rachels, James. "Naturalism." In *The Blackwell Guide to Ethical Theory*, ed. Hugh LaFollette, 74–91. Malden, MA: Blackwell, 2000.

Rapoport, Yossef. "Ibn Taymiyya's radical legal thought: rationalism, pluralism, and the primacy of intention." In *Ibn Taymiyya and His Times*, ed. Yossef Rapoport and Shahab Ahmed, 191–226. Karachi: Oxford University Press, 2010.

Rawls, John. "Two concepts of rules." *Philosophical Review*, 64 (1955), 3–32. Reprinted in *Theories of Ethics*, ed. Philippa Foot, 144–70. Oxford: Oxford University Press, 1967.

Al-Raysuni, Ahmad. *Imam al-Shatibi's Theory of the Higher Objectives and Intents of Islamic Law*, trans. Nancy Roberts. London: International Institute of Islamic Thought, 2005.

Reinhart, Kevin A. *Before Revelation: The Boundaries of Muslim Moral Thought*. Albany: State University of New York Press, 1995.

———. "Ritual action and practical action: the incomprehensibility of Muslim devotional action." In *Islamic Law in Theory: Studies in Jurisprudence in Honor of Bernard Weiss*, ed. Robert Gleave and Kevin Reinhart, 55–103. Leiden: Brill, 2014.

Saleh, Walid A. "Ibn Taymiyya and the rise of radical hermeneutics: an analysis of *An Introduction to the Foundations of Qur'ānic Exegesis*." In *Ibn Taymiyya and His Times*, ed. Yossef Rapoport and Shahab Ahmed, 123–62. Karachi: Oxford University Press, 2010.

Schacht, Joseph. *An Introduction to Islamic Law*. Oxford: Clarendon Press, 1964.

Schmidtke, Sabine. *The Theology of al-ʿAllāma al-Ḥillī (d. 726/1325)*. Berlin: Klaus Schwarz, 1991.

Schneewind, Jerome B. (ed.) *Moral Philosophy from Montaigne to Kant*. Cambridge: Cambridge University Press, 2003.

———. *Essays on the History of Moral Philosophy*. Oxford: Oxford University Press, 2010.

Schopenhauer, Arthur. *The World as Will and Representation*, trans. E. F. J. Payne. New York: Dover, 1969.

Schwarb, Gregor. "Muʿtazilism in the age of Averroes." In *In the Age of Averroes: Arabic Philosophy in the Sixth/Twelfth Century*, ed. Peter Adamson, 251–82. London: Warburg Institute, Nino Aragno, 2011.

Sebti, Meryem. "Avicenna's 'flying man' argument as a proof of the immateriality of the soul." In *De l'Antiquité tardive au Moyen Âge. Études de logique aristotélicienne et de philosophie grecque, syriaque, arabe et latine offertes à Henri Hugonnard-Roche*, ed. Elisa Coda and Cecilia Martini Bonadeo, 531–43. Paris: Vrin, 2014.

Sherif, Mohamed Ahmed. *Ghazali's Theory of Virtue*. Albany: State University of New York Press, 1975.

Shihadeh, Ayman. *The Teleological Ethics of Fakhr al-Dīn al-Rāzī*. Brill: Leiden, 2006.

———. "Theories of ethical value in kalām: a new interpretation." In *The Oxford Handbook of Islamic Theology*, ed. Sabine Schmidtke. Oxford: Oxford University Press, forthcoming.

Sidgwick, Henry. *The Methods of Ethics*. 7th ed. Indianapolis, IN: Hackett, 1981.

Singer, Peter. "Sidgwick and Reflective Equilibrium." *Monist*, 58 (1974), 490–517.

Starrett, Gregory. *Putting Islam to Work: Education, Politics, and Religious Transformation in Egypt*. Berkeley: University of California Press, 1998.

Swartz, Merlin. "A seventh-century (A.H.) Sunnī creed: the ʿAqīda Wāsiṭīya of Ibn Taymīya." *Humaniora Islamica*, 1 (1973), 91–131.

Tamer, Georges. "The curse of philosophy: Ibn Taymiyya as a philosopher in contemporary Islamic thought." In *Islamic Theology, Philosophy and Law: Debating Ibn Taymiyya and Ibn Qayyim al-Jawziyya*, ed. Birgit Krawietz and Georges Tamer, 329–74. Berlin: De Gruyter, 2013.

Vasalou, Sophia. "Equal before the Law: the evilness of human and divine lies—ʿAbd al-Ǧabbār's rational ethics." *Arabic Sciences and Philosophy*, 13 (2003), 243–68.

———. *Moral Agents and Their Deserts: The Character of Muʿtazilite Ethics.* Princeton, NJ: Princeton University Press, 2008.

———. "Ibn Taymiyya's ethics between Ashʿarite voluntarism and Muʿtazilite rationalism: a middle road?" In *Rediscovering Theological Rationalism in the Medieval World of Islam: New Texts and Perspectives,* ed. Gregor Schwarb, Sabine Schmidtke, and Lukas Muehlethaler. Leuven: Peeters, forthcoming.

Watt, W. Montgomery. "Ḥanīf." *Encyclopaedia of Islam.* 2nd ed. Leiden: Brill, 1960–2004. Vol. 3, 165–66.

Weiss, Bernard G. *The Search for God's Law.* Salt Lake City: University of Utah Press, 1992.

———. "Ibn Taymiyya on leadership in the ritual prayer." In *Islamic Legal Interpretation: Muftis and Their Fatwas,* ed. Muhammad Khalid Masud, Brinkley Messick, and David S. Powers, 63–71. Cambridge, MA: Harvard University Press, 1996.

———. *The Spirit of Islamic Law.* Athens: University of Georgia Press, 1998.

Zagzebski, Linda. "Morality and religion." In *The Oxford Handbook of Philosophy of Religion,* ed. William J. Wainwright, 344–65. Oxford: Oxford University Press, 2005.

Zysow, Aron. *The Economy of Certainty: An Introduction to the Typology of Islamic Legal Theory.* PhD dissertation, Harvard University, 1984.

———. "Two theories of the obligation to obey God's commands." In *The Law Applied: Contextualizing the Islamic Shari'a,* ed. Peri Bearman, Wolfhart Heinrichs, and Bernard G. Weiss, 397–421. London: I. B. Tauris, 2008.

Index